Stillman B. Pratt

The Plymouth County Directory, and historical Register of the Old Colony

Stillman B. Pratt

The Plymouth County Directory, and historical Register of the Old Colony

ISBN/EAN: 9783337132934

Printed in Europe, USA, Canada, Australia, Japan

Cover: Foto ©ninafisch / pixelio.de

More available books at **www.hansebooks.com**

THE PLYMOUTH COUNTY DIRECTORY,

—AND—

Historical Register of the Old Colony,

CONTAINING AN
HISTORICAL SKETCH OF THE
COUNTY, AND OF EACH TOWN IN THE
COUNTY; A ROLL OF HONOR, WITH THE NAMES
OF ALL SOLDIERS OF THE ARMY AND NAVY, FROM THIS
COUNTY, WHO LOST THEIR LIVES IN SERVICE; AN ALPHABETICAL
LIST OF THE VOTERS; A COMPLETE INDEX TO THE
MERCANTILE, MANUFACTURING, AND PROFES-
SIONAL INTERESTS OF THE COUNTY,
TOGETHER WITH MUCH VALUABLE
MISCELLANEOUS MATTER.

MIDDLEBORO, MASS:
PUBLISHED BY STILLMAN B. PRATT & CO.,
1867.

PREFACE.

This book, with its 425 pages, is the first attempt at a Directory and History, so far as Plymouth County is concerned. It has been our endeavor in this work to furnish:

1st. A condensed and yet a comprehensive Historical sketch of each town in the County.

2d. The names, residences and occupations of the voters of the County, as well as a General Business Directory of the same.

3d. A good advertising medium for the business men, both in and out of the County.

Had we realized at the outset—as we do now, the very large outlay of time and money the enterprise would require, we might have shrunk from engaging in it. We have aimed as far as possible at accuracy of information, but the reader will see that in such a work, dealing as it does mainly with strange names, there is peculiar liability to error.

It was our intention to have issued the book several weeks earlier, but owing to the procrastination of some of those upon whom we were dependent for information, as well as the unforeseen obstacles, its issue has been delayed.

Our advertising pages contain the cards of nearly every first class establishment throughout the County, as well as many good Houses elsewhere, and the reader will do well to consult that part of the work.

For three of the engravings of Manufacturing Establishments we are indebted to Hon. Benjamin Hobart, Author and Publisher of the History of Abington.

To the faithful agents who have been in our employ, as well as to large numbers of citizens who have aided us in many ways, as well as to the several gentlemen who have given us histories of their towns, we tender the cordial thanks of

THE PUBLISHERS.

ILLUSTRATIONS.

Frontispiece—C. Sprague's establishment, North Bridgewater.
Map.
Wm. L. Reed's Shoe Manufactory, opposite page 24, history.
Dunbar, Hobart & Whidden's Tack Factory, opposite page 33, history.
The Puritan Apple Tree, opposite page 56, history.
Indian Scene, page 66, history.
J. L. Nash's Shoe Factory, opposite page 124, history.
Hyland House, page 132, history.
Peirce Academy, page 162, history.
Jenkins Lane & Sons' Shoe Factory, page 165, history.
Harlow's Steam Mill, page 5, directory.
Lazell, Perkins & Co.'s Works, page 14, advertising department.

Historical Index.

	Page		Page
Abington,	23	Manufacturing Companies,	148
Agricultural Societies,	157	Marion,	61
Associations,	152	Marshfield,	59
Banks,	148	Masonic Lodges,	152
Bridgewater,	28	Mattapoisett,	65
Carver,	33	Middleboro,	66
Census,	156	Military,	145
Churches,	157	North Bridgewater,	73
Commissioners,	142	Pembroke,	78
Congressional Districts,	146	Plymouth,	81
County Officers,	141	Plymouth County,	17, 141
Courts,	141	Plympton,	97
Custom House Officers,	147	Representative Districts,	146
Duxbury,	36	Rochester,	102
East Bridgewater,	38	Savings Banks,	150
Good Templar Lodges,	152	Schools,	147
Halifax,	42	Scituate,	104
Halls,	154	Senatorial Districts,	146
Hanover,	45	Soldiers' Record, see sketch of each	
Hanson,	47	town, and	121
Hingham,	49	Sons of Temperance,	152
Hull,	52	South Scituate,	109
Insurance Companies,	155	State Constables,	145
Justices of the Peace,	142	Town Officers,	150
Kingston,	53	Wareham,	111
Lakeville,	57	West Bridgewater,	118

Index to General Directory.

	Page.		Page.
Abington,	9	Marshfield,	67
Bridgewater,	25	Mattapoisett,	71
Carver,	30	Middleboro,	74
Duxbury,	32	North Bridgewater,	83
East Bridgewater,	37	Pembroke,	92
Halifax,	42	Plymouth,	95
Hanover,	44	Plympton,	107
Hanson,	47	Rochester,	109
Hingham,	50	Scituate,	111
Hull,	59	South Scituate,	115
Kingston,	60	Wareham,	118
Lakeville,	63	West Bridgewater,	125
Marion,	65		

For Business Firms see 127th Page of Directory.

Index to Advertising.

☞ For Alphabetical list of Advertisers, see 2d page advertising department.

	Page.		Page.
Advertising Agencies.		J. M. Laippold, Middleboro,	21
Geo. P. Rowell & Co., New York,	141	**Boot & Shoe Manufacturers.**	
Agricultural Engineer.		W. O. Alger, Cochesett,	69
J. Herbert Shedd, Boston,	71	Lemuel Baxter, Boston,	63
Agricultural Implements.		**Boots, Shoes & Rubbers.**	
A. Vincent, New Bedford,	85	Andrew Bowker, Hanson,	20
Ambrotypes.		Chas. D. Brigham, No. Bridgewater,	53
(See Photographists.)		John S. Brooks, Hanover,	19
Apothecaries.		G. E. & H. L. Bryant, N. Bridgewater,	48
C. C. Bixby, No. Bridgewater,	27	Burges & Bailey, Kingston,	5
Benj. T. Crooker, Bridgewater,	51	Albert Chamberlain, No. Abington,	16
J. J. Estes, East Abington,	7	Darius Cushman, Bridgewater,	13
Benj. B Hubbard, Plymouth,	51	Benj. P. Davis, No. Bridgewater,	25
J. L. Hunt, Hingham,	18	E. Gushee, Bridgewater,	17
Chas. E. Monroe, Taunton,	60	J. Howland, Jr., Plymouth,	87
J. B. & J. Shaw, Middleboro,	33	Kingman & Hollywood, N. Bridgewater,	24
Attorneys.		I. N. & E. W. Nutter, E. Bridgewater,	39
Latham & Kingman, Bridgewater,	11	Geo. H. Pearson, South Abington,	10
Albert Mason, Plymouth,	36	H. C. Perry, Taunton,	85
Auctioneers.		J. A. Rice, East Abington,	10
N. S. Hoard, Taunton, previous to title		I. G. Stetson, South Hanover,	18
B. H. Holmes, Plymouth,	34	**Boxes and Trunk Wood.**	
Augers and Caulkers' Tools.		B. S. & E. H. Atwood, No. Abington,	10
C. Drew & Co., Kingston,	26	E. & J. C. Barnes, Plymouth,	45
Bakers.		Wm. B. Pratt, Hanover,	20
Hunt & Wilder, North Bridgewater,	55	Rock Mills, Middleboro,	91
John C. Tarry, Plympton,	20	Harlow's Steam Mills, Middleboro, directory, p. 5	
G. A. Whiting & Co., Plymouth,	51	**Bricks.**	
Belting.		M. Hooper & Co., Bridgewater,	12
Boston Belting Co., Boston, opp. h.	32	S. S. Paine & Bro., New Bedford,	61
L. D. Hawkins, Boston,	80	Charles M. Peirce, New Bedford,	61
H. C. Perry, Taunton,	85	S. P. Taylor & Co., Boston,	64
Blacking.		**Burning Oils.**	
Robert Farley, Jr. & Co., Boston,	72	Eureka Oil Co., Boston,	68
D. Whittemore, North Bridgewater, opp. h.	57	Folsom, Gilman & Pope, Boston.	64
Book Binder.		Lothrop Bearse & Co., Boston, prev. title	
J. G. Terry, Boston,	92	Marion Oil and Candle Co., Marion,	18
Books and Stationery.		**Calcined Plaster.**	
C. F. Copeland, No. Bridgewater,	30	E. & J. C. Barnes, Plymouth,	45
I. N. & E. W. Nutter, E. Bridgewater,	39	**Carriages.**	
J. B. & J. Shaw, Middleboro,	33	J. D. Bonney, Pembroke,	33
H. O. Thomas, No. Bridgewater, (embossed paper,)	26	Brownell, Ashley & Co., N. Bedford,	56
		H. G. O. Cole, New Bedford,	62
Boot and Shoe Makers.		Francis Sargent & Co., Boston,	65
Benj. P. Davis, No. Bridgewater,	25	S. L. Pratt, Cochesett,	77
Jonathan Hatch, So. Scituate,	39	**Carriage Robes.**	
J. E. Keith, Middleboro,	23	Kingman & Hollywood, North Bridgewater,	24

	Page
Carpetings.	
W. P. B. Brooks, Boston, prev. to title, and	78
Caleb Bryant & Son, Taunton,	60
S. M. Burbank, Plymouth,	83
Goldthwait, Snow & Knight, Boston,	after title.
Chemists.	
Berger, Shutts & Co., Troy, N. Y.,	73
Cigars and Tobacco.	
Wm. M. Judkins, East Bridgewater,	6
C. E. Richmond, Taunton,	60
Joseph B. Whiting, Plymouth,	36
Civil Engineer.	
J. Herbert Shedd, Boston,	71
Clairvoyants.	
H. A. Perrigo, Buffalo,	74
Mad. Remington, Troy,	73
E. F. Thornton, Hudson, N. Y.	76
Cloaks and Shawls.	
Brett Bros. No. Bridgewater,	29
Chas. Curtis, Taunton, previous to title	
Clocks and Jewelry.	
B. W. Atwood, Plymouth,	37
C. H. Carpenter, Middleboro,	23
L. F. Gurney, North Bridgewater,	47
Edward A. Hewitt, Bridgewater,	12
Heman Hewitt, North Bridgewater,	39
E. D. Tisdale, Taunton,	59
Coal and Wood.	
S. P. Taylor & Co., Boston,	64
Coffin Warehouses.	
Howard, Clark & Co., No. Bridgewater,	25
Wm. Prophett, Bridgewater,	24
Chas. Raymond, Plymouth,	34
Lothrop Shurtleff, N. Bridgewater,	24
George Soule, Middleboro,	34
Commercial College.	
J. H. Lansley, Poultney, Vt.,	58
Confectionery.	
A. L. Bliss, Taunton, prev. to title.	
B. Ellis, Plymouth,	86
Stephen Lucas, Plymouth,	51
C. E. Richmond, Taunton,	60
Harvey C. Ripley, Bridgewater,	11
F. B. Washburn, North Bridgewater,	30
Crockery.	
Andrew Bowker, Hanson,	20
John S. Brooks, North Hanover,	19
Dentists.	
C. W. Leach, Middleboro,	89
J. E. Packard, North Bridgewater,	26
Loring W. Puffer, North Bridgewater,	21
N. & C. Washburn, Bridgewater,	12
Distillers.	
D. Lawrence & Sons, Boston,	83
Doors, Sashes and Blinds.	
Cutter and Parker, Boston, prev. to title.	
John O. Foye, Weymouth Landing,	51
Augustus Hardy, Boston,	67
Mosher & Brownell, N. Bedford,	61
Draining Engineer.	
J. Herbert Shedd, Boston,	71
Drain Pipe.	
J. S. Bannister, Boston,	71
Wm. Mills, Boston, last cover.	
S. S. Paine & Bro., New Bedford,	61
Chas. M. Pierce, jr., New Bedford,	61

	Page
S. P. Taylor & Co., Boston,	64
Draughtsman.	
J. Herbert Shedd, Boston,	46
Dressing Blacking.	
D. Whittemore, No. Bridgewater, his.	57
C. L. Hauthaway & Son, No. Bridgewater,	26, 27
Drugs and Dyestuffs.	
Merrill Bros., Boston,	opp title
J. B. & J. Shaw, Middleboro,	33
Family Dye Colors.	
Howe & Stevens, Boston, history	21
Fancy Goods.	
E. L. Barnes, Plymouth,	129
B. C. Benner, North Bridgewater,	31
Brett Bros., " "	29
Charles C. Doten, Plymouth,last colored	
J. E. Dodge, Plymouth,	86
B. Ellis, Plymouth,	86
George Lincoln, Jr., Hingham,	20
Geo. H. Pearson, South Abington,	10
Harvey C. Ripley, Bridgewater,	11
Joseph B. Whiting, Plymouth,	36
Fertilizers.	
Geo. Davenport & Co., Boston,(guano)	62
S. S. Paine & Bro., New Bedford,	61
Chas. Pierce, Jr., " "	61
Dry Goods.	
B. C. Benner, North Bridgewater,	31
William Bodfish, Taunton,	59
Andrew Bowker, Hanson,	20
Brett Bros., No. Bridgewater,	29
S. M. Burbank, Jr., Plymouth,	83
Burges & Bailey, Kingston,	5
Geo. Lincoln, Jr., Hingham,	20
J. E. Luscomb, Taunton, previous to title	
I. N. & E. W. Nutter, E. Bridgewater,	59
J. A. Rice & Co., East Abington,	10
Roddick & McJennett, Middleboro,	21
N. H. Skinner, Taunton, prev to title	
File Manufacturer.	
Joseph Webster, Taunton,	57
Flour and Grain.	
A. & A. J. Ames, Boston,	63
John S. Brooks, North Hanover,	19
Andrew Bowker, Hanson,	20
F. H. Churchill, Plymouth,	41
T. W. Crocker, Bridgewater,	7
S. B. & G. E. Curtis, N. Bridgewater	23
W. B. Hathaway, Bridgewater,	22
L. Pratt & Co., Plymouth,	85
I. G. Stetson, South Hanover,	18
Fresco Painters.	
Brown & Strauss, Boston, outside cover.	
Furniture.	
W. P. B. Brooks, Boston, prev. to title.	
Burges & Bailey, Kingston,	5
Howard Clark & Co., N. Bridgewater,	25
Wm. Prophett, Bridgewater,	11
George Soule, Middleboro,	34
George W. Ware, Boston, hist.	25
Gents' Furnishing Goods.	
H. A. Brett, North Bridgewater,	54
G. E. & H. L. Bryant, N. Bridgewater,	48
Estes and Whiting, E. Abington,	10
B. R. Holt, Taunton,	59
E. Packard, New Bedford,	62
W. C. Reeves, Boston,	80
M. Toole, Middleboro,	53
Glass.	
J. M. Cook, Boston,	72

	Page.
Grindstones.	
Lombard & Co., Boston,	9
Read, Stevenson & Co., Boston,	91
Groceries.	
John S. Brooks, North Hanover,	19
Burges & Bailey, Kingston,	5
Wm. Burns, Plymouth,	33
F. H. Churchill, Plymouth,	41
T. W. Crocker, Bridgewater,	7
S. B. & G. E. Curtis, No. Bridgewater,	23
W. B. Hathaway, Bridgewater,	22
Southworth & Noyes, N. Bridgewater,	24
I. G. Stetson, South Hanover,	18
Hair Dressers.	
W. H. Barden, North Bridgewater,	25
Joseph B. Whiting, Plymouth,	36
Hair Restoratives.	
Berger, Shutts & Co., Troy, N. Y.,	74, 75
W. L. Clark & Co., Syracuse, N. Y.,	73, 76
Hammers.	
E. S. Morton,	81
Hardware.	
John O. Foye, Weymouth Landing,	57
John Hunt, No. Bridgewater,	14
Southworth & Noyes, N. Bridgewater,	24
A. Vincent, New Bedford,	85
Harnesses.	
J. Dean Bonney, Pembroke,	33
R. S. Rogers, Bridgewater,	13
F. Sargent & Co., Boston,	65
Hats and Caps.	
Wm. Atwood, Plymouth,	40
H. A. Brett, North Bridgewater,	54
G. E. & H. L. Bryant, N. Bridgewater,	48
B. R. Holt, Taunton,	59
Kingman & Hollywood,	24
Geo. H. Pearson, South Abington,	10
H. C. Perry, Taunton,	85
Hoop Skirts and Corsets.	
R. F. Thompson, N. Bridgewater & Middleboro,	69
Bradley, (hoop skirts), New York,	h. 16
Hotels.	
American House, Fitchburg,	78
Bay View House, Marion,	19
Hyland House, Bridgewater,	h. 132
Thompson's Hotel, Wareham,	56
House Furnishing Goods.	
George H. Doane, Middleboro,	32
J. H. Fairbanks, Bridgewater,	13, 77
N. S. Hoard, Taunton,	prev. to title.
Inks.	
W. C. Donald & Co., Boston, (printers')	8
Insurance Agents.	
Wm. S. Danforth, Plymouth,	82
J. Dwelley, Hanover,	19
J. T. Hall, Plymouth,	35
Henry B. Peirce, Abington,	13, 81
L. W. Puffer, North Bridgewater,	30
Insurance Companies.	
Ætna, Boston,	30
Berkshire, Pittsfield,	50
Columbus Accident,	70
North American,	outside cover.
Knickerbocker,	opp. hist. 33
Nails.	
E. W. Barstow, West Hanover,	83
Cobb & Drew, Plymouth,	84
Robinson Iron Co., Plymouth,	38

	Page.
Dunbar, Hobart & Whidden, South Abington,	opp. hist. 33
Japans and Varnishes.	
Dexter & Bro., Boston,	64
Merrill & Bro., Boston,	opp. title.
J. Porter & Co., Boston,	8
George H. Shaw, Middleboro,	81
Iron Foundries.	
Wm. R. Drew, Plymouth,	84
Lazell, Perkins & Co., Bridgewater,	14
Old Colony, East Bridgewater,	17
J. B. LeBaron, Middleboro,	53
Landscape Gardner.	
J. Herbert Shedd, Boston,	71
Lasts and Boot Trees.	
Gilson & Walker,	previous to title.
Leather Cutters.	
L. D. Hawkins, Boston,	80
Leather, Shoe Findings and Machinery.	
Lemuel Baxter, Boston,	63
Brooks & McCuen, "	65
Putterfield & Haven, "	67
L. D. Hawkins, "	80
E. S. Morton, Plymouth,	81
Phinney & Phillips, Boston,	65
Lamp Black.	
W. C. Donald, Boston,	8
D. W. Littemore No. Bridgewater,	opp. h. 57
Letter Cutters and Stencil Plates.	
Dodge & Power, Boston,	71
Frank L. Penney & Co., Boston,	79
F. E. Phelps, "	91
Lumber.	
S. P. Taylor & Co., Boston,	64
Machinists.	
E. T. Snell & Co., North Bridgewater,	44
Machinery.	
Industrial Iron Works, New Bedford,	77
Plymouth Mills, Plymouth,	88
Southern Cotton Gin Co., Bridgewater,	15
Union Machine Co., "	23
Lazell, Perkins & Co., Bridgewater,	14
Marble Workers.	
George W. Bryant, N. Bridgewater,	58
D. A. Burt, Taunton,	69
George H. Clapp, Hanover,	17
Robert Clark, Plymouth,	37
Melodeons.	
Philip Reynolds, No. Bridgewater,	30
George Soule, Middleboro,	34
Millinery.	
S. F. Barrows Middleboro,	57
Burges & Bailey, Kingston,	5
M. Burns "	21
M. R. Reynolds No. Bridgewater,	25
Mowing Machines.	
Heman Copeland, W. Bridgewater,	Directory 6
Newspapers.	
Standard, East Abington,	h 134
Journal, Hingham,	h 133
Memorial & Rock, Plymouth,	h 135
Gazette, Middleboro,	h 137
Nation, New York,	h 138
N. E. Farmer, Boston,	h 137
Tribune, N. Y.,	h 139

PLYMOUTH COUNTY HISTORY.   13

	Page		Page
Old Colony Sentinel, Plymouth,	h 136	**Provisions.**	
Pratt Bros., Middleboro,	h 133	P. C. Chandler, Plymouth,	41
Republican, Taunton,	directory, 6	F. H. Churchill, Plymouth,	43
Notary Public.		John Corthell, South Scituate,	47
James B. Bell, Boston,	63	Field's Market, No. Bridgewater,	44
Nurseries.		Union Market, No. Bridgewater,	28
Thos. Hooper, Bridgewater,	9	**Publishers and Booksellers.**	
B. M. Watson,	86	Gould & Lincoln, Boston,	78
Organs.		Briggs & Co., Boston,	directory, 6
A. B. Lincoln, Boston,	67	N. P. Kemp, Boston,	h 15
Philip Reynolds, N. Bridgewater,	30	Henry Hoyt, Boston,	directory, 126
S. D. and H. W. Smith, Boston,	66	Littell & Gay, Boston,	96
Geo. Soule, Middleboro,	34	S. B. Pratt & Co., Middleboro,	title page
Oyster Saloons.		A. Williams & Co., Boston,	directory 148
S. D. Ballard, Plymouth,	h 139	**Ready-Made Clothing.**	
J. E. Dodge, Plymouth,	96	Wm. Atwood, 2d, Plymouth,	40
G. L. Gilman, North Abington,	10	Andrew Bowker, Hanson,	20
Painters.		H. A. Brett, No. Bridgewater,	54
B. Loring Boomer, Middleboro,	19	G. E. & H. L. Bryant, "	48
J. G. Sparrow Middleboro,	directory 6	Burges & Bailey, Kingston,	5
Paints and Oils.		Burnes E. E. "	21
Banker and Carpenter,	prev. to title	Estes & Whiting, East Abington,	10
Dexter Bros.,	64	Kingman & Hollywood, N. Bridgewater,	23
Folsom, Gilman and Pope,	64	E. Packard New Bedford,	62
Lucas and Cook,	history, 129	M. C. Swift, Taunton,	prev. to title
Merrill bros.,	opp. title	M. Toole, Middleboro,	53
I. Washburn, Taunton,	outside cover	**Refreshment Saloons.**	
Paper Boxes.		J. E. Dodge, Plymouth,	86
Joseph R. Grose,	6	G. L. Gilman, North Abington,	10
Paper Hangings.		R. B. Grover, North Bridgewater,	57
S. M. Burbank, Jr.,	83	B. F. Tripp, Middleboro,	direc. 3
Geo. Lincoln, Jr.,	20	**Rivets.**	
I. N. and E. W. Nutter,	39	Cobb and Drew, Plymouth,	84
I. Washburn,	outside cover	J. Farris, Plymouth,	88
Patent Agency.		**Rubber Moulding.**	
J. H. Adams,	89	F. O. Raymond and Co., Boston,	92
Wm. Edson,	directory, 8	**Sale and Livery Stable.**	
Patent Medicines.		S. L. Pratt, Cohesett,	77
Turner's Neuralgia Pill, Boston,	57	**Scales and Balances.**	
Hembold's Sarsaparilla, N. Y.	h 15	Howe's "Standard,"	after title.
Holloway's Pill, N. Y.	directory 4	**Scrofula Remedy.**	
Pegging Machine.		H. O. Thayer,	31
D. Whittemore,	history 57	**Seed Sower.**	
Perfumes.		E. D. and O. B. Reynolds,	49
C. C. Cisby,	27	**Sewing Machines.**	
Robert Farley, Jr. and Co.,	72	L. L. Farber,	h 129
Benjamin Hubbard,	51	Butterfield and Haven,	67
Photographers.		Elliptic,	h 129
T. R. Burnham,	80	Florence,	h 129
D. T. Burrell,	13	L. Johnson and Co.,	last colored page.
J. J. Hawes,	79	A. S. Lincoln,	67, 87
Howard Bros.,	26	Walter Scott,	55
C. F. Richardson,	27	**Ship Chandlery.**	
Piano Fortes.		Ambrose Vincent,	85
A. M. Leland, Boston,	history, 129	**Shirt Manufacturer.**	
George Soule, Middleboro,	34	W. C. Reeves,	80
Woodward & Brown, Boston,	78	**Shoe Knives.**	
Plumbers.		W. Webster,	45
Wm. Mills, Boston,	last colored	**Shoe Tools.**	
Plumbers Materials.		E. T. Snell and Co.,	44
Wm. Mills, Boston,	last colored	**Soap.**	
Printers.		J. H. Burgess,	61
Geo. F. Andrews, Plymouth,	h 135	T. M. Davis,	last colored leaf
Avery & Cave, Plymouth,	h 136	**Second Hand Clothing.**	
J. Burrell, East Bridgewater,	89	S. R. Holt,	59
Blossom & Easterbrook, Hingham,	h 133	H. Norris,	57
S. B. Pratt, Middleboro,	h 137	**Spool Cotton.**	
T. S. Pratt, Abington,	h 134	Samoset Mills,	129

3

	Page		Page
Steam Engines.		Dunbar, Hobart and Whidden,	h. 33
J. C. Bradford,	previous to title.	Z. Keith and Co.,	43
L. D. Hawkins,	80	E. Y. Perry,	outside cover
Industrial Iron Works,	76	Phinney and Phalips,	65
Union Machine Co.,	23	Plymouth Rivet Works,	37
Steam Heating Engineer.		Alphonso Reed,	17
J. Herbert Shedd,	71	Sam'l Tolman and Bro.,	47
Straw Goods.		L. C. Waterman and Co.,	45
Bay State Straw Works,	56	**Taxidermist.**	
Lemuel Pitts,	28	S. H. Sylvester,	21
Schools.		**Tin Ware.**	
Ingleside,	h 25	Geo. H. Doane,	32
Peirce Academy,	21	J. H. Fairbanks,	13, 77
Sea Side,	h 25	Foster and Barnard,	59
State Normal,	12	L. D. Hervey,	71
Stoves.		W. Johnson,	16
Gardner Chilson,	last cover.	Walter Scott,	55
George H. Doane,	32	**Trunks and Valises.**	
Wm. R. Drew,	44	Wm. Atwood,	40
J. H. Fairbanks,	13, 77	H. A. rett,	54
L. D. Hervey,	71	G. E. and H. L. Bryant,	48
W. Johnson,	16	**Undertakers.**	
J. B. LeBaron,	53	Chas. Raymond,	34
A. Vincent,	85	Lothrop Shurtleff,	24
Whitten and Holmes,	52	George Scule,	34
Steam Heating Apparatus.		**Vinegar.**	
T. S. Clegston,	inside cover.	Poole Bros.,	directory, 8
Sleighs.		**Ventilating Engineer.**	
F. Sargent and Co.,	65	J. Herbert Shedd,	71
Surveyor.		**Well Windlass.**	
J. Herbert Shedd,	71	G. W. Holmes,	22
Tacks.		**Weather Strips.**	
Cobb and Drew,	84	F. O. Raymond,	92
Sam'l Salmond and Co.,	46	**Wood Turning.**	
B. D. Washburn,	80	A. B. Jaquith,	6
Tacks and Shoe Nails.		**Weather Vanes.**	
E. W. Barstow,	83	Jewell and Co.,	directory, 7
Cushing and Co.,	42		

HELMBOLD'S

Concentrated Fluid Extract SARSAPARILLA,

ERADICATES ERUPTIVE and ULCERATIVE DISEASES of the THROAT, NOSE, EYES, EYELIDS, SCALP, and SKIN.

Which so disfigures the appearance, PURGING the evil effects of mercury and removing all taints, the remnants of DISEASES, hereditary or otherwise, and is taken by adults and children with PERFECT SAFETY.

TWO TABLE-SPOONFULS of the Extract of Sarsaparilla, added to a pint of water, is equal to the Lisbon Diet Drink, and one bottle is equal to a gallon of the Syrup of Sarsaparilla, or the decoctions as usually made.

AN INTERESTING LETTER is published in the Medico-Chirurgical Review, on the subject of the Extract of Sarsaparilla in certain affections, by Benjamin Travers, F. R. S., &c. Speaking of those diseases, and diseases arising from the excess of mercury, he states that no remedy is equal to the Extract of Sarsaparilla; its power is extraordinary, more so than any other drug I am acquainted with. It is, in the trictest sense, a tonic with this invaluable attribute, that it is applicable to a state of the system so sunken, and yet so irritable as renders other substances of the tonic class unavailable or injurious.

Helmbold's Concentrated Extract Sarsaparilla,

Established upwards of 18 years. Prepared by
H. T. HELMBOLD, Druggist and Chemist, 594 Broadway, N. Y.

THEOLOGICAL
AND
Sabbath School Book Store,

No. 40 Cornhill, Boston,

In Addition to the Publications of the

AMERICAN TRACT SOCIETY,

The undersigned has made special arrangements to supply
Clergymen, Families and Sabbath Schools,
WITH

Commentaries, Theological Works, Reading for the Family,

AND

Libraries for Sabbath Schools.

A good variety of all works issued in this country designed for the purposes above named will be kept constantly on hand and sold on the best terms. Also a good supply of the publications of

The Presbyterian Board,
Am. Sunday School Union,
Am. Baptist Pub. Society,
R. Carter & Brother,
A. D. F. Randolph,
James S. Claxton,
J. P. Skelley & Co.

And other publishers of PHILADELPHIA, NEW YORK and BOSTON,

CLERGYMEN, FAMILIES AND SABBATH SCHOOLS,

Will be furnished with a larger amount of the best reading matter, including the

BIBLE AND BIBLE HELPS,

than can possibly be obtained from any other source, for the same money.

N. P. KEMP, 40 CORNHILL,

BOSTON, MASS.

FRUIT-TREES, GRAPE-VINES,

Small Fruits and Ornamental Stock.

We have imported from French Nurseries, and selected from the best stock we could find in New England and New York Nursery establishments, a large and choice assortment, consisting in part of

15,000 Standard and Dwarf Pear-trees, from 2 to 5 years old, about 100 varieties.
3,000 Standard and Dwarf Apple-trees, from 2 to 5 years old, about 25 varieties.
2,500 Standard Peach-trees, from 1 to 2 years old, about 15 varieties.
500 Standard Plum-trees, from 2 to 4 years old, about 10 varieties.
500 Standard Cherry, Apricot, Nectarine, and Quince Trees.
1,000 Extra large Pear-trees, *fruit-bearing*.
5,000 Grape-vines, 1 to 3 years old, including the newest varieties.
1,000 Choice Roses, Hybrids, Mosses, and Climbers.

SMALL FRUITS, consisting of Currants, Raspberries, Blackberries, Gooseberries, Strawberries, &c.

ORNAMENTAL STOCK.—Shade Trees, Evergreens, Shrubs, Climbing Vines, Bulbous Roots, Hedge Plants, Bedding, Border, and Hardy Herbaceous Plants.

A complete stock, strictly first-class, and warranted true to name.

Samples seen at our Salesroom, Basement 28 & 30 Water Street, Boston, during the season.

Descriptive Catalogues to applicants.

BENJAMIN T. WELLS & CO.,
Importers and Nursery Agents,

Office No. 7 Water Street, - - **BOSTON.**

SUB-AGENTS WANTED.

LATEST FASHIONS DEMAND
J. W. Bradley's Celebrated Patent
DUPLEX ELLIPTIC
OR
DOUBLE SPRING SKIRT.

The Wonderful Flexibility and great Comfort and Pleasure to any Lady wearing the Duplex Elliptic Skirt will be experienced particularly in all crowded Assemblies, Operas, Carriages, Railroad Cars, Church Pews, Arm Chairs, for Promenade and House Dress, as the Skirt can be folded when in use to occupy a small place as easily and conveniently as a silk or muslin dress, an invaluable quality in Crinoline, not found in any Single Spring Skirt. A lady having enjoyed the pleasure, comfort and great convenience of wearing the Duplex Elliptic Steel Spring Skirt for a single day will never afterwards willingly dispense with their use. For Children, Misses and Young Ladies they are superior to all others. They will not bend or break like the Single Spring, but will preserve their perfect and graceful shape when three or four ordinary Skirts would have been thrown aside as useless. The Hoops are covered with Double and Twisted Thread, and the bottom rods are not only double springs, but twice, or double covered, preventing them from wearing out when dragging down stoops, stairs, &c. The Duplex Elliptic is a great favorite with all ladies, and is universally recommended by the Fashion Magazines as the **Standard Skirt of the Fashionable World.** To enjoy the following inestimable advantages in Crinoline, viz: Superior Quality, Perfect Manufacture, Stylish Shape and Finish, Flexibility, Durability, Comfort and Economy, enquire for J. W. Bradley's Duplex Elliptic or Double Spring Skirt, and be sure you get the genuine article.

Caution.—To guard against imposition be particular to notice that Skirts offered as "Duplex" have the red ink stamp, viz: "J. W. Bradley's Duplex Elliptic Steel Springs" upon the waistband—none others are genuine. Also notice that every Hoop will admit a pin being passed through the center, thus revealing the two, or double springs braided together therein, which is the secret of their flexibility and strength, and a combination not to be found in any other Skirt.

For sale in all stores where First Class Skirts are sold, throughout the United States and elsewhere. Manufactured by the Sole Owners of the Patent,

WESTS, BRADLEY & CARY, 97 Chambers & 79 & 81 Reade Sts., N. Y.

SKETCH OF THE HISTORY OF PLYMOUTH COUNTY.

BY REV. JOHN A. VINTON.

THE History of the County of Plymouth dates back to the landing of the Pilgrims in 1620.

Rejecting the traditions of men, and adhering closely and resolutely to the teachings of inspired Scripture, a congregation of faithful men was formed for the worship of God and the enjoyment of his ordinances, at the village of Scrooby, in Nottinghamshire, England, in the year 1606. Of this church, John Robinson was the teacher, while Richard Clifton, a somewhat older man, was the pastor. Harrassed by persecution, they resolved to quit their native soil, and take refuge in Holland; a purpose which they accomplished in 1608. After sojourning in Amsterdam a few months, they removed to Leyden, where they remained about eleven years. A just concern for their children, who were liable, by a prolonged residence in Holland, to lose, not only their native tongue and their very name as English, but also to follow the evil practices which prevailed around them; this, together with an earnest desire to extend the bounds of Christendom, determined them at length to remove beyond the Atlantic, and to set up the banner of the Cross in the New World. After many disappointments, the plan was carried into execution in the latter part of the year 1620.

On Monday, the eleventh day of December in that year, reckoning according to the old style, corresponding to the twenty-first of that month, new style, an exploring party of ten men from the Mayflower, which had brought them across the ocean, landed at Plymouth. The party consisted of John Carver, William Bradford, and other leading individuals.* After a full examination of the locality, they determined

---

* The popular apprehension that the whole company of the Mayflower landed on the 11th [21st] of December, is founded in error. The pictorial representation of women and children on shore, and of the vessel as at anchor in Plymouth harbor *on that day*, has no just foundation. Only ten men—not one woman—landed from the shallop at that time, and only for the purpose of discovery. The Mayflower continued at her anchorage in Provincetown harbor—where she had been since November 11,—till the Saturday following Dec. 16, when she was brought to Plymouth. The landing of the entire company, then commenced, was not completed till March, 1621. There is no reason to doubt that the rock on which the landing took place, is historical. The rock is a bowlder, and must itself have travelled a long distance.

to begin there the new settlement. Having made report to their companions, the vessel was brought into the harbor a few days after, and the settlement commenced.

So severe were their sufferings, partly from the length of the voyage —they had been on ship-board since August 1—but more from the inclemency of the season, and from bad food, it came to pass that forty-six of the company, out of one hundred and two who came in the Mayflower, died before spring.

In March 1621, they were visited by a party of the natives, headed by Massasoit their chief sachem, from the borders of Rhode Island. A treaty of friendship and mutual succor was concluded, which remained in force fifty-four years.

The aboriginal inhabitants of Plymouth County, at the time of which we are speaking, were very few in number. A few years previous, a terrible pestilence had almost exterminated the powerful nation of the Pokanokets, who once overspread the whole region included between Narragansett Bay and the coast-line of Plymouth County. Instead of three thousand warriors whom they could have raised ten years before, scarcely five hundred could now be found. Within the bounds of this County, only the Namaskets, a small subdivision of Pokanokets, were to be found in 1620; they were seated in Middleboro.

In the following November, the infant colony was strengthened by the arrival of Robert Cushman and about thirty other emigrants, in the Fortune, a vessel of fifty-five tons burden. Their number was still further increased in July and August 1623, by the arrival of the Ann and Little James, two small vessels bringing about sixty passengers. To those who came in the four vessels already named, is now restricted, by correct usage, the appellation of PILGRIMS. During these three years, terrible hardships were endured without a murmur, by these heroic men and women, in the firm belief that God had sent them to these then inhospitable shores, for the maintenance of Gospel liberty, and for the advancement of his cause. When ten years had elapsed, the colony had increased to the number of only three hundred persons. With the exception of an outpost established at Manomet, in the present town of Sandwich, the population was confined, during those ten years, wholly to the town of Plymouth, including Kingston and Duxbury. The progress of settlement, from various causes, was far less rapid than in the neighboring colony of Massachusetts Bay.

A spirit of enterprise, however, was early awakened among the Plymouth people. About the year 1630, they had established a post for trading with the Indians on the Penobscot, and two or three years later, another on the Kennebec, and still another on the Connecticut, at Windsor. These establishments soon came to an end.

Sixteen years after the landing, there were eight towns within the colony. We will name them in the order of their establishment.

1. Plymouth, inclusive of the present towns of Kingston, Plympton, Carver, part of Halifax, and part of Wareham.

2. Duxbury is reckoned the second town in the colony, because its church, originally the second church in Plymouth, was gathered in 1632, though the town was not incorporated till 1637. It included Pembroke and Hanson.

3. Scituate, including Hanover, was incorporated in 1636.

4–7. Sandwich, Taunton, Yarmouth, and Barnstable, neither of which are now in Plymouth County, were incorporated in 1629.

8. Marshfield, taken from Duxbury, was incorporated in 1640. It was afterwards increased by adding a section of Scituate.

To these towns, Bridgewater was added in 1656, and Middleboro in 1669. We omit to mention ten or twelve other towns, incorporated between 1640 and 1690, and not now belonging to the County of Plymouth.

In 1646, the population of the town of Plymouth was greatly diminished by the removal of many of its inhabitants to Eastham on Cape Cod. Eastham then included Wellfleet and Orleans. Bridgewater was at first a mere extension of Duxbury, from which town it received its inhabitants.

The leading men, from the settlement till 1690, were William Bradford of Plymouth, Edward Winslow of Marshfield, Miles Standish and John Alden, of Duxbury, and Thomas Prince of Eastham, afterwards of Plymouth, all of the first generation. To these may be added of the second generation, William Bradford the younger, Josiah Winslow, Thomas Hinckley, Thomas and Constant Southworth. James Cudworth, Benjamin Church. Of the spiritual guides of the colonists, we may mention William Brewster of Plymouth, Ralph Partridge of Duxbury, Peter Hobart and John Norton of Hingham, (then in Suffolk County), Edward Bulkley and Samuel Arnold of Marshfield, Samuel Fuller of Middleboro, John Lothrop and Charles Chauncy of Scituate.

The early population were almost all cultivators of the soil. What little wealth there was, existed chiefly in lands and buildings. The iron manufacture was introduced into the Old Colony in 1652, by James and Henry Leonard, who had previously been connected with the forges at Lynn and Braintree. But their establishment was in the present town of Raynham, in the County of Bristol; and several generations passed before the manufacture of iron was commenced within the County of Plymouth. The first vessel constructed in the County was built in the year 1641, and measured but forty or fifty tons. The comparative poverty of the inhabitants kept them for many years behind their neighbors in Massachusetts.

The prosperity of the Old Colony in general, and of this portion of it in particular, was greatly checked by the great Indian War of

1675-6, commonly referred to as "Philip's War." We shall notice the events of this war no further than they immediately affected Plymouth County.

The war broke out in June 1675, in an attack made by the Indians on the town of Swanzey, which then included Barrington and Warren in Rhode Island. A small force was immediately collected from the Plymouth towns, and marched to the scene of blood. Being there joined by troops from Boston, they had little difficulty in driving Philip from his lair at Mount Hope, now Bristol, R. I.; but it was only that he might ravage and destroy in other places. Numbers of his men crossed the Bay in canoes, and fell upon the settlement at Middleboro, then recently commenced. This settlement, and Dartmouth in the present County of Bristol, they utterly destroyed. Those of the inhabitants who were not cruelly butchered, were driven off, and did not return till after the war.

The celebrated campaign against the Narragansett Indians, which utterly broke in pieces that powerful tribe, was conducted under the orders of Josiah Winslow of Marshfield, son of Governor Edward Winslow, and himself Governor of Plymouth Colony at this time. At the head of one thousand men, of whom more than half were from Massachusetts Colony, three hundred from Connecticut, and the remainder from Plymouth, he penetrated in the depth of winter into the heart of the Narragansett Country, in the present County of Washington, Rhode Island. Three thousand five hundred Indians of fierce and resolute spirit, had betaken themselves to a solid piece of upland, containing five or six acres, situated in the midst of a swamp, which at any other season of the year, would have been found utterly impassable. This natural defence the Indians had fortified by rows of palisades, making a barrier nearly a rod in thickness. The only entrance to this enclosure was over a bridge, consisting of a large tree which had been felled for the purpose, which could only be passed by men in single file. This bridge was defended by a block-house, or rude bastion made of logs. Such was the Narragansett fort.

The colonial army, having passed the night of the 18th of Dec. 1675, which was cold and stormy, without shelter, and with little food, marched at early dawn on the 19th, wading through the deep snow to attack this formidable fort, garrisoned by an enemy more than twice their own number. Men who were determined to conquer or die, entered the fort, and after a sharp conflict of two or three hours gained possession of it, inflicting a loss on the enemy of probably a thousand fighting men, besides women and children consumed in the burning wigwams; but themselves suffering the loss of seventy men killed, including six captains, and one hundred and fifty wounded. Such was the "Great Swamp Fight," never to be forgotten in the history of New England.

On the 13th of March, 1676, the Indians made an attack on the hamlet of Eel River, now Chiltonville, three miles south of the principal village in Plymouth, and killed eleven of its inhabitants.

The tide of war now rolling towards the Plymouth Colony, the authorities despatched Captain Michael Pierce of Scituate, with fifty of the English, and twenty friendly Indians from Cape Cod, to attack the remains of the Narragansett tribe, who, exasperated with their recent defeat, lost no opportunity of falling upon defenceless settlements. Capt. Pierce having been waylaid by a strong force of the enemy, near Pawtucket Falls, a severe action took place March 26, 1676, in which Capt. Pierce was killed, and all of his white companions, save one, met the same sad fate. The loss of the enemy was supposed to be nearly thrice as great. This was the most serious disaster sustained by the Plymouth Colony during the war.

Scituate was attacked April 20, and nineteen houses and barns burned. The inhabitants succeeded in repelling the enemy. Bridgewater was attacked May 8, but the assailants were repulsed. During the whole war, though Bridgewater was repeatedly attacked, and though Bridgewater men faced the enemy in battle, not a single inhabitant of that town was killed.

On the 12th, of August, 1676, Philip, the chief promoter of all this mischief, beset at his own home on the peninsula of Mount Hope by the forces of that brave partisan leader, Capt. Benjamin Church, was killed by a Saconet Indian, named Alderman, and the war substantially ended.

In this severe struggle, Plymouth Colony was nearly ruined. After many ineffectual attempts to obtain a charter—which it never possessed—Plymouth Colony was annexed to Massachusetts in 1692.

The history of the County since that time is merged in the history of Massachusetts. Until this day, however, some portion of the distinctive traits of the first settlers may be discerned among its population. To a remarkable degree, the old Pilgrim love of liberty, coupled with the determination to do right at all hazards, still exists among their descendants. During the long and arduous struggle, which so recently ended in the overthrow of slavery in our land, no portion of the American people were more outspoken, and perhaps none so nearly unanimous in their condemnation of that enormous wrong, as the people of the three southern counties of Massachusetts.

The County of Plymouth has furnished its full proportion of talent, of genius, of learning, and of enterprise; though men of eminence have often been drawn off to wider fields of action. Its sons have borne their full share of toil, of effort, and of suffering, in all the contests in which the country has been engaged, and have often been advanced to positions of honor and influence.

The County of Plymouth was organized in 1685, and then consisted of the following towns:

Plymouth, then including Plympton, Kingston, Carver, part of Halifax, and part of Wareham.

Duxbury, then including Pembroke and Hanson, and small portions of Kingston.

Scituate, then including Hanover.

Marshfield.

Bridgewater, then including West Bridgewater [the original settlement], North Bridgewater, East Bridgewater, and Bridgewater, the last having been known as the South Parish in Bridgewater.

Middleborough, including Lakeville, and part of Halifax.

Accord Pond Shares, } Plantations, parts of Scituate, Hanover,
Ford's Farm, } and the whole of Abington.

Accord Pond in Abington, [I think], was so named to commemorate the harmony of the Commissioners, who run the line between the Colonies of Massachusetts Bay and Plymouth.

There are no *data* from which we can learn the precise population of the County of Plymouth at that time, nor for a long time after. In 1675, the whole population of the Colony of Plymouth, including what in 1685 became the counties of Plymouth, Bristol and Barnstable, was estimated at seven thousand, five hundred, (7,500.) The population of those three counties did not in 1685, probably exceed 10,000. The population of Plymouth County at that time may be set down as not exceeding 4000.

Some estimate may be formed of the comparative population and importance of the several towns composing Plymouth County, from the following statement.

In 1690, a body of troops was raised in Plymouth Colony, to be under the command of Major Benjamin Church, and to march against the Indians, who were then ravaging our eastern frontier, or the portion of Maine which lies between the Piscataqua and the Kennebec. The soldiers who were to go, and the money to be raised were apportioned among the towns of Plymouth County as follows:

Plymouth was to pay 5 pounds and raise 4 men.
Duxbury, "   " 2.10 "   " 2 "
Scituate, "   " 8   "   " 6 "
Marshfield, "   " 4   "   " 3 "
Bridgewater, " " 3   "   " 3 "
Middleboro, "   " 1   "   " 1 "
                   ———   ——
                   £23:10   19

From this it appears that Scituate was then the most important town in the county. If a sufficient number of volunteers could not be obtained, the deficiency was to be supplied by impressment.

A portion of the force which was to go with Church, was raised in the other counties, Bristol and Barnstable. I believe also that a portion of Church's command was raised in the neighboring Colony of Massachusetts. In Plymouth Colony, all the able-bodied males between 16 and 60 were enrolled in the military companies, though clergymen and many others were exempted.

In 1692, the Colonies of Plymouth and Massachusetts Bay, were united, much to the dissatisfaction of the former.

Authorities consulted in the preparation of the foregoing sketch. Baylies' [Francis] Historical Memoir of the Colony of New Plymouth. Barry's [John Stetson] History of Massachusetts. Palfrey's [John Gorham] History of New England. Felt's [Joseph Barlow] Ecclesiastical History of New England. Drake's [Samuel Gardner] History of Boston. Hawe's [Joel] Tribute to the Memory of the Pilgrims. American Quarterly Register.

ABINGTON.

BY REV. H. D. WALKER.

THERE seems something prophetic in the naming of this town. It must always stand at the head of all alphabetical arrangments of the towns of Plymouth County, for none that might possibly be incorporated can so spell themselves as to take precedence. Yet those who gave it the name could hardly have anticipated that in one hundred and fifty years the almost wilderness they so designated would be the first town in the county in population, business and wealth.

Back from the shore and consequently having no harbors, having no considerable streams and no great water power because it is the almost level water shed between the bays on either side, it did not invite the early settlers of the county. There is nothing romantic or attractive in its scenery, and the soil though strong and productive is generally rough and hard. It is not strange therefore that at its incorporation in 1710, the town had probably less than 300 inhabitants, only three times the number Plymouth had, when, ninety years before, the Pilgrims had landed. At the first census in 1726, the number had increased only to 371.

At that period and long afterwards it was for the surrounding country a "lumbering region." "Saw mills" and "ship timber" were the business terms. Saw mills were erected in 1698, and the settlers looked to Hingham, Scituate, Hanover, Duxbury, Plymouth, where ships were built and commerce and trade prospered, as the old and wealthy towns upon which they depended for a market and supplies. The quality and quantity of the timber produced is illustrated by the fact, remembered by the old people with grateful pride, that the renowned frigate Constitution, the "Old Ironsides" was built in great part of Abington white oak. But the time came when *the soil* that produced this giant growth of timber must offer in its culture the principal business, and so agriculture be the dependence of the town. Very naturally there was at that period much emigration to regions that seemed better adapted to that pursuit than this hard, rough soil that demanded so much labor.

For a long period there was consequently very little growth. There had been some little manufacturing quite early, some rude "earthen ware," "meeting house bells," and "cannon and shot" for the war of the revolution. "Tacks," still an important item in the business of the town, were early made by hand, and a citizen, Mr. Jesse Reed, invented the machine which has given the business such impulse.

There were other home manufactures on a small scale by the industrious inhabitants who seem purposed that the town shall always be worthy of its old Indian name "Manamooskeagin" said to signify "many beavers." But the introduction of the Boot and Shoe business after 1820 or 30, and the turning to that manufacture the enterprise and energy of the people, gave a marked impulse to the prosperity and growth of Abington. Rapidly passing town after town in the county it has now nearly reached the point where it could claim incorporation as a city.

Fortunately or unfortunately there are four distinct centres of its business and population, and Centre, North, South and East Abington have perhaps less business intercourse with each other than with Boston. These three other villages are each about two miles distant from the Centre, and the Old Colony Rail Road, the avenue of trade for the four, opened in 1845, treating them quite impartially; touches and so fully accommodates none. The Hanover Branch, to be opened in the Summer or Fall of '67, will pass through the East village and perhaps give a new impulse to that already largest section of the town.

There are four Orthodox Congregationalist Societies, one in each village, a Baptist Society in the South and East, a New Jerusalem and Universalist at the Centre, all with good, and some with elegant houses of worship.

Perhaps no town in the State has so large a proportion of children to its valuation. With as many scholars as some towns that have many fold its wealth, and divided into so many different villages, it cannot foolishly attempt to vie with such towns in school buildings, and only by the most rigid and wise economy maintain good schools, which the people have always been most earnest to do. Such has always been the absorbing business activity and energy of the people, that very few of its young men have ever found their way to College. Their chosen path to usefulness and eminence has been that of manufacture and trade rather than literature.

BOOT AND SHOE FACTORY OF WILLIAM L. REED, SOUTH ABINGTON.

INGLESIDE
Boarding and Day School,
FOR YOUNG LADIES,

MIDDLEBORO,   -   -   -   MASS.

Designed as a School of the highest order, combining thorough individual instruction with all home influences and attractions.

Location beautiful. Grounds ample for all out-door exercises and recreations.

It will be the constant aim of the Principals to secure the welfare and improvement of their pupils in all respects.

MRS. REV. S. G. DODD,
MISS MARY E. MAXWELL, } Principals.

Mrs. E. W. Foss, Teacher of Vocal and Instrumental Music.

For Circulars, address as above.

Sea Side Boarding School
FOR YOUNG LADIES AND MISSES,
Mattapoisett, Mass.

MRS. H. B. PRATT, Principal.
MISS SARAH E. PRATT, Assistant.

Mrs. Pratt, in connection with the education of her own daughters, is prepared to receive into her family and school, a limited number of Young Ladies and Misses from ten to sixteen years of age.

The school is in a quiet, healthy locality, just beside the beach, with a southern outlook over the beautiful bay, making it popular as a Summer resort. Mattapoisett is in easy communication with New Bedford, Boston and Providence.

No effort will be spared to furnish a happy, joyous home. The system of instruction will be thorough and familiar, avoiding as far as possible the tendency of viewing study simply as an irksome task.

Special pains will be taken with the physical development of the Young Ladies. This branch will be under the charge of the Assistant Teacher, who has had previous experience as an instructor in accordance with Dio Lewis' popular system of Gymnastics. A judicious application in this direction, in connection with the ocean air and sea bathing, will aid essentially in the development of vigorous and healthy constitutions.

The moral and religious natures of the scholars will receive most careful attention.

EXPENSES.

Tuition, English Branches, and Board, per week, $5.00; Music, Piano Forte, per quarter, $12.00; Use of Piano, $3.00; Vocal Music, $3.00; Pencil Drawing, $4.00; Crayon Drawing, $5.00; Wax Flowers, $8.00; Latin, $5.00; French, $5.00.

The year is divided into three terms, 12 weeks each.

Spring Term commences Wednesday, April 3, closes June 25; Fall Term commences Sept. 4, closes Nov. 26; Winter Term commences Dec. 11, closes Mch. 4.

G. W. WARE & CO.,
12 CORNHILL AND 125 WASHINGTON STREETS,
BOSTON, MASS.

FURNITURE
—AND—
UPHOLSTERY GOODS,

Drapery Curtains, Window Shades, Feather Beds, Mattresses, Looking Glasses, Rich Drawing Room, Parlor, Library, Dining and Chamber

FURNITURE
OF
ROSEWOOD, MAHOGANY, WALNUT, OAK, CHESTNUT,
AND PAINTED IN EVERY VARIETY OF STYLE TO SUIT THE PURCHASER.

The best Invalid and Reclining Chair made. Call and see it.

FAMILY DYE COLORS,
PATENTED OCT. 13, 1867.
ALL SHADES, BOTH POWDER AND LIQUID.

Black,	Crimson,	Orange.
Black, for silk,	Dark Drab,	Pink,
Dark Blue,	Fawn Drab,	Purple,
Light Blue,	Lt. Fawn Drab,	Royal Purple,
French Blue,	Light Drab,	Salmon,
Dark Brown,	Dark Green,	Scarlet,
Claret Brown,	Light Green,	Slate,
Light Brown,	Maize,	Solferino,
Snuff Brown,	Maroon,	Violet,
Cherry,	Magenta.	Yellow.

For Dyeing Silks, Woolen and Mixed Goods, Shawls, Scarfs, Dresses, Ribbons, Gloves, Bonnets, Hats, Feathers, Children's Clothing, and all kinds of wearing apparel.

SILVERINE
An entirely new invention, for instantaneously
SILVER PLATING

Articles of Brass, Copper, German Silver, Bronze, &c. And for Cleaning and Polishing Silver and Silver Plated Ware. Applied to Silver Plated Ware, Fruit Dishes, Castors, Stair Rods, Harness Trimmings, Military Equipments, Door Knobs, and Plates, Metallic Window and Show Case Frames, &c., whose plating is worn off, it gives them all the beauty of new ware, which they will retain if the Silverine is applied as often as such articles are ordinarily cleaned.

HOWE & STEVENS, Manufacturers,
260 Broadway, Boston, Mass.

The citizens of Abington have however never fallen behind those of any other town in appreciating all the great issues of every period of our history. They were not tories in the war of the revolution, they were ready to defend their country in that of 1812, they rushed to save it when lately traitors would destroy.

It is not to the fact that the Boot and Shoe business of the town is now probably about $4,000,000 annually, the Tack and other branches most successfully prosecuted, to the general thrift and prosperity of the town, but to its record on the side of patriotism and right, that those who would know Abington are pointed. No town lost more by the breaking out of the rebellion. More than a million of dollars were at once sunk in debts at the South. The shock was fearful, but courage did not fail and money and men and goods were raised without stint for the country. A company from Abington was one of those that within twenty-four hours after the first call for 75,000 men, were on their way to Fortress Monroe. More than a full regiment, 1138 from this town enlisted during the war. The town furnished more than its quota of officers. Two Lieutenant Colonels, Three Majors, Twelve Captains, Seven 1st Lieutenants, Twelve 2d Lieutenants.

The present condition, the business prospects of the town, will best be learned from the Directory. Those who desire to know the particulars of its history are referred to "the History of Abington," published in 1866, by Benjamin Hobart, Esq., one of its oldest and most honored citizens. We are indebted to Mr. Hobart's work for valuable engravings as well as the following facts:—

The records of the first Church, earlier than 1724, cannot be found. At that time there were 49 members. The first house of worship stood in front of the old burying-ground. It had neither steeple, bell or pews. The second edifice was erected in 1751; the third in 1819; and the present house in 1849. The Pastors were Samuel Brown, 1714-1749; Ezekiel Dodge, 1750-1770; Samuel Niles, 1771-1814; Holland Weeks, 1815-1820; Samuel Spring, jr., 1822-1826; Wm. Shedd, 1829-1830; Melancthon G. Wheeler, 1831-1833; James W. Ward, 1834-1856; F. R. Abbe, present pastor, ordained Sep. 9, 1857.

The second Parish was formed in 1807, of inhabitants of South Abington and East Bridgewater, after strenuous opposition. The house of worship was dedicated and Rev. Daniel Thomas was ordained in 1808, dismissed in 1842. There were 16 members. Dennis Powers was minister eight years; Selden Hayes, and Alfred Goldsmith, one year each. H. L. Edwards, present pastor, installed in 1855.

The Third Church was formed at the house of Samuel Reed, Aug. 27, 1813. Pastors, Samuel W. Colburn, 1813-1830; Lucius Alden, 1832-1834; Horace D. Walker ordained in 1844.

4

The First Baptist Church was constituted Oct. 29, 1822, with 11 members. The settlements have been:—Willard Kimball L. 24-1826; David Curtis, 1825-1828; Silas Hall, 1830-1834; W. H. Dalrymple, 1835-1837; D. C. Messinger, 1837-1845; W. P. Stubbert, 1846-1852; Nath'l. Colver, D. D., 1852-1853; Horace T. Love, 1853-1854; F. A. Willard, 1854-1856; J. C. Wightman, 1857-1858; N. Judson Clark, present pastor, entered upon his labors, Dec. 11, 1860.

The First Society of the New Jerusalem, was organized in 1840, though Rev. Holland Weeks, pastor of the First Cong'l. Church was the first receiver of the doctrines, and began to preach them in 1820 In 1838, Joseph Pettee, was ordained pastor.

The First Universalist Society, dates its first meeting, April 6, 1836. Thompson Barron, was the first pastor, Mr. Hewitt, 1840-1845; Q. H. Howe, 1845-1846; Leander Hussey, 1846-1848; J. Whittier, 1848-1849; N. Gunnison, 1850-1853; E. S. Foster, 1855-1856; V. Lincoln, 1857-1860; J. Crehore was settled July, 1860.

The Congregational Church, North Abington, was organized Oct. 3, 1839, with 19 members. Pastors, Willard Peirce, 1849-1850; Isaac C. White, 1850-1859; Wm. Leonard and Benj. Dodge.

The Baptist Church in East Abington, was organized in May, 1854, with 22 members. Pastors, Horace T. Love, Wm. P. Everett, Wm. S. McKenzie, Jeremiah Chaplain, D. D., and Sereno Howe.

The Catholic Church was organized in 1854, by Rev. Mr. Roddan. In 1856, Rev. Mr. Roche, present incumbent was appointed. The church edifice, capable of seating more people than any similar building in the County, "was consecrated by the Right Rev. Bishop McFarland, of Hartford, under the invocation of St. Bridget, Patroness of Ireland."

The Semi-Centennial Celebration of the town was held June 10th, 1862, at Island Grove, (one of the most popular resorts for open-air meetings in the State.) The oration was delivered by Rev. D. Porter Dyer. Fifty soldiers of the war of 1812, appeared in procession, together with Bands, Military, Masonic, Sons of Temperance, and Public School organizations.

for breach of the Sabbath. In 1805, it was voted to divide the town, but this was soon after re-considered.

Slavery formerly existed in Abington. Isaac Hobart held several, previous to the Revolution. Rev. Mr. Brown had five. Some of these blacks lived to a great age.

No fire department or engine company has ever been organized in Abington, and there have been very few destructive fires, that of B. Hobart & Son's Tack Factory, was the most serious. Loss, $30,000.

Destructive tornadoes prevailed in Oct. 1804, and Sept. 1815. Thousands of fruit and forest trees were blown down, scores of barns and houses were unroofed, and many lives were lost.

Five natives of Abington became lawyers.

17 Abington men were lost in the Old French war, and in the Revolution, almost every man capable of bearing arms was in service for a longer or shorter period.

92 natives of Abington have received a college education, 13 of them becoming ministers.

The manufacture of earthen-ware was introduced in 1765, by Henry Benner. Meeting-house bells were cast for a number of years, at Col. Aaron Hobart's factory. During the Revolutionary war a large number of cannons were cast here.

The first tack factory was built by Benj. Hobart, in 1820, near the South Abington depot. The present factory, owned by Dunbar, Hobart & Whitten is built of brick, 188 by 18 feet, with L, 334 by 67 feet, besides adjoining buildings.

The Tack Factory of Henry H. Brigham, located a little east, was erected in 1865. The front building is 58 by 30 feet, with shop 180 by 36 feet, engine house, &c.

The Tack Factory of David B. Gurney, located at the Centre, is 110 by 30 feet.

The Shoe manufactory of J. Lane & Sons, East Abington, is a model building of its kind, 40 by 30 feet, three stories and basement, heated by steam. $350,000 worth of shoes manufactured here annually.

Leonard Blanchard's Shoe manufactory is located at the East. In 1865, $250,000 worth of goods were manufactured.

The Shoe Factory of Joshua L. Nash, at the Center, was formerly known as the "King House." Over 1200 pairs of shoes can be turned out per day. $300,000 worth of goods were manufactured in 1865.

There are many other extensive boot and shoe establishments in Abington, among them those owned by Washington Reed and A. Chamberlain, for making fur-lined goods.

NOTE.—For list of soldiers deceased in the late war, see Appendix.

BRIDGEWATER.

BY HOSEA KINGMAN, ESQ.

BRIDGEWATER was originally a plantation granted to Duxbury, by the Old Colony Court, in the year 1645, to compensate that town for its recent loss of territory by the incorporation of the town of Marshfield. The original grant to the inhabitants of Duxbury was of a competent proportion of land about Saughtuckquett (Satucket), towards the west "four miles every way from the place where they shall set up their center." This being a mere right to purchase of the natives, afterwards in 1649, a tract of land usually called Satucket, extending seven miles each way from the weir at Satucket, was granted to Miles Standish, Samuel Nash and Constant Southworth, in behalf of the town of Duxbury, by Ousamequin, who afterwards styled himself Massasoit.

Although the grant from the Court was only four miles every way from a center, yet for some unexplained reason, this purchase from the Indians embraced seven miles every way from the weir. No center was fixed upon during the time that Bridgewater remained a part of Duxbury. In June, 1656, this plantation was incorporated, by an order of Court, into a separate and distinct town under the name of Bridgewater. In the same year Miles Standish having been granted by the Court three hundred acres, with a competency of meadow at Satucket, provided it did not intrench upon Bridgewater, it became necessary that the center of that town should be fixed upon.

After several years of delay, urged by repeated orders from the Court, the town finally assented to the setting up of its center, about a mile and a half west of the old weir. The monument, now a stone near where the house of Thomas Hayward stood and near the East and West depot, was a small white oak tree bearing the initials of Constant Southworth, who was probably the Court committee appointed to fix the center. In 1662, in answer to a petition by inhabitants of the town dated 1658, the Court granted and confirmed to them the meadow north and west from the center, and within the seven miles granted by Ousamequin. In 1668, upon a petition praying for an enlargement "the whole six miles from the center, east, west, north and south" was granted, provided that grants of land formerly made by the Court be not molested. This was known as the two mile additional grant and the first as the old four mile grant. By this grant were secured two additional miles on the north towards the Massachusetts Colony line, and part on the south, but little if any on the east and west, as on the east six miles from the center would interfere with an earlier grant called the Major's Purchase. On the south six miles would extend into the Indian settlement of Titicut, and all of the land on the North side of Titicut river was within the six miles. In or about the year 1672, Nicholas Byram, Samuel Edson and William Brett were appointed to purchase, and did purchase, by a deed from Pomponeho *alias* Peter, all the lands lying on the north side of Titicut river and within the bounds of Bridgewater, excepting two parcels afterwards purchased of the Indians by individuals.

In 1685, all of these grants were confirmed by deed under the hand of Governor Hancock and the seal of the Government; about the same time another deed confirming the deed of Ousamequin was made by Josiah Wampatuck to Samuel Edson, John Howard and John Willis, agents for the town of Bridgewater. Thus the greater part of the town was twice purchased of the Indians, once of Massasoit and again of Wampatuck. With a small tract of land on the North, along the Colony line, purchased by individuals after the union of the Colonies, and annexed to Bridgewater in October 1730, these several grants and enlargements constituted all the territory, ever belonging to Bridgewater in its greatest extent. In this situation, containing about ninety six square miles, the town remained without diminution in its territorial limits until June 10, 1712, when the town of Abington was incorporated. Again on the seventh of June 1754, a large tract of land, now forming the greater part of Hanson, was taken from Bridgewater and annexed to Pembroke. Thus the town remained for nearly one hundred years, containing about seventy square miles. There were of course divisions in reference to church matters, made from time to time, five parishes being formed, the North, South, East, West, and Titicut. These parishes or precincts constituted the ground work of the subsequent divisions of the town.

As early as 1719, the South, only three years after its incorporation as a parish, applied to the General Court, to be made a distinct town, this although agreed to by the remainder of the town and granted by the House, was not concurred in by the Council; again, in 1738, the North precinct petitioned to be incorporated as a town; the remainder of the town at the same time consented and voted that the South and East should become separate and distinct towns—all these applications were however resisted and it was not until June 15, 1821, that any change was made. At this time the North, the youngest, but most populous parish, was incorporated by the name of North Bridgewater. The West, (the old town), was incorporated February 16, of the next year, by the name of West Bridgewater, and the East, by the name of East Bridgewater was incorporated June 17, 1823. Thus the South Parish, although the first to move in the matter was left with Titicut to retain the old name. And now, as it was then left, it remains, containing twenty-eight and one-eighth square miles, or 18,800 acres, bounded by East and West Bridgewater on the north, Halifax on the east, Middleboro on the south and Raynham on the west. The town is very pleasantly situated, about midway between Boston and Fall River, __ miles from Taunton and eighteen miles from Plymouth, on the Old Colony and Newport Railway.

The first settlements in this town, and also the first in the interior of the Old Colony, were commenced in the year 1650, upon the Town river, which flows from Nippenicket pond, in the present town of West Bridgewater, principally by inhabitants from Duxbury. House lots of six acres were granted these first settlers. The house lots were contiguous, and the settlement compact, to serve as a protection against the Indians. Among the names of these first settlers we find those of James Keith, the first minister, Deacon Samuel Edson from Salem, who built the first mill in the place, in about 1653, and Bassett, and Mitchell who were among the forefathers. The adjoining towns of Marshfield and Taunton were also represented in this settlement. From the west the town grew in a southerly direction towards the great pond on the road to Taunton, with which place the people had considerable intercourse. Until within a few years of the incorporation of the North precinct, the South and Titicut parishes were most populous; later, there was a rapid growth in the northerly part of the town. Now, the present town, although it has been slowly increasing in population, and within a few years there has been a rapid increase in a northerly direction about the iron works, has fallen considerably behind the other Bridgewaters, except perhaps the West. Its own children manifest a strong disposition to go abroad and take up their abode elsewhere, while their places are filled by a foreign population; still there yet remain descendants bearing the names of those ancient settlers, Hayward, Willis, Bassett, Washburn, Ames, Mitchell, Keith and Edson. And there are now in town, besides the numerous public buildings, manufactories, stores, workshops, &c., nearly six hundred dwelling houses, accommodating four thousand one hundred and ninety-six inhabitants. In wealth, it yields to no town of its size in the state, the amount of property assessed during the past year being 1,068,840 dollars.

The surface of the town is generally level, the only high ground, and even that not very high, is Sprague's Hill, in the eastern part. The soil is generally fertile and for the most part in a good state of cultivation. The people are very industrious and for a town of its size the number of idlers, and the number of places for their accommodation, is very small. Although considerable attention is paid to farming, yet this by no means constitutes the chief employment. Manufactures of various kinds are largely carried on. In the old town, in Titicut parish, were made, at the commencement of the revolution, small arm and cannons, probably the first ever made in the country. And now the manufacture of iron in the establishment of the Bridgewater Iron Manufacturing Company, incorporated in 1825, [the business having been previously carried on by Lazell, Carey & Co., and Lazell Perkins & Co.,] furnishing employment for hundreds of men and requiring the aid of some of the heaviest machines of the kind in the country, is the most extensive of any in the state. The heaviest work in the world is made in these works. Here also was built the greater part of the iron work for many of those "Yankee cheese boxes," the monitors. The manufacture of copper and yellow metal is also carried on extensively by this corporation. The manufacture of cotton gins was here commenced very early and is now largely carried on in the establishments of Bates, Hyde & Co., and Joseph E. Carver. Cotton Gins are sent from these two manufactories to nearly all parts of the world. Both of them are to be represented in the coming World's Fair, at Paris. There are also in town several foundries, [one new and very large recently erected by Henry Perkins], a paper mill, box and saw mills, and two brick-yards furnishing nearly three millions of bricks in a year and employing about fifty men.

Bridgewater is quite noted for its various institutions of learning, and as in former times, where it quite early in its history, subscribed liberally for the aid of the college at Cambridge, and was there largely represented, has paid great attention to education, both public and private. The first corporate action for the establishment of schools was taken in 1700, when Thomas Martin was engaged for four years, to keep a school in four places in town, each year. Its academy, established as early as 1799, is still maintained and is now in a most flourishing condition, under the able tuition of Horace Willard, a graduate of Brown University. This time-honored institution has received and sent forth into the world hundreds of pupils, scattering broadcast its influences throughout the land. Here also is established the State Normal School, the school of teachers. This institution has been largely patronized, and at present under the charge of Albert G. Boyden, attended by seventy-five pupils from various parts of the State, gives great promise for the future. And the last act of the town, when it abolished the school districts and established the town system, was one great step towards the accomplishment of that much desired result, a perfect system of public education.

The first meeting-house in the old town was built as early as 1663, in what is now West Bridgewater, and the first within the limits of the present town, was built in 1717. Now there are six churches in various parts of the town, each largely attended. Here also was built, in 1853, a State Alms-House, situated in the southern part of the town. Part of this is now being changed to a Work-House.

In its military history, Bridgewater has nobly sustained the honors it gained in its infancy, during the struggle with the Indians, (King

Philip's war.) Then, although removed from their friends, situated in the midst of the Indians' country, and numbering not more than fifty capable of bearing arms, urged by every possible inducement to retire to the sea shore, they still resolutely held out. They were the first to take up arms, and that, too, not only in defence of themselves, but to aid the town of Salem. The meeting-house was converted into a fortress, by means of palisadoes. In 1676, the Indians, about three hundred strong, having made an attack upon the easterly part of the town, were repulsed and overcome by the inhabitants issuing from the garrison. Nearly all the houses were burned on the borders of the town. Yet, notwithstanding the various encounters and the great courage and activity of the people, not one of this feeble settlement is known to have been killed. In the revolution, too, it stands forth as patriotic and as true to liberty as any of its neighbors, bearing its full proportion of its trials and burdens. During this time, the male population capable of bearing arms, did not exceed one thousand. In the Continuential service, exclusive of the Province and State service, during three years of the war, it furnished four hundred and twelve men, more than three thousand dollars, besides contributions of various supplies for the army. Among the number of killed are the names of Capt. Jacob Allen and Abner Robinson, who were killed at Saratoga, at the capture of Burgoyne, in 1777.

And in the last struggle for the maintenance of those principles of liberty and justice, in the establishing of which it had taken so active a part, it stands forth in all the strength of its riper years, and responds nobly to the country's call, furnishing forty men more than were required to fill its quota, paying out freely from its treasury thousands of dollars and sending to the relief of its soldiers, provisions and supplies of various kinds in abundance, withholding nothing even to the end of the war. Company K, of the third Massachusetts regiment was mainly composed of men from this town. Also a large portion of this company re-enlisted in the Fifty-Fourth regiment and there did good service at the battles of the Wilderness and before Petersburg. The town has sacrificed some of its best men upon the altar of its country, and we have but to mention the names of: —

Josiah Benson Jr., of Co. I, 58th Reg't. who died at City Point, Va.; Woodbridge Bryant, Co. E, 38th, Reg't. who died at Carrolton, La.; Philo Carver, who died at Baton Rouge, La.; Charles W. Clifford, Co. C, 29th Reg't, died in Bridgewater; Seth W. Conant, Co. D, 58th Reg't, killed at Petersburg, Va.; Lucius Conant, Co. D, 58th Reg't, killed; Frederick E. Fuller, died at Newbern, N. C.; S. C. Grovesnor, Co. C, 29th Reg't, killed near Petersburg, Va.; John T. Hartford, Co. D, 2d. Cavalry killed; Edwin A. Hayward, Co. I, 38th Reg't, who died at Baton Rouge, La.; Samuel Jones, Co. K, 3d Reg't, died at Newbern, N. C.; Corp. A. Bartlett Keith, Co. I, 7th Reg't, who died from

MACHINE BELTING.
STEAM PACKING,
AND ENGINE HOSE.

MANUFACTURED BY THE

Boston Belting Co.

(INCORPORATED 1845.)

This belting being made of HEAVY COTTON DUCK, coated with the BEST OF INDIA RUBBER, it is unaffected by HEAT, COLD, or MOISTURE, and is preferred to leather or that of any other material for

ELEVATORS, GIN BANDS, AGRICULTURAL MACHINES,
FLOURING MILLS,

And for every other purpose for which BELTING is used.

THE INDIA RUBBER HOSE

Is of all sizes, for CONDUCTING and HYDRANT purposes, and for LEADING and SUCTION HOSE for HAND and STEAM FIRE ENGINES, and is preferred by the Fire Departments and Engine Builders throughout the United States. *The Suction Hose is made by a greatly improved process,* INVENTED *and* PATENTED *by ourselves, and excels every other make for service and efficiency.*

THE STEAM PACKING

is used by the most skillful Engineers and Machinists in the world, for Manhole Plates, Piston Rods, Steam Joints, and for all parts of Machinery where packing is necessary. Also, all other articles of

VULCANIZED INDIA RUBBER,

used for mechanical and manufacturing purposes, made in the most skillful manner, and on the most favorable terms.

JOHN G. TAPPAN & CO., *General Agents,*
CORNER SUMMER AND CHAUNCY STREETS,
Boston, Mass.

$4\tfrac{1}{2}$

Established 1810, Dunbar, Hobart & Whidden, (successors to B. Hobart & Son,) manufacturers of Tacks, Brads, Shoe Nails, &c., South Abington, Mass. (See next page.)

(Established 1810)

DUNBAR, HOBART & WHIDDEN,

SUCCESSORS TO

B. HOBART & SON,

MANUFACTURERS OF

SWEDES & AMERICAN IRON,

TACKS, BRADS,

AND

PATENT BRADS,

Iron, Steel, and Zinc Shoe Nails, Finishing Nails, Trunk and Clout Nails, Cigar Box Nails, Copper Tacks and Nails, Brush Tacks, Shoe Tacks.

Silvered & Japanned Lining,

AND

SADDLE NAILS,

Leathered Head Carpet Tacks, Tinned Nails, and

TACKS OF ALL KINDS.

Also, Heel and Toe Plates, and Screw Head Nails for Boots and Shoes, Glaziers' Points, &c.

☞ Any variation from the above, in shape or size, or any new kinds made to order from sample.

SOUTH ABINGTON, MASS.

WM. H. DUNBAR.   HENRY HOBART.   H. F. WHIDDEN.

KNICKERBOCKER
LIFE INSURANCE CO.,
161 Broadway, N. Y.
ORGANIZED 1853.
ASSETS, 1867, $2,000,000.

ERASTUS LYMAN, President.

GEO. F. SNIFFEN, Secretary.

Directors.

ERASTUS LYMAN,	President.
CHARLES STANTON,	Merchant, 81 Front Street.
ISAAC KIP, Jr.,	Broker.
HUGH ALLEN,	Western Transp. Line, No. 1 Coenties Slip.
AARON WILBUR,	President Home Insurance Co., Savannah, Ga.
JOHN ANDERSON,	Tobacconist, 111 Liberty Street.
WM. B. HUNTER,	Merchant, 15 Old Slip.
GILMAN W. PRICHARD,	Merchant, 81 Front Street.
JAMES L. MORGAN,	Merchant, 17 Fulton Street.
SOLON F. GOODRIDGE,	Merchant, 32 Broad Street.
E. K. HAIGHT,	Merchant, 331 Broadway.
JOHN B. KITCHING,	25 Pine Street.
B. F. JOHNSON,	Manager of Western Branch Office, Chicago.
JOHN A NICHOLS,	Manager South Western Branch Office, Baltimore.

NEW ENGLAND BRANCH,
Under the management of
N. T. MERRITT,
GENERAL AGENT,
No. 113 Washington Street, Boston, Mass.

REFERENCES.

Hon. Oliver Warner, Secretary of State.
" S. N. Stockwell, 120 Washington Street.
" Jas. M. Usher, 27 Cornhill.
Messrs. Sewall, Day & Co., 83 Commercial Street.
" Baldwin, Bonme & Co., 10 City Wharf.
" Chase, Merritt & Blanchard, 20 and 22 Pearl Street.
" Lee & Shepard, 149 Washington Street.
" Cheney & Milliken, 1 Otis Street.
" Dodge, Collier & Perkins, 113 Washington Street.
" Stevens & Barrett, 196 Congress Street.
" Joyce & Richardson, 41 and 43 Fulton Street.
" William Haskins & Son, 129 State Street.
Edwin Pope, Esq., 282 Harrison Avenue.
Stephen M. Grant, Esq., 276 Harrison Avenue.
G. F. Burkhardt, Esq., Roxbury.
John W. Blanchard, Jr., Esq., 9 and 11 Haverhill Street.

wounds received at Chancellorsville; John C. Lambert, Co. C, 29th Reg't, killed at Blains' Cross Roads, Va.; Homer S. Leach, Co. I, 16th Reg't, killed; Frank R. Lee, Co. D, 38th Reg't, died at Bridgewater; Nathan Mitchell, Co. F, 38th Reg't, died at Poolesville, Md.; Lysander W. Mitchell, who died in prison; Wm. T. Murphy who died in rebel prison; Henry B. Rogers, Co. F, 12th Reg't, who died at Bridgewater; James H. Schneider, chaplain 2d U. S. colored troops, who died in Florida; Francis A. Tuttle, Co. K, 31st Reg't, who died at Port Hudson; Roscoe Tucker, Co. I, 1st Cavalry, who died in rebel prison; Henry A. Washburn, Co. D, 58th Reg't, killed at Petersburg, Va.; Joseph A. White, 11th Reg't, who died at Washington, D. C.; Benj. F. Winslow, 1st Battery, who died at Bridgewater; Rufus W. Wood, 18th Reg't, who died at Harrison's Landing Va.; William B. Wrightington, Co. K, 24th Reg't, who died at Annarundel, Md.

The fallen, lost during the rebellion, bring vividly to mind men of sterling virtues and great worth.

> "The gallant man, though slain in fight he be,
> Yet leaves his country safe, his nation free,
> Entails a debt on all the grateful state;
> His own brave friends shall glory in his fate,
> His wife live honored, and all his race succeed
> And late posterity enjoy the deed." —[POPE'S HOMER.

NOTE.—The writer is greatly indebted to Mitchell's History, for many facts.

CARVER.

BY DR. NATHANIEL B. SHURTLEFF.

THE portion of Massachusetts territory now called Carver, was settled about the year 1638, by families belonging to the Colony of New Plymouth. Towns in the Old Colony were formed in a peculiar manner; when a town became too large for one parish, a second was started, and in due course of time a new precinct was established; this in time was incorporated by the General Court of the Colony, on condition that a minister should be supported. Carver was therefore for many years a constituent part of the old town of Plymouth. On the 4th of June, 1707, the precinct in which Rev. Isaac Cushman, a son of the venerable Elder of the Plymouth Church, had gathered a church, and over which he was ordained in 1698, was incorporated as the town of Plympton. On the decease of Mr. Cushman, in 1732, another church was formed in the southern part of the town, and Rev. Othniel Campbell, a native of Bridgewater, and a graduate of Harvard College, was ordained over it in the year 1734. This new parish became the South Precinct, and on the 9th of June, 1790, was incorporated by the General Court as a town, and was named Carver, a very appropriate name, in honor of the memory of the first Governor of the Plymouth Colony, and very judiciously, as this very excellent man left no descendents to carry his name to posterity.

Carver is about eight miles S. S. W. of Plymouth, and about thirty-eight S. E. from Boston. The town is bounded on its north by Plympton on a line of about four miles; east by Kingston, one and a half miles, and by Plymouth seven miles; S. E. four miles by Plymouth; and S. W. by Wareham, about four miles; and west by Middleboro, about eight miles.

The town is not much noted for its rich soil and productions, the chief growth of wood being pitch pine, with a proportion of red and black oak. Nature, however, has in some degree compensated for this neglect by providing a large tract of about seven hundred acres of valuable white cedar swamp in the centre of the town. It is well supplied with streams, the South Meadow and Weweantic furnishing part of its boundary on Middleboro and Wareham. Wankonquag Brook on the Plymouth line, and Beaver Dam Brook and Cedar Brook meandering through its fields and forests. Sampson's Pond, near which is the "Charlotte Furnace" is rich with iron ore. Mohootset Pond with its brook, where is the ancient "Pope's Point Furnace," and Crane Brook Pond where was the "Federal Furnace," which was erected in 1794, are evidences of the well-watered condition of the town. Besides these are Wenham, Cooper's, Muddy, John's, Vaughan's, Flax, Clear, and Barrett's Ponds. The town is well supplied with necessary mills, and with workshops for the products of industry. It is said that the first cast-iron tea-kettle was made in Carver, not far from 1762; and it is certain that the furnaces have ever been famous for their hollow iron ware.

The succession of ministers of the old Congregational Church, have been, Othniel Campbell, 1734-1743; John Howland, 1746-1804; John Shaw, 1807-1815; Luther Wright, 1821-1825; Plummer Chase, 1828-1835; Paul Jewett, 1836-1839; Jona. King, 1839-1846; Ebenezer Gay, 1846-1851; Stillman Pratt, 1851-1854; William C. Whitcomb, who afterwards served as Chaplain in the army, where he died; Henry L. Chase, (present pastor.)

Of the other churches in Carver, the Baptist, at the Centre, was organized in 1791. Present Pastor, Wm. Leach. Their house of worship is very old, having been occupied one or more Sabbaths by Whitfield. There is in connection with the Society a fund for supporting Congregational preaching.

The Methodist Church at the South, was organized in 1831, and is in a flourishing condition.

The Union Society, at the South, was organized in 1853, and is composed of various denominations. They have a good house of worship.

When the town was incorporated in 1790, the most numerous names of the inhabitants were, Shurtleff, Cobb, Atwood, Shaw, Cole, Ransom, Dunham, Lucas, Vaughan, Sherman, Barrows, Savory, Hammond, Tillson, Murdock, Crocker, and Ellis; at the same time there were about one hundred and fifty families, which included eight hundred and forty-seven persons, twelve of whom were persons of color.

The South part of Carver, was for a long time known as "Sampson's Country," because in 1705, 200 acres, together with various special privileges, were reserved for the Sachem and his wife.

The people of South Carver have taken great pains in adorning and embellishing their Cemetery, until there are few, if any, more beautiful spots in the County. The first burial here was in 1776.

Carver lost severely in the late war. Among the Soldiers who died in service were :—

Lucius E. Griffith, died at Washington, D. C., Nov. 6th, 1863, of disease; James H. Stringer, died at Yorktown, Va., April 29th, 1862, of Typhoid Fever; George E. Bates, died at Baton Rouge, La., May 21st, 1863; Joseph F. Stringer, killed at second Bull Run, August 29th, 1862; William H. Barrows, killed at Gettysburg, Penn., July 2d, 1863; 1st. Serg't Bartlett Shaw, killed at Bull Run, Va., August 30th, 1862; Corporal Eli Atwood, Jr., died from wounds received at the Battle of Fredericksburg, Dec. 14th, 1862; Elbridge A. Shaw, died at Gains' Mills, Va., of Camp Fever, June 14th, 1862; Corporal Wilson McFarlin, killed at the Battle of Bull Run, Va., August 30th, 1862; Corporal Levi Shurtleff, Jr., died at Governor's Island, N. Y., of Camp Fever, Oct. 7th, 1862; Benj. W. Dunham, died at Alexandria, Va., of Chronic Diarrhœa, Oct. 26th, 1862; Allen S. Atwood, died at Washington, D. C., of wounds received at first Bull Run, Sept. 7th, 1862; Harry Finney, died at Campbell Hospital; John S. Robbins, killed at Bull Run, Va., August 30th, 1862; George H. Pratt, died from wounds received in battle, Oct. 19th, 1864—date of death unknown; Josiah E. Atwood, Brashear City, La., of Fever, July 11th, 1863; John Breach, died at New Orleans, May 11th, 1863; Alonzo D. Shaw, died at Newbern, N. C., of Measles and Chronic Diarrhœa, April, 18th, 1863; Corporal Lucien T. Hammond, died at Harrison's Landing, Va., Billious Dysentery, July 30th, 1862; Archibald Stringer; James McShea, died at Fortress Monroe, Va., of Small Pox, Jan. 13th, 1863; and Wm. H. O'Connell, died Sep. 30, 1863, of Consumption and Diarrhœa.

DUXBURY.

THE town was first settled about the year 1632, by the people of Plymouth, although it is probable, according to the records, that there were some settlers in Duxbury before this period. But they returned to Plymouth in the winter, to insure their better attendance at public worship, and also, to protect themselves from the attacks of the Indians.

The town was incorporated June 7th, 1637. It received its name, out of respect to Captain Miles Standish, from Duxbury Hall, the seat of the Standish family in England. Captain's Hill, formed a part of an early grant to Captain Standish, who settled near its base. The outlines of the foundation of his house are still visible.

The first tavern license was granted Francis Sprague in 1638. In 1678, the town licensed Mr. Seabury "to sell liquors into such sober minded naighbours, as hee shall think meet, see as hee sell not lesse then the quantitie of a gallon at a time to one person, and not in smaller quantities by retaile to the occasioning of drunkenss."

In 1643, there were 82 persons capable of bearing arms, this would show that the population was about 400. In 1800, there were 1664 inhabitants.

Among the earlier settlers of Duxbury, were some of the ablest men in the Colony, including John Alden, Wm. Brewster, Thomas Prence, George Soule and Joshua Pratt.

Inseparably connected with those early days will ever remain the story of the "Courtship of Miles Standish," so beautifully sung by Longfellow. The old warrior sent his fair-faced, stripling assistant, John Alden, to plead his case with Priscilla Mullins.

> "If the great Captain of Plymouth is so very eager to wed me,
> Why does he not come himself, and take the trouble to woo me?
> If I am not worth the wooing, I surely am not worth the winning!"
>
> * * * * * * * * *
>
> Archly the maiden smiled and, with eyes overrunning with laughter,
> Said, in a tremulous voice, "Why don't you speak for yourself, John?"

From John Alden, descended all of that name in the Old Colony.

Ralph Partridge, was settled over the Duxbury Church, in 1637. After a forty years, ministry he died at a good old age, and was interred in the first burying ground, on Harden Hill. John Holmes was his successor, who died in 1675. Ichabod Wiswall was settled in 1676, died in 1700. John Robinson, settled in 1702. He found great fault with his support and was dismissed, on this account, in 1738. Samuel Veasie was ordained in 1739, dismissed 1750. Charles Turner, 1752-1775; Zedekiah Sanger, 1776-1786; John Allyn, 1788-1825, after which date he had for colleague Benj. Kent, until his death in 1833. Rev. Josiah Moore, the present pastor, was settled in 1834.

The M. E. Church was organized in 1819. House of worship erected in 1823. The West Duxbury M. E. Church was organized in 1831. House erected in 1832. A chapel at North-West Kingston is connected with this church. The Wesleyan Methodist Church was organized about 1842, and house erected two years later.

"Partridge Academy" was founded by Hon. Geo. Partridge, who at the time of the Revolution, and afterwards, was a Member of Congress.

Hobomok, the Christian Indian, for twenty years the faithful friend of the Colony, lived here with Miles Standish.

Ship building was very extensively carried on at one time. In 1837, 11,711 tons were built. There was formerly a Bank and Insurance Office.

There were in the Army and Navy from Duxbury, 236 men. Thirty-five of these died in service, as follows:—

Charles E. Alden, Co. I, 4th Reg't, of Fever, at Quarantine Hospital, Mississippi River, March 9th, 1863; William Baily, Co. G, 38th Reg't, at Baton Rouge, of Diarrhœa, Mar. 29, 1863; James H. Bowen. Co. E, 18th, died June, 1864; Edward Bishop, Co. E, 18th Reg't, at Alexandria Hospital, Grace Church, Va., Nov. 10th, 1862, of Chronic Diarrhœa; Joshua T. Brewster, Co. I, 4th Reg't, of Chronic Diarrhœa, at Marine Hospital, New Orleans, August 2d, 1863; Geo. Bryant, Co. E, 18th Reg't, in Saulisbury Prison, Oct. 1st, 1864; Charles J. Chandler, Co. G, 38th Reg't, at General Hospital, Carrollton, La., of Bronchitis, Feb. 17th, 1863; David F. Church, Co. E, 18th Reg't, was killed at Bull Run, Aug. 30th, 1862; Stephen Clark, Jr., Co. I. 4th Reg't, of Disease, at Algiers, La., July 16th, 1863; John H. Crocker, Co. G, 38th Reg't, April 21st, 1863, at Berwick City Hospital, of wounds received at the Battle of Bisland; Daniel W. Delano, Co. I, 4th Reg't, of Chronic Diarrhœa, in Charity Hospital, New Orleans, March 22d, 1863; Oscar Delano, Co. I, 4th Reg't, of Diptheria, in Indianapolis, Aug. 15th, 1863; Francis B. Dorr, Co. G, 38th Reg't, at New Orleans, of Typhoid Pneumonia, May 13th, 1863; Harrison T. Glass, Co. I, 4th Reg't, of Congestive Fever, at Port Hudson, La., July 30th, 1863; Seth Glass, Co. G, 38th Reg't, at New Orleans, of wounds received at the Battle of Port Hudson, June 17th, 1863; Henry B. Paulding, Co. E, 18th Reg't, at Sharpsburg, Va., from wounds received at Bull Run; Walter Peterson, Co. I, 4th Reg't, of Typhoid Fever, at Port Hudson, August 3d, 1863; Daniel Rix, Co. E, 18th Reg't, was killed at the Battle of Bull Run, Aug. 30th, 1862; Bradford Sampson, Co. G, 38th Reg't, in New York City, of Typhoid Fever, Aug. 30th, 1864; Eden Sampson, Co. G, 38th Reg't, at Baton Rouge General Hospital, May 7, 1864; George B. Sampson, Co. I, 4th Reg't, of Chronic Diarrhœa, at Marine Hospital, New Orleans, July 11th, 1863; Aaron Snell, Co. E, 18th Reg't, was killed at

Bethesda Church, Jan. 3d, 1864; Aurelius Soule, Co. E, 18th Reg't. Feb. 28th, 1864, at Camp Hospital, Beverly Ford, Va., of Lung Complaint; John Southworth, Co. E, 18th Reg't, in 1864, in Rebel Prison; Daniel J. Simmons, at Berwick City Gen. Hospital, of wounds received at Battle of Bisland, La., May 10th, 1863; Joseph E. Simmons, Co. E, 18th Reg't, was killed at Bull Run, Aug. 30, 1862, he had been promoted Aug. 11th, 1862, as 1st Lieut. in the 38th Reg't, and had received his commission; Wilber F. Simmons, at Berwick City Gen. Hospital, of wounds received at Battle of Bisland, La., April 27th 1863; William Wadsworth, Co. I, 4th Reg't, at Court House Hospital, Baton Rouge, from wounds received in Battle at Port Hudson, July 24th, 1863; James H. Weston, Co. I, 4th Reg't, of Chronic Diarrhœa, in Charity Hospital, New Orleans, May 1st, 1863; Walter Weston, Co. E, 18th Reg't, was killed at Fredricksburg, Va., Dec. 14th, 1862; William Soule, Co. G, 38th Reg't, at Memphis, August 31st, 1863; William J. Keep, at Annapolis, Md., Mar. 16th, 1865, he had been a prisoner 7 months, and had just been released; Gershom Winsor, 54th Reg't, in New York, of Consumption, Dec. 29th, 1864; Elisha Swift, died in the service, not known when or where; Abel T. Lewis, Co. E, 4th Reg't, died June 26th, 1863. To perpetuate the memory of these fallen heroes, the citizens of Duxbury will erect a suitable Monument. Steps in that direction have already been taken, and nearly one thousand dollars have been secured for that purpose. The Monument will be located in the Cemetery, a lot having been already graded.

NOTE.—We are indebted to H. Barstow, for the soldier's list, and to Justin Winsor's very interesting history of Duxbury, published in 1849, for many facts.

EAST BRIDGEWATER.

BY WILLIAM ALLEN, ESQ.

ON the 23d of March, 1649, the Indian chief Massasoit deeded to Miles Standish, Samuel Nash, and Constant Southworth, Commissioners appointed by the Colonial government at Plymouth, a tract of land which now includes the four Bridgewaters, a part of Abington, and also of Hanson, for 7 coats, a yard and a half in a coat. 9 hatchets, 8 hoes, 20 knives, 4 moose-skins, and ten yards and a half of cotton. This contract was made and executed on a small hill in East Bridgewater, a little distance south-east of where the E. Carver & Co.'s Gin Works now stand, and on the farm now owned and occupied by Mr. Thomas Hewett. This territory was called Satucket.

The settlement of that part of the above described domain which is now called East Bridgewater, began in 1660, when Samuel Allen, jr., son of Samuel Allen of Braintree, emigrating hither, built a house a few rods from where the Bridgewater Branch of the Old Colony Railroad crosses Matfield river. The next settlers were Nicholas Byram, Thomas Whitman, William Brett, jr., and Robert Latham. These were the only inhabitants here previous to 1676, the time of King Phillip's war, when the dwelling houses of all the residents were burned by the Indians, except that of Nicholas Byram, which stood on the spot where is now the residence of Mr. Jotham Hicks.

On the 14th December, 1723, the east end of the North Parish of Bridgewater, which then included what is now the towns of West and North Bridgewater, together with 9 persons of the South Parish, (now Bridgewater), viz: Barnabas Seabury, Thomas Latham, Charles Latham, Nicholas Wade, Nathaniel Harden, Thomas Hooper, William Conant, Isaac Lazell, and Joseph Washburn, was made by the General Court, the East Parish of Bridgewater. The first meeting-house was built before the parish was formed, having been raised March 14th. 1720.

The church was gathered Oct. 28th, 1724, and consisted of thirty-three members, twelve male, twenty-one female. On the same day, Rev. John Angier, a native of Watertown, was ordained Pastor. He died April 14th, 1787, aged eighty-five years, and in the sixty-third year of his ministry. His son Samuel Angier, was settled as his colleague, Dec. 23d, 1767, and succeeded him as Pastor. He resigned his office March 25th, 1804, and died Jan. 18th, 1805, aged sixty-two years. The next Pastor, Rev. James Flint, was ordained 1806, and dismissed, 1821. His successors have been Rev. Benjamin Fessenden, ordained 1821, dismissed 1825; Rev. John A. Williams, ordained 1826, dismissed 1828; Rev. Eliphalet P. Crafts, ordained 1828, dismissed 1836. Rev. Nathaniel Whitman, installed 1844, dismissed 1852; Rev. Joseph H. Phipps, installed 1853, dismissed 1861; Rev. Silas Farrington, installed 1861, dismissed 1864. The present Pastor, Rev. Francis C. Williams, commenced his labors here 1865.

East Bridgewater was incorporated a town, June 14th, 1823. It is 25 miles south of Boston, and 17 from Plymouth, and contains 18 1-7 square miles. It has four villages, the Center, Joppa, Northville, and West Crooks, besides several other clusters of dwelling houses, which might perhaps properly be called villages. There have been eight religious societies within the limits of the town, in addition to the First Congregational, already mentioned, viz:

The Union Congregational, formed 1826.
The New Jerusalem, in Joppa village, formed 1831.
Universalist, formed 1834, not in operation.
Methodist, (Protestant), formed about 1843, not in operation.

Trinitarian Congregational, formed 1849, not in operation.

First Methodist Episcopal (in Northville), formed 1849, not in operation.

Second Methodist Episcopal (Centre Village), formed 1857.

Catholic, formed in 1862.

The town is generally rather level, but is well watered by rivers and brooks, and the soil is favorable for agriculture. There is a pond in the south-east part of the town called "Robin's Pond," about half a mile wide, with a small island near the central part, which, in Summer is a resort of pleasure parties. There are several small rivers in the town, the principal ones, the Satucket in the south-easterly part, and the Matfield in the westerly, unite near the Bridgewater line, on the southerly side, and form Taunton river. The Satucket is formed by a stream passing through Momponset Pond, in Halifax, and afterwards through Robin's Pond, and then uniting with Poor Meadow river, which flows through Abington and a part of Hanson, and enters this town on the east side, and with Black Brook. The Matfield, is formed by the union of Salisbury river, which rising in Stoughton, and flowing through North Bridgewater, enters East Bridgewater on the west side; Beaver Brook, which rises in East Randolph, and passing through North Bridgewater enters this town on the north-west, and with Snell Meadow Brook, which comes from Abington, on the north side.

This town has been famous for its early manufactures. Hon. Hugh Orr, who was born in Scotland in 1717, came to reside here at the age of twenty-one, constructed the first trip-hammer in this part of America, and began the manufacture of scythes. He was the first manufacturer of edge tools in this section. About 1748, he made five hundred muskets for the use of the Province of Massachusetts. Early in the Revolution he manufactured and furnished for the aid of the Colonies, in their struggles against the oppressions of the mother country, a great number of iron cannon and several of brass. These guns were cast solid, in Titicut, (the first of the kind in America,) and then taken and bored out at Mr. Orr's manufactory, which stood on the Matfield river a few rods from his house, now the residence of one of his decendents, Mr. William Vinton. Here, too, under the supervision of Mr. Orr, were made the first machines ever used in America for the carding, spinning and roping of cotton. The first nails ever made by machinery in this country were manufactured in this town "Probably the first nail completely cut and headed by machinery at one operation in the world, was made by the late Mr. Samuel Rogers," of this town.

To the inventive genius of Hugh Orr, Samuel Rogers, and Melville Otis, all residents of East Bridgewater, the civilized world is under lasting obligations.

In 1829, there were sixteen water privileges, on nearly all of which were manufactories of tacks or nails. The present number of mill-seats is eleven. In only one of these, tacks are now manufactured, in another nails. The forging of iron is carried on to a considerable extent. The chief business of the town for several years past has been the manufacture of boots and shoes.

The town paid for bounties to the soldiers, under all the calls for men from April 13th, 1861, to Dec. 19th, 1865,—$51,605.00.

Hartwell Atkinson, C, 22d, June 20th, 1862; Wm. W. Blanchard, A, 40th, of Chronic Diarrhœa, in hospital at Hampton, Va., Aug. 19th, 1864; George D. Brown, C, 29th, killed on picket duty at Fair Oaks, Va., June 15th, 1862, age 26; John Bryant, A, 1st H. A., killed at Spottsylvania, May 19th, 1864, age 37; Bertrand Burgess, D, 38th, of Scarlet Fever, in Marine Hospital, New Orleans, March 20th, 1864, age 20; William Curwin, in Navy, at Pensacola, on board ship Nightingale, 1862, age 27; Sergt. Alfred B. Cummings, C, 29th, taken prisoner at Morristown, Tenn., Nov. 1863, died at Andersonville, May, 1864, age 26; Allen B. Dunbar, E, 33d, at Chattanooga, June 22d, 1864; Charles E. Dyer, D, 38th, of Typhoid Fever, at Chesapeake Hospital, Hampton, Va., Nov. 16th, 1862, age 24; Myron Gould, D, 38th, at Baton Rouge, La., of sun-stroke, Aug. 29th, 1863, age 20; Charles Jaquith, 40th Reg't, killed near Fredericksburg, July, 1864; Aaron M. Keen, 1st Reg't Artillery, of wounds near Spottsylvania, May 19th, 1864, age 41; James Kingman, D, 38th, in Marine Hospital, at New Orleans, of Chronic Diarrhœa, June 14th, 1863, age 30; David H. Lincoln, C, 29th, of exhaustion on the battle field at Antietam, Sept. 18th, 1862, age 26; Charles McCarter, 1st Reg't, mortally wounded in battle near Spottsylvania, Va., May 19th, 1864, and died soon after, age 44; Lieut. Morton D. Mitchell, I, 38th, of Typhoid Fever, on board steamer City of Bath, June 17th, 1863, age 29; Color Sergt. William H. Mosher, B, 29th, killed in battle at Spottsylvania, May 12th, 1864, age 22; Patrick Mahoney, murdered at Washington; John M. Nason, C, 29th, at Convalescent Camp, Nicholasville, Ky., March, 1864; Peleg Osborne, jr., D, 38th, of Cholera Morbus, at Camp Stanton, Lynnfield, Mass., Aug. 29th, 1862, age 45; Sergt. Edmund T. Packard, C, 29th, of Chronic Diarrhœa, at Annapolis, Md., April 24th, 1864, age 37; Sergt. Josiah Richmond, E, 4th, of Congestive Chills, at Marion, Ohio, Aug. 15th, 1863, age 37; Wallace R. Ripley, Co. C, 29th Reg't, died of Typhoid Fever, at Newport News, Va., Aug. 9th, 1862, age 23 years; Eugene Sanger, Co. D, 38th Reg't, died of wounds received in battle of Bisland, April 13th, 1863, age 20; Charles F. Shaw, Co. E, 4th Reg't, died of Chronic Diarrhœa, at Memphis, Tenn., Aug. 9th, 1863, age 38; Sergt. J. F. Steingardt,

Co. C, 38th Reg't, died of Chronic Diarrhœa, at Baton Rouge, La., Sep. 2d, 1863, age 34; Sergt. Andrew J. Stetson, Co. D, 38th Reg't, was killed at Winchester, Va., Sept. 19th, 1864, age 27; Corporal Elijah H. Tolman, Co. C, 29th Reg't, died of wounds at Antietam, Sept. 18th, 1862, age 23; Color Corporal George H. Trow, Co. D, 38th Reg't, was killed in battle at Bisland, April 13th, 1863, age 22; James O. Underwood, Co. D, 58th Reg't, killed in battle at Shady Grove Church, June 3d, 1864, age 35; Horace Vosmus, 2nd Reg't, died of wounds at Hospital, Winchester, Va., June 4th, 1862, age 26; Benjamin F. Harden, 4th Cavalry; Daniel W. Harden, C, 29th, at U. S. General Hospital, Annapolis Junction, Sept. 22nd, 1862; Sergt. Silas N. Grosvenor, C, 29th, in battle before Petersburg, Va., June 16th, 1864, while carrying the colors of the Regiment, he was shot in the forehead and instantly killed; Nahum C. Hale, A, 10th, of Typhoid Fever, at Fort Ethan Allen, Md., Oct. 14th, 1862, age 32; Sergt. Calvin Francis Harlow, C, 29th, in battle at Fort Stedman, Va., March 25th, 1865, on the capture of the Fort he refused to surrender and was immediately shot down; Lieut. Elisha S. Holbrook, C, 29th, of Typhoid Fever, at Fortress Munroe, Aug. 20, 1861, age 21; Caleb L. Hudson, C, 29th, of Intermittent Fever, at Camp Dennison, Ohio, Sept. 11th, 1863, age 19; John Hudson, D, 38th, of Chronic Diarrhœa, while on a furlough at home, Nov. 1st, 1863, age 38; Galen Otis Hudson, D, 38th, mortally wounded in battle at Opequan Creek, Va., Sept. 19th, 1864, never heard from afterwards, aged 20; William W. Josselyn, K, 7th, of wounds, near Fredericksburg, Va., May 7th, 1863, age 31.

HALIFAX.

BY NATHANIEL MORTON.

GRAYWACKE and Granite is the geological formation of Halifax. Prof. Hitchcock says of the former that "it is capable of being made some of the best land in the State."

Halifax is located near the center of the county, 28 miles from Boston, and 12 miles from Plymouth Road. It contains 11,285 acres; 1700 of it water and about 200 swamp, abounding in beds of peat from 2 to 10 feet thick.

It was here in 1676, that Capt. Benj. Church "captured the Monponsetts and brought them in, not one escaping."

According to tradition, Mr. Sturtevant was the first settler, establishing himself near the residence of Thomas Holmes.

In 1733, a house of worship was built. This is now in use as a Town House. Halifax was incorporated July 4th, 1734, and was named for the Earl of Halifax.

John Cotton, a man of distinction, and author of the "History of Plymouth Church," was first pastor, succeeded by Wm. Patten, in 1757; Ephraim Briggs, 1769-1801; Abel Richmond, Eldridge G. Howe, Revs. Howland, Kimball and Brainard, and Wm. A. Forbes, present pastor, installed in 1866.

The people of Halifax were uncompromising patriots. Just before the Revolution, a soldier named Taylor deserted from the British company stationed at Marshfield and fled to Halifax, to the house of Mr. Thomas Drew. Three of the company were detailed to take the deserter back. In effecting this, a *ruse de guerre* was resorted to, and one of their number was sent in advance to pretend that he, also, had deserted, hoping to detain him, until his two comrades in arms should arrive. Mr. Drew saw through their arts and advised Taylor to flee for his life, into the woods, which was quickly done. When the other two had joined their comrade, and found to their chagrin that the bird had flown, they become exceedingly exasperated. They then went to the house of Noah Thompson, who was sick on his bed, and threatened to shoot him, with their pistols cocked, if he did not reveal the hiding place of the deserter, Taylor. Thompson, with sublime courage rose up in bed and took down his gun, which hung above his head on wooden hooks and brought it to his shoulder, while the fire flashed from his eyes, and said: "You are dead men, or leave my house."

They probably thought "discretion the better part of valor" and started on their way with disappointed hopes to join their company. In the meanwhile, the tidings of the affair flew in all sections like wild fire, and by the time they had got to the meeting-house, two minute men, Bradford and Bartlett, belonging to a company then organized in expectancy of trouble with the Mother Country, ordered them to stop and surrender, but their guns being *hors du combat*, the British soldiers cocking their pistols, ordered the minute-men into the road and marched them down to the house of Daniel Dunbar, who was a Tory, and placed them in the house as prisoners. It was not more than an hour before the house was surrounded by the whole company of minute men, and 'the surrender of their comrades demanded, which was refused. Upon this they threatened to break in and take them by force. The British soldiers retaliated by saying, that if they did so they would instantly kill the two prisoners, who entreated their friends, not to molest them as they felt sure the threat would be executed. It was finally determined upon to send for Josiah Sturtevant, who was a Justice of Peace, under the King, and he decided to bind the prisoners, Bradford and Bartlett, over to the court, to be tried for breaking the law upon the king's highway. Sturtevant subsequently, was driven away, shot at, and died, among the would-be enslavers of his country.

June 7th, 1777, the town voted to give $150, for men to fill the quota, provided they enlisted for three years, or during the war. Among the Revolutionary soldiers, was a slave owned by Caleb Sturtevant. Among the "Haligonians" who served in the Continental army, were Nathaniel Holmes, James Tillson, Josiah Thompson, Prince Witherel, Consider Pratt, Home Sears, Zebediah Thompson, Joshua Former, Elisha Faxon, Joseph Tillson, Richard Bosworth.

In 1812, the town furnished an entire military company, which was commanded by Capt. Asa Thompson, popularly known as the "tall Captain," who was 6 feet 6 inches in height, and it is said that people would collect around South Boston Bridge, to see him march his company over. This company is the oldest in the State, and was chartered by John Hancock, in 1792, and served in the late Rebellion. It is at present in a flourishing condition, and commanded by Capt. Charles P. Lyon. It will long be remembered by the people, how quickly this organization responded to the call of President Lincoln, April 16th, 1861; for which it was complimented by the Press of Boston.

This town suffered severely in the late war, and lost 22 men, out of a population of 739. Their names will be preserved to all coming time, on a monument, soon to be erected to their memory.

On the 5th of July, 1848, by fire, the manufacturing interests, of the town were ruined. In the conflagration, 1 woollen mill, and 3 houses, were destroyed, and thus about 50 males and females, were compelled to seek employment elsewhere. This was the greatest misfortune that ever befell this town, and from which it has never recovered.

There are 3 churches, 1 Orthodox, 1 Universalist, 1 Baptist, and 150 dwelling-houses. Present valuation, $365,471.00. One fact concerning the longevity of the citizens is worthy of mention. The average duration of life, up to the time of the late war, was 54 years, and of those who died, nearly one-half fell victims to consumption.

Perhaps in no town in Plymouth County, is wealth so equally divided. But *two* paupers are maintained at public expense. This is essentially an agricultural community, but there is no reason why, if the resources were properly developed by capital and enterprise, that we should not present a better spectacle than an increase in population of only 16 souls for the period of 36 years.

Monponsett Pond has always been a famous place of resort for wild fowl. In 1754, Mr. Drew, built a vessel here and floated it down the Winnetuxet to Newport.

John Thompson, who came from Wales in 1622, whose lineal issue to the eighth generation are now in Halifax, many of them residing on what was formerly his homestead, built a log house on the land now owned by Ephraim B. Thompson, which was burnt by the Indians during Phillip's war.

Soon after, in 1677, John Thompson, returned from the garrison at Middleboro, and built a frame house, (he being a carpenter), eight rods north of where the former house was burnt. It was lined with brick, originally, (with loop holes), so as to be proof against musket balls. This house was taken down in 1838. The site where the saw-pits, in which the boards and joist were sawed, with a whip-saw, is now extant. These houses were then in Middleboro, but now, within the limits of Halifax.

John Thompson, about the time his house was burnt, was commissioned by the Gov. and Council at Plymouth, as Lieutenant. Thus commissioned, he equipped himself with a gun, brass pistol and sword. The gun-stock and barrel, is 7 feet 4 1-2 inches : the length of the barrel is 6 feet, 1 1-2 inches; calibre, 12 balls to the lb.; lock, 10 inches long; whole weight of the gun, 20 lbs., 12 ounces. It is considered quite a muscular feat to hold it, and sight at arms length. The sword is 3 1-2 feet in length. These two have descended to Zadock Thompson, and the pistol to Ephraim B. Thompson.

John Thompson's customary hour of rising was at 4 o'clock, especially on Sabbath morning. The breakfast repast must be closed, even in summer, on or before the rising sun.

Either he or his wife, would go to church at Plymouth and return, every Sabbath, a distance of 13 miles.

NOTE. For list of Halifax soldiers, see Appendix.

HANOVER.

SETTLED in 1649, Hanover was not incorporated until 1727. Nearly all its territory was originally a part of Scituate. The town was named in honor of the Duke of Hanover, afterwards King George the First. The first settlement was at the Four Corners, and along the North and Indian Head rivers, William Barstow, ship-wright, being a pioneer. The outlines of his cellar are still visible. His grand-son Benjamin, had a family of twenty-one children. The piers of the first bridge built over North River, in 1662, may still be seen. Ship-building was commenced here as early as 1660, by the Barstow family, some of whom afterwards moved to Mattapoisett, and carried on the same business. Barstow's forge, (now Sylvester's), was erected in 1720. The Curtis Forge was erected in 1704, by the Burdens, who came from Scotland.

There were seven Indian nations in New England. The Wampanoags, divided into 32 tribes, with 3000 warriors, under Massasoit, occupied south-eastern Massachusetts. The Massachusetts, with 3000 warriors, under Chickatabut, occupied the territory from Duxbury mill to Titicut, thence to Nippenicket Pond, Bridgewater, and then in a straight line to Whitney's Pond in Wrentham. It was from the latter Sachem that Scituate and Hanover were purchased, in 1653. Jos. Barstow's house, in 1674, was garrisoned by twelve men. Indian burying grounds existed, on Pine Island and back of Assinippi Hall.

Religious services were held at private residences, in 1727. A building 48 by 38 feet, was erected in 1728. At this time common schools were kept in private houses.

Benj. Bass, was the minister of the First Parish, from 1728 till 1756; Sam'l. Baldwin, 1756-1789; John Miller, 1784-1805; Calvin Chaddock, 1806-1818; Seth Chapin, 1819-1824; followed by Ethan Smith, Abel G. Duncan and Joseph Freeman, present pastor.

The Episcopal services were first held in Scituate, 1725. St. Andrew's Church was established at Hanover "Corners," in 1810. Rectors, Joab G. Cooper, 1811-1816; Calvin Wolcott, 1818-1834; Samuel G. Appleton, 1835-1838; Eleazer A. Greenleaf, 1839-1841; Samuel Cutler, present incumbent.

In 1812, the Universalist Society, one of the first of the order in the County, was incorporated. H. C. Wood, present pastor.

The Baptist Church was constituted Feb. 17th, 1806. Present pastor, Andrew Reed.

Rev. James Aiken is pastor of the Second Congregational Church.

Few towns in the state can show a larger proportion of pleasant, attractive, country residences than Hanover. There is unmistakable evidence that the previous generation was one of thrift and success.

In 1807, the first Hanover Academy was erected, and in 1852, the present beautiful edifice.

Hanover soldiers did good service in the Revolution. The well-known Artillery Company was formed in 1798.

In 1754, there were eight male and nine female slaves in Hanover. Not only were blacks, but Indians held in bondage. Tradition says Job Tilden raised slaves for the market. Cuffee Josselyn a slave of Col. Joseph Josselyn, died in the almshouse, in 1831, aged 103.

David Prouty commenced here, the manufacture of the first cast-iron ploughs.

The burial ground at the Center, is the oldest in town. It has lately been much improved.

The new rail road, shown on our Country map, from No. Abington to Hanover Four Corners, was commenced in 1865.

NOTE.—From the History of Hanover, published by Rev. John S. Barry, in 1853, we glean the above items.

NOTE. For list of deceased soldiers and sailors see Appendix.

HANSON.

BY E. B. K. GURNEY, ESQ.

HANSON was incorporated Feb. 22d, 1820, and was formerly the "West Parish," of the town of Pembroke. Its size is comparitively small, containing an area of only 9730 acres, with a population of 1188, according to the last census. Its local early history, will, properly, be contained in the history of Pembroke. Like all other towns in Plymouth Co., it contains many relics of Indian settlements, such as remains of old orchards, cellars, &c., and rude implements of war, and articles for domestic use, &c. Nearly all its territory is embraced in the purchase of Major Josiah Winslow, of the Indian sachem, Josiah Wampatuck, as by deed, dated July 9th, 1662, known as the "Major's Purchase." There is a reserve made in said deed, of 1000 acres about the ponds at Mattakeset, (lying in Pembroke and Hanson,) to his son and George Wampy, which is still supposed, (a part of it at least,) to belong to their heirs, if any remains. Among the first settlers of Hanson, was a family by the name of Bourne, that located in the south part of this town, as early as about 1725, or before, as the name of Josiah Bourne is found in the records of the Proprietors of the "Major's Purchase," in 1732, May 12th, and from circumstances therein mentioned, he must have resided here some years before. The exact spot where he lived, is well known, and traces of the location yet remain to mark the spot, viz: old apple trees, old bricks, &c. In the north part of the town, a family by the name of Thomas, located, and the name of Edward Thomas, as being the clerk of the "Proprietors," is found in their book of records, as early as May 28th, 1759.

Rev. Gad Hitchcock, D. D., a man of talents, sociable, friendly, hospitable, and somewhat eccentric, was the first pastor, ordained in 1748, which office he held 55 years.

Rev. George Barstow was successor and colleague with Dr. Hitchcock, and continued the pastoral relation eighteen years, and died in 1821, aged 51 years. He was succeeded by the Rev. Mr. Howland.

The Baptist Church was organized in 1812, with Rev. Joseph Torrey as first pastor.

The well-known tack manufactory of E. Y. Perry & Co., is located in the limits of Hanson, although the post office address is South Hanover. Luther Howland, also, has a similar manufactory.

The "High-top" or "Summer Sweeting" apple-trees, yield now, as they did in the earliest days of the Colony, their prolific crop of golden fruit.

The name of the town, was one, out of many, that were suggested, and selected by vote. It has no particular derivation. Property is very equally distributed compared with many towns around. We have none of those persons, who from small beginnings, become noted, in a few years, as rich men, but each one makes slowly but surely. The town is very evenly settled.

No whole company was raised in this town, during the Rebellion, but a part of Co. A, 3d Reg't, went out to Fortress Monroe, April 16, 1861, for 3 months, and again to Newbern, N. C., for 9 months, Sept. 23d, 1862. Of those, all safely returned, and most of them again enlisted for 3 years.

Hanson raised for the Union service, 188 men; 6 for one hundred days; 14 for three months; 22 for nine months; 35 for one year, and 113 for three years, at an expense of $19,502, in addition to generous supplies through benevolent commissions.

The following men, lost in service, with one exception, belonged in this town:—

Thomas Drake, Co. D, 4th Cavalry, of starvation, at Andersonville. March 14th, 1865; Julius W. Monroe, Co. D, 38th Reg't of starvation, at Saulisbury, Feb. 15th, 1865; George Thompson, 11th Reg't, of starvation, at Andersonville, June 13th, 1864; Austin E. Luther, Co. F, 3d Cavalry, at Marine Hospital, New Orleans, of wounds, April 5th, 1864; Daniel Bourne, Co. D, 58th Reg't, killed, near Spottsylvania, Va., May 7th, 1864; Alfred G. Howe, Co. II, 18th Reg't, killed, near Spottsylvania, May 5th, 1864; Edward P. Mansfield, Co. C, 29th Reg't, killed near Spottsylvania, May 12th, 1864; Henry L. Ewell, 10th Battery, of wounds, at Washington, Nov. 20th 1864; George S. Golbert, Co. B, 22d Reg't, of Chronic Diarrhœa, at Fortress Munroe, August, 1862; Stephen Bates, Co. D, 38th Reg't, of Chronic Diarrhœa, at Baton Rouge, May 3d, 1863; Andrew W. Fish, Co. C, 38th Reg't, of Chronic Diarrhœa, at Baton Rouge, Aug. 3d, 1863; Joseph L. Fish, Co. D, 38th Reg't, of Chronic Diarrhœa, at home, Oct. 31st, 1863; John Lyons, Co. B, 41st Reg't, of Chronic Diarrhœa, at Port Hudson, Sept. 29th, 1863; Morton E. Hill, Co. C, 38th Reg't, of Chronic Diarrhœa, at Brashear City, April 13th, 1863; Horatio Foster, 1st R. I., of disease, at Catlett Station, Va., May 22d, 1862; Theodore L. Bonney, Co. E, 32d Reg't, of Fatigue and Fever, at Potomac Creek, Va., May 11th, 1863; Augustus F. Elmes, Co. K, 7th Reg't, of Fever, near Washington, Oct. 25th, 1861; John H. Perry, K, 7th Reg't, of Disease; James Coolican, Co. B, 41st Reg't, of Disease, La., Feb. 25th, 1863; George H. Bourne, Co. B, 40th Reg't, of Diarrhœa, near Folly Island, S. C., Nov. 28th, 1863; James A. Lyons, Co. D, 38th Reg't, of wounds, at Brashear City, La.

HINGHAM.

THE earliest record concerning the disposal of lands in Hingham, was in 1635. The first settlers came from Hingham, County of Norfolk, England, about two years previous.

Sept. 18, 1635, thirty inhabitants drew for house lots. The settlement was first called Bear Cove.

Rev. Peter Hobart was the first pastor. He died in 1679, leaving four sons who became ministers. Present Pastors, Joseph Richardson, and Calvin Lincoln.

The ancient Congregational Meeting-house erected in 1689, is now standing in good state of preservation, and is the oldest house of worship in New England, if not in the United States. The original size was 55 by 45 feet, with posts 20 feet, and cost $2,150, and the old house.

The Second Church was organized in 1745. Present minister, John Savary. The Third Church was formed in 1805. Pastor, Joshua M. Young.

The M. E. Church, located on North St., West Hingham, was organized 1818.

The First Baptist Church, Hingham, was organized, March 9, 1828, with 20 members. Present number 161. Jonathan Tilson is now in the sixteenth year of his settlement as pastor. The house of worship was dedicated Dec. 3, 1828. A vestry was built underneath, in 1832, and in 1851, the house was raised and a new vestry, committee room, pulpit, and other improvements were made.

The First Universalist Society was organized Nov. 1st, 1823.

The Evangelical Congregational Church, Main st., Hingham Center, was organized Dec. 21st, 1847. First Pastor, Rev. E. Porter Dyer, installed Jan. 4th, 1849. House of Worship dedicated Jan. 4th, 1849. Present Pastor, Rev. Henry W. Jones, installed May 24th, 1866.

The Derby Academy was incorporated, June 7th, 1797:—*President.*—Rev. Joseph Osgood, of Cohasset. *Trustees.*—Ebenezer Gay, Esq., of Dorchester; Rev. John L. Russell, of Salem; Rev. Calvin Lincoln, of Hingham; Benjamin Cushing, M. D., of Dorchester; John Q. Adams, Esq., of Quincy; Solomon Lincoln, jr., Esq., of Salem; Henry A. Clapp, Esq., of Dorchester; Rev. Joshua Young, of Hingham; Henry C. Harding, of Hingham; Charles C. Tower, M. D., Weymouth.

In 1676, John Jacobs was killed by the Indians, near his father's house, at Glad Tidings Plain. The next day they burned the houses of five settlers. Three forts and numerous garrison houses were early established.

Maj. Gen. Benjamin Lincoln, of Revolutionary fame, was born in Hingham, Jan. 23, 1733. He was second in command, of the army under Gen. Gates, that captured Burgoyne's forces. He was afterwards Secretary of War, Lieutenant Governor, &c., and died in the house in which he was born, in 1810.

The first Engine in town, was purchased in 1802, and was located at the Centre. It was private property and owned by a company of 15 men. "Precedent," was its name. During the war of 1812, when fire company membership exempted men from the draft, the proprietors made money out of it, by selling rights to persons liable to draft. Soon after this engine was obtained, in the same year, one was purchased at the lower part of the town. The Town first took control of the engines in 1819.

The soil in many sections of Hingham, is very fertile. The place has long been noted for its wooden box and bucket manufactories. Among the institutions of Hingham, we would mention its Banks, Insurance Company, Cordage Works, Tassel Factory, Nail Works, Furnaces, &c.

In 1865, Hingham had ten vessels employed in the mackerel and cod fisheries, with a tonnage of 790; taking 8,058 barrels of the former. Three small crafts also engaged in the coasting trade.

The "Hingham Journal" is a weekly paper established more than eighteen years ago. It is published by Blossom & Easterbrook.

The "Hingham Agricultural and Horticultural Society" has been in existence about nine years, and has held eight exhibitions. Meetings for discussions are held every month, and sometimes oftener. The Society owns an Agricultural Library, and has raised about $20,000, by subscription, and is about buying grounds with the view of building a large hall for its use. The officers are:—Hon. Albert Fearing, President; Hon. Solomon Lincoln, George M. Soule, Charles W. Cushing, Vice Presidents; DeWitt C. Bates, Recording Secretary; Fearing Burr, Corresponding Secretary; Joseph H. French, Treasurer; Lincoln Fearing, Librarian; Directors, David Whiton, John R. Brewer, Alfred Loring, Amasa Whiting, John Stephenson, John Lincoln, Bela Whiton, William Cushing, George Lincoln, jr., William B. Johnson of Cohasset, Dexter M. Wilcutt, of S. Scituate, Joseph Totman of Weymouth.

The First Social Library, founded in 1771, now contains about 1800 volumes, kept at Centre Hingham.

The Second Social Library was organized 1773. It is located at Ford's Building, North st., and contains 1300 volumes.

During the summer months, one or more steamers constantly ply between Hingham, Hull and Boston. Indeed, the town has more intimate business relations with Boston than with Plymouth County.

The soldiers' Record for Hingham, is as follows, so far as can now be ascertained:—Alvin Tower, Co. A, 20th, from wounds at battle of Fair Oaks, at Mill Creek Hospital, Fortress Monroe, June 8th, 1862, aged 30; Lieut. Nathaniel French, jr., 32d Reg't, at Harrison's Landing, August 9th, 1862, from Fever; Nelson F. Corthell, Co. A, 18th, at Battle of Second Bull Run, Aug. 28th, 1862; Lieut. Geo. W. Bibby, 32d Reg't, killed May 30th, 1864, at battle of Tolopotomy Swamp; Capt. Edwin Humphrey, Co. A, 11th, from wounds received at Gettysburg, July 3d, 1863, aged 31 years; James Haskell, Co. A, 32d, from wounds received at Gettysburg, July, 1863; Demerick Stodder, Co. F, 32d Reg't, killed at Gettysburg, July 3d, 1863, aged 23; William J. Stockwell, Co. I, 30th, from disease, at Baton Rouge, La., August 12th, 1863, aged 21; Michael Fee, Co. F, 16th, of disease, at Stanton Hospital, Washington, D. C., Sept. 25th, 1863, age 40; Sowell Pugsley, Co. F, 22d, from disease, at Mount Pleasant Hospital, Washington, D. C., Nov. 12th, 1863, 32 years; Sergt. William H. Jones, jr., Co. K, 18th, at Carver Hospital, Washington, D. C., Feb. 12th, 1864, 22 years; Richard J. Farrell, Co. G, 2d Reg't, U. S. Regular Artillery, from effects of wounds received at battle of Gaines Mill, March 17th, 1864, aged 22; George D. Gardner, Co. G, 39th Reg't, at City Point, August 5th, 1864, of Typhoid Fever; Jeremiah J. Corcoran, Co. A, 40th, June 8th, 1864; William H. Jones, Co. C, 4th Mass. Cavalry, at Magnolia, Florida, Sept. 19th, 1864; Henry F. Miller, Co. G, 39th Reg't, from wounds received at battle of Laurell Hill, May 25th, 1864, at Stanton Hospital, Washington, D. C.; William Breen, Co. A, 32d Reg't, at Salisbury Prison, from disease and exposure, Jan. 4th, 1864; Thomas Tinsley, Co. K, 1st Reg't, from wounds received in battle, May 11th, 1863, aged 42; John Q. Hersey, Co. E, 32d Reg't, from disease, at Hospital in Washington, D. C., Nov. 28th, 1863; Edward A. F. Spear, Co. G, 30th Reg't, at Salisbury Prison, from Pneumonia and exposure, Jan. 20th, 1865, aged 35; Charles E. French, Co. G, 39th Reg't, at Salisbury, N. C. Prison, from Chronic Diarrhœa and exposure, November 26th, 1864; Sergt. Henry C. French, Co. G, 39th Reg't, was shot by the rebel guard at Belle Isle, Richmond, Va., Aug. 26th, 1864; Gardner Jones, Co. F, 32d Reg't, from wounds received in battle, at Campbell Hospital, Washington, D. C., June 1st, 1864, aged 19 years; John S. Neal, Co. G, 39th Reg't, of Chronic Diarrhœa and exposure at Salisbury Prison, Jan. 16th, 1865; Albert S. Haynes, Co. G, 39th Reg't, in Hingham, from wounds received at Battle of Wilderness, June 11th, 1864, aged 22 years; Daniel L. Beal, 32d Reg't, at City Point Hospital, July 30th, 1864, from disease; Albert Wilder, Co. G, 39th Reg't, at Hospital, in Washington, June 1st, 1864, from wounds received at battle of Wilderness; Sergt. Peter Ourish, Co. E, 32d Reg't, from wounds received in battle of Wilderness, May 3d, 1864; James T. Churchill, Co. G, 39th Reg't, from exposure and starvation at Andersonville, June 23d, 1864; Charles E. Wilder, 32d Reg't, in Hingham, of disease, December 23d, 1864, aged 32 years; William H. Beal, Co. K, 24th Reg't, at Hingham, December 20th, 1865; Sergt. Charles Mead, Co. A, 32d Reg't, March 7th. 1864, aged 20 years; Samuel Spencer, 12th Reg't, July, 1864, aged 20 years; Dennis Sculley, Co. D, 4th, Mass. Cavalry; Washington J. Stoddard, Co. F, 32d Reg't, from wounds; Thomas Sprague, Co. G, 39th Reg't, died from disease; Wallace Humphrey, Co. E, 32d Reg't, from wounds; Jacob Gilkey Cushing, Co. F, 32d Reg't, died of wounds; Thomas Churchill; Don Pedro Wilson, last seen at Banks' retreat; James Fitzgerald; Henry B. Livingston, V. R. C.; John W. Gardner, 8th Maine Reg't, died July 24th, 1865, from disease and ill treatment in Rebel Prison; Lieut. Thomas Andrews, at New Orleans, in the Navy, from disease; Geo. Merrett, in the Navy, from disease.

HULL.

WAS incorporated in 1644, and in its early days was a place of some note.

The first minister settled in Hull, it is supposed, was Mr. Matthews. He was succeeded by Zachariah Whitman, settled in 1670; and Samuel Veasie, settled in 1753, dismissed 1763.

It is the smallest town territorially in the State, except Newburyport, and the smallest in population, except Gosnold. It is located on the peninsula of Nantasket, and nearly all the islands in Boston harbor belong to this town. Very few people realize how short a distance it is from Long Wharf, Boston, to Plymouth County. The town is formed of five small hills, connected by very narrow necks of land. The principal settlement is on Nantasket head.

Several large and popular summer hotels, among them the "Oregon" and the "Rockland House," have been erected here within a few years, and the town has become a popular resort.

For many years the vote of Hull indicated the relative strength of political parties, in Massachusetts elections, until it passed into a proverb:—"As goes Hull, so goes the State."

Hull did her whole duty in the war for the preservation of the Union, raising 22 soldiers and 2 sailors. Three men were lost in service. Sergt. Ansel P. Loring, E, 47th, killed on duty near New Orleans, June 24th, 1863, his body having been found floating in the Mississippi, with shot wounds through the head; Nathaniel R. Hooper, F, 20th, killed at Fredericksburg, Dec. 11th, 1862; and John M. Cleverly, A, 3d R. I. Cavalry, at Charity Hospital, New Orleans, of Chronic Diarrhœa.

KINGSTON.

BY REV. JOSIAH PECKHAM.

FOR more than a hundred years, Kingston was "The North End" of Plymouth. Twice it narrowly escaped being the most famous locality of the Old Colony. The day after the company from the Mayflower first landed, a party went, some by land, and some in the shallop, to look out a more desirable place for settlement. They reported "a great liking to plant" at Jones' River, but after prayer and reflection "the most voices" fixed upon Plymouth. In March, 1635-6, a project was set on foot, and was earnestly advocated by a viewing committee of the Court, consisting of some of the chief men in the Colony, to remove from both Plymouth and Duxbury, and to unite in a new town at Jones' River; but after long debating, and a reference to the two churches for a final decision, the matter was silently dropped.

Though at the time of the landing, all the region about was temporarily deserted of the natives, two burial-grounds, one where the Patuxet House now stands, and the other, in the ridge north of the Evergreen Cemetery, together with the frequent discovery of arrow-heads, mortars and hearth-stones, show that Kingston was a favorite resort, if not residence, of the Indians. The last one of the tribe dwelling here, as handed down by the "oldest inhabitant," was a woman, whose wigwam was at Blackwater, and who was famed the country around, for her superior cooking.

The earliest road from Plymouth to Duxbury, was nearer the shore than the present one, crossing Jones' River at the "Wading Place," near the Almshouse, and thence, passing over Abraham's Hill, through Stoney Brook, meeting another road which started near the Plymouth line, and crossed the river, at its mouth, by a ferry. Later, the main road passed by a bridge near Mr. Edward Holmes' fish-house. The present highway and bridge were opened in 1708. Both the ancient ferry and bridge were subjects of frequent legislation. At one time Capt. Standish was ordered, by the Court, to repair the bridge, even if he had to press men into the service. For a time, Gov. Bradford had his residence in Stoney Brook, near the dwelling of the late Francis Drew. The cellar of his house is still visible. His son, Deputy Gov. Bradford, lived, and died upon the same spot. A "High-Top Sweeting," the last tree of the orchard, set out by the son, is still standing by the lane leading to Dea. Foster's. Mr. Henry Colman speaks of it as "planted in 1669, and as bearing in 1838, thirty bushels of good fruit." If this account of its age is true, it bids fair soon to enter upon its third century. Joseph Bradford, another son of the Governor, settled a little south-east of the Landing. Isaac Allerton, for several years the Governor's sole Assistant, and afterwards the enterprising agent of the Pilgrims, and his son-in-law, "that precious servant of God," Elder Thomas Cushman, whose wife Mary, was the last survivor of the Mayflower band, lived a few rods north-east from the house of "Grandfather Cobb," who died in 1801, aged more than 107 years. John Howland and Elizabeth, his wife, ended their protracted pilgrimage, at the Nook, near the road to the old ferry. Samuel Fuller, the "beloved physician," and the deacon of the church, and Francis Cooke, the progenitor of an extensive race of Cooks, dwelt near Smelt Brook. Francis Billington, the discoverer of the "Sea," has left his name to the rocks in the bay near the town line, and Edward Gray, "the merchant," who came some years later, settled a little to the north of where his descendant and namesake now resides. Thus, if Kingston cannot claim to be a Pilgrim town, it has within its borders many Pilgrim memorials.

Deputy-Gov. Bradford was a Major, in King Philip's war. The house of his son John, who was doubtless in the service with him, was at the Landing; but, for the protection of his wife, to whom he had just been married, he temporarily removed to the guard-house, at Plymouth town. One day as he was returning to his house, with several soldiers, for the purpose of taking some of the goods he had left, he discovered it to be on fire, and saw an Indian, standing on the brow of Abraham's Hill, stationed as a sentinal to warn his comrades of the approach of the white man, waving his blanket and crying "Chockway, Chockway," (the white men are coming); but so intent were the Indians on plundering, that they heeded not their sentinel's cry, and were not aware of their danger, till Bradford rushed among them. They instantly fled, and made their way into a dense swamp at the foot of Abraham's Hill, and were pursued by Bradford, who fired at one of them, and supposed him killed, as he saw him fall. On reaching the spot he was greatly surprised at not finding the body of his enemy. He was at a loss how to account for this circumstance, till after the war, when an Indian made the fact known to him that he was the one fired at, giving evidence of this by the marks of the bullet shot through his side, and declaring that he had crept behind some logs to escape the notice of his pursuer. After the war, Mr. Bradford re-built on the same spot, and the house is now known as the Sampson house, in which for a long time was preserved his Grandfather's manuscript history of New Plymouth; but which, a short time before his death, in 1736, he loaned to Thomas Prince, who kept his library in the steeple of the Old South Church, in Boston. The manuscript, with other books, was carried to England, during the Revolutionary war, and lodged in the Fulham library, where, till 1855, it was concealed from the public, and for many years was supposed to be irrecoverably lost. It has since been published by the Mass. Historical Society, and is a most authentic and valuable contribution to the history of the first settlement.

The North End of Plymouth, was incorporated as a precinct in 1717, and as a town, in 1726. The greater convenience in the worship of God, and the better ordering of the schools, appear to be the reasons for the division. During the war of Independence, Kingston was thoroughly patriotic, furnishing its quota of men, paying in some instances, for less than six months' service, of a single soldier, more than ten thousand dollars of the currency of the times. Gen. John Thomas, who commanded at Roxbury, and subsequently succeeded Gen. Montgomery in Canada, where he died, was a prominent citizen of this town, as was also Maj. Seth Drew, who was an officer in the battles of Trenton, and Monmouth, and at the capture of Burgoyne. Gen. Peleg Wadsworth, commanded a company of minute men from Kingston, in the early part of the war.

The whole number of men furnished in the late war of the Rebellion, by this town, is one hundred and fifty-four. The following have died in connection with the service, viz:—Wm. O'Brien, Thomas Mullen, George Sampson, Melzor A. Foster, Lieut. Wm. Holmes, Allyn Holmes, jr., Nathaniel Washburn, jr., Waldo Peterson, George O. Beytes, E. Lyman Richardson, George F. Stetson, Harvey C. Pratt, Edward A. Pratt, also, Ensign Henry L. Ransom, of the Navy.

Kingston, at the time of its separation, probably contained about 300 inhabitants. By the census of 1865, the population was 1626, and 354 voters. Upon Jones' River and its branches, there are at the present time, eighteen mills, of different descriptions. It is a pleasantly located and healthy town, and according to population, is the richest in the county. The soil is mainly of the diluvial, or drift formation; or as Rev. Mr. Willis says "a red loam, intermingled with sand, gravel, and round stones in various degrees." It has a basis of granite or gneiss, which crops out both in valley and hill, and there are occasionally found veins of volcanic trap, thrown up in the ledges, so regular in their structure as to have the appearance of walls of masonry. Specimens of this may be seen in the "cut" on the Rail Road, and the "Devil's Stairway" in the fishing rocks at the Nook.

Kingston has three churches, (Unitarian, Baptist, and Trinitarian Congregationalist), a boarding school for boys, and eight public schools. The town abolished its school districts in 1866, and voted to erect a High School-house, which is nearly completed. It is a two story building, containing three rooms below and four above, together with the entries. When finished and occupied, few towns will have better facilities for good schools than Kingston.

*The College Graduates, natives of Kingston, are:—

Hon. William Sever, H, 1745, John Sever, M. D., sons of Nicholas,

*Those marked with H. graduated at Harvard, and with B. at Brown.

H, 1749; Gen. John Thomas, M. D., H, 1765; Crocker Sampson, H, 1771; William Sever, H, 1778, Commodore James Sever, H, 1782, John Sever, sons of William, H, 1787; Hon. Bezor Bryant, M. D., B. 1795; Rev. Oliver Cobb, D. D., B, 1796; Hon. John Holmes, U. S. Senator, B, 1796; Joseph Holmes, Ship Builder, B, 1796; Bartholomew Cushman, M. D., B, 1805; Henry Holmes, Lawyer, B, 1806; Hon. Thomas P. Beal, Lawyer, H, 1806; Daniel Cook, M. D., B, 1807; Wm. R. Sever, son of John, County Treasurer, H, 1811; John Thomas, son of Hon. John, Lawyer, B, 1813; Col. James W. Sever, son of James, H, 1817; Winslow W. Sever, son of John, H, 1818; Rev. Job Cushman, B, 1819; Samuel Stetson, Lawyer, B, 1820; Charles Washburn, Lawyer and Manufacturer, B, 1820; Joseph Sampson, Lawyer, B, 1821; Hon. Ezekiel Holmes, M. D., Editor, B, 1821; Samuel B. Parris, M. D., B, 1821; Rev. Caleb Stetson, H, 1822; Joseph S. Beal, Lawyer, Clerk O. C. R. R., H, 1835; Col. C. C. Holmes, M. D., H, 1837; Samuel Glover, jr., B, 1839; Paul L. Nichols, jr., M. D., H, 1845; Rev. Winslow W. Sever, son of James N., H, 1853; Joseph A. Holmes, son of Alexander, H, 1854; George C. Burgess, H, 1858; Albert Stetson, Prof. Normal School, Illinois, H, 1861;

The names of Professional men who have not graduated, natives of Kingston:—

Seth Stetson, Elisha Cushman, Wm. A. Drew, Editor, Martin Cushman, Job Washburn, Joseph F. Lovering, and Rev. John D. Sweet, jr., Hon. Joseph R. Chandler, Editor, Mem. of Congress, and Minister to Naples, and Erastus, Francis and Frederic W. Bartlett, and Seth Fuller, jr., Physicians.

Of successful business men, Kingston has furnished, Hon. Ichabod Washburn, of Worcester and Hon. Edward S. Tobey, of Boston, both men of wealth and widely known for their charitable gifts; Col. John Sever, first President of the O. C. R. R., and Alexander Holmes, late President of the same; Edward Holmes, Ship-builder, and Capt. Paraclete Holmes, late President of an Insurance Co., Boston. The last three, have handsome estates in Kingston, and are sons of Joseph Holmes, who died in 1863, aged 90 years, who built 80 vessels, and was reputed to be the richest man in the county, at the time of his decease; Nathaniel and Edwin Adams, Master-builders, Boston, Alexander Beal, Furniture dealer, Haymarket square; Hon. F. M. Johnson, and Albert Thompson, Leather Dealers, in Pearl st.; three Burgess brothers in Boston, and two in Portland, besides numerous sea Captains and other successful men who still have their residences in Kingston.

The first American nail-machine was patented by Col. Jesse Reed, then of Kingston. The first reaping-machine was invented by Samuel Adams of this town, while Caleb Bates is already famed for his

7½

A SAFE, CERTAIN, AND Speedy CURE —FOR—

NEURALGIA,

—AND—

Nervous Diseases in all Forms.

ITS EFFECTS ARE MAGICAL.

It is an UNFAILING REMEDY in all cases of Neuralgia Facialis; often effecting a perfect cure in less than twenty-four hours.

No other form of Neuralgia or Nervous Disease has failed to yield to this **Wonderful Remedial Agent.**

It is perfectly harmless, never producing the slightest injury.

It is in constant use by many of our most eminent Physicians.

The following, among many thousands of our best citizens, testify to its wonderful efficacy:—

"DR. T. LARKIN TURNER, BOSTON, MASS.—Dear Sir: I have prescribed the Pill prepared by you, and designed as a specific for the cure of Neuralgia Facialis, or Tic Douloureux, during the last fifteen years, to a large number of patients afflicted with that painful and tormenting condition of the nerves which has hitherto perplexed and baffled the skill of physicians; and I can assure you—and I do so with great pleasure—that in no instance, as yet, have they failed to relieve the patient immediately, frequently as by magic; and after the use of the number contained in from one to four boxes, effectually to remove the malady, much to the delight and astonishment of the sufferers, as invariably expressed. Very truly yours,

Framingham, July 18, 1864. O. O. JOHNSON, M. D."

"Having used Dr. Turner's Tic Douloureux or Universal Neuralgia Pill personally—and in numerous instances recommended it to patients suffering with neuralgia,—I have found it, without an exception, to accomplish all the proprietors have claimed.

12 Winter Street, Boston, Feb 18th, 1867. J. R. DILLINGHAM, Dentist.

MR. WYZEMAN MARSHALL—well known to all who are familiar with the dramatic art in its best displays—says: "Through the medium of this invaluable discovery, I am now happily rid of neuralgia."

MR. WM. CALDER, of the Boston Detective Police, says: "One package of Dr. Turner's Neuralgic Pill entirely cured me of severe neuralgia. I cannot commend it too strongly."

Price $1.00 Per Package.

Sent by mail for two Postage Stamps extra. It is sold by all Wholesale and Retail dealers in Drugs and Medicines throughout the United States, and by

TURNER & CO., Sole Proprietors,

120 Tremont Street, Boston, Mass.

LAKEVILLE.

BY HARRISON STAPLES, ESQ.

LAKEVILLE was incorporated May 13th, 1853. The most of its territory was embraced in the West Precinct of Middleboro. Its area is supposed to be about 19,000 acres, over 4,000 of which is water. The *chain* of Ponds or Lakes, parts of which are in Middleboro, Rochester and Freetown, have an area of about 6,000 acres being by far the largest Lake region in the State. They give to many places in this vicinity fine natural scenery, and have a perceptible influence on the climate of the locality, especially in the exemption from early autumnal frosts. Middleboro, before the division, was the largest township in the State, having a surface of nearly 100 square miles. Its large territory was one of the main causes of the separation of Lakeville.

The borders of its Ponds were famous resorts for the Indians. Here was a fine place to raise their maize and beans; to chase the deer, and catch their fish, and this was one of the last places they abandoned. At "Betty's Neck," on the south side of Assawampsett, quite a number of Indians lived within the memory of the present generation and there is some doubt whether all their titles to land are extinguished.

One of their number, Benjamin Simonds, is especially recollected as a noble specimen of his race; he was of fine physical proportions, weighing we should judge about 200. He was in the war of the Revolution, and after receiving a pension of $96 per annum, he moved to the north side of the pond, where he lived at a place known as "Ben's Island." He died in 1836, and was buried in the Cemetery, about a mile west of Lakeville Depot, where, by the enterprise of one of the citizens, a fitting monument marks his sepulchre.

The murder of Sausaman, a friendly and Christian Indian, on the Assawampsett, hastened Philip's war. During that war, the famous Captain Church had a severe skirmish with the Indians, on the west side of the same pond, resulting in their flight.

We think there was no settlement in the town till about 1700. One of the name of Peirce, came from Scituate and built near Myrickville, in 1705, whose descendants are very numerous. The Nelsons were the first white settlers on Assawampsett Neck, in 1717; the Southworths settled the part near Middleboro; Strowbridges, Richmonds, Canadys, Horrs, Sampsons and Pickenses, were early comers and large landholders.

There are in Lakeville, very considerable quarries of granite, that have already been worked quite extensively.

In 1688, the missionaries of the Society for the propagation of the Gospel among the Indians, reported: "There are at Assawampsit and Quitlaub twenty houses and eighty persons. John Hiacoomes, preacher and constant schoolmaster. Mr. Jocelyn preached at Assawampsit. At Kehtehticut are forty adults, to whom Charles Abram preached."

The first church was formed, ("The Precinct,") in 1725. Their first house was built a little east of the present one. Their second one near the present site. The last, was built in 1835. The succession of ministers have been Benjamin Ruggles, Caleb Turner, Thomas Crafts, John Shaw, Homer Barrows, Mr. Bragg, Calvin Chapman, Augustine Root, G. G. Perkins, and the present pastor James W. Ward. The ministry of the first three, covered nearly a century. The parish has always embraced a part of Taunton. The Second church, was Baptist, formed in the westerly part of the town, in 1757. Elder John Hinds, and Elder Simeon Coombs, each served many years as pastors. There were times when large congregations were gathered. After continuing about a century it became extinct.

In that vicinity, a Freewill Baptist Church was formed about 1828, through the labors of H. N. Loring. Rev. Mr. Steere preached at a more recent period. It is now extinct.

A second Baptist Church was formed about 1796. They built a fine house of worship on the west shore of the Assawampsett, their first pastor's name was Abbott, we believe, after which, the Rev. E. Briggs, held that relation for about forty years, till near the time of his death.

The Christian Church was formed February, 1812. Elders Shurtleff, Bryant, Tyler, Chadwick, and Jackson, have been pastors. E. W. Barrows is present pastor. Their house is in the westerly part of the town.

Three hundred and fifty volumes, the nucleus of the Lakeville Library, were donated to his native town, by Hugh Montgomery of Boston, in 1866.

Lakeville furnished 85 men for the Union Army, and 6 for the Navy.

NOTE.—For list, see Appendix.

MARSHFIELD.

BY REV. E. ALDEN, JR.

MARSH-FIELD indicates the nature of a considerable portion of the soil. Its three rivers, North, South, and Green's Harbor, popularly termed Cut, are navigable to some extent. Some small vessels were built in those days when ship-building was an important business on the South Shore. Its streams furnish considerable water-power. Two Cotton Factories were at one time in operation on the South River. Its water-power is now mostly employed in box-board mills. Agriculture is a leading occupation of its inhabitants. The recent successful inauguration of an Agricultural Fair, under the direction of a Farmer's Club, represents and promises to stimulate this branch of industry. Boots and shoes are made to some extent in Marshfield, though until recently, mostly for manufacturers out of town. The making of clothing for men and boys, furnishes employment for a large number of females.

The shore of Marshfield, has always been a favorite resort for sportsmen and for health and recreation. Brant Rock has been familiar to the people of the back towns for a century, and within a few years, Cut River and the island overlooking Marshfield Beach, have become no less so.

Marshfield was occupied during the summer, twelve years after the landing at Plymouth. The first church was organized in 1632, which may therefore be regarded as the date of the settlement of the town, which was made in its south-west part, then called Green's Harbor, and afterwards Rexham. The town was incorporated in 1641, and the Second, or North Parish, was organized in 1739. The Indian name of the place was Missaucatucket.

In 1658, occurred a death by lightning, and in 1666, three others from the same cause; which events at the time made a deep impression both in the community and abroad, upon a generation with whom divine providence was a doctrine of lively faith.

Edward Winslow, was the leading man among the first settlers. He called his place Careswell, in memory of the land of his birth. Of polished manners, as well as of thorough Puritan principles, Gov. Winslow, who married for his second wife, Susanna (Fuller) White, mother of Peregrine, after some years in the service of the Colony, both in the Old and New World, while on his way to the West Indies, with a commission from Cromwell, was lost at sea.

For several generations the Winslow's were a prominent family. A house built about 1635, still standing, is familiar to the public by prints. Josiah Winslow, son of Edward, was the first Gov. of Plymouth Colony, born in the country. His funeral was attended with public honors and military display.

NOTE—See appendix for list of Marshfield Soldiers.

Gen. John Winslow, noted in connection with the removal of the Acadians, commemorated by Longfellow, was of this family.

The ancient Winslow Burying Ground, contains the remains of the first child of the Pilgrims, the first mother, also the first bride, and the first native Governor.

Peregrine White, settled near the confluence of North and South River, and lived to an advanced age. May 22d, 1698, in his 78th year, he made a profession of his faith, which his pastor records as an illustration of Matt 20: 6, 7. The estate has continued in the family until recently. An ancient house stands upon it, and the famed apple-tree still bears fruit.

John Bourne, who died in 1859, a man of quiet manners and sterling worth, was a soldier of the Revolution, and lived to see one hundred years.

Gen. John Thomas, who fortified Dorchester Heights, was a native of Marshfield.

The most distinguished name connected with Marshfield, is that of Daniel Webster. He came for recreation to the place, which he afterwards made his home, in 1827, and became a resident of the town about 1832. He purchased the residence erected by Nath. Ray Thomas, the noted royalist, adjoining the Winslow estate. This house he re-modelled. The part containing the Library, was designed by his daughter, Julia. The grounds he enlarged, the Winslow estate comprising a part of them. By setting out trees, and enriching the soil, he changed the features of the place from a sterile waste of sandy hills, to a charming landscape of fertility and beauty. The tomb was built by himself, in the Winslow Burying Ground, within a lot abutting on his estate. The mouth of the river whence he went out in the Bay, on his favorite fishing excursions, is much changed since his day and is now well-known as Cut River.

William Carver, grand nephew of Gov. Carver, died Oct. 7th, 1760, aged nearly 102 years. On one occasion he worked in the field with members of three generations, while another was in the house in the cradle; five generations living at one time.

Col. Fletcher Webster, before his father's death, had a residence which he called Careswell, but afterwards occupied the Webster mansion.

Though in the Revolutionary war there was an influential Tory element in Marshfield, giving occasion for the stationing of a company of British Regulars, on the farm now associated with Webster, the town was active and outspoken on the patriotic side. In the recent struggle to put down the slaveholders' rebellion, Marshfield furnished for the Army and Navy, in 1861, for 3 months, 1 man; 1861, for 3 years, 43 men; 1862, 3 years, 26 men; 1862, 9 months, 33 men; 1864, 3 years, 9 men; 1864, 1 year, 19 men; 1864, 100 days, 5 men;

MARION.

BY J. BATCHELDER, M. D.

MARION was incorporated May 14th, 1852. Previous to this event it constituted a part of Rochester, and was called Sippican. Its corporate name was selected for no special reason. It was suggested merely for its euphony, and the facility of hailing vessels at sea by this name, this last circumstance rendering the former name objectionable. At various times, there had been exhibited some sectional differences between the two precincts of the town, which, in 1850, (or about that time), culminated in the repudiation, by the Rochester precinct, of all the Sippican candidates for town officers.

Marion is bounded on the north and east, by Wareham, Sippican and Weweantit rivers, which seperate it from Wareham, and Buzzard's Bay; on the south, by Buzzard's Bay, and Mattapoisett; on the west by Mattapoisett and Rochester. It is about four miles in medium length, and breadth, and therefore contains about sixteen square miles. Its outline is very irregular, following, to a considerable extent, the serpentine course of river and sea-coast. It is almost cleft into two nearly equal parts by Sippican Harbor. The land is low, level, and rocky. The soil is a marine deposit, and fertile, but requiring great expense and labor to clear it of rocks; hence but a small portion is under cultivation. This is divided into small lots by high stone fences. Dense forests of white pine and oak, cover nearly four-fifths of the town. One source of industry with the early settlers was the manufacture of tar, of which each resident was allowed by the proprietors, to make ten barrels from the undivided forest, and if he made more, he must pay a tax of one shilling per barrel to the proprietors. More recently, the manufacture of salt, and of late, box-boards, and fire-wood, constitute the principal exports.

The harbor is safe and commodious, and sheltered by several large islands. The channel, as far as opposite the upper wharf of the lower village, contains eleven feet of water. There are now owned in this place, four whalemen, (one brig, and three schooners), and two schooners engaged in the cod fisheries; there are also one or two smaller vessels engaged in the coasting business—aggregate tonnage 759. There are five wharves in the lower village, and two in the upper. Two of the former are not now in use. The imports from three whalemen and two fishermen, for the year 1865, were, for the former, $65,000, for the latter, $12,000. The people are generally mariners, a smaller portion mechanics and farmers. Formerly, they were extensively engaged in southern coasting, and many accummulated handsome fortunes. Now the fisheries are the chief industrial pursuit. There have been no persons of great public note belonging to this town. The citizens, however, have generally been enterprising, and successful in business, many of them eminently so. Among the prominent and useful citizens of this precinct, were, Seth Hiller, an extensive land-holder; Charles and George Blankinship, eminent ship-builders and owners; George B. Nye, a prominent business man; Stephen Hammond, an eminent mariner; Dr. W. N. Ellis, who, for nearly thirty years, was the principal medical and legal adviser. Many of the clergymen have been men of character and influence. The population of the town is about 1000, chiefly concentrated in two very pleasant villages, half a mile apart. There are four religious societies, one Protestant, Methodist, Episcopal Methodist, Universalist, and Congregationalist, each with a neat and commodious house of worship. There is one hotel, the "Bay View House," in the lower village, a boarding house in the upper, and another, called the "Marion House," on the extremity of Great Neck, of a capacity to accommodate three hundred boarders. All of these public houses will accommodate five hundred, and they are full to repletion every summer, at least a part of the time, besides several private houses owned by non-residents. Many private families also receive boarders. The are five stores, and one Petroleum Oil Factory, whose permanent stock amounts to $6500, and when in operation yields an income of about 50 per cent.

The salubrity of this town is above the average of towns in New England.

This town contributed 40 soldiers for the war of the Rebellion, four of whom died in the service, and one since, also 23 seamen, three of whom became officers. There are evidences of a remarkable change in the depth of water in the upper harbor. Where there is now considerable depth of water, during low ebbs there may be seen large trunks and stumps of trees, and there is a tradition, that the channel was once so narrow, that a person might step across at low water below the wharves, between Black Point and the ship-yard. The distance between these two points is about thirty rods.

The territory now called Marion, the greater part of Rochester, the westerly part of Wareham, and, (in many instances), Mattapoisett, was called Sippican, or, as it is more frequently spelt in the ancient records, Sepecan. It belonged to the territory of Massasoit, and afterwards, of his son and successor, Philip Metacomet, sachem of the Wampanoags. In 1632, Phillip entered into an agreement with the English not to dispose of any part of his territory without their consent. In 1666, he confirmed the title of the lands of Sepecan to two subordinate chiefs, Watachpoo and Sampson; with the provision in the deed corresponding with the above agreement. These lands had been held in the line of Watachpoo's ancestors, for at least six generations. On the 24th day of Dec., 1668, Philip gives his consent that Watachpoo may sell his lands, or a portion of them, to the English. The deed of his sale is not recorded. July 11th, 1667, two sachems of Sepaconit (probably Agawam Neck in Wareham), sold the westerly part of the present town of Marion, including what is called Charles' Neck to an Indian chief named Pompmunet, *alias* Charles of Ashimmit, "with libertie of Comanage for cattle and likewise to make use of any timber for fencing or building that is without this neck, with libertie of fishing or fowling or whatever priviledge is belonging thereunto as necessary." The consideration was eight pounds—$26.67.

The northern portion of Sepecan, including the north-west section of Wareham, and nearly the whole of Rochester, was granted to Thomas Besbeck, and others, Jan. 22d, 1638-9. In 1649, (June 6th,) "Libertie is granted unto the townsmen of Plymouth, to make use of the land at Sepecan for the herding and keeping of cattle, and wintering of them there as they shall see cause." This section included Great and Little Necks, and the vicinity bordering upon the sea-shore. For many years before and after this grant, herdsmen, with their herds, tenanted temporary habitations erected for their use, where the rich pasture lands and extensive salt marshes afforded ample sustenance for their charge. June 5th, 1651, the above grant was confirmed, and limited to the citizens of Plymouth; "and the bounds thereof to extend itself eight miles by the sea-side and four miles into the land." July 2d, 1655. "At this Court libertie was granted to the town of Plymouth, to purchase lands of the Indians at Sepecan, to winter cattle upon." June 3d, 1679. An Act was passed preliminary to the sale of those lands to certain persons, which was confirmed at the next Session of the Court in July, and the settlement commenced in 1680. The first house appears to have been erected by Samuel Briggs, who built about one fourth of a mile north-west of the residence of Abel Griffith. The names of some of the first principal settlers, as given by Barber, are:—Samuel Arnold, John Hammond, Moses Barlow, Samuel White, Samuel Hammond, John Wing, Aaron Barlow, Joseph Dotey, Jacob Bumpus, Joseph Burgess, John Haskell, —— Sprague, Abraham Holmes, Job Winslow.

The first settlement commenced near the entrance to Little Neck, and soon after extended to Great Neck, and towards Rochester center. Their first minister was Samuel Shiverick, from 1683 to 1687. He was succeeded in the latter year by Samuel Arnold, who died Feb. 11th, 1707. Timothy Ruggles was settled in 1710, who held the pastorate 57 years. The church was organized Oct. 13th, 1703. The first meeting-house was a building constructed for a "corn-house" by Samuel Briggs, and moved on to Little Neck, near a huge rock, around which the Indians used to perform their noisy demon-worship, sometimes at the same hour when the Christian worshippers were engaged in their service. The first burial-place was laid out, according to their usual custom, in the rear of the meeting-house. The first person buried there, is said to have been Eliza Briggs, aged 12 years. The next meeting-house was built in Rochester Center, not far from 1730. The first house built on Great Neck, was by John Allen, near the head of the Cove, between Stephen Allen's and Mrs. Bolles.

The first house in the lower village, was built by John Clark, where the store of J. C. Luce stands, about 1760.

The first house in the upper village was built by John Keen, where W. P. Delano's house stands. It was swept away by the great tide in 1815.

The Sepecan Indians do not appear very prominent in the history of Massachusetts. They were, at some remote period, very numerous, as the frequent and extensive shell-heaps indicate; though the interior tribes contributed largely to these relics, in their periodical excursions to the sea-shore. In Aug. 1677, while King Phillip's war was raging, the Sacoact tribe, near the eastern shore of Narraganset Bay, was detached from the Confederacy through the efforts of Captain Church, who advised queen Awashanks to go to Sandwich with her tribe and arrange terms of amity with the governor who resided there. Church, impatient at their delay, set out to find their camp. He passed through Agawam [Wareham], crossed the Weweantit river, and found Awashanks and her tribe encamped near the beach at Great Hill, on the spot where the "Marion House" stands. "Some were running races on horseback; some playing at foot-ball; some were catching eels and flat-fish; and others plunging and frolicking in the waves." The gallant queen received the English officer with the greatest respect and cordiality; entertained him with fried eels, bass, flat-fish, and shell-fish; and then, around a huge bonfire of pine knots, herself and warriors pledged their allegiance to the English, and thus sealed the fate of Philip.*

The list of Marion men, lost in service, so far as we can obtain it, is as follows:—Jesse L. Swift, C, 18th, of disease, Dec. 1, 1864; Nathan H. Weeks, C, 18th, of disease; Richard Gurney, A, 29th, killed; Benjamin D. Clifton, A, 20th, killed; Andrew T. Pratt, E, 3d, killed; Joseph Davis, 9th, N. H., Reg., Co. I, died in prison.

NOTE.—*See Abbott's History of King Phillip. Abbott calls the river which Captain Church crossed to reach Awashank's camp, Mattapoisett. If he has copied this name correctly, it is to be recollected, that, at this early period, the names of places, rivers, &c., had not became settled. Many instances of the interchange of names from ancient records might be quoted. The stream which bears this name at present, is an insignificant stream, near the western limit of Mattapoisett, ten miles beyond the Weweantit, and no bluff is found near it which commands "a wide prospect of Buzzard's Bay." If there is a spot near the former stream elevated enough to command a view of the water, only a portion of what is called Mattapoiset Harbor could be seen, a view incomparably inferior to that from Great Hill.

MATTAPOISETT

Was incorporated May 20, 1857. Previous to that time it had been for nearly one hundred and seventy-five years, a part of Rochester. The first town meeting was held in Purrington Hall, June 20, 1857. The Indian word Mattapoisett signified a place of rest. Mattapoisett was formerly justly celebrated for its extensive ship-building operations. For several years this important business has been very much depressed.

The following is a list of Mattapoisett citizens lost in the war of Rebellion :—Zaccheus M. Barstow, D, 3d Reg., at Newbern, N. C., Oct. 10, 1862, of congestion of the lungs. John T. Barstow, K, 1st Reg., at Washington, Dec. 20, '62, of diarrhœa. Edward F. Barlow, E, 18th Reg., of starvation, at Andersonville, Sept. 3, 1864. Wm. C. Dexter, E, 58th Reg., July 28, 1864, of fever, on board transport. Charles H. Hayden, C, 29th Reg. John A. LeBaron, H, 14th Reg., Point Lookout Hospital, Md., Oct. 6, 1861. Franklin A. Lobre, I, 3d Reg., Petersburg, Va., rebel hospital, Jan. 19, 1863. Geo. D. Snow, D, 18th, killed at Fredericksburg, Va., Dec. 13, 1862. Edward F. Snow, D, 18th Reg., at home, Sept. 6, 1864, of fever. Ebenezer Tripp, G, 20th Reg., killed at Balls Bluff, Oct. 21, 1861. Wm. H. Taber, C, 7th Pa. Cav., Munfordsville Hospital, Ky., of fever, March 18, 1862. Charles H. Tinkham, I, 3d Reg., Newbern, N. C., of fever, Nov. 30, 1862. Geo. W. Wilcox, D, 18th Reg., Christian Street Hospital, Phil., Aug. 23, 1862. Wm. S. Wilcox, 5th Battery, Falmouth Hospital, Nov. 28, 1862. John Bates, steamer Henry Andrew, killed at Mosquito Inlet, Fla., March 22, 1862. John S. Dennis, Acting Master, steamer Huntress, Feb. 22, 1865, at New Madrid, Mo., of fever. William H. Kinney, gunner, steamer Benton, killed at Grand Gulf, Miss., April 29, 1863. Elijah W. Randall, seaman, steamer Housatonic, off Charleston, S. C., April 19, 1863, of abscess.

MIDDLEBORO.

WE TRACE the first historical narrative we have of Middleboro, back to the account given by Captain Dermer, who visited this place the year previous to the first landing of the Pilgrims. He came here to restore Tisquantum or Squantum, a kidnapped Indian.

The first time the soil of Middleboro was ever pressed by the foot of a white man, so far as we know, was in 1616. A vessel was at that time wrecked at the north-east of Cape Cod, and from it a Frenchman escaped, was taken captive and brought to Namasket. Then tall primeval forests waved over the hills, and there must have been a native beauty and freshness about the whole scene.

> Here stood the Indian hamlet, there the lake
> Spread its blue sheet, that flashed with many an oar,
> Where the brown otter plunged him from the brake
> And the deer drank; as the light gale flew o'er,
> The twinkling maize field rustled on the shore."

Then the original lords of this fair heritage roamed in conscious dignity through the plains and valleys of Namasket. Would that the French sailor had left us a history of the three eventful years of his captivity, coming hither as he did before the blighting influence of civilization had been experienced, or the dusky ranks of the Indians had been thinned by pestilence. But a sad change was speedily manifest. The captive must have witnessed the ravages of that plague, which swept over all this region about the year 1617, when the inhabitants died so rapidly that there were not enough survivors to bury the dead; died as it is now believed, of the malignant yellow fever.

Three years later, Namasket was visited, for the first time, by an Englishman. It was a lovely spring morning—the birds carolled from the tree tops, amid expanding leaves and fragrant blossoms.

But a retrospective glance seems necessary in order to an understanding of this visit. In 1614, the famous John Smith, having charge of two vessels, explored the whole coast of New England, "from Penobscot to Cape Cod." Having secured 40,000 codfish and 1100 beaver skins, he returned with one vessel to England. The other was left in charge with Capt. Hunt, to fit himself for Spain with a load of dried fish. Having crossed over from Cape Ann to Cohasset and the South Shore, Hunt enticed 20 natives on board his craft, under the pretence of trade, and confining them in the hold, sailed for Malaga, where they were sold as slaves. Among them was one named Squanto, called also Tisquantum, a native, it is said, of Patuxet, or Plymouth.

After remaining in bondage, we know not how long, he is said to have been redeemed by Spanish monks and sent to London. Here he was shown for a wonder. He was then a goodly man, of brave aspect, stout and sober in demeanor, and could speak English so much as to say to those who came to see and to wonder at him, "Welcome, welcome."

Squanto was subsequently sent back to this country by Sir Ferdinando Gorges, in an exploring vessel.

In May, 1619, Capt. Dermer, commander of the craft, having searched every harbor on the coast, landed at Plymouth, and finding all dead there, he says—"I travelled alongst a day's journey to a place called *Nammasquyt*, where finding inhabitants, I dispatched a messenger a day's journey further west, to Poconoket, which bordereth on the sea; whence came to see me two kings, attended with a guard of 50 armed men, who being well satisfied, with that, my savage and I discoursed unto them, being desirous of novelty, gave me content in whatsoever I demanded. Here I redeemed a Frenchman, who, three years since, escaped shipwreck at the north-east of Cape Cod."

Capt. Dermer, however, came near losing his life at the hand of the Sachem Corbitant, who had been exasperated by the treatment some of his tribe had received from previous white visitors to the coast.

The "26 men's purchase," made of the Sachem Wampatuck, in 1662, and confirmed by the court at Plymouth in 1663, included all the land bounded by the Indian path on the south, Tippacunnecut and Hasnappit Brooks on the east, Winnatuxet River on the north, and Tetiquid and Nemasket Rivers on the west. The original settlement seems to have been made under this purchase, but many others soon followed until the whole town, (and more,) was clear of all Indian claims, except "Quittaub and part of Tetiquid," where there were remnants of tribes." The town was incorporated July 1, 1669.

Purchases continued to be made of the Namasket Indians during the succeeding ten years, even after the grant by the Court, until the settlers became the proprietors of the whole territory, except Quittaub and Tetiquid. We have records of the whole: some of them are from Wampatuck, some from Metispaquin, and one or more from Philip, chief sachem of the country of Pokanawkot. "The 26 men's, in March 1662; "the great men's," in 1663, ; "the 8 men's," "the Purchade," in 1662, July; "the major's, or 5 men's," in 1663; "the Little Lotmen's," in 1664; "Wood's," in 1667; "Prince and Coombs," in 1668; and the "Twelve men's," in 1672; "the south purchase," in 1673; "the 16 shilling," in 1695, and several small tracts and gores not named by any title.

In 1675, the town having been settled, and a mill and some twenty or thirty houses having been built, and "Philip's War" having broken out, the whole town was broken up and the mill and houses were all burnt.

In 1677 the settlement began to be renewed, but the town was not fully organized until 1680.

In 1680, an Indian war having broken out in Maine, the town was ordered to send two men to the service by the Council of War, and John Thompson and James Soule were impressed for the service; but they refused to attend the service, and were sentenced to pay four pounds each in money into the treasury of the town for their use, or to be imprisoned until they could pay the same with the fees.

In 1690 the population of the town was two hundred.

A considerable accession seems to have been made to our population just before or about the year 1690, one of the consequences of the prosecutions for witchcraft in the county of Essex, Mass. As nobody was safe, many fled into the Plymouth Colony, then a separate government, and where no witch was prosecuted, no Baptist whipped, no Quaker hanged: all the principles of the Pilgrims being opposed to things of this kind. The families of Thomas, Bennett, Smith, Morse and several others came in at this time to avoid these witch evils. There were two brothers by the name of Thomas, young men, who were drawn to serve on a witch jury, at Salem. They did not believe in witches, but knew if they expressed their disbelief, they would suffer persecution. They fled to this town, one settling on the Pond, and the other on the River—the descendants of the two families taking the names of the "Pond," and "River" Thomases.

In 1691 Plymouth was annexed by royal charter, to the colony of Massachusetts, much to their dissatisfaction, and the town, for a long series of years, sent no Deputies to Boston.

In 1776, the population of Middleboro was 4,479. The next winter, the males above sixteen years of age were 1066, embracing five Indians and eight negroes. In 1791 there were but 4526, being an increase of 47 in 15 years, showing an immense emigration. A large portion of the towns of New Salem and Shutesbury, Mass., and Woodstock, Vt., emigrated from Middleboro.

The different portions of Middleboro still bear some of the significant Indian names—Titicut signifies the place of the great river. Eliot, in his Indian Bible, uses, it is said, the same word in translating the great river Euphrates.

Namasket, a compound of Namusk, or as the Indian Bible has it, Namosog, and et, signifies the place of fish.

Assowamset signifies the place of white stones, and is expressive of the quartz locality in that vicinity.

Of the names, Namasket seems to have been the most comprehensive, and is sometimes used to embrace a large portion of the territory of Middleboro; as when the early writers speak of the "Kingdom of Namasket," in distinction from the "little town of Namasket."

That Middleboro was once densely populated with savages, is evinced by the following considerations:—

The fact that Taunton and Namasket rivers swarmed with bass, shad, and herrings; the brooks emptying into them with delicious trout, and all the great ponds with white perch and pickerel; while the deer, moose, wolves, bears, foxes, and wild fowl, filled these forests, served to make it an inviting residence for the red man.

That this was the stronghold of the Indians is evinced by the fact that Middleboro was not settled by the whites till 40 years after the landing of the Pilgrims at Plymouth, and was not organized into a town till years after Bridgewater and Taunton, and Sandwich, the latter including Wareham and Rochester, had been incorporated. The crowded state of the Indian cemeteries demonstrate the fact, that Namasket once teemed with multitudes of savages. In 1827, while digging down a small knoll, on the premises of Maj. John Shaw, in the village, more than eighty Indian skeletons were removed.

Middleboro constituted the occasional residence of the principal chiefs of the New England tribes. Here Massasoit, and Corbitant the proud sachem of his tribe were accustomed to resort with their chosen followers, to pass a portion of the hunting and fishing season.

At Titicut, dwelt the family of the great Chicataubut, whose sway extended to Neponset, where also he had a residence. His son, Wampatuck, sachem of the Monponsets, had an interest in this territory.

On the Assowamset Neck lived the mighty Tispaquin, surrounded with his 200 braves, the subjugation of whose tribe closed up the terrible war of King Philip in this vicinity.

9*

The Indians cultured the Indian corn in this vicinity in the following manner. Having tied the shoulder blade of a moose, or fastened a large clamshell to a stick, they dug small holes in the earth, four feet apart and placed therein a few herrings for manure. They then dropped in four or five clevels of corn and covered them up with the same rude instrument.

"What sort of a band should we make at farming with only the means of these settlers. True, they had fish and needed no other manure. But as to oxen and plows, they had to dig for the want of them, and as for shovels, there was not an *iron* shovel in town till within the age of a very elderly man now alive among us, and if they had a hoe they got it from England. Such a thing as digging and stoning a well was not so much as thought over. Their wooden shovels would perform no such service. All their houses must be built hard by some living spring. The springs and seats of their houses are many, if not all of them, now known and apparent."

Henry Wood and Ephraim Tinkham were two men who erected the first dwelling-houses at Namasket; Wood upon the Gen. Washburn farm, and Tinkham upon the Ichabod Wood place.

In 1675, the following are the names of those who were householders, and who were driven back to Plymouth by the Indians:— John Thompson, Isaac Howland, Francis Coombs, Samuel Fuller, John Morton, Nath'l Southworth, Ephraim Tinkham, Henry Wood, William Nelson, David Thomas, John Cobb, Jabez Warren, Edward Bump, Moses Simmons, Samuel Barrows, Samuel Eaton, Francis Billington, George Soule, Obadiah Eddy, Samuel Pratt, George Vaughan, John Shaw, Jacob Thompson, Francis Miller, John Holmes and John Alden.

The first meeting after the war, (the record of which is the first we have,) was in June, 1677, when they lament the loss of their records, and resolve upon the re-possession of their estates. The same families seem to have returned, attended by some others, of whom are the following: William Bartlett, John Haskell, Giles Ricard, Anthony Snow, Henry Warren, Jonathan Dunham, John Miller, David Wood, Benjamin Wood, Samuel Eddy, Zachariah Eddy, Jonathan Wood, Gershom Cobb, William Cushman.

Fortunately but one man was killed from Middleboro, in King Philip's war. His name was Robert Danson.

Until within 125 years there were very few neat cattle and few horses; and no grass except woods-grass and fresh meadow grass, and no vehicle on wheels except carts—not a wagon for ox or horse. Easy and warm spots of land were selected for their corn, and as for potatoes, it is not 150 years since they were first known among us.

In the Indian burying ground on Assowamset Neck, located between the Rochester road and Little Quittecus, are a number of graves with rough headstones. There are two, with regular head and foot stones of slate, with the following inscriptions.

"To the memory of Lidia Squeen, who died in 1811, age 72.

EPITAPH.
In God, the poor and helpless find
A judge most just, a parent kind.

The other was erected "to the memory of Jean Squeen, who died April 13th, 1794, in the 23d year of her age. Also of Benjamin, who died at sea, April 22d, 1790, in his 26th year, children of Lydia Squeen, a native."

EPITAPH.
When Earth was made and time began,
Death was decreed the fate of man.

In 1710, July 19, the West Precinct was incorporated, being nearly the same territory known as Lakeville, including a part of Taunton.

In 1743, the parish of Titicut was incorporated, and included all that part of Middleboro, west of Purchade Brook, (with the exception of a few families,) and northerly of Trout Brook, including a part of Bridgewater.

In 1783 the parish of North Rochester was incorporated, and included all that part of Middleboro south of a line from Pocksha Pond, due east to the town of Carver, with a part of Rochester and a part of Freetown.

The Herring question has always been an exciting one at the annual town meetings. In 1705, 6d a load was the price of fish. The size of the loads began to increase, owing to men's selfishness, until in 1725, it was voted that 8,000 fish be a load. For many years the herring privilege was sold by the Selectmen, at public vendue, to the highest bidder, and these officers were authorized to furnish liquor at the expense of the town.

Middleboro always took great interest in military matters, having furnished at different times, of commissioned officers for the militia service, enough to form a regiment. At one time there were in town nine infantry companies and one cavalry.

The first mill in town was for grining corn, and was located near the present site of the Star Mills. Two sawmills were early built on Bartlett's Brook, but we have no account of any manufacturing until 1734, when a slitting mill was built, by leave of the town, on Namasket River, at Oliver's Works. Strong objections were made to the work, on account of its apprehended detriment to the fishery—herrings being considered as indispensable to the raising of corn, as well as an article of food.

The best farming land in town is in the Titicut part. At present a large number of citizens are employed in the shoe business, Bay State Straw Works, Star Woolen Mills, and the various box and saw mills in different parts of the town.

Of antiquities, the most interesting is the Old Morton House, a part of which was erected about 200 years ago. For some years it served as a fort, to protect the settlers from the Indians, having been provided with port holes.

In 1833-4, the first newspaper was published in Middleboro. The name was the "Old Colony Democrat," Benj. Drew, editor and printer. The office was soon removed from the place. The "Namasket Gazette" was commenced Oct. 7, 1852, by Samuel P. Brown. In 1854, the establishment was purchased by Rev. Stillman Pratt, and the name changed to the "Middleboro Gazette and Old Colony Advertiser." Since the death of Mr. Pratt senior, Sept. 1, 1862, the paper has been published by his son, Stillman B. Pratt.

Of distinguished painters, Middleboro has produced Cephas Thompson, and his two sons, Cephas G. and Jerome B. Thompson; of musicians, Professor Oliver Shaw, of Providence, has been perhaps the most celebrated; of lawyers, the first rank has been accorded to Zachariah Eddy; while perhaps her most generous and wealthy merchant has been Enoch Pratt, of Baltimore, who has so munificently endowed the Pratt Free School, at Titicut.

Deborah Sampson, the well known female warrior of the Revolution, enlisted from this town, and served for about two years under the assumed name of Robert Shurtleff. Lavinia, wife of C. G. Stratton, (Gen. Tom Thumb) and Minnie Warren, the well known dwarfs, were natives and are now residents of Middleboro.

Luke Short, who died here in 1746, aged 116 years, was converted when about one hundred years old, as a result of a sermon he heard preached by John Flavel, about 80 years previous.

Moses Thompson, who died Dec. 2, 1858, aged 96 years, 5 months, was the last Revolutionary soldier from the town.

The oldest literary institution in town is Peirce Academy, Prof. J. W. P. Jenks, Principal. A very large cabinet and apparatus belongs to the institution. For a view of the building, as well as the First Baptist Church, see engraving. The Pratt Free School occupies the building formerly known as Titicut Academy.

The incorporated name of the town was Middleberry, and in the Old Colony records it was often written Middlebury. Afterwards the spelling of Middleborough was adopted, and by general consent the useless appendage of the *ugh* has of late years been usually dropped, leaving the name Middleboro.

NOTE.—Most of the foregoing facts were gathered by the late Messrs. Rev. Stillman Pratt and Z. Eddy, Esqr.

NORTH BRIDGEWATER.

THIS, the north-west town in Plymouth County, is located 20 miles south from Boston, and 25 miles from Plymouth. It is 5 1-2 miles in length and 5 in width, and contains 13,000 acres, with a total length of 67 miles of highway.

The villages in town are the "Centre," a thriving, energetic and attractive business locality; "Campello," signifying a small plain, noted for its manufactories of musical instruments, cabinet ware and boots and shoes; "Sprague's Village," where is situated the last factory and beautiful residence of Chandler Sprague, Esq., and "West Shares."

The facts connected with the old town of Bridgewater, before its division, are given elsewhere. The first settlers in the North Parish, came from the West Parish about 1700. Separate church organization was secured in 1738, and the town incorporation in 1821.

The first minister was John Porter, ordained in 1740. In 1800, Asa Meech was settled, as his colleague. Mr. Porter, died in 1802, and Mr. Meech was dismissed in 1811. The successors were Daniel Huntington, 1812-1833; Wm. Thompson, 1833-1834; Paul Couch, 1835-1859; Nathaniel B. Blanchard, 1861-1862; Edward L. Clark, 1863-1866; and Rev. J. W. Ward.

The Second Congregational Society was organized in 1825. John Goldsbury first minister.

The New Jerusalem Society, was formed in 1827, with ten members. Ministers, Eleazer Smith, 1827-1834; Haskell M. Carll; and Warren Goddard, settled in 1839. Their present Church Temple is 79 by 56 feet, Italian style, with a plain square tower. The seats are semi-circular, with pulpit and tabernacle of black walnut.

The South Congregational Church, Campello, was organized in 1837. John Dwight was settled in the same year, dismissed 1839. Daniel Huntington, settled from 1839 to 1853. In the great fire of that year, the church edifice and other buildings to the value of $50,000 were destroyed. A new edifice in the Romanesque style, with spire 135 feet high, was built at a cost of $16,000. D. Temple Packard, was settled two years, and in 1858, he was succeeded by Charles W. Wood, a native of Middleboro.

In 1830, 111 persons formed the First Episcopal Methodist Society, at West Shares. This is the only house that retains the elevated seats for colored people in each corner of the choir gallery.

The First Baptist Church was constituted Jan. 10th, 1850.

The Porter Evangelical Church, was composed of members who withdrew from the First Church, in 1850. The settlements have been John F. Norton, 1850-1851; Charles L. Mills, 1852-1862; Samuel H. Lee, 1862-1866; and J. V. Hilton.

The Catholics, previous to 1856, held meetings in private houses. Under the ministry of Thomas B. McNulty, a lot was bought for $5,225, and a splendid church edifice of the Romanesque style, 110 by 50 feet, was erected of brick, with tower and steeple 180 feet high. The chancel windows of stained glass have emblematic panes representing Matthew, Mark, Luke and John. Upon the walls are 14 Italian pictures of great value. The edifice cost $25,000.

The First Universalist Church was organized in 1857. W. A. Start was the first pastor, succeeded by Rev. S. L. Roripaugh.

The Second M. E. Church, was formed in 1842, and in 1853, the present attractive edifice was erected. It will thus be seen that the town may justly claim pre-eminence for the number as well as the beauty of its houses of worship.

In 1756, the precinct voted that "the rume on the womens side of the gallery should be for the women," showing that then, the men and women were seated in seperate pews. In 1772, a number of persons "larned" in the rules of "musick," were assigned seats in the gallery, which produced dissatisfaction. In 1789, it was voted to build pews in the porch and belfry for the negroes, and sell their present pews, which created ill feelings on the part of the colored population. In 1800, complaint was made that blacks occupied seats with white people, and they were instructed to sit in the porch gallery. In 1818, the subject of warming the church with stoves, was brought up, but was voted down as a sinful luxury. In 1833, the Parish voted that they would not accept a stove as a gift. In 1835, however, it was voted to warm the house. In 1827, while a new house was being built, precious meetings were held in the sheds on the green.

The Adelphian Academy, North Bridgwater Academy, and Mrs. Nathan Jones' School, were well known institutions in their day. Thirty-four natives of the town have been College graduates.

In 1845-6, the railroad from South Braintree to Bridewater was built, and was known as the Randolph and Bridgewater Co. Previous to this, the Fall River Branch had been built from Myrick's to Fall River. Another road was chartered from Bridgewater to Myrick's. These three lines were united as the Fall River road, and in 1854, this was united with the Old Colony road, and in 1864, the name was changed to the "Old Colony and Newport Railway."

The "Bridgewater Patriot and Old Colony Gazette," was commenced in 1835, by Geo. H. Brown. It was removed afterwards to East Bridgewater. The "Old Colony Reporter," was commenced in 1848, by Bartlett & Stetson. This continued till 1851. In the latter year, the "North Bridgewater Gazette" was commenced by George Phinney, now of the "Waltham Sentinel," who sold out to Augustus T. Jones, in 1853.

In 1690, there were but six tunes known in the Province; "Oxford," "Litchfield," "York," "Windsor," "St. David's" and "Martyr's," and no new tunes could be introduced without vote of the church. At present, the church music of North Bridgewater is of a high order.

At one time there were three Brass Bands in town. The Band of the 12th Regiment, was the favorite organization with Gen. Sherman.

The North Bridgewater Bank is one of the institutions of the past. The Savings Bank is in flourishing condition.

The first fire-engine was purchased by subscription, in 1827. The town bought the "Protector" and "Enterprise," in 1847. There has always been a laudable feeling of rivalry between the different Companies, and many trials of machines have been made.

The first burial-ground was located between the Center and Campello. The "Melrose" and "Oak Grove" and "St. Patrick's" Cemeteries, are the more modern ones.

Until 1823, the town's poor were put out at auction to the one who would support them the cheapest. In 1831, a poor-house farm was purchased. North Bridgewater has no Town House.

The Gas Light Company was organized in 1859.

In 1749, hay had to be brought from England on account of the severe drought. May 19th, 1780, a "dark day," when people were obliged to eat their dinners by the light of candles.

Archibald Thompson made the first spinning wheel in the country. The manufacture of lasts by Chandler Sprague, revolutionized that branch of business. E. D. & O. B. Reynolds are the inventors of a very ingenious and valuable Seed Sower. D. Whittemore, and C. L. Hauthaway & Son, are extensively engaged in the manufacture of blacking, and ink.

The Boot and Shoe Manufactories, Merchants, Musical Instruments, Photograph Saloons, Confectionary establishment and Marble Workers, of North Bridgewater, are favorably known in all the County.

The shoe trade of Massachusetts, may be said to have commenced about 1818, when the first cargo was shipped to New York. These were of the sewed kind. About this time, the uppers were riveted to the bottoms, using a steel plate for the purpose. Wooden pegs were first used by Joseph Walker, of Hopkinton. Micah Faxon, was the first manufacturer in town, coming from Randolph, in 1811. No one in town then could bind the vamps. He carried his first lot, of one hundred pairs, to Boston, on horseback. In 1865, with the aid of steam engines, sewing, pegging, cutting and scouring machines, 1,112,766 pairs of boots and shoes were manufactured, valued at $1,466,900, and employing 1267 persons.

Jesse Reed, born here in 1778, invented a new kind of trip hammer, at the age of nine. At twelve, he constructed a wooden clock. Since then, he has invented nail machines, pumps, cotton gins, boot and shoe machines, &c. He has made and lost several fortunes in his day.

Of the origin of some of the old families, we mention those of Ames, Alden, Bryant, Brett, Cary, Edson, Hayward, Howard, Packard, Pratt, Snow, Southworth, and Thayer, *English;* Dike and Keith, *Scotch;* Wilson, *Welsh;* Henry, *Irish.*

Fifty-five inhabitants of North Bridgewater served in the French and Indian wars. The record in the Revolutionary war was patriotic. In many instances the women of the town had to till the soil to obtain the necessities of life. In 1773, Bridgewater had 9 militia Co's.

At the conclusion of the Revolutionary war, the country was flooded with foreign goods, draining us of specie, and ruining our manufacturers. Our people, burdened under the great weight of taxation, and great numbers out of employment, became disheartened and were easily lead into the support of any scheme that would seem to relieve these burdens.

The result of a public meeting at Hatfield, Mass., August, 1786, so inflamed the people that a mob of fifteen hundred, gathered at Northampton, to prevent the sitting of the Courts. Daniel Shay, of Pelham, was one of the prime movers in the scheme, hence the name of "Shay's Rebellion." A gathering similar to the one at Northampton, was held at the Court House, Taunton, in September, but the insurgents were overawed by Lieut. Col. Orr's, and Capt. John Thompson's Companies, of the 3d Plymouth County Regiment. 54 of these soldiers were from North Bridgewater.

In the Rebellion war, the town shows a brilliant record. Co. F, 12th Mass. Reg't., Co, I, 1st Cavalry, Co, C, 69th Mass. Reg't., were mainly recruited here.

The list of deaths while in service, is as follows:—

Twelfth Regiment.

Capt. John S. Stoddard, killed at Spottsylvania, May 10th, 1864; Serg't. Francis P. Holmes, killed; Serg't James S. Tannett, of fever, at Manassas, July 13th, 1862; Serg't. Galen Edson, at Culpepper Court House, Feb. 20th, 1864; Geo. W. Childs, killed at Fredericksburg, Dec. 18th, 1862; Malcomb F. Dhalberg, from wounds at Antietam, Dec. 17th, 1862; Aaron B. Frost, battle of Bull Run, Aug. 30th, 1862; Andrew J. Frost, at Fairfax Court House, Aug. 28th, 1862; Linus P. Howard, killed at Bull Run, Aug. 30th, 1862; John S. Hamilton, of small pox, near Washington, Dec., 1862; Serg't Thaddeus Keith, killed at the Wilderness, May 6th, 1864; Francis N. Maroni, killed at Bull Run, Aug. 30th, 1862; Serg't Frank M. Stoddard, killed at Spottsylvania, May 10th, 1864; Francis A. Sanford, killed at Bull Run, Aug. 30th, 1862; Geo. B. Walker, died from wounds, Washington, Sept. 24th, 1862; Jerome R. Hodge, killed at Fredericksburg,

Dec. 13th, 1862; Lyman Allen, killed near Spottsylvania, May 10th, 1864; Henry L. Winter, killed at Wilderness, May 5th, 1864; John W. Burns, at Libby Prison, Feb. 24th, 1864; Richard Packard, killed at Fredericksburg, Dec. 13th, 1862.

First Mass. Cavalry.

Joseph T. Stevens, died at Hilton Head, Mar. 31st, 1862; A. W. Bartlett, from wounds, at Beaufort, Feb. 10th, 1864; Joseph P. Bisbee, died July 14th, 1862; Frederic M. Wortman, at Port Royal Harbor, Feb. 6th, 1864; John Sylvester, at Andersonville, Dec., 1864; Roscoe Tucker, at Florence, Jan. 29th, 1865; Horace F. Poole, while on his way home, from effects of starvation at Florence, Mar. 9th, 1865; Joel D. Dudley, killed at High Bridge, Va., April 6th, 1865. Ellis V. Lyon, died Sept. 24th, 1864.

Various Regiments.

Herbert C. Blood, C, 60th, at Indianapolis; Lieut. Geo. W. Pope, 29th, of wounds, at Georgetown Hospital, Aug. 5th, 1864; Quar. Sergt. John B. Cobb, 2d, H. A., of yellow fever, at Mansfield, N. C., Oct. 24th, 1864; Geo. E. Holmes, F, 58th, from rebel imprisonment, at Annapolis, May 28th, 1865; Harrison A. Hunt, at Danville prison, Nov. 22d, 1864; Samuel T. Packard, G, 56th, of wounds, Oct. 10th, 1864; Frank E. Drake, I, 1st H. A., at Andersonville, Nov. 18, 1864; Daniel W. Willis, D, 58th, killed in battle; John R. Mills, D, 58th, killed in battle; Walter D. Allen, 3d Cavalry, from wounds, at Philadelphia, Oct. 29th, 1864; John D. Sanford, K, 40th, at Andersonville, July 16, 1864; George M. Nash, 32d, wounded at Spottsylvania, died in an ambulance on the way to Fredericksburg; Charles W. Reynolds, D, 58th, fell at Petersburg; Dr. Charles H. Mason, Surgeon on gunboat Virginia, of yellow fever, near New Orleans, Oct. 13, 1864; Daniel P. Sherman, B, 1st Cavalry, killed at battle of Aldie, June 17, 1863; Capt. Enos W. Thayer, 26th, of wounds at Winchester, Oct. 19, 1862; George H. Thompson, F, 58th, at Andersonville, June 7, 1864; Ambrose Henry Hayward, D, 28th Pa., at Chattanooga, Tenn., June 15, 1864, of wounds received at Pine Knob; Austin Packard, 9th Battery, of wounds at Gettysburg, Sep. 21, 1864; Samuel Kimball, E, 18th, killed at Bull Run, Aug. 30, 1862; Wm. Flannegan, killed at Bull Run, Aug. 30, 1861; Ferdinand Robinson, killed at Bull Run; Joseph Beals, of wounds at Gettysburg, July 3, 1863; Edward F. Drohan, C, 29th, died Jan. 12, 1862; Charles F. Swanstrom, 33d, died Dec. 23, 1862; Henry Fenn, 9th Battery, killed at Gettysburg; and Andrew P. Olsom, C, 42d, died at New York.

NOTE.—Nearly all of the above facts are taken from the very valuable History of North Bridgewater, published in a large book of 700 pages, profusely illustrated, in 1866, by Bradford Kingman, Esq., member of the "New England Historic Genealogical Society;" Corresponding member of the "Wisconsin Historical Society," and author of "Kingman Memorial."

PEMBROKE.

BY I. COLLAMORE, M. D.

NOT much is known concerning what is now Pembroke, prior to its incorporation. Previous to 1712, all the territory that the limits of Pembroke now embrace, was Duxbury, except a small portion below Robinson's Creek. The western part of what is now Pembroke, was called Namattakeeset.

In March, 1641, the bounds of Duxbury were fixed at a court. *Ordered*, That the bounds of Duxburrow Township shall begin where Plymouth bounds do end, namely at a brook falling into Blackwater, and so along the Massachusetts path to the North River. This path was the regular line for travel between the Plymouth and Massachusetts Colonies.

Tradition says its crossed the Indian Head River near where Curtis's Iron Works now stand. It was at this place that James Ludden, an early settler of Weymouth, acting as guide to Gov. Winthrop and Rev. Mr. Wilson, while on their journey to Plymouth, in 1632, had the honor of taking their honors over the river, passback. From this fact, the Gov. named it Ludden's Ford. This name is now Lowden. That portion of Pembroke below Robinson's Creek, was included in the Two Mile purchase made by Mr. Hatherly and his associates of Scituate, of the Indian chief Josiah Wampatuck. In 1661, a grant was made to the towns of Duxbury and Marshfield, of a tract of land between Jones' River and Indian Head River. This was known as Marshfield upper lands. The "Major's purchase," an earlier grant to the town, included the Great Cedar Swamp, in the limits of Hanson now. Both these grants were included in the limits of Pembroke, at one time.

The tradition of the Barker family, is that in 1628 or 30, Francis Barker, and his brother, who were among the Plymouth adventurers, took a boat and coasted along the shore till they came to the North River, which they ascended as far as it was navigable, that they landed on a rock near the site of the present Herring weir and went in pursuit of a good place to locate. They built a house of brick, containing one room, and one story high. This, with the additions that have since been made, is the old garrison house, said to be the oldest house in the United States. In 1679, this dwelling-house was converted into a garrison and was a place of refuge for those who feared their savage neighbors.

Pembroke, at its incorporation, was bounded on the North by Scituate and Abington; on the East by Robinson's Creek, (separating it from Scituate). by Marshfield and Duxbury; on the South by Duxbury and Plymouth, and on the West by Bridgewater. It contained fifty-four families.

There were two places of public worship, one on the site of the present Unitarian Church, and the peaked meeting-house erected by the Friends.

The first Congregational meeting-house, was erected in 1703, the Friends' meeting-house in 1706.

Pembroke was incorporated in 1711. The prayer of the petition was that the new town should be called Brookfield. Why it was called Pembroke does not appear. It was probably named for Pembroke in England.

The Indians that lived in this vicinity, belonged to the Massachusetts, at one time a powerful tribe, numbering 3000 warriors and occupying the whole country from Neponset to Duxbury, and extending back from the shore to Bridgewater and Middleboro.

A large portion of this tribe were converted to Christianity and were known as praying Indians. At the breaking out of Philip's war, many of them were conveyed by Government to Clark's Island, where they might be secured from their hostile brothers. Chicatabut was their sachem. His father, Josiah Wampatuck, sold Scituate to Mr. Hatherly and his associates, for £14.

In 1684, there were about forty at Namattakeeset. The particular sub-division of this tribe that lived near the Indian ponds, was called Mattakeeset, and from these are descended Joseph Hyatt, Martin Prince, and William Joel.

David Fuller was descended from the Tumpum tribe. This was probably a family or patriarchal name.

It seems that Pembroke was not always considered out of the world. Indeed it was thought to be the very hub of Plymouth County, for in the year 1726, and for a number of subsequent years, endeavors were made to effect the removal of the county buildings here, and constitute it the shire town. If the Puritans had landed at Seabury Point instead of Plymouth Rock, it might have been.

It is a matter of history, that Pembroke was the first town in the Colonies, that publicly rebelled against the British Crown.

In 1740, the town protested against the efforts of the Prince to suppress the emission of bills of public credit, which had become depreciated on account of the large export of silver. The following is a very brief extract from the protest:—"Which instructions from the Crown are we presume a manifest infraction of our charter rights and privileges as well as that of our invaluable national constitution, so long enjoyed as well as so dearly obtained, whereby the people have a right of thinking and judging for themselves, as well as the Prince. And the representative shall be directed at all times strictly to adhere to the charter, rights, and privileges, which we are under, as also that of our English rights, liberties and constitutions, any royal instruction from his Majesty to the contrary notwithstanding."

Pembroke was noted for its patriotism. There was scarce a tory in the town. The town records are full of patriotic resolves passed by the town all along through the "times that tried men's souls."

In 1772, Dec. 28th, the following among other resolves, was passed. *Resolved*, "That this Province, and this town as part of it, hath a right whenever they think it necessary, to give their sense of public measures, and if judged to be unconstitutional and oppressive, to declare it freely and to remonstrate or petition as they may deem best."

Conspicuous among the leading spirits of those times were Josiah Keen, Esq., Dr. Jeremiah Hall, John Turner, Eleazer Hamlen, Seth Hatch, Josiah Smith, Capt. Freedom Chamberlain, Abel Stetson, Aaron Soule, Israel Turner, Capt. Ichabod Thomas, Asaph Tracy, Consider Cole, Asa Keen, and Nathaniel Stetson. Of these, Dr. Hall, Capt. Seth Hatch, Asa Keen, and Nathaniel Stetson had served in the French war. Dr. Hall was a Surgeon in the French war. Capt. Seth Hatch, commanded a supply ship, and at one time run the blockade of the St. Lawrence and furnished supplies to Gen. Wolf, and his army. For this he was publicly thanked by the General, and after the battle of Quebec, he was presented with some articles of the General's tent furniture.

John Turner, Dr. Hall, and Capt. Edward Thomas were members of the Provincial Congress. While attending this Congress, Dr. Hall was chosen on many important committees of that body. He was quite intimate with Dr. Joseph Warren, and thus described to a friend his last parting with him. "Being both members of the Provincial Congress, we left Concord at the dawn of day, June 17, 1775, and rode in company till our paths diverged, (Dr. Hall was going to the headquarters of the American army at Cambridge). Dr. Warren, at this interview, informed him that he had a Major General's commission in his pocket, but that he should not use it." Dr. Hall was afterwards Colonel of a Rhode Island regiment. He was a noted Surgeon. He held many public offices in the Colony. He had a son Jeremiah, who died while a soldier at Cambridge, according to the inscription placed on his tomb-stone by his patriot sire, "in the service of his country, opposing British tyranny and Britain's tyrants." Eleazer Hamlin, mentioned above, was grandfather to the Hon. Hannibal Hamlin.

Pembroke furnished one hundred and sixty-seven men for the war of the Rebellion, twenty-nine more than all its quotas. Of these the names of those who were killed or died in the service, are as follows, viz:—

Ansel F. Bonney, Co. E, 18th Reg't, wounded in the battles before

Richmond, June 3d, and died July 14th, 1864, at Washington, D. C.; Jacob Curtis, Co. E, 18th Reg't, wounded at Laurel Hill, and died at Washington, D. C., May 26th, 1864; Alfred G. Howe, Co. H, 18th Reg't, killed in the battle of the Wilderness, May 1864; Abel O. Stetson, Co. D, 38th Reg't, at Port Hudson, La., 1863; Hiram F. Stevens, Co. D, 38th Reg't, at Hampton Hospital, Va., Jan. 2d, 1863, of phthisis; Ansel W. Brown, Co. B, 40th Reg't, at Folly Island, S. C., Nov. 18th, 1863, of Diptheria; James T. Cummings, Co. B, 40th Reg't, wounded at Coal Harbor, Va., and died at Washington, D. C., June 21st, 1864. George M. Witherell, Co. I, 4th Reg't, at Baton Rouge, La., March 28th, 1863, of fever; John Bones, Co. I, 4th Reg't, June 11th, 1863, at Brashear City, La; James B. Curtis, Co. I, 4th Reg't, April 29th, 1863, at New Orleans, La ; Alden Howard, Co. I, 4th Reg't, July 15th, 1863, at New Orleans, La. ; Edwin Bosworth, Co. I, 4th Reg, Aug. 3d, 1863, at New Orleans. La., of chronic diarrhœa ; Robert Henry Cornell, Co. I, 4th Reg, April 21st, 1863, at Carrollton, La. ; Marcus M. Reed, Co. I, 4th Reg't, at Brashear City, La., June 8th, 1863, of chronic diarrhœa; Charles C. Clark, Co. I, 4th Reg't, at New Orleans, La., July 16th, 1863 ; George H. Ford, Co. I, 4th Reg't, at New Orleans, La., July 17th, 1863; Henry T. Stevens, Co. F, 28th Reg't, at Andersonville, Ga., Sept. 6th, 1864; Calvin S. Magoun, Co. A, 23d Reg't, died June 19th, 1862, on the cars between New York and Boston, of typhoid pneumonia; Marshall M. Chandler, Co.— 29th Reg't, died at Philadelphia, Penn., July 6th, 1862, of typhoid fever; Nathaniel B. Bishop, was killed June 2d, 1864, at Coal Harbor, Va., Co. B, 40th Reg't.

PLYMOUTH.

IN our preliminary sketch of Plymouth County we have given many facts that would otherwise appear in our history of this town.

Plymouth is thirty-seven miles south-west of Boston. The township is, we believe, the largest in the State, extending sixteen miles on the coast from north to south. The land, back from the village, is generally hilly and covered with pine woods. This wooded section extends many miles into Barnstable County, and is traversed by very few roads, and has scarcely any houses. The delicate fallow deer, still roams this territory, in his native wilderness, and every winter the hunter's rifle secures its antlered trophies.

The town is built on the shore, upon an easy declivity, about one-fourth of a mile in breadth and one and a half miles in length. The soil here is good.

The harbor is formed by a beach extending three miles northerly from the mouth of Eel river. This beach would long ago have been washed away by the ocean had not large appropriations been made by the town, state, and general government. At present there is not sufficient depth of water for the largest class of vessels, although a very considerable fleet of fishing and coasting vessels is owned here.

"There is considerable water-power in the town, and this mother of all the towns in the land, is setting her daughters a good example of domestic industry."

Numerous small streams cross the township, and there are upward of 200 lakes with an aggregate water surface of more than 3000 acres.

We give below an alphabetical list of passengers who arrived at Plymouth in the Mayflower, 180 tons burthen, Dec. 21st, 1620,—the Fortune of 55 tons, Nov. 9th, 1621,—the Ann, of 140 tons, and the Little James, of 44 tons, the last of July, or the beginning of August, 1623.

The letter attached to each name indicates the vessel in which the passenger came. M stands for the Mayflower,—F for the Fortune,—A for the Ann and Little James.

M Mr. Isaac Allerton, M John Alden, M John Allerton, F John Adams. A Anthony Annable, M Mr. William Bradford, M Mr. William Brewster. M John Billington, M Peter Brown, M Richard Britterige, F William Bassite, F William Beale, F Edward Bompasse, F Jonathan Brewster, F Clement Brigges, A Edward Bangs, A Robert Bartlett, A Fear Brewster, A Patience Brewster, A Mary Bucket, A Edward Burcher, M Mr. John Carver, M Francis Cook, M James Chilton, M John Crackston, M Richard Clarke, F John Cannon, F William Coner, F Robert Cushman, F Thomas Cushman, A Thomas Clarke, A Cuthbert Cuthbertson, A Christopher Conant, M Edward Doty, F Stephen Deane, F Philip de La Noye, A Anthony Dix, M Francis Eaton, M Thomas English, M Mr. Samuel Fuller, M Edward Fuller, M Moses Fletcher, F Thomas Flavell and son, F Widow Foord, A John Faunce, A Goodwife Flavell, A Edmund Flood, A Bridget Fuller, M John Goodman, M Richard Gardiner, M John Howland, M Mr. Stephen Hopkins, F Robert Hickes, F William Hilton, A Timothy Hatherly, A William Heard, A Margaret Hickes and her children, A William Hilton's wife and children, A Edward Holman, A John Jenny, A Manasses Kempton, M Edward Leister, A Robert Long, M Mr. Christopher Martin, M Mr. William Mullins, M Edmund Margeson, F Benet Morgan, F Thomas Morton, A Experience Mitchell, A George Morton, A Thomas Morton, Jr, F Austin Nicholas, A Ellen Newton, A John Oldham, M Degory Priest, F William Palmer, F William Pitt, F Thomas Prence, A Francis Palmer, A Mr. Perce's two servants, A Joshua Pratt, A Christian Penn, M Thomas Rogers, M John Ridgdale, A James Rand, A Robert Ratliffe, M Capt. Miles Standish, м George Soule, ғ Moses Simonson, ғ Hugh Statie, ғ James Steward. ᴀ Nicholas Snow, ᴀ Alice Southworth, ᴀ Francis Sprague, ᴀ Barbary Standish, м Edward Tilly, м John Tilly, м Thomas Tinker, м John Turner, ғ William Tench, ᴀ Thomas Tilden, ᴀ Stephen Tracy, м Mr. Edward Winslow, м Mr. William White, м Mr. Richard Warren, м Thomas Williams, м Gilbert Winslow, ғ John Winslow, ғ William Wright, ᴀ Ralph Wallen.

"Several names contained in the foregoing list, are differently spelt in modern times, namely: Bassite is now spelt Bassett; Bompasse, Bumpas, sometimes Bump; Burcher is probably the same as Burchard, the name of an early settler in Connecticut; De La Noye, Delano; Dotey is on our records called Dote, Dotey, and now frequently written Doten; Simonson, sometimes written Symons, is now Simmons."

Thomas Carlyle observes, in his recent work, "Look now to American Saxondom, and at that little fact of the sailing of the Mayflower, two hundred years ago. There were straggling settlers in America before; some material as of a body was there; but the soul of it was this. These poor men, driven out of their own country, and not able to live in Holland, determined on settling in the new world. Black untamed forests are there, and wild savage creatures; but not so cruel as a star chamber hangman. They clubbed their small means together, hired a ship, the little Mayflower, and made ready to sail. Hah! These men, I think, had a work. The weak thing, weaker than a child, becomes strong, if it be a true thing. Puritanism was only despicable, laughable, then; but nobody can manage to laugh at it now. It is one of the strongest things under the sun at present."

"Plymouth was the first town built in New England by civilized man; and those by whom it was built were inferior in worth to no body of men, whose names are recorded in history, during the last seventeen hundred years. A kind of venerableness, arising from these facts, attaches to this town, which may be termed a prejudice. Still, it has its foundation in the nature of man, and will never be eradicated either by philosophy or ridicule. No New Englander, who is willing to indulge his native feelings, can stand upon the rock, where our ancestors set the first foot after their arrival on the American shore, without experiencing emotions very different from those which are excited by any common object of the same nature. No New Englander could be willing to have that rock buried and forgotten."

"The institutions, civil, literary, and religious, by which New England is distinguished on this side the Atlantic, began here. Here the manner of holding lands in free soccage, now universal in this country, commenced. Here the right of suffrage was imparted to every citizen, to every inhabitant not disqualified by poverty or vice. Here was formed the first establishment of towns, of the local legislature, which is called a town meeting, and of the peculiar town executive, styled the selectmen. Here the first parochial school was set up, and the system originated for communicating to every child in the community the knowledge of reading, writing, and arithmetic. Here, also, the first building was erected for the worship of God; the first religious assembly gathered; and the first minister called and settled, by the voice of the church and congregation. On these simple foundations has since been erected a structure of good order, peace, liberty, knowledge, morals, and religion, with which nothing on this side the Atlantic can bear a remote comparison."

The first marriage in Plymouth, was May 12, 1621, of Edward Winslow and Widow Susanna White. The first mill in New England was erected near Billington Sea, by Stephen Dean, in 1632.

March 12, 1676, the house of Mr. Clark was attacked by the Indians and 11 persons belonging to two families killed, and the house burnt. May 11, the same year, eleven houses and two barns were burnt by the savages.

Plymouth is not the "rock-bound coast" that poets would make us believe. There is not known in the township a single ledge except those that the fishermen reach with their leads, off the coast, hence it is the more singular that a single, hard, grey-colored sienitic granite boulder should have become so celebrated as "Plymouth Rock." In 1774, some ardent whigs, attempted to remove this rock to town square with the intention of erecting over it a liberty pole. In the attempt, the rock split asunder, and the lower part was returned to its original bed, while the top part was drawn to the square, amid great excitement, by twenty yoke of oxen. July 4th, 1834, this part of the rock was placed in front of Pilgrim Hall. The part remaining at the water's side is about six and a half feet in diameter. Over this part, a substantial granite monument has been partially erected, by the Pilgrim Society, with funds contributed by the admirers of the Forefathers.

The honor of first stepping upon the Rock, has been claimed both for Mary Chilton and John Alden, by the descendants of each—resting upon tradition in both families.

Cole's Hill, the first burial place of the Pilgrims, is just back of the Rock. About 50 of those who came in the Mayflower, were buried here, including Gov. Carver, "with three vollies of shot fired over him," and Rose, the beautiful wife of Miles Standish.

Burying Hill, was originally called Fort Hill, because here was built the first defensive structure. This ancient fort is distinctly marked on the south-east part of the hill. The building was of good timber, strong and comely, with flat roof upon which the ordnance was mounted. It also served as a meeting-house. The hill was first used as a burying-ground soon after. The first stone erected, it is supposed, was that of Joseph Bartlett, who died in 1703, although there were many interments previous, including that of Edward Gray, in 1681. Within a few years, several costly monuments have been erected to the memory of the ancient worthies, by their descendants. The Cushman monument is one of the most noticeable. A stone has been erected in memory of the 72 seamen who perished from cold, in Plymouth Harbor, Dec. 26th, and 27th, 1778, on board the private armed brig General Arnold, of 20 guns, numbering 106 persons in all, 60 of whom were buried in one spot and 12 in other parts of the Hill. Quite lately numerous walks have been laid out in different parts of this burying-ground, and an effort to secure some degree of regularity of arrangement has been attempted. Any inhabitants of the town seem to have the free privilege of burying in any unoccupied sections of the lot, and many, even to this day, avail themselves of this privilege, although a large and beautiful cemetery has been consecrated at a little distance west from the village, under the name of "Oak Grove."

The corner stone of Pilgrim Hall, a monumental structure, was laid Sep. 1st, 1824, and the building completed ten years later. It is 70 by 40 feet, built of rough granite. On entering the Hall, the painting of the "Landing of the Pilgrims," generously presented to the Pilgrim Society, by Henry Sargent, Esq., of Boston, first challenges attention. The size is 13 by 16 feet. It was valued at $3000, aside from the frame, which cost $400. All the prominent characters in the Colony, are represented in the costume of their time, with the friendly Indian, Samoset, in the foreground. On the walls, are arranged portraits of Edward Winslow; Josiah Winslow, the first native Governor; his wife Penelope Pelham; Gen. John Winslow; Hon. Ephraim Spooner; John Alden of Middleboro, great-grand-son of John Alden the Pilgrim, who died in 1821, aged 102 years; Maj. Gen. Benj. Lincoln; Hon. John Trumbull; James Thatcher, M. D.; James Kendall. D. D.; and others. Among the antiquities are:—A chair which belonged to Gov. Carver; the sword, pewter dish, and iron pot, that belonged to Miles Standish; the gun-barrel with which King Philip was killed; the original letter of Philip to Gov. Prince, written in 1662; deeds bearing the signatures of Miles Standish, Josiah Winslow, Peregrine White, John Alden, and many other of the old notables; chairs belonging to Elder Brewster, and Gov. Wm. Bradford; a bead purse wrought by Mrs. Gov. Winslow, while on her voyage over; a gold ring owned by the Gov., and containing some of his hair; a commission from Oliver Cromwell to Edward Winslow, dated April, 1654; a clock belonging to Gov. Hancock, which was taken to West Bridgewater at the time of the siege; the "Fuller cradle;" besides many other valuable relics of the Pilgrims. There is also a large library.

In front of Pilgrim Hall, is an iron railing enclosing a part of Forefather's Rock on which are inscribed the 41 names of the signers of the compact in the Mayflower.

The "Old Colony Club" was formed in 1769. The first celebration of the Landing of the Forefathers, was held in 1769. A very plain dinner of the old-fashioned dishes was served. The succeeding year, in addition to the dinner, an address was delivered by Edward Winslow, the first of a long series of similar productions.

The "Pilgrim Society" was formed in 1820. In 1850, it was voted to erect a monument on or near the Rock.

The beach was formerly well wooded, and abounded with plums and grapes. The Gurnet, at the entrance of the harbor, containing about 27 acres of excellent land, was also well wooded. It is the extreme point of Marshfield beach.

The Province of Massachusetts erected a light house in 1768, which was destroyed by fire in 1801. The United States erected its successor in 1803. Saquish, the Indian for clams, is a headland containing 14 acres, and connected with the Gurnet. The "Cow Yard" is the good anchorage near by, so called because a cow whale was captured there in early days.

Clark's Island, so called in honor of the mate of the Mayflower, contains 86 acres, and was the place of the first landing of the Pilgrims in this section, and was where they spent their first Sabbath. It was formerly well covered with cedar trees. It has been owned by the town, and by the Watson family.

A large rock on the island called Election Rock, was long resorted to by holiday parties. Brown's Island was covered with trees when the Pilgrims landed. It is now under water.

The Court House, on Court House Square, is a very handsome building, fitted up in admirable style for the use of the various County Officers as well as Courts. The beautiful green in front, is enclosed with an iron fence. In the rear of the Court House are the geols and dwelling-house attached.

The Works for supplying Plymouth village with water from "South Ponds," which are situated some three miles south of the village, were constructed by the town in 1855, at a cost of about $82,000. The Constructing Engineer was Moses Bates, Esq. More than twelve miles of pipe, exclusive of service, was laid. The Plymouth Gaslight Co., is another city luxury that our people would hardly care to do without.

The seventy vessels employed in the Cod and Mackerel Fisheries, and coasting business, in 1865, with a tonnage of 20,733, employed 513 men. At the same date there were three cotton-mills, 1 spool-cotton mill, 1 woolen mill, 1 rolling mill, 2 tack manufactories, 4 cordage establishments, 2 rivet, and 2 neck stock and ties manufactories.

The first Indian with whom the Colonists had any intercourse, was Samoset, the Sagamore, whose home was probably in Maine. When he entered the settlement he was stark naked, except a leather about his waist, with a narrow fringe. The savage had picked up a few words of English from the fishermen who had occasionally visited the coast. It was a joyful day for the Pilgrim band when they heard in their own tongue the words "Welcome, Welcome Englishmen!" They gave him the best food they had and some strong water.

The Indian names of Plymouth were Umpame, Apaum or Patuxet.

No communication was opened between the Colony at Plymouth and the Dutch settlement at New York, until 1627.

The first cattle were imported in 1623.

Watson's Hill was the place where Massasoit appeared with sixty warriors, and exchanged hostages with the English, preliminary to the treaty of peace, in March, 1621. At this interview, Samoset appears again, for the last time in history, accompanied by Squanto, the only native of Plymouth, who had been captured and carried to England, and who also could speak a little English, accompanied by three others. These friendly natives acted as interpreters, and on that day a treaty of friendship and good will was effected that lasted for fifty years.

Billington Sea, is a lovely sheet of fresh water, two miles south-west of the town, which was discovered from a tree-top, by Francis Billington, in 1621. It is about one and a half miles long, and six miles in circumference.

Leyden street received its present name in 1823, out of grateful remembrance of the kindnesses received by the Pilgrims in the city of Leyden. It had previously been called First, Great, and Broad Street.

The first house of worship was built on the north side of Town Square. Richard Church, and John Thompson, afterwards of Middleboro, were the architects. This building was taken down in 1683, and another one built at the head of the square. A third house was built in 1744, being about 71 by 68 feet, with spire 100 feet high surmounted by a brass weather-cock. The Gothic edifice was built by the first church at a cost of $10,000. It is 61 by 70 feet. The church of the Pilgrimage was erected in 1840, and stands near the site of the first meeting-house. The Town House was built in 1749, and was formerly used as the County Court House.

In January, 1831, the snow was three feet deep in Plymouth woods, so impeding the movements of the deer, that with snow shoes the hunters captured 200, about 40 of them being taken alive.

The bi-centennial celebration of the landing, observed in 1820, was an occasion of great interest, Daniel Webster delivering the oration. "Among other affecting memorials, calling to mind the distresses of the Pilgrims, at the dinner, five kernels of parched corn were placed on each plate, alluding to the time in 1623, when that was the proportion allowed to each individual, on account of the scarcity."

The Samoset House, taking into account its location and management, is the most attractive summer home for the tourist in Plymouth County.

The first newspaper printed in the Old Colony, was at Plymouth, in 1786, by Nathaniel Cleverly. Since then, numerous hebdomadals have been established and gone to decay.

Two very superior weekly papers are now printed at Plymouth. "The Old Colony Memorial and Plymouth Rock" is published by Geo. F. Andrews. This paper was formed from the union of the old Democratic with the old Whig organ of the County, and is now in its forty-sixth year.

"The Old Colony Sentinel" is published every Saturday, by Moses Bates, Editor and Proprietor. "As an independent conservative journal, devoted to the interests of the people, the Sentinel claims to have no equal in the Old Colony."

The present officers of the Pilgrim Society are:—E. S. Tobey, of Boston, *President*; Wm. T. Davis, of Plymouth, *Vice President*; William S. Danforth, of Plymouth, *Rec. and Corresponding Secretary*; Isaac N. Stoddard, of Plymouth, *Treasurer*; Lemuel D. Holmes, of Plymouth, *Librarian*; Timothy Gordon, Wm. H. Whitman, Thomas Loring, Charles G. Davis, Samuel H. Doten, Charles O. Churchill, Geo. G. Dyer, and Benjamin Hathaway, of Plymouth, Samuel Nicholson, Isaac Rich, Edward S. Tobey, William Thomas, Nathaniel B. Shurtleff and Abraham Jackson, of Boston, George S. Boutwell, of Groton, Ichabod Washburn, of Worcester, William Savery, of Carver, George P. Hayward, of Hingham, *Trustees*.

The population of Plymouth in 1620, was 101; in 1720, it was 1206; in 1820, it was 4348, and in 1860, it was 6272.

The schools of Plymouth are many of them of a very high order. For several years the town has employed a Superintendent of public schools.

The corner-stone of a grand National Monument to the Forefathers, was laid on Monument Hill, Aug. 2d, 1859.

In 1627, Isaack De Raisiers, was sent from Manhattan to visit the Plymouth Colony. In his report to his own government, he gives the following very interesting sketch of the appearance of Plymouth at that early day:—

"At the south side of the town there flows down a small river of fresh water, very rapid, but shallow, which takes its rise from several lakes in the land above, and there empties into the sea; where in April and the beginning of May there come so many herring from the sea which want to ascend that river, that it is quite surprising. This river the English have shut in with planks, and in the middle with a little door, which slides up and down, and at the sides with trellice work, through which the water has its course, but which they can also close with slides. At the mouth they have constructed it with planks, like an eel pot, with wings, where in the middle is also a sliding door, and with trellice work at the sides, so that between the two [dams] there is a square pool, into which the fish aforesaid come swimming in such shoals, in order to get up above, where they deposit their spawn, that at one tide there are 10,000 to 12,000 fish in it, which they shut off in the rear at the ebb, and close up the trellices above, so that no more water comes in; then the water runs out through the lower trellices and they draw out the fish with baskets, each according to the land he cultivates, and carry them to it, depositing in each hill three or four fishes, and in these they plant their maize, which grows as luxuriantly therein as though it were the best manure in the world: and if they do not lay this fish therein, the maize will not grow, so that such is the nature of the soil.

"New Plymouth lies on the slope of a hill stretching east towards the sea-coast, with a broad street about a cannon shot of 800 [yards] long, leading down the hill; with a [street] crossing in the middle, northwards to the rivulet, and southwards to the land. The houses are constructed of hewn planks, with gardens also enclosed behind and at the sides with hewn planks, so that their houses and court yards are arranged in very good order, with a stockade against a sudden attack; and at the ends of the streets there are three wooden gates. In the centre, on the cross street, stands the Governor's house, before which is a square enclosure upon which four patereros [steen-stucken] are mounted, so as to flank along the streets. Upon the hill, they have a large square house, with a flat roof, made of thick sawn planks, stayed with oak beams, upon the top of which they have six cannons, which shoot iron balls of four or five pounds, and command the surrounding country. The lower part they use for their church, where they preach on Sundays and the usual holidays. They assemble by beat of drum, each with his musket or firelock, in front of the captain's door; they have their cloaks on and place themselves in order, three abreast, and are led by a sergeant without beat of drum. Behind comes the Governor, in a long robe; beside him, on the right hand, comes the preacher with his cloak on, and on the left hand the captain with his side arms and cloak on, and with a small cane in his hand,—and so they march in good order, and each sets his arms down near him. Thus they are constantly on their guard night and day.

"Their government is after the English form. The Governor has his council, which is chosen every year by the entire community by election or prolongation of term. In the inheritance they place all the children in one degree, only the eldest son has an acknowledgement for his seniority of birth.

"They have made stringent laws and ordinances upon the subject of fornication and adultery, which laws they maintain and enforce very strictly indeed, even among the tribes which live amongst them. They [the English] speak very angrily, when they hear from the savages that we should live so barbarously in these respects, and without punishment.

"Their farms are not so good as ours, because they are more stony, and consequently not so suitable for the plough. They apportion their land according as each has means to contribute to the Eighteen Thousand Guilders which they have promised to those who had sent them out; whereby they have their freedom without rendering an account to any one; only if the king should choose to send a Governor General they would be obliged to acknowledge him as sovereign chief.

"The maize seed which they do not require for their own use is delivered over to the Governor, at three guilders the bushel, who in his turn sends it in sloops to the North for the trade in skins among the savages; they reckon one bushel of maize against one pound of beaver's skin; in the first place, a division is made, according to what each has contributed, and they are credited for the amount in the account of what each has to contribute yearly towards the reduction of his obligation. Then with the remainder they purchase what next they require, and which the Governor takes care to provide every year.

"They have better means of living than ourselves, because they have the fish so abundant before their doors. There are also many birds, such as geese, herons, and cranes, and other small-legged birds which are in great abundance there in the winter. The tribes in their neighborhood have all the same customs as already above described, only they are better conducted than ours, because the English give them the example of better ordinances and a better life; and who, also to a certain degree, give them laws, by means of the respect they from the very first have established amongst them.

"The savages [there] practice their youth in labor better than the savages round about us; the young girls in sowing maize, the young men in hunting; they teach them to endure privation in the field in a singular manner to wit: when there is a youth who begins to approach manhood, he is taken by his father, uncle, or nearest friend and is conducted blindfolded into a wilderness, in order that he may not know the way, and is left there by night or otherwise, with a bow and arrows, and a hatchet and a knife. He must support himself there a whole winter, with what the scanty earth furnishes at this season, and by hunting. Towards the spring they come again, and fetch him out of it, take him home and feed him up again until May. He must then go out again every morning with the person who is ordered to take him in hand; he must go into the forest to seek wild herbs and roots which they know to be the most poisonous and bitter; these they bruise in water and press the juice out of them, which he must drink and immediately have ready such herbs as will preserve him from death or vomiting; and if he cannot retain it, he must repeat the dose until he can support it, and until his constitution becomes accustomed to it so that he can retain it. Then he comes home, and is brought by the men and women, all singing and dancing, before the Sackima; and if he has been able to stand it all out well, and if he is fat and sleek, a wife is given to him."

The following was the substance of the treaty of peace between the Colonists and Massasoit, made on Watson's Hill:—

"1. That neither he nor any of his should injure or do hurt to any of our people.

"2. And if any of his did hurt to any of ours, he should send the offender, that we might punish him.

"3. That if any of our tools were taken away, when our people were at work, he should cause them to be restored: and if ours did any harm to any of his, we would do the like to them.

"4. If any did unjustly war against him, we would aid him; if any did war against us, he should aid us.

"5. He should send to his neighbor confederates to certify them of this, that they might not wrong us, but might be likewise comprised in the conditions of peace.

"6. That when their men came to us, they should leave their bows and arrows behind them, as we should do our pieces when we came to them.

"Lastly, that doing thus, King James would esteem of him as his friend and ally.

"All which the King seemed to like well, and it was applauded of his followers. All the while he sat by the governor he trembled for fear. In his person he is a very lusty man, in his best years, an able body grave of countenance, and spare of speech; in his attire little or nothing differing from the rest of his followers, only in a great chain of white bone beads about his neck; and at it, behind his neck, hangs a little bag of tobacco, which he drank,* and gave us to drink. His face was painted with a sad red, like murrey, and oiled both head and face, that he looked greasily. All his followers likewise were in their faces, in part or in whole, painted, some black, some red, some yellow, and some white, some with crosses, and other antic works; some had skins on them, and some naked; all strong, tall men in appearance.

"So after all was done, the governor conducted him to the brook, and there they embraced each other, and he departed; we diligently keeping our hostages."

This visit of Massasoit's was returned by Edward Winslow and Stephen Hopkins. "They slept the first night at Namasket, now

---

* Or the same as smoking tobacco.

Middleboro, and arrived at Pockanocket the next day. The king was short of provision, but procured a couple of fish, of which he gave them part. They lodged upon a bed of plank, raised a foot from the ground, with a mat upon them; and upon the same lay also Massasoit, his wife, and two of his men, and so crowded them that they were more weary of their lodging than their journey. They set out for home the next day, fearing lest fasting, hard lodging, lice, fleas, and moschetoes, would render them unable to return.

In 1623, word came that Massasoit was sick nigh unto death, and Edward Winslow, and John Hambden visited him, accompanied by Hobamock as guide. Winslow in his account says:—

"In the way, Hobamock, manifesting a troubled spirit, brake forth into these speeches: *Neen womasu Sagimus, neen womasu Sagimus,* &c.,—My loving sachem, my loving sachem! Many have I known, but never any like thee." And, turning to me, he said whilst I lived I should never see his like amongst the Indians; saying he was no liar; he was not bloody and cruel, like other Indians. In anger and passion he was soon reclaimed; easy to be reconciled towards such as had offended him; ruled by reason in such measure as he would not scorn the advice of mean men; and that he governed his men better with few strokes than others did with many; truly loving where he loved; yea, he feared we had not a faithful friend left among the Indians; showing how he ofttimes restrained their malice, &c.; continuing a long speech, with such signs of lamentation and unfeigned sorrow, as it would have made the hardest heart relent.

"At length we came to Mattapuyst, and went to the *sachimo comaco,* for so they called the sachem's place though they call an ordinary house *witeo;* but Conbatant, the sachem, was not at home, but at Puckanokick, which was some five or six miles off. The *squa sachem,* for so they call the sachem's wife, gave us friendly entertainment. Here we inquired again concerning Massassowat: they thought him dead, but knew no certainty. Whereupon I hired one to go, with all expedition, to Puckanokick, that we might know the certainty thereof, and withal to acquaint Conbatant with our there being. About half an hour before sun-setting the messenger returned, and told us that he was not yet dead, though there was no hope we should find him living. Upon this we were much revived, and set forward with all speed, though it was late within night ere we got thither. About two of the clock, that afternoon, the Dutchman departed; so that in that respect our journey was frustrate.

"When we came thither, we found the house so full of men, as we could scarce get in, though they used their best diligence to make way for us. There were they in the midst of their charms for him, making such a hellish noise as it distempered us that were well, and therefore unlike to ease him that was sick. About him were six or eight women, who chafed his arms, legs, and thighs, to keep heat in him. When they had made an end of their charming, one told him that his friends, the English, were come to see him. Having understanding left, but his sight was wholly gone, he asked who was come. They told him Winsnow, for they cannot pronounce the letter *l*, but ordinarily *n* in the place thereof. He desired to speak with me. When I came to him, and they told him of it, he put forth his hand to me, which I took. Then he said twice, though very inwardly, *Keen Winsnow?* which is to say, Art thou Winslow? I answered, *Ahhe*, that is, Yes. Then he doubled these words: *Matta neen wonckanet namen, Winsnow!* that is to say, O Winslow, I shall never see thee again.

"Then I called Hobamock, and desired him to tell Massassowat, that the governor, hearing of his sickness, was sorry for the same; and though, by reason of many businesses, he could not come himself, yet he sent me with such things for him as he thought most likely to do him good in this extremity; and whereof if he pleased to take, I would presently give him; which he desired; and having a confection of many comfortable conserves, on the point of my knife, I gave him some, which I could scarce get through his teeth. When it was dissolved in his mouth, he swallowed the juice of it; whereat those that were about him much rejoiced, saying he had not swallowed anything in two days before. Then I desired to see his mouth, which was exceedingly furred, and his tongue swelled in such a manner as it was not possible for him to eat such meat as they had, his passage being stopped up. Then I washed his mouth, and scraped his tongue, and got abundance of corruption out of the same. After which I gave him more of the confection, which he swallowed with more readiness. Then he desired to drink. I dissolved some of it in water, and gave him thereof. Within half an hour this wrought a great alteration in him, in the eyes of all that beheld him. Presently after his sight began to come to him.------Then I gave him more, and told him of a mishap we had, in breaking a bottle of drink, which the governor also sent him, saying, if he would send any of his men to Patuxet, I would send for more of the same; also for chickens to make him broth, and for other things, which I knew were good for him; and would stay the return of his messenger, if he desired. This he took marvellous kindly, and appointed some, who were ready to go by two of the clock in the morning; against which time I made ready a letter, declaring therein our good success, the state of his body, &c., desiring to send such things as I sent for, and such physic as the surgeon durst administer to him.

"He requested me that, the day following, I would take my piece, and kill him some fowl, and make him some English pottage, such as he had eaten at Plymouth; which I promised. After, his stomach coming to him, I must needs make him some without fowl, before I went abroad, which somewhat troubled me; but being I must do somewhat, I caused a woman to bruise some corn, and take the flour from it, and set over the girt, or broken corn, in a pipkin, for they have earthen pots of all sizes. When the day broke, we went out, it being now March, to seek herbs, but could not find any but strawberry leaves, of which I gathered a handful, and put into the same; and because I had nothing to relish it, I went forth again, and pulled up a sassafras root, and sliced a piece thereof, and boiled it, till it had a good relish, and then took it out again. The broth being boiled, I strained it through my handkerchief, and gave him at least a pint, which he drank, and liked it very well. After this his sight mended more and more; ———— and he took some rest; insomuch as we with admiration blessed God for giving his blessing to such raw and ignorant means, making no doubt of his recovery, himself and all of them acknowledging us the instruments of his preservation. That morning he caused me to spend in going from one to another amongst those that were sick in the town, requesting me to wash their mouths also, and give to each of them some of the same I gave him, saying that they were good folk. This pains I took with willingness, though it were much offensive to me, not being accustomed with such poisonous savors.

"The messengers were now returned, but finding his stomach come to him, he would not have the chickens killed, but kept them for breed. Neither durst we give him any physic, which was then sent, because his body was so much altered since our instructions; neither saw we any need, not doubting now of his recovery, if he were careful. Many, whilst we were there, came to see him; some, by their report, from a place not less than a hundred miles. Upon this his recovery, he brake forth into these speeches: "Now I see the English are my friends and love me; and whilst I live, I will never forget this kindness they have showed me." Whilst we were there, our entertainment exceeded all other strangers."—*Good News from New England.*

There are fifteen towns with the name of Plymouth in the United States, besides "Plymouth Hollow," "Plymouth Meeting" and "Plymouth Rock," Iowa.

From the time of the first call for troops to suppress Rebellion, April 15th, 1861, to the close of the war, Plymouth promptly responded to the calls for men, and means. She furnished 69 three months' men, 42 for 9 months, 23 for 1 year, 478 for three years, and 108 for the Navy.

The following is the roll of the dead as published in the Town Report for 1866:—

John K. Alexander, E, 29th, killed at Spottsylvania, May 12th, 1864.
Wm. T. Atwood, E, 23d, at Newbern, of fever, July 20th, 1862.
Joseph W. B. Burgess, H, 8th N. H., died at Washington, Dec. 9th, 1864.

Thomas B. Burt, E, 29th, died at Washington, Oct. 31st, 1862.

Wm. Brown, a fugitive slave from Maryland, died on the naval ship "Constellation," Dec. 24th, 1864.

Victor A. Bartlett, of the steamer "Housatonic," captured in the naval attack upon Fort Sumter. died in Salisbury Prison, Mar. 25th, 1864.

Nathaniel Burgess, E, 29th, wounded at Fort Steadman, died July 1st, 1864.

Lawrence R. Blake, E, 29th, killed at Antietam, Sept. 17th, 1862.

Edward D. Brailey, E, 23d, killed on picket, at Newbern, April 27th, 1862.

George W. Burgess, G, 18th, transferred to regular artillery and died at Falmouth Hospital, March 8th, 1863.

George W. Barnes, Q. M. Serg't, 32d, at Harrison's Landing, Aug. 3d, 1862.

Jedediah Bumpus, C, 9th, killed June 30th, 1864.

Capt. Joseph W. Collingwood, 18th, wounded at Fredericksburg, died Dec. 24th, 1862.

Adj't. John B. Collingwood, 29th, at St. John's Hospital, Cincinnati, August 21st, 1863.

Thomas Collingwood, E, 29th, at Camp Parks, Ky., Aug. 31st, 1863.

John Carline, B, 23d, at Roanoke Island, Oct. 14th, 1864.

Joseph L. Churchill, E, 23d, killed at Newbern, March 14th, 1862.

Isaac Dickerman, 99th N. Y., died near Fortress Monroe, Nov. 12th, 1863.

Benj. F. Durgin, D, 38th, at Baton Rouge, Aug. 8th, 1863.

Seth W. Eddy, H, 58th, at Readville, August 13th, 1864.

William Edes, F, 11th, at Andersonville, Aug. 30th, 1864.

Theodore S. Fuller, E, 23d, captured Oct. 10th, 1863, and died in prison.

Melvin C. Faught, A, 32d, at Windmill Point Hospital, Va., Feb. 5th, 1863.

Lemuel B. Faunce, jr., G, 38th, at Goldsboro, N. C., April 23d, 1865.

Edward E. Green, E, 38th, at Baton Rouge, July 11th, 1863.

Lieut. Frederick Holmes, 38th, killed at Port Hudson, July 14th, 1862.

Thomas W. Hayden, E, 29th, at Crab Orchard, Sept. 4th, 1863.

Orin D. Holmes, E. 29th, killed at Fort Steadman, March 25th, 1864.

Edwin F. Hall, D, 58th, killed at Cold Harbor, June 3d, 1864.

George M. Heath, E, 32d, at Harrison's Landing, July 30th, 1862.

Justus W. Harlow, E, 29th, at Camp Hamilton, Sept. 16th, 1862.

Wm. N. Hathaway, G, 38th, at Convalescent Camp, Feb. 23d, 1863.

Thomas Haley, G, 38th, at St. James' Hospital, La., April 5th, 1863.

Lieut. Horace A. Jenks, E, 29th, at Mill Dale Hospital, Miss., July 24th, 1863.

Lieut. Thomas A. Mayo, E, 29th, killed at Gaines' Mills, June 27th, 1862.

Charles E. Merriam, at Harper's Ferry, Nov. 12th, 1862.

Lemuel B. Morton, E, 29th, killed at Spottsylvania, May 12th, 1864.

Gideon E. Morton, F, 7th, at Fredericksburg, May 3d, 1863.

J. T. Oldham, B, 24th, at Newbern, 1863.

Isaac H. Perkins, E, 23d, died of wounds, at Campbell Hospital, June 26th, 1864.

George T. Peckham, E, 29th, at Knoxville, Nov. 1st, 1863.

Wm. Perry, G, 38th, at New Orleans, June 5th, 1863.

Thomas Pugh, fugitive slave, 5th Cavalry, died at sea, Nov. 18th, 1865, while on his way home.

Lewis Payzant, date of death unknown.

Harvey A. Raymond, E, 23d, killed at Whitehall, N. C., Dec. 16th, 1862.

Henry H. Robbins, E, 29th, at Kalorama Hospital, Dec. 4th, 1863.

Albert R. Robbins, E, 29th, March 5th, 1864.

Edward Stevens, E, 23d, at Newbern, Jan. 19th, 1863, of wounds received at Whitehall.

Thomas S. Saunders, K, 23d, at Roanoke Island, March 11th, 1862.

William H. Shaw, E, 32d, Aug. 6th, 1865.

Edward Smith, E, 23d, captured, exchanged and died at Annapolis, May, 1862.

John Sylvester, 1st Cavalry, at Andersonville, Dec. 16th, 1864. His grave is No. 12,053.

Otis Sears, G, 38th, while at home on furlough, Jan. 5th, 1864.

E. Stevens Turner, Acting Master store ship "Relief," at Rio Janeiro, Aug. 5th, 1864.

Frank A. Thomas, E, 29th, at Camp Hamilton, Sept. 14th, 1862.

David A. Taylor, E, 32d, killed at Petersburg, June 22d, 1864.

Wallace Taylor, B, 24th, at Newbern, Nov. 23d, 1862.

Charles E. Tillson, E, 29th, at Andersonville, July 14th, 1864. His grave is No. 3,828.

Israel H. Thrasher, D, 38th, of wounds at Port Hudson, June 29th, 1863.

David R. Valler, I, 58th, at Alexandria, Oct. 6th, 1864.

Serg't George E. Wadsworth, 29th, at Camp Parks, Ky., Aug. 31st, 1863.

Charles E. Wadsworth, 12th, at Salisbury Prison, Nov. 29th, 1864.

David Williams, E, 29th, at Camp Dennison, Ky., Sept. 11th, 1863.

Benjamin Westgate, E, 23d, killed at Whitehall, Dec. 16th, 1862.

John M. Whiting, G, 38th, killed at Opequan Creek, Sept. 19th, 1864.

John Whitmore, Acting Master, of yellow fever, at sea, Aug., 1863.

A very large Monumental Association was formed in 1866, for the purpose of erecting a fitting memorial to the honored dead.

On the old forest road leading from Plymouth to Sandwich, may be seen the well-known "Sacrifice Rocks." They are within the limits of Plymouth. Tradition asserts that they have for ages been covered with sticks and stones. It was a habit with the Indians of the *Old Colony*, as well as of some portion of our own unlettered race, in early times, in both hemispheres, to thus mark certain spots with *their* sepulchral significance, and large *rocks* if lying on their path were selected for this purpose. In the absence of rocks, heaps of sticks accumulating through this simple rite of commemoration, attested their regard for the departed.

NOTE.—Among the authorities consulted in the preparation of the foregoing sketch, we mention "Russell's Pilgrim Memorials," "Barber's History," and "Hayward's Gazetteer."

PLYMPTON.

BY WM. PERKINS, ESQ.

BEFORE the incorporation of the town of Plympton, it was called the Western Precinct of Plymouth. The Indian name was Wenatuxet, and the principal stream, which runs through the town, is still called by that name. The territory was incorporated as a precinct, November 26th, 1695, "for the setting up of the worship of God, and the support of a learned and orthodox ministry" and the Rev. Isaac Cushman began to preach to the inhabitants of the Precinct, the same year. He was ordained in 1698, and continued his ministry here 37 years. His house stood a little southerly from where Thomas E. Loring lives. He was the son of Elder Thomas Cushman, of Plymouth, and grandson of Mr. Robert Cushman. He died in Plympton, October 21st, 1732, in the 84th year of his age. Before the Precinct was incorporated, the first settlers attended meeting at Plymouth, and men and women generally walked thither. Settlements were made here as early as 1680, and probably some years earlier. The following are the names of the first settlers, within the present limits of Plympton. John Bryant, who came from Scituate and set-

died near where the late Thomas B. Harrub lived; John Bryant, son of John Bryant of Plymouth, who lived where Zenas Bryant lives, and died in 1736; Stephen Bryant, who settled where Winslow Wright lives. Isaac King, who settled where James M. Harrub lives, and died in 1728; William Bonney, who lived where Daniel Churchill lives, and afterward near where Harvey Fuller lives; William Churchill, son of Joseph Churchill, of Plymouth, who settled where the late Seth Churchill lived, and died in 1722, aged 66 years,—he was the largest landholder in the town; Thomas, Elkanah, and Eleazer Cushman, brothers of the Rev. Isaac Cushman. Thomas lived where James S. Bonney lives, and died in 1726, aged 88 years. Elkanah, lived where George E. Wright does, and died in 1727. Benjamin Soule, son of John Soule, of Duxbury, who settled where the late Daniel McLean lived, and died in 1729. Joseph King, who settled near where Harvey Fuller lives. Nathaniel Harlow, who came from Plymouth and settled where George B. Fuller lives, and died in 1721, aged 57 years.

Samuel Fuller, son of Rev. Samuel Fuller, the first minister of Middleboro, who settled on the farm of the late Philemon Fuller, and died in 1728, aged 69 years. John, Samuel, Josiah, and Henry Rickard, sons of Giles Rickard of Plymouth. Henry settled where the late Henry L. Thomas lived, and died in 1726, and the other three brothers, settled in the section of the town called Annasnappet. Adam Wright, son of Richard Wright of Plymouth, who lived for a time near the site of Parker's Shovel Works, and afterward, where Daniel D. Wright lives, and died in 1724, aged 78 years. John, son of Adam Wright, was born here in 1680. Edmund Weston, who came from Duxbury and settled where the late Noah Weston lived, and died in 1727. Isaac and George Sampson, who came from Duxbury. They first settled where the late William M. Bisbee lived, and the latter, near the site of the Woolen Factory.

Daniel Pratt, who settled near Pratt's brook, on the road to Middleboro, and Mr. Dunham, who lived on Dunham's neck, near the residence of the late Ephraim Fuller. He lived in a cave, with a wooden roof, which took fire in the night and he was burned to death.

Plympton was incorporated as a town, June 4th, 1707. It then included the town of Carver, about three-quarters of Halifax, and a strip of Kingston, which contained 1306 acres. The territory of the town was afterwards reduced to nearly its present limits by the incorporation of Kingston, in 1726; of Halifax, in 1734; and of Carver, in 1790. It originally contained 55 square miles of territory. The present contents of the town is a little less than 14 square miles. The town contained 924 inhabitants according to the census of 1866.

A few rudely constructed mills, were built by the first settlers. The first grist mill was erected by Adam Wright, soon after he settled here. It was on Wenatuxet river, a little above the site of Parker's Shovel Works. The water wheel, with an upright shaft turned horizontally, and the mill-stone was attached to the upper end of the shaft and turned no oftener than the water-wheel did. The mill was called a gig-mill, and would grind four or five bushels a day, but as the inhabitants increased, it was found to be insufficient to meet their wants, and the owner built another mill, on a different construction, above the site of the Cotton Factory, near where he then lived. Iron works were erected in Plympton, about the year 1720. Two Forges were built on Wenatuxet river, one on the site of Parker's Shovel Works, owned by Joseph Mullerson, a merchant of Boston. The other was built on the site of the Cotton Factory, and was partly owned by Joseph Scott of Boston. Scott was a Tory, and during the Revolutionary war, the town took possession of his property here, and the Forge was fitted up and used to make cannon shot. Another Forge stood on the dam now occupied by Captain Martin Hayward's Sawmill. A Furnace, also stood a little westerly from this Forge, on the opposite side of the road. This Furnace was built about the year 1721, and stood until the Revolutionary war. Sometime during the war, cannon were cast in this Furnace, but they nearly all burst in proving, and not long after the Furnace was taken down. After the close of the Revolutionary war, for a period of twenty-five years, the water power of the town was not much employed except in sawing lumber and grinding grain, and manufacturing was confined chiefly to the domestic purposes of the inhabitants. But the war of 1812, by stopping the importation of foreign goods, gave manufacturing an impulse, and in that year the Cotton Factory was built, and during the fifteen years succeeding 1812, a Woolen Factory and Rolling Mill, and three factories for the manufacture of cut nails. The Woolen Factory was burnt in 1845, and the Rolling-mill run down, a few years after it was built. The Shovel Works of Parker & Co., built where the Rolling-mill stood, about the year 1840, together with one box manufactory, and one establishment for the making of tacks, complete the list of the principal manufactories of the town.

Rev. Jonathan Parker, was the second minister of Plympton. He was the son of Judge Daniel Parker of Barnstable, and was ordained as colleague with Rev. Isaac Cushman, in 1731, and preached in Plympton, 44 years. He died April 24th, 1776, in the 71st year of his age.

Rev. Ezra Sampson, was ordained in 1775, as colleague with Rev. Jonathan Parker, and preached in Plympton, nearly 21 years. He was dismissed by his request in the year 1796, and died in New York City in 1823.

Rev. Ebenezer Withington, was ordained in the year 1798, and preached in Plympton, about three years. He died in Boston, in 1831.

Rev. John Briggs, was installed in December, 1804, and preached here nearly seven years. He died in Richmond, N. H., in 1811.

Rev. Elijah Dexter, was ordained January 18th, 1809. After preaching here about 41 years, he died, October 19th, 1851, aged 65 years. He was the son of Elijah Dexter, of Rochester, Mass. Mary the second wife of Rev. Elijah Dexter, was the daughter of Nathaniel Morton, of Freetown, and sister of Governor Morton.

Dr. Caleb Loring, was the first physician who settled in Plympton. He came from Hull, in 1703, and bought Stephen Bryant's farm in the North part of the town. He was an eminent practitioner and much respected. He died in Plympton, in 1732, in the sixtieth year of his age. Quite a number of his numerous descendants are now living in Plympton.

Col. Seth Cushing, was the son of Seth Cushing of Hingham. He represented the town in the Provincial Congress, which convened at Watertown, in 1775. He was often chosen to represent the town during the Revolutionary war. He died in 1801, in his 78th year.

Elijah Bisbee, Esq., was the son of Elijah Bisbee, and was born September 4th, 1746. He was a Justice of the Peace, and of the quorum, and was much employed in business of a public nature. He was the Town Clerk for many years, and often held other offices in the town. He represented the town in the General Court for seven years in succession. He died April 21st, 1831.

John Avery Parker, was the son of Jonathan Parker, and grandson of the Rev. Jonathan Parker, the second minister of Plympton. He was born in Plympton, September 25th, 1769. He married a daughter of Shadrach Standish, and for a time followed the occupation of making wrought nails. Afterward he moved to Westport, and went into business there, but was unsuccessful and failed. He often told the story of his being warned out of Westport, by the Selectmen, to prevent his becoming a public charge to the town. From Westport he went to New Bedford, and there laid the foundation of an immense fortune, which at the time of his death amounted to some three millions of dollars. He died in New Bedford, in 1853, aged 84 years.

Jonathan Parker, Esq., brother of John Avery Parker, was born in Plympton, in the year 1774. He was widely known and much respected in Plymouth County. He often represented the town in the General Court, and occupied other positions of trust in the town and County. He died in 1851, in the 78th year of his age.

Dea. Lewis Bradford, was the son of Levi Bradford, of Plympton, born March 20th, 1768. Although a person of peculiar habits, he was a man of eminent piety. He was much devoted to antiquarian research, and was a member of the New England Historical and Genealogical Society. He was Town Clerk of Plympton, nearly forty years. He was killed by a fall from a carriage, near the Meeting-house in Plympton, on Sunday, August 10th, 1851. He was 83 years of age.

The original growth and variety of forest trees here was superior to anything within the ancient limits of Plymouth, this fact, together with the meadows, were the principal attractions to the earlier settlers. A noble white oak was cut in this town, some years since, containing seven tons and seven feet of ship-timber and two cords of fire-wood.

During the Revolutionary war, the cause of independence was constantly and earnestly supported by the town of Plympton. Town meetings were often held to raise men and money. At the one held May 25th, 1776, the town "voted unanimously independence of Great Britain."

The record of the town during the late war is of a similar character. Twenty-two Plympton men volunteered for three months' service. They served in company H, 3d Regiment, a Plympton Company, although not wholly composed of Plympton men.

Under the several calls made by the Government, the town was credited with 82 enlistments of three years' men, thirteen nine months' men, and with four men in the Naval service. A few of these were not residents of Plympton, and some of them re-enlisted, and were credited to the town more than once. Ninety of the town residents volunteered; of this number, fifteen were either killed in battle, or died in service.

John Haley, H, 18th, at Old Point Comfort, of fever, July 5th, 1862.

John G. Wright, B, 7th, of fever, on board Steamer Atlantic, July 5th, 1862.

Frederic S. Churchill, E, 18th, killed in the second battle of Bull Run, August 26th, 1862.

John Jordan, E, 18th, wounded at Bull Run, and died at Alexandria, Va., Sept. 14th, 1862.

Edward Turner, C, 18th, killed at Fredericksburg, December 13th, 1862.

Theodore P. Churchill, A, 32d, at Falmouth, of fever, December 14th, 1862.

Ephraim C. Ripley, jr., C, 18th, at Falmouth, of fever, December 14th, 1862.

Thomas Haley, G, 38th, at New Orleans, of fever, April 6th, 1863.

Bennet Soule, G, 38th, at Brashear City, of fever, June 6th, 1863.

William P. Eldridge, F, 32nd, mortally wounded at Gettysburg, and died in Hospital, July 4th, 1863.

George E. Harrub, E, 4th, on board steamer "North America," on the Mississippi, August 8th, 1863.

Jonathan Parker, K, 58th, wounded at Coal Harbor, and died in Washington, July 2nd, 1864.

Ezra B. Churchill, D, 2nd H. A., of sunstroke, at Newbern, July 2nd, 1864.

William P. Phinney, C, 24th, killed at Deep Bottom, August 16th, 1864.

John H. Thomas, C, 18th, at Baltimore, February 17th, 1865, of a wound received in battle.

Five of the above were single men; ten left widows, and six left children.

ROCHESTER.

BY CHARLES STURTEVANT, M. D.

ROCHESTER, called by the Indians *Menchoisett*, a large township of about fifty-eight square miles, distant 10 miles from New Bedford, and 20 from Plymouth; was settled by persons from Scituate, Marshfield, Plymouth and Sandwich, who in 1638, obtained a grant from the Provincial Court, at Plymouth "to locate a township and organize a religious Society in Sippican," an Indian locality near the head of Buzzard's Bay. They named their settlement Rochester, from the town of that name in Kent County, England, whence many of them emigrated. These settlers did not however actually take up their residence in Rochester, until 1651, when Rev. Samuel Arnold, John and Samuel Hammond, Moses and Aaron Barlow, Samuel White, John Wing, Joseph Dotey, Jacob Bumpus, Joseph Burge, (or Burgess), John Haskell, Abraham Holmes, Job Winslow, and ―― Sprague, with probably others whose names are lost, established themselves and erected their church in that part of the present town of Marion, known as Little Neck. At this place may be seen to this date, the traces of their primitive burial-place, and tradition has it that until their antique church was done, they worshipped upon and around a large flat rock, since known as Minister's Rock. Some time about this date a few families from the old town of Dartmouth, now Acushnet, who were friendly to the Indians in this vicinity, came and built a village between the Indian settlements of Sip-pi-can and Mat-ta-poisett. Here lived an old chief by name To-to-sin, a friend of King Philip, who frequently visited here. From him, the locality is called To-to-sin's, or Tow-ser's Neck.

Radiating from these centers the population spread to the North and West, making the next village at Rochester proper, especially at the locality since known as Leonard's Forge, or Handy's Mill. Here the first corn-mill in this part of the County was erected by the town, in 1704, having a perpendicular shaft, and attended by Peter Blackmer, who was appointed to that office and that of Town Clerk. The villages were yearly augmented by people coming from Boston, Salem, and Plymouth, and in 1709, Rev. Timothy Ruggles was ordained, the first minister in the town. In 1733, the settlers in Mattapoisett, were set off as a distinct parish under the pastoral care of Rev. Ivory Hovey. His immediate successor in 1772, was *Lemuel LeBaron. These two men continued in the ministry for 100 years. Rev. Thomas Robbins, D. D., the successor of Mr. LeBaron, possessed in his day the most valuable private library in the state. It consisted of over 3000 volumes and 4000 pamphlets, some of them rare. He also had an extensive collection of coins and manuscripts.

Still another religious society in the North village, or Snip-pa-tuit, was formed in 1748, under the ministry of Rev. Thomas West. These four precincts, agreed in 1670, to hold their town-meetings in the central village, thereafter to be known as Rochester town, the other villages retaining their Indian names till recently. In 1685, the town was incorporated, by the Provincial Court.

In 1775, Rochester voted to sustain the Continental Congress, whenever they might see fit to withdraw their allegiance from the crown, and in the succeeding struggle for Independence, this town furnished more men in proportion to territory or inhabitants, than any other town in the Old Colony. In 1816, the spotted fever made fearful ravages in the village of Mattapoisett, and in the western part of the central village. The population of the entire town being 2800, 61 heads of families were stricken down by this disease.

The surface of the town is level, the soil light, sandy, and not remarkably fertile, but bearing some fine pine and cedar forests. There are several large ponds, one of which, Snippatuit, together with its

---

*In 1696, a French privateer was wrecked in Buzzard's Bay, the crew were carried prisoners to Boston; the surgeon, Dr. Francis Le Baron, came to Plymouth, and having performed a surgical operation, the town being destitute of a physician, they petitioned Lieutenant Governor Stoughton for his liberation, that he might settle in their town. This was granted, and he married Mary Wilder, and he practised physic till he died, at the age of 36 years. Dr. Le Baron did not relinquish the Catholic religion, and was strongly attached to its ceremonies. He never retired to rest without placing the cross on his breast. He left descendants, and all those of his name in this country are descended from him.—*Thacher's History of Plymouth.*

There are other versions of this affair.

outlet to the sea, form a valuable herring privilege. The occupation of the people is chiefly agricultural, and considerable attention is paid in the winter, to the sawing and preparing for market of a large amount of box-boards. Rochester Academy was built and opened for educational purposes in 1839. It has always sustained an enviable reputation as a literary institution and continues to flourish under the present efficient management of Miss C. M. Rounseville. The educational standard has always been high in this town, and public spirit has liberally aided in whatever might elevate it.

SCITUATE.

BY HON. CALEB W. PROUTY.

SCITUATE, like most of the towns in Plymouth Colony, had been nearly depopulated of natives by the small-pox, a few years before the English made a permanent settlement on this coast.

They were the Matakeesetts and controlled by the chief or sachem of the Massachusetts.

Several places in the town still retain the ancient aboriginal names, viz: Musquasheut pond and Conihassett. The name of the town is the aboriginal name, derived from the brook that falls into the harbor. It was called by the Indians, Satuit, and the name of the town in the earliest records in 1633, was Satuit; shortly after it was written Seteat, then Cittewat, and about 1640, the present name Scituate was settled. The settlers at Scituate, extinguished the Indian title by purchase as per deed, dated June, 1653, from the chief of the Matakeesets, signed by Josias Wampatuck, and given to Mr. Timothy Hatherly, Mr. James Cudworth, Mr. Joseph Tilden, Humphrey Turner, William Hatch, John Hoar and James Torrey, for the proper use and behoof of the inhabitants of the town of Scituate. Prior to 1640, there was a deed given, which was subsequently destroyed. In the year 1727, a part of Scituate on the southerly side of the third herring brook, was incorporated by the name of Hanover.

In 1849, the southerly part of the town of Scituate, was incorporated by the name of South Scituate.

Scituate extends about eight miles on the sea shore, including the beach on the east, and the glades on the west. Nearly in the centre of this line is Scituate Harbor.

It affords about ten feet of water in ordinary tides. Here are several wharves, and the principal village of the town. The two points which form the harbor, are Crow point on the south-east, and Cedar point on the north-west. On this latter, a Light-house was erected in 1811. At the harbor the principal business carried on is fishing, mossing, lumber, grain and flour. Two regular packets run between Boston and Scituate.

Products of the sea, for the town of Scituate, for the year 1865: 465,989 lbs. Moss, value $22,558; 3,153 bbls. Herring, value $19,338; 123,999 Lobsters, value 4,753; 441 quintals of Cod Fish, value $2,956; 49 bbls. Mackerel, value $399, Mechanical Products, $164,878.

The earliest notice of a settlement at Scituate, was in 1628, by William Gillson, Anthony Annable, Thomas Bird, Nathaniel Tilden, Edward Foster, Henry Rowley, called "men of Kent," having come from that county in England.

A village was laid out Aug. 2nd, 1633. The principal street was called "Kent street;" it led from the bridge as it now lies, at the harbor, easterly to the third cliff. The first lot was at the corner, formed by Kent Street, and the road now called Central Street, which runs parallel with Satuit brook. This lot was assigned to Edward Foster, and his house stood on the premises, and is the same place occupied at the present time by Seth Webb, Esq., the house having been rebuilt.

Noted men.—John Cushing, jr., born April 28th, 1662, Chief Justice of the Superior Court of Plymouth, from 1702 to 1710; Councillor of Mass., 1710, to 1728; Judge of the Sup. Court, from 1728 to 1737.

John Cushing, 3d, Judge of Probate, from 1738 to 1746; Judge of the Sup. Court, from 1747 to 1771; also Councillor of the Province, from 1746 to 1763.

William Cushing, L. L. D., son of John 3d, graduated at Harvard University, 1751, commenced practice at Pownalboro', Me., 1755; Judge of Probate for County of Lincoln, 1768; appointed Judge of Sup. Court of Mass., (under the crown,) 1772, in which office he was the only member of the bench that adhered to the American cause. At the re-organization of the Court, 1777, he was appointed Chief Justice of that Court. At the organization of the U. S. Gov. in 1789, he was selected by Washington, for one of the Justices of the Court of U. S. In 1796, Judge Cushing was nominated to the Chief Justice office, and unanimously confirmed by the U. S. Senate. He died 1810.

Caleb Cushing, son of Jno. 1st, born 1772, graduated at Harvard College, 1692, ordained at Salisbury, 1697, married daughter of Rev. Jno. Cotton, widow of Rev. James Alling, of Salisbury. Hon. Caleb Cushing, of Newburyport, is his descendant, son of Judge Caleb Cushing.

Thomas Clapp, born 1703, graduate of Harvard College, 1722, was one of the most distinguished men of his time. He was ordained at Windham, Conn., 1726, chosen President of Yale College, 1740; continued in the chair until 1764, died at Scituate, 1765.

Charles Chauncy, (not born in Scituate), was a minister of the first Church of Scituate, for 13 years, from 1641 to 1654, when he was chosen President of Harvard College.

Henry Dunster, was also a minister of the first church and President of Harvard College, Aug. 27th, 1640; resigned 1654.

Samuel Woodworth, the late well known Editor and Poet, author of "The Old Oaken Bucket," was born in this town.

> "How dear to this heart are the scenes of my childhood,
>   When fond recollection presents them to view!—
> The orchard, the meadow, the deep-tangled wild-wood,
>   And every loved spot which my infancy knew!
> The wide-spreading pond, and the mill that stood by it;
>   The bridge, and the rock where the cataract fell;
> The cot of my father, the dairy-house by it,
>   And e'en the rude bucket that hung in the well—
> The old oaken bucket, the iron-bound bucket,
>   The moss-covered bucket that hung in the well."

The "orchard," the "meadow," the "deep-tangled wild wood," "wide spreading pond," the "mill," the "bridge," and the "rock where the cataract fell," all may be seen, as in the poet's "childhood," situated about two miles from Scituate harbor. "The cot of my father, the dairy-house by it, has been replaced by a modern-built house, by Mr. Joseph Northey, half brother of the Poet.

Ecclesiastical History.—The first church, Unitarian, in Scituate, was regularly gathered, January, 1634, O. S. This society have erected five churches, including the present one, which stands in the center of the town, on a high eminence, and is a noted land-mark, to the mariner in coming into Massachusetts Bay, and by the sailors, is called the "Old Sloop." The following are the ministers of the church, in the order as herein named:—

Giles Saxton, from 1631, to 1634, previous to the gathering of the church; Rev. John Lathrop, ordained 1634; Rev. Charles Chauncy, 1641; Rev. Henry Dunster, 1659; Rev. Nicholas Baker, 1660; Jeremiah Cushing, 1691; Rev. Nathaniel Pitcher, 1707; Shearjashub Bourn, 1724; Rev. Ebenezer Grosvenor, 1763; Ebenezer Dawes, jr., 1787; Nehemiah Thomas, 1792; Edmund Q. Sewall, 1822; Ephraim Nute, jr., 1848; Rev. Fisk Barrett, 1852; Rev. G. Babcock, 1860; Rev. Wm. S. Heywood, 1866, present pastor.

The Baptist Society was formed in 1825, church built same year and dedicated Aug. 17. Clergymen, Le Favor, Niles, Seagraves, Judson, Conant, Carpenter, and others. The Rev. Mr. Holmes is present pastor.

The First Trinitarian, formed 1825, church built in 1826, dedicated Nov. 16. Clergymen, Jewett, Wright, and others; the present pastor is the Rev. A. J. Sessions.

The Methodist E. Church, formed in 1825, church built near the Harbor, 1826. Clergymen, Avery, Barker, Keith, Holway, and others, the present pastor is the Rev. C. Nason. The church was burnt, July 4, 1865, and they are about erecting another on Central st.

Population of Scituate, May 1, 1865, 2,269; 1860, 2,227.

Names of soldiers who died in service during the late Rebellion:—

John Briggs Newcomb, Co. K, 7th Reg't, died of wounds May 7th, 1863.

Nathan Andrew Rogers, Co. B, 12th Reg't, died of wounds Nov. 13th, 1862.

Geo. Davis Brown, Co. G, 29th Reg't, killed June 15th, 1862.
Charles Henry Clapp, Co. F, 32d Reg't, died Feb. 21st, 1863.
Horace Lincoln Studley, Co. F, 32d Reg't, died April 1st, 1863.
James S. J. Andrews, Co. A, 35th Reg't, died Feb. 4th, 1863.
James Lufkins Brown, Co. G, 35th Reg't, died Aug. 4th, 1863.
David Otis Totman, Co. G, 38th Reg't, died April 18th, 1864.
Seth Kent Bailey, Co. G, 38th Reg't, died June, 1863.
Warren Studley Litchfield, Co. G, 38th Reg't, died Sept. 14th, 1863.
Andrew M. Hyland, Co. G, 38th Reg't, died Nov. 9th, 1863.
Warren Litchfield, jr., Co. F, 43d Reg't, died June 25th, 1863.
Albert Hutchinson, U. S. Eng., last heard from, July 1862.
Edwin White Damon, U. S. Eng., last heard from, July 1862.

No. of Drafted men that entered the army, 3; Drafted men paid commutation, 14; Volunteers for three years, 52; Volunteers for one year, 42; Substitutes, 2; Re-enlisted men for three years, 7; Seamen for three years, 7; Seamen at large, for three years, 15; Contrabands for three years, 4; Nine months' men, 17; Three months' men, 78.

Torrey's History of Scituate, says:—"Scituate, indebted to the substantial character of some of its founders, many of whom it is evident, came chiefly from Kent, in England, soon became a respectable town, early taking the lead in rates and levies of men, which superiority it maintained to the latest annals of the Colony. Are you a Kentish man, or a man of Kent? has its historical value, as it respects origin."

"Dean" gives this account of the Indian attack on Scituate:—

"They came into Scituate by the 'Indian path,' so called, which led from Scituate to the Matakeeset settlements at Indian head ponds, by 'the Cornet's mill,' on the third Herring brook, near the residence of the late Major Winslow. This saw-mill they burnt; and tradition tells that they wounded and burnt a man in it; but this is doubtful. They then proceeded to Capt. Joseph Sylvester's, and burnt his house. It stood north of the Episcopal Church hill, (now known as such,) and nearly on the same spot where stands the mansion of Mr. Samuel

Waterman. There was a garrison of twelve men at Joseph Barstow's, three-fourths of a mile south of Capt. Sylvester's, which they probably avoided, and proceeded down towards the town, burning as they went. But, unfortunately, we are able only to mention a few of the houses so destroyed, which we find incidentally mentioned in our town records. The next house which they burnt (of which we have certain record) was William Blackmore's. It stood where stands the house of the late Capt. Elijah Curtis, forty rods west of the head of the lane that leads to Union bridge, and on the north side of the street. William Blackmore was killed that day, but whether in attempting to defend his house or not, and what was the fate of his family, we have not learned, probably, however, they had escaped to the 'block-house' on the bank of the river, but fifty rods distant. The block-house was attacked, but not carried; John James, however, whose house was near the block-house, received a mortal wound, lingering about six weeks, and died. The Indians then hastened forward to attack the principal garrison at Charles Stockbridge's. Their path may be traced directly onward towards this garrison. The house of Nicholas (the Swede) was the next burnt, which stood on a small hill thirty rods north-east of Parker lane. We observe that the town voted the next year to allow him three pounds towards rebuilding his house. In their further progress they doubtless burnt other houses, as Wm. Parker's, Robert Stetson, Jr.'s, Standlake's, Sutliffe's, Holmes', John Buck's and others were nigh their path, but unfortunately the committee's report to Gov. Winslow is not extant, at least in full. They passed over Walnut Tree hill, on the northward of the late Judge William Cushing's, and entered Ewell's house, which stood at the 'turn of the road,' which spot may be known in modern times by saying it was nearly midway between Judge Cushing's mansion and farm-house. Ewell's wife was alone, save an infant grandchild, John Northey, sleeping in the cradle; the house being situated beneath a high hill, she had no notice of the approach of the savages until they were rushing down the hill towards the house. In the moment of alarm she fled towards the garrison, which was not more than sixty rods distant, and either through a momentary forgetfulness, or despair, or with the hope of alarming the garrison in season, she forgot the child. She reached the garrison in safety. The savages entered her house, and stopping only to take the bread from the oven which she was in the act of putting in, when she was alarmed, then rushed forward to assault the garrison. After they had become closely engaged, Ewell's wife returned by a circuitous path, to learn the fate of the babe, and, to her happy surprise, found it quietly sleeping in the cradle as she had left it, and carried it safely to the garrison. In a few hours the house was burnt. There was a considerable village around this place, and the houses of Northey, Palmer, Russell, Thomas King, Jr., and some others were doubtless burnt, though we are not able to quote record for it. That Ewell's house was burnt, we learn from his will, in which it was incidentally mentioned. The garrison-house of Stockbridge was palisadoed on three sides, the fourth being defended by the mill-pond. Besides this there was a small outwork near the mill, on a little island between the mill-stream and the waste-way, where a blacksmith's shop has for several years stood. It was thought to be a point of importance to the settlement to defend these mills. Here the Indians fought several hours, made many efforts to fire the buildings, and sustained heavy losses, from the well-directed shot from the garrison. They chiefly occupied the ground at the south end of the mill-dam. They were not repulsed until night close, when nearly the whole force of the town that was left at home was collected for the purpose. Lieut. Buck had mustered all the men below, and the veteran Cornet Stetson, had descended the river, with what people could be raised in the south part of the town. Unfortunately, Capt. John Williams, with thirty Scituate men, was absent, 'ranging the woods' about Namasket, (Middleborough)."

SOUTH SCITUATE.

BY SAMUEL TOLMAN, JR.

THE town of South Scituate was incorporated in 1849. It was originally a part of the town of Scituate, so that really a history of Scituate must be, to a great extent, a history of South Scituate.

Settlements were made on the coast, earlier than in that part of the town now within the limits of South Scituate. Cornet Robert Stetson, was probably the first person who permanently settled in South Scituate. He selected a beautiful plain near the river, and received a grant of a large tract of land, as early as 1634.

His house, as nearly as can be ascertained, occupied the site of that now owned by Mr. Clark Sampson; an unfailing spring of the purest water, gushes forth a few rods from the house, as it did more than two hundred years ago, having been, no doubt, one of the strong attractions which induced the early settler to make this spot his home. History speaks of him as possessed of considerable wealth, an enterprising and valuable man in the plantation, a deputy to court, a cornet of the first light horse corps raised in the Colony, a member of the

Council of war, a Colony Commissioner for settling the patent line, in short, he lived long and left a good name at last. In 1656, he, with others erected a saw-mill on the third Herring Brook. Remains of the dam, may now be seen near the residence of Samuel Tolman, jr. This mill was burned by the Indians, May 20th, 1676, who came into Scituate from Hingham, where the day before they had made depredations, and killed one man. They then passed on, and burnt a house situated nearly on the spot where now stands that of Lemuel C. Waterman, Esq. When preparing a site for a new mill, a few rods below the old dam, in 1838, the workmen discovered pieces of the old mill, completely charred, and in a perfect state of preservation, which are now in the possession of Col. Samuel Tolman.

South Scituate, affords remarkable instances of longevity, in the highly respectable name of Copeland. Joseph Copeland came into Scituate in 1730, and left twelve children, whose average age was eighty-six years. One of the daughters, Rhoda, the wife of Michael Ford, died at the age of ninety-three, from injuries occasioned by a fall. Five of her children are now living, the youngest of whom is more than *eighty-two* years of age. South Scituate is separated from the town of Marshfield by the North River, which has been noted for ship-building; indeed, it may well be called the nursery of ship-builders. North River ships were deemed the first-class, both as to beauty, and durability, being constructed entirely of the tough oaks of this vicinity. Many of the whale ships of Nantucket and New Bedford have been built here, rating from 300 to 400 tons. Mr. William Delano, built a merchantman in 1812, of 590 tons, which was at that time one of the largest. Scarce a ship-yard or Navy-yard, can be visited on our coast, where many workmen may not be found whose ancestors were employed at the North River. Especially may they be found in Medford, Chelsea, and East Boston. Curtis, Foster, Stetson, Taylor, James, Tilden, Delano; and many others, were here, all familiar names. Edward Delano, late Naval Constructor, at Charlestown, and Benjamin Delano, now Naval Constructor, at Brooklyn, N. Y., are sons of Mr. William Delano above named, and were born in South Scituate. This business, once so flourishing, is now almost entirely discontinued, partly because material is scarce, and larger ships are demanded, but chiefly on account of the increasing obstructions at the mouth of the river. An unsuccessful attempt was made a few years since to compel the waters to pass to the sea by an artificial channel.

South Scituate has been prompt in answering the calls of the government for men, during the late terrible but glorious war. The recruiting officers report from the records of the Provost Marshall. "Quotas all full, and a surplus for the "next call":—

She furnished under the call of April 16th, 1861, 9; May 3d, 1861.

15; June 17th, 1861, 22; May 28th, 1862, 22; July 4th, 1862. 22; August 4th, 1862, 34; July 1st, 1863, 21; October 17th, 1863, 21; February 1st, 1864, 15; March 15th, 1864, 14; July 19th, 1864, 26; December, 1864, 18; making 239 in all.

The following are the names of those who fell in battle, or died of wounds, or disease, contracted in the service:—

Wm. T. Sylvester, Edward Dover, Joseph Simmons, Clifton H. Vose, Henry H. Gardner, David W. Robinson, Sidney Gardner, Geo. Merritt, Henry Harlow, Josiah Stoddard, jr., Nathaniel W. Winslow, Samuel Freeman, Gustavus Jacobs, Beza W. Drake, Joshua S. Damon, Walter Foster, 2d, Abiel Farrar, Herbert Graves, William Whitcomb, Henry Currell, and Reuben H. Payne.

It would give us much pleasure, would the limits of the present work allow us to present the names of those who have been disabled by wounds, or are suffering from disease contracted in the service. Let us see to it, that our care for them, and the widows and orphans of the fallen, and our measure of gratitude for the services of our soldiers, equal, if possible, the magnitude of the blessings their sufferings have brought; remembering while we review the history of our towns and of our country, that whatever of prosperity the future historian may record, is based upon that universal liberty, which their sacrifices have established.

WAREHAM.

IN 1838, Silvanus Bourne, Esq., furnished a series of very interesting articles to one of the County papers, concerning the history of this town. He says:—The east part of the town, known as the "Agawam purchase," lay in the township of Plymouth, and the west part belonged to Rochester, until in 1739, these two tracts were incorporated as the town of Wareham, the name being borrowed from an old English town, once of some note. In 1827, Wareham was enlarged by the addition of a slice of Plymouth and Carver, known as Tihonet.

From 1739, until 1824, the people of the West end, and the inhabitants of Agawam, were mutually jealous of each others' rights, so much so that two constables, and two collectors, were always appointed, and even two sets of tax bills were always made.

Agawam probably derives its name from one of the Massachusetts tribes of that name. There are several Agawams in the State, and it is supposed that some one of these was the abiding place of the tribe, and that the others were temporary homes of parts of the same tribe. This tract was leased in 1678, for seven years, and in 1682, was sold by the town of Plymouth, in order to raise funds for building a new meeting-house in that town. The purchasers were ten in number, including John Chubbuck, Samuel Bates and John Fearing.

These early settlers began their colony as though they were a separate nation, laying out a mill lot, pound and grave yard, and would undoubtedly have built a pillory and whipping-post, but Plymouth was careful to reserve in the deed of sale, jurisdiction of the territory. Two lots of land and one of meadow, were reserved for the ministry, in 1701.

The first highway run nearly East and West, crossing the streams at the head of tide water. Other ways led to the house of every settler, some of them open, and some through gates and bars.

The land southerly of Agawam, is indented with many coves, forming numerous peninsulas, or necks, as they are here called. There are also numerous islands, among them Wickett's, named for the Indian who owned it; Ousett, on which the credulous believed money was buried, and where lights were formerly seen on stormy nights, and even the money chest has been seen by curious searchers! Little Bird, Tinis, besides the cluster of islands in Little Harbor. There are two beaches made by the waves of Buzzard's Bay, and the extensive flats yield many shell fish. There are several ponds, and numerous valuable streams of water, in this section, among them Red Brook, colored by the iron-ore bed over which it passes, and the Agawam river, a valuable manufacturing stream. The wood is mainly pitch-pine.

It is not known at what time the West end of the town was first settled. The lands were granted by the Virginia mode, called *shingling*. To each proprietor was given a warrant stating that he was entitled to a certain quantity of land. This warrant he could assign or locate it where he pleased, in one or more lots, or in any shape. Of course, all aimed to secure the best land, and one surveyor, not always knowing what another had done, some lots were often more than once covered, which led to litigation and trouble. There were also left many odd strips called gores.

At the time of the incorporation of Wareham, July, 1739, it is not known what its population was. At that time, every town containing forty qualified voters, was entitled to a representative, but for forty years after incorporation, the town voted that they were not qualified to send, and when they wished to be heard at General Court, they sent an Agent instead of a Representative.

In the French War of 1757-8, Wareham sent nine of her citizens to assist in the capture of Cape Breton, and Samuel Bosso lost his life there. Five others joined the Northern army, to capture Canada, besides Jo. Joseph, Sol. Joseph and Jabez Wickett, three Indians of the place, who fought against the hostile Indians.

Previous to the Revolutionary war, as early as Jan. 18, 1773, at the request of the town of Boston, a town meeting was held in Wareham to consider of matters of grievances the Provinces were under. Capt. Josiah Carver was moderator. In Feb. 1774, strong resolutions were adopted, insisting upon the rights of British Freedom. In Jan. 1775, they voted to allow every minute man 1s. 1d. per week, and refused to make any tax under the King's authority, but to pay the Province tax already made to Dr. Andrew Mackie, with instructions that he keep it till the town otherwise order. On March 17, they voted to purchase six guns for the town, and instructed Nathan Bassett to put the other guns in repair and make bayonets for them.

About the time of the battle of Lexington, it was rumored that the King's troops were at Marshfield, laying the country waste. Forty minute men immediately left for Plymouth, under the command of Capt. Israel Fearing, Lieuts. Ebenezer Chubbuck and Barnabas Bates.

Eight men served two months; eighteen enlisted for six months, and were stationed along shore. During their term of service, they went to an alarm at Nashuanu, rowing themselves in two whale boats. Nine were in the army near Boston, eight months, making thirty-six men sent into service the first year, from a town without voters enough to send a representative. In 1776, eighteen men enlisted, and in 1777, fourteen men enlisted for three years or the war, eight men enlisted for two months, to serve in Rhode Island, and in August, nearly every man in the militia went on the secret expedition to Newport.

In Sep., 1777, the town voted £33 for 100 lbs. of powder, and in Nov., £100 to supply the families of Continental soldiers with such articles as they should need. In Sept., 1778, the British burnt the shipping at New Bedford, and our militia turned out under Maj. Israel Fearing, and all concur in saying that he conducted the defences on the east side of the river, with good judgment and bravery, the fire of his men warding off a night attack. The militia went twice to Falmouth. Sep. 21st, 1780, voted £80. 17s. hard money, for beef to send to the army. Jan. 1781, voted to have a lottery to raise $280, hard money, to raise soldiers with. Eighty-six different individuals did service in the army, 13 of whom died.

"During the Revolutionary war, the operations of our patriotic citizens were not confined to the land. Capt. Barzilla Besse went out privateering under a commission from the State, in an armed sloop, and took one prize. He, together with John Gibbs, and some others of his crew, left his vessel at Nantucket, and went on board Capt. Dimmick of Falmouth, as volunteers, in a wood sloop borrowed at that place for the occasion, and running down towards the enemy's vessel, which was a shaving mill mounting six swivels. Dimmick was ordered to strike; he showed submission—but in running under her stern, he put his bowsprit over the enemy's taffrail, and, calling upon his men, they sprang on board, killed the English captain, and took his vessel in a few minutes.

"Also a 10 gun sloop, named the Hancock, owned by John Carver, Nathan Bassett, and others, was fitted out from this place as a privateer, commanded by James Southard. The first cruise, they went to the West Indies and took two prizes. The second cruise, they took 2 Grand Bank fishermen, both brigs, and brought them into Wareham.

"The enemy took from our citizens the schooner Lion, coming from the West Indies, with a load of salt—the schooner Desire, going to Brazil, and a sloop which was built for a privateer, and performed one unsuccessful cruise in that capacity, but was afterwards sent to Turks Island for salt, and was taken while returning."

In 1784, voted to vendue the colors belonging to the town. This vote is now much to be regretted.

Previous to the war of 1812, commerce flourished and many vessels were built at the Narrows. We had but one man in the regular army, Joseph Saunders, and he was killed at the battle of New Orleans. 13 of our sloops were captured by the enemy, among them:—

"The sloop Polly. Capt. Barrows, was taken on the 9th of June. 1814, off Westport. The Captain ransomed her for $200, and came home to get the money, leaving Moses Bumpus and James Miller with the British until his return.

"The same day, the sloop Polly was re-taken, by a party fitted out from Westport; but the two young men, Bumpus and Miller, had been taken on board the brig-of-war, Nimrod, and by their aid, as was supposed, in a few days, she run up the Bay to West's Island; here they landed, and took Samuel Besse on board for a pilot, as he says, by force, and compelled him to pilot the brig up the Bay. On the next day, June 13th, she was seen by Ebenezer Bourne, about nine o'clock A. M., off Mattapoisett, standing up the Bay; and at ten, came to an anchor about four miles southerly of Bird Island Light; and immediately manned six barges, which formed a line, two abreast. Each barge had a large lateen sail, and was rowed by six oars, double manned, with a fair wind and strong flood tide, and steered for Wareham. Bourne left his work, and ran to his boat, then lying at Crooked River, and sailed across to the lower end of the neck, where he took land, and in twenty minutes from the time he left home, gave information to the Selectmen, then assembled on other business, in the lower house, at the Narrows village. He and they passed quickly through the village, giving the alarm to the citizens, until they arrived at the house of Benjamin Fearing, Esq. Here the Selectmen ordered Maj. William Barrows to assemble the men and prepare their guns as fast as possible—then pass down the Narrows, and they would forward them ammunition as soon as it could be procured from the town stores, which were kept by Wadsworth Crocker, Esq. Bourne upon his first arrival at Fearing's, meeting with a gentleman, upon a smart horse, bound towards Agawam, requested him to quicken his speed, and stop at the next public house, then kept by Capt. Israel Fearing, and tell him to call out his men, and proceed forthwith to the east side of the Narrows—this the stranger promised, and performed. Maj. Barrows collected 12 men with arms, which he paraded; and the minister, Rev. Noble Everett, came from the Selectmen with a keg of powder, and balls. But while they were loading their guns, Wm. Fearing, Esq., and Jonathan Reed came to the Major, and told him to put his arms and ammunition out of sight, for they had made a treaty with the enemy, and had agreed to spare private property. The guns were hid under Capt. Jeremiah Bumpus' porch, and the keg of powder left near his house. The British came to the turn of the channel—here set a white flag, and proceeded to the lower wharf, where the marines landed—being about 200 in number—paraded on the wharf, and set a sentinel upon the high land back of the village, with orders to let no citizen pass from the village;—and about this time, Fearing and Reed approached the enemy with a white handerchief upon a cane, and made the treaty aforesaid. The enemy then marched up the street, detaching sentries upon the high land, at convenient distances, until they arrived at the Cotton Factory. This, they set on fire by shooting a Congreve rocket into a post in the middle of the first story, and returned, taking the arms and powder at Capt. Bumpus' house, and threatened to burn the house, if the town stores were not surrendered, which they thought were there.

"About this time, four schooners belonging to Falmouth, and one belonging to Plymouth, which had put into this port, for safety, were set on fire by the men left with the barges;—these, and the Factory, as they asserted, not being private property. As they passed up, they called at Wm. Fearing's store, took something to drink, and went into his kitchen, took a brand of fire, and proceeded to his ship-yard, immediately in front of his house, and here set fire to a new brig, nearly finished, upon the stocks, belonging to said Fearing, he remonstrating and reminding them of their treaty, but they asserting that she was built for a privateer, put her well on fire, so that she burnt to ashes. They fired also a ship and brig lying at the wharf, and five sloops, all of which, as well as the Cotton Factory, were put out. Six vessels were not set on fire. They next took twelve men as hostages, to prevent our citizens from firing upon them—and hoisting a white flag, and saying if a gun was fired the hostages would be massacred, embarked, having tarried on shore about two hours. About this time, Capt. Israel Fearing assembled 12 men on the opposite side of the Narrows, and showed fight. One of the barges dropped over that way, and the

Narrows citizens begged him not to fire, as a treaty had been made and hostages taken to insure its performance—whereupon he fell back, to watch their further movements, kept his men assembled, but as the hostages were not given up until they passed below him, he did not fire, and the enemy departed in peace, landing our citizens on Cromeset Point. The barges formed a line, fired a Congreve rocket into the air, fired a swivel from the bow of each barge, gave three cheers, and proceeded leisurely to the brig; landed Besse upon West's Island, and the young men at North Falmouth. Besse was taken up and examined before a magistrate, in New Bedford, and acquitted. Miller and Bumpus were examined and committed to prison for further examination and trial; and after being imprisoned about three months, were acquitted, and both shipped on board of a privateer, where Bumpus was killed, and Miller lost a leg by a cannon ball. The whole damage done by the expedition as estimated at the time, was $25,000."

The first settled minister was Rowland Thatcher, ordained in 1740, died 1773. His successors have been Josiah Cotton, 1774; Noble Everett, 1784-1820; Daniel Hemmenway, 1821-1828; Samuel Nott, ordained 1829; Homer Barrows, and Rev. T. F. Clary, present pastor. In 1830, the First Christian Society was formed, but not now in operation. The building on High Street, was purchased by the Catholics, about 1865, and is now occupied by them. In 1830, the M. E. Society was formed, and soon after a church built near the Center. Services have not been held there regularly, of late;—a good part of the membership being at Agawam, meetings are held there.

In 1780, the town paid their minister $240 per Sabbath—in the depreciated currency of the times. The town and parish records have been entered in separate books, since 1828, at which time the present church edifice was erected.

The first school was held in 1741, and the first Temperance Society was formed in Wareham, in 1824.

In 1742, Wareham sent out a colony of more than 100, which settled in Sharon, Ct. From 1739 to 1829, deer reeves were annually elected, to enforce the laws for the protection of these animals.

Wareham has long been celebrated for its iron and nail manufactories. The first machinery for making of nails, was introduced by I. & J. Pratt, & Co., in 1822.

In 1822, B. Murdock & Co., built the Washington Iron Works on the Weweantit river. In 1828, a second dam was erected, a half a mile above. In 1827, the "Poles Works" were erected; in 1828, the "Tihonet Works," and in 1836, the "Agawam Works."

Most of these establishments have been burnt out at various times. The Washington Works, now called Tremont, have lately been rebuilt in the best style. They are owned by Joshua B. Tobey. The Poles establishment is now owned by the Robinson Iron Co.

Besides the manufacture of nails, much attention has been given to iron casting and iron manufacturing. The "Franconia Works," on the wharf, below the Narrows, employ a large number of men in making merchantable iron. S. T. Tisdale, Esq., is at the head of the Agawam Works. The first blast furnace was erected in 1805, on the Weweantit river.

About 1820, the manufacture of hollow ware, in blast furnaces, was the most thriving business in the vicinity, although most of the furnaces were in Carver and Middleboro, yet the ore was brought from New Jersey, and landed at Wareham; from thence it was hauled to the different furnaces and the ware returned to Wareham, for shiping. Whole forests of pitch pine timber were felled, and converted into coal to melt the moulton masses with which these various furnaces were continually charged. The introduction of hard coal and pig iron, completely revolutionized this business, and blast furnaces were abandoned.

The manufacture of staves and nail casks has long been an important branch of business. The name of Lewis Kenney, is inseparably connected with this business, and in 1829, the first machinery for sawing the staves, was introduced by him, since which time he has added many valuable machines for sawing.

The first cotton factory here, was built in 1812. In 1816, Curtis Tobey built another, and in 1823, Benjamin Lincoln, added still another factory. Nothing is done in this line now.

The first paper mill was on the Weweantit, built in 1824, by Pardon Tabor. The new paper establishment, near the Tremont depot, was lately erected by Wheelwright & Co., of Boston. This, in 1865, employed 13 hands.

During the Revolutionary war, when salt was in great demand, our people embarked largely in its manufacture, by boiling the sea water in large kettles. From 1806, through the second war with England, great quantities of salt were made by evaporation.

The last native Indians died about 1830. When their ancestors sold the land here, one of the rights reserved was that of cutting broomsticks and basket stuff, wherever they chose.

The soil is diluvial, and our people have given much more attention to manufacturing than farming. Formerly there were many good orchards.

List of soldiers and sailors who died in the service of their country, in the late Rebellion:—

Geo. H. French, B, 24th, at Beaufort, N. C., Jan. 22d, 1863.
Joseph W. Tinkham, 3rd Reg.
Patrick Crim, K, 28th Reg't.
Thomas S. Hatch, C, 18th Reg't.
James F. Leonard, G, 18th Reg't.

Wm. Ashton. G, 18th Reg't.
Samuel Benson. G, 18th Reg't.
Theodore E. Paddock, G, 18th Reg't.
Arch. Stringer, G, 18th Reg't.
Patrick Cox, C, 58th, died Feb. 8th, 1865.
Jas. R. Russie, A, 20th, died in prison.
Stephen S. Russie, A, 24th Reg't.
Marcus Atwood, 18th Reg't.
Jas. Blackwell, A, 20th, died at Wareham.
Benj. F. Bumpus, A, 20th Reg't.
Daniel C. Bumpus, B, 24th Reg't, Sept. 30th, 1864.
John J. Carrol, A, 20th Reg't.
Benj. D. Clifton, 20th Reg't.
John A. Haskins, 6th Battery, died at Washington, D. C., Dec. 6th, 1864.
Joseph Hayden, B, 24th Reg't.
John D. Manter, B, 3d, at Newbern, N. C.
James Maddigan, A, 20th, at Wareham.
John R. Oldham, at Deep Bottom, Va., Aug. 14th, 1864.
John S. Oldham, B, 3d, Reg't, died at Newbern, N. C.
Isaac S. Oldham, B, 24th, died at Beaufort, N. C., Feb. 2nd, 1863.
David A. Perry, B, 24th Reg't.
Daniel Westgate, 1st Battalion, Co. D.
Julian W. Swift, A, 20th, killed at Petersburg.
Horatio G. Harlow, C, 58th, at Libby Prison.
Stephen H. Drew, 58th Reg't.
Geo. W. Besse, H, 58th, July 2d, 1864.
Geo. H. Loring, A, 20th, at Libby Prison.

WEST BRIDGEWATER.

THE early history of what is now the four Bridgewaters, was of course interwoven, so that previous articles on the other towns, have forestalled much that would otherwise have been mentioned in the sketch of this town.

Agriculture is the principal business in West Bridgewater, and the large farms of rich, mellow land, under the skillful management of our intelligent farmers, yield good returns. There are also several boot and shoe establishments, as well as good water power, used in the manufacture of iron.

Centre and Cochesett villages, in West Bridgewater, about two miles apart, are neat, and busy in the labors of domestic industry.

West Bridgewater lies twenty-five miles south from Boston, twenty north-west from Plymouth, ten north north-east from Taunton, and twenty-five north by east from Fall River.

The following were the names of the fifty-four original proprietors; those whose names are printed in *italics*, became permanent settlers.

William Bradford, William Merrick, John Bradford, Abraham Pierce, John Rogers, George Partridge, John Starr, William Collier, Christopher Wadsworth, Edward Hall, Nicholas Robbins, *Thomas Hayward*, Ralph Partridge, *Nathaniel Willis*, *John Willis*, Thomas Benney, Miles Standish, Love Brewster, John Paybody, Francis Sprague, *William Bassett*, *John Washburn*, *John Washburn, jr.*, *John Ames*, *Thomas Gannett*, *William Brett*, Edmund Hunt, William Clarke, William Ford, Constant Southworth, *John Cary*, Edmund Weston, *Samuel Tompkins*, Edmund Chandler, Moses Simmons, John Irish, Philip Delano, *Arthur Harris*, John Alden, *John Fobes*, Samuel Nash, Abram Sampson, George Soule, *Experience Mitchell*, Henry Howland, Henry Sampson, John Brewer, *John Haward*, Francis West, William Tubbs, James Lendall, Samuel Eaton, *Solomon Leonard*, Wm. Paybody.

Thus it will be seen that of the fifty-four original proprietors, only sixteen became inhabitants of the new settlement. The grant of the Bridgewater plantation, as we have seen, was in 1646, and the settlement made in 1650. The first settlers had a house-lot of six acres each on the town river, and the place was called Nuckatest, or Nunckotetest. The first lots were taken up at West Bridgewater; first houses built and the first improvements made there. The settlement was compact,—the house-lots being contiguous,—with a view for mutual protection and aid against the Indians; and, as a further protection from the natives, they erected a stockade or garrison on the South side of the river, and fortified many of their dwellings. From this original home, the settlers scattered into other portions of the town, extending their dwellings first into the South part of the town, toward Nippenicket Pond, on the road to Taunton, whither they were in the habit of going either to mill or to trade; and we are told they frequently went to that place on foot, with the grists upon their backs, a distance of several miles.

The West parish was never incorporated by an Act of the Legislature, but the parochial affairs were for many years, transacted by the old town. It was incorporated as West Bridgewater, Feb. 16th, 1822, thus leaving the South Parish to retain the old name of Bridgewater.

On the 3d of June, 1856, the four Bridgewaters, united in celebrating the two hundredth anniversary of the incorparation of the old town. An address was delivered by Hon. Emery Washburn, of Cambridge, and a Poem by Rev. James Reed, of Boston. A dinner was prepared for a thousand people, at which appropriate and interesting remarks were made by a number of distinguished gentlemen.

A hymn was sung at the celebration, written by William C. Bryant, Esq., of New York, and another by Rev. Daniel Huntington, of New London, which, after alluding in grateful terms, to our fathers, who—

> "Bought these fields of savage men,
> And reared their homes and altars here."

closed with the following stanzas:—

> "They left us freedom, honor, truth;
> Oh! may these rich bequests descend
> From sire to son, from age to youth,
> And bless our land till time shall end!
>
> So, as successive centuries roll,
> When we shall long have passed away,
> Here may our sons, with heart and soul,
> Still hail Bridgewater's natal day."

There were in the Army and Navy, from West Bridgewater, about 210 men. The persons named below, died in the service. There are several whom we have no account of. Probably others died.

Myron E. Alger, C, 29th Reg't.
George Colwell, K, 3d Reg't.
Patrick Cunningham, K, 9th Reg't.
Timothy Callahan, killed, E, 19th Reg't.
Alvan R. Coffin, in rebel prison, 2d Cavalry.
John B. Dunbar, of fever, H, 2d Reg't.
James E. Jacobs, killed in Navy.
Leonard Jones, D, 58th, of wounds, in hospital at Washington, June 30th, 1864.
Henry M. Folsom, D, 58th Reg't, of disease.
John B. Gould, K, 26th Reg't, killed Sept. 19th, 1864.
Eustace Howard, D, 58th Reg't, of wounds, at the Wilderness, June 30th, 1864.
Lyman E. Howard, K, 26th Reg't, killed Sep. 19th, 1864.
Granville Howard, K, 26th Reg't, killed Sep. 19th, 1864.
Charles H. Hayden, C, 29th Reg't, of disease.
Hector O. Kingman, C, 58th Reg't, of disease, Feb. 5th, 1865.
Francis Lothrop, K, 26th Reg't, of fever, Aug. 1863.
Timothy O'Leary, F, 12th Reg't.
Michael McMurphy, 59th Reg't, of disease.
Charles H. Parker, I, 40th Reg't, of disease.
Henry Quinley, H, 7th Reg't, killed.
Charles H. Turner, C, 29th Reg't, of disease.
Roscoe Tucker, I, 1st Cavalry, in rebel prison, Jan. 29th, 1865.
James Ryan, in Navy,
Asa F. Shaw, I, 40th Reg't, in rebel prison, Dec. 22d, 1864.
William Dewyre, in Navy.

Historical Appendix.

Containing additional list of Union Soldiers who died in service, etc.

Abington.

Henry W. Bebee, 7th, died of wounds received at battle of Fredericksburg, May 3, 1863.

Charles L. Baldwin, C, 38th, at Berwick City, May 3, 1863.

George E. Beal, C, 38th, Feb. 16, 1863.

Alson Bicknell, C, 38th, Marine Hospital, New Orleans, La., chronic diarrhœa, April 14, 1863.

Solon Bates, E, 4th, May 29, 1863.

Bradford W. Beal, 20th, May 28, 1864.

Sergt. Benj. F. Caswell, K, 18th, battle of Bull Run, Va., August 30, 1862.

Michael Coughlan, 18th, Aug. 12, 1864.

Frederick Cook, K, 7th, Oct. 12, 1862.

Timothy W. Crocker, S. C., at Boston, Dec. 18, 1864.

1st Lieut. Lysander F. Cushing, 12th, killed in action, September 17, 1862.

Benj. Curtis, G, 12th, killed in action, Sept. 17, 1862.

Wm. M. Campbell, 16th, killed at Fredericksburg, Dec., 1862.

Brine Downing, C, 38th, at Baton Rouge, of fever, June 21, 1863.

Daniel Dwyer, H, 18th, at Savannah, Ga., Sept. 18, 1864.

Edward L. Dyer, C, 38th, at Abington, Feb. 12th, 1864.

Daniel Daley, E, 4th, at Brashear City, Aug. 15, 1863.

Jason Duncan, E, 4th, May 25, 1863.

Walter R. Davis, G, 12th, at battle of Fredericksburg, December 25, 1862.

Calvin C. Ellis, C, 38th, at Baton Rouge, June 23, 1863.

James A. Fenno, A, 60th, at Indianapolis, Oct. 23, 1864.

S. Boardman Foster, G, 12th, Sept. 17, 1862.

Thomas Fuller, 18th.

George W. Folsom, 14th.

John A. Foster, 1st H. A., May 19, 1864.

Benj. W. Fernald, 58th, July 8, 1864.

Cornelius Foley, G, 59th, in Danville Prison, Jan 21, 1865.

James L. Glasier, 12th, Culpepper, Va., Dec. 25, 1863.

Winfield S. Gurney, Excelsior Brigade, 1862.
Henry S. Green, 4th Cavalry.
John B. Hutchinson, E, 4th, May 16, 1863.
George W. Harding, 30th.
Stephen Hayes, 7th, 1862.
Benj. F. Hutchinson, 7th, at Croney Island Hospital, Oct. 30, 1862.
Wm. F. Howland, K, 7th, at Abington, 1862.
Wm. F. Jacobs, G, 12th, killed in action, Sept. 17, 1862.
Charles J. Keene, 32d, May 10th, 1864.
Kyler Kennedy, G, 12th, killed Aug. 30, 1862.
Lowell W. Orcutt, 1st H. A., at Abington, Oct. 14, 1864.
Walter S. Oldham, 16th Bat., July 29, 1864.
Michael Luddy, E, 4th, Aug. 14, 1863.
Martin Loftus, 11th, June 29, 1864.
Emsley B. Means, 54th.
Henry C. Millett, C, 38th, at Baton Rouge, July 8, 1863.
Horace O. Matthews, E, 30th, on board Str. Iberville, Mississippi River, July 13, 1862.
James O'Connell, I, 2d H. A., at Newbern, N. C., May 6, 1865.
Henry Pratt, 23d, Aug. 14, 1864.
Richard Porter, G, 12th, Sept. 17, 1862.
Charles A. Parker, G, 12th, Sept. 17, 1862.
Elbridge G. Pool, G, 12th, Oct. 14, 1862.
John L. Quigley, E, 4th Cav., at Hilton Head, May 3, 1864.
Harvey A. Raymond, E, 23d, Dec. 16, 1862.
Capt. Ansel B. Randall, 56th, killed in action before Petersburg, April 2, 1865.
Nath'l L. Reed, 58th, June 18, 1864.
Wm. H. Robbins, E, 4th, June 7, 1863.
Simeon Ryerson, 12th, March 8, 1863.
Martin Shehan, 9th, May 23, 1864.
John M. Sewell, E, 23d, April 9, 1862.
Lieut. James G. Smith, 12th, at Spottsylvania, Va., of wounds, June 17, 1864.
Edward Saunders, 11th, August 7, 1863.
Nathan M. Stewart, C, 38th.
John Sullivan, E, 4th, June 26, 1863.
Charles Shaw 2d, E, 4th.
Charles E. Stetson, 4th Cavalry, Oct. 18, 1864.
Dexter Smith, G, 12th, at Andersonville, 1864.
George Soule, K, 7th, Sept. 29, 1862.
James H. Tucker, I, 1st Cav., at Hilton Head, April 30, 1862.
John G. Taylor, G, 12th, Dec. 30, 1862.
Randall Ward, 5th Cav.
John Mead, 19th Regt., 1862.

Gadlin Jordan, 5th Cav., December 1864.
Oscar E. Gould, 23d Regt.
James Lawless, Co. D, 56th Regt.
Franklin Williamson, Co. G, 12th Regt., Sept. 17th, 1862.
Hiram L. Whiting, 56th Regt.
Robert N. Hanson, Co. G, 12th Regt., May 6th, 1864.
Albert B. Smith, 1st Cav., So. Corolina.
Marcus N. Leavitt, Co. K, 7th Regt., Mary's Heights, May 3d, 1863.
John H. McNakin, K, 7th Regt., of wounds, May 3d, 1863.
Charles W. Reed, K, 7th Regt., Mary's Heights, May 3d, 1863.
Joseph Ripley, Co. C, 38th Regt., Oct. 9, 1864.
William T. Ewell, Co. C, 38th Regt.
William W. Knowles, Co. C, 38th Regt.
Joseph Merrow, Co. C, 38th Regt.
Erastus O. Prior, Co. C, 38th Regt.
Ebenezer G. Tuttle, Co. C, 38th Regt., Stoughton, 1866.
Rufus Robbins, Jr., Co. K, 7th Regt., Jan. 7th, 1863.
Barney F. Phinney, 18th Regt.
Charles L. French, 23d Regt.
Charles E. Ford, 4th Cav.

Halifax.

We failed entirely in our efforts to obtain in season for publication, from the Town Officers, the facts concerning the citizens of Halifax, who laid down their lives for their country. The Middleboro Gazette says:—

"The Soldiers' Monument was finished by the Quincy Granite Co. The base is four feet square, the second section three feet square, and the shaft 28 inches at the base and 16 at the top, with a total height of twenty feet. On a raised shield are the words, "Our Patriot Soldiers," and the date, 1867, to show when erected. On one side is a bronze plate, with the names, ages, dates, &c., of the twenty-four men lost from this town. It cost $1000, and is erected on the square in front of the Congregational church."

Hanover.

John Larkhum, 18th, G, Hospital, Va., of fever, Sept. 14, 1862.

James E. Stetson, 18th, G, Hanover, Mass. Discharged Dec. 18, 1862, for disability. Reached home and died Dec. 12, 1862.

Benjamin Curtis, 12th, G, Antietam, Md., killed in battle Sept. 17, 1862.

Marcus M. Leavitt, 7th, Fredericksburg, killed in battle May 3, '63.

Loammi B. Sylvester, 2d, Hospital, Va., wounds received in battle of Slaughter Mountain, Sept. 26, 1862.

Winfield S. Gurney, Sickles' Brigade. No account.
Hiram B. Bonney, 38th, K, Hospital, La., chronic diarrhœa, July 16, 1863.
Geo. R. Josselyn, 38th, K, Baton Rouge, La., chronic diarrhœa, Sept. 7, 1863.
Levi C. Brooks, 38th, K, Cane River, killed in battle April 23, '64.
Albert E. Bates, 38th, K, Morganza Bend, La., chronic diarrhœa and fever, June 23, 1864.
Joshua E. Bates, 38th, K, Baton Rouge, La., chronic diarrhœa, Aug. 10, 1863.
Arthur Shepherd, 38th, K, Carrolton, La., chronic diarrhœa, Feb. 26, 1863.
John H. Carey, 42d, strayed from camp, found dead, May 13, 1863.
Joseph D. Thomas, 2d, H. A., Andersonville, Sept., 1864.
Calvin S. Bailey, 3d Cav., Baltimore, Md., consumption, Sept. 24, 1864.
Francis A. Stoddard, 58th, Richmond, Va., Hospital, wounds received in battle near Pittsburg, Aug. 18, 1864.
John B. Wilder, 58th, Petersburg, Va., killed while returning from picket, Dec. 1, 1864.
Geo. W. Woodard, 58th, never heard from.
William Church, Jr., 58th, Beverly Hospital, N. C., Sept. 30, '64.
Joseph E. Wilder, 31st, Q. M.'s Serg't, Sabine Cross Roads, La., killed at battle of Sabine Cross Roads, April 8, 1864.
John W. Nelson, 18th, G, Virginia, killed at 2d days battle of the Wilderness, May 8, 1864.
Spenser Binney, 1st Bat. H. A., E, Hospital Fort Warren, small pox, May 23, 1865.
F. Willis, 1st H. A. wounds received in battle, March, 1865.

Lakeville.

Wm. H. Cole, C, 4th, at New Orleans, of chronic diarrhœa, August 19, 1863.
Benj. F. Holloway, C, 4th, of a wound received at Port Hudson, June 15, 1863.
Andrew J. Perkins, E, 40th, at Lakeville, Nov. 22, 1863.
Granville T. Record, F. 29th, of chronic diarrhœa, Sept. 13, 1862.
Michael Sullivan, I, 3d, killed at Plymouth, N. C., Dec. 12, 1863.
George W. Terry, A, 40th, killed at battle of Drury's Bluff, May 16, 1864.
Narcissus Williams, C, 4th, in Brashear City Hospital, of chronic diarrhœa, June 11, 1863.
Benj. L. Washburn, A, 40th, in Regimental Hospital, Folly Island, of dysentery, Sept. 20, 1863.
George Washburn, A, 40th, in Rebel Prison, 1864.

BOOT AND SHOE FACTORY OF J. L. NASH, (KING HOUSE), CENTER IRINGTON.

E. L. BARNES,

DEALER IN

FANCY GOODS,

Worsted Work,
   Edgings,
Embroidery,
    &c. &c.

Gloves,
   Hosiery,
     Insertions,
&c. &c.

Also, a large assortment of Ladies' and Gentlemen's COTTON AND WOOLEN

FURNISHING GOODS,

Constantly on hand and "Cheap for Cash."

14 MAIN STREET, PLYMOUTH, MASS.

☞ Stamping and Lettering for Embroidery done at short notice.

S. D. BALLARD'S
Oyster & Ice Cream Saloon.

OYSTERS

Are served up in this Saloon in every style, during the day and evening.

Ice Cream,
Pies,
Pastry,
Sauces,

Plain and Fancy
Cakes,
Fruit, Confec-
tionery.

Orders from **Families and Parties** filled at short notice.

This **First Class Restaurant** is designed to be worthy of the generous patronage it has gained.

No. 56 Main Street, Plymouth, Mass.

L. L. BARBER,

Machinist, and Dealer in all First Class

SEWING MACHINES,

All kinds of second-hand Family Sewing Machines bought, sold, exchanged and repaired. Shuttles, Bobbins, Needles, Gauges, Binders, Cast-Offs, Thread Guides, &c., on hand or made to order. **Boot and Shoe Machinery** made to order, for sale, exchanged and repaired. Particular attention paid to repairing all kinds of Wax Thread Machines, Pegging Machines, Eyelet Machines, and all kinds of machinery used in the manufacture of boots and shoes, at short notice.

NO. 9 GORE BLOCK, (opposite the Revere House,) **BOSTON.**

LUCAS & COOK,

STEAM GRINDERS AND MANUFACTURERS OF

House, Ship and Carriage Paints,

OILS, VARNISHES,

COACH, JAPAN AND LIQUID DRYER,

And dealers in all kinds of PAINTER'S MATERIALS. Also, Sole Manufacturers

of the celebrated

PERSIAN GREEN,

For **WINDOW BLINDS** and all kinds of Ornamental Work.

Factory and Store,   *New Bedford, Mass.*

Marshfield.

Samuel H. Ewell, E, 7th, Washington, Oct. 1, 1862.
Job L. Ewell, E, 7th, Alexandria, Va., June 5, 1864, of wounds.
Edmund Crossley, E, 7th, Washington, June 30, 1864, of wounds.
David Church, E, 7th, Virginia, May 6, 1864, killed.
Charles H. Cobbet, E, 7th, Virginia, August 5, 1863.
Joseph Joyce, E, 7th, October 14, 1862.
Nathan Sherman, jr., E, 7th, of disease.
Japhet S. Sampson, E, 7th, September 27, 1862.
Turner Ewell, jr., K, 38th, St. Louis, October 16, 1863.
James W. Fish, K, 38th, Savannah, June 14, 1865.
Andrew W. Hatch, K, 38th, New Orleans, August 22, 1864.
Robert Ames, K, 38th, Baton Rouge, June 2, 1863.
Wilbur F. Harrington, K, 38th, at New Orleans, June 10, 1863.
Freeman A. Ramsdell, K, 38th, at New Orleans, June 4, 1863.
Josiah C. Stoddard, K, 38th, at Baltimore, Dec. 4, 1862.
Sergt. Edwin Curtis, F, 43d, and 58th. June 19, 1864, of wounds.
S. Nelson Gardner, F, 43d, Newbern. N. C., June 4, 1863.
Josiah Thomas, F, 43d, and 2d H. A., Dec. 3, 1864.
James A. Wright, F, 43d, Newbern, N. C., May 7, 1863.
Col. Fletcher Webster, 12th, killed at Bull Run, Aug. 30, 1862.
Lucius L. Bonney, 2d H. A., of disease, in North Carolina.
Edwin R. Merry, Corp., G, 18th, Jan. 13, 1865.
George S. Lapham, navy, May 29, 1864.
Joseph E. Williamson, 1st H. A.
Hiram Butterfield, jr., Raleigh, N. C., May 15, 1865.

Middleboro.

Preston Soule, 18th, I, May 14, 1862, typhoid fever in N. Y. City Hospital.
William M. Atwood, 18th, C, Aug. 30, 1862, killed at 2d Bull Run battle.
Isaac Harlow, 18th, C, March 1, 1862, died at Camp Barnes.
Wm. R. Brightman, 18th, D, Sept. 18, 1862, in Libby Prison.
Henry M. Warren, 18th, D, Dec. 20, 1862, of wounds received at Fredericksburg.
Charles E. Hunt, 18th, D, June 1, 1864, at battle of Coal Harbor.
David H. Burgess, 4th, C, Aug. 28, 1863, of fever and diptheria, at home.
Adoniram Thomas, 18th, C, Sept. 2, 1862, from wounds received in Bull Run battle.
Sidney B. Wilbur, 40th, E, June 2, 1864, of wounds received in battle of Coal Harbor.

Cornelius G. Tinkham, 12th, A, Oct. 1, 1862, of wounds received at battle of Antetiam.

Francis S. Thomas, 4th, C, March 9, 1863, at Carrollton Hospital, of fever.

Washington I. Caswell, 1st Cav., K, Aug. 29, 1863, at Hospital in Washington, of fever.

Samuel Jones, 3d, K, May 26, 1863, in Hospital at Newbern, of diptheria.

Edward Jennings, 10th, E.

Williams Eaton, jr., 4th, C, June 21, 1863, of wounds received at Port Hudson.

Elbridge A. Maxim, 23d, E, July 25, 1864, at Newbern, of disease.

James H. Wady, 18th, D, Aug. 7, 1862, in Hospital at Phila.

George N. Gammons, 24th, D, March 8, 1862, at Roanoke Island, of fever.

Samuel M. Rider, 18th, D, Dec., 1862, of wounds received at Fredericksburg.

Ephraim K. Simmons, 4th, C. May 24, 1863, at Brashear City, of disease.

George Hinckley, 40th, E, Feb. 21, 1863, of wounds received at battle of Olustee.

George W. Paull, 18th, C, May 31, 1862, in Alexandria Hospital, of measles.

John L. Cobb, 58th, C, Aug. 12, 1864, in Hospital at Washington.

Daniel Handy, 4th, C, Sept. 10, 1863, in Centralia, Ill., of diarrhœa.

Ezra T. Westgate, 32d, E, June 4, 1864, killed in battle of Coal Harbor.

George Cummings, 3d Cav., B, July 23, 1864, died in Hospital at New Orleans.

George A. Thomas, 6th, F, Nov. 14, 1864, died at Middleboro.

Benjamin Chamberlain, 59th, G, Dec. 10, 1864, died in Hospital at Beverly, N. J.

James C. Record, 18th, D, Nov. 25, 1864, died in Hospital at Alexandria.

Albert Eddy, 4th Cav., D, Jan. 23, 1865, died of malaria fever in Middleboro.

Richard Cox, 58th, B, June 3, 1864, killed in battle at Shady Grove Church, Va.

Darius R. Clark, 18th, D, Dec. 13, 1862, killed in battle of Fredericksburg.

Myron E. Alger, 4th, C, July 10, 1863, died at Brashear City a prisoner.

Morrill Perkins, 18th, D, Dec. 20, 1862, died from wounds received in battle of Fredericksburg.

Martin V. Raymond, 18th, C, Aug. 30, 1862, killed in battle of Bull Run.
Stephen F. Thomas, 4th, C, May 1, 1863, died in Hospital of fever at New Orleans.
Cyrus White, 18th, H, Nov. 19, 1862, at Middleboro, of disease.
Frederic E. Atwood, 18th, C, Aug 26, 1862, killed in battle of Bull Run.
Peleg F. Benson, 18th, D, Nov. 17, 1862, in Hospital, of diarrhœa.
Francis B. Cushman, 18th, C, May 13, 1862, at Badloe's Island, of typhoid fever.
Ormel H. Churchill, 40th, E, Sept. 11, 1863, at Folly Island, of chronic diarrhœa.
J. Arthur Fitch, 40th, E, Sept. 30, 1864, killed at Fort Harrison, Virginia.
Cyrus Hall, 18th, D, Oct. 19, 1862, in Hospital at Washington, of typhoid fever.
Levi Hathaway, 4th, C, Aug. 20, 1833, at Indianapolis, of typhoid fever.
Francis M. Hodges, 40th, E, Oct. 27, 1833, at Beaufort, of chronic diarrhœa.
John K. Maxim, 18th, C, Jan. 27, 1865, at Parole Hospital, Md., of disease.
George H. Swift, 18th, C, May, 1863, of wounds received at Chancellorsville.
Timothy J. Sullivan, 40th, E, Aug. 22, 1864, of wounds received in battle of Petersburg.
Andrew E. Thomas, 4th, C, June 27, 1863, died near Brashear City, of chronic diarrhœa.
Joseph Thomas, 4th, C, Aug. 1, 1863, at Port Hudson, of chronic diarrhœa.
Alva C. Tinkham, 4th, C, July 15, 1863, at Brashear City, of chronic diarrhœa.
Samuel Mellen, 18th, D, Jan. 10, 1862, in hospital at Hall's Hill.
Henry L. McFarlin, 40th, E, June 10, 1864, of wounds received in battle near Coal Harbor.
Charles W. Wilmarth, 18th, D, July 18, 1864, in Andersonville Prison.
Henry L Shaw, 4th, C, Oct. 6, 1863, of wounds received at Port Hudson.
Nathan T. Tucker, 100 days, Nov. 18, 1864, at Middleboro, of disease contracted in service.
Ira E. Caswell, Feb. 7, 1865, in navy, died in U. S. Marine Hospital, Norfolk, Va.
Charles M. Tribou, Sept. 8, 1862, at Mound City Hospital, of disease.

Cyrus Perkins, 18th, D, Jan. 1, 1863, in Middleboro, of disease contracted in service.

Asa Shaw, 3d, B.

Rochester.

Pardon Gifford, died on board Receiving Ship, Boston.
John Phipps, Sergt., H, 38th, died in Hospital at New Orleans.
Wm. T. Bryant, H, 38th, died in Hospital at New Orleans.
George H. Clark, 33d, killed at battle of Lookout Mountain.
John A. Fuller, 33d, died at home, of disease contracted in service.
Lawrence Rankin, 58th, killed at battle before Petersburg.
Joseph F. Ryder, 33d, killed in battle.
Henry Kingman, died in Hospital.
Willard E. Clark, killed in battle.

HYLAND HOUSE,

Central Square,   *Bridgewater, Mass.*

The above House has been refitted and refurnished for Summer Boarders, and it is the aim of the Proprietor to make it a "Home" for all who may favor him with their patronage.

TERMS—$12 per week, through the Summer.

Moderate at all seasons of the year.

The Hyland House is very pleasantly situated, 25 miles from Boston, in the immediate vicinity of the Normal School, Academy and Churches, and within three minutes walk of the Depot.

A first class LIVERY STABLE is connected with the house.

N. FRANK DUNPHE,
Proprietor.

The Hingham Journal,

—AND—

SOUTH SHORE ADVERTISER.

IS PUBLISHED

EVERY FRIDAY MORNING,

—BY—

BLOSSOM & EASTERBROOK,

Office, Ford's Building, North St., Hingham.

TERMS—$2.50 a year, in advance, or $3.00 if payment is delayed until the end of the year.

TERMS OF ADVERTISING.

One square inserted from one to three weeks, $1.50. After the termination of three weeks, 30 cents per square for each subsequent insertion. Ten lines compose a square.

ADVERTISERS.

We wish to call the attention of the trade to the fact that we are interested in the publication of the

"*Middleboro Gazette,*"
"*Wareham News,*"
"*Bridgewater Banner,*" and
"*East Bridgewater News,*"

And that these combined papers give the most thorough circulation throughout the Old Colony.

PRATT & BROTHERS,

Middleboro, - - - **Mass.**

ABINGTON STANDARD

Book & Job Printing Office,

We have our office well stocked with all the latest styles of Fancy and Job Types, together with new and full Roman Fonts, so that we cannot be excelled by any country office, in

Plain or Fancy Printing!

We make a speciality of

POSTER WORK,

AND CAN PRINT

All Sizes,   Tinted Backgrounds,   Fancy Borders and Ovals,
All Colors of Ink,   White or Colored Paper.

PLAIN AND FANCY LABELS,

In Black, Blue or Red Inks, Gold or Silver Bronze, on White and Fancy Colored Papers. Particular attention given to the execution of every variety of

MERCANTILE PRINTING,

Wedding, Business, or Address Cards.

We are also fully prepared to do all kinds of

Book Work,

    Town Reports,

        Pamphlets,

            By-Laws, &c.

Orders by express or mail, as promptly attended to as though delivered in person.

OFFICE,

East Abington, - - **Mass.**

N. B.—All descriptions of Blank Papers and Cards constantly on hand.

THE MEMORIAL & ROCK,

Plymouth,

A FAMILY NEWSPAPER,

Published every Friday Morning, by

GEO. F. ANDREWS.

TERMS—Two Dollars and Fifty Cents a year in advance.

No papers discontinued until all arrearages are paid, except at the option of the publishers.

Rates of Advertising.

One square (12 lines) 3 insertions,	$1 50
Each subsequent insertion, per square,	50
One square one year,	10 00
One square six months,	7 00
One square three months,	5 00

SPECIAL NOTICES, leaded, 15 cents per line.
Transient and Legal Advertisements, CASH.

☞All advertisements, not otherwise marked in the copy, will be inserted until ordered out, and charged accordingly.

County Postmasters will act as Agents.

The Old Colony Sentinel.

PUBLISHED EVERY SATURDAY MORNING.

Office, No. 1 Court, cor. North Streets,

PLYMOUTH, MASS.

Terms.—$2.50 a year,—$2.00 if paid strictly in advance.

MOSES BATES, EDITOR AND PROPRIETOR.

THE SENTINEL

Is published every SATURDAY MORNING, and will be forwarded in season to reach subscribers in Plymouth County on the day of publication. The paper will be delivered to subscribers in town by carrier.

☞ Advertisements inserted at the usual rates.

☞ **Communications** of a local nature respectfully solicited from our friends in the County. Notices of Marriages and Deaths thankfully received.

AVERY & CAVE, *Printers and General Business Agents.*

Office, No. 3 Court Street, Bates' Building.

The Middleboro Gazette,

AND

Old Colony Advertiser,

Published every Saturday Morning, at $2.00 per annum.

Established in 1851, it long since became one of the most popular advertising mediums among country papers.

Advertising Rates, $1.25 per square of one inch, 3 weeks; 17 cents per square for each subsequent insertion.

THE JOB PRINTING OFFICE

Has just been supplied with

New Plain and Fancy Type.

Four Fast Presses for Job Work.

Personal attention given to the execution of **Books, Pamphlets, Newspapers, Circulars, Posters, Wedding, Visiting and Business Cards,** and all kinds of

LETTER PRESS PRINTING.

STILLMAN B. PRATT, Proprietor.

NEW ENGLAND FARMER.

Published Weekly by
R. P. EATON & CO.

No. 31 Merchants' Row,
BOSTON, MASS.

SIMON BROWN, Agricultural Ed.,
S. FLETCHER, Associate Ag. Ed.,
RUSSELL P. EATON, Gen. Editor.

TERMS—$2.50, per year in advance or if not paid in advance, $3.

MONTHLY NEW ENGLAND FARMER.

This is a magazine printed in large octavo page, on fine book paper, and contains all the Agricultural Matter published in the Weekly with none of the news or miscellaneous reading.

The terms of the **"MONTHLY FARMER"** are $1.50 per annum, in advance; 15 cents for single copies.

SECOND YEAR, THIRD VOLUME.

THE NATION.

An Independent Weekly Journal of

Politics, Literature, Science and Art,

Supported by the best talent of the country in every department, and having a truly national circulation and influence. It contains the most profitable reading for the FAMILY, the STUDENT, the PROFESSIONAL MAN, the MAN OF BUSINESS, the POLITICIAN, for all those of literary and scientific tastes, the lovers of the fine arts.

Every Congregation should supply its Pastor with a copy.
Every School teacher should have it.
Every Public Library.
Every College Boy.
The Young everywhere.

THE ORDER OF CONTENTS IS ABOUT AS FOLLOWS.

The Week—Brief comments on current events at home and abroad;

Literary, Scientific and Educational Notes;

Book Reviews—By the most accomplished writers;

Editorial Articles;

Articles on Social topics;

Art Criticisms—Music, Pictures, the Drama;

Correspondence—Special and occasional;

Books of the Day—A list of the latest publications with prices annexed.

TERMS :—Five Dollars per annum in advance.

A specimen number sent gratis on application to

E. L. GODKIN & CO., Publishers,
130 NASSAU STREET,
NEW YORK.

*** SUBSCRIPTIONS RECEIVED BY ALL BOOKSELLERS.

New York Tribune.

THE LARGEST AND CHEAPEST.

Notwithstanding the fact that the size of THE TRIBUNE has been increased more than one quarter, the price will remain the same. Now is the time to subscribe for

The Great Family Newspaper.

The New York Weekly Tribune

is printed on a large double-medium sheet, making eight pages of six broad columns each. It contains all the important Editorials published in the DAILY TRIBUNE, except those of merely local interest; also Literary and Scientific Intelligence; Reviews of the most interesting and important New Books; the Letters from our large corps of correspondents; the latest news received by Telegraph from Washington and all other parts of the country; a Summary of all important intelligence in this city and elsewhere; a Synopsis of the Proceedings of Congress and State Legislature when in session; the Foreign News received by every steamer; Exclusive Reports of the Proceedings of the Farmers' Club of the American Institute; Talks about Fruit, and other Horticultural and Agricultural information essential to country residents; Stock, Financial, Cattle, Dry Goods and General Market Reports; making it, both for variety and completeness, altogether the most valuable, interesting and instructive Weekly Newspaper published in the world.

The Full Reports of the American Institute Farmers' Club, and the various Agricultural Reports, in each number, are richly worth a year's subscription.

TERMS.

Mail subscribers, single copy, 1 year—52 numbers,	$2 00
Mail subscribers, Clubs of five,	9 00
Ten copies, addressed to names of subscribers,	17 50
Twenty copies addressed to names of subscribers,	34 00
Ten copies to one address,	16 00
Twenty copies to one address,	30 00

An extra copy will be sent for each club of ten.

The New York Semi-Weekly Tribune

is published every TUESDAY and FRIDAY, and contains all the Editorial articles not merely local in character; Literary Reviews and Art Criticisms; Letters from our large corps of Foreign and Domestic Correspondents; Special and Associated Press Telegraph Dispatches; a careful and complete Summary of Foreign and Domestic News; Exclusive reports of the proceedings of the Farmers' Club of the American Institute; Talks about Fruit, and other Horticultural and Agricultural Information; Stock, Financial, Cattle, Dry Goods and General Market Reports, which are published in THE DAILY TRIBUNE. THE SEMI-WEEKLY TRIBUNE also gives, in the course of a year, three or four of the BEST AND LATEST POPULAR NOVELS, by living authors. The cost of these alone, if bought in book form, would be from six to eight dollars. If purchased in the English Magazines, from which they are carefully selected, the cost would be three or four times that sum. Nowhere else can so much current intelligence and permanent literary matter be had at so cheap a rate as in the Semi-Weekly Tribune. Those who believe in the principles and approve of the character of the Tribune, can increase its power and influence by joining with their neighbors in forming Clubs to subscribe for the Semi-Weekly Edition. It will in that way be supplied to them at the lowest price for which such a paper can be printed.

Mail subscribers, 1 copy, 1 year—104 numbers,	$4 00
Mail subscribers, 2 copies, 1 year,	7 00
Mail subscribers, 5 copies, or over, for each copy	3 00

Persons remitting for 10 copies, $30, will receive an extra copy for six months.
Persons remitting for 15 copies, $45, will receive an extra copy 1 year.

THE NEW YORK DAILY TRIBUNE is published every morning and evening, (Sundays excepted) at $10 per year; $5 for six months.

TERMS, CASH IN ADVANCE.   Address,

THE TRIBUNE, New York.

GEO. P. ROWELL & CO.,
ADVERTISING AGENTS,
40 PARK ROW, NEW YORK.

ANY PART OF THE COUNTRY, CAN SEND THEIR ORDERS TO US

FOR ALL NEWSPAPERS IN THE UNITED STATES OR PROVINCES

WE ARE AUTHORIZED TO CONTRACT AT PUBLISHERS PRICES

BUSINESS MEN AND ALL OTHERS WISHING TO ADVERTISE IN

PLYMOUTH COUNTY.

Incorporated June 2, 1685.

SHIRE TOWN, - - - - PLYMOUTH.

County Officers.

Judge of Probate and Insolvency,	Wm. H. Wood,	Middleboro.
Register of Probate and Insolvency,	Daniel E. Damon,	Plymouth.
Clerk of Courts,	William H. Whitman,	Plymouth.
Register of Deeds,	William S. Danforth,	Plymouth.
County Treasurer,	William R. Sever,	Plymouth.
Overseers of House of Correction,	{ William H. Whitman,	Plymouth.
	D. J. Robbins,	Plymouth.
	Daniel E. Damon,	Plymouth.
Sheriff,	James Bates,	Plymouth.

Deputy Sheriffs.

Abington, Josiah Cushman ; Bridgewater, P. D. Kingman ; Duxbury, Wm. J. Alden ; Hingham, G. F. Hersey ; Marion, Daniel Hall ; Marshfield, John Baker ; Middleboro, Milton Alden ; North Bridgewater, Otis Hayward ; North Carver, Benj. Ransom; Plymouth, John Perkins, John Atwood ; Rochester, R. C. Randall ; South Scituate, Willard Torrey ; Scituate, J. O. Cole ; Wareham, Alexander Swift. .

Jailor and Master of House of Correction.

Plymouth, James Bates.

Sessions of Probate Courts.

At Abington, 4th Monday of May, August, and November.
At Bridgewater, 4th Monday of September.
At East Bridgewater, 4th Monday of February and December.
At Hingham, 4th Monday in March.
At Middleboro, 4th Monday of January, April, and 2nd Monday in July.
At Plymouth, 2d Monday of January, February, March, April, May, June, September, October, November and December.
At South Scituate, 4th Monday of June.
At Wareham, 4th Monday of October.

Sessions of Insolvency Court.

At Plymouth, 1st Monday in every month.

21

County Commissioners.

Wm. P. Corthell, Abington, term expires Dec., 1867; Charles H. Paine, Halifax, 1868; Harrison Staples, Lakeville, 1869.

Special Commissioners.—Alden S. Bradford, Kingston, term expires 1868; Jedediah Dwelley, Hanover, 1868.

Times of Meeting.—At Plymouth, 3d Tuesday in March, 1st Tuesday in August and January.

Commissioners of Wrecks.

Duxbury, Elisha Holmes; Hull, Nehemiah Ripley, jr.; Marshfield, John Baker, Otis Baker, George H. Hall; Plymouth, Josiah D. Baxter, Barnabas H. Holmes; Scituate, Perry L. Parker, John Tilden; North Scituate, John Damon.

Public Administrator.

Duxbury, Samuel Stetson.

Master in Chancery.

Plymouth, William H. Whitman.

Commissioners to Qualify Civil Officers.

Abington, Isaac Hersey, Jesse E. Keith; Bridgewater, Joshua E. Crane, Abraham Washburn, 2d; Duxbury, Samuel Stetson, Gershom B. Weston; East Bridgewater, Benj. W. Harris, Welcome Young; Hingham, Amos Bates, Solomon Lincoln; Middleboro, Everett Robinson, Eliab Ward; North Bridgewater, Franklin Ames, George W. Bryant, Jonas R. Perkins; Plymouth, Jacob H. Loud, John J. Russell, Wm. R. Sever, Wm. H. Whitman; Rochester, Joseph Haskell Theophilus King, James Ruggles; Scituate, John Beal, Elijah Jenkins; South Scituate, Anson Robbins, Samuel A. Turner; Wareham, Seth Miller; West Bridgewater, Austin Packard.

Justices of the Peace.

Including Justices of the Peace and Quorum, designated by a * ; and Justices throughout the Commonwealth designated by a †

Abington, Nath'l Fannce, Isaac Hersey, Charles W. Howland, Freeman P. Howland, Nath'l T. Hunt, Jesse E. Keith, Micah Nash, Holland W. Noyes, James Noyes, Bela Thaxter, Samuel B. Thaxter, John D. Wormell.

East Abington, Nath'l Beal, Charles Bearse, †Jacob B. Harris, Zenas Jenkins, †Levi Reed, Franklin Smith, Horace C. Totman.

North Abington, Jona. Arnold, Jr., James Ford, George W. Pratt, Edward P. Reed.

South Abington, Alexander Alden, William P. Corthell, Albert Davis, Benj. Hobart, George W. Reed, Wm. L. Reed, Spencer Vining, Jared Whitman.

Bridgewater, Horace Ames, Samuel Brock, Frederick Crafts, Joshua E. Crane, †Levi L. Goodspeed, Artemas Hale, Philip E. Hill, Caleb Hobart, *Lewis Holmes, Mitchell Hooper, Lafayette Keith, Hosea Kingman, *Williams Latham, Franklin Leach, Elisha G. Leach, Lewis G. Lowe, *Asa Millett, Eli Washburn.

Carver, Paine M. C. Jones, †Jesse Murdock, William Savery, Thomas Southworth, Benj. Ransom.

Duxbury, Benj. Alden, Nath'l Ford, John Holmes, John S. Loring, Samuel Loring, Samuel Stetson, Joshua W. Swift, †Gershom B. Weston.—*West Duxbury*, Elbridge Chandler, George B. Standish. —*South Marshfield*.—Benjamin Boylston, Henry B. Maglathlin.

East Bridgewater, Joseph Chamberlain, Benjamin W. Harris, Aaron Hobart, jr., Henry Hobart, B. W. Keith, Thomas Keith, Ezra Kingman, †James H. Mitchell, Wm. H. Osborne, *Isaac Pratt, Calvin Reed, John Reed.

Halifax, Edwin Ingles, Charles H. Paine, Ira L. Sturtevant, Dexter C. Thompson, Ephraim B. Thompson.

Hanover, Robert S. Curtis, Jedediah Dwelley, Perez Simmons.

Hanson, Freeman P. Howland, Jr., Edward Y. Perry, George F. Stetson, Joseph Smith, Thomas Smith, Isaiah Bearce, Eben B. K. Gurney.

Hingham, Quincy Bicknell, *Edward Cazneau, Henry Hersey, James S. Lewis, *Solomon Lincoln, Caleb B. Marsh, Charles N. Marsh, Charles W. Seymour, Elijah Shute, Atherton Tilden, *Joseph B. Thaxter, Jr., Israel Whitcomb.

Hull, Robert Gould, Jr.

Kingston, Frederic C. Adams, Joseph S. Beal, Alden S. Bradford, Philander Cobb, Samuel E. Cushman, James Foster, Edward Gray, Noah Prince, Edwin Reed, Joseph Stetson.

Lakeville, Reuben Hatford, Abizier T. Harvey, Eleazer Richmond, Warren H. Southworth, Harrison Staples, Henry L. Williams, Asa T. Winslow.

Marion, Daniel Hall, Barnabas Hiller, Joseph S. Luce, Moses H. Swift, Bartholemew W. Tabor.

Marshfield, John Baker, John Ford, *Luther Hatch, Henry P. Oakman, †Hiram A. Oakman, Seth Weston.

Mattapoisett, Winslow Barstow, Amittai B. Hammond, Noah Hammond, Thomas Nelson, Noah C. Sturtevant.

Middleboro, Ichabod F. Atwood, John Bennett, Stillman Benson, Sylvanus Hinckley, John Q. Morton, Noah C. Perkins, Andrew J. Pickens, Ebenezer Pickens, Stillman B. Pratt, Zebulon Pratt, Everett Robinson, Augustus H. Soule, Andrew L. Tinkham, Eliab Ward, Benjamin P. Wood, Cornelius B. Wood, George W. Wood, William H. Wood, Andrew L. Alden, Joshua M. Eddy, Sidney Tucker, Wm. B. White.

North Bridgewater, Jonathan Ames, George W. Bryant, George Clark, David L. Cowell, Daniel Crocker, Nelson J. Foss, Francis M. French, Sumner A. Hayward, Nathan Jones, Arza B. Keith, Edwin H. Kingman, Charles Lincoln, *Jonas R. Perkins, William Perry. Galen E. Pratt, Loring W. Puffer, Isaac E. Snell, Edward Southworth, Jr., Chandler Sprague, Rufus L. Thacher, †Jonathan White. —*Campello*, Josiah W. Kingman.

Pembroke, *Martin Bryant, Wm. H. H. Bryant, Joseph Cobb, Francis Collamore, George F. Hatch, John Oldham, 2d, James H. Whitman.—*East Pembroke*, Andrew E. Poole.—*North Pembroke*, Horace Collamore.

Plymouth, Aaron Bartlett, Gustavus D. Bates, James Bates, William Bishop, Lemuel Bradford, Charles O. Churchill, Nathaniel Clark, James Cox, Daniel E. Damon, Allen Danforth, †William S. Danforth, Charles G. Davis, William T. Davis, Samuel H. Doten, Charles H. Drew, George G. Dyer, Timothy Gorden, John T. Hall. †Robert B. Hall, John Harlow, 2d, Benjamin Hathaway, Barnabas H. Holmes, Charles H. Howland, Thomas Loring, Jacob H. Loud. Leander Lovell, Albert Mason, John Perkins, Thomas Pierce, Daniel J. Robbins, Edmund Robbins, †John J. Russell, Thomas B. Sears. William R. Sever, †Eleazer C. Sherman, Isaac N. Stoddard, *William Thomas, Ezekiel C. Turner, *William H. Whitman, Oliver T. Wood. —*Chiltonville*, George Bramhall.

Plympton, Isaiah Churchill, James C. Ellis, Josiah S. Hammond. Zaccheus Parker, Martin Perkins, William Perkins, Wm. H. Soule.

Rochester, John Blackmer, Joseph W. Church, Thomas Ellis, Chas. Hooper, Theophilus King, James H. Look, Israel F. Nickerson, Geo. Peirce, James Ruggles, William Sears.

Scituate, George M. Allen, George H. Bates, *John Beal, Elijah Jenkins, Ezekiel Jones, Caleb W. Prouty.

North Scituate, Joseph O. Cole, George C. Lee, Dexter Merritt, Geo. W. Merritt, Shadrack B. Merritt.

South Scituate, Henry J. Curtis, Ebenezer T. Fogg, David B. Ford, Elisha Jacobs, Samuel Tolman, Jr., George H. Torrey, Samuel A. Turner, William Turner, Lemuel C. Waterman.

Wareham, William Bates, Stephen Ellis, Joseph P. Hayden, Darius Miller, Seth Miller, Adolphus Savery, Thomas Savery, Nath'l Sherman, James G. Sprout, Joshua B. Tobey.
East Wareham, John M. Kinney.
West Bridgewater, Dwelley Fobes, James Howard, Austin Packard.
Cochesett, Orin F. Gray.

Trial Justices.

Abington, Isaac Hersey; Bridgewater, Lewis Holmes, Elisha G. Leach; East Bridgewater, William H. Osborne; Hingham, James S. Lewis; Middleboro, Ebenezer Pickens; North Bridgewater, Rufus L. Thatcher; Plymouth, Albert Mason; Scituate, Caleb W. Prouty; Wareham, William Bates; West Bridgewater, Austin Packard.

Notaries Public.

Abington, Jesse E. Keith; Bridgewater, Samuel Brock; East Bridgewater, Moses Bates; Hingham, Henry C. Harding; Marshfield, Luther Hatch; Mattapoisett, Thomas Nelson; North Bridgewater, Jonas R. Perkins; Plymouth, Moses Bates, William S. Danforth, Jacob H. Loud, John J. Russell; Scituate, John Beal; Wareham, Wm. Bates.

Coroners.

Bridgewater, Philip D. Kingman; Carver (North), Benjamin Ransom; Duxbury, Jonathan Y. Gross; Hanson, Melzar Sprague; Marshfield, Charles L. Tilden, Eliot R. Tilden; Middleboro, Ebenezer W. Drake; North Bridgewater, Benjamin A. Packard; Scituate, John Beal.

Deputy State Constables.

North Abington, Mr. Pratt.
East Bridgewater, George H. Morse.
Plymouth, Joshua D. Baxter.

Third Regiment of Infantry.

Colonel, Mason W. Burt, of Taunton.
Lieut-Colonel, Thomas J. Borden, of Fall River.
Major, G. Hubert Bates, of Scituate.
Adjutant, John H. Church, of Taunton.
Quartermaster, Phil. W. Williams, of Taunton.

Companies.

A.—Halifax, Capt., Charles P. Lyon.
   1st. Lieut., Morton V. Bonney.
   2d Lieut., Lysander M. Thompson.
C.—Scituate, Capt., John E. O. Prouty.
   1st Lieut., Henry O. Cole.

SENATORIAL DISTRICTS.

Plymouth County—Two Senators. Average Ratio, 5,925.

First District.—Carver, Duxbury, Kingston, Lakeville, Marion, Mattapoisett, Middleborough, Plymouth, Plympton, Rochester and Wareham. Legal voters, 5,973.

Second District.—Abington, Bridgewater, East Bridgewater, Halifax, Hanson, North Bridgewater, Pembroke and West Bridgewater. Legal voters, 5,878.

Norfolk and Plymouth District.—Cohasset, Hanover, Hingham, Hull, Marshfield, Scituate, South Scituate, Braintree and Weymouth. Legal voters, 5,904.

REPRESENTATIVE DISTRICTS.
Plymouth County.

	Voters.	Reps.
1. Cohasset, Scituate,	1,064	1
2. Hingham, Hull.	931	1
3. South Scituate, Hanover, Hanson.	1,166	1
4. Marshfield, Pembroke, Halifax.	1,029	1
5. Duxbury, Kingston.	985	1
6. Plymouth, Carver, Plympton.	2,034	2
7. Wareham, Marion.	855	1
8. Mattapoisett, Rochester, Lakeville.	987	1
9. Middleboro.	1,112	1
10. Bridgewater, West Bridgewater.	1,019	1
11. East Bridgewater, North Bridgewater.	2,120	2
12. Abington.	1,833	2
Total,	14,643	15

CONGRESSIONAL DISTRICTS.
AS ESTABLISHED BY CHAPTER 226 OF THE ACTS OF 1862.

District 1.

The several towns in the counties of Barnstable, Dukes County, and Nantucket, together with the cities of New Bedford and Fall River, and the towns of Acushnet, Dartmouth, Fairhaven, Freetown and Westport, in the County of Bristol; and the towns of Carver, Duxbury, Halifax, Kingston, Lakeville, Marion, Mattapoisett, Middleboro, Pembroke, Plymouth, Plympton, Rochester and Wareham, in the County of Plymouth.

District 2.

The towns of Attleborough, Berkley, Dighton, Easton, Mansfield, Norton, Raynham, Rehoboth, Seekonk, Somerset, Swanzey, and the city of Taunton, in the County of Bristol; and the towns of Abington, Bridgewater, East Bridgewater, Hingham, Hanover, Hanson, Hull, Marshfield, Scituate, South Scituate, North Bridgewater and West Bridgewater, in the County of Plymouth; and the towns of Braintree, Canton, Cohasset, Dorchester, Milton, Quincy, Randolph, Sharon, Stoughton and Weymouth, in the County of Norfolk.

State Almshouse at Bridgewater.

Joseph B. Thaxter, Hingham; James Ford, Fall River; James H. Mitchell, East Bridgewater, *Inspectors.* Levi L. Goodspeed, *Superintendent.*

Custom House Officers—District of Plymouth.

Port of Plymouth.—Thomas Loring, Collector; Charles O. Churchill, Deputy Collector and Inspector.

Port of Duxbury.—Harvey Soule, Deputy Collector and Insp.

Port of Kingston.—Stephen Holmes, 2d, Deputy Collector and Inspector.

Port of Scituate.—Joseph S. Drew, Deputy Collector and Insp.

Bridgewater State Normal School.
(Established, 1840.)
FOR BOTH SEXES.

Albert G. Boyden, A. M. Principal; Elisha H. Barlow, A. B.; Geo. H. Martin. Male applicants for admission must be at least 17 years of age. Female applicants, 16. Tuition, free. See advertisement.

Bridgewater Academy, Bridgewater.

Incorporated 1799. Horace M. Willard, Principal; Mrs. S. C. W. Gammell, Miss Elizabeth Crafts, Assistants.

Derby, Hingham.

Incorporated 1797. Henry F. Munroe, Principal; Elizabeth A. Andrews, Assistant.

Hanover Academy, Hanover.

Incorporated 1861. P. L. Woodbury, Principal.

Ingleside School for Young Ladies, Middleboro.

Established in 1866. Mrs. S. G. Dodd, Principal. (See card.)

Middleboro Boarding School for Boys.

Rev. P. L. Cushing, Principal.

Partridge, Duxbury.

Incorporated 1629. Capital, 20,000. Rev. J. Moore, Principal.

Peirce Academy, Middleboro.

Incorporated 1808. J. W. P. Jenks, A. M., Principal; C. A. Cole, Assistant; A. G. Pickins, Music. (See card and engraving.)

Pratt Free School, North Middleboro.

Incorporated 1865. M. C. Mitchell, Principal; Miss Martha Keith, Assistant.

Rochester, Rochester.

Incorporated 1838. Cornelia Rounseville, Principal; Catharine L. Barker, Assistant; Harriet S. Clapp, Painting; F. B. Pitcher, Music.

Sea Side Boarding School for Misses, Mattapoisett.

Established in 1865. Mrs. H. B. Pratt, Principal. (See card.)

Abington National Bank.

Organized July 1, 1865; Capital, $150,000. President, Baxter Cobb; Directors, Baxter Cobb, Jenkins Lane, Sumner Shaw, Asaph Dunbar, Martin S. Stetson, Bela Thaxter, and Joshua Whitmarsh; Cashier, J. N. Farrar. Discount Mondays.

Hingham National Bank.

Organized April 24, 1865. Capital, $200,000. President, David Lincoln; Directors, David Lincoln, Crocker Wilder, Alfred Loring, P. L. Whiton, T. L. Whiton, Wm. Fearing, 2d, E. W. Burr; Cashier, John O. Lovett. Discount, Mondays.

The Old Colony National Bank.

Organized Feb. 27, 1865. Capital, $210,000. President, Eleazer C. Sherman; Directors, E. C. Sherman, J. H. Loud, J. Farris, L. Lovell, W. H. Nelson, W. R. Drew, W. S. Danforth; Cashier, George G. Dyer. Discount, Mondays.

The Plymouth National Bank.

Organized Dec. 22, 1864. Capital, $200,000. President, William T. Davis; Directors, Isaac Brewster, Franklin B. Cobb, William T. Davis, Timothy Gordon, Benjamin Hathaway, Isaac L. Hedge, John J. Russell, Isaac N. Stoddard, of Plymouth, and William Savery, of Carver; Cashier, I. N. Stoddard. Discount, Fridays.

The National Bank of Wareham.

Organized June 26, 1865. Capital, $100,000. President, J. B. Tobey; Directors, Jesse Murdoch, Curtis Tobey, M. S. F. Tobey, William Savery, Stephen Ellis, Isaac Pratt, Jr.; Cashier, T. R. Miles. Discount, Mondays.

Manufacturing Companies.

Bridgewater Iron Manufacturing Co., Bridgewater, commenced 1825; Nahum Stetson, Treas., Sec'y, and Resident Agent; Lazell, Perkins & Co., Boston, Selling Agents; Capital, $96,000; Articles Manufactured: Castings, Rolling Mill, Machinery. (See card.).

East Bridgewater Iron Co., East Bridgewater; K. E. Sheldon, Resident Agent; Rogers & Sheldon, Boston, Selling Agents; Articles Manufactured: Nails, Tacks and Shovel Plates.

E. Carver Co., East Bridgewater; Aaron Hobart, Jr., Treasurer; Aaron Hobart, Boston, Selling Agent: Articles Manufactured: Cotton Gins.

Hingham Cordage Co., Hingham, commenced 1853; David Fearing, Treasurer; John Rider, Resident Agent; Whiton Brothers & Co., Boston, Selling Agents; Capital, $59,000; Manufacture Cordage.

Hingham Wooden Ware Co., Hingham, commenced 1866; Fearing Burr, Treasurer.

Old Colony Batting Co., Plymouth; John T. Stoddard, Treasurer; S. Pember, Sup't and Resident Agent; Manufacture Batting.

Old Colony Duck Co., Plymouth; Isaac Thacher, Treasurer; Fearing, Thacher & Co., Boston, Selling Agents; Capital, $50,000; Manufacture Duck.

Parker Mills, Wareham, commenced 1845; Nahum Stetson, Treasurer; C. C. Sprague, Resident Agent; Nahum Stetson, Boston, Selling Agent; Capital, $200,000; Manufacture Cut Nails.

Plymouth Cordage Co., Plymouth, commenced 1824; Bourne Spooner, Treasurer and Resident Agent; Capital, $200,000; Manufacture Cordage.

Plymouth Iron Foundry, Plymouth; W. R. Drew, Treasurer; Capital $25,000; Manufacture Castings and Stoves.

Plymouth Mills, Plymouth, commenced 1846; Jeremiah Farris, Treasurer and Resident Agent; N. E. James & Co., New York, Selling Agents; Capital, $46,000; Manufacture Rivets and Water Wheels.

Plymouth Tack and Rivet Works, Plymouth; S. Loring, Proprietor; Manufacture Tacks and Rivets.

Plymouth Woollen and Cotton Factory, Plymouth; Isaac Thacher, Treasurer; E. B. Hayden, Resident Agent; Fearing, Thacher & Co., Boston, Selling Agents; Manufacture Duck.

Plymouth Woollen Mills, Plymouth, commenced 1863; Dwight Faulkner, Treasurer and Resident Agent; Frothingham & Co., Boston, Selling Agents; Capital, $80,000; Manufacture Flannels.

Robinson Iron Co., Plymouth; F. H. Russell, Treasurer; Capital, $100,000; Manufacture Nails and Tack Plate.

Russell Mills, Plymouth, commenced 1855; Edward S. Tobey, Treasurer; D. H. Gilbert, Resident Agent; N. Boynton & Co., Boston, Selling Agents; Capital, $125,000; Manufacture Cotton Duck.

Star Mills, Middleboro, commenced 1863; George Brayton, Treasurer; T. L. Dunlap, Resident Agent; Capital, 180,000; Manufacture Fancy Cassimeres.

Tremont Nail Co., West Wareham, commenced 1858; J. B. Tobey, Treasurer and Resident Agent; Horace P. Tobey, Boston, Selling Agent; Capital, $100,000; Manufacture Cut Nails.

TOWN OFFICERS.

Abington.—Town Clerk, N. T. Hunt. Selectmen and Overseers of Poor, Marcus Reed, Henry A. Noyes, Brainerd Cushing. Treasurer and Collector, Bela E. Faxon.

Bridgewater.—Town Clerk, Lewis Holmes. Selectmen, Van R. Swift, Spencer Leonard, I. Sanford Wilbur. Collector and Treasurer, Van R. Swift.

Carver.—Town Clerk, Wm. Hammond. Selectmen, Assessors and Overseers of the Poor, Thomas Vaughan, Andrew Griffith, Frederick Cobb. Treasurer and Collector, Thomas Cobb.

Duxbury.—Selectmen and Assessors, Samuel Atwell, George Bradford, George B. Standish. Town Clerk, Josiah Peterson. Treasurer, Frederic P. Sherman.

East Bridgewater.—Town Clerk, Jacob A. Rogers. Selectmen, Jacob Bates, George Bryant, Eliab Latham. Treasurer, I. N. Nutter. Collector, E. S. Whitmarsh.

Halifax.—Town Clerk, Edwin Inglee. Selectmen, Assessors and Overseers of the Poor, Edwin Inglee, Abram Bourne, Nathaniel Morton. Treasurer, Nath'l Morton.

Hanover.—Town Clerk and Treasurer, Albert Stetson. Selectmen and Overseers of Poor, J. Dwelley, J. G. Stetson, Robert Ellis.

Hanson.—Town Clerk and Treasurer, Joseph Bryant. Selectmen and Overseers of Poor, E. B. K. Gurney, Joseph Smith, C. L. Howland.

Hingham.—Town Clerk, Charles N. Marsh. Selectmen and Overseers of Poor, Caleb Gill, Seth Sprague, Demerick Marble. Treasurer, Wm. Fearing, 2d. Collector, Andrew J. Gardner.

Hull.—Town Clerk, Andrew D. Cook. Selectmen, Assessors, and Overseers of Poor, John Reed, Francis McKann, Orlando D. Cook. Treasurer and Constable, Edward G. Knight.

Kingston.—Town Clerk, Nathan Brooks. Selectmen and Assessors, Alden S. Bradford, Edward Gray, John F. Holmes. Treasurer and Collector, Nathan Brooks. Overseers of Poor, Edward Gray, Alden S. Bradford, John F. Holmes, Lysander Bartlett.

Lakeville.—Town Clerk, Treasurer and Collector, C. T. Westgate. Selectmen and Assessors, W. H. Southworth, Leander Winslow, Josiah B. Bump. Overseers of Poor, Job Peirce, J. P. Peirce, C. E. Jenney.

Marion.—Town Clerk, W. P. Delano. Selectmen and Assessors, Jos. S. Luce, Geo. H. Kelley, Samuel H. Elder. Treasurer and Collector, Silas B. Allen.

Marshfield.—Town Clerk and Treasurer, Daniel Stevens. Selectmen, Warren Kent, Robert H. Moorehead, William C. Oakman. Overseers of Poor, Chas. T. Hatch, Solomon Little, Nath'l Church. Collector, Charles T. Hatch.

Mattapoisett.—Town Clerk, Thomas Nelson. Selectmen, Overseers and Assessors, Franklin Cross, Wilson Barstow, Josiah Holmes, jr. Treasurer and Collector, Henry Taylor.

Middleboro.—Town Clerk, Treasurer and Collector, Cornelius B. Wood. Selectmen, Jos. T. Wood, J. M. Eddy, Thos. Smith. Overseers of Poor, C. B. Wood, Jos. S. Barden, S. Hinckley.

North Bridgewater.—Town Clerk, Welcome H. Wales. Selectmen, R. L. Thatcher, N. J. Foss, Isaac Kingman. Treasurer, Oakes S. Soule.

Pembroke.—Town Clerk, Francis Collamore. Selectmen, Assessors and Fence Viewers, John Oldham, 2d, Wm. Whiting, Julius Cushman. Treasurer, Seth Whitman. Collector, Hector Monroe. Overseers of Poor, J. Oldham, 2d, Wm. Whiting, Julius Cushman, Willard Pool, Briggs Ford, Luther Magoun, Horace Hall, Job H. Beal, John W. Bryant, John Holmes, Ezekiel Bemis.

Plymouth.—Town Clerk, Leander Lovell. Selectmen, Albert Mason, E. C. Turner, Lysander Dunham, T. B. Sears, Hosea Bartlett. Treasurer, James Cox. Collector, Lemuel Bradford. Overseers of Poor, John H. Harlow, Wm. H. Whitman, Lemuel Bradford, L. T. Robbins, J. C. Hovey.

Plympton.—Town Clerk and Treasurer, Wm. Perkins. Selectmen, Assessors and Overseers of the Poor, Zaccheus Parker, Wm. Perkins, Ira Holmes. Collector, Lemuel Cobb, jr.

Rochester.—Town Clerk, Theophilus King. Selectmen, John Blackmer, Thomas Ellis, George H. Peirce. Treasurer and Collector, John S. Rider.

Scituate.—Town Clerk, Jas. L. Merritt. Selectmen and Assessors, Geo. C. Lee, T. Tilden, F. Damon. Treasurer, Roland Turner.

South Scituate.—Town Clerk, E. T. Fogg. Selectmen and Overseers of Poor, Samuel Tolman, Jr., Ziba Litchfield, Edward Stowell. Treasurer and Collector, E. T. Fogg.

Wareham.—Town Clerk, Treasurer and Collector, Alvin Gibbs. Selectmen, A. S. Hathaway, George Sanford, P. N. Bodfish. Assessors and Overseers of Poor, George Sanford, Wm. A. Caswell, John M. Kinney.

West Bridgewater.—Town Clerk, Austin Packard. Selectmen, Caleb Copeland, jr., Shepard L. Pratt, James Howard. Treasurer and Collector, George M. Pratt.

SOCIETIES.

Lodges of F. A. M. in Plymouth County.

Fellowship, Bridgewater, 1797, Monday, on or b. f. m.
Social Harmony, Wareham, 1823, 2d Friday.
Plymouth, Plymouth, 1825, Monday, on or b. f. m.
Old Colony, Hingham, 1792, Tuesday, on or b. f. m.
Corner Stone. Duxbury, 1801, Saturday, b. f. m.
Paul Revere, No. Bridgewater, 1857, Tuesday, on or b. f. m.
John Cutler, Abington, 1860, Monday, on or a. f. m.
Pythagonian, Marion, 1862, Tuesday, on or b. f. m.
May Flower, Middleboro, 1864, Tuesday.

Lodges of I. O. of G. T. in Plymouth County.

Adelphian, No. 13, Abington, Monday, Templars Hall.
Fraternal, No. 25, No. Bridgewater, Friday, Fraternal Hall.
The Old Oaken Bucket, No. 75, North Scituate.
Social Harmony, No. 86, East Abington, Tuesday.
Pilgrim, No. 117, South Abington, Wednesday.
Monponsett, No. 138, Halifax, Saturday.
Good Hope, No. 141, Kingston, Tuesday.
Speedwell, No. 147, Middleboro, Wednesday, Soule's Hall.
Ironside, No. 165, Duxbury, Friday.
Plymouth Rock, No. 166, Plymouth, Wednesday.
Perseverance, No. 172, Hanover, Thursday.
King Philip, No. 192. Eel River, Friday.
Weweantit, No. 222, Marion, Friday.
Massasoit No. 223, Mattapoisett, Wednesday.
Amaranth, No. 125, East Bridgewater.

Divisions S. of T. in Plymouth County.

Assinippi, 31, West Scituate, Friday.
Assawampsett, 34, Middleboro, Monday.
Indian Head, 48, South Hanson, Wednesday.
Home, 49, Abington, Friday.
King Philip, 66, South Scituate, Monday.
Fraternal, 77, West Abington, Monday.
Annawon, 85, Hanson, Thursday.
Sumner, 99, North Abington, Wednesday.
Wareham, 108, Wareham, Saturday.
Agawam, 125, East Wareham, Tuesday.
Wankinco, 135, South Carver, Thursday.

Wellspring, 139, East Bridgewater, Monday.
Sparkling Water, 151, West Wareham, Monday.
Mattapoisett, 164, Mattapoisett, Friday.
Corner Stone, 165, Hingham, Wednesday.
Silver Lake, 167, Kingston, Saturday.

Association Meetings.

Mayflower Lodge, I. O. of O. F., Plymouth. Regular Meetings Tuesday evenings, at the Hall on High Street.

Y. M. L. I., Plymouth. Regular Meetings for Literary Exercises every Friday evening, at Institute Hall, Exchange Block, Middle St.

Young Men's Christian Association, North Bridgewater. Reading Rooms open every evening.

Young Men's Christian Association, Plymouth. Rooms open every evening; Religious meetings Friday and Sunday evenings.

Christian Union, Plymouth. Leyden Hall, Main St. Open every evening; Religious meetings Monday and Thursday evenings.

Savings Banks in Plymouth County.

Abington Savings Bank—Abington.
Incor. 1853. President, Jenkins Lane; Treas., J. N. Farrar.

Hingham Institution for Savings—Hingham.
Incor. 1833. President, A. Tilden; Treas., H. C. Harding.

Middleboro Savings Bank—Middleboro.
Incorporated 1867.

North Bridgewater Savings Bank.
Incor. 1851. Pres., Henry W. Robinson; Treas., Edward Southworth, jr.

Plymouth Five Cents—Plymouth.
Incor. 1855. Pres., Robert B. Hall; Treas., Daniel J. Robbins.

Plymouth—Plymouth.
Incor. 1828. Pres., N. Russell; Treas., A. Danforth.

Scituate Savings Bank—Scituate.
Incor. 1854. Pres., Elijah Jenkins; Treas., C. W. Prouty.

South Scituate Savings Bank.
President, Moses T. Rogers. Vice President, Geo. H. Wetherbee. Secretary, Thomas J. Gardner. Treasurer, C. T. Fogg.

Wareham Savings Bank—Wareham.
Incor. 1847. Pres., J. B. Tobey; Treas., Thomas R. Miles.

Public Halls in Plymouth County.

Abington.—Hatherly Hall, Centre, seats 300; price $6; J. French, agt. Manson Hall, East Abington, seats 500; price $6; G. C. Soule, agt. Culver Hall, North Abington, seats 400; price $10; J. M. Culver, proprietor.

Bridgewater.—Agricultural Hall, Broad street, seats 3000; Van R. Swift, J E. Crane, Lafayette Keith, committee. Town Hall, Central Square, seats 500; price $10; Eli Washburn, Lewis Holmes, Lafayette Keith, committee. Music Hall, Hyland House, Central Square, seats 250; price $8.

Carver.—Bay State Hall, South Carver; $1 per hour; W. Savery, K. C. Freeman, agents.

Duxbury.—Town Hall, seats 600. Masonic Hall, seats 150. Odd Fellows' Hall, seats 150. Academy Hall, seats 200. Temperance Hall, seats 100. Union Hall, at Ashdod, seats 125. Price of above halls, $3 to $5.

East Bridgewater.—Town Hall, seats 400; price $5; I. N. Nutter, agent.

Halifax.—Town Hall, seats 400; price $3.00; Selectmen.

Hanover.—Town Hall, seats 500; price, $5 to $10; Town Clerk. Academy Hall, seats 300; Rev. S. Cutler. Hanover Hall, seats 200; F. Howard.

Hanson.—Elysium Hall, seats 200; price $2.50; Julius Josselyn, agent. Soper's Hall, seats 300; price $2.00; Jeremiah Soper, agent.

Hingham.—Town Hall, seats 450; price, for lectures, &c., when the public are admitted free, $3 00 in summer and $3.50 in winter; for shows, &c., when an admission fee is charged, $6.00 in summer and $6.50 in winter. Loring Hall, Main St., seats between 500 and 600; Isaac Hersey, agent. Liberty Hall.

Kingston.—Town Hall, Town Clerk; Holmes' Hall, Alden White, agent; Fuller's Hall, Frank Fuller, agent.

Lakeville.—Sausaman Hall, seats 200.

Marion.—Hadley's Hall, seats 400; price $3.00; Andrew J. Hadley, agent.

Marshfield.—Agricultural Hall, seats 300; price $5 to $8; Charles P. Hatch, agent.

North Marshfield.—Concert Hall, seats 200; price $2 to 6; George M. Baker, agent. Roger's Hall, seats 350; price $5 to $10; Wales Rogers, agent. Tilden's Hall, seats 150; price $2; let only for lectures and meetings; Henry Tilden, agent.

Mattapoisett.—Purrington Hall, seats about 250; price, $4 to $8.

Middleboro.—American Hall, seats 600; price $6 to $12; George

Waterman, proprietor. Soule's Hall, seats 200; price $2 to $3; Geo. Soule, proprietor.

North Bridgewater.—Central Hall, Church St. seats 750; price $12; George R. Whitney, agent. New Church Hall, Main St., seats 500; price $15; George E. Bryant, agent. Hauthaway's Hall, Chapel St.. seats 400; price $5 to $10; C. L. Hauthaway, proprietor. Satucket Hall, Hotel, Main Street, seats 250; Tyler Cobb, proprietor.

Pembroke.—Town Hall, seats 300; price $2.50; Nathan B. Simmons, agent.

Plymouth.—Davis' Hall, the best arranged in the County, seats about 1000.

Plympton.—Union Hall, seats 500; price $3; Martin Perkins, agent. Town Hall, seats 500; price $2; Noah Simmons, agent.

Scituate.—Allen's Hall, seats 200; Wm. P. Allen, agent. Union Hall, seats 200. Town Hall, seats 500; price $12.50; Geo. W. Elliot, agent. Armory Hall.

Wareham.—Webster Hall, seats 500; price $8 for one evening, $15 for two evenings; Stephen Ellis, agent.

East Wareham.—Weston's Hall, seats 250; price $5; Samuel T. Tisdale, agent.

West Bridgewater.—Town Hall, seats 500; price $5 to $10. Copeland's Hall, seats 200; price from .75 to $2; Nathan Copeland, agt.

Insurance Companies.

ABINGTON.

Abington Mutual Fire Insurance Company.—Incorporated 1856. President, Baxter Cobb. Directors, Baxter Cobb, William Brown, Edward W. Cobb, Albert Chamberlain, Judson N. Farrar, Sumner Shaw, Joshua L. Nash, Joseph Vaughan, William Ripley, Z. N. Whitmarsh, William P. Corthell, all of Abington; Philip D. Kingman, Bridgewater, and Chandler Sprague, North Bridgewater. Secretary, Freeman P. Howland.

HINGHAM.

Hingham Mutual Fire Insurance Company.—Incorporated 1826. President, Seth S. Hersey. Directors, Seth S. Hersey, John Leavitt, Wm. Foster, Caleb Gill, Amos Bates, Atherton Tilden, of Hingham; Jacob H. Loud, of Plymouth; Benj. Kingman, of North Bridgewater. Secretary, David Harding.

Census of Plymouth County.

Towns,	Date of Incorporation,	Popul'n 1865
Abington,	June 10, 1712,	8,576.
Bridgewater,	June 3, 1656,	4,196.
Carver,	June 9, 1790,	1,059.
Duxbury,	June 7, 1637,	2,377.
East Bridgewater,	June 14, 1823.	2,977.
Halifax,	July 4, 1734,	739.
Hanover,	June 14, 1727,	1,545.
Hanson,	Feb. 22, 1820,	1,195.
Hingham,	Sept. 2, 1635,	4,176.
Hull,	May 29, 1644,	260.
Kingston,	June 16, 1726,	1,626.
Lakeville,	May 13, 1853,	1,110.
Marion,	May 14, 1852,	960.
Marshfield,	Mar. 2, 1640,	1,810.
Mattapoisett,	May 20, 1857,	1,451.
Middleboro,	June —, 1669,	4,525.
North Bridgewater,	June 15, 1821,	6,335.
Pembroke,	Mar. 21, 1711,	1.488.
Plymouth,	Dec. 11, 1620,	6,075.
Plympton,	June 4, 1707,	924.
Rochester,	June 4, 1686,	1,156.
Scituate,	Oct. 5, 1636,	2,269.
South Scituate,	Feb. 14, 1849,	1,578.
Wareham,	July 10, 1739.	2,842.
West Bridgewater,	Feb. 16, 1822,	1,825.
Plymouth County,	June 2, 1685,	63,074

Agricultural Societies.

Plymouth County Agricultural Society.—Incorporated in 1819. Located in Bridgewater. Grounds in Broad street comprise 63 acres. Valuation of property, $26,000. President, Charles G. Davis, of Plymouth. 1st Vice President, Allen S. Bradford, of Kingston. 2d Vice President, Chandler Sprague, of North Bridgewater. Secretary, Lafayette Keith, of Bridgewater. Treasurer, Van R. Swift, of Bridgewater. Trustees, J. E. Crane of Bridgewater, Eliab Latham of East Bridgewater, Pardon Copeland of West Bridgewater, William A. Thompson of North Bridgewater, Stillman Benson and Joshua M. Eddy of Middleboro, James E. Sproat of Wareham, Thomas M. Nelson of Lakeville, Ephraim B. Thompson of Halifax, Thomas O. Jackson of Plymouth, William H. H. Bryant of Pembroke, Samuel B. Thaxter of Abington. Number of members, 850.

Hingham Agricultural and Horticultural Society.—A. Fearing, President. This Society has been in operation several years, and is in a most flourishing condition. We were not able to get a list of officers in season.

Marshfield Agricultural Society.—This Society meets in Agricultural Hall once a week. It was organized Nov. 19, 1864. President, Geo. M. Baker. Secretary, John Baker. Treasurer, Robert H. Moorehead. Auditor, Warren Kent. Trustees, Stephen Henry, Charles P. Hatch, Henry T. Crossley. The Annual Fall Exhibitions have been very successful.

Churches in Plymouth County.

For other particulars see the Historical Sketch of each town. Alphabetical list of Clergymen, in the Directory.

Bridgewater.

First Congregational, organized June 1, 1716. Lewis Bryant, Dea.

Trinity Church, organized 1748; Rev. Charles Clark Harris, Rector; Franklin Leach, George L. Edson, Wardens.

Central Square Trinitarian Church, organized in Scotland Village, Oct. 17, 1821; removed to Central Square 1836; present house of worship erected 1862; Abiel Bassett, George W. Holmes, Deacons.

New Jerusalem Church, organized May, 1833; J. A. Hyde, Secretary, E. H. Sprague, Treasurer.

Scotland Trinitarian Congregational Church, organized July 4, 1836; Ezra Fobes, Deacon.

St. Thomas Aquinas Church, (Roman Catholic,) instituted in 1852; Rev. M. T. Maguire, Pastor.

Carver.

First Congregational Church, Green; Thomas Cobb, William Atwood, Deacons.
Baptist, Centre, H. A. Lucas, Ephraim Dunham, Deacons.
Methodist, South: Supt. Sabbath School, Charles Ryder.
Union Society, South; Trustees, Jesse Murdock, Wm. Savery, S. F. Jenkins, Wm. B. Gibbs, George P. Bowers, Daniel Shaw, D. M. Bates, A. P. Kinney, Perez Smith; Wm. Savery, Sec'y; Joseph Barrows, Treasurer.

Duxbury.

First Church, organized in 1632; church membership about 20.
Methodist Episcopal; Church membership 66.
West Duxbury M. E.; Church membership, 82.
Wesleyan Methodist: Church membership, 100; Jabez Keep, Clerk.

East Bridgewater.

First Congregational: Francis Cary, Azor Harris, Deacons.
Union Church of East and West Bridgewater: Rufus A. Littlefield, Stephen Harlow, Deacons.
New Jerusalem Church, Joppa: Mrs. L. W. Richards, Organist; L. W. Richards, Chorister; S. W. Keen, Sexton.
Second M. E.: R. M. Smith, Geo. T. Mitchell, Joham H. Hicks, Waldo Hayward, Franklin Edson, William Keen, Sam'l F. White, Chas. H. Brown, Trustees.
St. Bridget's, (Roman Catholic); Rev. M. T. Maguire, Pastor.

Halifax.

First Cong; Eben. Fuller, Clerk; Eben. Fuller, Darius Holmes, Deacons.
First Baptist; organized 1821; Z. L. Britton, Jabez Smith, Deacons.

Hanover.

St. Andrews Episcopal; L. C. Waterman, George Curtis, Wardens.
First Cong.; S. S. Church, F. Chamberlain, Deacons.
Second Cong.; H. B. Barstow, James Tolman, Deacons.
Universalist; S. O. Jacobs, Clerk; I. B. Sanborn, Treasurer; H. J. Curtis, Charles Jacobs, Amasa Whiting, Assessors.
Baptist; William Church, John Brooks, Deacons.

Hanson.

Cong'l; Thomas Smith, Seth Gannett, Deacons.
Baptist; Jonathan R. Gurney, Josiah Barker, Deacons.

Hingham.

First Parish; organized 1635; Pastors, Joseph Richardson and Calvin Lincoln; Supt. S. School, Henry Siders; No. of scholars, 185.
Second Parish; South: Supt. S. School, Joseph Jacobs, Jr.; No. of scholars, 128.
Third Cong'l; organized 1805; 75 S. School Scholars.
Evangelical Church; Deacon and Supt. of S. S., Caleb S. Hunt.
Methodist Episcopal; West Hingham; organized 1818; has a Sabbath School of 81 scholars; John Gardner, Supt.

First Universalist Society; Supt., Edmund Hersey, 2d; 67 scholars and 14 teachers.
First Baptist; organized in 1828, with 20 members; present number, 161; Mr. Joshua Thayer, only surviving Deacon; Caleb Marsh, Church Clerk.

Kingston.

First Cong. Unitarian; James Foster, Deacon.
Second Cong. Trinitarian; Nath'l Cushman, S. M. Andrews, Guilford S. Newcomb, Deacons.
Baptist; Henry Cobb, Ira Chandler, Deacons.

Marion.

Congregational; organized Oct. 13, 1703, with 87 members; James Wittett, Moses H. Swift, Deacons.
Protestant Methodist; organized in 1831.
Universalist; organized in 1833.
M. E. Church; organized July, 1865, with 29 members; Daniel Hall, William H. Briggs, Charles C. Dean, Ezra J. Parlow, Joshua W. Dean, Thomas Bourne, Sumner Ryder, Amos Hadley, Stewards.

Marshfield.

First Congregational; Elijah Ames, Lewis Simmons Deacons; David P. Hatch, Supt. S. School.
North Baptist; Lincoln Damon, Deacon.
South Baptist; Ambrose Magoun, Amos Sherman, Deacons.
Unitarian Church; Hiram Oakman, Benj Hatch, Deacons.
Methodist; Luther Magoun, Benj. Baker. Wm. Baker, Zenas Thomas, John Sprague, Charles Williamson; Harvey Stetson, Wm. Harrington, Stewards.

Mattapoisett.

Congregational; organized July 27, 1736, as the "First Parish in Rochester;" Amittai B. Hammond, Nath'l A. Crosby, Noah Hammond, Solomon K. Eaton, Deacons; S. K. Eaton, chorister; Henry Taylor, Supt. S. School.
First Christian Church; organized about 1820; was formerly a branch of church at Long Plain; Joseph Purrington, Wm. L. Bourne, Gideon Barlow, Deacons; Philip A. Barrows, chorister; Wm. R. Randall, Supt. S. School.
Universalist Church; organized April 25, 1859; Ivory Snow. Alden Dexter. Deacons; James H. Purrington, Supt. Sabbath School.
Friends' Meeting; belonging to Long Plain Preparative Meeting, and to New Bedford Monthly Meeting.

North Bridgewater.

First Congregational; John W. Hunt, Jeremiah Beals, Joel T. Packard, Deacons; Francis French, Clerk; Oliver F. Leach, Treasurer.
First New Jerusalem; William Faxon, Henry French, Daniel Crocker, Committee; Elisha Washburn, Secretary.
First M. E. Church; Bradford Packard, Supt. S. School; John Hall, Clerk; Samuel Clark, Treasurer.
South Cong. Church, Campello; George Sawyer, S. F. Packard, Galen Pratt, Cary Howard, Deacons.

Porter Evangelical; Simeon Packard, Elbridge H. Packard, Geo. H. Cushman, S. W. S. Howard, Deacons.

Second M. E. Church; Sanford Alden, Philip Reynolds, Darius C. Place, George R. Whitney, Thomas Hathaway, John Montgomery. Uriah Macoy, Edward J. Benner, John Ellis, Trustees.

St. Patrick's (Roman Catholic) Church; Rev. T. B. McNulty, Pastor; Arthur Dimond, Organist; Wm. O'Neil, Chorister; John Owens. Supt. S. School.

First Universalist Society; L. D. Hervey, David Hall, T. L. Gifford, Deacons; Nelson Mace, Supt.

Pembroke.

Friend's Meeting; organized previous to 1658; Nathan T. Shepherd, Clerk of the Monthly Meeting.

Methodist Episcopal; organized 1829; Chas. N. Hinkley, Supt. S. School; Official Members, Abel Stetson, Hiram Munroe, John D. Mason, Josephus Bryant, John B. Chandler, Greenleaf Kilbrith; Clerk, Josephus Bryant.

Unitarian; organized in 1712; Peter Salmond, Seth Whitman. Deacons.

Plymouth.

Unitarian; Lemuel D. Holmes, Samuel T. Talbot, Deacons; Wm. H. Whitman, Supt. S. School.

Third Congregational; organized 1801; Timothy Gordon, Jesse Harlow, G. G. Dyer, Deacons.

Baptist; organized 1809; Peleg Faunce, A. J. Whiting, Deacons.

Plympton.

Congregational; Rufus Wright, Perez Packard, Deacons.

Rochester.

First Congregational, Centre; organized Oct. 13, 1703; John H. Clark, George W. Haskell, Deacons.

Congregational, No. Rochester; organized in 1755; Abner Braley. John B. Dornin, Deacons.

Christian Baptist, Pine Grove; organized Dec. 11, 1850; Jonathan Hathaway, Deacon.

Union Protestant Methodist; organized April, 1866.

Scituate.

Methodist Episcopal; Franklin Damon, Frederick Howard, James Taylor, Michael Welch, E. P. Welch, G. H. Bates, Judah Chandler, Henry Chubbuck, Wm. Manson, Stewards.

South Scituate.

Unitarian; Ebenezer Stetson, George Tilden, Deacons;

Universalist; incorporated 1812; Stephen O. Jacobs, Clerk.

Wareham.

First Congregational; Hiram Barrows, E. N. Thompson, Deacons.

St. Patrick's Church; Rev. Peter Bartoldi, Parish Priest; James Griffin, Deacon,

West Bridgewater.

First Cong'l Unitarian; organized 1662; for 167 years it had but three pastors; F. E. Howard, Deacon; Simeon J. Dunbar, Supt. S. School.

Baptist; organized 1789; Alba Howard, P. E. Hill, Deacons.

Methodist; organized 1841.

ELLIPTIC SEWING MACHINE CO.'S HIGHEST PREMIUM.
Wonderful Simplicity. Unequalled Capacity.
Lock Stitch Sewing Machines.

(Formerly Sloat's Elliptic.) Incomparably the best for family use. Their superiority vindicated by the highest authorities. GOLD MEDAL. Fair Maryland Institute, 1866. All the highest premiums at the Maryland Institute, New York and Pennsylvania State Fairs in 1866, given on Sewing Machines, except one given to a Manufacturing Machine at the N. Y. Fair, were awarded after a most severe and impartial test, to the ELLIPTIC LOCK STITCH MACHINE, as follows: At the Maryland Inst. Fair, as the BEST FAMILY SEWING MACHINE, and at the N. Y. State Fair as the BEST FAMILY SEWING MACHINE, BEST DOUBLE THREAD SEWING MACHINE. *These two completely covering all the ground*, and for the BEST SAMPLE OF SEWING MACHINE WORK:

As can be seen by the following comprehensive and conclusive report of the committee of practical and experienced mechanical experts appointed by the State Board to investigate into the merits of the different sewing machines: "We, the committee on Sewing Machines, after a careful and thorough investigation into the respective merits of the various machines submitted for examination, find the *Elliptic Lock-stitch Sewing Machine* to be *superior* to *all others* in the following points, namely: Simplicity and Thoroughness of Mechanical construction. Ease of Operation and Management. Noiselessness and Rapidity of movement. Beauty, Strength and Elasticity of Stitch. Variety and perfection of Attachments, and range of Work. Compactness and beauty of Model and Finish. Adaption to material of any thickness by an Adjustable Feed Bar, and in the Unequalled Precision with which it executes the Lock-Stitch, by means of the Elliptic Hook, and we therefore award it the First Premium as the BEST FAMILY SEWING MACHINE, and also for the above reasons the First Premium as the BEST DOUBLE THREAD SEWING MACHINE.

C. E. PETERS, HECTOR MOFFAT, Committee.

Liberal arrangements made with parties of energy, good standing and capital, who may wish to engage in the sale of these machines, as agents, in such territory as yet remains unoccupied; for further information in regard to which, and private circular address   CHAS. H. COFFIN, N. E. AGENT,
292 Washington St., Boston.

A. M. LELAND,
Dealer in
SECOND HAND
Piano Fortes
Of Every Description.

No. 289 Washington St., (Up Stairs,)   **BOSTON.**

FLORENCE SEWING MACHINES.
C. Patch & Co. New England Agents.

Also Manufacturers and Dealers in **Sewing Machine Needles, Shuttles, Bobbins, Screw Drivers, Oil Cans and Oil,** and every variety of Sewing Machine Trimmings, Machine Twist, Sewing Silk & Threads.

141 Washington Street.

Manufactory, Haymarket Square,
Corner of Charlestown Street,   **BOSTON.**

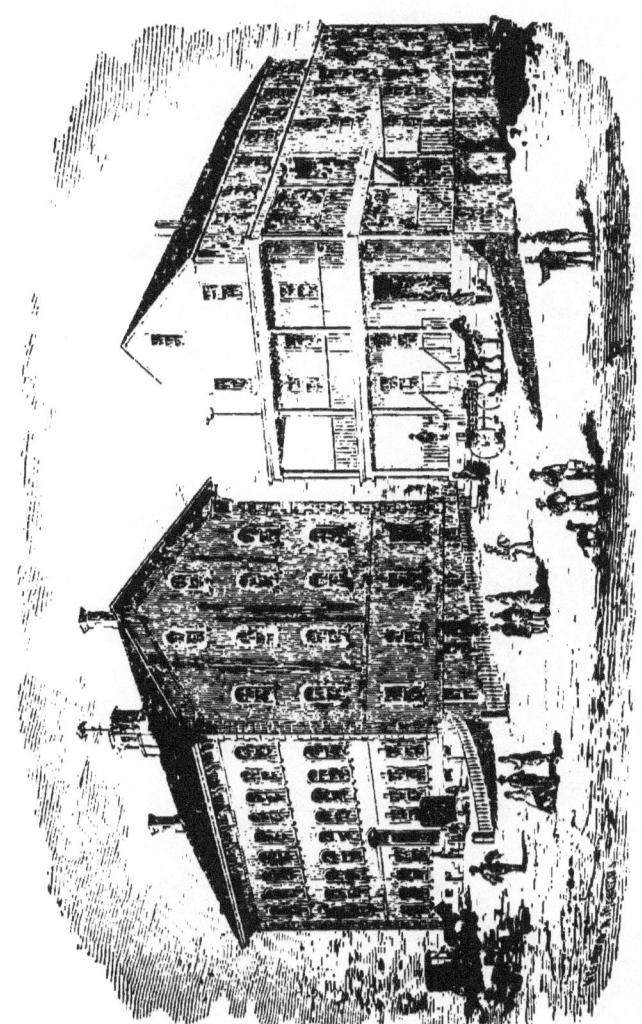

BOOT AND SHOE FACTORY OF JENKINS LANE AND SONS, EAST ABINGTON.

GENERAL DIRECTORY

OF

PLYMOUTH COUNTY.

Halifax Soldiers.

The following are the names of those who died in the service from Halifax. The list was received too late for classification under its proper head:—

Martin S. Morse, James D. Fuller, Z. L. P. Britton, Wm. H. Fuller, Frederic E. Fuller, Horatio W. Cornish, killed, Herbert P. Bosworth, John Wood, killed, Benj. F. Durgin, Edward Bishop, Nathaniel B. Bishop, killed, Lewis S. Wade, Edward A. Richmond, rebel prison, Joseph S. W. Richmond, Charles W. Soule, Lorenzo A. Tower, James A. Lyon, Joseph L. Melton, Joseph T. Bourne, Abel T. Bryant, died in navy, Oliver E. Bryant, George Drew 3d, killed, Cyrus Thompson, Luther Hayward.

B. F. TRIPP,

POST OFFICE BLOCK, - - - - - - MIDDLEBORO.

REFRESHMENT SALOON,

Oysters, Fruit, Confectionery and Ice Cream.

H. F. CORNWALL,

PHOTOGRAPHER,

Centre Street, Middleboro.

A superior quality of Photographs, Porcelain Pictures, Ambrotypes, &c. Particular attention paid to copying from Ambrotypes and Tintypes, into photographs of any size, and finished in ink or colors.

Frames, Cases, Cord and Tassels for sale.

JAMES H. HARLOW,

132 Main Street, - - *Middleboro, Mass.,*

Manufacturer and Dealer in

Carriages,
Harnesses,
Sleighs,
and Robes.

A. M. EATON,

(Successor to Lothrop Shurtleff.)

Cor. Water and Clifford Streets, MIDDLEBORO,

UNDERTAKER.

Coffins, Caskets, Robes, Hearses, Funeral Flowers,

furnished, and every duty appertaing to funerals attended to, on the most reasonable rates.

FURNITURE REPAIRING PROMPTLY ATTENDED TO.

HELMBOLD'S EXTRACT OF SARSAPARILLA cleanses and renovates the blood, instils the vigor of health into the system, and purges out the humors that make disease.

THE SCIENCE OF HEALTH.
Every Man his own Physician.

HOLLOWAY'S PILLS,
AND
HOLLOWAY'S OINTMEMT.

Disorders of the Stomach, Liver and Bowels.
The Stomach is the great centre which influences the health or disease of the system—abused or debilitated by excess—indigestion, offensive breath and physical prostration are the natural consequences. Allied to the brain, it is the source of headaches, mental depression, nervous complaints and unrefreshing sleep. The Liver becomes affected and generates bilious disorders, pains in the side, &c. The bowels sympathize by Costiveness, Diarrhœa and Dysentery. The principal action of these Pills is on the stomach, and the liver, lungs, bowels and kidneys participate in their recuperative and regenerative operation.

Erysipelas and Salt Rheum.
Are two of the most common and virulent disorders prevalent on this continent, to these the Ointment is especially antagonistic, its *"modus operandi"* is first to eradicate the venom and then complete the cure.

Bad Legs, Old Sores and Ulcers.
Cases of many years standing, that have pertinaciously refused to yield to any other remedy or treatment, have invariably succumbed to a few applications of this powerful unguent.

Eruptions on the Skin.
Arising from a bad state of the blood or chronic diseases, are eradicated, and a clear and transparent surface regained by the restorative action of this Ointment. It surpasses many of the cosmetics and other toilet appliances in its power to dispel rashes, and other disfigurements of the face.

Female Complaints.
Whether in the young or old, married or single, at the dawn of Womanhood, or the turn of life, these tonic medicines display so decided an influence that a marked improvement is soon perceptible in the health of the patient. Being a purely vegetable preparation, they are a safe and reliable remedy for all classes of Females in every condition of health and station of life.

Piles and Fistula.
Every form and feature of these prevalent and stubborn disorders is eradicated locally and entirely by the use of this emolient; warm fomentations should precede its application. Its healing qualities will be found to be thorough and invariable.

Both the Ointment and Pills should be used in the following cases:—
Bunions, Burns, Chapped Hands, Chilblains, Fistula, Gout, Lumbago, Mercurial Eruptions, Piles, Rheumatism, Ringworm, Salt Rheum, Scalds, Skin Diseases, Swelled Glands, Sore Legs, Sore Breasts, Sore Heads, Sore Throats, Sores of all kinds, Sprains, Stiff Joints, Tetter, Ulcers, Venereal Sores, Wounds of all kinds.

CAUTION.—None are genuine unless the words "Holloway, New York and London," are discernable as a *Watermark* in every leaf of the book of directions around each pot or box; the same can be plainly seen by holding the leaf to the light. A handsome reward will be given to any one rendering such information as may lead to the detection of any party or parties counterfeiting the medicines or vending the same, knowing them to be spurious.

☞ Sold at the manufactory of Professor Holloway, 80 Maiden Lane, New York, and by all respectable Druggists and Dealers in Medicine throughout the civilized world.

☞ There is considerable saving by taking the larger sizes.

N. B.—Directions for the guidance of patients in every disorder are affixed to each pot and box.

☞ Dealers in my well-known medicines can have show cards, circulars, &c., sent Free of Expense, by addressing **Thomas Holloway, 80 Maiden Lane, New York.**

I. H. HARLOW & CO.,

MANUFACTURERS OF

Barrel, Half-Barrel, and Quarter Barrel Heads,

Nail Casks, Boxes, &c., &c.,

STEAM MILLS,

Middleboro,

Mass.

THE Bristol County Republican,

Published at Taunton, Mass.

Has the largest circulation of any newspaper in the Second Congressional District, which comprises thirty-three towns and the city of Taunton.
We insert advertisements at one dollar per square of ten lines, each insertion. Advertisements by the year at less rates.
Subscription price of the *Republican*, $2 per year.

DAWES, WILBAR & DAVOL, Proprietors.

JACOB G. SPARROW,
House, Sign, & Carriage
PAINTER,

Water Street, Middleboro, Mass.

Glazing, Paper Hanging, Graining & Varnishing,
PROMPTLY ATTENDED TO.

☞ Contracts for large Manufactories, Churches and Public Buildings, taken on the most favorable terms.

KNIFFEN MOWING MACHINE,
THE BEST MOWER IN THE WORLD.

THE FARMERS' WANTS FULLY SATISFIED.

One-Horse Mowers Practicable.

Some of the Many Points of Excellence of the Kniffen Machine.

The Wheels are lighter and higher; Fewer Bolts, and no Spring Keys; Less Shafting; The Kniffen combines greater strength and lightness than any other Machine; The gearings are the most perfect in adjustment, and the draft is adjustable and reduced to a lower point; Better adapted for elevations and depressions of surface; In economy of power it is unsurpassed; There is never any strain or cramping of the cutters, whatever position they may be placed in.

EVERY MACHINE WARRANTED.

For Circulars, or other information, send to

Heman Copeland, Campello, Mass.

☞ Also, Agent for Reynolds' Eagle Seed Sower; Packard's Wringing Machine; The Horse Pitch Fork; and for the various Sewing Machines.

BRIGGS & CO.,
DIRECTORY PUBLISHERS,

NO. 25 KILBY ST., BOSTON, MASS.

JUST ISSUED, THE NEW ENGLAND CITIES

Business Directory for 1867.

PRICE $3.00.

Also Publishers of Connecticut State Directory,

Essex Co., Mass. Directory,

WORCESTER CO. DIRECTORY,

Middlesex County Directory, &c., &c.

☞ Directories furnished for any part of the United States.

A. L. JEWELL & CO.,

Manufacturers of 78 varieties of

COPPER

Weather Vanes.

Horses, Cattle, Sheep, Eagle, Church Vane, Arrows, Scrolls, &c.

ALL KINDS OF VANES

MADE TO ORDER.

Old Vanes bought or exchanged, and repaired.

Second Hand Vanes Sold Cheap.

ORDERS ANSWERED AT ONCE.

BILLS C. O. D.

SEND FOR CATALOGUE.

Waltham, Mass.

GEO. F. HARTWELL,
MERCHANT TAILOR,

And Dealer in

GENTS' FURNISHING GOODS, HATS, CAPS,

UMBRELLAS, CARPET BAGS, &C.,

Centre Street,   -   -   MIDDLEBORO, MASS.

WILLIAM EDSON,

SOLICITOR OF

American & Foreign Patents,

ROOM NO. 10,

STUDIO BUILDING,

110 Tremont Street,   -   -   -   -   BOSTON.

A. F. & C. POOLE,

Wholesale Dealers in

White Wine and Cider Vinegar,

Pure Cider Vinegar, Pickles, Cider, Ketchups, Sauces,

MUSTARD, TOMATOES, PEACHES, HERBS, &c.

No. 237 North Street,   -   -   -   BOSTON.

ALSON F. POOLE.   CALEB POOLE, JR.

☞ Also old and new Cider bought of Farmers. ☜

THE LARGEST COLLECTION OF SEEDS
EVER OFFERED IN AMERICA.

Full and explicit directions for cultivation are given in our new **AMATEUR CULTIVATOR'S GUIDE** to the Kitchen and Flower Garden. Now Ready. A descriptive work of 140 pages, fully illustrated with a beautiful colored plate and 100 engravings, containing a list of over 2,500 varieties of Flower and Vegetable Seeds; also 150 varieties of the choicest French Hybrid Gladiolus. All the Novelties, both of Flower and vegetable, for 1867, will be found described in the above work.

Mailed free, to any address, on receipt of 25 cents.

WASHBURN & CO., Seed Merchants,

Horticultural Hall, Boston, Mass.

Abington General Directory.

(Canvassed under the direction of C. A. Gould.)

Locality of Streets.

We give in the following list, the locality of some of the principal streets of Abington:—

Adams Street, North Abington.
Ashland Street, Centre Ward.
Bedford Street, Centre Ward.
Belmont Street, Centre Ward.
Beulah Street, South Ward.
Bigelow Avenue, East Ward.
Birch Street, North Abington.
Brighton Street, North Abington.
Central Street, Centre Ward.
Centre Avenue, from Centre to East Ward.
Cork Street, East Ward.
Cross Street, North Abington.
Deering Square, East Ward.
Dove Street, South Ward.
Dublin Row, East Ward.
Dunbar Square, Centre Ward.
Elm Street, Centre Ward.
Exchange Street, East Ward.
Franklin Street, South Ward.
Glen Street, South Ward.
Groveland Street, Centre Ward.
Hancock Street, North Abington.
Harvard Street, South Ward.
Hingham Street, East Ward.
Liberty Street, East Ward.
Lincoln Street, North Abington.
Market Street, East Ward.
Niles Street, Centre Ward.
North Avenue, from North to East Ward.
Orange Street, Centre Ward.
Pearl Street, North Abington.
Plain Street, East Ward.
Pleasant Street, South Ward.
Plymouth Street, North to South Ward.
Pond Street, East Ward.
Progress Street, Centre Ward.
Rail Road Street, North Abington.
Randolph Street, North Abington.
Rockland Street, Centre Ward.
Salem Street, East Ward.
School Street, South Ward.
South Avenue, South Ward.
Spring Street, South Ward.
Summer Street, Centre Ward.
Summit Street, South Ward.
Temple, Centre Ward.
Thaxter Avenue, Centre Ward.
Union Street, East Ward.
Vernon Street, East Ward.
Washington Street, from Centre to South Ward.
Walnut Avenue, Centre Ward.
Water Street, East Ward.
Webster Street, East Ward.
Winter Street, South Ward.

Policy Holders in the BERKSHIRE LIFE INSURANCE COMPANY of Pittsfield, Mass., DO NOT FORFEIT THEIR POLICIES by reason of FAILURE TO PAY their premiums. (See page 50.)

ABBE REV. FREDERICK R. cor. Bedford and Groveland
Adams George, (Reed & Adams)
Additon Z. R. shoemaker, r Belmont
Ager Wilbar F. shoemaker, r Randolph
Agnew John, merchant tailor, Central
Alden Alexander, manufacturer, r School
Alden Amos, shoe manuf. r Washington
Alden Belah, shoemaker, r South Avenue
Alden J. farmer, r South Avenue
Alden Jared, shoemaker, r Plymouth
Alger Frank, laborer, South avenue
Allen C. F. boot & shoe manuf. r Temple
Allen C. W. shoemaker, r Temple
Allen Daniel W. stitcher, r Centre av
Ames Frank, shoemaker, r Union
Ames Jacob, shoemaker, r Union
Ames Joshua, shoemaker, r Liberty
Ames jr. Joshua, shoemaker, r Liberty
Ames Joshua F. shoemaker, r Union
Ames Wm. T. shoemaker, bd Liberty
Anderson James, shoemaker, Groveland
Andrews J. laborer, bds Plymouth
Arnold Briggs, shoemaker, r North ave
Arnold E. A. clerk, (J. E. Estes), Union
Arnold Edward, shoemaker, Union
Arnold Ezra, shoemaker, North ave
Arnold Ezra D. shoemaker, r Liberty
Arnold Jonathan, shoemaker, r Liberty
Arnold jr. Jonathan, shoemaker, r Adams
Arnold Leonard, last maker,
Arnold Leonard P. last maker, 1 Adams.
Arnold Moses N boot and shoe manuf. r Adams.
Arnold N. last maker.
Arnold N. W. last maker, r Adams.
Arnold William B. shoemaker, bd Adams.
Arnold William D. shoemaker, No. ave.
Atwood B. S. (B. S. & E. H. Atwood,) r North ave.
Atwood E. H. (B. S. & E. H. Atwood,) r Brighton.
Atwood Elijah, boxmaker, r Brighton.
Atwood S. S. farmer, r Washington.
Atwood Timothy S. shoemaker, r Dunbar Sq.
Averell Louis C. laborer, r Plymouth.

BAILEY JAMES, shoemaker, r Washington
Bailey John, shoemaker, r Centre ave.
Bailey Thos. H. shoemaker, r Union
Bailey Thos. H. jr. shoemaker, r Union
Baker Amos H. carpenter, r Vernon
Baker Calvin L. carpenter, Dunbar sq
Baker Horatio, blacksmith, r Market
Baker Paul, blacksmith, r Market
Baker Porter, shoemaker, r Market
Baldwin Barney, shoemaker, r Central
Baldwin Gilbert, shoemaker, r Centre ave
Ballard James, shoemaker, r Rockland
Ballou Francis D. shoemaker, r Progress
Barber John A. r Liberty
Barnes Sylvanus, engineer, r Quincy
Barrell Chas. H. shoemaker, r Washington
Barrett James, laborer, r Salem
Barrett Simeon, shoemaker, r Union
Barrows Gustavus, at Wm. L. Reed's
Barry David, shoemaker, r Union
Barry David F. shoemaker, r Washington
Barry James, shoemaker
Barry John, laborer, r North ave

Bass Alden, shoemaker, r Linden ave
Bass Quincy, blacksmith, r Liberty
Bass Robert, blacksmith, r Liberty
Bates Alvin, shoemaker, r Bedford
Bates Asa, wheelwright, r School
Bates Charles, shoemaker, r Union
Bates Cyrus, carpenter, r South ave
Bates Daniel W. cutter, r Centre ave
Bates David, shoemaker, r School
Bates David B. shoemaker, r Harvard
Bates Eliphalet R. shoemaker, r Randolph
Bates Henry A. grocer, r Washington
Bates Jacob P. shoemaker, r Union
Bates James, machinist, r Dover
Bates James A. machinist, r Nursery lane
Bates John, shoemaker, r Washington
Bates Louis D. shoe manuf. r Plymouth
Bates Nahum, provisions, Washington
Bates N. B. cutter, (H. Hunt), r North Abington
Bates Oscar, shoemaker, r Union
Bates Samuel, shoemaker, bds Central
Bates Wm. H. shoemaker, r Union
Baxter Thomas, shoemaker, r Salem
Baxter Willard, shoemaker, r Salem
Beaty James, shoemaker, Dover
Beal Asahel, farmer, r Salem
Beal Benj. farmer, r Union
Beal Benj. shoemaker, Centre ave
Beal Benj. 2d, shoemaker, r Centre ave
Beal Benj. 3d, agent, r North ave
Beal Boylston, shoemaker, r North ave
Beal Daniel W. shoemaker, r North ave
Beal Danl. W. 2d, r North ave
Beal David, merchant, r Bedford
Beal David, shoemaker, r Water
Beal David H. shoemaker, r Water
Beal Ezekiel, shoemaker, r Webster
Beal G. A. bookkeeper, r Centre ave
Beal Gridley, cutter, r Plymouth
Beal John A. shoemaker, r Progress
Beal John Q. musician, r Central
Beal John W. shoemaker, r Webster
Beal Josiah, shoemaker, r Progress
Beal N. shoemaker, r Beulah
Beal Nathan, farmer, r Water
Beal Nathan jr. farmer, r Water
Beal Nathan A. shoemaker, bd Water
Beal Nath'l, shoe manuf. r Webster
Beal Nath'l jr. shoe manuf. r Webster
Beal Nelson, cutter, r Centre ave
Beal Noah, farmer, r Water
Beal Samuel C. cutter,
Beal Walter, shoemaker, r Union
Beal Webster, shoemaker, r Centre ave
Bearce Chas. clerk, r Union
Bearce H. D. clerk, r Temple
Belcher Leonard, shoemaker, bds Randolph
Bennett B. V. clerk, r Union
Bennett Chas. mason, bds Plymouth
Bennett Nath. B. mason, r Plymouth
Bennett Nath. E. shoemaker, bds Plymouth
Bennett S. D. cutter, r Union
Bennett Seth, lastmaker,
Bennett Seth W. farmer, r Plymouth
Bennett Seth W. jr. shoemaker, r Plymouth
Benson Calvin B. shoemaker, r Brighton
Benson E. S. shoemaker, r North ave
Benson Leonard, cutter, r Adams

The "ABINGTON STANDARD" is published in the largest town in Plymouth County, and is a Good Advertising Medium.

ABINGTON DIRECTORY.   11

Benson Thomas B. cutter, r Adams
Bermingham Richard, shoemaker, bds Union
Bemis Frank, carpenter, b ds Vernon
Berry Michael, shoemaker, r North ave
Bessey Hassard N. stitcher, for B. Wilks s, r Plymouth
Beverly James B. shoemaker, r Salem
Bickford Edward, shoemaker, r School
Bicknall Wm. H. bds Washington
Bigelow David, grocer, r Union
Bigelow James F. shoe manuf. r Union
Blake Chas. works at Lane's
Blake Nathaniel, boot manufac. r South
Blake Samuel, gentleman, r S. Abington
Blakeman Thomas, shoemaker, r Liberty
Blanchard Benj. S. stone cutter, r Adams
Blanchard Dan. boot and shoe manuf. r Union
Blanchard Danl. H. boot and shoe manuf. r Union
Blanchard Dean, farmer, r Adams
Blanchard Edmund, farmer, r Union
Blanchard jr. Edmund, shoemaker, bd Union
Blanchard Edward, clerk, r Washington
Blanchard Elwin, provision dealer, Washington
Blanchard jr. Eli, shoemaker, r Washington
Blanchard E. N. foreman, r Hancock
Blanchard Jos. shoemaker, bd Union
Blanchard Leonard B. shoe manuf. r Union
Blanchard Thos. shoemaker, r Washington
Blanchard V. butcher, r Washington
Blanchard Vinson, boot and shoe manuf. Washington, r Hancock
Blaisdell Alexander, shoemaker, r Union
Blaisdell Moses, farmer, r Union
Blaisdell Wm. H. shoemaker, r Union
Blaisdell Wm. P. farmer, r Union
Blaney Chas. H. last maker, r Adams
Blaney Henry, last maker
Blaney John, last maker
Blood Noah O. clerk, r Water
Boise Timothy, tailor, r Union
Boud John S. hair dresser, r Washington
Bosworth Ambrose, machinist, at H. H. Brigham's
Bosworth John C. shoemaker, r Harvard
Bolzer Thos. shoemaker, r Water
Bower Luke H. shoemaker, r North ave
Bourne Francis, (Bourne & Ring), bds Washington
Bowles William, shoemaker, r Glen
Bowler John, shoemaker, r Cork
Boynton Edward, book keeper, r North avenue
Bradbury C. W. clerk
Bradley James S. shoemaker, r Liberty
Bradman Florentine K. shoemaker, bds Dunbar sq.
Bressingham John, oyster saloon, r Beulah
Brew John, laborer, r North ave
Brewster Henry O. harness maker, r Union
Brian Henry, shoemaker, bd Lincoln
Briggs Jefferson, shoemaker, r Webster
Briggs John, ship carpenter, r cor. of Walnut and Thaxter ave

Briggs Jos. W. shoemaker, r Plain
Briggs Jos. N. W. shoemaker, bd Plain
Briggs Nath'l B., shoemaker, bd Vernon
Brigham Andrew C. tack maker, r Winter
Brighon Henry H. nail and tack manuf. South ave
Brigham Sabina, last maker.
Brock Michael, shoemaker, r Salem
Brooks Benj. F. shoemaker, r Union
Brooks Edward, shoemaker, r Union
Brooks Henry A. stitcher, r Washington
Brooks Spencer, cutter, r Union
Brooks Theodore, mason, r Union
Brow John, tack maker, r Hanson
Brown Alfred, stone cutter, r Beulah
Brown Austin, shoemaker, r Belmont
Brown Austin, shoemaker, r Elm
Brown Beh, wheelwright, r Bedford
Brown Benjamin, boot cutter, r Washington
Brown E. E. shoemaker, r Brighton
Brown G. A. cutter, bds Center ave
Brown Gilbert, shoemaker, r Union
Brown Harry H. shoemaker, bds Belmont
Brown H. L. shoe manuf. r Washington
Brown J. Willard, (Soule & Brown)
Brown Peleg, tack maker, r South ave
Brown William, shoe manuf. (Brown & Hunt), r Washington
Bryant J. F. shoemaker, r South ave
Bryant Saml. M. shoemaker, r Liberty
Burbank Walter, shoe finisher, r North avenue
Burbee J. G. packer, r South ave
Burgess Baldwin B. engineer, r Centre avenue
Burgess Emery, gentleman, r North ave
Burgess Josiah, shoemaker, r Centre av
Burke David, shoemaker, r Biglow ave
Burke James, shoemaker, r Central
Burke John, laborer, r Liberty
Burke Michael, shoemaker, r Harvard
Burns Matthew, shoemaker, r Elm
Burrell Adna, stable keeper, r Webster
Burrell Benj. shoemaker, r Webster
Burrell C. M. shoemaker, r Union
Burrell Daniel, farmer, r High
Burrell Elias, jobber, r Vernon
Burrell Harvey C. shoemaker, r Webster
Burrell Henry, shoemaker, r Webster
Burrell Hiram, shoemaker, r Hingham
Burrell John, shoemaker, r Union
Burrell John 2d, shoemaker, r Webster
Barrell Lucius, shoemaker, r Hingham
Burrell Reuben, shoemaker, r Water
Burrell Stephen, shoemaker, r Webster
Butler John H. hairdresser, r Dover
Butler Otis H. shoemaker, r School
Butterfield Moses shoemaker, r Plain

CAHOON WILLIAM, boot and shoe manuf. Railroad st
Cain Francis, farmer, r Central
Cain Ambrose, farmer, r Central
Calkins Jesse H. harnessmaker, r cor Brighton and North ave
Callahan Cal, shoemaker, r North ave
Callahan Mike, shoemaker, r Bedford
Callahan Thos. dresser, r Groveland
Callings Charles H. farmer, r Liberty
Campbell John, shoemaker, Dublin row
Campbell Peter, shoemaker, cor Vernon and Liberty
Cancannon Martin, laborer, r Central

ANNUAL CASH DIVIDENDS in the BERKSHIRE LIFE INS. CO.,
Pittsfield, Mass.   Boston Office 95 1-2 Washington St.   (See page 50.)

PLYMOUTH COUNTY DIRECTORY.

Cannaway William, cutter, r North ave
Canterbury Aug. shoemaker, r Adams
Canterbury George, shoemaker, r Adams
Canterbury Geo. D. shoemaker, r Adams
Caplice James, shoemaker, r Deering sq.
Caplice John, shoemaker, r Vernon
Cary Matthew, shoemaker, r North ave
Cary Thomas, laborer, r Dublin row
Cary Thomas, shoemaker, r Union
Cary Wm. shoemaker, r Salem
Carney Richd. shoemaker, r cor. Salem and Union
Carter John W. tack maker, bd South ave
Carter L. M. shoemaker, r Temple
Casey Francis, shoemaker, bds Central
Cassidy Thos. J. painter, bds Union
Ceary Morris, shoemaker, r Deering sq.
Chamberlin Albert, shoe manuf. Plymouth,
Chamberlin Aug. boot maker, r Adams
Chamberlin Edward, merchant, Plymouth
Chamberlin Edward, shoemaker, r Plymouth
Chamberlin John N. boot maker, r Adams
Chamberlin J. P. cutter, r Adams
Chandler Julius B. painter, bds Cottage
Chandler Seth, shoemaker, r Liberty
Chase A. F. box maker, r Bedford
Chase Henry, shoemaker, r Union
Childs Edward, shoemaker, bds Centre avenue
Chubbuck Chas. shoemaker, r Liberty
Chubbuck Francis H. shoemaker, r Webster
Chubbuck Hosea, shoemaker
Chubbuck Thos. A. shoemaker, r Liberty
Churchill Benj. shoemaker, r Washington
Churchill Chas. E. shoemaker, bds Bedford
Churchill Freeman, shoemaker, r Washington
Churchill Otis, cutter, r Washington
Churchill Milliard F. shoemaker, r Hancock
Churchill N. clerk, (N. Rosenfeld,) r Vernon
Clapp Geo. B. shoemaker, r Union
Clark ——, farmer, r Chesnut
Clark James H. shoemaker, r Union
Clark James W. shoemaker, r Bedford
Clark Lemuel F. shoemaker, r Vernon
Clark Patrick, laborer, r Plymouth
Clark Silas, shoemaker, r Salem
Clark Thomas, shoemaker, r Bedford
Clark William P. farmer, r Bedford
Cleverly Geo. grocer, r North Abington
Cleverly Joseph, manuf. r Adams
Cleverly Seth H. shoe manuf. r North Av.
Clift Belas, blacksmith, r School
Clift Ezra V. shoemaker, r Washington
Clift Richard, blacksmith, r School
Cloud Harvey H. tinman, North avenue
Cobb Baxter, leather dealer, r Washington,
Cobb Chas. N. (Cobb & Thompson), r Washington
Cobb Dana, foreman, r Washington
Cobb Edward W. merchant, r Walnut
Cobb Henry, cutter, r Groveland
Cobb Horace B. shoemaker, r Plymouth
Cobb John F. carpenter, r Belmont
Cobbett James, clerk, r Union
Cobbett James E. shoemaker, bd Union
Cobbett Lewis, wheelwright, r Liberty
Cobbett Philip, shoemaker, r North ave
Cochran John, boot treer, r Central
Coffey Tim, shoemaker, r Liberty
Cole B. shoemaker, r Dover
Cole Ephraim, shoemaker, r Glen
Cole E. T. shoemaker, r Beulah
Cole Levi, express, r South ave
Cole Owen, shoemaker, r School
Cole Patrick, shoemaker, r Union
Collins John, shoemaker, r Temple
Colliver Albert, clerk, r Market
Colson Charles, stitcher, r Groveland
Colson Henry, cutter, r Rockland
Colson Samuel, dealer, r Groveland
Colson Samuel jr. dealer, r Groveland
Conant Albion, cutter, r Bedford
Conant C. F. r Bedford
Conant J. Greenleaf, stitcher, bd Thaxter ave
Conant John, shoemaker, r Bedford
Condit Mike, farmer, r Webster
Condon James, shoemaker, r Hingham
Condon John, shoemaker, r Hingham
Condon John, shoemaker, r Liberty
Condon Morris, shoemaker, r Liberty
Condon Michael, shoemaker, r Cork
Condon Mike, shoemaker, r Hingham
Condon Thos. laborer, r Liberty
Coulin James, shoemaker, r Liberty
Conley John, shoemaker, r Dover
Connell Jerry, shoemaker, r Plain
Connelly Patrick, shoemaker, r Adams
Connors Morris, shoemaker, r Salem
Connors Patrick, shoemaker, r Union
Comy John, shoemaker, bds Groveland
Conry James, shoemaker, r School
Conry Luke, shoemaker, r School
Constine Michael, shoemaker, r Centre avenue
Conway Dennis, laborer, r South ave
Conway James, farmer, r Spring
Cooney John, shoemaker, r Liberty
Cooney Patrick, shoemaker, r Liberty
Cook Davis H. shoemaker, r Harvard
Cook Edwin B. tack maker, bd Winter
Cook Geo. W. shoemaker, bds Plymouth
Cook Joshua, auctioneer
Cook Levi, shoemaker, cor. Progress st and Central ave
Cook Randall, groceries, South ave
Cook Randall W. clerk, bd Plymouth
Cook Robt. shoemaker, r cor. Summit and Liberty
Cook Thomas H. shoemaker, r Plymouth
Coombs J. B. circus actor, r Plymouth
Corliss Chas. M. last maker, r Dunbar sq.
Corn Edward, shoemaker, bds Central
Corthell James L. clerk, r Washington
Corthell Jeremiah, shoemaker, r Washington
Corthell J. E. clerk, r Washington
Corthell Merritt, shoemaker, r Washing'n
Corthell Sam'l N. shoemaker, r S. Ward
Corthell Wm. P. county commissioner, r Washington
Cortery Daniel, shoemaker, r Dublin row
Coughlin Daniel, shoemaker, r Bedford
Coughlin John T. laborer, Central
Coughlin John 2d, shoemaker, r Central
Coughlin Timothy, shoemaker, bds Bigelow ave

The "ABINGTON STANDARD," established in 1853, is published by Thos. S. Pratt & Co.

Cox Edwin, shoemaker, bds Washington
Cox Enos, shoemaker, r Centre ave
Cox Hiram, shoemaker, r High
Cox James F. clerk, r Centre ave
Cox Samuel, merchant, r Centre ave
Coy Geo. W. tobacconist, r Union
Coy William, foreman, r from Howard
Crocker A. shoemaker, r Hingham
Crocker E. shoemaker, r Hingham
Crocker Henry, shoemaker, r Webster
Crossfield, Geo. J. shoemaker, r Bedford
Crowell Joel, mechanic, r North Ave
Crowley James, shoemaker, r Union
Culver Albert, book-keeper, (J. Lane & Sons,) r Market
Culver C. H., (Culver & Cleverly,) r Railroad st
Culver John M., grocer, r Railroad st
Cummings Alfred A., stitcher, r Washington
Cunningham Edward, shoemaker, r Central
Cunningham John S., shoemaker, bds Plymouth
Cunningham Patrick, laborer, r Plain
Curtis Abner, shoemanuf. r Union
Curtis Albert, shoefitter, r Summit
Curtis Charles, shoemaker, r Market
Curtis Chas. A. shoemaker, r Union
Curtis Chas. H. shoemaker, r Vernon
Curtis E. B. shoemaker, r Hingham
Curtis Edward E. shoemaker, bd. Union
Curtis Geo. E. shoe manuf., r Market
Curtis Geo. teamster, r Union
Curtis Henry B. mercht. r Union
Curtis H. Stanton, shoemaker, r Webster
Curtis Job, shoemaker, East Ward
Curtis John H. shoemaker, r Union
Curtis jr. Joshua, shoe manuf. r Union
Curtis Leander, shoe manuf. r Union
Curtis Peter, shoemaker r Union
Curtis Samuel G. teamster, r Union
Curtis Warren C. shoemaker, r Liberty
Cushing Brainard, shoemaker, r Water
Cushing David, trunkmaker, r Wa er
Cushing Davis, butcher, r Market
Cushing G. farmer, r Washington
Cushing Galen P. shoe manuf. Washington, r Walnut
Cushing Gilbert A. shoemaker, r Bedford
Cushing Henry L. shoemaker, bd. Washington
Cushing John, shoemaker, r Walnut
Cushing Josiah, shoemaker, r Washington
Cushing Ogden, carpenter, r Linden Av.
Cushing Samuel B. broker, r Washington
Cushing Sylvanus, shoemaker, r Randolph
Cushing 2d Sylvanus, shoe manuf. r Walnut
Cushing Sylvanus E. shoemaker, bd. Randolph
Cushing W. H. shoe cutter, (G. P. Cushing) r Walnut
Cushing W. W. cutter, r Walnut
Cushing Zatto, farmer, r Water
Cushman Isaiah, cutter, r Bedford
Cushman Josiah, deputy sheriff, r Bedford
Cushman Sam'l, shoemaker, r Centre Av.

DAGNAN, FRANCIS, shoemaker, r Central
Dailey Jeremiah, carpenter, r near R. R.
Daily Cornelius, tailor, r Union
Damon Chas. shoemaker, r Pond
Damon Henry, shoemaker
Damon Howard, shoe finisher, r Quincy
Damon Joseph, farmer, r Hingham
Damon Joseph E., farmer, bds Randolph
Damon Joseph J., marketman, r Randolph
Damon Joshua, shoemaker, bds Cross
Damon Martin W., pattern maker, r Union
Damon Pyam, shoemaker, bds Vernon
Damon Samuel A., section master, r Adams
Damon Thomas W. shoemaker, r Webster
Damon Washington, shoemaker, bd Vernon
Damon Wm. W., shoemaker, r Liberty
Daniels William, shoemaker, bds Centre Avenue
Daniels Wm. H., shoemaker, r Randolph
Darling Marcus, jeweller, r Water
Darrow Rev. G. R., r Washington
Davis Albert, postmaster, r Washington
Davis James, shoemaker, r Central
Davis John, shoemaker, r Liberty
Davis Walter S., farmer, bds Vernon
Davis Wm. H., painter, Washington
Davy Alonzo M., shoemaker, r Granite
Davy Wm. A., clerk, bds Granite
Dawes Nath. machininst, r South Ave
Dawes Sylvester H., shoemaker, r Union
Dean Lindley M., shoemaker, r Centre Avenue
Dempsey John, laborer, r near R. R.
Denham Edwin H., bootmaker, r Randolph
Denham Henry, shoemaker, r Randolph
Denly Thorne, shoemaker, r Union
Denley William D. blacksmith, r Liberty
Denel Thorne, cutter, r Union
Devlyn Geo., shoemaker, bds Groveland
De Vols James, carpenter, r West
Dill Chas. H. 1st, shoemaker, Hingham
Dill Chas. H., 2nd, boot and shoe manufacturer, r Union
Dill Joseph, shoe manuf., Webster
Dill Jos., shoe manuf., r Liberty
Dill Joseph jr., shoemaker, bds Webster
Dill J. W. shoemaker, r Hingham
Dill Wesley, shoemaker, r Union
Doane Jesse, shoe pedler, r Market
Dodge Rev. Benj. r Randolph
Doherty Joseph, shoemaker, r Deering sq
Doherty Patrick, shoemaker,
Donahoe James, boot and shoemaker, r Central
Donahue Michael C. shoemaker, bds Central
Donahue Patrick, shoemaker, bds cor. Vernon and Liberty
Donahue Timothy, shoemaker, bds Plain
Donahue John, shoemaker, r Central
Donahue Timothy, shoemaker, bds Central
Donan Patrick, shoemaker, r Centre ave
Donovan B. shoemaker, r Hingham
Donovan Charles, clerk, bds Liberty

DIVIDENDS ADDED to the POLICY in the BERKSHIRE often exceed the premium paid; are NON-FORFEITABLE and will be redeemed in CASH ON DEMAND. (See page 50.)

Donavan Cornelius, dry goods, r Liberty
Donavan Danl. shoemaker, r Bigelow
Donavan Henry, shoemaker, r Union
Donavan Henry D. stitcher, r Union
Donavan Jerry, shoemaker, r Deering sq
Donovan Michael, shoemaker, Webster
Donavan Timothy, shoemaker, r Liberty
Donham George E. Dr. dentist, bds Liberty
Doagherty John, shoemaker, r Central
Douglas William, eating house, Union
Downey Dennis A. shoemaker, r Union
Driscoll Jeremiah, shoemaker, r North avenue
Driscoll John, shoemaker, r Hingham
Driscoll Mike, crimper, r near Railroad
Driscoll Timothy, laborer, r Central
Doane Edward, boot treer r Rockland
Dudley Dr. Henry W. r Centre ave
Dunbar Asaph, gentleman, r Washington
Dunbar Geo. C. shoemaker, r Union
Dunbar Henry, shoemaker, r Hingham
Dunbar Lucius E. shoemaker, bds Washington
Dunham Andrew, shoemaker, r Washington
Dunham Brackley C. cutter, r Washington
Dunham C. A. merchant, r Groveland
Dunham Cornelius, merchant, r Centre avenue
Dunham Cornelius L. grocer, (Dunham & Pratt,) r Centre ave. near R. R.
Dunham E. shoe cutter, r Orange
Dunham Henry, shoe manuf. r Centre ave
Dunham jr. Henry, shoe manuf. bds Centre ave
Dunham Henry L. bds Centre ave
Dunham Jesse, shoe cutter, r Orange
Dunn Michael, shoemaker, Hingham
Dunn Jos. shoemaker, r Liberty
Durant Andrew, last maker
Durant D. F. last maker
Dyer Bela, farmer, r South Avenue
Dyer Christopher, gentleman, r Washington
Dyer Henry B. shoe cutter, r Orange
Dyer James B. gentleman, r Washington
Dyer James B. jr. dentist, r Washington
Dyer N. N. groceries, hardware and varieties, cor. So. Av. and Washington
Dyer Sam'l, farmer, r High
Dyer Sam'l, periodicals, Washington
Dyer Samuel 2d, butcher, r South Avenue
Dyer Samuel B. gentleman, r Washington
Dyer Sam'l N. clerk, r Washington
Dyer jr. Sam'l N. com mercht. r Washington

EASTERBROOK CHAS. G., printer, r cor. Walnut & Thaxter
Eaton Shepard, shoemaker, r North Av
Edson George, crimper, r Rockland
Edwards Rev. Henry L., r Washington
Ellis Benj. F., oyster saloon, r Market
Ellis Freeman, tack maker, r Boston
Ellis Horatio, machinest, r Washington
Ellis John, shoemaker, r Dover
Ellis N. B., shoemaker, r Market
Ellis Reuben, shoemaker, r Liberty
English Thomas, shoemaker, r Washington

Erskine M. A., shoemaker, r Washington
Erskine J. S. painter, r Washington
Erskine Valentine, shoemaker, r Washington
Estes Daniel B. watchmaker, r Union
Estes Edward, shoemaker, r Spring
Estes Elijah, carpenter, r Union
Estes J. J., druggist, Union
Estes Robert, blacksmith, r Market
Estes R. T., (Estes & Whiting,) at West Hanover
Estes Warren, shoemaker, r Market
Eustice Edward W., shomaker, bds Liberty
Eustis Thomas F., shoemaker, r Liberty
Everson Geo. N., shoemaker, r Randolph
Everson Isaac, shoemaker, r Hingham
Everson L. F., shoemaker, r Plain
Everson Seth C., carpenter, r Plymouth
Everson Wilmot V., shoemaker, bds Plymouth

FAIRBANKS C. W. (Fairbanks & Poole) r Temple
Fairbanks William, shoemaker, r Plain
Farrar Greenleaf, finisher. r Centre Av.
Farrar Job P. shoe manuf. r Dunbar Sq.
Farrar J. P. (Floyd & Farrar) r Columbus Square
Farrar John C. finisher, (S. Vaughan) r Washington
Farrar Judson N. cashier, r Washington
Farrar Lucian W. jeweler, r Dunbar Sq.
Farrington J. pedlar, r Washington
Faunce Arthur M. carpenter, bds. Walnut
Faunce Elijah, carpenter, Thaxter Av.
Faunce Ichabod W. mason, r Centre Av.
Faunce Quincy A. mason, r Centre Av.
Faxon Alfred W. shoemaker, r Belmont
Faxon Andrew, bds. cor. Washington and Rockland
Faxon B. E. grocer, Washington, bds. same
Faxon Calvin, shoemaker, r Belmont
Faxon Lucius, shoe manuf. cor. Washington and Rockland
Faxon William, stitcher, r Bedford
Fay Patrick, shoemaker, bds. Plain
Fenner ——, silversmith, r Washington
Fenno James, shoemaker, r Liberty
Fenno James H. shoemaker, r Webster
Ferris H. hotel, Centre Abington
Fickett Elbridge L. shoemaker, bd. Union
Fitzgibbon James, shoemaker, r Dover
Fielding J. F. gentleman, r Temple
Fitzgerald John, laborer, r Central
Fish Lee B. shoemaker, r Washington
Fitzgerald William H. marble worker, r Central
Flanegan Thomas, laborer, r Plymouth
Flemming Edward, shoemaker, Liberty
Fleming William, cutter, r North ave
Floyd Ira, shoe manufacturer, (Floyd & Farres), Washington
Floyd John A. shoemaker, r Orange
Flynn ——, laborer, r Centre ave
Flynn Jeremiah, shoemaker, bds Central
Flynn Michael, shoemaker, r Salem
Flynn Patrick, laborer, r Union
Flynn Wm. laborer, r Central
Foley Cornelius, shoemaker, r Dunbar sq
Foly Patrick, shoemaker, r Plain

The "ABINGTON STANDARD" is published in the largest town in Plymouth County, and is a Good Advertising Medium.

Foley Patrick, shoemaker, r Summit
Folsom Hiram, harness maker, r Belmont
Forbes Wm. shoemaker, r Union
Ford Augustus N. shoemaker, r Randolph
Ford Austin, shoemaker, r Randolph
Ford Austin A. shoemaker, bds Randolph
Ford B. F. painter, r Union
Ford Daniel A. farmer, r Centre ave
Ford David, farmer, r Randolph
Ford Eldridge G. expressman, r Washington
Ford Gilbert, shoemaker, r Union
Ford James, groceries, r Bedford
Ford James, shoemaker, r Market
Ford James, carpenter, bds Vernon
Ford J. L. shoemaker, r Union
Ford John, cutter, r North Abington
Ford John, shoemaker, r Bedford
Ford John, shoemaker, bds Union
Ford John, shoemaker, r Liberty
Ford John C., shoemaker, r North Ave
Ford Jos. E., shoemaker, r Randolph
Ford Oscar, shoemaker, bds Union
Ford Lewis, carpenter, bds Vernon
Ford Lucius, shoemaker, r Randolph
Ford Lucius, bootmaker, bds Bedford
Ford Lucius jr., shoemaker, bds Bedford
Ford Solomon, bds Randolph
Ford Thomas, shoemaker, r Market
Ford Wilson, shoemaker, cor Randolph & Hancock
Ford Wilson, shoemaker, bds Plymouth
Foster Alonzo T., shoemaker, r Liberty
Foster Freeman, cutter, r Washington
Foster Freeman, shoemaker, r Washington
Foster Hiram, shoemaker, r Cottage
Foster Lorenzo, shoemaker, r Liberty
Foster Nathan B., clerk, bds Market
Foster Samuel, shoemaker, r Washington
Foster Solomon, currier, r Market
Foster Thomas, stitcher, r Liberty
Fox ——— laborer r near R. R.
Francis Thos. F., clerk, r Exchange
Freeman Noah, shoemaker, bds Liberty
French Chas., shoemaker, r Market
French Edwin F., clerk, bds Birch
French Francis M., clerk, r Union
French Francis M., shoemaker, r Liberty
French Joseph, grocer, Water, r Union
French Joseph E., shoemaker, r Water
French Wm., laborer, r Washington
French Joseph, painter, r Washington
Friar John, shoemaker, r Spring
Friar William, shoemaker, r Spring
Fuller John, shoemaker, r West
Fuller Josiah F. clerk bds. Union
Fuller J. K. boot manuf. (Fuller & Blanchard) r Union
Fuller Josiah K. shoemaker, r Union
Fullerton Edward, shoemaker, r High
Fullerton Harvey, shoemaker, r Harvard
Fullerton Henry W. shoemaker, r Washington
Fullerton Lysander N. shoemaker, r High
Fullerton Nahum, shoemaker, r Washington
Fullerton Noah, shoemaker, r Washington
Fullerton Samuel, shoemaker, r Glen
Fulton Daniel M. shoemaker, r Temple

GAINS WM. shoemaker, r Centre Av.

Gannett Thomas, tackmaker, r So. Av.
Garcelon Peter, carpenter, r Randolph
Gard Peter, shoemaker, r Cross
Gardner James C. shoemaker, r Liberty
Gardner Richard, shoemaker, r Union
Gardner Saunders, shoemaker, r Liberty
Gardner Washington, shoemaker, r Pond
Garrity Lawrence, shoemaker, r No. Av.
Gary Zephaniah, tackmaker, r Quincy
Geardon John, shoemaker, r Bigelow
Geary Thomas, shoemaker, r Salem
Gifford Chas. T. shoemaker, bd. Cross
Gibbs Henry L. shoemaker, bds. Washington
Gibbs Leonard, engineer, r Washington
Gibbs Warren S. shoemaker, bds. Washington
Gilbert Judson, shoemaker, r Centre Av.
Gilbert Julius C. shoemaker, r Washington
Gilbride Bernard, shoemaker, r Centre Av.
Giles Jesse H. last manuf. r Centre Av.
Giles J. H. machinist, r School
Giles John, tailor, r Bedford
Gilman Caleb, r Water
Gilman George H. eating and billiard saloon, Railroad st., r same
Gilson B. shoemaker, r Rockland
Gilson Jonas, carpenter, r Birch
Gilson Lorenzo C. painter, r Union
Gilson William R. mechanic, r Centre Av.
Glover Cyrus J., shoemaker, bds Washington
Gloyd Daniel, shoemaker, r Plymouth
Glover Luther, shoemaker, r Washington
Gloyd Spencer, shoemaker, r Belmont
Gorman John, patent agent, r Brighton
Gorman Morris, shoemaker, bds Groveland
Gormley John, dresser, r Washington
Goss Henry, shoemaker, r Hingham
Goss Walter S. shoemaker, r Washington
Gould Henry, shoemaker, r Union
Gowell William, stone cutter, r Adams
Grace William, shoemaker, r Hingham
Graham Thomas, shoemaker, r Hancock
Gray John, shoemaker, r Webster
Gray Joshua S. shoemaker, r Union
Green James J. shoemaker, bds Liberty
Green Jerentiah, laborer, r Centre ave
Green Michael, shoemaker, r Bigelow
Green Patrick, shoemaker, r Centre ave
Green Patrick, shoemaker, r Liberty
Groce Byron, student, r Liberty
Groce Dexter, shoe manuf. North ave
Groce Nath. shoemaker, r Liberty
Groce Wm. shoemaker, r Liberty
Grover Almon F. expressman, r Union
Grover Chas. H. grocer, r Union
Grover D. H. grocer, r Union
Grover J. O. express, r North ave
Gurney Albert, shoemaker, r Hancock
Gurney Andrew, shoemaker, r School
Gurney Chandler, farmer, r Washington
Gurney Cyrus, tack manuf. r South ave
Gurney Davis, shoe manuf. cor. South ave, and Washington
Gurney D. B. tack manuf. Centre ave. r at South Abington
Gurney D. B. tack manuf. r Washington
Gurney Edmund, farmer, r Washington
Gurney Edwin, shoemaker, r South ave

The terms for **ENDOWMENT**, and **TEN ANNUAL LIFE POLICIES** in the **BERKSHIRE** are peculiarly favorable, and rates lower than in any Note Company. (See page 50.)

Gurney E. L. music teacher, r South ave
Gurney Francis, shoemaker, r Hancock
Gurney Fredk. H. clerk, bds Washington
Gurney Henry, shoemaker, r Washington
Gurney James C. shoemaker, r Vernon
Gurney James S. shoemaker, r Webster
Gurney J. H. sole cutter, r Washington
Gurney John, shoemaker, r Washington
Gurney Jos. W. shoemaker, r cor. Webster and Hingham
Gurney Richd. shoemaker, r Washington
Gurney Samuel, shoemaker, r Washington
Gurney Thomas, cutter, r Liberty
Gurney Thos. W. r Webster
Gurney Wesley, stitcher, r Webster
Gurney Wm., shoemaker, r Hancock
Gurney Wm. H., clerk, r School

HACKETT EDMOND, laborer, r Liberty
Hackett Joseph H., mill hand, r Adams
Hackett Seth H., mill hand, r Adams
Hackey Daniel, shoemaker, r Cross
Hall Silas W., shoemaker, bds Washington
Hallett H., shoemaker, r Liberty
Hallett Amasa, cutter, r East Ward
Hammond Chas. F., shoemaker, r Liberty
Hammond David, shoemaker, bds Union
Hanlen Timothy A., shoemaker, bds Groveland
Hannan John, laborer, r Union
Harden James F., painter, r Washington
Harding Frank, shoemaker, r Harvard
Harding Morton E., painter, r Dunbar
Hardy J. W. grocer, (Noyes & Hardy) r Washington
Harlow A. H. clerk, r Washington
Harlow Frank B., shoemaker, r Washington
Harlow George, carpenter, r Washington
Harlow Geo., carpenter, bds Bedford
Harlow Zaccheus, carpenter, r Centre Av
Harper John, clerk, r Union
Harrington Dan'l, shoemaker, bd. Union
Harrigan James, shoemaker bd. Water
Harris Jacob B. lawyer, r Union
Harris James H. shoe manuf. r Central
Harris John H. farmer, r Centre Avenue
Harris Dr. John T. cor. Elm and Rockland
Hart Matthew, shoemaker, r Union
Hartleff John, laborer, r Linden Av.
Harvell Elisha, cutter, at Lane's
Hastings B. F. physician, r Union
Hatch Geo. shoemaker, r cor. Bigelow Av. and Union
Hatch J. Warren, shoe manuf. r cor. Progress St. and Centre Av.
Hatch Samuel G. shoemaker, r Webster
Hatch Thos. cooper, r Water
Hayes Dennis, shoemaker, r North Av.
Hayes John, laborer, r near R. R.
Hayes John, shoemaker, r Bigelow Av.
Hayes Michael, shoemaker, r Central
Healy Aaron, shoemaker, r Harvard
Healy Oliver G. carpenter, r Beulah
Hedge, J, shoemaker
Henderson M. H. shoemaker, r Plymouth

Herring John E. blacksmith, r Dearing
Herron Patrick, shoemaker, r Union
Hern John, farmer, r Liberty
Hersey Avery, r Plymouth
Hersey George E. clerk, bd. Washington
Hersey I. trial justice, r Plymouth
Hersey Jason, livery stable, r Washington
Hersey Timothy, shoemaker, r Bedford
Hetherington Chas. carpenter, b.ds. Washington
Heywood William, shoemaker, bds. Centre Av.
Hibbard Albert, shoemaker, r Union
Hibbard Chas. A. shoemaker, r Union
Hibbard Harrison, shoemaker, r Union
Hibbard Wm. H. shoe manuf. r Webster
Hickey Cornelius, laborer, r North ave.
Higgins Patrick, shoemaker, r North ave.
Hiland Morgan, shoemaker, r Union
Hill Frank, shoemaker, r South ave.
Hill Isaac, shoemaker, r Washington
Hill I. F. clerk, r South Avenue
Hill Roger, laborer, r near R. R.
Hobart Albert, shoemaker, r East Ward
Hobart Hon. Benj. r South ave.
Hobart Caleb, r East Ward
Hobart Elbert F. shoemaker, r Brighton
Hobart John, shoemaker, r Hingham
Hobart Walter H. clerk, r at E. Bridgewater
Hobbs John, fireman, r Deering sq.
Hobson Robert, barber, Union, r Plain cor. Water
Holbrook Amos L. shoemaker, bds. Union
Holbrook David, shoemaker, bds. Union
Holbrook Dexter, shoemaker, r Salem
Holbrook Enos, shoemaker, r Salem
Holbrook Franklin, shoemaker, bds. Salem
Holbrook Jerome A. shoemaker, r Bedford
Holbrook Loring, furniture, r Washington
Holbrook O. M. undertaker, r Market
Holbrook Otis, shoemaker, r Walnut
Holbrook Quincy, shoemaker, r Salem
Holbrook Quincy 2d, shoemaker, r North Ave.
Holbrook Richard, shoemaker, r Union
Holbrook Soranus, shoemaker, bds. Union
Holbrook Turner, shoemaker, r Cross
Holbrook Turner R shoemaker, r Union
Hollis Edwin, shoemaker, bds. Bedford
Hollis Edwin F. shoemaker, bds. Bedford
Hollis John, shoemaker, r Temple
Hollis Wm. F. shoemaker, r Randolph
Holmes Abraham, clerk, r Washington
Holmes Bradford R. shoemaker, r Randolph
Holmes Farrell, laborer, r Washington
Holmes Isaac K. shoemaker, Centre ave.
Holt John F. supt. alms house, Central
Holt Meltiah E. shoemaker, bds Hancock
Hook Chas. O. shoemaker, r Union
Hooker Edwin B. shoemaker, bds. Plymouth, near N. A.
Hooker Joseph, shoemaker, bds. Central
Hopkins Isaac, shoemaker, r Market
Hough George, machinist, bds North ave
House James, grocer, r Liberty
House Julius jr., shoemaker, r North Av.
House J. L. clerk, r Webster

The "ABINGTON STANDARD," established in 1853, is published by Thos. S. Pratt & Co.

Howard Elijah C., cutter, r Washington
Howe Charles, shoemaker, r School
Howe David, butcher, r School
Howe Rev. Sereno, r Linden Avenue
Howland Caleb, shoemaker, r Glen
Howland Chas. W., clerk, r Bedford
Howland Freeman P., insurance, r Bedford
Howley Patrick, shoemaker, r near R. R.
Howley Thomas, shoemaker, r near R. R.
Hughs R. J. shoemaker, r Hingham
Hunt Benj. N. r Washington
Hunt Chas. H. shoemaker, bds. Randolph
Hunt David, shoemaker, r Union
Hunt David F. shoemaker, r Union
Hunt Ebenezer, farmer, r Bedford
Hunt Ed. G. shoemaker, bds. Union
Hunt Emerson, laborer, bds. Plymouth
Hunt Fredk. W. shoemaker, r Union
Hunt Geo. H. shoemaker, r Union
Hunt Gilbert, farmer, r Union
Hunt Gridley, shoemaker, r Union
Hunt Henry, boot and shoe manuf. Washington
Hunt Horace M. shoemaker, bds. Union
Hunt John W. *(Brown & Hunt)*, r Ashland
Hunt Jos. W. shoemaker, r Union
Hunt Kingman, shoemaker, r Hancock
Hunt Leander, shoemaker, r Union
Hunt Marcus N. shoemaker, r Hancock
Hunt N. T. town clerk, r Washington
Hunt Orlando, shoemaker, r Hancock
Hunt Reuben, drover, r Union
Hunt Seth, farmer, r High
Hunt Thomas, shoe manuf. r Washington
Hunt T. J. boot and shoe manuf. r Washington
Hunt Ward, stitcher, r Groveland
Hunt Washington, cutter, r Washington
Hunt Wm. shoemaker, r Union
Hunt Wm. E. farmer, bds. Bedford
Hunter William, shoemaker, Dover
Hunting Chas. farmer, r Washington
Hurd Wm. A. shoemaker, r Bedford
Hylan Thos. shoemaker, r Summer
Hylett Chas. shoemaker, r Union
Hyslop John, shoemaker, r Belmont
Hyslop jr. John, carpenter, bds. Belmont

JACKSON ARTHUR, shoemaker, r Cottage
Jackson Francis E. machinist, Dunbar Square
Jackson Isaac R. farmer, r Randolph
Jackson Luther, farmer, r Randolph
Jackson Winslow, shoemaker, r Bedford
Jacobs David, shoemaker, r Water
Jacobs jr. David, shoemaker, r Water
Jenkins Chas. S. shoemaker, r Washington
Jenkins David, shoemaker, r Plymouth
Jenkins Isaiah, shoemaker, r Union
Jenkins Lemuel, shoemaker, r Union
Jenkins Nathan S. shoe manuf. r Union
Jenkins Warren, shoemaker, r Linden Avenue
Jenkins Woodbridge, mercht. r Washing'n
Jenkins Zenas, selectman, r East Ward
Johnson Dan'l, shoemaker, r Union
Johnson jr. Dan'l, shoemaker, bds. Union
Johnson Jacob, bootmaker, bds. Cross
Johnson Jacob, wood cutter, r Washington
Johnson James B. shoemaker, r Washington
Johnson John A. shoemaker, bds. Union
Johnson Joseph F. shoemaker, r Washington
Johnson William, shoemaker, r Hingham
Jones Christopher B. trader, r Pond
Jones Ebenezer W. shoemaker, r Plymouth
Jones Geo. W. shoemaker, r Pond
Jones John, shoe cutter, r Plymouth
Jones Sam'l, shoemaker, bds. Randolph
Jones Winslow L. mariner, r Centre Av.
Jones Wm. shoemaker, r Washington
Joslyn Eleazer, shoemaker, r Market
Josselyn Marquis F. tack maker, r Harvard
Joy Benj. F. shoemaker, bds. Bedford
Joy Martin, cutter, r Washington

KALEHER JOHN, laborer, r Central
Kamel James, shoemaker, r near R. R.
Kannelly John, shoemaker, bds. Plymouth
Kanneally John, shoemaker, r Adams
Kanneally Timothy, laborer, r Adams
Kanney Augustus, cigar maker, r Market
Keath E. shoemaker, r Temple
Kearing James, shoemaker, r Union
Keith J. E. lawyer, Centre ave r Washington
Kendrigan John, blacksmith, r Union
Kennedy, shoemaker, r Dover
Keene Bradley J. shoemaker, r Centre ave
Keene Geo. R. carpenter, r Walnut
Keene James, shoemaker, r Central
Keene J. clerk, r Union
Keene John F. pedlar, r Market
Keene Josiah, farmer, r Randolph
Keene Julius, shoemaker, r Market
Keene Melzer, shoemaker, r Water
Keene Saml. shoemaker, cor. Liberty and Market
Keloe William, fish dealer, r Adams
Kelleher Daniel, shoemaker, r Centre ave
Kelleher Jeremiah, shoemaker, r Washington
Kelley Albert F. clerk, r Union
Kelley Edward, farmer, r Plymouth
Kelley Patrick, shoemaker, r Centre ave
Kelley Thos. shoemaker, r Plymouth
Kenney Charles, shoemaker, r Plymouth
Kenney John, shoemaker, r Plymouth
Kennedy Hugh, shoemaker, r Deering sq
Kennedy Patrick, shoemaker, r Cork
Kennedy Timothy, boot treer, North Abington
Kepen Goddard, shoemaker, r Glen
Kilbride Thomas, shoemaker, r Central
Kimball E. A. machinist, Central ave r same
Kimball Jos. E. shoemaker, r cor. Orange and Washington
Kindregon John M. shoemaker, bds Central
King A. P. express, r South ave
King William, carpenter, r South ave
Kingman Lucius, shoemaker, r Hancock
Kingston J. R. shoemaker, r Dover
Knox Ellis, expressman, r Webster
Lane Albert, shoemaker, r North Av.
Lane Alonzo, merchant, bds. cor. Union and Market

Policy Holders in the BERKSHIRE LIFE INSURANCE COMPANY of Pittsfield, Mass., DO NOT FORFEIT THEIR POLICIES by reason of FAILURE TO PAY their premiums. (See page 50.)

Lane Ceron P. pedlar, r Market
Lane Chas. H. shoemaker, bds. Liberty
Lane E. (*Lane & Sons*) r at New Orleans
Lane Eldridge, shoemaker, r Union
Lane Jenkins, (*Lane & Sons*) shoe manuf.
Lane John, merchant, r Union.
Lane John F. shoemaker, cor. Washington and Rockland
Lane Marshall, shoemaker, r Union
Lane Patrick, shoemaker, r Dublin Row
Lane Thomas, shoemaker, r Liberty
Lane Richmond J. (*Lane & Sons*) mercht.
Lane Z. N. shoe manuf. r Union
Lane Z. M. (*Lane & Sons*) r Union
Lang Andrew, shoemaker r Centre Av.
Lannin Rob't, shoemaker, r Union
Lannin Wm. shoemaker, r Union
Lapham Andrew, shoemaker, r Union
Lapham Melzer, shoemaker, r Vernon
Lawrence Albert H. painter, bds. Washington
Lawrence Franklin N. shoemaker, r Linden Av.
Lawrence Geo. R. shoemaker, bds. Union
Leach A. cutter, bds. Liberty
Leach John, machinist, r Havard
Leahy Cornelius, laborer, r Salem
Leahy John, shoemaker, r Deering Sq.
Lean Wm. M. blacksmith, r Washington
Leavitt Geo. E. shoemaker, bds. Plymoath
Leavitt Harry, shoemaker, r Water
Leavitt Winslow, farmer, r South Av.
Lee Michael, shoemaker, r Spring
Leighton ——, shoemaker, r North Av.
Lewellen Henry, shoemaker r Vernon
Lewellan John, laborer, r Union
Lewellen Wm. shoemaker, r Liberty
Lewis George, carpenter, r Plain
Lewis Henry M. shoemaker, r Union
Lewis John F. shoemaker, bds Hancock
Lewis Wm. carpenter, r Summer
Lincoln James B. cutter, r Centre Av.
Lincoln James P. shoemaker, r Centre
Lincoln Matthew, shoemaker, r Harvard
Lincoln Samuel B. painter, r Brighton
Lincoln W. P. shoemaker, r Temple
Lincoln W. W. shoemaker, r Brighton
Lindsay Martin, shoemaker, r Plain
Linnell Josiah, shoemaker, r Centre Av.
Litchfield L. Elwin, shoemaker, r Vernon
Litchfield N. P. stitcher, r Orange
Locke James, shoemaker, r Vernon
Locke Parmelius, cutter, r Washington
Looby Jeremiah, shoemaker, r Liberty
Lord Geo. school teacher, bds. Randolph
Loring Edwin, shoemaker, r Washington
Loring James E. shoemaker, r Bedford
Loring Jos. carpenter, bd Vernon
Loring Morton, carpenter, bd Vernon
Loud Alden S. grocer, r Rockland
Loud Chas. shoemaker, r Union
Loud C. G. boot manuf. Rockland
Loud John M. shoemaker, r Dunbar sq
Loud Joshua B. shoemaker, r Walnut
Loud Lem. shoemaker, bd Liberty
Loud Livingston W. shoemaker, r Bedford
Loud Loring, carpenter, r Rockland
Loud Percie, carpenter, r Bedford
Loud Rueben, farmer, r Salem
Loud Samuel, boot maker, r Centre ave
Loud S. T. packer, r Rockland
Loud Tyler, shoemaker, r Spruce

Lovell Marcena, shoemaker, r Union
Lovell W. S. clerk, bds Union
Lowell Elihu B. cutter, r North ave
Lowell Ira F. boot and shoe manuf. Noav
Lowell Nelson, shoemaker, r North ave
Lucas Albert, shoemaker, r Union
Lucas Daniel, shoemaker, bds Washing.
Luddy Patrick, boot treer
Lufkin Albert, shoemaker, r Washington
Lydon John, shoemaker, r Adams
Lyon John P. carpenter, r Adams
Lyons Henry, laborer, r Central
Lyons James, shoemaker, r Union
Lynch James, shoemaker, r Central

MAGUIRE JOHN, shoemaker, r Bedford
Maguire Owen, shoemaker, r Union
Mahan Hugh, shoemaker, r Salem
Mahoney Timothy, laborer, r Central
Maloy John, shoemaker, r Washington
Malumpy John, laborer, r Salem
Manley Carlos, shoemaker, r Lincoln
Manley Edward F. shoemaker, bd Wash.
Manley jr. Patrick, shoemaker, r Wash.
Mann Gustavus N. shoemaker, r Liberty
Mann Horace E. shoemaker, bd Union
Mann John, farmer, bd Summit
Mann jr. John, shoemaker, r Summit
Mann Josiah, shoemaker, r Union
Mangan Michael, laborer, r Liberty
Manson A. J. shoemaker, r Union
Maragan Michael, laborer, r Central
Maragan Timothy, shoemaker, bd Liberty
Maguire James, shoemaker, r Bigelow ave
Macooney James, shoemaker, r Cross
Mackin John, shoemaker, r Salem
Magney John, shoemaker, r Liberty
Mara James, shoemaker, r Salem
Marsh jr. E. shoemaker, r School
Maxie William H. tinsmith, r Adams
Maxwell Chas. W. shoemaker, r Adams
McAuroa Anthony, shoemaker, r Cork
McAuroa, Michael, farmer, r Cork
McAvoy Joseph, shoemaker, r North ave
McCarter Chas. H. blacksmith, bds Wash.
McCarter M. C. blacksmith, r Washington
McCarty Callahan, laborer, r Washington
McCarty Charles, shoemaker, bds cor. Bigelow ave and Union
McCarty Dennis, tailor, r Liberty
McCarty Daniel, shoemaker, r Centre ave
McCarthy John, laborer, r Plain
McCarthy John, shoemaker, r Salem
McCarthy John, shoemaker, r Deering sq
McCarthy Patrick, shoemaker, r Union
McCarthy Simon, farmer, r Plain
McCarthy Thomas, farmer, r Plain
McClintock George, laborer, r Temple
McConney James F. shoemaker, cor. Washington and Bedford
McCreight Rogers, laborer, r Union
McDevitt Wm. shoemaker, r Groveland
McElvine Samuel, cutter, r North ave
McGovern Philip, shoemaker, r Central
McGrath James, shoemaker, r Vernon
McGuire James, laborer, r Spruce
McHugh Brian, shoemaker, r Central
McIlveen Andrew, shoe cutter, r North
McKenna A. W. shoe cutter, Centre ave
McKenna Jerry, cutter, r Union
McKenney Frank, shoemaker, r North
McKenney Henry, shoe maker, r Bedford
McKenney John D. clerk, r Dunbar sq

The **"ABINGTON STANDARD"** is published in the largest town in Plymouth County, and is a Good Advertising Medium.

McKenney Moses, shoemaker, r Washington
McKenney S. shoemaker, r Orange
McKensie Danl. shoemaker, r Chestnut
McMakins Geo. shoemaker, North ave
McMakins John, shoemaker, r Randolph
McMorrow John, shoemaker, r Union
McNamara Michael, shoemaker, r Liberty
McNamara Thomas, shoemaker, bds Central
McNary Timothy, laborer, r North ave
McPherson Henry M. shoemaker, Haucock
Mearty Timothy, harness maker, Temple
Mears Samuel T. shoemaker, r Bedford
Meigs Wm. F. painter, r Washington
Mellefort Robert, shoemaker, r Central
Mera Cornelius, shoemaker, r Cork
Merrett Charles, sailor, r Plain
Merritt Edward, mechanic, bds Washington
Merritt Francis, shoemaker, r High
Merritt Ira, tool manuf. r Washington
Merritt Jos. shoemaker, r Vernon
Merritt Whitman B. shoemaker, r Niles
Meserve Alonzo, student, r Adams
Meserve Chas. shoe manuf. r Adams
Meserve Cushing, shoe finisher, r Washington, N. Abington
Meserve Justin, shoemaker, r Adams
Millet Benj. shoemaker, r Centre ave near R. R.
Millet Chas. A. shoemaker, bds Centre ave near R. R.
Millet Herbert M. shoemaker, bds Centre ave near R. R.
Mitchell Chas. farmer, r Market
Mitchell Chas. W. shoemaker, r Market
Mitchell John, shoemaker, r Washington
Mitchell John, B. shoemaker, r Washington
Mone Francis, shoemaker, cor. Vernon and Liberty
Mone Francis, shoemaker, r Union
Monroe James, shoemaker, bd Union
Monroe James A. shoemaker, bd Union
Monroe Joshua L. shoemaker, bd Union
Moncoe Saml. shoemaker, r Spring
Moran Felix, boot maker, r Central
Moran James, shoemaker, r Vernon
Moreland Thomas, shoemaker, r Dover
Morey Chas. shoemaker, r School
Morrey Saml. carpenter, r Market
Morris Elijah G. shoemaker, r Washington
Morrissey John, shoemaker, r Union
Morse Job L. shoemaker, cor. Granite and Cottage
Morton Edwin, shoemaker, r Central
Morton Geo. H. shoemaker, r Centre ave
Moulton Henry, market, r Water
Mullally James, shoemaker, r Union
Mulreedy Luke, shoemaker, r Union
Murphy Dennis, laborer, r Plain
Murphy John, laborer, r Dublin row
Murphy Thomas, shoemaker, r Bedford
Murphy Thomas, shoemaker, r North av
Murphy Patrick, shoemaker, bds Water
Murray Cyrus D. shoemaker, bds Groveland
Murray Wm. shoemaker, r Chestnut
Murrell Jerry, shoemaker, r Market

NASH AUGUSTINE, shoemaker, r Central
Nash A. M. manuf. r Washington
Nash Bela G. shoe manuf. r Washington
Nash Bela T. shoe manuf. r Washington
Nash Chas. D. clerk, bds Washington
Nash E. Dexter, shoemaker, r Washington
Nash E. M. broker, r Washington
Nash Francis A. clerk, r Washington
Nash Francis H. shoemaker, r Washington
Nash Gridley, shoe manuf. bds Washington
Nash James D. shoemaker, r Centre av
Nash Gridley T. (M & G. T. Nash,) r Washington
Nash James E. oyster saloon, Centre ave
Nash James O. shoemaker, r Washington
Nash J. B. farmer, r Washington
Nash Joshua H. bds Washington
Nash Joshua L. shoe manuf. r Washington
Nash Leonard, shoemaker, r Washington
Nash Louis A. cutter, r Central
Nash Lysander, shoemaker, r Brighton
Nash Lysander B. shoemaker, r Plymouth
Nash Merritt, clerk, r Washington
Nash Micah (M. & G. T. Nash,) shoe manf. r Thaxter ave
Nash Minot, farmer, r Central
Nash Sylvanus, apothecary, r Washington
Nash Sylvanus, shoemaker, r Walnut
Nash Wm. Capt. carpenter, r Washington
Nash Wm. H. shoemaker, bds Washington
Navins Patrick, laborer, r Washington
Neate Joseph, shoemaker, r Randolph
Nears Saml. P. shoemaker, r Bedford
Nelson Cyrus, shoemaker, r Progress
Nevins Martin, shoemaker, r School
Newton Geo. shoemaker, r Randoph
Newton John C. engineer, bds Winter
Nichols J. M. dresser, r Washington
Norton Benj. shoemaker, r Washington
Norton Samuel, manuf. r cor Temple and Washington
Norton Samuel, shoemaker, r Washington
Noyes Avery, shoemaker, bds Washington
Noyes Cephas D. shoemaker, r Washington
Noyes Daniel, shoemaker, r Belmont
Noyes Eliab, shoemaker, r Harvard
Noyes Henry, music teacher, r Belmont
Noyes Henry, school teacher, r Groveland
Noyes Isaiah, jeweller, Washington
Noyes Jacob, 2d, shoemaker, r Washington
Noyes John N. coal and grain dealer, Centre ave, r Walnut
Noyes Josiah, shoemaker, r cor Walnut and Dunbar sq
Noyes L. B. grocer, (Noyes & Hardy,) r Beulah
Noyes Lorenzo D. ice dealer, r Progress
Noyes Lonis, ——, r Groveland
Noyes Luke B. shoe manuf. r Washington
Noyes Silas C. shoe manuf. r Dunbar sq

ANNUAL CASH DIVIDENDS in the BERKSHIRE LIFE INS. CO., Pittsfield, Mass. Boston Office 95 1-2 Washington St. (See page 50.)

O'BRIEN DAN'L. shoemak'r, bds Central
O'Brien Daniel, shoemaker, Salem
O'Brien James, boot-treer, r Rockland
O'Brien James, laborer, r Summer
O'Brien James, shoemaker, r Washington
O'Brien John, shoemaker, r Randolph
O'Brien John, shoemaker, r Bigelow ave
O'Brien Michael, shoemaker, r Salem
O'Brien Mike, shoemaker, r North ave
O'Connell Daniel, shoemaker, r Plain
O'Connell Daniel, shoemaker, r Market
O'Connell Dennis, laborer, r Salem
O'Connell Dennis, shoemaker, bds Liberty
O'Connell Jeremiah, shoemaker, r Cork
O'Connell Philip, student, bds Union
O'Donnell Thos. farmer, bds Union
O'Donnell Thos. shoemaker, r Deering sq
O'Donnell Patrick, laborer, r Spring
O'Hearn James, laborer, r Union
O'Hearn Patrick, shoemak'r, r Dublin row
O'Hearn Timothy, shoemaker, r Plain
O'Neil Denis, shoemaker, r Cross
Orcutt Abial, farmer, r Chesnut
Orcutt Asa, shoemaker, r Hancock
Orcutt Bela, farmer, r Chesnut
Orcutt Cyrus, clerk, r Randolph
Orcutt Elisha V. shoemaker, r Hancock
Orcutt Emerson, farmer, r Randolph
Orcutt Franklin E. shoemaker, r Hancock
Orcutt Jabez, shoemaker, r Hancock
Orcutt Lewis, shoemaker, r Chesnut
Orcutt Walter, shoemaker, r Washington
Orcutt William, shoemaker, r Bedford
Osborn James, shoemaker, r School
Osborn Moses, hairdresser, r Union
Osgood Gilman, shoe manuf. r Washington

PACKARD CHARLES H. shoemaker, r Washington
Packard Dan'l. grocer, r Washington
Packard Hiram, shoemaker, r Glen.
Packard Jos. shoemaker, bd Water
Packard Z. farmer, r Washington
Page Jos. N. shoemaker, r Union
Parker John, shoemaker, r Dublin row
Parlin Robinson, mason, r Central
Parmeter John, shoemaker, r Central
Parsons Joseph, farmer, r Market
Pastor Lanar, shoemaker, r Liberty
Payn Stephen, shoemaker, r Union
Pearson Benj. F. shoemaker, bds Groveland
Pearson G. H. merchant, South Ward
Pearsons H. C. clerk, r Rockland
Peckham, J. K. farmer, r Washington
Penney Augustus, butcher, r Market
Peirce Alexander E. r Randolph
Peirce Henry B. ins. agent, r Centre ward
Peirce Henry G. last maker,
Peirce Martin B. carriage manuf. r Washington
Peirce Henry G. last maker,
Peirce Martin B. carriage manuf. r Washington
Peirce William H. wagon maker, r Washington
Peirce William M. carriage painter, r Washington
Peirce William N. carriage maker, r Washington

Penniman Cornelius, cutter, r Washington
Penniman James, shoemaker, r Hancock
Penniman Lewis, shoemaker, r Washington
Penniman Lewis B. shoemaker, r Washington
Percy Jacob, baker, r Washington
Perham Wm. S. shoemaker, r Liberty
Perkins George, engineer, r Liberty
Perkins J. R. carpenter, r Washington
Perry Joseph, merchant, r Market
Perry William, boot and shoe manuf. Market, r Market
Peterson Edward B. shoemaker, r Harvard
Peterson Franklin, farmer, r School
Peterson Jabez, mason, r Plymouth
Peterson Luther, shoemaker, r Harvard
Peterson Washington, cutter, r Harvard
Pettee Joseph, clergyman, r Bedford
Pettee Joseph jr. book-keeper,
Pettee Michael, shoemaker, r Adams
Phelon Dewit, machinist, bds Washington
Phelps E. A. shoemaker, r Union
Phillips Chas. tack maker, r Washington
Phillips Gideon B. stone cutter, r Webster
Phillips jr. Gideon B. shoemaker, bd Webster
Phillips James B. tack maker, r Quincy
Phillips Nathan, shoemaker, r Webster
Phillips Nathaniel, shoemaker, r Webster
Phillips Wm. S. shoemaker, r Webster
Phinney Benjamin, shoemaker, r Brighton
Platts Andrew H. grain, r North ave
Pool Benjamin F. clerk, r Union
Pool C. C. shoemaker, r North ave
Pool Chas. H. shoemaker, r Liberty
Pool Cyrus, shoemaker, r Union
Pool 2d Cyrus, shoemaker, r Water
Pool David S. shoemaker, r Water
Pool Elias, cutter, r at East Abington
Pool Elias, shoemaker, r Liberty
Pool Elias A. shoemaker, r Liberty
Pool Francis W. shoemaker, r Water
Pool Franklin, grocer, r Union
Pool F. H. shoemaker, r North ave
Pool Geo. T. clerk, bd Union
Pool Henry W. shoemaker, bd Union
Pool Hiram, mason, r Harvard
Pool Horace M. shoemaker, bd Union
Pool Jacob, shoemaker, r Harvard
Pool James, watchman, r Harvard
Pool John C. shoemaker, r Liberty
Pool Ludo, farmer, r Union
Pool Ludo A. shoemaker, r Webster
Pool Luther, shoemaker, r Harvard
Pool Micah H. shoemaker, r Union
Pool Nahum, variety, (*Fairbanks & Pool*), r Harvard
Pool Nath. shoe manuf. r Webster
Pool Stillman, shoemaker, r Water
Pool Thaxter, butcher, r Market
Pool Wm. shoemaker, r Harvard
Pool W. W. shoemaker, r Webster
Porter Abner, shoemaker, r Beulah
Porter Chas. farmer, r Groveland
Porter John, shoemaker, r Dublin Row
Porter John E. farmer, r Groveland
Powers Calvin P. cutter, r Plymouth
Powers Enoch, stone cutter, r Washington

The "ABINGTON STANDARD," established in 1853, is published by Thos. S. Pratt & Co.

Powers Henry, clerk, r Beulah
Powers Henry W. clerk, bd Beulah
Powers John, shoemaker, r Centre ave
Powers Saml. A. shoemaker, bd Washington
Powers Thomas, shoemaker, r Deering square
Powers William, stitcher, r Bedford
Pratt Benj. H. express, r Randolph
Pratt Danl. farmer, r High
Pratt George C. shoe manuf. r North ave
Pratt George W. state constable, r Washington
Pratt Henry, (*Dunham & Pratt*), r Centre ave near R. R.
Pratt Henry J. shoe manuf. cor. Central and Plymouth
Pratt H. J. clerk, for (B. Wilkes),
Pratt Isaac R. shoemaker, r Bedford
Pratt Leander, artist, r Spring
Pratt jr. Nath, nail maker,
Pratt Samuel, boot maker, r Bedford
Pratt Saml. L. shoemaker, r Bedford
Pratt Thos. S. publisher of Abington Standard, and job printer, r Union
Prouty Henry, shoemaker, r Water
Purcell Danl. clerk, r Plain

QUINN JAMES, shoemaker, r Water
Quinn John, shoemaker, r Salem
Quinlan Danl. shoemaker, bd Cross
Quinlan Danl. shoemaker, bd Randolph
Quinlan Michael, shoemaker, r Randolph
Quinlan Patrick, shoemaker, r near R. R.
Quinlan Richard, shoemaker, r near R. R.

RAMSDELL GIDEON, shoemaker, r Washington
Ramsdell Gilbert, shoecutter, r Washington
Ramsdell Henry, shoemaker, r Washington
Ramsdell Henry A. shoemaker, r Washington
Rand Erastus R. shoecutter, r Plymouth
Rand Wm. laborer, r Union
Randall Chas. shoemaker, bds Lincoln
Randall Joseph, shoemaker, r Bedford
Randall Joseph W. shoemaker, r Washington
Randall Stephen D. shoemaker, r Adams
Randall Warren, shoemaker, r Washington
Raymond F. T. stitcher, r Central
Raymond Herbert, shoemaker, bds Bedford
Raymond H. L. shoemaker, r Bedford
Raymond W. A. shoemaker, r Bedford
Raymond Winslow, shoemaker, r Adams
Reardon Daniel, shoemaker, North ave
Reardon Michael, shoemaker, r Deering square
Reardon Timothy, shoemaker, r Plain
Reardon William, laborer, near R. R.
Reed Aaron, shoemaker, r Washington
Reed Abiah, carpenter, r Spring
Reed A. N. grain dealer, (*A. N. Reed & Co.*), r North ave
Reed A. S. (*A. S. Reed & Co.*), r Market
Reed Bela, farmer, r Centre ave
Reed Chas. C. hostler, bds Washington
Reed Dexter, shoemaker, r Plain

Reed Ebenezer, stonecutter, r Washington
Reed Edward P. flour and grain, (*A. N. Reed & Co.,*) r North ave
Reed Edwin, farmer, r Washington
Reed Edwin R. clerk, bds Hancock
Reed Ezekiel, farmer, r Centre ave
Reed Frederick, shoemaker, r Plain
Reed Geo. cutter, r Centre ave
Reed Geo. A. mercht. r Washington
Reed Geo. F. shoemaker, r Centre ave
Reed G. W. shoemaker, r Glen
Reed Harvey T. shoemaker, bds Hancock
Reed Henry H. clerk, r Union
Reed Henry W. shoemaker, bds Plymouth
Reed Hiram, bootmaker, r Centre ave
Reed Horace, clerk, r Pleasant
Reed Isaac, shoemaker, r Plymouth
Reed Jacob, farmer, bds Centre ave
Reed Jesse, farmer, r Plymouth
Reed Jesse, jr. shoemaker, r Plymouth
Reed Joseph, butcher, r Spring
Reed J. P. shoemaker, r Temple
Reed Levi, gentleman, r Union
Reed Lewis, shoemaker, r School
Reed Lloyd, shoemaker, r Harvard
Reed Lorenzo, (*Curtis & Reed*), r Union
Reed Lorenzo, shoemaker, r Union
Reed Lewis, shoemaker, r Plain
Reed Marcus, selectman, r Washington
Reed Marcus, jr. shoemaker, r Washing'n
Reed Philip, painter, r Harvard
Reed Saml. boot and shoe manuf. Union
Reed Saml. farmer, r Market
Reed Saml. farmer, r Temple
Reed Saml. shoemaker, r Harvard
Reed Saml. jr. shoe manuf. r Union
Reed Seth, farmer, r Washington
Reed Seth D. shoemaker, r Bedford
Reed Theodore, farmer r Market
Reed Turner, farmer, r Plymouth
Reed Washington, shoe manuf. r Union
Reed Wm. E. shoemaker, r Union
Reed Wm. H. grocer, (*Bates & Reed*), r Washington
Reed W. L. shoe manuf. r Pleasant
Remington Jacob S. farmer, r Thicket
Reynolds Griffin C. shoe manuf. r Bank
Richmond Elijah, shoemaker, r Dunbar
Ridlington Henry M. shoemaker, r Randolph
Riley James, shoemaker, r Liberty
Ring Charles, bootmaker, r Brighton
Ring Saml. E. (*Bourne & Ring*), bds Hotel
Ripley Wm. hardware, Washington
Riply Wm. laborer, r Washington
Roarty James, tailor, r Liberty
Robbins Rufus, shoemaker, r High
Roberts Hiram, stitcher, r Bedford
Robinson John, shoemaker, bds Dunbar
Roche Rev. A. L. near Catholic Church
Rochforto F. W. stitcher, r near Washing'n
Rockwood John, dresser, r Plymouth
Rogers Geo. shoemaker, r Cottage
Rose John, machinist, South ave
Rosenfeld Nathan, dry goods, Union, r at South Braintree
Rouke Peter, shoemaker, r Central
Ronke James, shoemaker, r Central
Rounds Chas. shoemaker, bds cor. Walnut and Dunbar
Rowe Z. W. shoemaker, r Temple
Rush John, shoemaker, r North ave

The terms for **ENDOWMENT**, and **TEN ANNUAL LIFE POLICIES** in the **BERKSHIRE** are peculiarly favorable, and rates lower than in any Note Company. (See page 50.)

Russell Christopher, shoemak'r, r Central
Russell John, carpenter, r Elm
Ryan John, shoemaker, r Deering square
Ryan Philip, shoemaker, r King road
Ryan Thos. laborer, r Union

SAMPSON A. HARRIS, packer, r Winter
Sampson Chas. shoemaker, r Webster
Sanborn Quincy A. shoemaker, r Wash.
Sanborn Simeon S. teacher, bds Centre ave near R. R.
Saville Alonzo F. shoemaker, bds Plymouth
Sears E. last maker,
Seavey ———, shoemaker, r Salem
Sharpe Alfred, shoemaker, South ave
Sharpe Eldridge, shoemaker, r Washington
Sharpe Gibens, farmer, r Washington
Shaler John T. shoemaker, r North ave
Shannahen Patrick, shoemaker, r Deering sq
Shaw Abraham, shoemaker, r Union
Shaw Alden N. shoemaker, r Union
Shaw Arthur, shoemaker, bds Union
Shaw Brackley, drover, r Union
Shaw Brackley W. boot maker, r Bedford
Shaw Calvin, shoemaker, r Bedford
Shaw Chas. farmer, r High
Shaw Chas. F. shoemaker, bd Bedford
Shaw Danl. shoemaker, r Bedford
Shaw E. A. boot and shoe, Union, r Linden
Shaw Jacob 2d E. A. hotel and livery stable, r Union
Shaw Edmund A. shoemaker, r Union
Shaw Elias A. shoemaker, r Union
Shaw Elijah, shoe manuf. r Linden ave
Shaw Ezra, carpenter, r Randolph
Shaw Francis, shoemaker, r Orange
Shaw Henry, shoemaker, bd Union
Shaw Henry N. shoemaker, r Randolph
Shaw Howard W. shoemaker, r Union
Shaw Jacob, boot manuf. Bedford, r same
Shaw Melvin, shoe manuf. r Union
Shaw Micah P. cutter, r Union
Shaw M. Roland, shoemaker, r Union
Shaw Noah, shoemaker, r Bedford
Shaw Nath. shoemaker, r High
Shaw S. sewing machines, Union, r same
Shaw Sumner B. shoe manuf. r Webster
Shea James, shoemaker, r Rockland
Shea James, shoemaker, r Groveland
Shea Jerry, shoemaker, r Deering sq
Shea Morris, shoemaker, r Liberty
Shea Wm. shoemaker, bds Union
Sheehan Jeremiah, shoemaker, r Dublin row
Shell jr. Saml. L. shoemaker, bd Randolph
Sheridan Wm. laborer, r North ave
Sherman Benj. clothing store, r Union
Sherman Thomas, shoemaker, r Dover
Shields John, treer, r Bedford
Shoery Eli, farmer, r Market
Shurtleff Micah, shoemaker, bd Market
Simmons Alfred F. tack maker, Quincy
Simms Alexander, shoemaker, r Centre avenue
Simmons Geo. carpenter, bd Vernon
Sisk Wm. shoemaker, r Liberty

Slaughtery Patrick, laborer, r Rockland
Smith Albert, shoemaker, r Union
Smith A. Thos. shoemaker, bd Cross
Smith Bela, cutter, r Centre ave
Smith B. H. B. cutter, r Centre ave
Smith Dana, shoemaker, r Liberty
Smith David B. carpenter, r Plymouth
Smith Davis, farmer, r North ave
Smith Everett J. dry goods dealer, Centre avenue
Smith Franklin, claim agent, r Union
Smith James, farmer, r Central
Smith James E. confectioner, r Bedford
Smith John, farmer, r Liberty
Smith John, shoemaker, bds Central
Smith John, cutter, r Central
Smith Joseph, teamer, r Adams
Smith Joseph 2nd, carpenter, r Adams
Smith Nath. R. shoemaker, bd Union
Smith Nehemiah, shoemaker, r Union
Smith Nicholas, r Rockland
Smith Owen, shoemaker, r Lincoln
Smith Pat, laborer, r Groveland
Smith Patrick, shoemaker, r Central
Smith Peter, shoemaker, bd cor. Vernon and Liberty
Smith Philip, boot maker, r Summer
Smith Robt. shoemaker, r Bigelow ave
Smith Terrance, shoemaker, r Hancock
Smith Thomas, shoe finisher, r North Abington
Smith Zenas, shoemaker, r Webster
Snell Nat. B. cutter, r Liberty
Snell Thomas J. shoemaker, bd Randolph
Snell Saul. L. shoemaker, r Randolph
Somers Samuel, farmer, r North ave
Somers Saml. shoemaker, r Hancock
Soule Danl. (Soule & Brown), r Washington
Soule G. C. grocer, r Union
Soule James P. shoemaker, r Glen
Soule Josiah, gentleman, r Union
Soule jr. Josiah, clerk, r Union
Soule Louis, shoemaker, r Washington
Soule Otis W. dept. collector, r Washington
Spence John, shoemaker, r Plain
Spence Michael, carpenter, r Deering sq
Spence Robert, saloon, r Union
Spooner J. tack maker, r South ave
Sprague Elbridge, grocer, r Birch
Sprague Seth C. farmer, r Randolph
Sprague jr. Seth C. shoemaker, r Bedford
Sproul John, tailor, r Washington
Sproul J. W. tailor, r Washington
Sproul Saml. shoemaker, r Dove
Squier A. F. bds corner Elm and Rockland
Standish Stephen, carpenter, r Market
Stebbins John D. nail maker,
Stetson Andrew, carpenter, r South ave
Stetson Chas. shoemaker, r Bedford
Stetson ———, farmer, r Beach Hill
Stetson Oliver, fish dealer, r Union
Stevens David, groceries, r Union
Stevens Everett T. clerk, bds Union
Stewart ———, teacher, r Liberty
Stewart John E. engineer,
Stimson Martin, com. mer, r South ave
Stockbridge Jos. C. stage driver, r Plain
Stoddard Benj. shoemaker, r Union
Stoddard Geo. W. shoemaker, r Webster

The "ABINGTON STANDARD" is published in the largest town in Plymouth County, and is a Good Advertising Medium.

Stoddard Melvin, shoemaker, r Liberty
Stoddard Samuel, carpenter, r Union
Stoddard Samuel, shoemaker, r Union
Stoddard William, shoemaker, r Union
Strout Geo. H. farmer, bd Union
Studley Andrew, butcher, r Vernon
Studley Andrew H. shoemaker, r cor. Union and Salem
Studley Austin, shoemaker, r Vernon
Studley Ezekiel R. shoemaker, r Water
Studley Gideon, box manuf. Birch, r E. Abington
Studley Gridley, shoemaker, r Vernon
Studley Hilton, shoemaker, r Union
Studley Jacob, shoemaker, bd Market
Studley James B. shoe manuf. bd Union
Studley John A. shoemaker, bd Webster
Studley Nathan, shoemaker, r Water
Studley Reuben, butcher, r Market
Studley W. B. jeweler, r Union
Studley Wm. shoemaker, r Market
Studley William A. clerk, r North ave
Sullivan Daniel, shoemaker, r Washington
Sullivan Dennis, shoemaker, r Central
Sullivan James N. shoemaker, r Liberty
Sullivan Jeremiah, shoemaker, r Central
Sullivan Jerome, shoemaker, r Central
Sullivan John, shoemaker, r Adams
Sullivan John, shoemaker, r Vernon
Sullivan Michael, shoemaker, r Market
Sullivan Patrick, shoemaker, bds Central
Sweeny John, laborer, near R. R.
Swain Levi, shoemaker, r Dover
Sylvester Nelson, carpenter, r Randolph

TAGGARD DAVID, carpenter, r Washington
Tangney J. shoemaker, r Cork
Tanner Dr. N. B. North Abington
Tanner N. B. jr., carriage maker, r Washington
Taylor Willis, carpenter, bds Washington
Teatue Lysander, shoemaker, r School
Temple John, cutter, r Adams
Terry Enoch, farmer, r Bedford
Terry Enoch E. shoemaker, bd Liberty
Thaxter Bela, gentleman, bds Washington
Thaxter Gridley, farmer, r Washington
Thaxter Saml. merchant, r Washington
Thayer Albert M. tack maker, r Plymouth
Thayer Francis P. shoemaker, bd Randolph
Thayer Henry W. shoemaker, bd Lincoln
Thayer Isaac F. tack maker, r South ave
Thomas David, shoemaker, r Webster
Thompson ———, carpenter, School
Thompson Arioch, mason, cor. Water and Central
Thompson Arioch, A. shoemaker, cor. Water and Central
Thompson E. photographer, r Union
Thompson Edwin, machinist, r Washington
Thompson Edwin, tack maker, r Washington
Thompson Gilbert, shoemaker, r Central
Thompson Guy, shoemaker, r Union
Thompson Horatio, shoemaker, r Centre avenue
Thompson James F. shoemaker, bd Liberty
Thompson Josiah, carpenter, r Washington
Thompson Luke, shoemaker, r Central
Thompson Rinaldo, shoemaker, r Cottage
Thompson Rufus D. shoemaker, bd Liberty
Thompson Samuel E. carpenter, r Central
Thompson S. G. r Central
Thompson William A. (*Cobb & Thompson*) r Washington
Thompson Wm. F. shoemaker, bd Liberty
Thorpe Joshua, shoemaker, r Glen
Thorp Thos. H. shoemaker, r Washington
Tibbetts A. F. boot maker, r Bedford
Tirrell Americus, shoemaker, r Rockland
Tirrell Edwin S. shoe manuf. r Union
Tirrell Gideon, shoemaker, r Brighton
Tirrell John H. shoemaker, r Brighton
Tirrell Major, shoemaker, r Brighton
Tirrell Saml. shoemaker, r Salem
Tirrell Thos. A. shoe finisher, r Progress
Torrey Chesterfield, farmer, r Washington
Torrey C. W. boot and shoe manuf. r Union
Torrey David, furniture and dry goods, (*D. & E. P. Torrey*), r Union
Torrey Edward P. (*D. & E. P. Torrey*), r Union
Torrey James H. soap pedlar, r Market
Torrey Josiah, farmer, r Market
Totman George, shoemaker, r Centre ave
Totman George N. shoemaker, r Centre avenue
Totman Horace C. shoemaker, r Market
Tower James A. shoemaker, r Plain
Towle James, expressman, r Washington
Townsend Chas. A. shoemaker, bd Union
Townsend E. shoemaker, r Adams
Townsend Ezekiel, farmer, r Adams
Trufer Ezra, farmer, r High
Trumball Howard M. shoemaker, r Union
Tracey Mike, shoemaker, r North ave
Tribon William, boot finisher, Birch
Tribou Wm. E. shoemaker, bd Plain
Tribou Wm. shoemaker, r Cross
Tucker Lemuel, farmer, r Market
Tufts Charles, shoemaker, r Temple
Turner Alonzo, shoemaker, r Adams
Turner Chas. shoemaker, bd Webster
Turner Ezekiel, laborer, r Webster
Turner George W. shoemaker, r Washington
Turner George W. jr., shoemaker, r Washington
Turner John, shoemaker, bd Webster
Turner Jos. S. shoe manuf. r Webster
Turner Noah, laborer, r Water
Twombly H. E. clerk, r Webster

UNDERHAY JOHN, shoemaker, r Orange
Underhay Wm. shoemaker, r Orange
Underwood James M. physician, r Union

VALEGE BERNARD, carpenter, bds Plain
Varney George, blacksmith, North ave
Vaughan A. B. V. boot and shoe manuf. (*J Vaughan & Sons*), r Washington
Vaughan Alvin B. shoe manuf. bds Washington

DIVIDENDS ADDED to the POLICY in the BERKSHIRE often exceed the premium paid; are NON-FORFEITABLE and will be redeemed in CASH ON DEMAND. (See page 50.)

Vaughan Francis L. bookkeeper, bds Plymouth
Vaughan Geo. D. mercht. bds Plymouth
Vaughan J. A. V. (J. Vaughan & Sons), r Orange
Vaughan Joseph, (J. Vaughan & Sons), r Washington
Vaughan Stetson, boot and shoe manuf. r Plymouth
Vining Benj. shoemaker, r Liberty
Vining Elmer H. shoemaker, r Union
Vining J. Q. shoemaker, r Union
Vining Richard, cutter, r Washington
Vining Spencer, gentleman, r Washington
Vining Wm. shoemaker, r Liberty
Vining Wm. R. shoe manuf. r School
Virgin Samuel, carpenter, r Washington
Wade Henry, shoemaker, r Chesnut
Wade Henry A. carpenter, r Plain
Wade John, shoemaker, r Plain
Wade John, gentleman, r Dover
Wade Wm. shoemaker, r School
Wales Cyrus M. shoe manuf. r Bedford
Wales Ira W. cutter, r Washington
Wales Simeon, shoe manuf. r Plymouth
Wales S. R. shoe manuf. r Adams
Wales W. S. boot and shoe manuf. r Adams
Waters James, shoemaker, r Dublin row
Watts Samuel, shoemaker, r Liberty
Walker Rev. H. D. r Union
Walker Silas N. school teacher, bds Centre ave
Wall Hugh, shoemaker, r Liberty
Walch Lawrence, tailor, Washington, r same
Ward Patrick, shoemaker, r Central
Warren Augustus N. shoemaker, r Spring
Warren Robt. D. cutter, r Washington
Warner Henry, shoemaker, r Linden av
Washburn Jerome, shoemaker, r Temple
Washburn Wm. R. shoemaker, bds Central
Waterman Seth, blacksmith, r cor. Centre ave. and Quincy
Welch James, shoemaker, bds cor. Bigelow and Union
Welch Wm. shoemaker, r Cork
West James, farmer, r High
West John, shoemaker, r Washington
Weston Elias E. express, r Temple
Wetherbee Joseph, stonecutter, r Liberty
Wetherbee Jos. M. stonecutter, b Liberty
Wheeler Danl. G. shoemak'r, r Hingham
Wheeler E. A. shoe dealer, r Union
Wheeler E. B. shoemaker, r Webster
Wheeler Geo. trader, r Liberty
Wheeler John, shoemaker, Vernon
Wheeler John F. boxmaker, r Elm
Wheeler L. F. shoemaker, r Webster
Wheeler Wm. shoemaker, r Webster
Whidden Frank, tack manuf. South ave
Whitcomb Jacob, farmer, r Bedford
Whitcomb Jacob H. clerk, r Union
White John, laborer, r Union
White Thos. laborer, r School
White Wm. merchant, r Union
White Wm. shoemaker, bds Centre ave
Whiting Chas. H. farmer, r Liberty
Whiting E. Edwin, shoemaker, bds Bedford
Whiting Edwin W. mercht. r Vernon
Whiting Eleazer, ———, r Webster
Whiting E. W. (Estes & Whiting), r Vernon
Whiting E. Y. shoemaker, r Market
Whiting Franklin T. livery at E. Abington, bds cor. Groveland and Elm
Whiting Jacob, shoe manuf. r Webster
Whiting Leonard, shoe manuf. r Webster
Whiting Loring, farmer, r Spring
Whiting P. Alonzo, shoemaker, r Webster
Whiting Simeon D. shoemaker, bd Webster
Whiting Stephen, shoemaker, r Webster
Whiting Thomas, shoemaker, r Hingham
Whiting Wm. H. livery, cor. Elm and Groveland
Whitman A. shoemaker, bds Plymouth
Whitman Jared, lawyer, r Washington
Whitman S. drover, r Union
Whitman Theron, shoemaker, r Union
Whitmarsh Henry M. shoe cutter, r Orange
Whitmarsh J. boot maker, r South ave
Whitmarsh James, boot and shoe manuf. Thaxter ave r Washington
Whitmarsh J. F. L. broker, r Bedford
Whitmarsh Joshua, shoe manuf. r Washington
Whitmarsh Joshua, merchant, r Orange
Whitmarsh T. W. clerk, bds Washington
Whitmarsh Z. N. merchant, r Washington
Whitmarsh Z. T. clerk, bds Washington
Wiginton ———, farmer, r Beach Hill
Wilkes Bela, boot and shoe manuf. r Centre ave near R. R.
Wilkes Joseph, merchant, r Centre ave
Wilkes Orange, shoemaker, r Washington
Wilkes Wm. W. shoemaker, bds Centre avenue
Willey Chas. B. cabinet maker, r Dunbar sq
Willey James H. painter, r Dunbar sq
Williams Charles, shoemaker, r Adams
Williams Chas. H. shoemaker, r Adams
Williams John, laborer, r Centre ave
Williams Horatio, farmer, r South ave
Williamson Lorenzo, shoemaker, r Washington
Willis ———, laborer, r Spring
Willis Frank, shoemaker, r Centre ave
Wilson Chas. L. shoemaker, r Plain
Wilson Nathaniel, shoe cutter, r Washington
Windsor James H. shoemaker, r Liberty
Windsor Josiah T. shoemaker, bd Liberty
Winslow John E. shoemaker, r Water
Winslow Joshua, shoemaker, r Washington
Witherell George, shoemaker, r Temple
Wood Ezra L. baker, r Centre ave
Wood G. W. livery stable, r Union
Worington ———, blacksmith, r Liberty
Wornell Benj. school teacher, r Orange
Wornell J. D. r Orange cor. Bedford
Wright Lorenzo, shoemaker, r Water
Wright Nolan, shoemaker, bd Water
Wright Stephen, machinist, r Washington

YOUNG GEO. W. shoemaker, r Plymouth
Young Harrison, shoemaker, r Plymouth
Young Jacob K. machinist, Market, r
Young Wm. laborer, r Washington

The "ABINGTON STANDARD," established in 1853, is published by Thos. S. Pratt & Co.

Bridgewater General Directory.

ADAMS WILLIAM H. farmer, Auburn
Akins Charles W. machinist, bd Bedford
Alden Caleb, laborer, bds High
Alden Cromwell, farmer, r High
Alden Elijah, farmer, bds Vernon
Alden Ezra H. expressman, r School
Alden Horatio, farmer, r Conant
Alden Isaac F. watchman, r Walnut
Alden Isaac R. clerk, bds Bedford
Alden James S. painter, r Bedford
Alden John C. merchant, r South
Alden Lewis T. farmer, r Titicut
Alden Leander M. machinist, bds Plymouth
Alden Oliver, farmer, r High
Alden Samuel, physician, r South
Alden Walter H. teacher, r Oak
Alden William S. farmer, r Summer
Alden William S. jr., farmer, bds Summer
Aldrich Henry C. laborer, Beach
Alger Adin, farmer, r Pleasant
Alger James M. butcher, Main
Alger Stillman, commission merchant, r Main
Alger William H. butcher, r Main
Ames Horace, farmer, r South
Ames Jotham, farmer, r North
Ames Virgil, farmer, r South
Ames Washington L. farmer, r North
Andrews Manassah, machinist, r Plymouth
Andrews M. Lloyd, machinist, r Plymouth
Andrews Perez F. shoemaker, r Plymouth
Andrews Thomas F. L. r Plymouth
Armstrong Charles J. laborer, r Main

BAKER GEORGE, shoemaker, r Walnut
Baker Phineas, farmer, r Main
Ball Merrill W. laborer, Plymouth
Barnes Harrison F. r Pleasant
Barney Mark F. butcher, Summer
Barney Cyrenus, blacksmith,
Barstow Edwin W. r Pleasant,
Bartlett Elijah, tack manuf. r Green
Bartlett Horace, tack manuf. r Green
Bartlett John A. tack manuf. r Green
Bassett Abiel, farmer, r North
Bassett Abigence W. farmer, r Pleasant
Bassett George, farmer, r Pleasant
Bassett George W. merchant, r Main
Bassett Josiah L. cor. Main and Broad
Bates George W. farmer, South
Bates Joshua, farmer, South
Bates Samuel W. farmer, South
Beals Thomas A. machinist, r Oak

Beebe William, merchant, r Summer
Benson Alonzo P. farmer, r Conant
Benson Hubbard D. shoemaker, r Auburn
Benson Jonah, farmer, r Auburn
Benson Jonathan, farmer, r Auburn
Benson Thomas, shoemaker, r Auburn
Berry Aaron, watchman, r Main
Bottomer Dennis, laborer,
Boyden Albert G. teacher normal school, r School
Bradbury Samuel, mechanic, r Whitman
Bradford Peleg S. machinist, r High
Brailey Bradford, mechanic, r Broad
Braman Henry F. painter, r Mt. Prospect
Braman John G. painter, r School
Braunon Thomas, heater, r High
Breck Samuel, farmer, r South
Brigham John, carpenter, r Summer
Briggs Jeremiah, laborer, r Oak
Briggs John, farmer, r Spring Hill ave
Briggs William T. farmer, r Vernon
Broadhurst Thomas, mechanic, r Broad
Brown Daniel E. soap maker, r Pleasant
Brown David, laborer,
Brown Jason P. engineer, r Plymouth
Bryant Benjamin, shoemaker, Walnut
Bryant Charles L. shoe finisher, r Walnut
Bryant Dion, farmer, r South
Bryant George A. laborer, Hayward Place
Bryant Lewis, miller, r Walnut
Bump Alden B. farmer, r Furnace Place
Bump Ansel B. shoemaker, r Vernon
Bump Isaac F. shoemaker, r South
Bump Noble P. farmer, r Oliver Place
Butterworth Lloyd N. carpenter, r Titicut
Burrell David T. photographer, r Grove
Burr Laban, stage driver, bds Hyland House
Burt George H. carpenter, r Main
Burt Matthias T. pattern maker, r Main

CAGNEY DANIEL, laborer, r Centre
Cagney William, laborer
Carr Nelson O. shoemaker, r Plymouth
Carver Francis, shoecutter, r Laurel
Carver Grenville, shoemaker, r Conant
Carver John, farmer, r Laurel
Carver Jos. E. cotton gin manuf. r Broad
Case William, shoemaker, r South
Cashon Patrick, laborer, r High
Chamberlain A. J. shoemaker, r Cherry
Chamberlain N. W. blacksmith, r Orange
Chipman George, postmaster, Scotland, r Pleasant
Christian Caleb, mechanic, r Summer
Church Hezekiah W. farmer, r Vernon

Policy Holders in the BERKSHIRE LIFE INSURANCE COMPANY of Pittsfield, Mass., DO NOT FORFEIT THEIR POLICIES by reason of FAILURE TO PAY their premiums. (See page 50.)

Clark Thos. A. laborer, bds Main
Clear Lawrence, clerk, Bolton place
Clifford Luther, iron-puddler, r Centre
Cole Samuel K. heater, r Main
Coll John, laborer, r Alger
Conant Andrew, farmer, r Forrest
Conant Galen, farmer, r Titicut
Conant Ira, farmer, r Pleasant
Conant Ira M. hoop skirt manuf. r School
Conant Isaac, laborer, r Main
Conant Marcus, mechanic, r Spring hill av
Conant Seth, farmer, r [mant]
Conant Virgil V. farmer, r South
Connor Thomas O. laborer
Connor Michael, laborer
Copeland Asa, machinist, r Plymouth
Copeland Asa E. yard-master, Eagle Cotton Gin Co., r Union
Copeland C. D. mechanic, r South
Copeland Cyrus, farmer, r South
Copeland Francis, farmer, r South
Copeland Geo. A. machinist, r Plymouth
Copeland Joseph, farmer, r Forrest
Copeland Lorenzo, mechanic, r Summer
Copeland Valentine, mechanic, r Summer
Cornell Emmor K. paper manuf. r Plymouth
Cornell Mark H. paper manuf. r Plymouth
Cottle Charles E. laborer, r Oak
Crafts Frederick, teacher, r Main
Crane Joshua E. merchant, r Broad
Crapo Henry, manuf. Crapo's Lin. r Oak
Creighton David, machinist, r Wall
Creighton Nathan R. machinist, Bolton pl
Crocker John W. clerk, r Grove
Crocker Jonathan, merchant Central sq
Crocker Thomas W. merch't, r Central sq
Crocker Walter, r Centre
Crocker Walter B. bds Centre
Cromolly Timothy, laborer, r High
Cropper John, machinist, r Main
Curtis Lyman H. carpenter, Summer
Cushing Jonathan, r Main
Cushing Ransom J. machinist, r South
Cushman Darius, shoedealer, r Bedford
Cushman Isaac N. farmer, r Elm
Cushman Nathaniel T. farmer, r Fruit
Cushman Thomas, farmer, r Broad
Cutter William P. carpenter, r South

DAMON ISAAC, clerk, r School
Danneher John, laborer, r Bedford
Darling Benj. wheelwright, r Plymouth
Darling Daniel, wheelwright, r Plymouth
Donnovan Daniel, laborer
Donnovan John, laborer
Dorr Amos L. laborer, r Summer
Douglass Ebenezer, clergyman, r South
Dove Alexander, machinist, r Wall
Duckworth Geo. engineer, r Plymouth
Dunbar Amasa A. butcher, r Titicut
Dunbar Darius, farmer, r Titicut
Dunbar Darius H. grocer, r Spring hill av
Dunbar Eliab F. farmer, r Titicut
Dunbar Geo. F. shoe manuf. r Titicut
Dunbar Lewis B. mechanic, r South
Dunbar William, mechanic, Dunbar pl
Dunham Henry C. butcher, r Centre
Dunphe Havillah W. mechanic, r Plymouth
Dunphe Hiram, mechanic, r Main
Dunphe James M. mechanic, r Plain

Dunphe John A. mechanic, r South
Dunphe Jotham, mechanic, r Plain
Dunphe Nathan H. cotton gin manuf. r Main
Dunphe N. Frank, proprietor of Hyland House

EAGAN DANIEL, laborer,
Edmondson James, machinist, r Wall
Edson Josiah W. wheelwright, r Main
Ellis Thomas, laborer, r South
Elms Lazell, farmer, r Pleasant
Eltz William H. druggist, bds Main
Enwright John, laborer,
Estes Calvin, stable keeper, Hyland House

FAIRBANKS JOHN H. tinman, Central square
Ferguson James, (supt L. P. & C. Iron Works), r High
Ferguson James jr., machinist, bds High
Ferguson Robert, furnace man, r Main
Fish Isaac L. farmer, r Oak
Fobes Addison, r Vernon
Fobes Albert S. wheelwright, r Vernon
Fobes Arctas, farmer, r Pleasant
Fobes Bela, farmer, r Vernon
Fobes Ezra, farmer, r Pleasant
Fobes Franklin, farmer, r Pleasant
Fobes Joseph B. physician, r Pleasant
Fobes Joshua, mason, r South
Fobes Laban, farmer, r Fobes Place
Fobes Willard W. r Spring Hill ave
Foley Thomas, laborer
Folsom George W. shoe manuf. r Summer
Ford Darius C. pattern maker, r South
Fraher Patrick, laborer
Frawley David, moulder, r Main
Frawley John, heater, Mt. Prospect
Frawley Michael, laborer, Mt. Prospect
Frawley Michael 2nd, moulder, r Centre
Frawley Patrick, laborer, Centre
Frawley William J. moulder, r Main
Fuller John, restorator, r Wall

GAMMONS RUFUS, heater, r Main
Gardner William, furnace man, r Oak
Gassett Walker, watchman, r Main
Gay Ebenezer, clergyman, r Pleasant
Gibbs Samuel B. painter, bds Broad
Gilbert Grenville, bds cor Main and Broad
Godfrey Hozea R. r Titicut
Goodspeed Levi L. supt. state alms house
Gould Lorenzo L. clerk, bds Hyland House
Gould Theodore B. mechanic, r Broad
Grabrant Isaac ——, tailor, r Pleasant
Griffeth James W. moulder, bds Hyland House
Gurney Charles, farmer, r Laurel

HALE ARTEMUS, r Central sq.
Hall Alfred, machinist, bds Spring Hill avenue
Hall Charles T. forgeman, r High
Hall Ebenezer, farmer, r Plymouth
Hall Jona. L. r Titicut
Hall Henry A. merchant, r Main
Hall Maximilian, music teacher, r Wentworth Place
Ham Joseph L. pattern maker, bds Main
Harden Albert, mechanic, r Walnut
Harden Benjamin, farmer, r Plymouth

J. A. JACKSON, 101 COURT STREET, BOSTON, DEALER IN HATS, CAPS, AND FURS.

BRIDGEWATER DIRECTORY. 27

Harden George P. peddler, r Walnut
Harden Jabez, carpenter, r Walnut
Harlow Columbus, blacksmith, r Pleasant
Harlow Lewis, farmer, r Cherry
Harlow Southworth, blacksmith, r Union
Harris C. C. clergyman, r Main
Hartwell Charles, shoemaker, r Conant
Hawes Samuel, shoe cutter, r Central sq
Hayden Aaron, shoemaker, bds Plymouth
Hayden Lewis, machinist, r Main
Hayden Lewis W. machinist, r Main
Hayward Alden, nailer, r Broad
Hayward Ariston M. farmer, r Oliver Place
Hayward Benjamin B. carpenter, r Plain
Hayward Caleb T. shoemaker, r High
Hayward Charles, mechanic, r Bedford
Hayward Daniel L. farmer, r Pine
Hayward Edwin, machinist, r Pearl
Hayward Elijah F. shoemaker, r High
Hayward John C. mechanic, r Main
Hayward Solomon, mechanic, Hayward Place
Hayward Tilley B. clergyman, bds Pleasant
Hayward Thomas J. nailer, r Broad
Hayward Wales, farmer, Pine
Healy Barney, laborer, r Plymouth
Hewett Edward A. jeweller, bds Pleasant
Hill Horace W. shoemaker, r Plymouth
Hill James H. laborer, r South
Hill Philip E. ins. agent, r Elm
Hill Warren, jobber, bds Hyland House
Hobart Caleb, merchant, r Main
Holmes Bradford C. shoemaker, Conant
Holmes Calvin, shoemaker, r East
Holmes Cornelius, farmer, r Conant
Holmes Gaius, shoemaker, r Conant
Holmes George W. farmer, r Conant
Holmes John, shoemaker, r East
Holmes Lewis, post master, r Bedford
Holmes Lewis J. general agent, Central square
Holmes Martin D. farmer, r High
Holmes Soranus, shoemaker, r Summer
Holmes Thomas, shoemaker, r Summer
Hooper Arthur, painter, bds Spring Hill avenue
Hooper George M. clerk, r Plymouth
Hooper Joseph, bds Plymouth
Hooper Joseph C. tack maker, r High
Hooper Levi, farmer, r South
Hooper Mitchell, brick manuf. r Plymouth
Hooper Philo, farmer, r South
Hooper Preston, painter, bds Spring Hill avenue
Hooper Thomas, florist, r Spring Hill ave
Hopkins Lewis G. physician, r Summer
Howard John J. farmer, r High
Howard Joseph, forgeman, r Wall
Howard Marcellus G. butcher, Whitman
Howe Martin, shoemaker, r Walnut
Howe Philip H. machinist
Howes Phineas, tailor, r Grove
Howland Robert, carpenter, r Main
Hull Curtis J. restorator, r Grove
Hull Sewell, forgeman, r Broad
Hunter John, mechanic, bds Bolton Place
Hyde Joseph A. cotton gin manuf. r Cedar

IRISH HANSON L. moulder, r Bedford

JACOBS EDWARD S. laborer, bds South

Jewett Charles H. tinman, r Summer
Jewett Jesse G. clerk, bd Pleasant
Jewett Thomas G. capt. steamer, r Pleasant
Johnson Job H. shoemaker
Johnson Nahum, shoemaker, r Centre
Jones Franklin, shoemaker, r Summer
Jones Freeman, mechanic, r Summer
Jordan Simeon, mechanic, r Whitman
Jordan Simeon P. mechanic, bds Whitman
Josselyn Hervey, r Main

KEITH ADNA P. farmer, r Forrest
Keith Albert, farmer, r Fruit
Keith Ambrose, carpenter, r Summer
Keith Benjamin, farmer, r Pleasant
Keith Dennis, laborer, North
Keith E. Harrison, mechanical engineer, Main
Keith George F. shoemaker, South
Keith Henry A. farmer, Keith Place
Keith Holden W. farmer, r South
Keith Israel, heater, r Main
Keith Joseph H. clerk, r Main
Keith Lafayette, ast. assessor, int rev. r Bedford
Keith Lloyd, carpenter, r Spring Hill ave
Keith Lemuel M. grocer, r High
Keith Oliver, farmer, r Pleasant
Keith Otis, farmer, r Pleasant
Keith Philo, machinist, r Pleasant
Keith Royal, r Pleasant
Keith Salmon, farmer, Keith Place
Keith Samuel D. farmer, r Green Place
Keith Solomon, carpenter, r Summer
Keith Sumner, carpenter, Spring Hill ave
Keith Sumner 2nd, (Supt. Eagle Cotton Gin Co.) r Main
Keith Sylvanus, farmer, r Fruit
Keith Thomas, nailer, r Wall
Keith Thomas M. book keeper, r Main
Keith Vassal, carpenter, r South
Keith Zephaniah, farmer, r South
King Francis D. stable keeper, Washburn Court
Kingman Benj. S. ins agent, r Pleasant
Kingman Bradford S. jeweller, bds Broad
Kingman Hosea, lawyer, bds Central sq
Kingman Philip D. dept. sheriff, r Broad
Knapp Zenas, carpenter, r Cross

LAMBERT CHARLES E. forgeman, r South
Lambert Edward H. r Oak
Latham Williams, lawyer, r Summer
Lathrop Avery, farmer, r Conant
Lathrop John A. teacher, r Conant
Lazell William, farmer, r Summer
Leach Andrew C. laborer
Leach Alphens, farmer, r Fruit
Leach Caleb D. farmer, Elm
Leach Elisha G. farmer, Titicut
Leach Franklin, carpenter, r Pleasant
Leach Horace, shoemaker, r South
Leach James C. carpenter, Spring Hill ave
Leach James F. farmer, r South
Leach James K. carpenter, r Pleasant
Leach James W. r Pleasant
Leach Jonathan S. farmer, r Elm
Leach Philander, farmer, r Elm
Leach Peleg, shoemaker, r South
Leach Shepard H. farmer, r Pleasant

ANNUAL CASH DIVIDENDS in the BERKSHIRE LIFE INS. CO., Pittsfield, Mass. Boston Office 95 1-2 Washington St. (See page 50.)

Leach Unite R. farmer, r North
Leach Zadoc, farmer, r Beach
Leach Zadoc W. farmer, r Beach
Leavitt Calvin, drover, r Whitman
Leavitt Franklin, laborer, r Centre
Lee George H. shoemaker, r Plain
Lee James E, mechanic, r Walnut
Leonard Cary M. machinist, r Plymouth
Leonard Elmer, machinist, r Curve
Leonard Geo. F. machinist, r Pleasant
Leonard H. P. clergyman, r Prospect
Leonard Isaac, farmer, r Cherry
Leonard James M. farmer, r Fruit
Leonard James M. 2d, depot-master, r Pleasant
Leonard Lucius K. shoemaker, r Curve
Leonard Martin, farmer, r Auburn
Leonard Philander D. teacher, r Union
Leonard Samuel, farmer, Auburn
Leonard Samuel L. mechanic, r Auburn
Leonard Seth, farmer, r Summer
Leonard Seth H. farmer, r Summer
Leonard Spencer, farmer, r Whitman
Leonard Wallace, bootmaker, r Auburn
Loring Edward S. mason, r Summer
Lovell John C. r Main
Lovell Lucius W. moulder, r Main
Lowe Lewis G. physician, r Pleasant
Lynch James, laborer, r High
Lynch Michael, laborer, r High
Lynch Terrence, laborer, r Oak

MAINE THOMAS, forgeman
Makepeace Jason T. L. mechanic, r Bolton pl
Marrer Edward, machinist, r Main
Martin Geo. H. teacher, bds South
McLaughlin E. Kirby, farmer, r Summer
McLaughlin Hervey W. fireman, r Oak
Millet Asa, physician, r Main
Mitchell Bela, mechanic, r Pleasant
Mitchell Caleb, farmer, r High
Mitchell Henry M. carpenter, r Plymouth
Mitchell James W. expressman, r Pleasant
Mitchell Leonard, farmer, Auburn
Mitchell Oreb, farmer, r Plymouth
Mitchell Philo, farmer, r Mt. Prospect
Mitchell Simeon W. farmer, r Auburn
Mitchell William, farmer, r High
Morgan Benj. D. r Wall
Morse Edwin, laborer, bds Oak
Morse Obediah, millwright, r Main
Munroe David B. machinist, bds Plymouth
Munroe Nathan, blacksmith, r Oak
Munroe Snow W. laborer, r Oak

NEWTON MARTIN V. mercht. r Wall
Norton Joseph C. farmer, r High
Norton Joseph C. jr., machinist, High

O'CONNOR RICHARD, laborer, r High
O'Leary James, laborer, r High
O'Hara Patrick, blacksmith, r Bolton pl
Oldham Miller S. forgeman, r Pleasant
Osborne Almanzor, shoemaker, r Plain

PARSONS LLOYD, cotton gin manuf. r South
Padelford Joshua, farmer
Perkins Aaron, engineer, r Centre
Perkins Alfred H. moulder, r Main
Perkins Asa, machinist, r High

Perkins Asa M. butcher, bds Centre
Perkins Calvin, fish-peddler, r Plymouth
Perkins Henry, ironfounder, r Main
Perkins Isaac, machinist, r Main
Perkins James, machinist, r Main
Perkins John, machinist, r Main
Perkins Simeon, ma on, r Main
Perkins Solomon, furnaceman, r Centre
Pierce Albert, bootmaker, r Bedford
Pierce Marcus, laborer, r North
Pocheron Chas. E. painter, bds Laurel
Pope Nahum, mechanic, r High
Pope Sylvanus P. mechanic, r Walnut
Porter Francis W. machinist,
Pownall George, harness maker, Wall
Pratt Anthony S. shoemaker, r South
Pratt Ebenezer, farmer, r Auburn
Pratt Ebenezer A. farmer, r Auburn
Pratt Edwin, machinist, r South
Pratt Gustavus, clerk, bds Broad
Pratt Henry T. cotton gin manuf. r School
Pratt Joseph, mechanic, r Auburn
Pratt Leonard, farmer, r Auburn
Pratt Seth, blacksmith, r South
Pratt Seth jr., machinist, r Broad
Pratt Silas, shoemaker, r Cherry
Pratt Sylvanus, shoemaker, r Auburn
Price Benjamin H. shoemaker, r Plymouth
Price Benj. W. shoemaker, r Plymouth
Prophett Wm. furniture dealer, Spring Hill ave

RAMSDEN WILLIAM, shoemaker, r East
Randall Henry M. laborer, r Pleasant
Randall Henry W. laborer, r Pleasant
Reed Alden A. conductor, r Pearl
Reed Charles M. merchant, r Main
Reed James, gardner, r Bedford
Reiser William H. hairdresser, bds Central sq
Revere Paul, clerk, r Main
Richmond Israel, r Green
Richmond James, r Green
Richmond Nath'l W. farmer, r Pleasant
Richmond Zadoc, blacksmith, r Green
Riley Patrick, laborer, r High
Riley Peter, laborer, r High
Ripley Henry W. mechanic, r Pleasant
Ripley Hervey C. restoraior, r Bedford
Robbins Charles, carpenter, r South
Robbins Silas, farmer, r South
Robinson Dyer, r Main
Robinson Floyd, shoemaker, r Curve
Robinson Gad, r Main
Robinson Hillman, mechanic, Spring Hill avenue
Robinson Jacob H. expressman, r Main
Robinson Jared, forgeman, r Main
Robinson John E. machinist, r Main
Robinson William H. nailer, r Wall
Rogers Bartlett, laborer, bds Summer
Rogers Royal S. harness maker, r South

SAMPSON GEORGE, machinist, r South
Sampson Passon H. machinist, r High
Sanford Henry D. clerk, r School
Sanger Samuel T. farmer, r Summer
Sawyer Edward, physician, Central sq
Scanlan James, laborer, r Broad
Scott Charles, laborer, r Plymouth
Shaw John A. teacher, r Plymouth

Shockley William, farmer, r Summer
Smith Christopher C. farmer, Titicut
Smith James W. trapper, r Summer
Smith Robert E. mechanic, r Auburn
Smith Thomas, farmer, r Bedford
Snell Henry C. farmer, r Summer
Snell Isaac H. farmer, r Summer
Snow Linus W. farmer, r Pine
Sprague Ephraim H. mechanic, bds South
Sprague Fisher A. (Lazell, Perkins & Co), r Grove
Sprague Holmes, mechanic, bds South
Sprague Jackson, mill wright, r High
Sprague Waterman, iron worker, Bolton Place
Sprague William H. forgeman, r Wall
Standish Job, mason, r Main
Stetson George B. (Lazell, Perkins & Co), r Broad
Stetson Nahum, (Lazell, Perkins & Co), r Summer
Stetson William, grocer, bds Broad
Sturtevant Dexter M. farmer, r South
Sturtevant Isaac, farmer, r Plymouth
Sturtevant William, mechanic, r Plymouth
Sturtevant Zadock, farmer, r Titicut
Sullivan Thomas, laborer, South
Summer Charles H. machinist, bds Broad
Sweeney Morris, laborer,
Sweeney William, laborer,
Swift James, shoemaker, r North
Swift Martin, farmer, r Ozier Place
Swift Melvin, farmer, r Summer
Swift Orrin B. moulder, r Summer
Swift Thomas, machinist, r Main
Swift Van R. farmer, r Summer

TALBOT AMERICA P. shoemaker, r Crescent
Thomas Luther, heater, r Oak
Thompson Charles H. bds Broad
Thompson Jacob, farmer, r Summer
Thompson Marshall, laborer, r Broad
Thurber Benjamin, engineer, r Oak
Tillson Ephraim, farmer, r Plymouth
Tillson Moses L. shoemaker, r Plymouth
Tolman Joel, farmer, r Pleasant
Tootle Richard, engineer, Bolton Place
Townsend Jeremiah H. brick manuf. Plymouth
Townsend John P. machinist, bds Plymouth
Tucker Jeremiah, station agent, r Titicut
Tucker Stillman, farmer, r Titicut
Turner John T. machinist, r Main
Turner William T. mechanic, r Broad

UPPMAN ANTONIO, laborer

WADE JOHN W. shoemaker, r High
Wadsworth Dura, carpenter, r Centre

Walker Levi, farmer, r North
Washburn Abram, mechanic, r Summer
Washburn Albion K. mechanic, r Plymouth
Washburn Azel, stone cutter, bds Ozier Place
Washburn Cephas, farmer, r Plymouth
Washburn Christian, dentist, Central sq
Washburn Clinton, farmer, r Summer
Washburn Eli, r South
Washburn Hosea, farmer, r South
Washburn Nahum, dentist, r Central sq
Washburn Rothens, mechanic, r Summer
Washburn Seth, farmer, r South
Washburn Willard, farmer, r Plymouth
Waterman Walter L. mason, r Main
Welch Alexander, laborer, r Bedford
Wentworth Hiram, farmer, r South
Wentworth Horace, mechanic, r Pleasant
Wentworth Horace E. shoemaker, r Pleasant
Wentworth John M. mechanic, r Wentworth
Wentworth Lewis, farmer, r Bedford
Wentworth Lucin F. shoemaker, r Pleasant
Weston Franklin C. machinist, r Auburn
Weston Joseph L. carpenter, bds Union
White Hiram H. engineer, r Summer
Wilbar Charles W. shoemaker, r South
Wilbar David H. shoemaker, r Winter
Wilbar David W. farmer, r Cherry
Wilbar Florencins, carpenter, r Pleasant
Wilbar Gardner, farmer, r Pleasant
Wilbar George, farmer, r Vernon
Wilbar George S. farmer, r Vernon
Wilbar Henry F. shoemaker, r South
Wilbar Horace, shoemaker, r South
Wilbar Isaac S. butcher, r Cross
Wilbar Kilea, mechanic, r Summer
Wilbar Oliver C. farmer, r Union
Wilbar Richard W. shoemaker, r School
Wilbar Sanford, farmer, r South
Wilbar Seth O. shoemaker, r Green Place
Wilbar Theodore C. carpenter, r Pleasant
Wilbar Winslow C. artist, bds Summer
Wiley Robert, machinist
Willard H. M. teacher, bds Main
Willis Nathan, shoemaker, r Main
Wing Philip H. farmer, r Plymouth
Winslow John B. mechanic, r Broad
Winslow Kenelm, mechanic, r Plymouth
Winsor Francis, shoemaker
Winsor Samuel G. shoemaker
Witherell Jabez, farmer, r Oak
Witherell James F. heater, r Main
Witherell John, heater, r Main
Wood Henry, farmer, r Titicut
Wood Martin, farmer, r Curve
Wood Nahum B. farmer, r Curve
Wood Simeon D. shoemaker, r High
Worcester Charles F. moulder, r North

Carver General Directory.

ATWOOD CHARLES H. farmer, Centre
Andrews Robert W. moulder, r South
Appling Geo. H. moulder, North
Atwood Bartlett S. farmer, Centre
Atwood Eli, farmer, Centre
Atwood George, farmer, North
Atwood George W. farmer, Centre
Atwood Gustavus, farmer, South
Atwood Elbridge E. farmer, Centre
Atwood Jacob, farmer, Centre
Atwood John S. shoemaker, North
Atwood Joseph, moulder, South
Atwood Josiah W. farmer, South
Atwood Lucius, farmer, Centre
Atwood Luther, farmer, South
Atwood Marcus, farmer, South
Atwood Oren, farmer, Centre
Atwood Salmon, laborer, South
Atwood Stephen, farmer, Centre
Atwood Sumner, farmer, South
Atwood Tillson, moulder, Centre

BARROWS ASA, laborer, North
Barrows Andrew F. moulder, Centre
Barrows John B. moulder, South
Barrows Joseph, farmer, South
Barrows Lothrop, moulder, Centre
Barrows Nelson, machinist, South
Barrows P. W. moulder, Centre
Bates David M. stove-mounter, South
Bates Nathaniel B. shoemaker, South
Bennett Allen, blacksmith, South
Bennett Charles, japanner, South
Benson Jabez, laborer, South
Bent Geo. W. grate manuf. South
Bent Ira C. moulder, Centre
Bent John, farmer, Centre
Bent John, jr. sawyer, Centre
Bent Joseph F. laborer, South
Blake Edson C. peddler, Centre
Blake Hiram A. shoemaker, North
Bosworth James H. stove-mounter, South
Bowers Geo. P. manuf. South
Breech Isaac P. sailor, North
Breech James, basketmaker, North
Breech William, basketmaker, North
Brett Rufus J. trader, North
Brett William, farmer, Centre
Bumpus Daniel, moulder, South
Bumpus Edmond P. farmer, South
Bumpus Edward, farmer, South
Bumpus John, laborer, South
Bumpus Philander W. farmer, North

CARNES EDWARD S. r North

Carter John S. teamer, r South
Chace Charles H. peddler, North
Chace Henry L. orthodox minister, North
Chace John, farmer, Centre
Chamberlain B. blacksmith, South
Chamberlain B. A. blacksmith, South
Chandler Job C. farmer, North
Chandler Job C. jr., box maker, North
Chandler John B. moulder, North
Chandler Joseph S. box maker, North
Chandler Josiah, shoe maker, North
Chandler William B. shoe maker, North
Cobb Charles, carpenter, North
Cobb Frederic, shoemaker, North
Cobb Joseph F. laborer, North
Cobb Levi, farmer, North
Cobb Sydney, clerk, North
Cobb Thomas, peddler, North
Cobb Walter B. shoemaker, North
Cole Ansel, shoemaker, North
Cole Bartlett B. peddler, North
Cole Harrison G. box manuf. North
Cole Hezekiah, carpenter, North
Cole Theron M. box maker, North
Copeland Ralph, shoemaker, North
Cornell Charles P. shoemaker, North
Crowell Jeremiah, carpenter, Centre
Cushman Jacob, moulder, South
Cushman Stephen, farmer, South

DEMPSEY ROBERT M. shoemaker, South
Drew Atwood, caulker, North
Drew Atwood R. shoemaker, North
Dunham Benjamin, farmer, South
Dunham Daniel, teamer, North
Dunham Ebenezer, farmer, South
Dunham Ebenezer jr., farmer, South
Dunham Ellis D. shoemaker, North
Dunham Elisha M. clerk, South
Dunham Isaac L. farmer, North
Dunham James, shoemaker, North
Dunham John, shoemaker, North

EAMES ANDREW R. box maker, North
Eaton Calvin H. shoemaker, North
Eames Luther, box maker, North
Ellis Matthias, iron foundry, South
Ellis Joseph M. iron foundry, South

FAUNCE JAMES V. farmer, North
Finney Benjamin D. farmer, North
Freeman Rufus C. machinist, South
Frees William, laborer, North
Fuller Ansel, shoemaker, North
Fuller Benjamin F. shoemaker, North

J. A. JACKSON, 101 COURT STREET, BOSTON, DEALER IN HATS, CAPS, AND FURS.

GIBBS THOMAS, laborer, South
Gibbs William B. farmer, South
Griffeth Albert, laborer, South
Griffeth Andrew, moulder, South
Griffeth Charles W. moulder, South
Griffeth Ellis, farmer, South
Griffeth Ephraim, farmer, South
Griffeth John, moulder, South
Griffeth Thomas B. manuf. South

HACKETT ELKANAH, laborer, North
Hammond Benjamin, farmer, North
Hammond Henry T. sailor, North
Hammond William, farmer, Centre
Harlow Benjamin, carpenter, South
Harlow Ephraim T. peddler, North
Harlow Simeon, carpenter, South
Hatch John B. sawyer, Centre
Hathaway Geo. moulder, South
Hathaway William E. peddler, North
Herd Manoah, farmer, Centre
Holmes Jacob, farmer, Centre

JENKINS S. F. braid manuf. South
Jones P. M. C. farmer, North

KING GEO. M. shoemaker, North
King Luther S. W. teamster, North
Kinney Amos P. machinist, South

LEACH WILLIAM, clergyman, Centre
Leonard Benj. F. machinist, South
Lucas Ebenezer S. farmer, North
Lucas Harvey, farmer, North
Lucas Horatio A. farmer, North
Lucas Jesse, laborer, North
Lucas Jesse F. shoemaker, North
Lucas John B. shoemaker, North
Lucas Samuel F. farmer, North

MANSFIELD MICHAEL, farmer, South
Manter Everett T. sailor, North
Maxim Ellis, blacksmith, South
Maxim John, farmer, South
Maxim Nathan B. sawyer, Centre
Maxim Thomas, farmer, South
McFarlin John B. moulder, South
McFarlin Joseph T. moulder, South
McFarlin Sampson, farmer, South
McFarlin Solomon F. moulder, South
McFarlin Thomas H. farmer, South
McFarlin William S. moulder, South
Merritt Andrew D. shoemaker, North
Morse Geo. shoemaker, North
Morse Harrison D. shoemaker, North
Murdock Elisha, moulder, South
Murdock Henry C. sailor, South
Murdock Jesse, grate manuf. South

NICKERSON ZIBA, laborer, South
Norrell Charles, laborer, South

PARSONS CHARLES, carpenter, South
Perkins Albert, carpenter, Centre
Perkins Alvin, farmer, Centre
Perkins Alvin S. carpenter, South
Peterson Daniel M. shoemaker, North
Pierson William, farmer, North
Pierson William S. W. shoemaker, North
Pratt E. Tillson, teacher, North
Pratt Frederick A. moulder, South
Pratt Lewis, iron foundry, North
Pratt Matthias, iron foundry, North

Pratt Wm. B. moulder, North
Pratt Winslow, farmer, North
Purrington Elias, carpenter, North

RAMSDELL CORNELIUS, shoemaker, North
Ransom Benj. merchant, North
Ransom Levi, farmer, North
Richards Erastus, shoemaker, Centre
Richards Luther, farmer, Centre
Richards Rufus L. shoemaker, Centre
Richards Wm. stone cutter, Centre
Rider Charles, merchant, South
Rider Nathan, farmer, Centre
Rickard Benj. W. shoemaker, North
Rickard L. Warren, farmer, North
Ripley Calvin, farmer, North
Robbins Benj. W. farmer, North
Robbins Chandler, jr. farmer, North
Robbins Ephraim P. farmer, North
Robbins Josiah P. farmer, North

SANBORN JOHN D. shoemaker, North
Savery Benjamin H. shoemaker, North
Savery William, iron foundry, South
Savery William S. merchant, North
Sears Edmond, carpenter, North
Sears Edmond L. carpenter, North
Shaw Atwood, farmer, Centre
Shaw Charles S. blacksmith, North
Shaw Daniel, farmer, Centre
Shaw Daniel A. merchant, Centre
Shaw Ebenezer D. moulder, Centre
Shaw Edward W. farmer, Centre
Shaw Elijah, farmer, North
Shaw Elkanah, moulder, South
Shaw E. Howard, shoemaker, South
Shaw E. Watson carpenter, Centre
Shaw George, moulder, Centre
Shaw George H. moulder, Centre
Shaw Isaac, farmer, North
Shaw Isaac 2nd, moulder, South
Shaw Jesse, laborer, Centre
Shaw John F. moulder, South
Shaw John, farmer, Centre
Shaw John 2nd, moulder, Centre
Shaw Linus A. moulder, Centre
Shaw Lorenzo N. teamer, North
Shaw Jason, laborer, North
Shaw Marcus M. moulder, South
Shaw Nathaniel, farmer, Centre
Shaw Nathaniel jr. moulder, North
Shaw Stillman, laborer, South
Shaw Samuel, clerk, South
Shaw Samuel 2d, clerk, South
Sherman Albert, moulder, North
Sherman Andrew B. farmer, North
Sherman Earl, farmer, North
Sherman Ebenezer, farmer, North
Sherman Frederic C. shoemaker, North
Sherman Henry, farmer, North
Sherman Joseph W. shoemaker, North
Sherman Levi V. shoe express, North
Sherman Nelson, farmer, North
Shurtleff Abial, moulder, North
Shurtleff Albert, farmer, North
Shurtleff Albert T. clerk, North
Shurtleff George, sailor, North
Shurtleff Henry F. shoemaker, North
Shurtleff Ichabod, farmer, South
Shurtleff Ichabod jr., farmer, South
Shurtleff James F. scholar, North
Shurtleff Levi, farmer, North

DIVIDENDS ADDED to the POLICY in the BERKSHIRE often exceed the premium paid; are NON-FORFEITABLE and will be redeemed in CASH ON DEMAND. (See page 50.)

Shurtleff Perez, farmer, Centre
Shurtleff Peter, moulder, South
Shurtleff Seth, farmer, North
Smith Perez B. H. dyer and bleacher,
  South
Smith Perez, stone cutter, South
Southworth Eli, farmer, Centre
Southworth Thomas, surveyor, South
Southworth Thomas M. South
Southworth Jason, carpenter, South
Stanley William, foreman of factory,
  South

THOMAS LEVI, blacksmith, South
Threshie Charles, iron foundry, South
Tillson Augustus F. clerk, South
Tillson Freeman F. moulder, South
Tillson H. Bartlett, moulder, South
Tillson John, farmer, South
Tillson Marcus M. moulder, South
Tillson William, shoemaker, North
Tillson Zenas, moulder, South

VAIL, ISAAC B. agent, North
Vaughan Daniel, shoemaker, North
Vaughan J. C. architect, Centre

Vaughan Ezra, wheelwright, North
Vaughan Levi C. clerk, Centre
Vaughan Thomas, farmer, Centre

WARD ANSEL, laborer, South
Ward Ansel B. shoemaker, North
Ward Austin, butcher, North
Ward Benjamin, farmer, Centre
Ward Stillman, butcher, North
Ward Stillman jr., sailor, North
Washburn A. F. farmer, South
Washburn Asaph, farmer, South
Washburn Henry C. farmer, South
Washburn Jacob, farmer, North
Washburn Joseph M. painter, North
Washburn Joseph G. shoemaker, Centre
Washburn Marshall A. laborer, South
Waterman John, North
Westgate Ephraim C. blacksmith,
White Henry, shoemaker, North
Williams George, farmer, North
William John, stone cutter, South
Wood Geo. F. physician, North
Wrightington Henry, laborer, South
Wrightington Thomas, foreman farmer,
  South

Duxbury General Directory.

Prepared by Henry Barstow.

ADAMS JOHN, farmer
Alden Benjamin, auctioneer
Alden Henry, laborer
Alden Ichabod, laborer
Alden James, farmer
Alden John, trader
Alden John, jr. master mariner
Alden Samuel, boat-builder
Alden Thomas, farmer
Alden William J. deputy sheriff
Alden William J. jr. shoemaker
Ames Thomas R. shoemaker
Armstrong John, shoemaker
Arnold Abel C. shoemaker
Arnold Gamaliel, shoemaker
Arnold Orson M. shoemaker
Atwell George, farmer
Atwell Samuel, selectman

BAKER ALVEN, carpenter,
Baker Daniel, farmer
Baker George
Baker Geo. L.
Baker Granville, shoemaker
Baker Harvey, ship carpenter
Baker Herbert, shoemaker
Baker Sumner B. farmer

Baker Walter, shoemaker
Bailey Edgar H. shoemaker
Bailey George H. house carpenter
Bailey Louis M. farmer
Bancroft Kirk H. physician
Barstow Augustus P. mason
Barstow Benjamin, mason
Barstow Daniel W. boot maker
Barstow Henry, shoe cutter
Barstow Henry W. mason
Barstow Hiram W. farmer
Barstow Ichabod, ship carpenter
Barstow Lewis, mason
Barstow Lewis B. mason
Barstow William, ship carpenter
Bemis Benjamin C.
Belknap Scott, shoemaker
Bisbee Benjamin F. trowel worker
Bisbee Joseph F. mechanic
Bisbee Franklin, manuf. of trowels
Boylston Benjamin, trader
Bosworth Joseph P. carpenter
Bosworth Joseph P. jr. shoemaker
Bowen William, shoemaker
Bradford Daniel, master mariner
Bradford George, selectman
Bradford Gershom, trader

J. A. JACKSON, 101 COURT STREET, BOSTON, DEALER IN HATS, CAPS, AND FURS.

Bradford Ephraim, rope maker
Bradford William, spar maker
Brett Royal T. butcher
Brewster Asa, fisherman
Brewster Charles E. trader
Brewster Daniel W. master mariner
Brewster John W. farmer
Brewster Joseph, fisherman
Brewster Melzar, farmer
Brewster Melzar jr., farmer
Brewster Nathan, carpenter
Briggs Samuel P.
Brown Charles H. farmer
Brown George H. bootmaker
Brooks Peleg T. stage proprietor and expressman
Bryant Franklin, farmer
Bryant Fredric, shoemaker
Bryant Hiram, shipcarpenter
Bryant John, farmer
Burditt Andrew, master mariner
Burgess Charles G. farmer
Burgess Consider, farmer
Burgess Daniel, lobster-dealer
Burgess James
Burgess James K. farmer
Burgess Nathaniel, farmer
Burgess Nathan A. farmer
Burgess Spencer, painter
Burns John, fisherman

CHANDLER AARON, rigger
Chandler Alden, painter
Chandler Alonzo, farmer,
Chandler Asa, shoemaker
Chandler Bailey, farmer
Chandler Calvin
Chandler Charles H. box-mill proprietor
Chandler David, jr. shoemaker
Chandler Ebenezer, farmer
Chandler Edwin P. carpenter
Chandler Elbridge, farmer
Chandler Elbridge H. mason
Chandler Eli, farmer
Chandler Emmons A. shoemaker
Chandler Francis A. farmer
Chandler George, stone mason
Chandler George, 2d, shoemaker
Chandler George T.
Chandler George T. 2d
Chandler Harrison, shoemaker
Chandler Henry
Chandler Hiram, shoemaker
Chandler Hiram W. boat-builder
Chandler Horatio
Chandler Howard, house-carpenter
Chandler Ichabod D
Chandler Ichabod W. laborer
Chandler Isaac
Chandler Isaac W
Chandler Jerome, house-carpenter
Chandler Joseph, farmer
Chandler Joseph, 2d, trader
Chandler Judah, keeper of alms-house
Chandler Julius B. farmer
Chandler Levi, farmer
Chandler Martin S. farmer
Chandler Nathaniel, jr.
Chandler Nathaniel L. farmer
Chandler Noah J. shoemaker
Chandler Otis, stone mason
Chandler Pelham
Chandler Philip, farmer

Chandler Proctor
Chandler Richard B. farmer
Chandler Rufus G. house-carpenter
Chandler Seth D. farmer
Chandler Thaddeus W
Chandler Thomas, shoemaker
Chandler Thomas, 2d farmer
Chandler Wadsworth, farmer
Chandler Willard R
Chandler William, farmer
Childes George W. farmer
Church Martin, ship-carpenter
Church Samuel T.
Clapp Lewis
Clark Willard, stove and tin ware manuf.
Coggeshall Samuel W. clergyman
Collins William, fisherman
Cook Peleg, ship-carpenter
Cox Charles, shoemaker
Crocker George P. shoemaker
Curtis George W. fisherman
Curtis James, farmer
Curtis Julius, master mariner
Cushing Benj. D. shoe carter
Cushing John, farmer
Cushing John W. shoemaker
Cushing Levi H. farmer
Cushing Nathaniel, master ship-builder
Cushing Seth C. farmer
Cushing William H. shoemaker
Cushman Alden, ship carpenter
Cushman Benjamin,
Cushman Briggs,
Cushman David, master mariner
Cushman George, farmer
Cushman Henry L. carpenter
Cushman John,
Cushman Peleg,

DAMON PROCTOR A.
Davis John,
Davison George, shoemaker
Dawes Abraham, farmer
Dawes Albert A.
Dawes Josephus, master mariner
Delano Albert,
Delano Alden, fisherman
Delano Asa S. ship carpenter
Delano Briggs B. ship carpenter
Delano Charles, carpenter
Delano Charles 2d, farmer
Delano Charles C.
Delano Charles H.
Delano Elijah, ship joiner
Delano Elijah 2d,
Delano Elisha, box manufacturer
Delano Henry,
Delano Henry M. carpenter
Delano Hiram, blacksmith
Delano Hiram T. fisherman
Delano Hiram T. 2d, fisherman
Delano James S.
Delano Jesse,
Delano John jr., farmer
Delano Joseph S. farmer
Delano Judah, shoemaker
Delano Nathaniel, blacksmith
Delano Otis, shoemaker
Delano Samuel, fisherman
Dorr Nathan, mason
Door Rufus B. blacksmith
Drew Alfred, master mariner
Drew Henry, painter

Policy Holders in the BERKSHIRE LIFE INSURANCE COMPANY of Pittsfield, Mass., DO NOT FORFEIT THEIR POLICIES by reason of FAILURE TO PAY their premiums. (See page 50.)

Drew Joshua E.
Drew Lyman, organist
Drew Spencer, ship carpenter
Drew William B. master mariner
Driscoll Daniel, farmer
Dunster Henry J. fisherman

ELDRIDGE EVERETT, mariner
Ellis John, fisherman
Ellis Nathaniel, farmer
Estes Charles, farmer

FARRAR AUSTIN,
Faunce George, farmer
Faunce Geo. A. mariner
Faunce Zenas, blacksmith and gunsmith
Fish Henry P.
Fish Joseph, peddler
Fleming William, farmer
Ford Benjamin P. shoemaker
Ford Ezra J. shoemaker
Ford George W. trader
Ford Jonathan S. trader
Ford Joshua O.
Ford Joshua T. tanner
Ford Levi, shoemaker
Ford Nathaniel, trader
Ford Peleg, farmer
Frazar Samuel A. ship carpenter
Frazar Walter D.
Frazar William S. farmer
Freeman Albert,
Freeman Arnold, caulker
Freeman Bradford, fisherman
Freeman David C. shoemaker
Freeman David H. shoemaker
Freeman Enoch, shoemaker
Freeman Eugene S. shoemaker
Freeman George P. master mariner
Freeman Harrison G. O. shoemaker
Freeman James H. shoemaker
Freeman Joseph
Freeman Joshua S. ship joiner
Freeman Martin, carpenter
Freeman Nathan D.
Freeman Sprague, box maker
Freeman Theodore P. shoemaker
Freeman Walter D.
Freeman Walter H. farmer
Freeman Weston, carpenter
Freeman Winfield S. shoemaker
Frost Alonzo, shoemaker
Frost Charles, farmer
Frost Edward F. shoemaker
Frost George W. shoemaker
Frost William W. farmer
Furnell Sumner F. painter
Furness Charles H. farmer

GARDNER LUTHER T. shoemaker
Gardner Merlin, farmer
Gerry Joseph D. farmer
Gifford Stephen N. Clerk of Senate, Boston
Glass Abram P.
Glass Daniel F. caulker
Glass Daniel P. caulker
Glass Eugene, caulker
Glass Horace, peddler
Glass John, farmer
Glass Jonathan jr.,
Glover John, caulker
Gorham Thomas,

Goodspeed David, mariner
Goodspeed Joseph, shoemaker
Graves Augustus A. peddler
Gross Jonathan, carpenter
Gulliver Bailey, caulker
Gulliver John, ship carpenter
Gulliver Peleg
Gurdy Samuel H. butcher

HAMILTON JOHN E.
Harris Lebbeus, shoemaker
Harriman Elihu A. shoemaker
Hatch Jabez, fisherman
Hathaway Joshua W. painter
Harlow Judah, farmer
Harlow Judah jr.,
Harlow Briggs,
Hathaway Rufus, farmer
Higgins George L. carpenter
Holliday Rufus, master mariner
Hollis John B. State Deputy Constable
Holmes Allen, ship carpenter
Holmes Elisha, fisherman
Holmes George W. fisherman
Holmes Gershom, ship carpenter
Holmes Henry,
Holmes John,
Holmes Rufus,
Holmes Samuel,
Holmes William,
Holmes William E.
Holmes William W. farmer
Howland Benjamin, farmer
Hunt Barker, farmer
Hunt Cassius, fisherman
Hunt Charles W. shoemaker
Hunt Edwin, fisherman
Hunt Henry A. fisherman
Hunt Hiram,
Hunt John H.
Hunt John T.
Hunt Joseph W. fisherman
Hunt Melzar, fisherman
Hunt Oscar E. mariner
Hunt Samuel W.
Hunt Wadsworth, master mariner
Hunt William F. fisherman
Hunt Ziba, blacksmith
Hutchings Nelson V. blacksmith

JACKSON STEPHEN H. fisherman
Joice Samuel H.
Joice William, teamster
Jones William W. fisherman
Joseph Antonio, stevedore
Josselyn Calvin, ship carpenter
Josselyn George, mariner
Josselyn Issachar, shoemaker
Josselyn Lyman, ship carpenter
Josselyn Walter L. mariner

KEEN ISAAC, farmer
Keen Nahum, carpenter
Keen Nathan C. box maker
Keen Nathaniel P.
Keep Jabez, peddler
Kenned Robert B. tailor
Kingman Ziba,
Knowles Samuel, merchant

LANE ALEXANDER, fisherman
Lane George W. fisherman
Leonard Augustus C. farmer

J. A. JACKSON, 101 COURT STREET, BOSTON, DEALER IN HATS, CAPS AND FURS.

Lewis Alonzo, mason
Lewis George G. mariner
Lewis Henry H.
Lewis John C. farmer
Lewis John J. shoemaker
Lewis Joseph, carpenter
Lewis Joseph H. carpenter
Lewis Martin K.
Loring Perez, farmer
Loring Samuel, tack manufacturer
Louden George, ship joiner and carpenter
Loring Edgar F. peddler
Loring John S. oil petroleum

MAGLATHLIN DANIEL S. farmer
Maglathlin Henry B. mathematician
Magoun Edward
Magoun Seth S.
Mann Marcus M.
McDonald Alexander J. trader
McNaught John, shoemaker
McNaught Thomas, shoemaker
Meehan David C. shoemaker
Metcalf Edward G. shoemaker
Moore Josiah, clergyman
Morton Otis, sailmaker
Myrick Albert C. fisherman
Myrick William, farmer

NICKERSON GEORGE, master mariner
Northey Andrew, mason

OLDHAM CHANDLER, ship-carpenter
Oldham Manton, mason

PACKARD ALPHEUS,
Paine Calvin B. farmer
Paine Eugene W.
Paine Isaac M. farmer
Paine Roland G
Partridge John
Partridge Ralph, teacher
Paulding Alfred, ship-carpenter
Paulding Henry, ship-carpenter
Paulding Wm. master ship-builder
Perkins Chesley
Perry James, fisherman
Peterson Alfred, shoemaker
Peterson Alfred, 2d
Peterson Alonzo S.
Peterson Briggs, farmer
Peterson Clark, ship-carpenter
Peterson Daniel B. farmer
Peterson David L. fisherman
Peterson Edwin, rigger
Peterson Elijah, farmer
Peterson Elisha,
Peterson Ellis, fisherman
Peterson Geo. P. shoemaker
Peterson Gilbert M. fisherman
Peterson Hiram,
Peterson Jabez, farmer
Peterson Josiah, town clerk
Peterson Lewis, clerk
Peterson Martin, shoemaker
Peterson Nehemiah, shoemaker
Peterson Otis, shoemaker
Peterson Reuben, ship-carpenter
Peterson Samuel S. boat builder
Peterson Stephen, farmer
Peterson Stephen F. farmer
Peterson Stephen S. fisherman
Peterson Stillman S. farmer

Peterson Walter S. fisherman
Peterson Willam B. fisherman
Phillips Augustus, carpenter
Phillips Luther T. carpenter
Pierce John, farmer
Pierce Leander B. shoemaker
Pierce Luther, farmer
Pierce Rufus, fisherman
Pratt Bryant, butcher
Pride Frank, farmer
Prior Allen, flour and grain dealer
Prior Charles, shoemaker
Prior Eliphaz, flour and grain dealer
Prior George C. master mariner
Prior George P. fisherman
Prior Joseph,
Prior Sylvanus, farmer
Pryor William, master mariner
Prior William, jr. master mariner

RANDALL JAMES, farmer
Randall Jason H. farmer
Randall Josiah D. farmer
Randall Josiah D. jr. farmer
Randall Francis J. trader
Randall Robert T.
Randall Rufus, farmer
Randall Seth D. farmer
Randall Thomas,
Randall William,
Richardson Geo. P. master mariner
Rider Geo. F. shoemaker
Rider Geo. R. shoemaker
Rider Gilbert M. shoemaker
Rider Nathaniel C. ship-carpenter
Ripley Obed, farmer
Rogers Charles A. mariner
Russell Matthew,
Rutledge Joseph M.

SAMPSON ALFRED,
Sampson Alfred jr., painter
Sampson Andrew, caulker
Sampson Charles, caulker
Sampson Daniel,
Sampson Eden, carpenter
Sampson Eden 2d,
Sampson Eden S. livery stable and ship joiner
Sampson Elisha jr., master mariner
Sampson Ellis,
Sampson George,
Sampson George, ship carpenter
Sampson Geo. F.
Sampson Henry L. post master
Sampson Henry R. painter
Sampson Isaac L.
Sampson John, trader
Sampson Nathan, carpenter
Sampson Nahum, farmer
Sampson Rufus, farmer
Sampson Rufus jr.,
Sampson Studley, caulker
Sampson Sylvanus, farmer
Sears William, fisherman
Sennott Peter A. laborer
Shedd Sylvanus, shoemaker
Sheldon William, farmer
Sherman Fredric P. town treasurer
Sherman Luther, farmer
Sherman Luther W.
Simmons Aaron,
Simmons Abram P. shoemaker

ANNUAL CASH DIVIDENDS in the BERKSHIRE LIFE INS. CO., Pittsfield, Mass. Boston Office 95 1-2 Washington St. (See page 50.)

Simmons Chas. W.
Simmons Edmond F. house carpenter
Simmons Edward F.
Simmons Francis W.
Simmons George,
Simmons Geo. A.
Simmons James,
Simmons James A. trader
Simmons Jesse,
Simmons Joseph W.
Simmons Joshua W.
Simmons Levi, farmer
Simmons Lewis,
Simmons Lewis jr.,
Simmons Lyman,
Simmons Peleg, farmer
Simmons Samuel J. house carpenter,
Simmons Warren M.
Simmons William,
Simmons William H.
Simmons William W. shoemaker
Smith Hamilton E. at Custom House Boston
Smith William, shoemaker
Snell Charles, shoemaker
Snell Charles H. box maker
Snell Elijah F.
Soule Charles, master mariner
Soule Charles 2d, laborer
Soule Daniel L. farmer
Soule Edwin A. fisherman
Soule Enoch, farmer
Soule Freeman, master mariner
Soule Harvey, trader
Soule James, ship carpenter
Soule James O. farmer
Soule John A. shoemaker
Soule Joseph A. farmer
Soule Lot, pump and block maker
Soule Micah A. shoemaker
Soule Nathan, pump and block maker
Soule Nathan 2d,
Soule Nathan T. teacher
Soule Oscar H. shoemaker
Soule Samuel P.
Soule Simeon, clerk in Boston
Soule Stephen, master mariner
Soule Thomas, carpenter
Southworth Henry,
Southworth Jacob, master mariner
Southworth James,
Southworth John,
Southworth Walter,
Sprague Ezekiel, farmer
Sprague George,
Sprague Jacob, freight agent, office in Boston
Sprague Joseph, farmer
Strang Peter S. laborer
Standish Bailey G. farmer
Standish Geo. B. selectman
Steel Robert, fisherman
Stetson Andrew, shoemaker
Stetson Nelson, wheelwright
Stetson Samuel, counsellor
Stickney Samuel jr., clerk
Sturtevant Lewis,
Swift Joshua W. stage and express proprietor
Swift Lot, farmer
Symmes Daniel W.
Symmes Isaac, caulker

TAYLOR CHASE, clergyman
Thomas Briggs, master mariner
Thomas James, farmer
Thomas Nathaniel, master mariner
Thomas Nehemiah, farmer
Thomas William H. shoemaker
Thompson Thomas,
Thompson Walter, farmer
Tisdale William R. clergyman
Torrey George H. fisherman
Torrey Isaac, farmer
Trask James, farmer
Tretheway Robert J. farmer
Turner Daniel, ship carpenter
Turner Hezekiah, fisherman
Turner Jonathan F. fisherman
Turner William, ship carpenter
Turner William K. fisherman

VINAL JAMES B. stage and express proprietor
Vinal James C. blacksmith
Vinal Henry G. blacksmith

WADSWORTH ALEXANDER, master mariner
Wadsworth Daniel, boat builder
Wadsworth Dura, carpenter
Wadsworth Eden, master mariner
Wadsworth Gamaliel, fisherman
Wadsworth Hamilton, shoemaker
Wadsworth Harrison, shoemaker
Wadsworth Henry, trader
Wadsworth Seth, farmer
Wadsworth William,
Walker David P.
Walker Isaiah jr., lobster dealer
Washburn James B. clergyman
Waterman Nathaniel,
Watson George,
Watson William, farmer
Welsh William,
Weston Alden B. merchant, retired
Weston Alden B. 2d,
Weston Augustus, farmer
Weston Bradford, carpenter
Weston Briggs T.
Weston Charles H. fisherman
Weston Charles S. fisherman
Weston Edward B. master mariner
Weston Edward R. fisherman
Weston Harrison G. carpenter
Weston Henry,
Weston Hiram,
Weston Geo. P.
Weston George S. fisherman
Weston Gershom B. merchant
Weston Jabez P. shoemaker
Weston James, carpenter
Weston James H. carpenter
Weston James M. carpenter
Weston John F.
Weston Joseph, house carpenter
Weston Joseph jr., house carpenter
Weston Nathaniel, ship carpenter
Weston Otis, shoemaker
Weston Thomas,
Weston William E. caulker
Weston William H.
Weston Wyman
White Benjamin
White Daniel W.

J. A. JACKSON 101 COURT STREET, BOSTON, DEALER IN HATS, CAPS AND FURS.

White Edward
White Jonathan F.
White Otis, farmer
Whiting Geo. L.
Whiting Henry T. farmer
Whiting Nathan G.
Whitmarsh John
Whitmarsh Samuel G.
Wilde James, physician
Wilde John, carpenter and singing teacher
Winslow George, ship joiner
Winsor Alden
Winsor Bailey D. fisherman
Winsor Calvin G. fisherman
Winsor Charles, fisherman
Winsor Corindo, shoemaker
Winsor Eden, farmer
Winsor Edward W.
Winsor George
Winsor George 2d, master mariner
Winsor Geo. H.
Winsor Harvey D.
Winsor Henry O. 2d.
Winsor Hiram, master mariner
Winsor James E.
Winsor James H. shoemaker
Winsor James H. jr., shoemaker
Winsor Joshua, shoemaker
Winsor Lewis, master mariner
Winsor Lorenzo D. master mariner
Winsor Martin, master mariner
Winsor Richard H.
Winsor Samuel, farmer
Winsor Samuel A.
Winsor Seth
Winsor Spencer T. master mariner
Winsor William G. fisherman
Winsor William H. fisherman
Witherell Amos
Witherell Gershom W. livery stable proprietor
Woodard Henry H.
Woodard Ozro W. mariner
Woodard William, fisherman

East Bridgewater General Directory.

ACKERMAN BENJ. M. farmer, Black Brook
Adams Bethuel, mechanic, Pearl
Adams Rufus, mechanic, Satucket
Alden Abner L. shoemaker, Village
Alden Bartlett R. carpenter, Village
Alden Benjamin R. Village
Alden Joseph, mechanic, Village
Alden Samuel G. lumber dealer, Village
Alger Ebenezer, farmer, Beaver
Alger Orlando M. farmer, Beaver
Allen Bailey, carpenter, Village
Allen David, shoemaker, Beaver
Allen Galen, shoemaker, Beaver
Allen George, clerk
Allen George W. shoe cutter, Shaw's Mill
Allen Henry, machinist
Allen James S. shoe manuf. Beaver
Allen John A. shoe cutter, Shaw's Mill
Allen Samuel B. tailor, Joppa
Allen Samuel B. 2d, shoemaker, Satucket
Allen Samuel P. teacher, Joppa
Allen Sidney, farmer, Shaw's Mill
Allen William, teacher, Satucket

BAILEY LEVI P. shoemaker
Bailey William S. Village
Baker Ansel G. teamer
Bancroft Edwin W. shoemaker, Shaw's Mill
Barrell George W. shoemaker, Beaver
Bartlett Ezekiel R. shoemaker
Bates Irving, shoe manuf. Joppa
Bates Jacob, farmer, West Crook
Bates Moses, manuf. and editor, Village
Bates Reuben, shoemaker
Bates Samuel, confectioner, Northville
Bates William H. H. machinist
Beal Alonzo, shoemaker, Robbins Pond
Beal Asaph, stitcher, Robbins Pond
Beal Blaney P. shoemaker, Black Brook
Beal Nathaniel, farmer
Beal Samuel, shoemaker, Birch Swamp
Bell John, shoemaker, Beaver
Bell Leander, shoemaker
Bennett Chas. W. machinist, Satucket
Bennett Eleazer C. machinist, Satucket
Benson Albion K. forgeman
Benson George, carpenter, Joppa
Bird Cushing, shoemaker, Satucket
Bird Edmund, shoemaker, Satucket
Bird Elijah, farmer, Satucket
Bird Elijah S. tack maker, Satucket
Bird George E. shoemaker
Bird William, shoemaker, Village
Bisbee Joseph E. shoemaker
Bisbee Otis, forgeman
Blackman Andrew G. shoe finisher
Blanchard Augustus W. shoemaker, Birch Swamp
Blanchard Daniel T. shoemaker, Northville
Blanchard Eli, shoemaker, Northville
Blanchard George W. shoemaker, Northville

The terms for TEN ENDOWMENT, and TEN ANNUAL LIFE POLICIES in the BERKSHIRE are peculiarly favorable, and rates lower than in any Note Company. (See page 50.)

Bonney Charles H. carpenter
Bonney Gladden, carpenter, West Crook
Bonney Lucius, millwright
Bosworth Ambrose, machinist
Bottemore Alfred, farmer, Satucket
Bouldry Nathaniel S. laborer
Bourne Isaac F. mechanic, Satucket
Bourne Isaac N. mechanic, Satucket
Brett Royal F. mason, Joppa
Brett William U. tack maker, Village
Brown Charles, wheelwright
Brown Charles H. shoemaker, Robbins Pond
Brown David W. farmer, Northville
Brown Edwin, heater, Northville
Brown Isaac, shoemaker, Northville
Brown John E. shoemaker, Northville
Brown Warren, mechanic, Satucket
Bryant George, nurseryman, Joppa
Bryant Francis C. Joppa
Bryant Seth, shoe manuf. Joppa
Bullock Jabez, furnaceman
Burgess Silas, machinist, Village
Burrill Jarvis, agent and printer, Village
Byram Branch L. mechanic, Robbins Pond
Byram George H. mechanic, Village
Byram Harrison G. mason, Birch Swamp
Byram Lorenzo G. moulder
Byrnes Arthur S. nailer, Village

CARLTON GEORGE H. carpenter, Shaw's Mill
Carney Edward, laborer, Village
Carroll John, shoemaker, Village
Cary Francis, farmer, Joppa
Casey Edmund, laborer, Beaver
Chadwick John H. laborer
Chamberlain Francis B. peddler, Northville
Chamberlain Joseph, farmer, Village
Chamberlain Nathan, laborer
Chandler Hervey, hairdresser, Village
Chandler Nymphas M. mechanic, Village
Chandler Samuel V. shoemaker
Chaplin Daniel, physician, Village
Chapman John, foreman, O. C. Iron Foundry
Churchill Abisha S. shoe finisher, Joppa
Churchill Caleb S. shoemaker, Northville
Churchill Frederick S. shoe finisher, Joppa
Churchill Levi, merchant, Joppa
Churchill Luther, farmer, Birch Swamp
Churchill Luther jr., shoemaker
Churchill Newton, stitcher, Joppa
Churchill Warren K. post master, Joppa
Clark Elijah L. foreman iron works
Conant John, shoe cutter, Joppa
Conant John A. merchant, Village
Conant Seth P. shoemaker, Satucket
Conant Thomas, shoe cutter, Joppa
Cook John, laborer, Village
Cooper James H. carpenter, Harmony
Copeland Roland F. farmer, Black Brook
Costello John, cigar maker, Village
Crooker Elbridge, box maker, Beaver
Crowley Patrick, laborer, Village
Cummins Thomas, laborer, Harmony
Curtis Elbridge, shoe cutter, Joppa
Curtis Elbridge B. carpenter, Joppa
Curtis Minot S. painter, Joppa
Curtis Robert, clerk, Joppa

Cushing Joseph W. shoemaker, Satucket

DAVENPORT ELIPHALET, laborer, Village
Davenport Geo. H. shoemaker
Davenport John E. painter, Joppa
Dee James, mechanic, Satucket
Delano Lewis, shoemaker
Desmond Daniel, laborer, Village
Dickerman Lucius, nailer
Dickerman Lucius F. nailer
Doody Michael, furnaceman, Peaver
Drake Ira, farmer, Northville
Drake Ira W. peddler, Northville
Drake Timothy, farmer, Birch Swamp
Dunbar Lemuel, shoemaker, Beaver
Dunn Jeremiah, laborer, Village
Dyer Albert H. shoemaker

EDDY ALLEN P. cigarmaker, Village
Edson Albert C. shoemaker
Edson Benj. F. carpenter
Edson Daniel P. mechanic, Satucket
Edson Franklin, shoedealer, Village
Edson Henry, shoedealer, Joppa
Edson Jonah, brassfounder, Joppa
Edson Nahum, nailer, Village
Edson Plyma, nailer, Village
Edson Seth B. shoemaker
Edson William, shoemaker
Ellis Barzilla F. laborer, Village
Elwell George E. mechanic, Satucket
Erskine Hiram H. mechanic, Village
Estes Alanson, shoemaker
Eustis William H. box-maker, Pearl

FARRINGTON WILLIAM F. clergyman
Feeney Michael, laborer, Village
Field Edward F. shoemaker
Field William G. carpenter, Joppa
Fish Adoniram J. mechanic, Satucket
Fisher Elisha P. mechanic, Satucket
Fisher Jeremiah, mechanic, Satucket
Flagg Francis R. shoemaker, Black Brook
Flynn John, shoemaker, Harmony
Folsom Jacob, Village
Ford Arunah T. Joppa
Ford Edmond, laborer, Beaver
Foster Joseph, butcher
Freeman Enoch, laborer, Satucket
Freeman Josephus, laborer, Beaver
Freeman Theodore C. shoemaker
French Daniel, furniture dealer, Joppa
French Nathaniel W. farmer, Northville
French Samuel, hostler, Village
Fuller Ezra T. carpenter
Fuller Isadus, carpenter, Village

GALLAGHER JOHN, shoemaker, Harmony
Gammons Rufus K. forgeman, Village
Gardner Thomas C. mechanic, Village
Gardner William C. carpenter, Village
Gardner William W. carpenter, Village
Gilbert William J. hammersman, Village
Gould Clarence C. stitcher, Village
Gould Henry K. painter, Village
Gould Morris C. painter, Village
Goss Caleb, box maker, Beaver
Goss Charles H. box maker, Beaver
Griffin Alfred, stable keeper, Village
Griffin Jeremiah, laborer, Village
Griffin Michael, laborer, Village

J. A. JACKSON, 101 COURT STREET, BOSTON, DEALER IN HATS, CAPS, AND FURS.

Griggs Charles, shoemaker, West Crook
Griggs Stephen, shoemaker, West Crook
Griggs Thomas, shoemaker, West Crook
Gross George, carpenter, Shaw's Mill
Grover Otis, shoemaker, Shaw's Mill
Grow Henry A. painter, Village
Gurney Alfred, laborer, West Crook
Gurney Almon, farmer, West Crook
Gurney Almon A. shoemaker, West Crook
Gurney Cyrus, farmer, West Crook
Gurney David H. shoemaker, Village
Gurney David S. teamer
Gurney Henry, farmer, West Crook
Gurney Levi T. shoemaker, West Crook
Gurney Seth P. shoemaker, West Crook

HALE ZACCHEUS, shoemaker, Beaver
Hall Stephen, shoemaker, West Crook
Hall William B. shoemaker, Village
Harden Albert, machinist, Satucket
Harden George W. shoemaker, Black Brook
Harden Harlow, carpenter, Village
Harden Jehial B. shoemaker, Black Brook
Harden John B. shoemaker, West Crook
Harden Lucius, West Crook
Harden Luther, shoemaker, Black Brook
Harden Noah, West Crook
Harden Noah T. West Crook
Harden Reuben, West Crook
Harden Willis, shoemaker, West Crook
Harden Zenas, laborer, West Crook
Harlow Calvin H. blacksmith, Joppa
Harlow Stephen, farmer, Village
Harlow Timothy S. mechanic, Satucket
Harris Arthur, carpenter, Williams st
Harris Azor, farmer, Williams st
Harris Benjamin W. lawyer, Village
Harris Samuel, laborer, Satucket
Hatch Isaac, shoemaker, Black Brook
Hathaway John H. shoemaker, Satucket
Hathaway Josiah, shoemaker
Hathaway Seabury C. farmer, Black Brook
Hathaway Seabury C. jr., farmer, Black Brook
Hathaway William B. merchant
Hathaway William R. farmer
Hayward Benj. S. Village
Hayward Edward, well digger, Village
Hayward Edward Y. farmer, Beaver
Hayward Francis, clerk, Beaver
Hayward George F. shoemaker, Beaver
Hayward Leonard H. peddler, Beaver
Hayward Waldo, shoemaker, Beaver
Healey Reuben, carpenter, West Crook
Henisee Morris, laborer, Village
Herrick Thomas A. pattern maker, Village
Hersey William W. farmer, West Crook
Hewitt Thomas, blacksmith, Satucket
Hickey James, laborer
Hicks Jotham, grocer, Village
Hicks Jotham H. overseer of forge, Village
Hill Henry G. farmer, Joppa
Hill Leonard, seed grower, Village
Hinckley Elijah, shoe cutter, Village
Hobart Aaron, merchant, Village
Hobart Henry, tack manuf. Village
Hobart Israel, farmer, Black Brook
Hobart John, Village

Hobart Theodore, carpenter, Beaver
Hodgson William, forgeman, Village
Holbrook Arvin, shoe cutter, Joppa
Holbrook Silas, shoe cutter, Joppa
Holland John O. shoemaker, Black Brook
Holmes Alonzo L. shoemaker, Village
Holmes Ellis, farmer
Holmes Ellis W. machinist, Village
Holmes Ellis W. 2d, teacher, Black Brook
Hooper Cornelius C. farmer, Beaver
Horton Ira, shoemaker, Joppa
Howard David, West Crook
Hoyt Damon, shoe cutter, Joppa
Hoyt Samuel J. Joppa
Hubbard David G. farmer, Robbins Pond
Hudson Caleb L. seaman, Joppa
Hudson Mark P. farmer, Robbins Pond
Hunting Amos, merchant, Village
Humble Marshall N. West Crook
Howland George B. shoemaker, Black Brook

JACKSON ABNER C. carpenter, Robbins Pond
Jackson Andrew, carpenter, Village
Jenkins Merritt, farmer, Village
Jenkins William, fish peddler, Satucket
Jenness John S. shoemaker, Village
Johnson Willard, tinman, Village
Jones John, wheelwright, Village
Jordan Charles, carpenter, Joppa
Jordan Charles E. carpenter, Joppa
Josselyn James E. Village
Joyce Isaac T. shoemaker, Depot st

KALEY PATRICK, laborer, Village
Keen Caleb, laborer, Satucket
Keen Judah C. nurse, Joppa
Keen Leonard L. engineer, Village
Keen Newton M. shoe cutter, Joppa
Keen Samuel, machinist, Joppa
Keen Samuel D. machinist, Joppa
Keen Simeon W. machinist, Joppa
Keen William, shoemaker, Black Brook
Keen William W. farmer, Joppa
Keith Benjamin, r Pleasant
Keith Benjamin W. post master, r Pleasant
Keith Edward S. clerk, Village
Keith Franklin, Village
Keith Freedom, shoemaker, Satucket
Keith George, farmer
Keith George M. shoemaker
Keith Henry M. tack manuf. Satucket
Keith Heman, farmer
Keith Hezekiah, carpenter, Satucket
Keith Kezekiah H. machinist, Satucket
Keith Isaac, shoe cutter, Joppa
Keith Isaac 2d, shoemaker, Satucket
Keith Isaac N. clerk, Joppa
Keith James, Beaver
Keith Levi, farmer, Village
Keith Lewis, expressman, Village
Keith Marcus M. grocer, Village
Keith Nahum P. shoemaker, Harmony
Keith Parley, farmer, Beaver
Keith Perez, farmer, Satucket
Keith Robert C. shoe manuf. Williams st
Keith Samuel, tack manuf.
Keith Simeon C. shoe manuf. Williams st
Keith Scott, farmer, Village
Keith Thomas, surveyor, Beaver
Keith Willard, nailer, Village

DIVIDENDS ADDED to the POLICY in the BERKSHIRE often exceed the premium paid; are NON-FORFEITABLE and will be redeemed in CASH ON DEMAND. (See page 50.)

Keith William F. clerk, Village
Keith Zebina, tack manuf. Satucket
Keith Zebina jr., tack manuf. Satucket
Keith Zenas, farmer, Village

Kennon John W. merchant, Joppa
Kingman David, laborer, Village
Kingman Edward, shoe manuf. Joppa
Kingman Ezra, shoe manuf. Joppa
Kingman Francis M. painter, Satucket
Kingman Jacob, nailer, Village
Kingman Nathan, tackmaker, Pearl
Kingman Nathan, 2d, stitcher, Joppa
Kingman Otis, nailer
Knapp James G. carpenter, Joppa

LAHEY WILLIAM, laborer, Village
Lang Stephen, carpenter, Satucket
Latham Azor H. farmer, Williams
Latham Charles A. farmer, Black Brook
Latham Eliab, farmer, Williams
Latham Galen, farmer, Williams
Lazell Caleb G. carpenter, Joppa
Leonard Herman, carpenter, Joppa
Lincoln Charles, shoemaker, Williams
Lincoln Charles W. shoemaker, Williams
Lincoln Isaac, shoemaker, Black Brook
Lincoln Isaac H. shoemaker, Black Brook
Lincoln Matthew, W. shoemaker, Beaver
Lincoln Reuel, farmer, Beaver
Lincoln Reuel A. shoemaker, Williams
Littlefield Rufus A. farmer, Beaver
Lovell James P. butcher, Williams
Luby Edmond, shoemaker, Village
Luby John, laborer, Village
Lucas Harvey, shoemaker, Joppa
Lucas Levi, Depot st
Luzarder Geo. E. shoemak'r, West Crook
Luzarder Samuel, shoemaker, Joppa
Lyon Elbridge G. farmer, Birch Swamp
Lyon Isaac K. shoecutter, Shaw's Mill

MAHONEY JEREMIAH, furnaceman, Beaver
Maine Wm. H. shoemaker, Birch Swamp
Mann Frederick C. carpenter, Joppa
McCarter James, shoemaker, Village
Mellam Amos W. laborer, West Crook
Mellam Geo. W. shoemaker, West Crook
Millett Daniel E. shoemaker, Beaver
Millett Samuel G. shoemaker, Beaver
Millett Solomon, farmer, Beaver
Milliken Heard, baker, Village
Mitchell Cushing, Main
Mitchell George, Joppa
Mitchell George T. forgeman, Willow Grove
Mitchell James H. merchant, Village
Mitchell Timothy, farmer, Williams
Mitchell William L. forgeman, Village
Morey Daniel, laborer, Village
Morey Patrick, laborer, Village
Morse Geo. H. state constable, Harmony
Morse Joseph, blacksmith, Shaw's Mill
Mullen James, shoemaker, Village
Munroe Ethan, nailer, Black Brook
Munroe Franklin, Village
Munroe Granville H. shoecutter, Village
Munroe James, shoemaker, Black Brook

NASH DANIEL L. shoemaker
Neville Andrew, watchman, Village
Newhall Geo. S. stitcher, Village
Newhall George W. clerk, Village
Newhall Horace W. engineer, Village
Newhall Samuel P. saddler, Harmony
Newhall Samuel R. carpenter, Village
Noonan John, laborer, Village
Noyes Josiah E. farmer, West Crook
Noyes Levi W. Joppa
Nute Jotham, nailer, Village
Nutter Edmond W. merchant, Village
Nutter Isaac N. merchant, Village

O'BRIEN ANDREW, shoemaker, Village
O'Brien Thomas, laborer, Village
Orr Hector O. A. Main st
Orr Samuel A. physician, Main st
Osborne George, stitcher, Joppa
Osborne Galen, shoemaker, Robbins Pond
Osborne Henry A. painter, Village
Osborne Joseph R. shoe cutter, Joppa
Osborne William H. lawyer, Village
Osborne William L. shoemaker, Beaver
Otis Cushing, machinist, Black Brook

PACKARD RUFUS E. shoemaker, Black Brook
Packard Sidney, undertaker, Joppa
Paine Timothy O. clergyman, Joppa
Parker Levi B. shoe cutter, Joppa
Parris Martin, farmer, Robbins Pond
Peck Horace M. overseer shoe factory, Northville
Perigo James M. Shaw's Mill
Perkins James S. shoemaker, Robbins Pond
Perkins Nathaniel, shoemaker, Robbins Pond
Perry Otis B. furnaceman, Shaw's Mill
Peterson Asaph, tackmaker, Satucket
Peterson James B. tack maker, Satucket
Phillips Mark, millwright, Black Brook
Phillips Wadsworth, millwright, Black Brook
Pool Lawrence V. stitcher, Village
Pool Nathan M. shoe cutter, Shaw's Mill
Pool Peregrine W. carpenter, Satucket
Pool Samuel, carpenter, Birch Swamp
Pool Samuel R. shoe cutter, Birch Swamp
Porter Allen M. farmer, Black Brook
Porter Cephas A. farmer, Black Brook
Porter John B. farmer, Black Brook
Porter Nathaniel, farmer, Black Brook
Potter J. Henry, jeweller, Main st
Pratt Addison, farmer, Black Brook
Pratt David, farmer, Birch Swamp
Pratt David H. shoemaker, Northville
Pratt George H. shoemaker, Birch Swamp
Pratt Isaac, farmer, Birch Swamp
Pratt John T. shoemaker, Village
Pratt Josiah J. Village
Pratt Oliver, shoemaker, Birch Swamp
Pratt Philander, shoe cutter, Joppa
Pratt William F. machinist, Joppa

QUIGLEY O'BRIEN, laborer, Village
Quigley Patrick, laborer, Village

RAMSDALL AARON, shoemaker, Birch Swamp
Ramsdall Joseph, farmer, Northville
Ramsdall Nath'l, farmer, Birch Swamp
Ramsdall William, shoemaker, Harmony
Reed Calvin, shoemaker, West Crook

J. A. JACKSON, 101 COURT STREET, BOSTON, DEALER IN HATS, CAPS AND FURS.

Reed Daniel, shoemaker, West Crook
Reed Daniel N. farmer, Beaver
Reed Isaac, farmer, West Crook
Reed Isaac jr., shoemaker, West Crook
Reed James T. shoemaker, West Crook
Reed John, farmer, Beaver
Reed John N. box maker, Beaver
Reed John P. mason, Northville
Reed Joseph, farmer, West Crook
Reed Joseph jr., shoemaker, West Crook
Reed Marcus S. shoe manuf. West Crook
Reed Quincy, shoe manuf. West Crook
Reed Timothy K. machinist, Shaw's Mill
Reed William, shoemaker, Harmony
Remmick Lucius, shoemaker, Village
Reymond Charles W. shoemaker, Black Brook
Reymond Lewis P. shoemaker, Black Brook
Reymond Samuel D. shoemaker, Northville
Reynolds David P. farmer
Reynolds David P. 2d, shoemaker
Riadon James, forgeman
Richards Luther W. merchant, Joppa
Richards Zeba, farmer, Shaw's Mill
Richmond Simeon, farmer, Beaver
Richmond Simeon W. stone cutter, Beaver
Ripley William B. shoemaker
Robinson Amasa L. shoemaker, Beaver
Robinson Benjamin R. farmer, Harmony
Robinson Perez, stone mason, Beaver
Rogers Charles, Main st
Rogers Jacob A. tack maker, Main st
Rogers Thomas, liquor agent, Village
Rogers Wales, merchant, Main st
Rollins James, shoe cutter, Joppa
Rosenfield G. merchant, Village
Rouch David, laborer, Village
Round Martin, shoemaker, Village
Round William F. shoemaker, Village
Rust Wallace, farmer, Village

SAMPSON A. P. expressman, Joppa
Sampson Ezra F. shoemaker, Black Brook
Sampson William S. shoemaker, Robbins Pond
Sanford Baalis, clergyman, Village
Savory George H. shoemaker, Northville
Scribner John H. shoemaker, Joppa
Severance James F. machinist, Village
Severance Walter, machinist, Village
Sharp Alonzo, shoemaker, Black Brook
Sharp Oliver M. shoemaker, Birch Swamp
Shaw Jerome B. shoemaker, Northville
Shaw John J. merchant, Shaw's Mill
Shaw Joseph, laborer, Village
Shaw Martin, shoe cutter, Joppa
Shaw Minot C. shoe manuf. Joppa
Shaw Samuel, shoe manuf. Joppa
Shaw Samuel jr., shoe manuf. Joppa
Shaw Samuel D. grain dealer, Shaw's Mill
Shaw William N. shoe cutter, Joppa
Sheldon Kimball E. manuf. nails, &c., Village
Siddall Benjamin, carpenter, Village
Siddall Charles, blacksmith, Village
Siddall James, blacksmith, Village
Smith Charles J. nailer, Village
Smith Christopher B. shoe manuf. West Crook

Smith David H. tack maker, Village
Smith Lebbeus, farmer, West Crook
Smith Nahum B. shoemaker, West Crook
Smith Nahum N. shoemaker, West Crook
Smith Richard M. farmer, Village
Smith Samuel C. forgeman, Black Brook
Snell Edwin L. shoemaker, Village
Snow Nathaniel S. shoemaker, Village
Southworth Nathaniel, teamer, Village
Soule James W. shoe manuf. Joppa
Soule John, shoemaker, Shaw's Mill
Soule Nathan P. gunsmith
Soule William H. shoemaker, Joppa
Sprague George, shoemaker, Joppa
Standish David, shoe cutter, Harmony
Staples Jasper N. shoemaker, Beaver
Starbuck Henry J. farmer, West Crook
Steingard Daniel N. shoemaker, Northville
Steingard Joseph A. shoemaker, Northville
Stetson Thomas G. stone mason, West Crook
Stran Hugh, painter, Joppa
Strong Fredrick S. Agent Cotton Gin Co. Joppa
Sturtevant Jabez H. shoemaker, Village
Sturtevant Joshua, blacksmith, Black Brook
Sturtevant Zenas W. shoemaker, Village
Summer Martin, tack maker, Village
Swallow Clark, machinist, Satucket
Sweeting James N. farmer, Birch Swamp
Sweetser Rufus, farmer, Black Brook

THAYER JOHN, farmer, Beaver
Thayer John B. farmer, Beaver
Thomas Abiel, blacksmith, Harmony
Thompson Charles, painter, Joppa
Thompson Peleg, farmer, Joppa
Thompson Seth, brick maker, Village
Thompson Seth jr., brick maker, Village
Thrasher Charles, farmer, Black Brook
Thrasher Cyrus, farmer, Black Brook
Thrasher Daniel W. shoemaker, Black Brook
Thurlow Jeremiah D. shoemaker, Northville
Tillson Samuel W. farmer, Black Brook
Tinkham Sylvanus, shoemaker, Shaw's Mill
Tirrell Williams, shoemaker, Beaver
Tisdall Ebenezer, farmer, Beaver
Tribou Daniel, stone cutter, Harmony
Trow Bartholemew, wheelwright, Village
Tyson William H. farmer, Northville

UNDERWOOD JOSEPH, mason, Black Brook

VINTON JOSEPH, shoe manuf. Village
Vinton Josiah O. shoe manuf. Village
Vinton William, shoe manuf. Matfield
Vosmus John H. carpenter, Black Brook

WADE CALVIN, shoemaker, Satucket
Wade John, farmer, Robbins Pond
Wade Nicholas, farmer, Robbins Pond
Wade Oliver H. carpenter, Satucket
Wade Robert, shoemaker, Satucket
Walker Eugene, shoemaker, Joppa
Ward Benjamin, butcher, William st
Washburn Allen, farmer, Black Brook

Policy Holders in the BERKSHIRE LIFE INSURANCE COMPANY of Pittsfield, Mass., DO NOT FORFEIT THEIR POLICIES by reason of FAILURE TO PAY their premiums. (See page 50.)

Washburn Benj. H. millwright, Black Brook
Washburn Isaac, millwright, Main st
Washburn Lysander, shoemaker, Joppa
Washburn Noah A. millwright, Village
Washburn Orace, shoemaker, Village
Washburn Seldon, farmer, Satucket
Washburn Seldon M. shoemaker, Joppa
Washburn Theodore, Main st
Waterman John, stable keeper, r Pearl st
Waterman John E. depot master, Pearl st
Waterman Melzer, shoemaker, Black Brook
Wentworth Clark, painter, Village
West George A. shoe cutter, Joppa
West Obadiah, shoe manuf. Joppa
Wheeler Albert D. shoemaker, West Crook
Wheeler George A. teacher, West Crook
Whitcomb Ward, farmer, West Crook
White Benjamin, shoemaker, Black Brook
White Benjamin M. shoemaker, Village
White Cushing, shoemaker, Village
White Cushing jr., shoemaker, Satucket
White Harrison H. machinist, Joppa
White Nehemiah, currier, Joppa
White Samuel C. shoemaker, Village
White Samuel F. farmer, Beaver
Whiting John A. mason
Whiting John B. merchant, Black Brook
Whiting John M. mason
Whiting Martin, farmer
Whitman Asa T. farmer, Northville
Whitman Asa W. shoemaker, Village
Whitman Calvin S. Black Brook
Whitman Charles C. shoe manuf. Joppa
Whitman Daniel, farmer, West Crook
Whitman Eleazer, farmer, Harmony
Whitman Josiah, farmer, Joppa
Whitman Mereena A. mason, Village
Whitman Willard, farmer, Village
Whitman William E. farmer, Beaver
Whitmarsh Asaph, farmer, Northville
Whitmarsh Eben'z'r, farmer, Black Brook
Whitmarsh Ezra, farmer, Black Brook
Whitmarsh Ezra S. farmer, Black Brook
Whitmarsh James R. farmer, Birch Swamp
Whitmarsh Levi, shoemaker, Beaver
Whitmarsh Simeon G. farmer, Black Brook
Whitmarsh Thomas, farmer, Black Brook
Wilbur Gideon, carpenter, Joppa
Williams John A. clergyman, Village
Williams F. C. clergyman, Village
Willis Daniel E. farmer, Beaver
Willis Galen, farmer, Beaver
Willis Galen, 2d, shoemaker, Beaver
Winsor Elbridge, peddler, Robbin's Pond
Wood Charles G. nailer, Village
Wood Greenough, peddler, Joppa
Wood Simeon, nailer, Matfield
Woodward Cyrus C. restorator, Depot st
Worcester Horace, shoemaker, Village
Worcester Luke, shoemaker, Village
Wright George A. nailer, Village
Wright John W. shoemaker
Wright Levi, nailer, Matfield
Wright Levi C. nailer, Matfield

YOUNG ROBERT, Village
Young Welcome, lawyer, Village

Halifax General Directory.

ALDEN REUEL T. shoemaker
Allen Jarad B. shoemaker
Allen John, shoemaker

BIRD HENRY W. shoemaker
Bishop Charles R. carpenter
Bishop Nathaniel, carpenter
Blake Daniel P. shoemaker
Bonney Elbridge P. painter
Bosworth Daniel, teamster
Bosworth Henry M. teamster
Bosworth Libbeus, farmer
Bosworth Martin, farmer
Bosworth William H. shoemaker
Bourne Abram, farmer
Bourne Josiah, shoemaker
Bourne William N. laborer
Briggs Benj. shoemaker
Briggs G. W. shoe cutter
Britton Z. L. farmer

Bryant Thomas H. B. farmer

CARVER CHARLES G. laborer
Carver Samuel, farmer
Churchill Edmond, shoemaker
Churchill Samuel, shoemaker
Clark Stephen, farmer
Cobb Lewis A. farmer
Cook John, painter
Cornish Ellis, farmer
Crooker Melvin, carpenter
Crooker Melvin, jr., farmer
Crooker Wm. H. clerk
Cushman Nahum W. farmer
Cushman Noah, farmer

DABEY WILLIAM S.
Drew George, farmer
Drew James T. farmer
Dyson William A. shoemaker

J. A. JACKSON 101 COURT STREET, BOSTON, DEALER IN HATS, CAPS AND FURS.

FEARING SETH, shoemaker
Fisher George A. laborer
Fobes Wm. A. pastor Cong. Church
Fuller Alfred, farmer
Fuller Charles H. shoemaker
Fuller Chipman, farmer
Fuller Cyrus, farmer
Fuller Eben, farmer
Fuller Eustace, shoemaker
Fuller Granville C. farmer
Fuller Isaac, farmer
Fuller John, farmer
Fuller Marshall, shoemaker
Fuller Nathan, farmer
Fuller Nathan, jr., farmer
Fuller Richard, shoemaker
Fuller Samuel, farmer
Fuller Thomas S. shoemaker

HARLOW GEORGE, shoemaker
Harlow Joseph, shoemaker
Harlow Stephen, farmer
Hatch Nahum, shoemaker
Harriman Abel A. shoemaker
Hayward Geo B. laborer
Hayward Kinsley, laborer
Hayward Kinsley, jr., shoemaker
Hayward Lysander, laborer
Hayward Wm. T. farmer
Holmes Darius, soapmaker
Holmes Darius E. farmer
Holmes Jabez S. seaman
Holmes Jabez W. peddler
Holmes John, shoemaker
Holmes Martin, shoemaker
Holmes Nathaniel T. farmer
Holmes Thomas, farmer
Howland Martin, farmer

INGLEE EDWIN, W. I. & dry goods and auctioneer
Inglee Lucius, farmer
Inglee S. S. farmer

JACKSON GEORGE W. farmer
Jackson George W. jr., farmer

KEEVY PETER, shoemaker

LULL STEPHEN P. shoemaker
Lyon Alpha, farmer
Lyon Charles P. boot maker
Lyon Edwin, shoemaker
Lyon George F. periodical dealer
Lyon Sylvanus W. shoemaker
Lyon William A. sawyer

MORTON CYRUS, physician
Morton E. G. farmer
Morton Nathaniel, farmer
Marston William T. shoemaker
Mitchell George W. blacksmith
Moody Robert, farmer
Morse Levi, shoemaker

OSBORNE MARTIN, shoemaker

PACKARD ANSEL, farmer
Packard Harrison D. farmer
Packard Horace F. farmer
Packard Jesse, farmer
Paine Charles H. county commissioner
Parris B. F. H. shoemaker

Parris I. N. shoemaker
Parris Jonathan, farmer
Parris Matthew, laborer
Peasley William A. farmer
Peasley William A. jr., carpenter
Penniman William, cotton batting
Perkins Friend S. peddler
Perkins James, shoemaker
Perkins Jason, farmer
Poole Alsen, merchant
Poole Caleb, farmer
Poole Caleb jr., merchant
Poole Eliab, farmer
Pope Josiah S. farmer
Porter Chipman, farmer
Porter Henry M. farmer
Pratt Abner C. laborer
Pratt Otis, farmer
Pratt Stillman, laborer

RICHMOND ABEL, farmer
Richmond Andrew, farmer
Richmond Cyrus, farmer
Richmond E. P. farmer
Richards Reuben, heel maker

SAMPSON HENRY G. shoemaker
Sears William H. shoemaker
Smith Reuben, shoemaker
Soule Amasa S. farmer
Soule Jabez, farmer
Soule Jacob, farmer
Soule John M. farmer
Soule Nathaniel, farmer
Standish Shadrach, farmer
Stetson Ephraim, cranberry cultivator
Sturtevant Calvin, farmer
Sturtevant George F. shoemaker
Sturtevant Ira L. farmer and surveyor
Sturtevant Isaac T. laborer
Sturtevant Isaac W. laborer
Sturtevant John, farmer
Sturtevant John jr., farmer
Sturtevant John 3d, laborer
Sturtevant Simeon, farmer
Sturtevant Stafford
Sturtevant Thomas, farmer
Sullivan Timothy, farmer
Swasey James, farmer
Sylvester Joseph, farmer

THAYER EDWARD, shoemaker
Thayer Ellis P. shoemaker
Thomas Horace, iron worker
Thomas Sylvanus, shoemaker
Thompson Adam, farmer
Thompson Albert, carpenter
Thompson Asaph P. shoemaker
Thompson D. C. farmer
Thompson Ephraim B. farmer
Thompson Horace O. farmer
Thompson Ichabod, farmer
Thompson Jacob P. shoemaker
Thompson John T. Z. farmer
Thompson Lewis, farmer
Thompson L. H. farmer
Thompson Marcus M. shoemaker
Thompson Morton, teacher
Thompson Otis, farmer
Thompson Shepard, farmer
Thompson Soranus, shoemaker
Thompson Varnum M. shoemaker
Thompson Ward, farmer

**ANNUAL CASH DIVIDENDS in the BERKSHIRE LIFE INS. CO.,
Pittsfield, Mass. Boston Office 95 1-2 Washington St. (See page 50.)**

Thompson Ward jr., farmer
Thompson Zadock, farmer
Thompson Zedediah, farmer
Thrasher B. B. farmer
Tillson William, farmer
Tillson William M. farmer
Tolman Benjamin, shoemaker

VAUGHAN CORNELIUS P. shoemaker
Vickery Ebenezer, shoemaker

WADE JAMES, shoemaker
Wade Leavitt, iron worker
Waterman Isaac, shoemaker
Waterman J. B. farmer

Watson Daniel, boot maker
Watson John, boot maker
Washburn John L. farmer
White Charles, farmer
White Josephus, farmer
Whitney Charles T. shoemaker
Wills Cyrus, shoemaker
Wood Alvinzer, farmer
Wood Asaph S. farmer
Wood Cyrus, shoemaker
Wood Elihu, teamster
Wood Frederic, farmer
Wood Isaac, farmer
Wood Martin, farmer
Wood Timothy F. farmer

Hanover General Directory.

AIKEN JAMES, clergyman, 2d Cong'l

BAILEY A. H. laborer
Bailey Benjamin, farmer
Bailey Benjamin W. shoemaker
Bailey Edwin, shoemaker
Bailey G. J. shoemaker
Bailey J. D. keeps Alms House
Bailey J. Q. shoemaker
Bailey M. C. house painter
Bailey Stephen, shoemaker
Bailey S. W. clerk
Barker Joshua, iron caster
Barstow Daniel, farmer
Barstow Edward, master mariner
Barstow H. B. farmer
Barstow Nathaniel, master mariner
Barstow Robert, acting master in navy
Barstow Samuel, farmer
Bass Elisha, ship joiner
Bates Enos, stone cutter
Bates G. M. tack maker
Bates E. J. shoe stitcher
Bates Hira, farmer
Bates H. S. merchant
Bates H. W. shoemaker
Bates Joshua, shoemaker
Bates J. S. farmer
Bates L. F. shoemaker
Bates L. T. tack maker
Bates M. S. machinist
Bates Rufus, farmer
Bates S. W. shoemaker
Bates T. M. shoemaker
Bates T. O. mason
Bates Walter, mason
Beal Zadoc, farmer
Benner H. G. shoemaker
Benner J. H. shoecutter
Blanchard E. merchant

Blanchard Eben, merchant
Bonney A. F. shoemaker
Bonney Josiah, farmer
Bonney J. W. farmer
Briggs C. B. shoemaker
Briggs E. B. shoemaker
Briggs J. G. farmer
Briggs Joseph, farmer
Briggs William S. farmer
Brooks Ara, shoemaker
Brooks A. S. shoemaker
Brooks E. G. shoemaker
Brooks Gilbert, shoemaker
Brooks James, farmer
Brooks John, farmer
Brooks Joseph, shoemaker
Brooks Joseph, jr., shoecutter
Brooks J. S. merchant
Brooks J. W. shoecutter
Brooks Thomas D. shoecutter
Bryant Snow H. painter
Buffum Samuel F. shoemanuf.
Burgess B. F. shoemaker

CALLAHAN JOHN, shoemaker
Capell William, shoemaker
Cashman James, farmer
Chamberlain A. B. mason
Chamberlain Francis, shoecutter
Chamberlain Josiah, shoecutter
Chamberlain J. Warren, shoecutter
Chamberlain J. Warren, jr., shoecutter
Chamberlain L. E. shoemaker
Chamberlain M. F. mason
Chamberlain Norman, shoemaker
Chamberlain N. P. shoemaker
Chapman Daniel, farmer
Chapman L. shoemaker
Christy M. laborer
Church Benj. farmer

J. A. JACKSON, 101 COURT STREET, BOSTON, DEALER IN HATS, CAPS, AND FURS.

Church Martin, farmer
Church R. S. shoe cutter
Church S. H. anchor smith
Church S. S. caulker
Church Wm. tanner
Churchill Job,
Clark Andrew, shoemaker
Cushing John, sea captain
Clark Joshua M. shoemaker
Cooley Pat. laborer
Corbin Francis, house painter
Corthell David, shoemaker
Crane Rufus, shoe manuf.
Crocker C. E. shoemaker
Crocker Ensign, road builder
Cudworth John, ship carpenter
Curtis Benj. N. clerk
Curtis C. L. shoemaker
Curtis Enos, farmer
Curtis E. R. shoemaker
Curtis Geo. anchor smith
Curtis G. M. shoemaker
Curtis George W. farmer
Curtis Hiram, farmer
Curtis H. J. merchant
Curtis John, farmer
Curtis Loring, farmer
Curtis R. S. merchant and p. m.
Curtis W. H. fish monger
Curtis W. H. 2d, shoemaker
Curtis William, farmer
Curtis William 2d, clothing maker
Cutler Samuel, Episcopal clergyman

DAMON ALBERT, shoemaker
Damon Alfred, shoemaker
Damon A. T. shoemaker
Damon Bernard, shoemaker
Damon C. H. shoemaker
Damon Daniel, farmer
Damon Ellis, shoemaker
Damon George, farmer
Damon Geo. F. shoe manuf.
Damon James E. shoemaker
Damon John, laborer
Damon Joseph, farmer
Damon Rector, shoe manuf.
Damon Thomas, carpenter
Darling David, farmer
Davis D. jr., farmer
Davis J. T. shoe stitcher
Dawes William
Dennis William, farmer
Digan Bernard, laborer
Donley E. iron worker
Downs Nathaniel, physician
Dwelley C. H. farmer
Dwelley E. B. cattle dealer
Dwelley Jedediah, shoe cutter
Dwelley J. H. shoemaker
Dwelley J. M. mason
Dwelley Joseph, farmer
Dwelley J. S. shoemaker
Dwelley Lemuel, farmer
Dwelley Nathan, farmer
Dyer Charles, farmer
Dyer Charles jr., tack maker
Dyer Theodore, farmer

EELLS J. P. ship painter
Eells Robert, wheelwright
Ellis F. B. shoemaker
Ellis Joseph, shoemaker

Ellis J. T. shoemaker
Ellis N. B. shoemaker
Ellis Spooner, farmer
Estes H. C. shoemaker
Estes John, shoemaker
Estes John W. shoemaker
Estes Zaccheus, farmer

FINNEY BENJAMIN, shoemaker
Fish F. H. shoemaker
Ford Charles jr., shoemaker
Foster Joshua, farmer
Foster Otis, blacksmith
Freeman Joseph, clergyman
French J. O. druggist

GARDNER GEORGE B. shoemaker
Gardner Hiram, farmer
Gardner J. H. fisherman
Gardner J. B. expressman
Gardner Noah, laborer
Gardner T. B. saw and grist mill
Gates Joshua, farmer
Green Francis, shoemaker
Goodrich T. B. shoe manuf.
Gurney J. R. tack maker

HAMMOND H. M. laborer
Hanson R. A. tinman
Harding S. W. shoemaker
Hatch John, carpenter
Hatch J. jr., leather cutter
Hayden M. H. shoemaker
Holbrook Josiah, laborer
Hollis Samuel, shoemaker
Hollis Silas, carpenter
Howard Frank, Hotel keeper
Howes Julius, shoe cutter
Howes Julius jr., shoemaker
Howes J. W.
Howes William, shoemaker
Howes W. R. physician
Howland Alonzo, shoemaker
Howland C. A. shoemaker
Howland H. W. shoemaker
Hurley John, shoemaker

JACOB CHARLES, farmer
Jacob S. O. farmer
Josselyn Charles, shoemaker
Josselyn C. B. shoemaker
Josselyn Cyrus, shoemaker
Josselyn E. C. carpenter
Josselyn Eleazer, farmer
Josselyn E. M. carpenter
Josselyn Ira, farmer
Josselyn Lewis, shoemaker
Josselyn Oren, anchor smith

KEENE P. T. teamer
Keene P. T. jr., clerk
Keene Samuel, shoemaker
Killam C. H. shoe manuf.
Killam R. W. clerk
Kingman J. W. tack maker

LEAVITT KINSMAN, stone cutter
Lindsey Jerome, shoemaker.
Litchfield Luther, shoemaker
Litchfield L. jr., shoemaker
Little E. E. shoemaker
Little Peabody, shoemaker

The terms for ENDOWMENT, and TEN ANNUAL LIFE POLICIES in the BERKSHIRE are peculiarly favorable, and rates lower than in any other Company.   12   (See page 50.)

MANN A. G. farmer
Mann C. G. carpenter
Mann David, farmer
Mann Henry, shoemaker
Mann H. F. farmer
Mann Joshua, farmer
Magoun Abner, farmer
Magoun A. B. merchant
Magoun H. B. merchant
McLaughlin G. J. shoemaker
Merrill Isaac jr., farmer
Moore J. C. laborer
Morse Marcus, shoe manuf.
Morse Quincy, shoe dresser
Munroe Elbert, shoemaker
Munroe F. M. shoemaker
Munroe Hiram, shoemaker
Murch C. B. furrier
Murphy Daniel, laborer

NILES T. E. shoemaker
Nott Hugh, merchant

OAKMAN N. S. house carpenter

PAINE A. D. shoemaker
Perkins Lewis, anchor smith
Perkins Ozias, farmer
Perry Elijah, peddler
Perry Ethan, farmer
Perry E. T. trader
Perry Franklin, shoemaker
Perry Jerome, nail timmer
Perry Josiah, caster
Perry Josiah F. shoe cutter
Perry Kilborn R. shoemaker
Perry Levi, shoemaker
Perry P. E. shoemaker
Perry Samuel, farmer
Perry Seth, laborer
Phillips Albert, shoemaker
Phillips C. B. shoemaker
Phillips Edmund, farmer
Phillips Ezra, tack manuf.
Phillips M. A. merchant
Phillips William, shoemaker
Pool B. B. shoemaker
Pool John, shoemaker
Pool S. A. shoemaker
Pratt B. C. ship carpenter
Priest A. C. shoemaker
Puffer John, shoe cutter

REED ANDREW, Baptist clergyman
Reed S. H. shoemaker
Ripley W. shoemaker
Rogers Edwin, farmer
Rogers Reuben, house carpenter
Rose Charles, farmer
Rose Edwin, farmer
Rose J. S. shoemaker
Russell Lucius, shoemaker
Russell Lyman, shoemaker
Russell Marcus P. shoemaker
Russell Solomon, anchor smith
Russell William P. shoemaker

SEARLES WILLIAM H. shoemaker
Sheldon Francis, shoemaker
Sherman W. S. tack maker
Simmons Ebenezer, carpenter
Simmons Perez, Attorney
Simmons Warren, farmer

Smith Charles, laborer
Smith J. M. tack maker
Smith J. S. shoe dresser
Smith W. F. shoemaker
Soule Abisha, shoemaker
Stetson Albert, town clerk
Stetson Benjamin, laborer
Stetson B. L. farmer
Stetson C. T. tack manuf.
Stetson Harrison, shoemaker
Stetson J. G. merchant
Stetson Jeremiah, shoemaker
Stetson J. F. tack maker
Stetson Joshua, ship carpenter
Stetson J. Q. shoemaker
Stetson H. M. farmer
Stetson M. W. farmer
Stetson Reuben, farmer
Stetson S. C. shoemaker
Stetson Turner, shoemaker
Stetson W. F. shoemaker
Stetson W. W. shoemaker
Stockbridge Lebbeus, tanner
Stockbridge William, farmer
Stoddard C. C. shoecutter
Stoddard D. H. shoemaker
Stoddard D. T. carpenter
Stoddard Francis, shoemaker
Stoddard H. A. shoe manuf.
Stoddard J. A. carpenter
Stoddard L. M. shoedresser
Stoddard William B. shoemaker
Studley B. F. shoemaker
Studley David, farmer
Studley E. H. shoe manuf.
Studley George, carpenter
Studley Jabez, farmer
Studley J. H. shoe manuf.
Studley Joshua, farmer
Studley Judson, shoemaker
Studley J. W. shoemaker
Studley Philander, shoecutter
Studley Robert, clerk
Studley William, shoemaker
Sturtevant G. shoemaker
Sturtevant R. M. shoemaker
Sturtevant Z. G. farmer
Sylvester E. Q. tack manuf.
Sylvester E. W. shoemaker
Sylvester G. F. tackmaker
Sylvester James, farmer
Sylvester J. B. anchor-smith
Sylvester L. C. farmer
Sylvester Michael, farmer
Sylvester M. R. tackmaker
Sylvester Robert, farmer

THAYER C. E. shoecutter
Thayer Ebenezer, farmer
Thayer M. C. shoemaker
Thomas Charles, shoemaker
Thompson Lyman, stonecutter
Torrey Dexter, shoemaker
Tower C. L. shoemaker
Tower John, shoemaker
Tower Reuben, shoemaker
Tribou A. T. shoemaker
Tribou John T. shoemaker
Tribou L. W. fisherman
Tubbs Joseph, farmer
Turner C. E. shoemaker
Turner E. J. shoemaker
Turner G. W. farmer

J. A. JACKSON 101 COURT STREET, BOSTON, DEALER IN HATS, CAPS AND FURS.

HANOVER DIRECTORY. 47

Turner J. M. mason
Turner James, shoemaker
Turner Luther, carpenter
Turner S. N. shoe manuf.
Turner S. S. carpenter
Turner Thomas, carriage-maker
Turner William F. shoe manuf.

VINAL JOSEPH, shoemaker
Vining A. D. shoemaker
Vining C. C. shoemaker
Vining Joseph, shoemaker
Vining Judson, shoemaker
Vining L. L. shoemaker
Vining W. H. shoemaker
Vining William J. shoemaker

WHITING E. M. fisherman
Whiting G. B. shoemaker
Whiting G. C. auctioneer
Whiting G. D. shoemaker
Whiting Jared, farmer
Whiting J. S. sole leather-cutter

Whiting L. A. shoemaker
Whiting L. C. shoecutter
Whiting Nathan, shoemaker
Whiting O. T. shoemaker
Whiting Sylvanus, shoemaker
Whiting T. B. shoemaker
Whiting William, farmer
Wilder J. M. merchant
Wilder J. C. farmer
Winslow Charles, shoemaker
Winslow D. W. shoemaker
Winslow E. B. shoemaker
Winslow H. T. shoecutter
Winslow J. B. shoemaker
Winslow Josiah, farmer
Winslow Oliver, tackmaker
Winslow Richmond, farmer
Witherell C. S. anchor-smith
Wood Alex. merchant
Wood E. F. trader
Wright Henry, shoemaker
Wright Warren, blacksmith

Hanson General Directory.

ADAMS RUSSELL W. farmer
Aldridge Stillman, farmer
Ames John C. box maker
Ames Marcus, farmer
Ames Marcus F. peddler
Arnold Caleb, shoemaker

BANICAN PATRICK, farmer
Bailey George C. shoemaker
Baldwin C. H. farmer
Barker Benjamin, farmer
Barker Bowen, physician
Barker John, farmer
Barker Josiah, farmer
Barker Lot P. farmer
Barker Philip H. shoemaker
Barrows Alfred, supt. almshouse
Barrows George L.
Bates Andrew H. shoemaker
Bates Cyrus A. carpenter
Bates Elbridge G. shoemaker
Beal Alden, farmer
Beal Bernhard C. shoemaker
Beal Charles M. shoemaker
Beal George P. farmer
Beal Gibson, shoemaker
Beal Henry A. shoemaker
Beal John, farmer
Beal William L. shoemaker
Beal William O. shoemaker
Bearce Benjamin H. shoemaker
Bearce Isaiah, farmer
Bearce Joseph, moulder
Bearce Virgil P. shoemaker

Bearce William W. shoemaker
Beggen Francis, farmer
Bonney Ezekiel, farmer
Bonney Josiah, shoemaker
Bonney Josiah 2d, boot maker
Bonney Morton V. clerk
Bonney Otis L. teacher
Bonney Seth, laborer
Bosworth Ichabod, shoemaker
Bourne Abel, farmer
Bourne Calvin F. shoemaker
Bourne Charles, farmer
Bourne Charles W. laborer
Bourne Ebenezer B. farmer
Bourne Ephraim B. shoemaker
Bourne Ferdinand A. shoemaker
Bourne Francis, farmer
Bourne Francis W. farmer
Bourne Isaac, shoemaker
Bourne James A. farmer
Bourne John T. moulder
Bourne Martin W. shoemaker
Bourne Samuel T. shoemaker
Bourne William, farmer
Bowker Andrew, dry-goods and groceries
Bowker Benjamin H. teamster
Bowker Gad, farmer
Bowker George T. clerk
Bowker John, shoemaker
Bowker Luther, shoemaker
Bowker Richard, laborer
Branning John, shoemaker
Brewster James B. farmer
Brewster Philip, farmer

DIVIDENDS ADDED to the POLICY in the BERKSHIRE often exceed the premium paid; are NON-FORFEITABLE and will be redeemed in CASH ON DEMAND. (See page 50.)

Briggs Samuel, farmer
Briggs Seth M. dancing-master
Briggs Zalmon, farmer
Brown David, nailer
Brown Richmond, shoecutter
Bryant Abijah, farmer
Bryant Bradley S. paper dealer
Bryant Charles E. farmer
Bryant Josephus, shoemaker
Burnham Francis A. sea captain

CARR ALFRED W. shoemaker
Carr Moses, farmer
Chapman Luther, carpenter
Chapman Luther W. boot maker
Clark Edwin, shoemaker
Clark Thomas G. wheelwright
Clark Thomas G. jr., shoemaker
Cobb Henry F. shoemaker
Cobb Theodore, shoemaker
Colton Alonzo, newspaper agent
Cook John, hatter
Cook Joshua, tack maker
Cook Jonah G. shoemaker
Courtney Alfred, farmer
Cox Albert F. shoemaker
Cox Ephraim, shoemaker
Cox Joseph H. shoemaker
Cox Levi S. shoemaker
Cox Samuel, shoemaker
Cox Samuel O. shoemaker
Cox William, farmer
Cushing Charles, agent
Cushing Elijah, farmer
Cushing George, box maker
Cushing Nathaniel W. farmer
Cushing Theodore, box maker

DALAND DANIEL, shoemaker
Damon Elijah, farmer
Damon William, farmer
Delano George, shoemaker
Delano George T. shoemaker
Delano Nathaniel, shoemaker
Delano Thomas B. sailor
Denham Charles W. shoemaker
Denham Silas, teamster
Doten John, zinc worker
Dow Joseph E. shoemaker
Drayton John, grocery
Drayton Joseph W. farmer
Drew Cyrus, dry goods and grocer
Drew Thomas, clerk

ELLIOTT GEORGE W. carriage painter
Elmes Daniel R. wood and lumber
Elmes George, shoemaker
Elmes John L. shoemaker
Estes F. shoemaker
Estes Stephen H. farmer
Emerson Barnabas, farmer
Everson Calvin, shoemaker
Everson Frederic O. shoe maker
Everson Henry H. shoemaker
Everson Joseph H. shoemaker
Everson Lysander W. shoemaker
Everson Richard, farmer
Everson Sylvanus, farmer
Everson Sylvanus B. shoemaker
Everson William F. shoemaker

FARRELL JAMES, laborer
Fisher John B. medical student

Foster Isaac, shoemaker
Fuller Lucius T. shoemaker
Fuller Nathan T. shoemaker

GANNETT SETH, tack maker
Gurney Ebenezer B. K. surveyor and conveyancer
Gurney Ebenezer H. music teacher
Gurney Jonathan R. farmer
Gurney Joseph J. shoemaker
Gurney Thomas, shoemaker

HALE M. M. shoemaker
Hammond Joshua T. shoemaker
Harding Alpheus C. farmer
Harding Amos, farmer
Harris Seth L. mason
Hatch Nathaniel T. box maker
Hathaway Joseph T. corn and flour
Hewett James E. peddler
Hill Charles R. shoemaker
Hill George H. shoemaker
Hill Lorenzo F. shoemaker
Hill William C. shoemaker
Hobart Isaac, farmer
Holmes Edward, farmer
Holmes Luther, farmer
Hood William W. shoemaker
Howard Willard, shoemaker
Howes Augustus M. painter
Howland Albert, shoemaker
Howland Albert B. groceries
Howland Asa, farmer
Howland Calvin L. 2d, station agent
Howland E. P. moulder
Howland Freeman P. jr., farmer
Howland Friend W. farmer
Howland Isaac J. farmer
Howland James H. shoemaker
Howland John, moulder
Howland Joseph B. farmer
Howland Calvin L. station agent
Howland Luther, tack manuf.
Howland Richard, egg dealer
House Albert, shoemaker
House Samuel T. shoemaker
Howland Lewis T. moulder

JEWETT JOHN, shoemaker
Johnson James G. shoemaker
Johnson William H. tack maker
Jordan James P. shoemaker
Josselyn Albert, carpenter
Josselyn Benjamin, farmer
Josselyn Benjamin W. carpenter
Josselyn Carl P. shoemaker
Josselyn Edgar A. carver
Josselyn Julius, shoemaker
Josselyn Luther A. shoemaker
Josselyn Samuel W. farmer
Joyce T. shoemaker

KEENE CHARLES, shoemaker
Keene David L. farmer
Keene Ebenezer B. farmer
Keene Frank F. shoemaker
Keene John A. farmer
Keene Luther, farmer
Keene Nahum, farmer
Keene Orren, farmer
Keene Thatcher, shoemaker
Keene William B. farmer
Kiley Patrick, shoemaker

J. A. JACKSON, 101 COURT STREET, BOSTON, DEALER IN HATS, CAPS, AND FURS.

HANSON DIRECTORY.   49

Kiley Thomas, laborer

LANE IRVIN, shoemaker
Leary John, laborer
Leavitt Hiram, shoemaker
Leonard Joseph, jeweller
Lewis Leander, shoemaker
Lincoln Cyrus, machinist
Lincoln Rufus W. shoemaker
Loring Joseph B. carpenter
Loring Joseph T. carpenter
Loring Morton M. carpenter
Luther Edward Y. shoemaker
Luther Herbert M. shoemaker
Lyon Josiah T. shoemaker

MACOMBER GEORGE, tackmaker
Magoun Ezra E. shoemaker
Mann Josiah, zinc-worker
Mann Josiah C. tackmaker
McGough Lawrence, laborer
McSweeney Edward, nailer
Monroe Charles, shoemaker
Monroe Cyrus, farmer
Monroe George W. farmer
Monroe Hiram, shoemaker
Monroe Hiram F. shoemaker

OAKES R. B. shoemaker
Osborne Barak, farmer
Osborne Frank, shoemaker
Orcutt Edward, shoemaker

PARRIS ORIN, laborer
Percival Gustavus, seaman
Perkins Joshua L. shoemaker
Perkins Daniel H. shoemaker
Perry Edward Y. tack and nail manuf.
Perry Henry J. shoemaker
Perry James H. shoemaker
Perry Joshua, farmer
Perry Otis, carpenter
Perry Robert, farmer
Phillips Calvin T. shoemaker
Phillips Calvin T. 2 l. clerk
Phillips Lot, millwright
Poole Elias C. blacksmith
Pratt Edwin W. farmer
Pratt Isaac, soapmaker
Pratt Jacob D. shoemaker
Pratt John S. nailer
Pratt Joshua S. laborer
Pratt Nathaniel, carpenter
Pratt Nathaniel, jr., tackmaker
Pratt Seth, shoemaker
Pratt Thomas, shoemaker
Pratt Thomas, jr., shoemaker
Prouty Joseph E. shoemaker
Prouty William H. shoemaker

RAMSDELL ELBRIDGE, shoemaker
Ramsdell Elijah W. shoemaker
Ramsdell Isaac, shoemaker
Ramsdell Levi, farmer
Ramsdell Lyman S. carpenter
Ramsdell Samuel D. carpenter
Ramsdell Silas D. shoemaker
Reed Hezekiah, R. R. express
Reed Isaac T. tackmaker
Reinhardt Charles H. laborer
Robbins E. shoemaker
Roberts John C. painter
Rogers Samuel L. shoemaker

SAMPSON ANDREW, shoemaker
Sampson Augustus M. shoemaker
Sampson Bartlett, shoemaker
Sampson Byram, farmer
Sampson George T. farmer
Sampson Turner, shoe cutter
Senlley Michael, seaman
Shaw Zenas, shoemaker
Simmons John F. shoemaker
Smith Aaron, shoemaker
Smith Joseph, civil engineer
Smith Thomas, farmer
Soper Hervey A. shoemaker
Soper James B. clerk
Soper Jeremiah, custom shoemaker
Soper John S. farmer
Soper Nathaniel, shoemaker
Southworth Benjamin, pastor Cong'l. Church
Sprague Charles H. shoemaker
Sprague Melzer, farmer
Stebbins John D. tack maker
Stetson Aden, farmer
Stetson Charles H. shoemaker
Stetson Edwin L. shoemaker
Stetson George, shoe manuf
Stetson George F. shoemaker
Stetson Hiram, millwright
Stetson Isaiah, moulder
Stetson Jeremiah, carpenter
Stetson Nahum, millwright
Stetson Thomas, millwright
Stevens Albert W. shoemaker
Stevens Benjamin H.
Stevens Frederic A. shoemaker
Stevens Frederic R. tack maker
Stevens Howes, tack maker
Stoddard James P. farmer
Stoddard Richard, farmer
Stoddard Joseph E. shoemaker
Studley George, farmer
Sturtevant George W. shoemaker

TAFT ANDREW J. carpenter
Thatcher Samuel G. seaman
Thomas Benjamin, farmer
Thomas Benjamin H. shoemaker
Thomas Charles, shoemaker
Thomas Ebenezer, laborer
Thomas Elihu, moulder
Thomas Elijah C. gentleman
Thomas Gershom B. shoemaker
Thomas Heman, farmer
Thomas Isaac, farmer
Thomas John, farmer
Thomas Levi Z. shoemaker
Thomas Lewis L. farmer
Thomas Nathaniel B. farmer
Thomas Nelson, farmer
Thomas William —
Thomas William O. shoemaker
Thompson Lysander M. shoemaker
Tubbs Erastus, farmer
Turner George W. shoemaker
Turner Seth, farmer
Turner Seth F. shoemaker

VICKERY DANIEL, shoemaker

WATSON WOODMAN H. Pastor Baptist Church
White Benjamin, shoemaker
White Caleb, shoemaker

Policy Holders in the BERKSHIRE LIFE INSURANCE COMPANY of Pittsfield, Mass., DO NOT FORFEIT THEIR POLICIES by reason of FAILURE TO PAY their premiums.   (See page 50.)

White Clayton, horse and carriage dealer
White Cornelius, farmer
White Cyrus, tack maker
White Ezra, shoemaker
White Joel, farmer
White Joseph, horse and carriage dealer
White Welcome, farmer
Whiting Charles H. shoemaker
Willet Isaac, shoemaker
Willis John, laborer

Whiting Charles H. W. shoemaker
Whiting John A. millwright
Whiting Thomas F. machinist
Whitmarsh William F. shoemaker
Whitten John O. shoemaker
Willett John, carpenter
Willis Reuben, shoemaker

YOUNG ELISHA, laborer

Hingham General Directory.

ADAMS GEORGE, shoecutter, r North
Adams George M. shoemaker, r Hull
Anderson Miles D. mariner, r Beal
Andrews Benjamin, clerk, r South
Andrews Henry, gentleman, r Whiting
Andrews John, gentleman, r Whiting

BAILEY CALEB, livery stable, Summer
Baker James L. merchant (Boston), bds Main
Baker John, gentleman, r Main
Ballentine William, ropemaker, r Cedar
Barnard John, variety and fancy goods, North
Barnes Benjamin, farmer, r North
Barnes Caleb B. house-carpenter, r East
Barnes Edwin, carpenter, r Summer
Barnes George, carpenter, r North
Barnes Henry, farmer, r Weir
Barnes Isaac, gentleman, r Summer
Barnes James, shoemaker, r Hull
Barnes Kilburn W. farmer, r Summer
Barnes Lemuel, laborer, bds North
Barnes Lincoln, iron moulder, r Weir
Barnes Lyman, cooper, r Main
Barrett Michael, farmer, r North
Barry John, peddler, r Hobart
Barry Patrick, currier, r High
Barry Patrick, laborer, r Friend .
Barry William, laborer, r Friend
Barstow Joseph O. shoemaker, bds North
Barstow Samuel B. boot maker, r North
Bartlett Daniel, bucket maker, r Main
Bartlett L. A. Mrs. dry goods, r North
Bassett Caleb, vest maker, r North
Bassett Charles H. clerk, bds Main
Bassett Daniel, coal and wood dealer, r Summer
Bassett George, livery stable, Elm cor. Main

Bassett George L. clerk, bds Elm cor. Main
Bassett John, real estate agent, Boston, r North
Batcheldor John B. cooper, r Main
Bates Amos, gentleman, r Main
Bates Amos B. *(Whitcomb & Bates)*, boot and shoe manuf. r Main
Bates Benjamin, shoemaker, r Whiting
Bates David, shoemaker, r Hersey
Bates David F. box maker, bds Hersey
Bates De Witt C. school teacher, r East
Bates E. shoemaker, r High
Bates George H. boot and shoe manuf. r Ship
Bates Joseph H. shoemaker, bds Hersey
Bates Urban, shoemaker, r Hersey
Bates William, shoemaker, r Hersey
Battles Martin, laborer, r Fort Hill
Bayley George, house carpenter, r Main
Bayley Samuel G. house carpenter, r Main
Beach Ambrose, shoemaker, r Summer
Beal Abner L. farmer, r Hull
Beal Caleb, merchant, Boston, r Lincoln
Beal Caleb G. salesman, Boston, bds Hull
Beal Christopher, laborer, r East
Beal Daniel, farmer, r Hull
Beal Edwin H. shoemaker, r Garden
Beal Edwin W. shoemaker, bds Hull
Beal Elijah, mariner, r North
Beal James, farmer, r East
Beal James S. house-carpenter, r Main
Beal John, shoemaker, r North
Beal Laban, shoemaker, r Hull
Beal Leavitt, shoemaker, r North
Beal Lewis, shoemaker, r Hull
Beal Luther V. shoemaker, r East
Beal Martin, shoemaker, r Hull
Beal Robert, laborer, r Middle
Beal Wilder F. merchant, Boston, bds East
Beal William, mariner, r Summer

J. A. JACKSON 101 COURT STREET, BOSTON, DEALER IN HATS, CAPS AND FURS.

HINGHAM DIRECTORY.   51

Bender John, farmer, r Beal
Bicknell Ezra, shoemaker, r Fort Hill
Bicknell Ezra L. shoemaker, r Fort Hill
Bicknell Lincoln B. farmer, bds West
Bicknell Quincy, farmer, r West
Binney Henry, farmer, r Fort Hill
Blanchard Alvin, farmer, r Pleasant
Blanchard Alvin jr., shoemaker, bds Pleasant
Blossom E. D. carpenter, bds Main
Blossom Edward C. painter, r Main
Blossom Thomas D. (*Blossom & Easterbrook*), printers, r Main
Booth Curtis, rope maker, r South
Booth William, rope maker, bds South
Botting Fielder, shoemaker, r Leavitt
Botting Fielding jr., shoemaker, r Leavitt
Boullard Joel S. shoe manuf. r South
Bowditch William N. butcher, r Main
Bowker Perez G. mason, r Main
Braintle Lorenzo, laborer, r Hersey
Branch Charles, laborer, r Hersey
Breen John, farmer, Crow Point Lane
Brendly Lawrence, laborer, r Elm
Brett Mareena, mason, r Prospect
Brown Benjamin F. (*Burr, Brown & Co.*) r Boston
Bronsdon James E. farmer, bds South
Bronsdon Samuel, musician, r South
Buck Cyrus M. farmer, r Lazel
Bullard Joel S. (*Whiton & Bullard,*) r South
Bullen Garason, mariner, r North
Burbank Abraham, farmer, r East
Burbank Ephraim, house carpenter, r South
Burbank Samuel, farmer, r Jones
Burch Richard, farmer, r Beal
Burdenshaw Henry, Cooper, r North
Burke John, laborer, r Main
Burns John, laborer, r Elm
Burns Michael, laborer, r Elm
Burr Arthur A. draughtsman, Boston, r Leavitt
Burr Charles T. Supt. Tassel Factory
Burr Daniel, farmer, r South
Burr David, teamster, r Back
Burr Elijah W. (*Burr, Brown & Co.*) manuf. of tassels, r South
Burr Elisha, boot and shoe maker, r Leavitt
Burr Fearing, (*F. Burr & Co.*) dry goods and groceries, r Main
Burr Jacob, (*M. H. & J. Burr*), groceries bds Main
Burr John W. shoemaker, bds Leavitt
Burr Lincoln, tailor, r Leavitt
Burr Matthew H. (*M. H. & J. Burr*), groceries, r Main
Burr Peter, (*F. Burr & Co.*) dry goods and groceries, r Main
Burr Pyam C. box manuf. r Leavitt
Burr Samuel, farmer, bds Main
Burr Seth L. blacksmith, r Main
Burrell Jotham, teamster, r Summer
Burrell J. Webster, shoe manuf. r Fort Hill
Burrell Stephen, farmer, r Friend
Burrell Lemuel, laborer, r South
Burrell Martin, shoemaker, r Fort Hill
Burrell Warren, shoemaker, r Fort Hill
Buttemore John, gardner, r Summer
Buttemore Thomas, gardner, r Summer

Byrnes Michael, r Elm
Byrnes Patrick, ropemaker, bds Hersey

CABOT FREDERICK S. merchant, Boston, r Lincoln
Cain Alphonzo, bootmaker, bds North
Cain Daniel, shoemaker, r Fort Hill
Cain David, grocer, r South
Cain Eben W. expressman, r Fort Hill
Cain Joseph, cordwainer, r Fort Hill
Cain Leonard, boot maker, r North
Cain Leonard O. boot and shoe manuf. r South
Cain Thomas, house carpenter, r Pleasant
Caldwell Calvin, cabinet maker, r Hersey
Callahan Dennis, laborer, r Main
Callahan John H. farmer, r Main
Campbell Charles, nail maker, bds Fort Hill
Carter James D. cooper, r Hull
Carter William M. mariner, r Fort Hill
Carver Justin A. shoemaker, r Whiting
Caryl Aaron, farmer, r Back
Casey John, gardner, r Green
Casey Jonas A. rope maker, r Hersey
Casey Michael, laborer, r Summer
Casey Richard, laborer, bds Hersey
Cazneau Edward, cabinet maker, r South
Chamberlain Artemas W. gentleman, r Hersey
Chamberlain George A. W. lawyer, r Hersey
Chamberlain Kinsman S. cabinet maker, r Fort Hill
Champlin David H. shoemaker, r Summer
Chandler Martin, photographer, r South
Childs James, ship carpenter, r Water
Chittenden Israel, silk cord maker, r South
Chubbuck Annis, shoemaker, r Garden
Chubbuck Eleazer, farmer, r Garden
Chubbuck Eleazer jr., shoemaker, r Garden
Chubbuck Washington, shoemaker, Garden
Clapp Michael F. bucket maker, r High
Clark Andrew J. silk cord maker, bds North
Clark Melzar W. baker, r North
Clement James F. lumber dealer, r Summer
Clery George C. hair dresser, r North
Cloudman Marcellus, boot and shoe manufacturer, r Short
Cloudman M. C. (*Hutchings & Cloudman*) boots and shoes, r Leavitt
Cobb David, house painter, r Summer
Cobb Elisha, fisherman, r North
Cobb Silas H. engineer, r North
Colbarth Charles, stone mason, r East
Coleman John, laborer, r Green
Condon B. laborer, r Prospect
Condon William, teamster, r Green
Cook Charles R. blacksmith, r Main
Copeland Charles H. boot maker, r Fort Hill
Corbett Charles, house carpenter, bds Summer
Corbett John M. clerk, Boston, bds South
Corcoran Patrick, laborer, r Hersey
Corcoran Thomas, blacksmith, r Whiting
Corthell Elijah C. box maker, r Hersey
Corthell Elijah L. box maker, bds Main

ANNUAL CASH DIVIDENDS in the BERKSHIRE LIFE INS. CO. Pittsfield, Mass. Boston Office 95 1-2 Washington St. (See page 50.)

Corthell Gustavus P. cooper, r Hersey
Corthell John, merchant, Boston, bds Leavitt
Corthell Levi, gentleman, r Back
Corthell Loring, trader, r Main
Corthell Nelson, cooper, r Hersey
Corthell Reuben H. foreman Hingham wooden ware manuf. r Main
Coughlin James, tanner, r High
Coughlin William, currier, r High
Coughnihan Matthew, laborer, r Thaxter
Craig Matthew, laborer, bds Hersey
Crane Lawrence, laborer
Crane Patrick, laborer, r Summer
Crehan Lawrence, teamster, r Elm
Creswell James, laborer, r Green
Creswell John, shoemaker, r Leavitt
Crocker Ellery C. clerk, bds Fort Hill
Crocker Ezra, machinist, r Leavitt
Crosby Alanson, shoemaker, r Leavitt
Crosby Joshua, farmer, r Lazel
Crosby Joshua, jr., shoemaker, r Scotland
Crosby Saml. T. jeweller, Boston, r North
Cross Moses, housepaint'r, (Cross & Lane) r Main
Crowe John, ironmoulder, r Hersey
Churchill Jesse, woodturner, r Hersey
Churchill Moses, shoemaker, r North
Curtis Samuel C. patternmaker, r Main
Cushing Allyne, house-carpenter, Water
Cushing Alonzo, dry goods and groceries, r Main
Cushing Andrew, farmer, r Main
Cushing Andrew C. merchant, Boston, r Main
Cushing Caleb, farmer, r Main
Cushing Charles Q. farmer, r Main
Cushing Charles W. farmer, r Main
Cushing David, farmer, r Pleasant
Cushing David, lumber dealer, r North
Cushing David jr., expressman, r Main
Cushing David 2d, lumber dealer, r Summer
Cushing Delmont O. carpenter, r Whiting
Cushing Edmund, harness maker, r Main
Cushing E. L. (foreman A. Loring), r Main
Cushing E. S. shoemaker, r Main
Cushing Ferdinand, farmer, r South Pleasant
Cushing George, gentleman, r Main
Cushing George, stage driver, r Main
Cushing George L. shoe cutter, bds Back
Cushing George P. clerk, r Main
Cushing George R. shoemaker, r Main
Cushing George R. (Cushing & Kelley), shoe stitcher, bds Main
Cushing George W. gentleman, r Main
Curtis Henry, farmer, bds High
Cushing Henry, harness maker, r Main
Cushing Henry B. butcher, bds Main
Cushing Isaac, carpenter, r Main
Cushing Jacob, farmer, bds Pleasant
Cushing James, farmer, r South Pleasant
Cushing John, boot and shoe maker, r Main
Cushing John Q. shoemaker, r High
Cushing Laban, farmer, r South Pleasant
Cushing Leonard, farmer, r Main
Cushing Loring H. shoemaker, r High
Cushing Pyam, bucket maker, r Main
Cushing Stephen, laborer, r So. Pleasant
Cushing Theophilus, farmer, r Main

Cushing W. A. (Cushing & Kelley), shoe manuf. bds Main
Cushing William, painter, r Main
Cushing William C. shoemaker, r North
Cushing William G. bucket maker, r Main
Cushing W. G. jr., shoemaker, r Main

DALEY JOHN, laborer, bds Beal
Daley Daniel, laborer, r Summer
Daley James M. (Daly & Rolfe), r Boston
Daley John, laborer, r Thaxter
Daley Patrick, farmer, r Beal
Damon Galen F. cabinet maker, r Back
Damon Isaac, harness maker, r South
Damon Isaac N. blacksmith, r Water
Damon John J. farmer, r Main
Datha Timothy, laborer, r New Bridge
Davis William, pump and block maker, r Summer
Davis W. R. laborer, r High
Dawes John G. shoemaker, r North
Dawes John P. mason, r North
Dawes William L. boot and shoemaker, bds North
Dayton Bela, fisherman, r Wear
Dean George H. paperdealer, r South
Dolan Patrick, laborer, r Ship
Donavan Bartholemew, boot maker, r Summer
Donavan James, laborer, r Green
Donavin Patrick, laborer, bds Fort Hill
Dower James, ropemaker, r Hersey
Downer George, laborer, r Main
Downey John, laborer, r Hersey
Drezil Thomas, laborer, r Hobart
Dunbar A. W. currier, r Main
Dunbar John M. shoemaker, r Main
Dunbar Eleazar P. merchant, Boston, r Fort Hill
Dunbar George, shoemaker, bds Main
Dunbar Martin D. shoemaker, r South
Dunbar Seth, boot and shoemaker, r Main
Dunbar William, laborer, r Summer
Dunn Alexander, currier, r So. Pleasant
Dunn Cornelius, laborer, r North
Dunn John, laborer, r Friend
Dunn Thomas, laborer, r Friend
Durgan Nailan, farmer, r Main
Dyer Solomon L. shoemaker, r North

EASTERBROOK JOSEPH, (Blossom & Easterbrook), printers, r Elm
Easterbrook Samuel, grocer, r Cottage
Easterbrook Samuel H. clerk, bds Cottage
Eastman Herman R. W. trader, r Hersey
Eaton Osgood, boot and shoe manuf. r Hull
Edes Robert T. physician, bds North
Eldridge Charles H. iron moulder, r Green
Eldridge John C. house painter, r South
Eldridge John W. house painter, r South
Eldridge Reuben, grocer, r Green
Ewell Charles F. carpenter, r Main
Ewell Walter H. carpenter, r Main

FANNING JAMES, laborer, bds East
Farmer, Jedediah, printer, r North
Farwell Samuel, alms house keeper, r Beal
Fee James, laborer, Crow Point Lane
Fee John, laborer, r Thaxter
Fee Patrick, laborer, r Cedar

Fee Patrick, laborer, r Pleasant
Fee Thomas, stone mason, r Cedar
Fearing Abel, shoemaker, r Lazel
Fearing Albert, merchant, Boston, r North
Fearing Andrew, farmer, r Lazel
Fearing David, Treas. Hingham Cordage Company, r Main
Fearing David jr., yeoman, r Main
Fearing Eben, bucket maker, r Main
Fearing E. C. (*Hutchings & Chadman*), shoemaker, bds Union
Fearing Henry, blacksmith, r High
Fearing John, farmer, r Lazell
Fearing Lincoln, agent Hingham woodenware Co. r Main
Fearing Martin, gentleman, r Main
Fearing Morris, farmer, r Main
Fearing S. L. farmer, r Lazel
Fearing Thomas, farmer, r Free
Fearing Thomas, jr., shoemaker, r Free
Fearing William, laborer, r Main
Fearing William, 2d, groceries and drugs, r Main
Fletcher Henry L. nailmaker, r Fort Hill
Flint Willard, upholster, r West
Flynn Dennis, farmer, r Green
Foley Cornelius, laborer, Crow Point lane
Ford James, laborer, r Hersey
Ford Joshua, currier, r Main
Fortler Peter, farmer, r Beal
Foster William, house-carpenter, r Water
French Brosard, tapmaker, r Lincoln
French Ezra, shoemaker, r South
French George, jr., shoemaker, r South
French Thomas L. shoemaker, bds North
French James R. carpenter r North
French Joseph H. boot and shoe dealer, bds Main
French Levi, house-carpenter, r North
French Nathaniel, mariner, r Main
Fuller George E. Rev. r Fort Hill
Fuller John E. publisher, r South
Fuller Tilson, clerk, Bank, r Water

GALE W. ALLAN, artist, r South
Gardner Aaron, laborer, r Hobart
Gardner Albert, farmer, r Whiting
Gardner Alfred, hostler, Cottage
Gardner Andrew J. shoemaker, r Fort Hill
Gardner Andrew W. shoemaker, r Fort Hill
Gardner Calvin, grocer, r Water
Gardner Charles, farmer, r Whiting
Gardner Charles A. boot-treer, r Main
Gardner Edwin D. shoemaker, r Main
Gardner Elijah L. shoemaker, r Main
Gardner Francis A. shoemaker, r Whiting
Gardner Franklin, shoe maker, r New Bridge
Gardner George, boxmaker, r Hersey
Gardner G. L. house-carpenter, r Summer
Gardner H. C. shoemaker, bds Main
Gardner Hiram, farmer, r Main
Gardner Howard, mason, r Main
Gardner Isaac, clerk, bds Water
Gardner Isaac, shoemaker, r Garden
Gardner Isaac, 2d, grocer, r North
Gardner Isaiah, shoemaker, r Garden
Gardner Jacob, laborer, r Main
Gardner J. L. shoemaker, r Main
Gardner John C. paperhanger, r Main
Gardner John C. machinist, bds Lincoln
Gardner Josiah, farmer, r Garden
Gardner Josiah Q. boot-treer, r Main
Gardner Leonard, bucketmaker, r Garden
Gardner Lewis, farmer, r Garden
Gardner Russell D. shoemaker, r Cushing
Gardner Tobias O. merchant, Boston, r North
Gardner Warren, farmer, r Garden
Gardner Winslow D. shoemaker, r Garden
Germyn Francis, farmer, r Green
Gilles Alexander, ropemaker, bds Hersey
Gill Caleb, gentleman, r South
Gill Charles, stove and tin ware dealer, r North
Goodwin I. F. farmer, r Weir
Gorman Michael, ironmelter, r Thaxter
Gough Francis W. willow ware, r Fort Hill
Gould Lincoln, shoemaker, r Thaxter
Glasur John D. farmer, r Leavitt
Glover Theodore, gentleman, r Thaxter
Glover T. R. merchant, r Lincoln
Graham James, ropemaker, r Main
Grover A. H. carpenter, r Scotland
Grovner ———, farmer, r Prospect
Greeley William, fisherman, r Elm
Green Charles T. pastry ped ler, r North
Gross Nelson, shoe manuf. r Main
Gould Lincoln, shoemaker, r Thaxter
Gould Stephen P. foreman, r Thaxter
Gould William K. truckman, r Hersey
Guild Ira, farmer, r Main
Gunn Owen, laborer, r Main

HALL C. S. shoemaker, r North
Halero Edward W., U. S. N. r Back
Hally Patrick, baker, r Thaxter
Hally Patrick, hostler, r North
Hapgood Charles, Lostler, r Hull
Harding David, secretary Ins. Co. r Main
Harding Ephraim, fireman, r South
Harding Henry C. treas. Savings Ins. bds Main
Harding Wm. F. foreman at Seth L. Hobart's, r South
Harlow J. E. physician, r Main
Harvey Peter, mariner, r Green
Hatch Frank, merchant, Boston, r North
Hatch Warren, cooper, r Cedar
Hatch Warren, jr. shoemaker, r Cedar
Hatchfield Joseph, peddller, r West
Hanglif Chas. F. master machinist Hingham Cordage Co. r Main
Hawkes James, farmer, r Beal
Hayden Wm. shoemaker, r Scituate
Hays James, blacksmith, bds Water
Helme Charles, laborer, r Main
Henderson Saml. J. shoemaker, r Leavitt
Hersey Albert, teamster, r Hobart
Hersey Albert F. stagedriver, r Hersey
Hersey Alfred C. mer't. Boston, r Summer
Hersey Pela F. cidermaker, r Hersey
Hersey Caleb, farmer, r Main
Hersey Caleb S. cooper, r Hersey
Hersey Charles C. peddler, r Elm
Hersey C. F. hotel-keeper, r Main
Hersey C. L. grocer, r North
Hersey Cotton, cooper, r Hersey
Hersey Cushing, cooper, r Hersey
Hersey David A. carriage and harnessmaker, r Main
Hersey David R. ship-chandler, Boston, r Main

The terms for ENDOWMENT, and TEN ANNUAL LIFE POLICIES in the BERKSHIRE are peculiarly favorable, and rates lower than in any Note Company.   (See page 50.)

Hersey Edmund, fruit and pill box manuf. r Hersey
Hersey Edmund, 2d, dry goods and groceries, r South
Hersey Edwin, carpenter, r Thaxter
Hersey Francis, cooper, r Hersey
Hersey Franklin, cooper, r Hersey
Hersey Franklin H. cabinetmak. r Hersey
Hersey George, gentleman, r South
Hersey Geo. jr. groceries, (Geo. Hersey, jr. & Co.) r South
Hersey George L. mariner, r Fort Hill
Hersey George W. cordmaker, r Elm
Hersey Gridley F. dept. sheriff, r Thaxter
Hersey Henry, Rev. r Summer
Hersey Henry A. clerk, Boston, bds Summer
Hersey Henry F. house-carpenter, r Hersey
Hersey Henry M. clerk, r South
Hersey Hosea B. shoemaker, r North
Hersey Isaac, groceries and provisions, r South
Hersey Isaac L. box-maker, r Hersey
Hersey Isaiah, farmer, r Hersey
Hersey Jacob, bucketmaker, r Main
Hersey John P. house-painter, r Hersey
Hersey Laban, gentleman, r North
Hersey Levi, works Boston, r South
Hersey Loring, mariner, r Elm
Hersey Nathaniel, bucketmaker, r Hobart
Hersey Noah, mason, r South
Hersey Peter, boot and shoemaker, r Main
Hersey Reuben, toy ware and boxmaker, r Hersey
Hersey Samuel, toy ware and box manuf. r Hersey
Hersey Samuel T. clerk, Boston, r Main
Hersey Seth S. gentleman, r Main
Hersey Seth S. jr. carpenter, r Main
Hersey Thomas J. gentleman, bds Union Hotel
Hersey Warren A. mason, r South
Hersey William H. cooper, bds Hersey
Hersey William H. shoemaker, bds South
Hersey William, jr. shoemaker, r Thaxter
Hersey William, 2d, sailmaker, r Thaxter
Hersey William J. farmer, r Prospect
Hersey Zadock, gentleman, r South
Hickey Edward, laborer, r North
Hickey James, ironmoulder, r South
Hickey Lawrence, currier, r Main
Hickey Thomas, blacksmith,
Higgins Ezra, yacht-keeper, r Ship
Higgins Geo. O. provisions, (J. L. Higgins & Co.) bds Pleasant
Higgins Herman L. shoemak'r, bd Leavitt
Higgins Joshua L. provision, (J. L. Higgins & Co.) r Pleasant
Hill Christopher, laborer, r Free
Hill Daniel, farmer, r Elm st. ave
Hines Edward, farmer, r Main
Hines Thomas, farmer, r Prospect
Hitchborn Frank L. shoemaker, r Fort Hill
Hitchborn William, painter, r Fort Hill
Hobart Daniel H. housepainter, r North
Hobart Eben, shoemaker, r Main
Hobart Ebenezer, hostler, r Main
Hobart Edmund, bootmaker, r Main
Hobart Elijah, farmer, r Cushing
Hobart George, shoemaker, r Hersey

Hobart George F. butcher, bds Fort Hill
Hobart Leavitt, gentleman, r Hersey
Hobart Peter, farmer, r Main
Hobart Peter, jr. cabinetmaker, bds South
Hobart Seth L. cabinet manuf. r South
Hobart Seth S. bootmaker, r Main
Hobart William, butcher, r Fort Hill
Hobart William M. fishdealer, r West
Hobart William T. bootmaker, bds Main
Holbrook William, draw-tender, r Beal
Hopkins George W. cooper, r Ship
House H. M. cordwainer, r Main
Howard Alfred, cabinetmaker, r Elm
Howard Charles, iron foundry, (Charles Howard & Co.) r Main
Howard Hiram P. shoemaker, r North
Howard Waters, bait mill manut. r Main
Hudson Augustus L. cabinetmak'r, r North
Hudson Eben H. shoemaker, r Hersey
Hudson George M. cabinetmaker, r North
Hudson Jotham J. shoe manuf. bds North
Hudson Martin, shoemaker, r South
Hudson William, artist, bds North
Humphrey Abner, cooper, r Ship cor. Cottage
Humphrey Charles, mason, r North
Humphery Davis, shoemaker, r Hersey
Humphrey Francis, dyer, r Hersey
Humphrey Joshua, shoemaker, r South
Humphrey Leavitt, gentleman, r Cottage
Humphrey Marcellus, mariner, r South
Humphrey Ned, boot crimper, r South
Humphrey Peter, shoemaker, r North cor. West
Humphrey Thomas C. book-keeper, Boston, bds North
Humphrey William, mason, r North
Humphrey William, jr. mason, r North
Hunt Caleb N. mariner, r South
Hunt George, Boston, North
Hunt J. L. druggist, South

JACKSON WILLIAM, laborer, r Lincoln
Jacobs David, clerk, r Back
Jacobs David F. cooper, r Pleasant
Jacobs Hosea S. hatchetmaker, r High
Jacobs Joseph, edge tool manuf. (Joseph Jacobs & Son.) r Main
Jacobs Joseph, jr. edge tool manuf. (Joseph Jacobs & Son.) r Main
Jacobs Joshua, works hatchet factory
Jacobs Joshua, jr. shoemaker, r Main
Jacobs Lincoln, basketmaker, r Back
Jacobs Loring, dry goods and groceries, r Back
Jacobs Peter H. bootmaker, r North
Jacobs Warren, shoemaker, r Main
Jacobs William, wheelwright, r Main
Jacobs William H. edge toolmak'r, r Main
Jeffries John, ironmoulder, r Green
Jernegan William, periodical dealer, 4 Lincoln's building, r South
Jerrald O. F., R. R. track repairer, r East
Jones Benjamin, farmer, r Jones
Jones Benjamin L. house-carpenter, bds Jones
Jones Gardner M. stonemason, r Hull
Jones Henry, shoemaker, bds Back
Jones Henry W. Rev. bds Back
Jones Moses, farmer, r Back
Jones Seaver, farmer, r Weir
Jones Thomas, blacksmith, r Friend
Jones William, shoemaker, bds Back

J. A. JACKSON 101 COURT STREET, BOSTON, DEALER IN HATS, CAPS AND FURS.

KARNES JOHN, laborer, r Ship
Keating Redmond, moulder, r Thaxter
Keefe Patrick, laborer, r Elm
Keeshan John, ironmoulder, r Main
Kelegar John, laborer, r Cedar
Kelley Michael, shoe manuf. *(Cushing & Kelley.)* r So. Pleasant
Kelsey Joseph B. shoemaker, bds North
Kelsey William P. shoemaker, bds North
Kenerson Eli H. expressman, r North
Kenison Isaac L. farmer, r Main
Kent Morris, laborer, r Thaxter
Keyes John, laborer, r South
Kilburn George, mason, r Garden
King James S. farmer, bds Back
King George W. farmer, bds Back
King Thomas, cooper, r Back
Kurz Samuel, sawyer, r South

LANDERS GARRETT, laborer, r Ship
Landers Patrick, laborer, r Thaxter
Lane Chas. B. W. laborer, r North
Lane Isaac, farmer, r North
Lane Josiah, grocer, r Main
Lane Josiah, farmer, r Free
Lane Leavitt, cooper, r Back
Lane Morallus, farmer, r High
Lane Rufus, merchant, Boston, r South
Lane William, house-painter, *(Cross & Lane.)* r Back
Leavitt Abner L. ship-steering wheels, r Main
Leavitt Charles, house painter, r Main
Leavitt David, house-carpenter, r Leavitt
Leavitt Elijah, farmer, r Main
Leavitt Jacob, laborer, r Main
Leavitt Jerome, farmer, r Leavitt
Leavitt John, millwright, r Middle
Leavitt Levi, farmer, r Main
Leavitt Martin, farmer, r Leavitt
Leavitt Martin, machinist, Pleasant
Leavitt Thomas J. turner, r Pleasant
LeBarron Russell, farmer, r Ship
Lewis Elijah W. teamster, r Main
Lewis George, house-carpenter, r Pleasant
Lewis George F. shoemaker, r Hersey
Lewis George F. jr. shoemaker, r Hersey
Lewis Jacob, laborer, bds Main
Lewis James S. boxmaker, r Pleasant
Lewis John B. boxmaker, bds Pleasant
Lincoln Allen A. merchant, Boston.
Lincoln Alexander, merchant, Boston.
Lincoln Arthur, lawyer, Boston, bd Main
Lincoln Bela, merchant, r Fort Hill
Lincoln Benjamin S. fisherman, r North
Lincoln Calvin, Rev. r North
Lincoln Calvin A. merchant, Boston, r North
Lincoln Charles, cooper, r Lincoln
Lincoln Charles, shoemaker, r North
Lincoln Charles, jr. shoemaker, r North
Lincoln Cornelius, farmer, r East
Lincoln Daniel, shoemaker, r Fort Hill
Lincoln Daniel S. nailmaker, r Fort Hill
Lincoln Daniel W. expressman, r Main
Lincoln David, Pres. of Hingham Bank, r Lincoln
Lincoln Edward, fireman, r Lincoln
Lincoln Edward, hatter, r North
Lincoln Ensign, baker, r North
Lincoln Francis H. bds Main
Lincoln Francis M. shoemaker, r Beal

Lincoln George, Rev. r Garden
Lincoln George, jr. dry goods dealer, 2 Lincoln, r Main
Lincoln Gorham, farmer, r East
Lincoln J. B. merchant, Boston, r North
Lincoln John, farmer, r Pleasant
Lincoln John, jr. farmer, bds Pleasant
Lincoln Joseph H. shoemaker, r Fort Hill
Lincoln Martin, carver, r South
Lincoln Revere, clerk, r North
Lincoln Samuel, butcher, r Main
Lincoln Solomon, Cash. W. Bank, Boston, r Main
Lincoln Sydney, cabinetmaker, bds South
Lincoln Thomas H. carpenter, r North
Lincoln William, farmer, bds South
Lincoln William, solecutter, r Fort Hill
Lincoln William O. farmer, r North
Lincoln Wm. O. jr. U. S. Army, r North
Litchfield F. H. bootcrimper, r Main
Litchfield Frank, farmer, r Union bridge road
Litchfield Joseph H. butcher, r Main
Litchfield Samuel, farmer, bds Fort Hill
Litchfield Samuel H. farmer, r Fort Hill
Long Dennis, laborer, r Elm
Lording Timothy, laborer, r Green
Loring Abner, shoemaker, r Prospect
Loring Alfred, tanner and currier, Main
Loring Albert, farmer, r Main
Loring Albert B. farmer, r Prospect
Loring Enos, stove and tin ware dealer, *(E. & I. W. Loring.)* r South
Loring Fuller, mason, r Main
Loring Hawkes, carriagepainter, r Cedar
Loring Isaiah W. stoves and tin ware, *(E. & I. W. Loring.)* r Main
Loring Job O. farmer, r Main
Loring John, farmer, r Pleasant
Loring Meditah, currier, r Main
Loring Peter, stagedriver, r Main
Loring Pyam, farmer, r Pleasant
Loring Samuel W. farmer, r Main
Loring Zenas, blacksmith, r Cedar
Loud Charles H. shoestitcher, r South
Lovett Jno. O. Cash. of Hingham Bank, r North
Lowery James, laborer, r Hersey
Lowery William, laborer, r Hersey

MAFFAT JOHN, farmer, r Hobart
Mahoney Patrick, laborer, r Green
Maloney John, laborer, r West
Manning George A. machinist, bds Hersey
Marble Demerick, *(B. H. Whiton & Co.)* r Leavitt
Margetts Edward, shoemaker, bds South cor. Hersey
Marsh Caleb, foreman, r South
Marsh Caleb B. coal and wood dealer, r Main
Marsh Charles N. clerk, r South
Marsh Josiah, butcher, r Fort Hill
Marsh Samuel, shoemaker, r Main
Marshall John, ropemaker, bds Hersey
McCarty Charles, laborer, r Thaxter
McFern George, nailmaker, r Fort Hill
McGuire Charles, hostler, r Main
McGuire George, ropemaker, r Pleasant
McGuire George H. harness maker, bds Pleasant
McGuire Joseph C. shoemaker, bds Pleasant

DIVIDENDS ADDED to the POLICY in the BERKSHIRE often exceed the premium paid; are NON-FORFEITABLE and will be redeemed in CASH ON DEMAND. (See page 50.)

McKean Joseph, laborer, r South
McKenna Daniel, blacksmith, r Main
McNeil Paul, fisherman, r North
Mead F. K. R. R. station agent, r Lincoln
Mead Walter V. works Boston, r North
Mears James S. boot-treer, r Main
Merchant James, printer, bds North
Merchant John F. tailor, r North
Merns John, farmer, r Ship
Merritt Henry, jr. blacksmith, r Leavitt
Merrit Paul B. teacher, bds North
Meservey Benj. F. watchmaker, r Ship
Moore Patrick, laborer, r Elm
Morrissey Thomas, laborer, r Elm
Morse Benjamin C. farmer, r Main
Morse Daniel, farmer, r Rockland
Morse Edward, farmer, r Hull
Morse Edward E. shoemaker, bds Hull
Morse Henry G. teamster, r Hersey
Morse Joshua, engineer, r Main
Morton Benj. B. shoemaker, bds Main
Morton John T. blacksmith, r Main
Munroe Henry F. teacher, r Main
Murphy Jeremiah, farmer, r Crow Point lane
Murphy John, farmer, r North
Murphy John, laborer, r Fort Hill
Murphy Thomas, laborer, r East
Murphy Thomas R. shoemaker, bds North
Murray Thomas, blacksmith, r Thaxter

NASH REUBEN, shoestitcher, r North
Nash Reuben H. shoestitcher, r South
Newcomb Enoch, mariner, r East
Newcomb Jedediah, mariner, r East
Newcomb Samuel, 2d, mariner, r Green
Newcomb Silas, mariner, r East
Newcomb Stephen, cabinetmak'r, r Pleasant
Newhall Geo. A. cabinetmaker, r Thaxter
Newhall Joseph A. furniture manuf. (*Ripley & Newhall.*) r South
Nelson Alexander, farmer, bds Main
Nelson James, icedealer, r Green
Nelson William J. carpenter and builder, r Summer
Nelson William T. shoemaker, r North
Nichols Alfred, laborer, r Main
Nichols George W. asst. clerk Supreme Court, Boston, r Lincoln
Nickerson Anderson, merchant, N. Y. r Middle
Nooning Thomas, laborer, r Green
Norris Dennison S. Propr. Union Hotel, r North
Noyes A. W. boot and shoemaker, r Cedar
Noyes J. Henry, boot and shoemaker, bds Main
Nye Atkinson, sailmaker, r Ship
Nye Henry, sailmaker, Commercial wharf
Nye John, inspector of fish, bds Ship
Nye John Sturgis, gentleman, r Main

O'HARRA JEREMIAH J. rope maker, bds Middle
O'Harra Simon, laborer, r Middle
O'Hart John, hatchet maker, r Main
O'Rourk Barnard, provisions, North
Osborn Henry, shoemaker, r Hersey
Our Isaac W. farmer, r Fort Hill,
Overton Frank, refreshment saloon, r North

PALMER BENJAMIN S. gentleman, r Hersey
Palmer Hartwell, house carpenter, r Green
Palmer Hartwell A. house carpenter, bds Green
Palmer Solon, engineer, r Leavitt
Parker Benjamin, door blind and sash manuf. r South
Price James, shoemaker, r Leavitt
Peirce John W. house carpenter, r Main
Peirce Thomas S. laborer, r Ship
Peri Horace, boot maker, r North
Perkinson Wm. laborer, r South
Phinney Seth, shoemaker, r Hull
Pike John, farmer, r Main
Poole George S. shoemaker, r Scotland
Poole Joseph M. baker, r Elm
Poole Theron, shoemaker, r Main
Powers John, shoemaker, r Hull
Pratt Abner, farmer, r High
Pratt B. F. shoemaker, r Main
Pratt Harvey M. shoemaker, r Main
Pratt J. M. boot treer, r South
Pratt Lewis, shoemaker, r North
Prouty George, shoemaker, r Hersey
Prouty James B. shoemaker, r North
Prouty Nathaniel, blacksmith, r North
Puffer John, farmer, r Main
Pyne David, laborer, r Green
Pyne Edward, laborer, r Lincoln
Pyne John, laborer, r Elm
Pyne Patrick, laborer, r Lincoln
Pyne Walter, laborer, r Ship

QUINN BARTHOLEMEW, teamster, r Thaxter
Quinn Charles, farmer, r Beal

RAFFERTY THOMAS, laborer, r Summer
Ray Caleb, cabinet maker, r Pleasant
Ray Charles N. cooper, r Summer
Read George, farmer, bds Main
Reed George R. house painter, bds Short
Reed Horace F. house painter, bds Short
Reed John A. house carpenter, bds Short
Reed Reuben M. mariner, r Short
Remington Bela, laborer, r Lincoln
Remington Foster, nail maker, r Ship
Remington John D. stone mason, r Fort Hill
Remington John O. salesman, Boston, r South
Remington Josiah S. shoemaker, r Fort Hill
Remington Martin, laborer, bds Fort Hill
Remington Wendell F. cabinet maker, bds South
Richardson Frank, shoemaker, r Elm
Richardson Joseph Rev. r Main
Richardson Smith, shoemaker, r Elm
Richardson Thaddeus, shoemaker, r Elm,
Rider John, Sup't Hingham Cordage Co. r Main
Riley Francis, rope maker, r Cedar
Riley Wm. edge tool maker, r Thaxter
Ripley Ebenezer, butcher, r Main
Ripley Elijah S. farmer, bds Pleasant
Ripley George R. butcher, r Main
Ripley Henry, butcher, r Main
Ripley Henry W. farmer, bds Main

J. A. JACKSON, 101 COURT STREET, BOSTON, DEALER IN HATS, CAPS, AND FURS.

Ripley Joseph, (Ripley & Newhall) furniture manuf. r South
Ripley Justin, house carpenter, r Main
Ripley Justin jr. house carpenter, r Leavitt
Ripley Justin E. house carpenter, bds Leavitt
Ripley Levi B. mason, r Leavitt
Ripley Obed, farmer, r Main
Ripley Roland C. provisions, bds Main
Robb Daniel J. blacksmith
Roberts Ebenezer, shoemaker, r North
Robinson Nahum, blacksmith, r New Bridge
Rolfe Enoch C. (Daly & Rolfe) r Boston
Ryan Edward, tanner, r Lazel

SCHMIDT CHARLES, bl'ksmith, r Main
Sculley Charles, shoemaker, r Whiting
Sculley John, blacksmith, r Whiting
Sears Orin, farmer, r Lincoln
Sears Orin B. machinist, r Lincoln
Seymour Charles W. S. overseer box factory, r Main
Shea Thomas, laborer, r Main
Shea Timothy, laborer, r New Bridge
Sherman Samuel, carver, r Hersey
Shuck F. A. engineer, r Main
Shute Daniel, edge toolmaker, r Main
Shute Daniel, shoemaker, r Main
Shute Elijah, farmer, r Main
Shute Henry, blacksmith, r Main
Shute Isaiah, carpenter, bds Main
Shute William, farmer, r Main
Siders Charles, agent, Boston, r Main
Siders Henry F. clerk, Boston, r Main
Siders John, foreman, r Hersey
Siders John T. engineer, r Hersey
Silvia Frank, shoemaker, r Beal
Simmons Samuel, gentleman, r South
Sloane John, woodturner, r Scituate
Smith Amos, fisherman, r Ship
Smith Charles W. shoemaker, r Main
Smith Thos. D. house-painter, r Scotland
Snell John E. stonemason, r North
Soule Nathan T. teacher, bds Main
Southark Martin, ropemaker, r Main
Souther Benj. S. ropemaker, r Leavitt
Souther Charles, ropemaker, r Main
Souther David, musician, Boston, r Ship
Souther Elijah, ship-carpenter, r Leavitt
Souther James, ropemaker, r Leavitt
Souther John S. cooper, r Leavitt
Souther Martin, layer, Hingham Cordage Co. r Main
Souther Samuel, laborer, r Hobart
Spalding Henry E. homeopathic physician and surgeon, bds Union Hotel
Spencer David, shoemaker, r Free
Spooner George H. shoemaker, r West
Spooner Ichabod, laborer, r Fort Hill
Spooner Warren, shoemaker, r Hersey
Sprague Artemus, cabinetmaker, r North
Sprague Bela, farmer, r Mount Blue road
Sprague Blossom, shoemaker, r Main
Sprague B. T. grocer, r Main
Sprague Charles, house-painter, r Middle
Sprague Daniel, currier, r Back
Sprague D. W. shoemaker, bds Back
Sprague Obed, farmer, r Leavitt
Sprague Elijah, trader, r Main
Sprague Franklin, carpenter, bds Back
Sprague Henry, laborer, bds Back

Sprague Jairus, caulker, r Summer
Sprague Joseph, clerk, Boston, r South
Sprague Joseph C. blacksmith, r Pleasant
Sprague Joseph T. carriage painter, r Main
Sprague Josiah, (J. & S. Sprague), house painter, r Pleasant
Sprague Leavitt, jig sawyer, bds South
Sprague Leavitt, trader, bds Main
Sprague Luther, blacksmith, bds North
Sprague Luther, jr., house carpenter, r North
Sprague Martin, box maker, r Middle
Sprague Moses, cooper, r Pond
Sprague Peter, shoemaker, r Main
Sprague R. O. stair builder, r Main
Sprague Samuel, clerk, r North
Sprague Seth, (I. & S. Sprague), house painters, r Back
Sprague Seth M. farmer, r Main
Sprague Sidney, clerk Hingham Insurance Co.
Sprague Thomas L. clerk, Boston, bds South
Sprague Timothy, carpenter, r Thaxter
Sprague William, painter, bds Main
Spring Charles, fish market, r South
Spurr W. R. boot maker, r South
Stacy Wm. rope maker, bds Main
Stanton John, blacksmith, r New Bridge
Stanton Michael, laborer, r New Bridge
Steele Charles, carpenter, r Hersey
Stephenson E. physician, r Main
Stephenson Charles, shoe dealer, Boston, r Water
Stephenson Henry, blacksmith, r Middle
Stephenson John, balance manuf. r Middle
Stephenson Luther, (L. Stephenson & Co), balance manuf. r Middle
Stephenson Luther jr., insurance agent, r Water
Stephenson Thomas E. C. clerk, Boston, bds Main
Stockwell Alonzo, expressman, r North
Stockwell Otis, iron moulder, r North
Stoddar Caleb, iron-smith, r Main
Stoddar Caleb S. boot maker, r High
Stoddard Charles, fisherman, r South
Stoddard Charles H. F. shoemaker, r Fort
Stoddard Jacob, shoemaker, r North
Stoddard James M. rope maker, r Pleasant
Stoddard John H. farmer, bds West
Stoddard Laban, tanner, r Main
Stoddard Martin, mariner, r North
Stoddard Martin B. boot maker, r Fort Hill
Stoddard Matthew, mariner, r Fort Hill
Stoddard Melzar, mariner, r North
Stoddard Obed S. shoemaker, r Fort Hill
Stoddard Quincy, fisherman, r North
Stoddard Thomas W. shoemaker, r Fort Hill
Stoddard William T. cord maker, r Cottage
Stodder Thomas, mariner, r Green
Stodder Zadock, mariner, r Green
Stowell Hersey, farmer, r North
Stowell Jared, farmer, bds North
Stowell Stephen, stone mason, r Fort Hill
Strong John, keeper hotel, N. Y. r South

Policy Holders in the BERKSHIRE LIFE INSURANCE COMPANY of Pittsfield, Mass., DO NOT FORFEIT THEIR POLICIES by reason of FAILURE TO PAY their premiums. (See page 50.)

Studley Benjamin, silk cord maker, bds South
Studley Benj. G. express, r Main
Studley George, works Boston, r South
Studley Thomas, blacksmith, bds Leavitt
Sturgis Sumner
Sullivan Daniel, laborer, r Main
Swan Aaron A. shoe manuf. r Scotland
Sylvester Nathaniel, farmer, r Prospect

TAFT SILAS W. livery and boarding stable, bds Union Hotel
Tarbell George G. physician, bds Lincoln
Taylor William, shoemaker, r North
Thaxter David, lawyer, Boston, r North
Thaxter Joseph B. merchant, Boston, r Main
Thaxter Norton Q. farmer, r South
Thayer A. E. grocer, bds South
Thayer Benj. D. mariner, r Main
Thayer Elihu, provision dealer, r South
Thayer Joshua, gentleman, r Elm
Thomas Benjamin, farmer, r Lazel
Thomas David, (B. Thomas & Co.), iron foundry, r Kilby
Thomas Joseph, superintendent foundry, r Rockland
Thomas Reuben, (B. Thomas & Co.), r Union
Thomas W. H. painter, r Pond
Thomas William, clerk, Boston, r Pleasant
Thompson A. boot maker, r North
Thompson Daniel P. laborer, r North
Thompson Dominick, drover, r North
Thompson John, engineer, r North
Thompson Michael F. carpenter, r North
Thompson Patrick, laborer, r Hersey
Tilden Atherton, r Main
Tilden Edward F. shoemaker, r Pleasant
Tilden Edwin F. boot treer, bds Pleasant
Tilden Elijah, cooper, r Pleasant
Tilden Elijah D. clerk, r Summer
Tilden Elijah D. flour and grain dealer, r North
Tilden George W. house carpenter, r Middle
Tillson Jonathan Rev. r Cottage
Tirrell Alfred, iron moulder, r Rockland
Tirrell Edwin F. cutter, r North
Todd John, tailor, r Lincoln
Torrey F. J. poultry dealer, r Main
Torrey Henry O. blacksmith, r Main
Torrey William, laborer, r Main
Torrey William C. butcher, bds Main
Totman Charles H. shoemaker, r Fort Hill
Totman William H. shoemaker, r Fort Hill
Tower Cushing, farmer, r Back
Tower Edwin, bucket maker, r High
Tower George F. shoemaker, r Main
Tower John, shoemaker, r Hobart
Tower John M. shoemaker, r Hobart
Tower Joshua, gentleman, r High
Tower Leavitt, cooper, r High
Tower Reuben, clock and watch maker. r Main
Tower William, variety store, r Main
Tower William S. bucket maker, r Main
Trowbridge Henry, butcher, bds Main
Trowbridge Roswell, flour and grain, r Main
Tulley Hubert, laborer, r Main
Turner G. R. livery and stage stable, r Leavitt
Turner Joshua D. wheelwright, r Whiting
Tuttle James, shoemaker, r Ward
Tuttle John, shoemaker, r Ward

URIC JOHN, dyer, r North

VOGELL GEORGE, rope maker, bds Main

WADE JOHN, boot and shoemaker, r Short
Wall Henry, rope maker, bds Hersey
Wall John J. rope maker, bds Hersey
Wall Nicholas, rope maker, r Hersey
Wall Thomas F. rope maker, bds Hersey
Wallace Morris, laborer, r Summer
Wallace Thomas, laborer, r Green
Walper Charles, currier, r Main
Walper John C. tanner, r Main
Waters George H. cabinet maker, r Ship
Waters John, cooper, r Water
Webber Daniel, woodcarver, r East
Weeks Ellis, shoemaker, r Pine
Weimer Christian, laborer, r Hersey
Wells A. E. plateman Hingham Cordage Co. r Main
Wells Edward A. ropemaker, r Main
Welsh John, laborer, r Ship
Welsh John F. gentleman, r High
Wilder Alden, wooden ware manuf. (C. & A. Wilder.) r Main
Wilder Alfred, shoemaker, r Main
Wilder Bradford C. boot and shoemaker, bds Main
Wilder Crocker, wooden ware manuf. (C. & A. Crocker,) r Main
Wilder Daniel, dry goods and groceries, (D. & J. Wilder,) r Main
Wilder Edward, Supt. Hingham Wooden Ware Co. r Main
Wilder Edward C. shoemaker, bds North
Wilder Edwin, livery stable, r Lincoln
Wilder Edwin, 2d, post-master, r North
Wilder Ezra, watch and clockmaker, cor. Main and Friend
Wilder George, carpenter, r Lincoln
Wilder Henry, mariner, r North
Wilder Isaac H. shoemaker, bds North
Wilder John, grocer, r Main
Wilder John, shoemaker, r New Bridge
Wilder Joseph, gentleman, r Main
Wilder Joseph D. shoemaker, r Main
Wilder Joseph H. tailor, r Main
Wilder Martin, shoe manuf. r Lincoln
Wilder Nathaniel, 2d, shoemaker, r North
Wilder William C. bucket manuf. r Main
Wilder William W. merchant, Boston, r Lincoln
Wingfield Thos. M. hairdresser, bds South
Winslow Isaac, U. S. dept. collector of customs, r North
Wolfe George A. shoemaker, r Lincoln
Woodbury Daniel W. shoemaker, r Fort Hill
Woodward Joseph, book agent, bds Pleasant
Woodward Thos. K. boxmaker, r Pleasant

J. A. JACKSON, 101 COURT STREET, BOSTON, DEALER IN HATS, CAPS, AND FURS.

Worrick Paul B. gentleman, r Hull
Whitcomb E. B. boot and shoe manuf. (*Witcomb & Bates,*) r High
Whitcomb Israel, farmer, r Lazel
White Caleb C. shoecutter, bds Middle
Whiting Alfred B. carpenter, r Whiting
Whiting Albert, gentleman, r Main
Whiting Amasa, axe manuf. r Main
Whiting Charles, gentleman, r Main
Whiting Dexter, farmer, r Garden
Whiting Hosea, farmer, r Gardner
Whiting Hosea, jr. shoe manuf. r Whiting
Whiting Joseph N. farmer, r Garden
Whiting Richard, shoemaker, r North
Whiting Sylvanus, farmer, r Garden
Whiton Albert, printer, r Thaxter
Whiton Alvan, farmer, r Main
Whiton Bela, flour and grain, r Cottage
Whiton B. H. carriagemak'r, (*B. H. Whiton,*) r Main
Whiton Charles F. clerk, Boston, r Main
Whiton Dexter B. cabinetmaker, r North
Whiton E. L. hats, caps, boots and shoes, r North
Whiton Elijah, gentleman, r Main
Whiton Erastus, teamster, r Main
Whiton Isaiah, mariner, r South
Whiton Job S. farmer, r South
Whiton L. B. (*Whiton & Bullard,*) r South
Whiton Lyman B. boot and shoe manuf. bds South
Whiton Peter L. inspector of fish, bds Lincoln
Whiton Royal, drugs and groceries, r South
Whiton Thomas, mercht. Boston, r Main
Whiton Thomas F. ship chandler, r Lincoln
Whiton Thomas L. farmer, r Lincoln
Whiton William, mercht. Boston, r Main
Whitney Jason W. supt. r North
Wright George, clerk, Boston, r Ship
Wyman Christian, laborer, r Elm
Wyman John, laborer, r Elm

YOUNG CALVIN H. bootmaker, r Main
Young James K. shoemaker, r Whiting
Young Joshua, Rev. r Cottage

Hull General Directory.

ANDERSON JAMES, fisherman
Anderson Lewis, mariner
Augustus George T. fisherman
Augustus John, mariner
Augustus John jr., fisherman

BATES MARSHALL, fisherman
Bates Thomas, keeper of Boston Light

CARNEY WILLIAM B. house carpenter
Carter Charles A. fisherman
Cleverly John M. pilot
Cobb Elisha T. mariner
Cobb Joseph, mariner
Cook Orlando D. telegraph operator

DILL DAVIS W. fisherman

GOULD ROBERT, house carpenter

HAYDEN JOHN, fisherman
Hillier James, fisherman
Hobbs George, fisherman
Hooper Charles J. asst. light keeper
Hooper Nathaniel R. spit light keeper

JAMES JOSHUA, fisherman
James Riennier, mariner
James Samuel, mariner
James William, mariner
James William W. mariner

KNIGHT CHARLES H. farmer
Knight Edward G. house carpenter
Kimball Noah, fisherman
Knight Martin, farmer

Knight John G. school teacher
LORING LEWIS P. farmer
Loring Samuel, farmer
Lowe James jr., fisherman

MATTHEWS GIDEON, house carpenter
McKann Francis, fisherman
Milleken Clement, laborer
Mitchell Alonzo L. fisherman
Mitchell Harrison, mariner
Mitchell Henry O. farmer
Mitchell Nicholas, fisherman

POPE ANDREW F. fisherman
Pope Benjamin F. fisherman
Pope James W. fisherman
Pope Joseph, grocer
Pope Joseph, post master
Pope Joseph, telegraph operator
Pope William, fisherman

REED DANIEL D. fisherman
Reed John, fisherman
Ripley Nehemiah, Prop'r Rockland house

SAWYER SAMUEL H. pilot
Shore Robert, asst. light keeper, Boston Light
Sirovich Lewis G. fisherman
Sirovich Nicholas, fisherman

TOWER JOHN W. farmer
Turner James, fisherman

VINING ALEXANDER, Proprietor Mansion House

ANNUAL CASH DIVIDENDS in the BERKSHIRE LIFE INS. CO., Pittsfield, Mass. Boston Office 95 1-2 Washington St. (See page 50.)

Kingston General Directory.

ADAMS CHARLES, farmer
Adams Frederic C. butcher
Adams George, butcher
Adams George T. butcher
Adams Henry L. sea captain
Adams William S. sea captain
Ames Benj. F. clerk
Andrews Samuel M. overseer in Co. Mill

BAGNELL FREDERIC, farmer
Bagnell John C. shoemaker
Baker L. C. pattern maker
Baker Levi, sea captain
Baker Otis jr., sea captain
Bailey Caleb E. blacksmith
Bailey Justus A. seaman
Bailey Nahum, organ manuf.
Bailey Nahum jr., variety store
Bailey Thomas, organ maker
Bailey W. B. seaman
Bartlett C. A. ship joiner
Bartlett Lysander, ship carpenter
Bartlett Uriah, farmer
Bartlett Walter S. house carpenter
Bates Caleb, farmer
Bearse Ichabod, farmer
Bearse John, farmer
Beal Joseph S. attorney
Beal Thomas, clerk
Berry Roscoe G. laborer
Beytes A. M. rope maker
Bicknell George T. seaman
Bicknell Thomas, tack maker
Bisbee Daniel, organ maker
Bisbee Daniel jr., shoemaker
Bonney John A. shoemaker
Bonney John, shoemaker
Bonney Wallace, house painter
Bowker Davis W. marble cutter
Bradford Alden S. farmer
Bradford Alpheus, shoemaker
Bradford Amos, tack maker
Bradford George A. tack maker
Bradford George B. shoemaker
Bradford H. S. road master
Bradford Jason, fish merchant
Bradford Orin W. earthenware manuf.
Bradford Peleg, farmer
Bradford Stephen, box board and shingles
Bradford William, farmer
Brewster Elisha, farmer
Brewster Spenser, farmer
Briggs Seneca F. wheelwright
Brooks Nathan, town clerk
Bryant C. E. shoemaker
Bryant George B. laborer
Bryant James H. farmer
Bryant Nathaniel, carpenter
Bryant O. E. laborer
Bryant Peleg, farmer
Bryant Sylvanus, farmer
Bryant Sylvanus jr., box board manuf.
Bryant William B. laborer
Burkell M. rope maker
Burgess William H. merchant
Bunker Edward, rope maker
Barnes E. E. tailor

CALLAHAN THOMAS, mason
Carey Dennis, laborer
Chandler A. S. farmer
Chandler David, farmer
Chandler E. D. farmer
Chandler H. J. laborer
Chandler Ira, farmer
Chandler Ira jr., clairvoyant doctor
Chandler J. H. laborer
Chandler J. S. blacksmith
Chandler Nathan, teamster
Churchill A. R. farmer
Churchill Ebenezer, shoemaker
Churchill George D. farmer
Churchill Henry, shoemaker
Churchill James T. shoemaker
Churchill Otis, shoemaker
Churchill Prince, farmer
Churchill S. E. farmer
Cobb Benjamin, rivet manuf.
Cobb Henry, farmer
Cobb John W. clerk
Cobb Martin, farmer
Cobb Nathaniel, pastor evangelist
Cobb Philander, merchant
Cobb Seth, rope maker
Cole James, basket maker
Cole Josiah T. anchorsmith
Cole Leander S. rivet maker
Cole Samuel P. rivet maker
Cole Thomas E. moulder
Cook Ase, farmer
Cook Benjamin, sea captain
Cook Edwin, shoemaker
Cook Henry F. shoemaker
Cook Josiah T. anchor smith
Cook Martin, shoemaker
Comer Joseph, rope maker
Corey Gustavus, laborer
Cunningham T. B. sea captain
Cushing S. W. ship carpenter
Childs Abner P. wheelwright
Cushman Arthur L. clerk
Cushman Asa, blacksmith
Cushman Daniel S. carpenter
Cushman Edwin, cabinet maker
Cushman F. D. iron moulder
Cushman George, farmer
Cushman George 2nd, shoemaker
Cushman James H. farmer
Cushman John, shoemaker
Cushman Joseph, shoemaker
Cushman Joseph P. farmer
Cushman Josiah, hotel keeper
Cushman Nathaniel, farmer
Cushman S. E. farmer
Cushman William, baker

DAVIE SOLOMON, tinman
Dawes J. H. sea captain
Delano Benj. fish merchant
Delano David, house-carpenter
Delano Joshua, fish merchant
Delano Lewis S. blacksmith
Dergon Patrick, ropemaker
Drake Marden, shoemaker
Drew Cornelius, ship-carpenter

J. A. JACKSON 101 COURT STREET, BOSTON, DEALER IN HATS, CAPS AND FURS.

Drew Cornelius Jr., ship carpenter
Drew C. P. organmaker
Drew Eli C. farmer
Drew Job W. blacksmith
Drew John, ship-carpenter
Drew John N. fisherman
Drew N. D. ship-carpenter
Drew Robert A. laborer
Drew Seth, organmaker
Doneley James S. ropemaker
Doneley John, ropemaker
Dorcey Patrick, laborer
Doten E. L. shoemaker
Doten Isaac, laborer

EAGER ROBERT, laborer
Eldridge D. G. wheelwright
Ellis Wyllie R. boarding-school
Evans Green, soap manufacturer
Everson Charles, house-carpenter
Everson James O. shoemaker
Everson Warren N. shoemaker

FAUNCE ALBERT, house-carpenter
Faunce C. A. expressman
Faunce C. C. mason
Faunce C. T. mason
Faunce E. farmer
Faunce Elmer, house-carpenter
Faunce George, house-carpenter
Faunce John, farmer
Faunce Martin, farmer
Faunce S. W. mason
Faunce W. H. teacher
Foster A. B. stable keeper
Foster C. T. farmer
Foster James, farmer
French Timothy, farmer
Fuller Alexander, farmer
Fuller C. H., U. S. Navy
Fuller Daniel W. laborer
Fuller Ephraim, farmer
Fuller Frank, clothing manuf.
Fuller James, seaman
Fuller John, fish monger
Fuller John A. tackmaker
Fuller Josiah, cooper
Fuller Ezra, farmer
Fuller Samuel, laborer
Fuller Smith, laborer
Fuller T. H. farmer

GREY EDWARD, edge tool manuf.
Grey S. W. shoemaker
Griffeth H. C. iron moulder
Griffeth James W. iron moulder
Griffeth Wilson, iron moulder

HAGGERTY WILLIAM, laborer
Hall John F. farmer
Hamilton H. M. coachman
Hammond Asa C. house carpenter
Haney Dennis, laborer
Harlow James M. rope maker
Hayward Lucius, shoemaker
Holmes Alexander, anchor manuf.
Holmes Allyn, house carpenter
Holmes Cornelius
Holmes Edward, ship builder
Holmes E. H. seaman
Holmes Ephraim, farmer
Holmes F. H. anchor manuf.
Holmes Gaius, anchorsmith

Holmes Gaius jr., anchorsmith
Holmes George, anchorsmith
Holmes Ira, farmer
Holmes James W. anchorsmith
Holmes John F. farmer
Holmes Joseph, ship joiner
Holmes Joseph A.
Holmes Robert W. farmer
Holmes R. E. farmer
Holmes Samuel, farmer
Holmes S. N. farmer
Holmes Stephen, house carpenter
Howe A. F.
Howland D. F. farmer
Hunt Henry, merchant

JOHNSON JOHN, farmer
Jones Henry N. physician
Jones John A. rope maker
Jones Leander L. bucket manuf.
Joyce Eli, shoemaker

KEITH HENRY K. merchant
Kennedy Frank, seaman
Kennedy James, rope maker
Kennedy James jr., rope maker

LANMAN THOMAS, farmer
Leach Erastus, depot master
Leach M. G. shoemaker
Lucas H. F. farmer

MAHONEY JOHN, laborer
McGrath Michael, laborer
McGrath Tom, shoemaker
McGrath William, laborer
McLaughlin Elisha, blacksmith
McLaughlin George W. anchorsmith
McLaughlin P. W. caulker
McLaughlin R. B. anchorsmith
McLaughlin S. W. tack maker
Mitchell Ezra, shoemaker
Mitchell Harvey, shoemaker
Mitchell John, shoemaker
Mitchell Ransom, shoemaker
Morse E. G. shoemaker
Morse Francis, shoemaker
Morse George, shoemaker
Morton Franklin, shoemaker
Morton George H. shoemaker
Myrick William H. tinware and stoves

NEWCOMB G. S. book keeper
Newcomb Thomas, cotton thread manuf.
Nichols Paul L. physician
Nutter S. J. farmer

O'BRIEN PATRICK, laborer
Oldham A. J. mason
Oldham John, carpenter
Owens G. E. shoemaker

PAINE R. C. farmer
Peckham Joseph, clergyman
Peirce J. B. laborer
Peirce Moses, rope maker
Perkins Ezra, blacksmith
Perkins H. F. cigar maker
Peterson Esias, shoemaker
Peterson Ichabod, ship rigger
Peterson William, sea captain
Pezzy Tom, fisherman
Phillips G. L. carpenter

The terms for ENDOWMENT, and TEN ANNUAL LIFE POLICIES in the BERKSHIRE are peculiarly favorable, and rates lower than in any other Company. (See page 50.)

Phipps J. H. clergyman
Powers Edwin, sea captain
Prince Noah, box board manuf.
Prince Tom, cigar maker

RANSOM HARVEY, lobster dealer
Ransom Winslow, lobster dealer
Reed Alphonzo, tack manuf.
Reed Edmund, tack maker
Reed Edwin, mackerel kit manuf.
Reed Franklin, tack manuf.
Reed P. C. tack manuf.
Richardson Edwin, seaman
Richardson E. P. shoemaker
Ring D. W. farmer
Ring D. W. jr., farmer
Ring Samuel, farmer
Ripley C. W. machinist
Ripley Lewis, house carpenter
Ripley Obed, house carpenter
Ripley S. E. house carpenter
Ripley Tom, ship carpenter
Robbins Charles, merchant
Robbins Charles T. merchant
Robbins Joseph S. carpenter
Robbins William A. sea captain
Russell Thomas, tack maker
Ryan John, laborer

SAMPSON AZEL, farmer
Sampson Azel H. post master
Sampson Benjamin, farmer
Sampson C. H. shoemaker
Sampson Columbus, farmer
Sampson Constant, caulker
Sampson Elbridge, farmer
Sampson George, farmer
Sampson George H. miner
Sampson Oliver, farmer

Sampson Walter S. mason
Sampson William A. shoemaker
Sedgley Dexter E. soap maker
Sever J. N. merchant
Simmons Augustus, shoemaker
Simmons Charles, farmer
Simmons E. F. anchor smith
Simmons F. O. anchor smith
Simmons Henry, house carpenter
Simmons Henry jr., seaman
Simmons Nahum, blacksmith
Simmons Peleg, laborer
Shaw S. B. laborer
Smith John, cotton thread maker
Soule Henry, tack manuf.
Soule Henry jr., tack maker
Soule James C. anchor smith
Soule William F. miller
Southworth Tom, shoemaker
Stetson Charles, sea captain

Stetson Elisha, farmer
Stetson George, farmer
Stetson H. T. farmer
Stetson J. H. mason
Stetson Joseph, harness maker
Stetson K. W. tack manuf.
Stetson W. S. shoemaker
Stranger A. R. shoemaker
Stranger J. A. shoemaker
Stuart David, cooper
Sturtevant Henry, farmer
Symmes William, sea captain

THOMAS AUGUSTUS, farmer
Thomas William A. farmer
Thomas William R. moulder
Thompson J. S. house-carpenter
Tribble William T. seaman
Tupper Seth, liquor agent

VINAL C. A. blacksmith

WADSWORTH GEORGE, ropemaker
Wadsworth W. A. shoemaker
Walker A. mason
Washburn A. W. lobster dealer
Washburn A. H. laborer
Washburn Caleb F. anchorsmith
Washburn Cephas, depot master and p. m.
Washburn C. F. laborer
Washburn C. H. laborer
Washburn Charles, laborer
Washburn Francis, lobster dealer
Washburn George, iron melter
Washburn G. L. rivetmaker
Washburn Henry, wiremaker
Washburn John, shoemaker
Washburn M. P. blacksmith
Washburn Philip, ropemaker
Washburn W. D. hatter
Waterman A. B. shoemaker
Waterman E. E. house-carpenter
Waterman Nathaniel, farmer
Waterman Thomas E. house-carpenter
Webb Fred
Weston T. R.
White Alden, farmer
Willis Edward, wool dealer
Willis Foster, seaman
Willis George F. insurance agent
Willis Jonah, soap manufacturer
Willis Jonah, jr. shoemaker
Willis N. T. farmer
Willis William H. shoemaker
Wilson Eli, overseer, cotton thread manf.
Winsor E. G. sea captain
Winsor William D. farmer
Witherell E. C. laborer
Wixon O. F. seaman
Wright J. L. shoemaker

J. A. JACKSON 101 COURT STREET, BOSTON, DEALER IN HATS, CAPS AND FURS.

Lakeville General Directory.

ALDRICH JOHN R. shoemaker
Allen Clothier, farmer
Allen John, farmer
Allen John F. farmer
Andrews Gustavus G. carpenter
Andrews Stillman S. carpenter
Ashley Abraham, tanner
Ashley David, farmer
Ashley John C. farmer
Ashley John E. farmer
Ashley Joseph, farmer
Ashley Josiah R. cooper
Ashley Luther, mason and farmer
Ashley Silas P. farmer

BACK GEORGE, shoemaker
Baker Abisha, farmer
Baker Freeman, farmer
Baker Josiah, farmer
Baker Marcus, farmer
Baker Simeon, farmer
Baker William, farmer
Baker William, 2d. farmer
Barney George, farmer
Barney William, farmer
Barrows Elijah W. clergyman
Bassett Charles H. shoemaker
Benton William H.
Bishop Dexter, hack-driver
Booth Henry B. farmer
Briggs Jonathan C. farmer
Briggs Joseph H. carpenter
Briggs Peltiah, farmer
Brown Edward, shoemaker
Bump Josiah B. shoemaker
Bump Thomas W. shoemaker

CANEDY ALEXANDER, laborer
Canedy Elkanah W. farmer
Canedy John W. farmer
Canedy William, farmer
Carpenter Henry G. hotel-keeper
Carpenter William H. hotel-keeper
Carver Gilbert W. laborer
Caswell Abraham, shoemaker
Caswell Abraham H. shoemaker
Caswell Eliab, farmer
Caswell Horatio, trader
Caswell Martin L. shoemaker
Caswell Nathaniel, laborer
Caswell Solomon, farmer
Caswell William H. farmer
Caswell Stetson, trader
Churchill George W. farmer
Churchill Libbeus, painter
Clark Stephen, farmer
Cole Charles G. laborer
Cole Job N. laborer
Cole Samuel, farmer
Cole Thomas F. shoemaker
Coombs Clarence A. shoemaker
Coombs Hopestill B. shoemaker
Coombs James M. farmer
Coombs Simeon, mason
Coombs William A. farmer
Crane Ebenezer, farmer
Crane Luther, carpenter

Cudworth Elisha G. farmer
Cudworth John, farmer
Cudworth Joseph S. shoemaker
Cummings Jason, farmer

DEAN ALLEN, brick burner
Dean Barney T. shoemaker
Dean Henry A. shoe manuf.
Dean James A. shoemaker
Dean John, shoemaker
Dean Philip C. farmer
Dean William, shoe manuf.
DeMeranville Josiah, farmer
DeMeranville Josiah jr.,
Dunham Edward E. shoemaker
Durfee William N. laborer

ELMES HIRAM, shoemaker
Elmes Royal, farmer
Emerson John L. shoemaker

FARMER CHARLES, cooper
Fisher Obed T. laborer
Freeman Alexander H. shoemaker

GODFREY JOB M. farmer
Goff Joseph W. machinist
Griffith William, dry goods packer

HACKETT EDWARD W. farmer
Hackett Peleg S. farmer
Hafford Reuben, farmer
Hafford William F. farmer
Hall Levi, farmer
Harlow William, farmer
Harvey Abiezer T. farmer
Haskins Austin, shoemaker
Haskins Bartlett, shoemaker
Haskins Cephas, station agent
Haskins Edmund, tailor
Haskins Franklin, carpenter
Haskins Gilbert T. laborer
Haskins Ira, laborer
Haskins Irvin
Haskins Levi H. farmer
Haskins Martin K. carpenter
Haskins Myrick, carpenter
Haskins Orin E. farmer
Haskins Thompson R. laborer
Haskins John C. farmer
Hinds John, sawyer
Hinds Stephen V. sawyer
Hinds Sumner, farmer
Hoard George S. farmer
Hopkins William H. com. merchant
Hopkins William H. jr., com. merchant
Horr Elijah, shoemaker
Horr Job, farmer
Howland James M. farmer

JACKSON ABRAHAM, clergyman
Jenney Charles E. farmer
Jenney Edwin, farmer
Jones Ebenezer, laborer
Jones Paul L. shoemaker

DIVIDENDS ADDED to the **POLICY** in the **BERKSHIRE** often exceed the premium paid; are **NON-FORFEITABLE** and will be redeemed in **CASH ON DEMAND.** (See page 50.)

KEEN SETH, farmer
Keith Joseph W. laborer
Kinsley John, carpenter

LEACH CHARLES W. dentist
Leonard Abiatha, farmer
Leonard Ezra S. shoemaker
Leonard Frederick, farmer
Leonard Gideon, farmer
Leonard Henry B. shoemaker
Leonard James, farmer
Leonard J. J. C. farmer
Letcher John W. laborer
Loner William E. shoemaker
Lovell Thomas J. straw manuf.

McCULLEY EZRA, farmer
McCulley Stephen, farmer
McGee Andrew, farmer
Meach John, seaman
Meach Lawson, farmer
Miller Samuel, shoemaker
Montgomery John, farmer
Montgomery John F. farmer

NANCE FREDERICK A. cooper
Nelson Cyrus, farmer
Nelson Horatio, farmer
Nelson John H. farmer
Nelson Sidney T. farmer
Nelson Thomas M. farmer
Norveill Levi, farmer
Nye L. farmer

OSBORN ANDREW, shoemaker
Osborn George, nail manuf.
Osborn Joseph C. nail worker

PARKHURST WALTER B. farmer
Parris Abner, laborer
Parris Enos, farmer
Parris Moses, laborer
Parris William C. trader
Parry John E. farmer
Paul Roger, cooper
Paul William, farmer
Pawn David S. farmer
Pawn John, farmer
Pawn John H. seaman
Peirce Abram, laborer
Peirce Anson L. farmer
Peirce Charles T. carpenter
Peirce Ethan E. farmer
Peirce Enos, farmer
Peirce Henry, farmer
Peirce Isaac, farmer
Peirce James P. farmer
Peirce Job, farmer
Peirce John, farmer
Peirce Levi, farmer
Peirce Philip H. farmer
Peirce James, trader
Pickens Benjamin A. farmer
Pickens Davis, teamer
Pickens Edward P. farmer
Pickens Henry C. painter
Pickens Jonathan, farmer
Pickens Josephus, farmer
Pickens Silas, farmer
Pickens Silas D. shoemaker
Pickens Zaccheus, farmer
Pickens Zattue, farmer

REED BENJAMIN H. stonecutter
Reed Henry B. laborer
Reed John C. farmer
Reed John E. farmer
Reed Levi, stonecutter
Reed Milton, laborer
Richmond Benjamin, farmer
Richmond Charles R. box manuf.
Richmond Eleazer, box manuf.
Richmond Hiram L. shoemaker
Richmond Leonard, trader
Richmond William, laborer
Robbins Joseph W. farmer
Robbins Lemuel, farmer
Robbins Lemuel, jr. farmer
Robbins Orin S. laborer
Roberts Austin J. farmer
Robinson Adoniram J. butcher
Rogers Harris, farmer
Rogers Hiram, shoemaker

SAMPSOM ABIEL M. farmer
Sampson Charles H. farmer
Sampson Ebenezer, farmer
Sampson Francis E. farmer
Sampson Horatio N. farmer
Sampson James M. farmer
Sampson Nathaniel, farmer
Sampson Nathaniel M. farmer
Sampson Sylvanus W. carpenter
Sampson Uriah, farmer
Sears Abner J. farmer
Sears John W. farmer
Shaw Abraham, farmer
Shaw Francis T. shoemaker
Shaw Jarius H. carpenter
Shaw John, shoemaker
Shaw Zebulon, farmer
Shockley Andrew J. farmer
Shockley Charles, farmer
Southworth Abiel, farmer
Southworth Albert, farmer
Southworth Alvarius C. farmer
Southworth Enoch, blacksmith
Southworth James, farmer
Southworth Otis, carpenter
Southworth Thomas, farmer
Southworth Warren H. carpenter
Spooner George H. farmer
Spooner Thomas jr., farmer
Staples Charles W. shoemaker
Staples George B. shoemaker
Staples Harrison, farmer
Staples James, farmer
Staples James M. peddler
Staples Job M. shoemaker
Staples William B. farmer
Stetson Sprague S. farmer
Strowbridge Benjamin H. farmer

TERRY S. farmer
Thresher Cyrus, farmer
Thresher George E. shoemaker
Thresher Israel, farmer
Thresher Job, farmer
Thresher Stephen M. shoemaker
Tinkham Dennis, laborer
Tinkham Francis M. sawyer
Tinkham Horatio, shoemaker
Tinkham Josiah F. farmer
Tinkham Otis, shoemaker
Tobey Job T. farmer
Tolman Nicholas W. farmer

J. A. JACKSON, 101 COURT STREET, BOSTON, DEALER IN HATS, CAPS, AND FURS.

Townsend John, shoemaker
VAILS ADONIRAM, laborer
Vails Joseph W. laborer
WARD JAMES W. clergyman
Washburn Charles E. farmer
Washburn Cyrus, trader
Washburn Francis, farmer
Washburn Hiram, cooper
Washburn Leonard, carpenter
Washburn Salmon, farmer
Westgate C. T. farmer
White Benjamin, farmer
White George M. farmer
White Henry C. shoemaker
Williams Elkanah, farmer
Williams Eli, farmer
Williams Eli W. farmer
Williams Elisha, farmer
Williams Elisha H. farmer
Williams George, farmer
Williams George W. shoemaker
Williams Henry L. farmer
Williams John, farmer
Williams Samuel, laborer
Winslow Asa, farmer
Winslow Asa T. farmer
Winslow Jirah, farmer
Winslow Leander, farmer

Marion General Directory.

ALLEN ANDREW M. carpenter
Allen Bartholomew G. mariner
Allen Charles A. laborer
Allen Charles C. teamster
Allen George D. mariner
Allen Henry D. farmer
Allen Henry M. agent for whaling vessels
Allen John D. carpenter
Allen John M. architect
Allen Silas B. carpenter
Allen Reuben, farmer
Allen Stephen, farmer
Allen Weston, farmer
Atwood Alexander A. mariner
Atwood George W. mariner
Atwood Warren, farmer

BACHELDER JOHN, physician and surgeon
Barden Frederick, master mariner
Barden Jordan B. prop'r. Marion and New Bedford stage
Bartlett William H. farmer
Bates George S. farmer and trader
Bates Jared, farmer
Bates John S. merchant
Bates Prince H. carpenter
Benson Consider, farmer
Blankinship Albert C. mariner
Blankinship Andrew M. laborer
Blankinship Charles W. mariner
Blankinship David W. mariner
Blankinship James W. mariner
Blankinship Job, farmer
Blankinship John B. farmer
Blankinship Joseph, master mariner
Blankinship Peleg, master mariner
Blankinship Seth, mariner
Blankinship Walter F. carpenter
Blankinship Warren, carpenter
Bolles Charles D. mariner
Bolles Charles M. farmer
Bolles Leonard, master mariner
Bolles Leonard A. mariner
Bolles Richard E. shoemaker
Braley Elijah, carpenter
Briggs Barnabas A. mariner
Briggs Benjamin S. master mariner
Briggs Charles H. carpenter
Briggs Elnathan, farmer
Briggs Hallet, carpenter
Briggs Howard S. carpenter
Briggs Isaac D. farmer
Briggs Jedediah, mariner
Briggs John B. pilot
Briggs John, 3d. master mariner
Briggs Joseph W. teamster
Briggs Josiah K. farmer
Briggs Justus A. mariner
Briggs Nathan, master mariner
Briggs Oliver E. master mariner
Briggs Paul W. carpenter
Briggs Peleg T. laborer
Briggs Philip, laborer
Briggs Reuben A. mariner
Briggs Roswell K. mariner
Briggs Roland, farmer
Briggs Rufus F. blacksmith
Briggs Seth H. laborer
Briggs Silas, blacksmith
Briggs Timothy, mariner
Briggs William H. carpenter
Briggs Zenas M. mariner
Brown George H. mariner
Bruce J. E. clergyman
Burgess John, laborer

CANNON HENRY, mariner
Chase Benjamin F. farmer
Chamberlain James, blacksmith
Clark Charles A. carpenter
Clark Joseph W. mariner
Clark William, ship-carpenter
Clifton Jirah, teamster

Policy Holders in the BERKSHIRE LIFE INSURANCE COMPANY of Pittsfield, Mass., DO NOT FORFEIT THEIR POLICIES by reason of FAILURE TO PAY their premiums. (See page 30.)

Clifton Obed D. farmer
Clifton Timothy, farmer
Cobb Edward W. teamster
Cobb Leander, clergyman
Cobb Oliver, carpenter
Coffin Shubael C. farmer
Coffin William J. farmer
Coleman Hezekiah, mechanic
Cowing Leander, mason and bricklayer
Crowell Francis, master mariner

DEAN ABIEL, miller
Dean Charles C. oysterman
Delano Benjamin, farmer
Delano Charles H. mariner
Delano Clark, master mariner
Delano Ebenezer, shoemaker
Delano Harper, master mariner
Delano Henry D. master mariner
Delano James, master mariner
Delano James H. mariner
Delano John, carpenter
Delano Obed, master mariner
Delano Ward P. merchant, Landing
Dexter Sumner, painter
Dexter Zoath, caulker
Dorr Richard H. clergyman, dentist
Dorr Charles H. butcher
Dryer Henry C. baker

ELDER SAMUEL H. merchant
Ellis Charles D. farmer
Ellis Stephen, farmer
Ellis Stephen A. carpenter

FAUNCE DAVID, laborer
Faunce David jr. laborer

GRAY HENRY, mariner
Gray Rufus, master mariner
Gray Russell, master mariner
Gray Russell jr. mariner
Gifford Henry W. fisherman
Griffith Josiah S. oysterman
Griffith Obed, farmer
Gurney Ansel H. trader
Gurney Barnabas H. farmer
Gurney Charles B.

HADLEY AMOS, farmer
Hadley Andrew J. merchant, Sippican
Hadley Byron, farmer
Hadley Stephen D. master mariner
Hadley Stephen W. mariner
Hall Charles D. farmer
Hall Daniel, sheriff and constable
Hall Sylvanus W. post master and merchant, Sippican
Hamblin Harvey M. teamer
Hammond Charles A. mariner
Hammond Clement, mariner
Hammond Ed. E. master mariner
Hammond George, carpenter
Hammond John, shoemaker
Hammond M. V. B. mariner
Hammond Stephen, carpenter
Handy Augustus, carpenter
Handy Benjamin B. master mariner
Handy Charles, farmer
Handy Ebenezer, laborer
Handy Frederick P. carpenter
Handy Leonard, laborer

Handy Noah D. carpenter
Handy Osmer
Handy Pardon, carpenter
Handy William, master mariner
Handy William H. carpenter
Hardy William W. trader
Haskell Andrew J. laborer
Hathaway Alexander, mill sawyer
Hathaway Franklin L. master mariner
Hathaway Isaac N. master mariner
Hathaway John K. master mariner
Hathaway William C. master mariner
Hiller Barnabas, ship carpenter
Hiller Matthew, mariner
Holmes Barnabas, teacher
Holmes Ebenezer, farmer
Holmes Ebenezer, jr., farmer
Holmes Peter A. butcher
Howard Lucius, hotel keeper

JACKSON ANDREW, mariner
Jenney James E. mariner
Jenney Job, mill sawyer
Jenney Job T. mariner

KEEN CLIFTON, mariner
Keen George H. master mariner
Kelley George H. painter and glazier
Kelley Henry H. tinman and caulker
Kelley John, master mariner
Kelley Lucius C. caulker
Kent Joseph C. architect

LEONARD SETH C. proprietor of Marion and New Bedford express
Look Frederick B. mariner
Look Hiram H. mariner
Lovell Austin, expressman
Luce George A. pilot
Luce George L. master mariner
Luce James, carpenter
Luce John, master mariner
Luce Joseph S. proprietor of Bay View House
Luce Rowland L. mariner
Luce Samuel W. master mariner
Luce Shubael K. mariner
Luce Stephen C. master mariner
Luce Weston, trader

MAHONEY JOHN, laborer
Maxim Jesse, oysterman
Mendall Elbridge G. painter
Mendall Ezra J. farmer
Mendall Frederick A. stone cutter
Mendall Jonathan, merchant
Mendall Joseph C. laborer
Mendall Nathan H. carpenter
Mendall James B. mariner
Mendall Seth G. carpenter
Mendall William C. master mariner
Miner Henry, axe maker
Miner John W. dentist

NYE GEORGE B. farmer
Nye John B. B. farmer, Proprietor Marion Strawberry Gardens

PARKER ALFRED L. mariner
Parker Robert, carpenter
Parlow Charles H. mill sawyer
Parlow Ezra, miller
Parlow Nathan, miller

J. A. JACKSON 101 COURT STREET, BOSTON, DEALER IN HATS, CAPS AND FURS.

MARION DIRECTORY.   67

Parlow George W. stone cutter
Parlow George Wilson, painter and glazier
Phinney Stephen C. peddler
Pitcher James S. H. master mariner
Pitcher John, master mariner
Portagues Job, mariner
Potter William H. laborer

RUGGLES CHARLES H. Proprietor Aroostock express
Ryder John C. carpenter
Ryder Jonathan, farmer
Ryder William H. H. mariner

SAVERY RUFUS L. mariner
Sherman Edward, carpenter
Sherman Edward F. carpenter
Sherman Eli, shoemaker
Sherman Humphrey, shoemaker
Sherman Humphrey L. master mariner
Simmons John H. clerk
Smith Augustus, clerk
Snow Ebenezer, farmer
Stone Dwight, farmer
Sullivan Patrick, laborer
Sweeney Richard, laborer
Swift Anderson, carpenter
Swift Moses H. merchant

Swift Richard N. farmer
Swift Samuel, nailer

TABER ALBERT W. mariner
Taber Bartholomew W. tailor
Taber Jabez, mariner
Tallman Alfred carpenter
Tripp Pardon, master mariner
Turner Charles W. merchant

VAIL WILLIAM, stone mason
Vose Henry C. clergyman and homeopathic physician

WATERS SAMUEL, peddler
Washburn Horatio, farmer
Washburn Peleg, farmer
Weeks George S. laborer
Weeks Henry, mariner
Weeks James D. nailer
Weeks Paul M. mariner
Willett James, sailmaker
Willett James T. sail maker
Wing Charlton H. carpenter
Wing Charlton H. Jr., carpenter
Wing George W. mariner
Wing Jabez, painter
Wing James R. laborer

YOUNG JAMES A. clerk

Marshfield General Directory.

ALDEN EBEN, jr. Clergyman
Ames Edwin, farmer
Ames Elijah, farmer
Ames George, shoemaker
Ames Isaac, shoemaker
Ames Tilden, farmer
Arnold F. P. shoe manufacturer
Atwell Charles, soldier
Atwell Edwin
Atwell Seth, laborer

BAKER ARTEMUS, shoemaker
Baker Benjamin, shoemaker
Baker Dwelley, laborer
Baker George M. trader
Baker Horace E. carpenter
Baker James, farmer
Baker James E. farmer
Baker John, auctioneer
Baker Otis, farmer
Baker Quincy A. shoemaker
Baker Samuel, farmer
Baker Thomas, shoemaker
Baker William, shoemaker
Bailey Charles, laborer
Bailey Charles W. shoemaker
Bailey George, laborer
Bates Albert, shoemaker

Bates Henry S. teacher
Bates Marshall, stone cutter
Bonney Cephas, farmer
Bonney Cephas W. fisherman
Bonney Henry B. shoemaker
Bonney Lucius L. shoemaker
Bowen John, farmer
Bowen John H. farmer
Blackman T. Bradford farmer
Brown Daniel, carpenter
Brown David, blacksmith
Brown T. C. shoemaker
Butterfield Hiram, laborer

CARVER BARSTOW, ship-wright
Carver David, farmer
Carver Frank E. laborer
Carver Hatch, ship-wright
Carver Israel, farmer
Carver Israel H. carpenter
Carver John, carpenter
Carver Silas, house-carpenter
Chandler John, farmer
Chandler Simeon B. sawyer
Church Nathaniel, farmer
Clapp James, ship-wright
Clark Albert, shoemaker
Clark Amos O. shoemaker

ANNUAL CASH DIVIDENDS in the BERKSHIRE LIFE INS. CO., Pittsfield, Mass. Boston Office 95 1-2 Washington St.   (See page 54.)

Clark Hiram, shoemaker
Clift Edwin, teamster
Clift Wales R. farmer
Conant Winslow, soap manufacturer
Cook Henry O. laborer
Corlan F. A. shoemaker
Cox Eben, laborer
Creed John, ship-wright
Crossley H. T. trader
Crowell Josiah C. shoemaker
Cudworth Elijah F. shoemaker
Cudworth Laban, ship-wright
Curtis Samuel, farmer
Cushing William B. shoemaker
Cushing William P. farmer

DAMON ALFRED C. shoemaker
Damon Amos F. shoemaker
Damon Andrew L. shipwright
Damon Edward N. shoemaker
Damon Frederic N. carriage maker
Damon George S. shoemaker
Damon Granville D. confectioner
Damon Hiram A. laborer
Damon James L. carriage maker
Damon John, carpenter
Damon Lincoln, shipwright
Damon Moses K. laborer
Damon Nathaniel, farmer
Damon Nathaniel, jr., shipwright
Damon Samuel, shipwright
Davis Jacob, clergyman
Deeral Seth, farmer
Delano George
Delano Henry C. carpenter
Delano Nathaniel C. laborer
Dingley Israel P. farmer
Doane Reuben, sailor
Drew William B. farmer
Dunham Henry G. miller

EAMES GEORGE W.
Eames William, sawyer
Estes William S. laborer
Ewell Abijah, shoemaker
Ewell Allen, farmer
Ewell Allen, 2d, carpenter
Ewell Charles, laborer
Ewell Daniel E. shoemaker
Ewell Ezra D. farmer
Ewell Frederic H. shoemaker
Ewell George H. shoemaker
Ewell Zenas T. laborer
Ewell Zenas T. jr., laborer
Ewell John, shoemaker
Ewell Judson, blacksmith
Ewell Lewis, shoemaker
Ewell Marshall, shoemaker
Ewell Quincy A. shoemaker
Ewell Thatcher, shoemaker
Ewell Turner, farmer

FORD A. farmer
Ford Calvin, shoemaker
Ford Edwin, shoemaker
Ford Ezra, shoemaker
Ford Frank, farmer
Ford Gera, shoemaker
Ford Henry F. shoemaker
Ford Henry G. farmer
Ford Hiram A. carpenter
Ford James, farmer
Ford John, surveyor

Ford John E. peddler
Ford Nathan, house carpenter
Ford Samuel, farmer
Ford Thomas P. carpenter
Ford William H. carpenter

GOODELL CURTIS B. farmer
Gardner Henry D. farmer
Gardner L. A. shoe manuf.
Gardner Stephen, shoe manuf.
Groce Nathaniel, shoemaker

HAGAR JOSEPH, physician
Hall Elisha W. trader
Hall George H. manuf.
Hall Harvey, shipwright
Hall Henry, laborer
Hall James, laborer
Hall Samuel, shipwright
Hall Tilden, shoemaker
Hall Warren, farmer
Hall William, carpenter
Harlow Charles M. peddler
Harlow John A. farmer
Harrington Lorenzo D. shoemaker
Harrington William, shoemaker
Hatch Anson, expressman
Hatch Austin, laborer
Hatch Benjamin, carpenter
Hatch Calvin O. shoemaker
Hatch Charles, farmer
Hatch Charles R. box manuf.
Hatch Charles T. farmer
Hatch Clinton, farmer
Hatch David P. box manuf.
Hatch Edward, carpenter
Hatch Elisha, farmer
Hatch Elisha C. farmer
Hatch Emmons, shipwright
Hatch Frederic, carpenter
Hatch George, farmer
Hatch Henry W. farmer
Hatch Ichabod, farmer
Hatch Israel H. carpenter
Hatch John F. box manufacture.
Hatch Jotham, carpenter
Hatch Lewis, laborer
Hatch Luther, farmer
Hatch Marcellus, farmer
Hatch Perez, farmer
Hatch Samuel, sawyer
Hatch Samuel F. farmer
Hatch Thomas D. laborer
Hatch Winslow F. stagedriver
Hatch William, blacksmith
Henderson William L. shoemaker
Henry Stephen, dentist
Hewitt Asa, farmer
Holmes Ellis, farmer
Holmes Thomas, farmer
Holmes Thomas, jr., ship-wright
Hopkins Nathan S. shoemaker

INGLEE ROBERT, farmer

JONES CHARLES, shipwright
Josselyn Charles S. shoemaker
Josselyn Henry W. shoemaker
Jennings Nathaniel, farmer
Joyce Calvin, shoemaker
Joyce Elisha, shoemaker

KEEN B. F. H. caulker

J. A. JACKSON, 101 COURT STREET, BOSTON, DEALER IN HATS, CAPS, AND FURS.

MARSHFIELD DIRECTORY.

Keene Cornelius, laborer
Keene Elisha, fisherman
Keene Nathaniel, shipwright
Keene Nathaniel jr., shoemaker
Keene Samuel, laborer
Keep Samuel, caulker
Keith James, farmer
Kent Andrew, shoemaker
Kent Elisha, farmer
Kent Elisha W. ship carpenter
Kent James W. shoemaker
Kent Martin, shoemaker
Kent Peleg, farmer
Kent Peleg S. shipwright
Kent Warren, carpenter
Kent William, shipwright
Kent William M. blacksmith
King Samuel B. shoemaker
Knox Joseph, farmer

LAPHAM ALLEN, farmer
Lapham Church C. blacksmith
Lapham Constant C. shoemaker
Leonard George, clergyman
Leonard George E. shoemaker
Leonard Otis, teacher
Lewis Albert, mariner
Lewis Benjamin J. shoemaker
Lewis Calvin, mariner
Lewis Charles, farmer
Lewis Francis P. laborer
Lewis Jesse L. shoemaker
Lewis Roger, shipwright
Lewis William T. shoemaker
Little Charles M. carpenter
Little Constant, farmer
Little Henry H. type maker
Little Melvin, farmer
Little Solomon, farmer
Little William F. carpenter
Little William F. farmer
Lombard James, shoemaker
Loring George W. carpenter
Loring Winslow, farmer
Lowe Samuel, farmer and blacksmith

MITCHELL ALDEN B. shoemaker
Magoun Ambrose, box manuf.
Magoun Andrew T. peddler
Magoun Charles H. master mariner
Macomber Charles W. farmer
Merrill Erastus A. shoemaker
Macomber Israel H. farmer
Morehead Robert H. farmer

NASH WILLIAM F. shoemaker
Nichols Robert, shoemaker

OAKMAN CHRISTOPHER, carpenter
Oakman Constant, farmer
Oakman Hiram, farmer
Oakman Hiram A. teacher
Oakman Henry P. carpenter
Oakman Israel, carpenter
Oakman Roswell E. carpenter
Oakman Thomas R. mariner
Oakman William C. carpenter
Osborne George, laborer
Osborne Levi, farmer

PACKARD LEMUEL, mill-wright
Paulman Martin, gardener
Paine Briggs T. shoemaker

Paine Ezekiel, shoemaker
Paine Isaac, physician
Paine Israel H. laborer
Paulding Joshua T. ship-wright
Pease Benjamin F. clergyman
Peirce Enos, farmer
Perry Charles F. shoemaker
Peterson George J. shoemaker
Peterson William C. carpenter
Phillips Alfred, gentleman
Phillips Alfred, jr. farmer
Phillips Edwin, farmer
Phillips James, trader
Phillips James C. shoemaker
Phillips Nathaniel, farmer
Phillips Nathaniel, 2d, farmer
Phillips Wendall A. farmer
Porter Alvin, laborer
Porter Nathaniel J. clerk
Porter Nicholas, farmer
Porter Nicholas, jr. shoemaker
Porter William S. mariner

RAMSDELL FREEMAN A. carpenter
Ramsdell Martin, jr. shoemaker
Randall Josiah, carpenter
Randall Ethan A. shoemaker
Reed Jesse, machinist
Roberts Davis B. farmer
Robinson Increase, gentleman
Rogers Abijah, carpenter
Rogers Alden, carpenter
Rogers Arthur, pump maker
Rogers Arthur F. fisherman
Rogers Avery, shoemaker
Rogers Charles, shoemaker
Rogers Charles E. shoemaker
Rogers Clift, merchant
Rogers Edwin P. shoemaker
Rogers Elisha, shoemaker
Rogers George H. farmer
Rogers George W. shoemaker
Rogers Howland, farmer
Rogers Isaac T. peddler
Rogers James L. farmer
Rogers Marcellus W. blacksmith
Rogers Wales, blacksmith
Rogers Wales A. shipwright
Rogers William, painter

SAMPSON AARON, farmer
Sampson Charles, farmer
Sampson Charles, 2d, peddler
Sampson Charles L. laborer
Sampson Harrison F. shoemaker
Sampson Joseph, laborer
Sampson Sidney W. shoemaker
Sears Charles, fisherman
Sears Francis, keeper saloon
Sears George fisherman
Sherman Albion P. farmer
Sherman Amos, farmer
Sherman Asa, farmer
Sherman Asa jr., farmer
Sherman Augustus F. fisherman
Sherman Josiah H. shipwright
Sherman Leander, farmer
Sherman Moses, shoemaker
Sherman Peleg S. shipwright
Sherman Spencer W. shoemaker
Sherman Stephen, farmer
Sherman Stephen C. fisherman
Sherman William, farmer

The terms for ENDOWMENT, and TEN ANNUAL LIFE POLICIES in the BERKSHIRE are peculiarly favorable, and rates lower than in any Note Company. (See page 50.)

Simmons Byron, shoemaker
Simmons Ezra H. shoemaker
Simmons Hewitt, wheelwright
Simmons James H. blacksmith
Simmons Jonathan, shoemaker
Simmons Moses T. shoemaker
Simmons Nathaniel, farmer
Smith Ezra, farmer
Sprague Albert T. mariner
Sprague Barker, fisherman
Sprague Chillingworth, farmer
Sprague Edward, carpenter
Sprague Elisha C. teacher
Sprague Elisha P. master mariner
Sprague Harvey, farmer
Sprague Horatio B. mariner
Sprague James, farmer
Sprague John, sawyer
Sprague John jr., master mariner
Sprague Seth F. master mariner
Sprague Stephen C. master mariner
Stephens Daniel, carpenter
Stephens Ray, farmer
Stevens Charles, shoemaker
Stevens Peleg, shoemaker
Stevens Thomas, shoemaker
Stetson James H. shoemaker
Stetson James H. jr., shoemaker
Stetson Samuel, farmer
Stetson Samuel C. shoemaker
Stoddard Martin, shoemaker
Stoddard Wallace A.

TAYLOR LEWIS, farmer
Taylor Nathaniel, mariner
Taylor William, shipwright
Taylor William H. mariner
Thomas Caleb, carpenter
Thomas Charles W. laborer
Thomas Eben S. shoemaker
Thomas Luther, farmer
Thomas Peleg, farmer
Thomas William F. farmer
Thomas Zenas, farmer
Thompson Daniel H. peddler
Tilden Atwood H. carpenter
Tilden Charles L. master mariner
Tilden Charles M. carpenter
Tilden Corrington, farmer
Tilden Elliot R. shoemaker
Tilden George, farmer
Tilden Henry, trader
Tilden Horatio N. carpenter
Tilden John, farmer

Tilden Luther H. shoemaker
Tilden William M. carpenter
Tolman Henry, shoemaker
Tolman William P. carpenter
Turner Horace, laborer

VENTRESS GEORGE W. peddler

WADSWORTH ICHABOD, farmer
Wadsworth Luke, farmer
Walker Asa, farmer
Walker Charles A. carpenter
Walker Edwin, shoemaker
Walker Ephraim H. carpenter
Walker Ephraim H. jr., farmer
Walker Henry A. carpenter
Walker Levi, farmer
Waterman Nathaniel, farmer
Waterman Nathaniel, jr., shoemaker
Weston George, carpenter
Weston George P. shoemaker
Weston Ichabod, carpenter
Weston Seth, farmer
Weston Seth, jr., carpenter
Weston William A. shoemaker
Wetherbee G. H. jr., trader
White Benjamin, shoemaker
White G. shoemaker
White Lewis E. shoemaker
White Luther, carpenter
White Martin, shoemaker
White Thomas, farmer
White Warren, carpenter
White Warren F. shoemaker
Whiting N. H. clerk
Williams Albert B. laborer
Williamson Abner, laborer
Williamson Calvin, shoemaker
Williamson Calvin, jr., shoemaker
Williamson Charles, shoemaker
Williamson Elijah, peddler
Williamson George H. blacksmith
Williamson Job, shoemaker
Williamson John, mariner
Williamson Joshua, farmer
Williamson Peter, shoemaker
Williamson Samuel, farmer
Williamson Timothy, laborer
Williamson William, shoemaker
Wright Abner, farmer
Wright Allen, farmer
Wright Charles P. farmer
Wright Daniel, farmer
Wright Ezra, butcher
Wright Nathaniel, laborer

J. A. JACKSON 101 COURT STREET, BOSTON, DEALER IN HATS, CAPS AND FURS.

Mattapoisett General Directory.

AIKEN WARREN, cooper
Aiken Warren, jr., machinist
Allen James S. ship-wright
Allen James S. jr., shoemaker
Ames Daniel H. carpenter
Ames Nathaniel F. ship-wright
Ames Theodore, rigger
Atsatt John T. merchant
Atsatt Philip, shoemaker
Atsatt William, shoemaker

BACON BENJAMIN, ship-wright
Barlow Franklin, rigger
Barlow Gideon B. rigger
Barlow Gideon B. jr., mariner
Barlow George, rigger
Barrows Alphens, blacksmith
Barrows Andrew J. painter
Barrows Joseph L. painter
Barrows Philip A. mariner
Barrows Samuel, painter
Barstow Benjamin, ship-wright
Barstow Calvin, joiner
Barstow Charles B. mariner
Barstow Elijah W. Lieut. 5th Reg. Art'y.
Barstow Henry, box mill
Barstow Henry W. joiner
Barstow James, rigger
Barstow James, 2d, joiner
Barstow John, ship-wright
Barstow Nathan H. box mill
Barstow Solomon, mariner
Barstow Wilson, farmer
Bates Joshua T. ship-wright
Beal Charles C. farmer
Blankenship James R. mariner
Bolles Charles E. dentist
Bolles Job A. mariner
Bolles John D. mariner
Bolles Joseph W. mariner
Bolles Joshua, farmer
Bolles Prince, cooper
Bolles Solomon E. mill
Bolles William E. cooper
Bowles Resolved W. auctioneer
Bowles Stephen W. farmer
Bowles William T. farmer
Boodry Dennis S. carpenter
Boodry Nathan, ship-wright
Bourne Edmund L. mariner
Bourne George W. mariner
Bourne William L. carpenter
Bowlin Josiah, blacksmith
Bowlin William H. seaman
Bowman Alexander B. mariner
Bowman Benjamin, mariner
Bowman Luther A. mariner
Bowman Macy, mariner
Briggs Nathan, mariner
Brightman Henry G. farmer
Brown James L. shoemaker
Brownell Ezra, farmer
Buck Charles H. mariner
Buell Edward, ship-wright
Bumpus Henry F. farmer
Burbank Charles M. ship-wright
Burbank Ezra, ship-wright
Burbank Joseph, ship-wright

Butts Joseph A. farmer
Butts Patrick M. farmer

CANNON ARVIN, ship-wright
Cannon David H. ship-wright
Cannon David H. 2d
Cannon Elisha, caulker
Cannon Elisha, 2d, mariner
Cannon Frederick J. mariner
Cannon George H. mariner
Cannon Hallet M. ship-wright
Cannon James, ship-wright
Cannon Thomas J. mariner
Carr John P. auctioneer
Carter James, mariner
Caswell Elbridge G. stonecutter
Caswell Elbridge G. jr. cooper
Clark Elijah M. mariner
Clark James M. mariner
Clark Jonathan M. farmer
Cleavland John P., D. D.
Coleman Andrew, clerk
Cowin Abner P. ship-wright
Cowin George D.
Cowin Isaac L. carpenter
Cowin Seth, mason
Crosby David, expressman
Crosby Nathaniel A. ship-wright
Cross Franklin, farmer
Cushing William R. ship-wright

DAVIS GEORGE H. machinist
Davis Lemuel L. B. mariner
Davis Thomas M. mariner
Davis William L. machinist
Delano Thomas S. mariner
Denham Andrew, farmer
Denham Charles W. ship-wright
Denham Nathaniel H. farmer
Dexter Alden, caulker
Dexter Benjamin F. ship-wright
Dexter Caleb, ship-wright
Dexter Calvin, ship-wright
Dexter Charles, mariner
Dexter Elisha, miller
Dexter Elisha L. miller
Dexter Ephraim, caulker
Dexter Ephraim A. caulker
Dexter George H. mariner
Dexter Gideon, ship-wright
Dexter Horace, mariner
Dexter James W. painter
Dexter John, ship-wright
Dexter John 2d, caulker
Dexter John S. carpenter
Dexter Joseph, farmer
Dexter Leonard, mariner
Dexter Samuel, caulker
Dexter Samuel jr., caulker
Dexter Sumner, mariner
Dexter Thomas, caulker
Dexter Warren, ship-wright
Durfee Edward

EATON SOLOMON K. architect and surveyor
Ellis Albert, mariner
Ellis Daniel S. farmer

DIVIDENDS ADDED to the POLICY in the BERKSHIRE often exceed the premium paid; are NON-FORFEITABLE and will be redeemed in CASH ON DEMAND. (See page 50.)

Ellis Jarvis, farmer
FAUNCE REV. WILLIAM,
Faunce William T. shoemaker
Forbes James D. clerk
Freeman Seth, mariner
Friedhoff James, mariner

GIBBS CHARLES M. butcher
Gifford David, farmer
Gifford Ephraim
Gifford John L. mariner
Gifford Sylvanus, carpenter
Gilbert Benjamin D. ship-wright
Goodspeed Hiram H. mariner

HALL LARNET, jr., lighthouse and depot keeper
Hall Martin, blacksmith
Hallett Eben A. hotel
Hammond Amnittai B. farmer
Hammond Charles B. mariner
Hammond E. farmer
Hammond George F. mariner
Hammond Hiram M. farmer
Hammond John M. farmer
Hammond Joseph J. farmer
Hammond Larnet H. merchant
Hammond Nathaniel, ship-wright
Hammond Noah, farmer
Hammond Roland, student
Hammond Thomas P. farmer
Hammond William, soap manuf.
Handy Elisha B. mariner
Harlow William, mariner
Harris Joseph, blacksmith
Harris William jr., mariner
Haskins Lorenzo D. carpenter
Hathaway Edwin F. mariner
Hathaway Isaac, farmer
Hathaway Philip D. farmer
Hiller Alpheus B. joiner
Hiller Benjamin E. joiner
Hiller Caleb, ship-wright
Hiller David P. mariner
Hiller Edward B. farmer
Hiller Isaac, farmer
Hiller Isaac jr., farmer
Hiller Jonathan, joiner
Hiller L. farmer
Hiller Nathan D. carpenter
Hiller Nathaniel, farmer
Hiller Nathaniel P. ship-wright
Hiller Seth, carpenter
Hiller Prince, joiner
Holmes Jonathan H. ship-builder
Holmes Josiah, jr., ship-builder
Holmes Heman G. moulder
Howes Marshall, stone cutter
Howland Roland, shipwright
Howland Thomas, ship-wright
Howland Weston, ship-wright
Hoxie Asa, mariner
Hudson Joseph, sail-maker
Hudson Wilson B. sail-maker

JACKSON ANDREW, mariner
Jenney Alonzo M. ship-wright
Jenney Elisha C. peddler
Jenney John, sawyer
Jenney Joseph R. mariner
Johnson Charles H. cabinet maker
Johnson Thomas, mariner

Jones Ebenezer, painter
Jones Lot N. butcher
Jones Sylvanus T. mariner

KEENE FREEMAN C. mariner
Keith Benjamin F. carpenter
Keith Charles, express
Keith Charles F. mariner
Keith Marshall, mariner
Keith William H. mariner
King Caleb, clerk
King James, mariner
Kinney Charles F. mariner
Kinney Charles F. 2d, mariner
Kinney Jireh, shoemaker
Kinney Jireh jr., saloon
Kinney Jonathan, mason
Kinney Samuel, mason
Knobb William, farmer
Konkiel Christian, farmer

LANDERS THOMAS C. mariner
Lawson Elias, mariner
LeBaron Albert S. jeweller
LeBaron Edward, farmer
LeBaron Enoch H. patent halters
LeBaron Frederick L. patent halters
LeBaron James, farmer
LeBaron Lemuel, merchant
LeBaron Marcus B. sawyer
Lewis George W. ship-wright
Lobdell George W., R. R. contractor
Luce Charles O. ship-wright
Luce Shubael K. mariner
Luce Thomas, farmer
Luce William, merchant

MACOMBER JOSHUA L. mariner
Mendall Ellis, shoemaker
Mendall Nathan H. mariner
Merrithew Edmund, jr
Merrithew Russell, mariner
Merrithew Stephen, mariner
Merrithew William W. mariner
Morse Ansel, ship-wright
Morse Edward A. mariner
Morse George F. mariner
Morse Theodore S. mariner
Murray John, farmer

NELSON THOMAS, cabinet maker
Nye Charles H. mariner
Nye Charles F. mariner
Nye Francis, ship-wright
Nye Francis L. mariner
Nye George B. mariner
Nye Ichabod, ship-wright
Nye Joseph J. farmer
Nye Prince M. mariner

PARKER JOHN, shipwright
Parker Nathaniel D. shipwright
Payne Abraham, shipwright
Payne Daniel H. shipwright
Payne Francis M. mariner
Payne James A. mariner
Polly Jacob, farmer
Purrington Henry J. carver
Purrington Henry W. shipwright
Purrington George, carpenter
Purrington George, jr., merchant
Purrington Isaiah, mariner
Purrington James H. carpet sweeper

J. A. JACKSON, 101 COURT STREET, BOSTON, DEALER IN HATS, CAPS, AND FURS.

Purrington Joseph, shipwright
Purrington Samuel, shipwright

RANDALL CHARLES, caulker
Randall Charles A. mariner
Randall Clement, caulker
Randall Fayette E. farmer
Randall George W. farmer
Randall Joseph S. caulker
Randall Lemuel, farmer
Randall Leonard, farmer
Randall Lewis, farmer
Randall Stephen, farmer
Randall Thomas, farmer
Randall William R. caulker
Ransom James B. farmer
Ransom James B. jr., mariner
Ransom Joseph H. mariner
Ransom Nathaniel C. mariner
Ransom Sidney, mariner
Robinson Benjamin F. mariner
Robinson Joseph H. mariner
Robinson Josiah, miller
Robinson Josiah, jr., mariner
Robinson William, sawyer
Rounceville Job P. mariner

SAMPSON ANDREW C. mariner
Sampson Benjamin F. mariner
Sampson Joseph T. mariner
Sampson Thomas C. shipwright
Sanford Edward C. mariner
Shaw Bruce F. farmer
Shaw James, farmer
Shaw John A. farmer
Shearman Job, shipwright
Shearman Noah, teacher
Shurtleff Alvah H. farmer
Shurtleff Henry A. farmer
Silva Edgar S. mariner
Sisson Andrew F. farmer
Smith Charles W. shipwright
Smith John, shipwright
Smith Joseph E. sawyer
Snow Allen W. mariner
Snow Dennis F., R. R. agent
Snow Eliot K. mariner
Snow Ephraim, wheelwright

Snow Harrison, mariner
Snow Harvey, shipwright
Snow Henry A. wheelwright
Snow Henry L. mariner
Snow Ivory, shipwright
Snow Joseph W. carpenter
Snow Levi, grocer
Snow Martin, grocer
Snow Prince, shipwright
Snow Rufus D. machinist
Snow Russel E. mariner
Snow Silas W. mariner
Snow Stephen, shipwright
Snow William, shipwright
Snow Wiatt, shipwright
Snow Wiatt, jr., grocer
Southworth Andrew, mariner
Sparrow William E. apothecary and physician
Spooner William, farmer
Stevens Thatcher C. blacksmith
Sturtevant Noah C. mason
Sturtevant Samuel, jr., merchant
Sturtevant Samuel L. carpenter
Sweat William W. physician

TABER JOSEPH R. mariner
Taber William L. mariner
Taylor Henry, merchant
Tinkham Abraham, farmer
Tinkham Clark, farmer
Tinkham Isaac D. farmer
Tinkham James H. shipwright
Tinkham James W. shipwright
Tinkham Nelson B. farmer
Tripp Job P. farmer

WASHBURN JAMES M. shipwright
Washburn John, shipwright
Washburn John M. shoemaker
Weeks Ansel, surveyor
Welch John, mariner
Westgate Edward A. farmer
Willis Elijah, merchant
Winslow Benjamin, shipwright
Winston Orsamus, peddler
Winters James
Wright Alfred M. farmer

Policy Holders in the BERKSHIRE LIFE INSURANCE COMPANY of Pittsfield, Mass., DO NOT FORFEIT THEIR POLICIES by reason of FAILURE TO PAY their premiums. (See page 50.)

Middleboro General Directory.

☞ There are five Post Offices in the town, as follows: "Middleboro," "North Middleboro" or Titicut, "South Middleboro," "East Middleboro," and "Rock."

Locality of some of the Principal Streets.

Beach, South.
Bedford, North, (Titicut).
Benson, South.
Brook, East.
Carver, East.
Cedar, East.
Centre, from Centre to East.
Cherry, Centre.
Chestnut, Centre.
Clay, Titicut.
Courtland, Centre.
Elm, Centre.
East, South.
France, South.
Fuller, East.
Grove, Centre.
High, Centre.
Highland, Rock to South.
Jackson, Centre.
Main, Centre.
Miller, Rock.
Montello, Centre.
Namasket, Centre.
Neck, Centre to South.
North, Centre.
Oak, Centre.
Pearl, Centre.
Peirce, Centre.
Perry, Rock.

Pine, South.
Plain, North.
Pleasant, Titicut.
Plymouth, from Bridgewater line at Titicut, to Carver.
Plympton, East.
Precinct, Centre.
Prospect, Centre.
Purchade, Titicut.
Purchase, Rock to Carver line.
River, North.
Rock, Centre.
Rocky-Meadow, East.
School, Centre.
Smith, Rock.
Soule, East.
South, South.
Spruce, South.
Stone, East.
Taunton, Centre.
Thomas, Centre.
Thompson, Centre, (Lowlands).
Tispaquin, Centre.
Vaughan, Centre.
Vernon, Titicut.
Wareham, Centre to South.
Water, Centre.
Winter, East.
Wood, Centre.

J. A. JACKSON 101 COURT STREET, BOSTON, DEALER IN HATS, CAPS AND FURS.

MIDDLEBORO DIRECTORY. 75

ABBOTT LEVI A. clergyman, r School
Adams Asa, farmer, r Wareham
Adams Edward, farmer, r Plymouth
Adams James, farmer, r Plymouth
Alden Albert, Bay State Straw Works, r Main
Alden Andrew, mechanic, r Plymouth
Alden Andrew L. farmer, r Plymouth
Alden Apollos G. merchant, r Pearl
Alden Charles E. mechanic, r Bedford
Alden Daniel, insurance agent, cor. Centre and Bedford
Alden Elijah, farmer, r Purchade
Alden George L. peddler, r Fuller
Alden James M. farmer, r Plymouth
Alden Jared, farmer, r Purchade
Alden Jared F. insurance agent, r Pleasant
Alden John C. teacher, r Plymouth
Alden John F. teacher, r Plymouth
Alden Leander M. mechanic, r Plymouth
Alden Milton, deputy sheriff, r Centre
Alden Sidney H. mechanic, r Plymouth
Alden Thomas J. section master, r Clay
Alden William C. shoemaker, r Pleasant
Aldrich Daniel W. shoemaker, r Centre
Aldrich Ezekiel H. shoemaker, r Taunton
Aldrich Hosea, farmer, r Vernon
Aldrich Solomon, farmer, r Centre
Aldrich William C. star mills' hand, r Star ave
Alger Isaac, shoemaker, r School
Allen Wm. miller, Namasket
Andrews Justin, carpenter, r Pleasant
Andrews William S. merchant, r Main
Arnold Henry, shovelmaker, r Namasket
Arnold Orlando B. shoemaker, r North
Ashley Charles W. blacksmith, r Jackson
Ashley Cornelius G. engineer, r Courtland
Ashley David M. shoecutter, r Peirce
Ashley William C. laborer, r North
Atkins Joshua, ship master, r Main
Atwood Charles N. sawyer, r Miller
Atwood Daniel L. peddler, r Elm
Atwood Daniel W. laborer, r Elm
Atwood Eben H. teamster, r Vine
Atwood Emery F. teacher, r Miller
Atwood F. Austin G. farmer, r Beach
Atwood George, farmer, r Thompson
Atwood H.N. general agent, Rock vill'ge
Atwood Harrison W. r Thompson
Atwood Ichabod F. Supt. Rock Mills, r Miller
Atwood Jacob, farmer, r Cedar
Atwood John S. laborer, r Beach
Atwood Levi, farmer, r Carver
Atwood Loranus, farmer, r Thompson
Atwood Reuel, carriagemk'r, r Plymouth
Atwood Reuel, 2d, horse dealer, r Jackson
Atwood Shadrack F. W. farmer, r Beach
Atwood William F. farmer, r Cedar
Atwood William W. shoemaker, r Wall

BACKUS JOSEPH A. farmer, Plymouth
Baker Jonathan W. railroad overseer, Elm
Baker John S. assistant dentist, Jackson
Barden John C. carpenter, Water
Barden Joseph S. butcher, Water
Barden Stephen F. box maker, Rock
Barden T. Frank, box manufacturer, Water
Barden Walter S. box maker, Water

Barrows Edward N. farmer, Neck
Barrows George, shoe manuf. Centre
Barrows George W. painter, Water
Barrows G. L. farmer, Plymouth
Barrows Harrison, farmer, Neck
Barrows Horatio, shoe manuf. Main
Barrows Jacob T. farmer, Plymouth
Barrows LeRoy, shoemaker, Main
Barrows Lewin, farmer, Neck
Barrows Lewin A. laborer, Neck
Barrows Nathaniel L. farmer, Neck
Barrows Reland F. straw manuf. Main
Barrows William O. stone mason, Smith
Beals Eber, blacksmith, Plymouth
Beals Joseph E. book-keeper, Pearl
Beals Solomon, shoemaker, Summer
Beals Solomon F. shoemaker, Plymouth
Bearse James I. printer, Water
Belcher Frederic T. straw manuf. Main
Bennett Earle, mechanic, Water
Bennett George, laborer, Chestnut
Bennett Grover, farmer, Plympton
Bennett Henry, mariner, Wareham
Bennett James, mariner, Wareham
Bennett John, farmer, Plympton
Bennett Nehemiah, farmer, Wareham
Benson Andrew, farmer, South
Benson Asa, farmer, Highland
Benson Elisha, farmer, Highland
Benson Gilbert M. farmer, Plymouth
Benson John S. farmer, Spruce
Benson Stillman, box manuf. Wareham
Bent Otis, moulder, East Village
Bisbee Andrew A. shoemaker, Cherry
Bisbee Augustine W. teacher, Rock
Bisbee Hopestill, farmer, Neck
Bisbee Ichabod W. laborer, Walnut
Bisbee Joseph H. farmer, North
Bisbee Sylvanus, farmer, Neck
Bishop Andrew A. star mills, Main
Bishop Alpheus K. farmer, South
Bishop Augustus W. farmer, South
Bishop Zenas, farmer, Smith
Bolles Charlton H. farmer, Main
Bonney Ezekiel C. shoemaker, Purchase
Boomer B. Loring, painter, Plymouth
Bosworth Andrew B. station agent, Courtland
Boucher Thomas, farmer, Precinct
Bowen Henry, laborer, Plymouth
Bowman John L. straw worker, Elm
Bradford Charles W. paint maker, Main
Bradford DeWitt C. shoemaker, Winter
Bradford Harry, hostler, Rock
Braley Job, mason, North
Brayton George, Treasurer of star mills, Main
Briggs Elijah, retired, Centre
Briggs James W. stable keeper, Plymouth
Briggs Otis, horse dealer, Plymouth
Briggs Roland, shoemaker, Main
Brightman William H. tailor, Oak
Brown Charles I. shoemaker, Plymouth
Brown Jarvis, laborer, Brook
Brown Theophilus S. farmer, Spruce
Bryant Abraham, farmer, Wool
Bryant A. Walter, clerk, Wool
Bryant Arad, wheelwright, Plymouth
Bryant Henry E. shoemaker, Plympton
Bryant Ira, farmer, Main
Bryant Isaac, farmer, Raven
Bryant James W. shoemaker, Plymouth
Bryant Joseph O. A. shoemaker, Summer

ANNUAL CASH DIVIDENDS in the BERKSHIRE LIFE INS. CO.,
Pittsfield, Mass. Boston Office 95 1-2 Washington St. (See page 50.)

Bryant Loring, wheelwright, Plymouth
Bryant William E. shoemaker, Wood
Bump Benjamin W. shoemaker, Plymouth
Bump Isaac D. shovel maker, North
Bump James S. farmer, Plymouth
Bump Sylvanus W. shoemaker, Plymouth
Bumpus Alden B. farmer, Plymouth
Bumpus Linus, laborer, Beach
Bumpus Marcus, laborer, Beach
Bunker Roland, carpenter, Pleasant
Burgess Bradford C. shoemaker, Summer
Burgess Elijah, shovel maker, North
Burgess Frederic O. shoemaker, North
Burgess James A. shoemaker, Namasket
Burgess Thomas A. shoe cutter, Plymouth
Butterworth Alfred D. mechanic, Summer
Butterworth John N. laborer, River

CARPENTER CHARLES H. jeweller, Main
Carter James, shoemaker, Plymouth
Carter Richard, straw worker, Plymouth
Carter William, shoemaker, Plymouth
Carver John, farmer, Wareham
Carver Orlando W. farmer, Wareham
Case G. engineer, Centre
Case James H. engineer, West
Caswell Abiatha, carpenter, Main
Caswell Eleazer, farmer, Main
Caswell Eleazer R. farmer, Main
Caswell William R. engineer, Vine
Champlin H. straw worker, Centre
Chase Bradford, shoemaker, Wareham
Clapp Sylvester, clergyman, Water
Clark Abisha T. farmer, Neck
Clark Abner J. shoemaker, Neck
Clark Avery L. farmer, Neck
Clark David, carpenter, Pleasant
Clark David 2d, farmer, Highland
Clark David R. shoemaker, Pleasant
Clark Elisha, farmer, Neck
Clark George S. laborer, Pleasant
Clark Harrison, farmer, Plympton
Clark Isaac, drover, Water
Clark John, farmer, Neck
Clark Joseph, farmer, Main
Clark Maltiah, teamer, Tispaquin
Clark Noah, farmer, Neck
Clark P. Otis, clerk, Plymouth
Clark Samuel, farmer, Main
Clark Samuel W. farmer, Walnut
Clark Warren, carpenter, Miller
Clark Zebulon L. farmer, Neck
Cobb Allen, farmer, Soule
Cobb Ansel A. shoemaker, Murdock
Cobb Daniel, shoemaker, Wareham
Cobb George E. farmer, Plympton
Cobb George S. farmer, Tispaquin
Cobb Heman, farmer, Plympton
Cobb Jabez, farmer, Wareham
Cobb John, mariner, Plymouth
Cobb John B. shoe manuf. Waterville
Cobb Jonathan, farmer, Smith
Cobb Nelson, shoemaker, Thompson
Cobb Nelson jr. shoemaker, Plympton
Cobb Otis, farmer, Soule
Cobb Sylvester, laborer, Tispaquin
Cobb Sylvester F. farmer, Smith
Coffin Charles W. farmer, Thompson
Coffin Samuel C. farmer, Thompson

Cole Charles A. stitcher, Main
Cole Cyrus A. teacher, School
Cole Edward W. farmer, Purchase
Cole Edwin M. shoe cutter, Plymouth
Cole James, farmer, Walnut
Cole James jr., livery stable, cor. Main and Rock
Cole Nathaniel W. tin peddler, Rock
Cole Nelson, shoemaker, Thompson
Cole Robert V. carpenter, Main
Collins Thomas C. shoemaker, Namasket
Comstock W. W. physician, cor. Peirce and Oak
Coombs Henry C. clergyman, School
Coombs Levi H. carpenter, Main
Coombs William A. shoemaker, Walnut
Cornish Charles F. farmer, Thompson
Cornish Josiah T. farmer, Thompson
Cornwall H. F. daguerreotypist, Centre
Covington Arad, farmer, River
Covington Henry D. student, River
Cox Elisha, farmer, Fuller
Cox George, box manuf., Fuller
Cronan Andrew, watchman, near Courtland
Crosby William H. currier, Fuller
Crossman Alpha, farmer, Main
Curtis David L. carpenter, Wood
Cushing Josiah C. fish dealer, Centre
Cushing Matthew, farmer, France
Cushing Matthew H. merchant, Main
Cushing Nathaniel S. teacher, France
Cushing Rev. P. Lincoln, teacher, Grove
Cushman Abner, farmer, Highland
Cushman Abraham H. horse dealer, Neck
Cushman Abraham M. farmer, Neck
Cushman Adoniram J. carpenter, North
Cushman Alexander H. sawyer, Plymouth
Cushman Earl H. farmer, Vernon
Cushman Elbridge, nursery agent, Neck
Cushman Elias, farmer, Walnut
Cushman George, farmer, Vaughan
Cushman Isaac, farmer, Wareham
Cushman Isaac S. farmer, Miller
Cushman James E. shoemaker, Plymouth
Cushman James G. saw mill, Plymouth
Cushman Samuel, shoemaker, Precinct
Cushman Venus, farmer, Neck

DARLING ALANSON, farmer, r River
Darling George, shoemaker, r Plympton
Darling Linus, collector, r Oak
Darling Thomas, farmer, r River
Davis Enoch, farmer, r Neck
Davis Enoch R. peddler, r Neck
Davis Nehemiah, shoemaker, Peirce
Davis Timothy M. laborer, r Peirce
Davis William, farmer, r Plymouth
Dean Edwin M. shoemaker, r Plymouth
Dean William L. saloon, Main
Deane Edmund W. shovelmaker, r Namasket
Deane Eliab, farmer, r Thompson
Deane Orien E. farmer, r Thompson
Deane Seth, farmer, r Precinct
Dunham Elijah, farmer and shoemaker, Water
Dunham Henry, farmer, r Main
Dunham Israel H. straw worker, r Centre
Dunham T. Fred. merchant, Main
Dunlap A. saloon-keeper, Water
Dunlap Wm. L. works Star Mills
Doane George H. hardware dealer, Oak

J. A. JACKSON, 101 COURT STREET, BOSTON, DEALER IN HATS, CAPS, AND FURS.

Doane Jeremiah, clerk, Oak
Dodd S. G. clergyman, Main
Dorrence E. B. machinist, Main
Downing Silas, teamster, Vine
Drake Ebenezer W. physician, Main
Drake Enoch, carpenter, Centre
Drake Enos, mechanic, Pleasant
Drake Ezra, tailor, Pleasant
Drew Stephen D. shoemaker, Plympton
Drew Stephen D. jr. shoemaker, Peirce
Driggs Leonard, farmer, Plymouth
Dunlap T. L. Supt. Star Mills, Main
Durfee H. W. straw manuf. Oak

EATON ANDREW M. wheelwright, and undertaker, Clifford
Eaton Barzilla, farmer, Centre
Eaton Francis F. laborer, Cross
Eaton Frank R. shoe cutter, Rock
Eaton George F. mechanic, Bedford
Eaton Henry A. shoemaker, Murdock
Eaton Lewis, carpenter, Plymouth
Eaton Oliver, carpenter, Centre
Eaton Reuel W. farmer, Purchade
Eaton Solomon K. carpenter
Eaton Williams, carpenter, Bedford
Easterbrook Mason C. printer, Water
Eddy Joshua M. post-master, Plympton
Eddy Nathaniel, manuf. Plympton
Eddy William C. shovel manuf. Plympton
Eddy William S. shovel manuf. Plymouth
Edwards Shubael G. farmer, Thompson
Edwards Shubael P. farmer, River
Eldridge Benjamin F. spinner, North
Eldridge George W. mill overseer, North
Elliott James, laborer, Jackson
Elliott John, shoe cutter, Lincoln
Ellis Rufus H. tinman, Main
Ellis Thomas S. merchant, Plympton
Ewer Seth, clergyman, Rock village

FARRINGTON GEORGE B. shoemaker, Precinct
Field Lysander W. laborer, Thomas
Finney George L. shoemaker, North
Finney Lewis, straw worker, Wareham
Finney Nelson, farmer, North
Fittz George B. teacher, Oak
Fittz Hervey, clergyman, Oak
Forbes Laban P. painter, Main
Foss Edward F. (*Rosenfeld & Foss*), dry goods, Main
Foster Edward, upholsterer, Plymouth
Freeman Andrew, carpenter, Thompson
Freeman Benjamin, farmer, Fuller
Freeman Harrison, carpenter, Fuller
Freeman Morton, shoemaker, Fuller
Freeman Samuel, carpenter, Thompson
Fuller Abiel, farmer, Spruce
Fuller Amos S. shoemaker, East p. o.
Fuller Ansel, laborer, South p. o.
Fuller Charles E. shoemaker, Fuller
Fuller Charles T. shoemaker, Fuller
Fuller Consider, farmer, Fuller
Fuller Harrison, shoecutter, Fuller
Fuller Marcus, livery stable, Jackson
Fuller Seth, farmer, Pleasant
Fuller Thomas, laborer

GAMMONS C. M. mechanic, Wareham
Gammons Curtis, peddler, Wareham
Gammons Darius, mill worker, Wareham

Gammons Eph. H. works in mill, Wareham
Gammons Ferdinand C. farmer, France
Gammons George T. M. farmer, Perry
Gammons John, clergyman, Wareham
Gammons Roland E. farmer, Wareham
Gammons Samuel N. farmer, France
Gay Charles F. woolworker, North
Gay Erastus E. straw worker, Centre
Gay Henry B. shoemaker, Namasket
Gay L. W. shoe stitcher, Rock
Gibbs Abiel, laborer, Water
Gibbs Ansel E. laborer, Gibbs pl
Gibbs Charles F. laborer, North
Gibbs Daniel, mule spinner, Lincoln
Gibbs Francis B. hotel clerk, Main
Gibbs Marshall F. butcher, Tispaquin
Gibbs Moses C. farmer, Gibbs pl
Gibbs Reuben, farmer, Miller
Gibbs Stephen B. mariner, High
Gibbs William T. farmer, Gibbs pl
Gifford Stephen W. shovel maker, Water
Gilmore Samuel, laborer
Gisby Thomas, farmer, Plympton
Gisby Thomas, jr. shoemaker, Plympton
Gisby William, farmer, Plympton
Glasse Seth, laborer, Water
Glidden Benj. R. baggage master, Rock
Gooding Charles H. shoemaker, Main
Goss Warren L. author and lecturer, North
Goss William W. canvasser, School
Grant H. L. M. shoemaker, Plymouth
Grew Isaac G. conductor, Main
Gurney Marcus A. shoemaker, Wareham

HACKETT ALEXANDER, laborer, Water
Hackett Elijah, farmer, Tispaquin
Hagan Charles, shoemaker, Thompson
Hall Caleb, farmer, Bedford
Hall Stillman, shoemaker, Benson
Harlow Bradford G. farmer, Main
Harlow Chester I. steam mill workman, Oak
Harlow Ezra A. laborer, Main
Harlow Foster A. book keeper, Main
Harlow Isaac, farmer, Thompson
Harlow Ivory H. steam mill, Main
Harlow Ivory H. 2d, farmer, Thompson
Harlow James H. carriage dealer, Main
Harlow Obed, farmer, Summer
Harlow R. A. shoemaker, Centre
Harlow Reuben, teamer, Centre
Harlow R. Kendrick, student, Main
Harlow Solomon L. farmer, France
Harlow Thomas S. blacksmith, Summer
Hartwell George, shoe cutter, Summer
Hartwell George F. merchant tailor, Centre
Haskell John T. straw worker, Water
Haskell Josiah, section master, West
Haskins Charles T. laborer, North
Haskins George, laborer, Spruce
Haskins Harrison, straw worker, Cherry
Haskins Job R. farmer, Plympton
Haskins Sebra, laborer, Murdock
Hathaway Jacob, sawyer, Water
Hathaway Joseph, chemist, Bedford
Hathaway Otis W. carpenter, Pleasant
Hathaway Rufus J. machinist, East
Hathaway Silas, farmer, Pleasant
Hathaway Simeon, boot maker, Water
Hathaway Warden, boot maker, Jackson

The terms for **ENDOWMENT**, and **TEN ANNUAL LIFE POLICIES** in the **BERKSHIRE** are peculiarly favorable, and rates lower than in any Note Company.   21   (See page 50.)

Haven Perley, shoemaker, Chestnut
Hazeltine Ebenezer, farmer, Centre
Hazeltine Ebenezer jr., mechanic, Centre
Hazelton Henry A. cigar maker, Clay
Herrick Daniel C. laborer, Grove
Hill Emerson S. clergyman, Rock village
Hill Ellis, clerk, Rock village
Hinckley Sylvanus, auctioneer, Plymouth
Hinckley Sylvanus jr., saloon, Water
Hinds William S. steam mill workman, West
Holmes Charles H. painter
Holmes Edwin, farmer, Plymouth
Holmes Jesse, shoemaker, Main
Holmes Lewis W. shoemaker, Main
Holmes Luther G. H. farmer, Wareham
Holmes Richard B. machinist, Main
Holmes Richard H. shoe cutter, Centre
Holmes Theo. P. harness maker, Water
Holmes William L. farmer, Miller
Hooper Avery F. merchant, Plymouth
Howes Charles A. shoemaker, Murdock
Hunt Ephraim, gardner, North
Hunt Eph. A. shoemaker, Wareham
Hutchinson Joseph, clergyman, Plymouth
Hutchinson Thomas, laborer, East village

IVES WILLIAM, laborer, Water

JACKSON ADNAH, farmer, North
Jackson Joseph, farmer, Main
Jackson C. S. physician, Main
Jackson Wm. A. lecturer, South
Jefferson Earle F. laborer, Beach
Jefferson Martin F. stone cutter, Spruce
Jefferson Walter T. farmer, Beach
Jenks Elisha T. machinist, Main
Jenks John W. P. Principal of Academy, Main
Jenks Nicholas, physician, Peirce
Jenney James L. teamster, Peirce
Johnson Emory A. shoemaker, Vernon
Johnson E. Arnold, shoemaker, Vernon
Johnson Henry E. shoemaker, Purchade
Johnson Jacob, shoemaker, Cherry
Jones B. F. music teacher, Main
Jones George W. shoemaker, Plymouth
Jones Watson F. wheel-wright, Water

KEEFE JOHN O. factory hand, North
Keith Allen, box maker, Peirce
Keith Foster A. farmer, Highland
Keith Justin E. shoemaker, Peirce street
Keith Nahum, shoe manuf. Plymouth st
Keith Nahum W. shoemaker Pleasant st
Keith Samuel P. farmer, Forest st
Keyes Samuel S. steam mill workman, Vine street
King Nathan, merchant, Main street
King William A. salesman, Main street
Kingman Calvin D. shoe manuf. Oak st

LAMB AMASA, shovel maker, Main
Lane Benjamin F. blacksmith, Plain
Lane Isaac H. express driver, Main
Lawrence Charles H. laborer, Purchade
Leach Arnold, farmer, Water
Leach Arnold A. shoe-dresser, Rock
Leach Edwin J. shoe cutter, Pearl
Leach George M. shoe manuf. Cedar
Leach George M. jr., shoe stitcher, Plymouth

Leach Otis, farmer, Summer
Lebaron Charles E. farmer, Wareham
Lebaron Cyrus, cooper, Wareham
Lebaron John, farmer, Water
Lebaron John B. iron-foundry, Water
Lebaron J. Baylis, moulder, Centre
Lebaron Joshua, Supt. Alms House
Lebaron Theophilus B.
Lebaron Thomas M. farmer, Wareham
Leonard Benjamin, forgeman, Grove
Leonard Benjamin F. shoemaker, Grove
Leonard Charles E. shoe manuf. High
Leonard George, North
Leonard George jr., shoe manuf. Oak
Leonard George C. laborer, Cherry
Leonard George S. farmer, Chestnut
Leonard Henry D. butcher, Water
Leonard Joseph M. straw bleachery, Centre
Leonard Lemuel M. shoemaker, Plymouth
Leonard Lewis, farmer, River
Leonard Nathaniel W. straw bleachery
Leonard Richard W. laborer, Cherry
Leonard Zebedee, farmer, Centre
Lewis Nathaniel, laborer, Peirce
Lincoln Erastus M. shoemaker, Wareham
Lincoln Lewis, blacksmith, Water
Lincoln William L. blacksmith, Water
Little Elbridge G. clergyman, Plymouth
Littlejohn A. Buell, blacksmith, Main
Littlejohn Ira O. shoemaker, Wood
Littlejohn Orsamus, blacksmith, Main
Loring Southworth, box maker, Rock
Lovell Augustin M. watchman, Water
Lovell Benjamin P. W. farmer, Vaughan
Lovell Galen E. H. straw worker, Water
Lovell Samuel L. shoemaker, Wood
Lovell Thomas, farmer, Wood
Lucas Caleb, farmer, Carmel
Lucas Daniel, express messenger, Main
Lucas F. A. B. saloon keeper, Plymouth
Lucas Isaac, shoe cutter, Centre
Lucas Job, carpenter, Main

MACOMBER ELBRIDGE H. shoemaker Plymouth
Macomber Isaac E. shoemaker, Vernon
Makepeace Frank A. optician, Summer
Marchant Charles, farmer, Highland
Marchant George, farmer, Highland
Marshall Josiah P. laborer, Wareham
Marshall Ponsonby, farmer, Sachem
Marshall W. H. laborer, Wareham
Mason Albert T. tack maker, Pleasant
Maynard Henry N. farmer, Benson
Maxim Henry F. farmer, Carver
Maxim Ezra, farmer, Benson
McAllister James, blacksmith, Plymouth
McAllister William, blacksmith, Plymouth
McCrillis John, nursery agent, Plympton
McCrillis John S. shoemaker, Pearl
McCully Joseph P. shoemaker, Pearl
McJennett J. M. *(Roddick & McJennett)*, dry goods, Main
McLathlin Freeman T. farmer, Purchase
McMann James E. furnaceman, Vine
Mendall Sylvanus, carpenter, Pearl
Merrick John R. heel maker, Water
Miller Abishai, farmer, Wareham
Miller Alden, carpenter, Oak
Mitchell Leonard, farmer, River

J. A. JACKSON, 101 COURT STREET, BOSTON, DEALER IN HATS, CAPS, AND FURS.

Mitchell Leonard C. carpenter, River
Mitchell Moses G. farmer, River
Mitchell Ophir D. shoemaker, River
Monroe L. D. grocer, (*Cushing & Monroe*), Water
Morrill Nathan S. overseer, Star ave
Morse Artemus, peddler, Miller
Morse B. Albert, shoemaker, Tispaquin
Morse Cephas, farmer, Rocky Meadow
Morse Charles, laborer, Wareham
Morse Ezra, farmer, Titicut
Morse Horatio, teamer, South p. o.
Morse John P. shoemaker, Tispaquin
Morse John Q. A. farmer, Wareham
Morse Levi, farmer, Pleasant
Morse Levin S. laborer, Wareham
Morse Sylvanus, boarding house, cor. School and Peirce
Morton John Q. teamer, Miller
Murdock Calvin, farmer, Plymouth
Murdock Philo S. shoe manuf. Plymouth
Murdock William, farmer, Plymouth

NANCE ALLEN F. cooper, Main
Newell Frederic C. clergyman, North
Nichols Darius M. farmer, Cedar
Nichols James G. sawyer, Cedar
Norton Lot, mariner, Rock p. o.
Noyes Ira, shoemaker, Thompson
Noyes William shoemaker, Thompson

OSBORN EDWARD N. station agent, Centre
Osborn William, conductor, Centre

PACKARD F. W. musician, North
Packard Isaiah, farmer, North
Packard J. H. clerk, Main
Packard L. Frank, musician, North
Parker N. M. straw worker, Wareham
Paty Lemuel B. farmer, Highland
Paul Charles A. farmer, Wareham
Paul Luther, farmer, Wareham
Pease Alvin, carpenter, North
Pease Joseph L. gardener, Plymouth
Pease Samuel N. carpenter, Wapenucket
Peirce Charles F. merchant, North
Peirce Edwin, moulder, Carmel
Peirce James E. merchant, Main
Peirce Job C. merchant, Main
Peirce Thomas S. merchant, Main
Peirce Tyler, farmer, Miller
Peirce William R. farmer, Main
Penniman Prince, shoemaker, Fuller
Penniman Prince E. saloon, Main
Perkins Abraham, farmer, Plymouth
Perkins Andrew M. shoemaker, Summer
Perkins Cyrus, miller, Water
Perkins D. Sumner, shoe manuf. Plymouth
Perkins Edward G. miller, Water
Perkins Elijah E. shoe manuf. Plymouth
Perkins Isaac E. farmer, Plymouth
Perkins J. H. carpenter, Plymouth
Perkins John C. farmer, Plymouth
Perkins John J. shoemaker, Plymouth
Perkins Lloyd, soap maker, Water
Perkins Lothrop, retired, Centre
Perkins Nathaniel C. farmer, Highland
Perkins Noah C. shoe manuf. Pearl
Perkins Thompson, shoemak'r, Plymouth
Perry Andrew B. shoecutter, Plymouth
Pettee Calvin, straw worker, Elm

Pettee Wm. E. M. musician, North
Phinney Zenas C. shoemaker, Fuller
Phinney Zenas P. shoemaker, Fuller
Pickens Albert G. music teacher, Main
Pickens Andrew J. straw worker, Main
Pickens Ebenezer, trial justice, Main
Pickens George, merchant, Main
Pickens James M. music teacher, Main
Pickens Philo H. carriage maker, Water
Pickens Samuel, tinman, Main
Pickens Wilkes W. straw worker, Main
Porter Oliver C. farmer, Lowlands
Pratt Albert G. farmer, Vernon
Pratt Allen, shoemaker, Vernon
Pratt Arvin N. farmer, Spruce
Pratt Augustus, farmer, Plymouth
Pratt C. C. K. farmer, Pleasant
Pratt Ebenezer, shovel maker, Plymouth
Pratt F. Girard, shoemaker, Vernon
Pratt Francis G. clergyman, Plympton
Pratt H. jr. merchant, Plymouth
Pratt Harrison O. shoemaker, Vernon
Pratt Jared, farmer, Plymouth
Pratt Jeremiah K. auctioneer, Plymouth
Pratt John H. farmer, Spruce
Pratt Jonathan C. farmer, Plymouth
Pratt Martin V. bookseller, Plymouth
Pratt N. F. C. farmer, Plymouth
Pratt Otis, wheelwright, Plymouth
Pratt Simeon M. farmer, Main
Pratt Stillman B. publisher, Main
Pratt T. Jefferson, farmer, Plymouth
Pratt Thomas A. peddler, Main
Pratt Thomas B. shoemaker, Plymouth
Pratt William W. straw worker, Courtland
Pratt Winslow, jr. butcher, Tispaquin
Pratt Zebulon, auctioneer and farmer, Plymouth
Putnam Israel W. clergyman, Plymouth

RAMSDELL JAMES H. shoemaker, School
Ramsdell John B. farmer, Plain
Raymond Aaron, switchman, Elm
Raymond Alexander, shoemaker, Soule
Raymond Isaac E. shoemaker, Soule
Raymond John, laborer, Rocky Meadow
Raymond Solomon, laborer, Wareham
Raymond Zeph. E. farmer, Soule
Redding Cheney, farmer, Ash
Reed Charles E. laborer, Vernon
Reed Jeremiah W. farmer, Neck
Reed John C. farmer, Centre
Reed Nathaniel W. farmer, Peirce
Reed Sylvanus W. carpenter, Pearl
Reed Thomas D. farmer, Wareham
Reed William, shoemaker, Cross
Rich George W. hack owner, Main
Richmond Edward, farmer, Clay
Richmond Hercules, farmer, Taunton
Richmond Lysander, shoe manuf. Plymouth
Robbins James, shoemaker, Purchase
Robbins Jos. M. shoemaker, Wood
Robbins Philander, farmer, Sachem
Robinson Everett, lawyer, Main
Robinson-Morrill, physician, Plymouth
Rogers Charles M. painter, Oak
Rounsville Martin, stone mason, Peirce
Ryder Charles H. farmer, Neck
Ryder Henry K. W. farmer, Highland

DIVIDENDS ADDED to the POLICY in the BERKSHIRE often exceed the premium paid; are NON-FORFEITABLE and will be redeemed in CASH ON DEMAND. (See page 56.)

Ryder Horace N. farmer, South
Ryder Lucas, farmer, South
Ryder Nathaniel F. salesman, Highland
Ryder Samuel, farmer, Highland
Ryder Samuel W. farmer, Highland
Ryder Standish, farmer, Highland
Ryder Standish jr., farmer, Highland
Ryder Stephen C. farmer, Highland
Ryder Wilson C. farmer, Highland
Ryder W. Clarkson, teacher, Miller

SADDLER WILLIAM, farmer, Cherry
Sampson Joseph, farmer, Main
Sampson Obediah, shoemaker, Plymouth
Sampson P. Miller, farmer, Plymouth
Sampson Samuel B. farmer, Rocky Meadow
Sampson Shadrach, farmer, Plymouth
Sampson Thomas W. marketman, Rocky Meadow
Sanford Arnold B. mill supt. Main
Sanford John A. overseer, Centre
Savery Albert A. farmer, Taunton
Savery Albert T. shoemaker, Rocky Meadow
Savery Everett W. shoemaker, Main
Savery George S. straw worker, Spring
Savery James, carpenter, Miller
Savery Luther W. shoemaker, Tispaquin
Savery Peregrine W. farmer, Rocky Meadow
Sawyer R. M. clergyman, Plympton
Scanlin John, shoemaker, Summer
Sears Ivory H. carpenter, Cherry
Shaw Alfred, farmer, Plymouth
Shaw Asael A. farmer, Summer
Shaw Benoni, moulder, Tispaquin
Shaw Cephas, farmer, France
Shaw Charles F. farmer, Thompson
Shaw Eben A. farmer, Rocky Meadow
Shaw Ebenezer, carpenter, Pleasant
Shaw Ebenezer C. farmer, Rocky Meadow
Shaw Elbridge G. farmer, Bedford
Shaw Elisha T. laborer, Neck
Shaw Ezra, farmer, Rocky Meadow
Shaw George, stone mason, Wood
Shaw George H. japan manuf. Rock
Shaw Henry, straw worker, West
Shaw Henry H. express messenger, Main
Shaw Ira, butcher, Thompson
Shaw Jacob B. apothecary, School
Shaw John A. shovel maker, Plymouth
Shaw John jr., apothecary, Peirce
Shaw Joseph A. carpenter, Pleasant
Shaw Josiah C. farmer, Thompson
Shaw Lewis R. straw bleacher, Centre
Shaw Luther, farmer, Tispaquin
Shaw Orlando H. carpenter, Pleasant
Shaw Thomas F. farmer, near Carver
Shaw Thomas J. farmer, near Carver
Shaw William, farmer, North
Shaw William, farmer, Pleasant
Shaw William A. mariner, Plymouth
Shaw William B. straw worker, West
Shaw William N. shoemaker, Main
Sherman Abner W. farmer, Neck
Sherman Benjamin H. carpenter, Smith
Sherman Charles, farmer, Neck
Sherman Charles W. farmer, Neck
Sherman Elnathan, farmer, Smith
Sherman Erastus F. farmer, Neck
Sherman Frank M. shoe cutter, Jackson

Sherman J. H. homoeopathic physician,
Sherman Joshua, carpenter, Main
Sherman Nathan, farmer, Miller
Sherman Simeon A. carpenter, Miller
Shiverick William, harness maker, Oak
Shurtleff Benjamin, shoemaker, Plymouth
Shurtleff Clark, farmer, Miller
Shurtleff Gideon, shoemaker, Wall
Shurtleff Isaac S. furnaceman, Tispaquin
Shurtleff Nathaniel, laborer, Thomas
Shurtleff Nathaniel 2d, mill owner, France
Shurtleff Nathaniel 3d, furnaceman, Tispaquin
Shurtleff Nathaniel F. farmer, South p.o.
Shurtleff Salem, laborer, France
Shurtleff Seth, farmer, Beach
Simmons Charles, farmer, East Village
Simmons George E. mariner, Water
Simmons James H. mariner, Water
Simmons Reuben K. shoemaker, Water
Sisson George, carpenter, Neck
Smith Adoniram J. farmer, Wareham
Smith Ansel, farmer, Wareham
Smith Chandler R. farmer, Spruce
Smith Cyrus, farmer, Fuller
Smith Daniel, laborer, Wareham
Smith Darius, farmer, Fuller
Smith Earle T. shoemaker, Plympton
Smith Ebenezer, farmer, Wareham
Smith Ebenezer 2d, farmer, Wareham
Smith Elbridge G. farmer, Wareham
Smith George L. shoemaker, Centre
Smith G. Sumner, shoemaker, Centre
Smith Harvey, farmer, Wood
Smith Henry W. farmer, Wareham
Smith Hercules, straw worker, Water
Smith Hiram S. shoemaker, Smith
Smith Ira, farmer, Water
Smith Israel, station agent, Miller
Smith Jabez, shoemaker, Fuller
Smith James, drover, Fuller
Smith Lorenzo, farmer, Spruce
Smith Moses T. farmer, Fuller
Smith Richard C. stone mason, Neck
Smith Thomas, farmer, Wood
Smith Thomas F. painter, School
Smith William, farmer, Neck
Snow Elisha N. mariner, Main
Snow George W. physician, Highland
Snow James, carpenter, Plymouth
Snow Thomas, farmer, Carver
Snow Venus, wheelwright, Summer
Soule Augustus H. teacher, Soule
Soule Charles, farmer, North
Soule Charles W. furniture, Oak
Soule Ebenezer T. shoe cutter, Oak
Soule Edward L. shoemaker, Water
Soule Edwin, shoe cutter, Cedar
Soule George, undertaker and cabinet ware, Oak
Soule George L. music teacher and furniture dealer, Oak
Soule Isaac, carpenter, Cedar
Soule James, blacksmith, Cedar
Soule J. Horace, clerk, Cedar
Soule John A. laborer, Cherry
Soule John M. mariner, Main
Soule Jonathan, farmer, Cedar
Soule Marcus, shoemaker, Oak
Soule Otis, farmer, Soule
Soule William H. shoemaker, Cedar
Southworth Calvin, farmer, Neck
Southworth Rodney E. painter, Water

J. A. JACKSON 101 COURT STREET, BOSTON, DEALER IN HATS, CAPS AND FURS.

Sparrow Hartley A. painter School
Sparrow Jacob G. painter, Water
Sparrow James P. carpenter, Plympton
Standish A. Otis, laborer, Chestnut
Standish Ethan A. shoe cutter, North
Standish George E. peddler, Montello
Standish Martin P. salesman, High
Standish Simeon R. straw worker, Main
Stansell Charles C. merchant, Plymouth
Straffin David F. shoemaker, Centre
Swett Sargent S. painter, Water
Swift Daniel L. mariner, Peirce
Swift Gustavus L. shoemaker, Plymouth
Swift Henry A. shoemaker, Plymouth
Swift Isaiah S. shoe cutter, Oak
Swift Jabez, farmer, Carmel
Swift Lorenzo R. harnessmaker, Water
Swift William, farmer, Clay
Swift William C. farmer, Carmel
Sylvester S. H. hair dresser and taxidermist, Centre

FABER ADMIRAL D. peddler, Spruce
Taylor Geo. W. stage driver, Centre
Taylor William, dyer, Star Mills
Thatcher Allen, merchant, Main
Thatcher Charles T. express clerk, Centre
Thatcher Francis, shoemaker, Thompson
Thatcher Israel F. farmer, Thompson
Thatcher John, hunter, Thompson
Thatcher Lewis, shoemaker, Thompson
Thayer Granville L. straw goods packer, Oak
Thomas Abraham, carpenter, Cherry
Thomas A. Clement, bootmaker, Main
Thomas Albert, farmer, North
Thomas Arad, farmer, Purchase
Thomas Arad, jr. farmer, Purchase
Thomas Augustus W. moulder, Purchase
Thomas Bartlett, farmer, Chestnut
Thomas Benjamin, farmer, Plymouth
Thomas Benjamin, 2d, moulder, Purchase
Thomas Charles H. shoemaker, Purchase
Thomas Eleazer, farmer, Purchase
Thomas Eleazer, jr. moulder, Purchase
Thomas Eliphalet, farmer, Centre
Thomas Elmer,
Thomas Elisha, teamster, Peirce
Thomas George, shoemaker, Plymouth
Thomas Harrison, shovel maker, Plymouth
Thomas Harvey C. farmer, Tispaquin
Thomas Horatio N. butcher, Smith
Thomas Ira, merchant, Main
Thomas Ira M. clerk, Centre
Thomas Lothrop, moulder, Purchase
Thomas Lothrop S. farmer, Wareham
Thomas Nelson, farmer, Tispaquin
Thomas Robert M. engineer, Rock
Thomas Seneca, farmer, Purchase
Thomas Seneca R. farmer, Purchase
Thomas Stephen, moulder, Thomas
Thomas William, farmer, Wareham
Thompson Benj. F. shoemaker, Thompson
Thompson Charles L. carpenter, Thompson
Thompson Edmund, shoemaker, Wood
Thompson Edward, farmer, Plymouth
Thompson Elkanah, laborer, Precinct
Thompson Franklin S. farmer, Thompson

Thompson Henry A. shoemaker, Thompson
Thompson Isaac, farmer, North
Thompson Israel W. merchant, North
Thompson Ivory H. grocer, Thompson
Thompson Lewis H. peddler, Thompson
Thompson Martson, mason, Cross
Thompson Oliver, carpenter, Oak
Thompson Philander, farmer, Thompson
Thompson Philander W. farmer, Thompson
Thompson R. F. hoop skirt manuf. Main
Thompson Reuel, farmer, Thompson
Thompson Venus, farmer, Thompson
Thrasher A. P. farmer, Plymouth
Thrasher Benj. G. laborer, Plymouth
Tillson Benj. O. teamster, North
Tillson Charles T. shoemaker, North
Tillson George L. shoemaker, North
Tillson James B. carpenter, Centre
Tillson Thomas, farmer, North
Tinkham Alva, farmer, Precinct
Tinkham Andrew L. post master, Centre
Tinkham Benj. F. shoecutter, Pleasant
Tinkham Calvin, farmer, Neck
Tinkham Charles C. farmer, Wood
Tinkham Ebenezer, teamster, Precinct
Tinkham Enoch, farmer, Centre
Tinkham Foster, jeweller, Namasket
Tinkham George C. butcher, Cherry
Tinkham George F. farmer, Glass pl
Tinkham John, farmer, France
Tinkham Joseph, Rock village
Tinkham Josiah, farmer, Wood
Tinkham Leander A. farmer, T st
Tinkham Levi F. teamster, Oak
Tinkham Lorenzo, carpenter, Elm
Tinkham Otis L. carpenter, School
Tinkham Sylvanus, farmer, Main
Tobey Alfred A. shoemaker, Water
Tobey Frank H. carpenter, Oak
Tobey Joel W. carpenter, Oak
Tobin Richard, laborer, Jackson
Toole Michael, gent's clothing, cor. Main and Water
Tribou Charles W. fish peddler, Oak
Tribou Henry R. farmer, Plymouth
Tribou Josiah C. straw worker, Peirce
Tribou Nahum M. horse dealer, Plymouth
Tripp Benjamin F. saloon keeper, Water
Tucker David A. fish dealer, Centre
Tucker Elisha, merchant, Main
Tucker Sidney, pension agent, Main

VAUGHAN A. C. farmer, Vaughan
Vaughan Alvin P. carpenter, Main
Vaughan Charles F. agent, Plymouth
Vaughan David C. carpenter, Thomas
Vaughan Harrison W. mason, Plymouth
Vaughan Isaac N. blacksmith, Vaughan
Vaughan John C. straw manuf. Centre
Vaughan John G. saw mill, Summer
Vaughan Josiah H. farmer, Vaughan
Vaughan Nathan H. carpenter, Vaughan
Vaughan Peter, farmer, Vaughan
Vaughan Sylvanus H. hotel keeper, Main
Vaughan William H. wheelwright, North
Vining David, shoemaker, Plymouth

WALDRON ROSWELL, farmer, Centre
Ward Calvin B. cotton mill workman, School
Ward Eliab, lawyer, Main

Warner Frederic C. works Star Mills
Warren James, miller, North
Warren James W. shoemaker, North
Warren John M. farmer, Summer
Warren Lewis F. heel maker, Main
Warren Nathaniel, laborer, Summer
Warren Sylvanus, laborer, Summer
Washburn Azel, planer, Pearl
Washburn Bradford S. merchant, Oak
Washburn Charles L. shoemaker, Plain
Washburn John T. mason, Plain
Washburn Peter, lumber dealer, Pearl
Washburn Philander, merchant and manuf. Main
Washburn Solomon L. mason, Plain
Washburn Thomas, farmer, Plain
Washburn William, lumber dealer, Centre
Waters Eldred R. laborer, Wareham
Waterman Edward H. wheelwright, Summer
Waterman Elisha, farmer, Plymouth
Waterman George, merchant, Centre
Waterman James H. laborer, Plymouth
Waterman Thomas E. shoemaker, Plymouth
Wentworth Soranus, peddler, Plymouth
Westgate David, farmer, Neck
Westgate Edward S. shoemaker, Neck
Westgate Elisha P. shoemaker, Neck
Westgate Joseph, laborer, Wareham
Westgate Sylvanus F. shoemaker, Neck
Weston Andrew, farmer, Clay
Weston Dura, farmer, Purchase
Weston Dura T. farmer, Purchase
Weston Ellis, carpenter, Sachem
Weston Enoch, farmer, Bedford
Weston Erastus D. moulder, Purchase
Weston Frederic, farmer, Purchase
Weston James H. carpenter, Centre
Weston Robert F. shoemaker, Thompson
Weston Robert W. shoemaker, Thompson
Weston Sanford, farmer, Bedford
Weston Thomas, farmer, Summer
Weston Thomas 2d, furnaceman, Purchase
Wetherbee Thos. P. shoemaker, Vaughan
Whitcomb Henry, laborer, Water
Whitcomb William R. teamster, Water
White Chauncey D. carpenter, Mill
White Daniel E. shoemaker, Centre
White Samuel, farmer, Centre
White Silas, farmer, Plymouth
White Solomon, merchant, Plymouth
White William B. carpenter, Mill

White William Emery, carpenter, Clay
Whitmarsh George, shoe cutter, Plymouth
Whitmarsh Joshua, shoe cutter, Centre
Wilbur Charles C. heel maker, Centre
Wilbur Nahum D. gas works, Oak
Wilbur Simeon D. station agent, Wareham
Wilbur Horatio N. carpenter, Plymouth
Wilbur Nelson, mariner, Plymouth
Wilbur Perry A. farmer, Plymouth
Wilder Parker P. whitewasher, Grove
Wilder Thomas, gardner, North
Williams Joseph, mariner, Grove
Williams Nathan, farmer, Vernon
Williams Samuel, clergyman, Peirce
Willis Marcus M. laborer
Winslow Isaac, shoemaker, Centre
Withington William T. laborer, Spruce
Wood Abiel, shoe cutter, Main
Wood Abner, farmer, Neck
Wood Albert J. shoe cutter, Thompson
Wood Alfred, merchant, Main
Wood Andrew C. lumberman, Peirce
Wood Benjamin F. farmer, Wood
Wood Benjamin P. farmer, Wood
Wood Cornelius B. town clerk, North
Wood Daniel F. painter, Wareham
Wood Eliab, building mover, Wood
Wood Frederic E. painter, Centre
Wood George W. farmer, Summer
Wood Hartley, farmer, Grove
Wood Isaac, farmer, Walnut
Wood Jacob, laborer, Cherry
Wood Joseph T. farmer, Main
Wood Joshua, painter, Wood
Wood Lorenzo, farmer, Plymouth
Wood Samuel N. straw worker, School
Wood Thomas, farmer, Wood
Wood Thomas J. farmer, Thompson
Wood Warren, straw worker, Plymouth
Wood Willard, farmer, Summer
Wood William B. gentleman, Main
Wood William H. Judge of Probate, Main
Wood William T. farmer, Neck
Wood Charles A. Plymouth
Wright Charles B. farmer and agent, Wood
Wright Charles L. farmer, Wood
Wright F. F. farmer, Plymouth
Wright William, laborer, Namasket
Wrightington Edward jr., farmer, Thomastown
Wrightington S. G. farmer, Chestnut

YOUNG JOHN, laborer

J. A. JACKSON, 101 COURT STREET, BOSTON, DEALER IN HATS, CAPS, AND FURS.

North Bridgewater General Directory.

ALDEN LUCAS W. provision dealer
Alden Luther E. shoecutter, r Montello
Alden Russell, shoe manuf. r Main
Alden Samuel F. butcher, r Quincy
Alden Sanford, farmer, r Quincy
Alden Sanford O. bootmaker, r Quincy
Allen Benjamin C. shoecutter, r Belmont
Allen F. E. shoemaker, r Centre
Allen Horatio G. shoecutter, r Turnpike
Allen James A. mechanic, bds Hotel
Ames Edwin C. shoecutter, r Pleasant
Ames Francis, farmer, r Cary
Ames Franklin, r Main
Ames Horace, bootmaker, r Ames
Ames John, bootmaker, r Belmont
Ames Luther, shoecutter, r Court
Ames Theron, farmer, r Cary
Andrews Alpheus C.
Andrews George, mechanic, r School
Andrews Leander B. mechanic, r School
Andrews Tyler, shoecutter, r Main
Arnold Albert L. shoemaker
Ashport Calvin, laborer, r Bryantville
Averill William, cabinet maker, r Pond

BACON CHARLES W. bds Montello
Bacon Willard, r Montello
Bailey Ephraim, box maker, r Main
Baker Horace, grocer
Bancroft Rinaldo, laborer
Barden William H. hairdresser, bds Main
Barnes Willard A. butcher
Barry Edward, shoemaker
Bartlett Orin, cabinet maker, r Court
Bates Elijah, shoecutter
Bates Isaac, shoemaker
Bates Lorenzo D. shoemaker, r Main
Battles Ansel, shoecutter, r Pleasant
Battles Benjamin F. shoemaker, r Battles
Battles Hiram, mason, r Pond
Battles John, shoecutter, r Main
Battles, Josiah O. shoecutter, r Main
Battles Nahum, mason, r Battles
Baxendale John, shoe manuf. r Pleasant
Baxter Freeman, farmer, r Main
Beals Jeremiah, farmer, r Turnpike
Beals John F. carpenter, r cor. Church and Montello
Beals Martin, cabinet maker, r Chapel
Belcher J. A. shoecutter, r Crescent
Benner E. J. merchant, r Belmont
Bennett Edward E. livery stable, r High
Bennett James, mechanic, r High
Billings Jesse, blacking manuf. r Pond
Bird Lemuel T. harness maker, Pond
Bisbee Jefferson, blacksmith, r Pleasant
Bixby Charles C. druggist, r Main
Bixby Jonathan, farmer, r West Shares
Blanchard Cyrenus W. stitcher
Blanchard Frederick C. clerk, Centre
Blanchard Junius M. shoecutter
Bliss L. C. grocer, r Main
Blodget Moses, shoemaker
Bloomstrand Poter, shoemaker, r Main
Bonney Watson, shoemaker, r Cottage
Borden George K. shoemaker, bds High

Boucher John, shoemaker, r Main
Boucher William, laborer, r Main
Bowles Samuel, shoemaker
Boyle James, laborer, r Grove
Brackett E. R. peddler, r Pond
Brackett Loring, laborer, bds Belmont
Bradford Waldo, blacksmith, r High
Brailey James H carpenter, r Main
Brett David, r Prospect
Brett Edward, shoemaker, r Bartlett
Brett Ellis, farmer, bds Pleasant
Brett Ephraim, farmer, r Pleasant
Brett Francis, shoemaker, bds Main
Brett Fred. L. *(Brett Bros.)* r Main
Brett Henry A. merchant, r cor. Main and Elm
Brett Joel P. shoecutter, r Quincy
Brett Pliny, shoe manuf. r Main
Brett Rufus E. *(Brett Bros.)* bds cor. Main and Church
Brett Samuel S. shoe manuf. r Montello
Brett Samuel T. farmer, r Main
Brett Zenas, r Main
Brett Zibeon, farmer, r Battles
Brigham Charles D. merchant, r Elm
Brooks John, machinist, r Crescent
Brooks Joseph, blacksmith
Brown Bela T. shoefinisher, r Short
Brown John, peddler, r Crescent
Brown Van R. bootmaker
Bryant George E. merchant, r Elm
Bryant George W. *(G. W. B. & Co.)* Main
Bryant Harrison, shoecutter, r South
Bryant Henry L. merchant, Main
Bryant Horace, shoe manuf. r Montello
Bryant Ira, farmer, r Cary Hill
Bryant Ira A. farmer, r Cary
Bryant Willard, r South
Bryant Ziba, laborer, r Cary
Buck S. N. shoe manuf. r Pond
Bullard Lewis L. box maker, r Crescent
Bunker Eli, shoemaker, r Battles
Bunker Henry L. shoemaker, r Battles
Burden Alexander, farmer
Burgess Leonard, tinman
Burke David, farmer, r Main
Burke Edward, shoemaker, r Crescent
Burke James A. shoemaker, r Court
Burke John T. shoe manuf. r Quincy
Burrell Henry, clerk, bds Grove
Burrell Nicholas, shoemaker, r Grove
Burtman John P. shoe manuf. r Battles

CALDWELL BENJAMIN O. clerk, bds Belmont
Calkins Clarence, boot maker
Campbell Oscar A. shoemaker, Battles
Carr Alpheus, farmer, Pleasant
Carr Henry, Centre
Carr James L. butcher, Main
Carr Lysander, boot maker, Turnpike
Carr Simeon, shoe cutter, Turnpike
Carr Simeon D. Turnpike
Carr William B. carpenter, bds Church
Cary Barzillai, shoe cutter, Main

ANNUAL CASH DIVIDENDS in the BERKSHIRE LIFE INS. CO.,
Pittsfield, Mass. Boston Office 95 1-2 Washington St. (See page 50.)

Cary Charles, Cary
Cary Charles H. shoemaker, Winter
Cary Daniel H. carpenter, Cary
Cary George C. shoe cutter, Main
Cary Howard, shoemaker, r Cary
Cary Nathan S. farmer, Main
Cary Williams, farmer, Winter
Chamberlin Robert M. mechanic, Centre
Chesman Noah, shoe manuf. Elm
Chesman Zachariah, shoe cutter, Pleasant
Childs Thomas W. shoemaker, Campello
Churchill Solomon S. mechanic
Clapp Benjamin R. merchant, Main
Clapp Otis F. surveyor, Main
Clark A. Clinton, clerk, Pleasant
Clark Benjamin, vineyard, Main
Clark Benjamin S. vineyard, r Main
Clark George, liquor agent, Pleasant
Clark Herman B. clerk, bds Pleasant
Clark Lemuel, peddler, Montello
Clark Lyman, cabinet manuf. Main
Clark Samuel, peddler, r Montello
Clark Samuel J. boot maker, r Church
Cleveland Walter F. teamer
Cobb David, merchant, r Main
Cobb David H. merchant, r Main
Cobb George P. hotel
Cobb Lyman E. grocer, r Centre
Cobb Otis, carpenter, r Chestnut st, Campello
Cobb Tyler, merchant, Main
Cole Charles, r Campello
Cole Charles H. r Campello
Cole Eleazer, machinist, r Summer
Cole George W. shoe cutter, Campello
Cole John H. r Campello
Collier Stephen N. bootmaker
Colwell Benjamin O. clerk, r Belmont
Colwell H. B. shoe manuf. r Belmont
Commons William jr. shoe finisher, r Crescent
Connerty Patrick, shoemaker, Main
Coombs Joseph C. shoe cutter, r Campello
Cooper Francis, mechanic, r L.
Cooper James H. clerk, r Pleasant
Coots Henry R. shoemaker, r Montello
Copeland Caleb, farmer, r Summer
Copeland Cyrus F. telegraph operator, r 15 L.
Copeland Cyrus P. boot maker, r Summer
Copeland Ephraim, shoemaker, r Summer
Copeland Fisher, shoe cutter, r Montello
Copeland George M. turner, r L.
Copeland Ira, grocer, r Pine
Copeland Lawrence, farmer, Centre
Copeland Marcus, shoe cutter, r Campello
Copeland Rufus, stitcher, r L.
Corcoran Christopher, shoemaker, r Battles
Corcoran Philip, shoemaker, r Battles
Cowell David L. ast. p. m. r Green
Crafts F. A. clergyman, r Church
Crane George J. watchmaker, r Centre
Creeden Daniel, marble worker, Main
Crimmin Philip, bootmaker
Crocker Allen, blacksmith, r Ward
Crocker Charles B. shoe cutter, Ash
Crocker Daniel, r Main
Crocker Edward, farmer, Ash
Cross Henry, shoe manuf. r Main

Crosby Asa F. mechanic, r Main
Crosby John, mechanic, r Main
Crosby John W. mechanic, r Main
Curtis Charles H. farmer, bds Crescent
Curtis Edmund, laborer, r Plain
Curtis George E. grocer, bds Crescent
Curtis Isaac, farmer, r Crescent
Curtis John W. farmer, r Pine
Curtis Levi S. clerk, bds Crescent
Curtis Sylvanus B. grocer, bds Crescent
Curtis Theodore L. farmer, Crescent
Cushing Elisha A. shoemaker, r Main
Cushing George, farmer, r Main
Cushman George H. carpenter, r Main
Cushman John J. carpenter, r Pine
Cushman Nelson, bootmaker
Cushman O. B. shoemaker, r Crescent
Cushman William H. shoecutter
Cushman Winslow B. carpenter, r L.

DALTON PETER, stitcher, Campello
Davenport Nathaniel, r South
Davenport Nathaniel, jr. peddler, r South
Davis Benj. P. boot and shoe dealer, r Pond
Davis Stephen, shoecutter, Campello
Dearborn S. F. druggist, r Main
Dean Edgar E. physician, r Centre
Dexter Freeman, carpenter,
Dickerman Nahum, bootmaker, r L st
Diamond Patrick, laborer, Campello
Doyle Thomas, farmer
Dow Alexander, stitcher, r Court
Drake Aaron B. merchant, r Campello
Drake Albert, bootmaker, r Turnpike
Drake Charles F. bootmaker, r Pond
Drake Jonathan W. bootmaker, r Turnpike
Drake Reuben, bootmaker, r West Shares
Drake Stafford, cabinetmaker, r Campello
Drayton Thomas gardener, r Main
Drew Francis D. r Belmont
Dunbar Bradford, clerk, r Pleasant
Dunbar Charles A. peddler, r Crescent
Dunbar Charles H. farmer, r Linwood
Dunbar Daniel, shoe finisher, r Plain
Dunbar David, shoemaker, r Rockland
Dunbar Geo. B. broker, r Montello
Dunbar Heman, butcher
Dunbar Henry S. laborer, r School
Dunbar Henry T. bds School
Dunbar Hiram, bootmaker, r Pleasant
Dunham Benjamin F. stitcher
Dunham Cornelius H. shoe finisher, r Prospect
Dunham Isaac A. mechanic, r Centre
Dunham M. V. B. bds Prospect
Dunham Soranus, mechanic, r Cottage
Dunham Stillman, farmer, Turnpike
Dyer Henry, Campello

EAMES EPHRAIM N. shoe cutter, r Main
Eames Daniel, teamer, r Crescent
Eames Isaac, farmer, r Main
Eaton Apollos, mechanic, r L.
Eaton Benjamin H. shoemaker, r Belmont
Eaton John E. r Eaton
Easton Caleb, bootmaker, r Oak
Easton George W. farmer, r Oak
Easton John C. H. wheelwright, r Eaton
Eddy Henry, farmer, r Main

J. A. JACKSON 101 COURT STREET, BOSTON, DEALER IN HATS, CAPS AND FURS.

Eddy Henry T. bds Main
Eddy Willard, bds Main
Edson Amasa, farmer, r Winter
Edson Bartlett C. shoemaker
Edson Daniel W. r Summer
Edson David, farmer, r Pine
Edson David, 2d, farmer, r Summer
Edson Josiah, shoemaker
Edson Seth, carpenter, r Pleasant
Edson Simeon W. farmer, r Summer
Eiffe Thomas, baggage master, r Pond
Eldred David, jr. shoe manuf. r Pond
Eldred Daris R. mason, r Pond
Elliot Leonard, shoecutter
Ellis John, r Main, Campello
Emerson John O. shoe manuf. Campello
Emerson William, shoemaker
Emery John, bootmaker, r Chestnut
Emmes John B. shoecutter, r Cottage

FARNHAM GEO. painter, r Crescent
Farrar Gustavus A. peddler, r Crescent
Farrell James, shoemaker, r Quincy
Farrell John, shoemaker, r Montello
Farrell John 2d, shoemaker, Montello
Farrell William, shoemaker, r Quincy
Faunce Enos E. bootmaker, r Main
Faunce Hiram, bootmaker, r Howard
Faxon William, awl manuf. r Main
Faxon William H. music teacher, r Main
Faxon Micah, r Crescent
Feeley Mark, marble worker, r Pond
Fellows Lewis, r Pond
Field Bazillai, r Prospect
Field Charles C. market, r Main
Field Charles T. shoecutter, r Prospect
Field Daniel, farmer, r Oak
Field Franklin, farmer, r Pleasant
Field George, clerk, bds Main
Field Jabez, carpenter
Field Waldo, shoemaker, r West Shares
Field William L. farmer, r Main
Filon John, shoemaker, r Crescent
Filoon H. H. clerk
Filoon Veranus, shoecutter, r Prospect
Fisher George, expressman
Fitzpatrick John, r Campello
Fletcher Ephraim S. wheelwright, r Court
Foley James, blacksmith, r Grove
Ford Charles R. shoe manuf. r Main
Ford Daniel, shoemaker, r Main
Ford Henry A. r Montello
Ford Hiram, shoemaker, r Main
Ford Josiah W. carpenter, r Belmont
Ford Lewis, shoemaker, r Elm
Ford Noah, shoecutter, r Main
Foss Nelson J. r Campello
Fowle James A. painter, bds Court
Foye Isaac M. carpenter, r Cottage
Foye Josiah W. carpenter, r Cottage
Freeman A. J. shoecutter, r Montello
Freeman Henry W. bootmaker
Freeman Hiram, stitcher
Freeman J. B. shoecutter, r Main
Freeman Joseph W. bds Main
Freeman Rufus C. shoemaker, r Main
Freeman Weston, shoecutter, r Main
French Edward C. merchant, r Main
French Francis, book dealer, r Elm
French Francis M. boot manuf. r Main
French Henry, post master, r Main
French J. Herman, clerk, bds. Main
French Levi, farmer, r Summer

French Marcus M. r Summer
French Merritt, farmer, r cor. Pleasant and Summer
French Samuel, farmer, r South
French Seth L. r Campello
French Walter D. shoe manuf. r Main
French William, farmer, r Main
French Zibeon, shoemaker, r Elm
Frobisher Benjamin C. bootmaker, r Cary
Fuller John S. clerk, r Belmont
Fullerton Daniel F. r Campello
Fullerton Marcus, peddler
Fullerton Richard M. shoecutter

GALLUCIA SAMUEL, lastmaker r Crescent
Gardner Andrew G. shoemaker, r Belmont
Gardner Charles W. shoedresser, r Main
Gardner F. B. shoecutter
Gardner Henry, shoecutter, r Pleasant
Gardner Hugh, shoemaker, r Belmont
Gardner Samuel P. shoedresser, r Main
Gegan John, shoemaker, r Centre
Gegan Thomas, shoemaker, r Centre
Gegan William, shoemaker, r Quincy
Gibbs Andrew, mechanic
Gifford Charles A. laborer, r Belmont
Gifford Thaddeus E. farmer, r Belmont
Gilmore John, grocer, r Grove
Gilson Frank G. machinist, bds Elm
Glass Spencer B. shoecutter, r Main
Glover Amasa S. shoecutter, r School
Goddard Warren, clergyman, r Pond
Gorham Jesse R. shoecutter, r Montello
Gould Charles A. shoemaker, r Crescent
Graves David W. peddler, r Belmont
Gray Barnabas H. shoecutter, r Main
Grew James L. merchant, r Wales ave
Grover R. B. restaurant, r Main
Gunn Charles W. S. blacksmith
Gurney Alpheus, grocer, r Main
Gurney Azel E. shoemaker, r Pond
Gurney George H. shoe manuf. r Pond
Gurney Joshua V. music teacher
Gurney Linus, shoemaker, r Main
Gurney Lucius, shoecutter, r Main
Gurney Lucius, 2d, shoecutter, r Green
Gurney Lysander, jeweller, r Pond
Gurney Nathan, shoecutter
Gurney N. Norton, musicteach'r, r Franklin
Gurney Thos. J. music teacher, Franklin
Gurney Warren S. jeweller, bds Main

HALE E. Z. boot maker, r Summer
Hale Fredrick, shoemaker, r Pine
Hale Henry Z. shoemaker, r Summer
Hull Asa O. boot maker, r Crescent
Hall Daniel jr., carpenter, Pine
Hall Domino, mason, r Main
Hall David, last maker, r Belmont
Hall Fredrick, last maker, r Grove
Hall Hiram E. laborer, r Pine
Hall John, carpenter, r Turnpike
Hall John A. boot maker, r Turnpike
Hall Oliver W. farmer, r Elm
Hamilton Elijah, fish dealer, r Main
Hamilton W. D. merchant, Main
Hancock Moses W. expressman, r Church
Handy Joseph A. mechanic, r Centre
Hannigan Patrick, shoemaker, r Eaton
Hanson Frederick, (G. W. B. & Co.)

The terms for ENDOWMENT, and TEN ANNUAL LIFE POLICIES in the BERKSHIRE are peculiarly favorable, and rates lower than in any Note Company. (See page 50.)

Harden Peleg S. farmer, r Pine
Harlow Aaron S. shoe cutter
Harris Isaac, farmer, r Quincy
Harris Isaac K. Summer
Harris Marcus, shoemaker, r Prospect
Harris Roland, shoemaker, r Prospect
Harris Samuel, Howard
Harris Samuel B. soap dealer, Howard
Harris Sidney, shoemaker, r Prospect
Hartwell Charles A. shoe cutter, r Belmont
Hartwell Clarence E. boot maker, r Belmont
Hartwell Isaac H. farmer, r Turnpike
Hartwell John, bootmaker, r Belmont
Hatch Charles P. carriage builder, Factory Village
Hauthaway Charles L. blacking manuf. r Montello
Hauthaway Charles M. blacking manuf. r Montello
Hauthaway Fred W. shoemaker
Haven Curtis, farmer, r Battles
Haven George A. r Campello
Haven Henry R. r Campello
Hayden Albert W. shoemaker
Hayden George L. shoemaker, r Centre
Hayden Isaiah, farmer, Howard
Hayden Luther, farmer, r Howard
Hayward Albert F. clerk, bds Main
Hayward Ambrose, grocer, r Green
Hayward Bela B. boot maker, r Belmont
Hayward Daniel, grocer, r School
Hayward Joseph, carpenter, r Stone Hill
Hayward J. W. bread peddler, r Church
Hayward Otis, dept. sheriff, r Wales ave
Hayward Sumner A. insurance agent, r Main
Hayward Zina, farmer, r Plain
Hayward Zina 2d, farmer, r Plain
Henderson Robert, shoe dresser, bds Montello
Herod James, cutter, bds Battles
Herod Samuel A. shoe manuf. r Main
Hervey Lorenzo D. tinman, r Centre
Hervey Oliver B. tinworker, r Pond
Hewett Herman, jeweller, r Main
Hewett Joseph, farmer, r Prospect
Hewett S. Myron, jeweller, bds Main
Higgins Harrison L. mechanic, r Belmont
Hodge Nehemiah, shoemaker, r Montello
Holbrook Levi B. mechanic, r Pond
Holbrook Levi W. mechanic, r Crescent
Holbrook Samuel A. clerk, bds Main
Holbrook Samuel W. shoemaker, r Main
Holbrook William, shoe cutter, r Spring
Holbrook William H. mechanic, r West End
Holland Richard, painter, r Main
Hollis Elisha, bootmaker
Hollis John E. shoe cutter, bds Elm
Hollis John L. shoe manuf. r Elm
Hollis Levi, bootmaker
Hollis Luther H. bootmaker, r Winter
Hollis Royal, boot maker, r Winter
Hollywood Peter F. tailor, r Main
Holmes Abner, peddler, r Belmont
Holmes Alpheus, shoemaker, r Belmont
Holmes Edward F. stitcher, r Summer
Holmes Francis P. mechanic, r Main
Holmes Fredrick E. carver, r Centre

Holmes Freeman, shoemaker, r South
Holmes George N. shoe manuf. North End
Holmes Lorenzo, mechanic, r Crescent
Holmes Marcus, shoe manuf. r Pine
Holmes Marcus 2d, shoe cutter, r Main
Holmes Nathan, r Summer
Holmes Nehemiah S. carpenter, r Main
Holmes Warren A. shoemaker, r Belmont
Howard Adoniram J. shoemaker, r Howard
Howard Austin, farmer, r Quincy
Howard Cary, carpenter, r Main
Howard Charles, needle manuf. r Centre
Howard Charles 2d, shoe finisher, r Belmont
Howard Charles jr., stitcher, r Church
Howard Cyrus, farmer, r Howard
Howard Cyrus jr., boot maker, r Belmont
Howard Daniel S. shoe manuf. r Montello
Howard Darius, boot and shoe manuf. r Chapel
Howard David, boot manuf. r Main
Howard Edwin, r Campello
Howard Edwin, farmer, r Howard
Howard Eliakim, soap maker, r Winter
Howard Embert, merchant, r Main
Howard Ephraim, mechanic, r Pleasant
Howard Franklin O. boot manuf. r Main
Howard Fredrick, r Green
Howard Gorham B. merchant, r Main
Howard Hovenden L. farmer, r Howard
Howard John A. r Campello
Howard John S. boot manuf. r Elm
Howard Linus, shoe cutter, r Main
Howard L. Bradford, (Howard Bros.), r Green
Howard Nathan C. shoe manuf. r Turnpike
Howard Rufus E. shoe cutter, bds Main
Howard Samuel F. shoe dresser
Howard Samuel H. overseer of the poor
Howard Samuel W. S. (Howard Bros.), r Church
Howard Thomas J. farmer, r Belmont
Howard Webster, farmer, r Winter
Howard Warren A. shoe manuf. r Montello
Howard Welcome, farmer, Belmont
Howard Welcome A. shoemaker, bds Belmont
Howard Willard, farmer, r Main
Howe Alvin, shoemaker, r Main
Howland E. P. painter
Howland N. T. shoe cutter, r Pine
Hunt Albert D. boot maker
Hunt Charles D. shoemaker
Hunt John W. baker, Centre
Hunt Jonathan, shoemaker

JACKSON ANDREW, mechanic, r Pond
Jackson Benjamin F. farmer, r East
Jackson Ephraim, stone mason, r Wales avenue
Jackson Henry, bootmaker, r South
Jackson Henry M. shoemaker, r Centre
Jackson Laban, farmer, r East
Jackson Thomas, farmer, r South
Jacobs Edward E. hair dresser, r Elliot
Jacobs William H. hair dresser, r Elliot
James Melvin F. shoemaker, r Turnpike
Jameson Joel P. r Quincy

J. A. JACKSON, 101 COURT STREET, BOSTON, DEALER IN HATS, CAPS, AND FURS.

NORTH BRIDGEWATER DIRECTORY.   87

Jameson William, farmer, r Quincy
Jenks George A. mechanic, r Main
Jenney Ansel E. mason
Jennegan Cyrus, shoe cutter, r Green
Jennegan Hiram, shoe cutter, r Green
Jocoy Isaac H. shoemaker, r Court
Johnson Andrew M. shoemaker, r Main
Johnson Charles S. carpenter, r Main
Johnson Edwin, drug clerk
Johnson George P. shoe dresser, r Elm
Johnson Henry, expressman, r Pond
Johnson Jacob, r Campello
Johnson Nahum, shoe manuf. r Pond
Johnson Patrick, laborer
Johnson Richard F. carpenter, r Main
Jones A. Dexter, shoemaker, r Montello
Jones Alfred W. shoemaker
Jones Augustus, farmer, r Main
Jones Augustus T. printer, r Main
Jones F. G. shoemaker, r Main
Jones John B. carriage painter, r Lincoln
Jones Nathan, grocer, r Main
Jones Pelham, boot maker, r Main
Jones S. Gardner, boot maker, r Belmont
Joslyn Elisha H. expressman, r Main
Joslyn Elmar, expressman, r Main

KEEN AUGUSTUS W. r Prospect
Keen Isaac, r Prospect
Keith Aberdeen, manuf. counters, r Prospect
Keith Adelbert, shoe manuf. r Main
Keith Albert, shoe manuf. r Main, Campello
Keith Arza B. shoe manuf. r Campello
Keith Bela, carpenter, r Main, Campello
Keith Calvin, r Pleasant
Keith C. P. shoe manuf. Main, Campello
Keith Daniel N. shoe finisher, r Main
Keith Edwin, bds Belmont
Keith Elmer L. shoe manuf. r Main
Keith Franklin, shoe manuf. r Main
Keith Hartwell, carpenter, r Pleasant
Keith Howard, shoecutter, r Elliot
Keith Howard P. shoemaker, r Montello
Keith James, laborer
Keith Jonathan, farmer, r Ames
Keith Joshua A. r North End
Keith Levi W. shoemaker, r Campello
Keith Lucius, shoemaker, r Summer
Keith Nathan, farmer, r Summer
Keith Robert, shoemaker, r West End
Keith Samuel D. shoecutter, r Main
Keith Sylvanus, shoe manuf. r Main
Keith William, laborer, r Crescent
Keith Williard, shoe manuf. r Montello
Kendrick Hiram D. mechanic, r Pond
Kenney William, mechanic
Kent Charles H. shoe finisher
Keough Daniel, shoemaker, r Prospect
Kimball Rufus C. (Howard, Clark & Co.) r Main
Kingman Abel W. physician, r Crescent
Kingman Albert, farmer, r Centre
Kingman Benjamin, farmer, r Main
Kingman Benjamin F. tack manuf. r Main
Kingman Charles E. shoemaker, r Summer
Kingman Cyrus B. shoe manuf. r Summer
Kingman Damon, shoecutter, r Campello
Kingman Edwin H. farmer, r Pine
Kingman Elbridge, shoemaker, r Pine
Kingman Eliphalet, farmer, r Summer

Kingman Emerson, shoemaker, r Main
Kingman Gardner I. shoe manuf. r Campello
Kingman Isaac, farmer, r Summer
Kingman John W. mechanic, r Belmont
Kingman Josiah W. shoe manuf. r Main
Kingman Lewis A. wheelwright, r Mill
Kingman Rufus P. merchant, r cor. Belmont and Main
Kingman Thomas B. farmer, r Pine
Kinsley John P. bootmaker

LANDERS EDMUND, shoecutt'r r Pond
Langmaid John, laborer
Lawson Daniel F. shoemaker, r Main
Lawson Peter, shoemaker, r Main, Campello
Lawson William A. shoemaker, r Main
Leach Daniel H. shoe manuf. r Quincy
Leach Edward B. expressman, r School
Leach Geo. W. carpenter, r Cary
Leach Levi, farmer, r Elm
Leach Lucian B. shoemaker, r Crescent
Leach Lucius, shoe manuf. r Pine
Leach Marcus, shoe manuf. r Pine
Leach Oliver, shoe manuf. r Quincy
Leach Oliver F. shoe manuf. r Centre
Leach Peleg S. shoe manuf. r Elm
Leavitt Jeremiah, bread peddler, r Crescent
Leonard Seth, boot maker, r Winter
Leonard Thomas, mechanic, r Church
Lewis Benj. F. shoemaker, r Wales av
Lewis Horatio P. shoemaker, r Cottage
Lewis Joseph C. boot and shoe manuf. r Main
Lewis Wm. painter, Main
Lilley Theodore, bootmaker, r South
Lincoln Augustus, cabinet-maker
Lincoln Charles, mechanic, r School
Lincoln Charles B. peddler, r School
Lincoln Henry E. clerk, Green
Linnell Nathan, clerk, Main
Littlefield Charles A. clerk, bds Pond
Littlefield Henry M. shoe manuf. r Pond
Loring A. B. stitcher, Pleasant
Loring George, stitcher, Pleasant
Lothrop Caleb H. shoecutter, Summer
Lothrop Nahum P. shoemaker, r Summer
Lovell Daniel, grocer, r School
Lovell Daniel B. clerk, r Elm
Lucas Benjamin P. mechanic, r Pond
Lucuden Isaac, bootmaker, r Cottage
Lunn Albert N. shoecutter
Luther Job, peddler
Lynch Michael, boot former, r North
Lyon Danforth T. r Campello
Lyon Vinal, carpenter, r Main, Campello

MACE NELSON, last maker, r Pine
Mackey Wm. shoemaker, r Main
Macoy Uriah, r Main
Maguire David, shoemaker, r Montello
Maguire Edward, shoemaker, Grove
Maguire Terrence, shoemaker, r Grove
Manchester Isaac F. shoemaker, r Chapel
Manley Galen, farmer, r Liberty
Manley Milo, farmer, r Manly
Marshall Albert L. farmer, r Turnpike
Marshall Hayward, farmer, r Turnpike
Marshall H. Tisdale, farmer, r Turnpike
Marshall Perez, farmer, r Turnpike

DIVIDENDS ADDED to the POLICY in the BERKSHIRE often exceed the premium paid; are NON-FORFEITABLE and will be redeemed in CASH ON DEMAND.   (See page 50.)

Marston Arthur B. melodeon manuf. r Campello
Marston Z. L. melodeon manuf. r Campello
Mattis Benjamin K. bootmaker, r Marshalls Corner
Mason Albert H. wheelwright, r bet. Belmont and Elm
Mason Charles, mason, r Centre
Mason Harland R. last turner, r Grove
Martland William J. mechanic, r Lincoln
Mathison John, expressman
McCall John, laborer, r Court
McCann M. L. upholster
McCarty John, shoemaker, r Court
McDonald Francis, bootmaker
McDonald Thomas, shoemaker, r Montello
McFarland Isaac, teamer
McGowan John, farmer, r Montello
McInerny John, shoemaker, r Quincy
McLaren Andrew, marble worker, r Factory Village
McLaughlin Samuel, carpenter, r Pleasant
McSherry James, laborer
Merchant George A. mechanic, r Cottage
Merchant Nathaniel, miller, r School
Merritt George, farmer, Belmont
Merritt Isaac, carpenter, r Turnpike
Messenger Jason L. shoemaker, Rockland
Mitchell Benjamin G. shoemaker, r Montello
Mitchell William A. shoecutter, bds Elm
Montgomery John shoemaker, r Campello
Moore Michael, bootformer, r Charles
Moran Patrick, marbleworker, r Main
Morey Dennis, shoemaker, r Quincy
Morey Isaac S. r Pleasant
Maroni Francis L. carpenter, r Ash
Morse Elbridge W. merchant, r Church
Morse Harrison, shoecutter, r Montello
Morse John W. confectioner, r High
Mowery Albert, peddler, r Prospect
Murphey John, shoemaker, r Grove
Myrick Gideon H. shoemaker, r School
Myrick William H. fireman r Centre

NASH FRANCIS H. boot maker, r Howard
Nash Henry F. boot maker
Nason Stephen, laborer, r Grove
Nightingale Henry M. hostler, r Pond
Nevins Rapha H. farmer, r Main
Newman Gustavus, shoemaker, r Bartlett
Newman James S. shoe manuf. r Campello
Noyes Alva, farmer, r Centre
Noyes Edward O. merchant, r Ward
Noyes Rufus S. farmer, r Centre

O'BRIEN PATRICK, r Montello
O'Neill Peter, shoemaker, r Main
O'Neill Terrence, laborer
O'Neill William H. mechanic, r Main
O'Riley James, shoemaker, r Campello
Orr Melvin, cabinet maker, r Court
Orr Thomas M. shoe cutter, r Court
Orr Wilson, shoe finisher
Osborn Isaac P. shoemaker, r Rockland

Owens Edward, shoemaker
Owens John, shoemaker, Montello
Owens John 2d, carpenter
Owens Michael, shoemaker, bds Pond
Owens Robert, shoemaker, Montello

PACKARD ALDEN, r Belmont
Packard A. Morton, shoemaker, r bet. Pond and Main
Packard Ambrose, boot manuf. r Prospect
Packard Azel, farmer, Crescent
Packard Benjamin, farmer, r Prospect
Packard Benjamin, sexton, r Main
Packard Benj. A. shoemaker, r Belmont
Packard Bradford, butcher
Packard Caleb H. r Main
Packard Chas. J. F. peg dealer, r Centre
Packard Charles T. r Main
Packard Charles N. farmer, r Ashland
Packard David, laborer, r Main
Packard Davis S. counter manuf. r Pond
Packard D. W. C. stitcher
Packard E. Austin, shoecutter, r Main
Packard Edward B. farmer, r Cary
Packard Ed. C. shoecutter, r Hammond
Packard Edwin, laborer, r Crescent
Packard Edwin, 2d, farmer, r Pleasant
Packard Elbridge H. farmer, r Cary
Packard Ellis, grain dealer, Pleasant
Packard Frederick, farmer, r Linwood
Packard Frederick C. mechanic, r Centre
Packard Frederick W. shoecutter, r Prospect
Packard Galen, farmer, r Prospect
Packard George A. grocer, r Turnpike
Packard Henry, mechanic
Packard Henry A. mechanic
Packard Henry B. boot manuf. r Prospect
Packard Henry C. shoemaker, Centre
Packard Isaac, farmer, r Prospect
Packard Isaac, 2d, shoemaker, r Main
Packard Jas. A. shoecutter, r North End
Packard Jason, shoemaker, Crescent
Packard Joel, bootmaker, r Court
Packard Joel T. grocer, r Main
Packard John, r Crescent
Packard John L. shoecutter, r Main
Packard Josiah E. dentist, bds Main
Packard Josiah P. r Centre
Packard J. Wallace, needle maker, r Lincoln
Packard Lemuel, shoecutter, r Main
Packard Liberty, mechanic, r Pond
Packard Lorenzo E. shoe cutter, r Centre
Packard Manley, farmer, r Turnpike
Packard Marcus, farmer, r Ashland
Packard Martin, farmer, r Main
Packard Martin T. shoe kit dealer, r Crescent
Packard Melvin, shoemaker, r Turnpike
Packard Moses, farmer, r Battles
Packard Moses A. shoemaker, r Main
Packard Nathan, farmer, r cor. Centre and Quincy
Packard Nathan 2d, farmer, r Turnpike
Packard Nathan F. farmer, r Turnpike
Packard Nathaniel R. shoe manuf. r Centre
Packard Nelson, farmer, r Ashland
Packard Ransom, farmer, r Turnpike
Packard Robert, farmer, r Plain
Packard Robert H. farmer, r Plain

J. A. JACKSON 101 COURT STREET, BOSTON, DEALER IN HATS, CAPS AND FURS.

Packard Rodney B. r Elm
Packard S. Franklin, clerk, Montello
Packard Simeon, farmer, r Hammond
Packard Thomas B. r Centre
Packard Washburn, shoe manuf. r Pond
Packard Walter D. shoe dresser, r Franklin
Packard Willard, shoemaker, r Pleasant
Packard Zenas, shoe cutter, r Belmont
Page Samuel A. shoe cutter, r Main
Paine William A. stitcher, r Main
Parker Benjamin, mechanic, r Main
Parker Gould E. shoe finisher
Parker John B. shoemaker, r Main
Parks Henry, shoe manuf. r Main
Patten Oliver O. r Pond
Payton Patrick, shoemaker, r Battles
Peck Hiram F. blacksmith, bds Lincoln
Peck Horatio W. blacksmith, bds Centre
Peirce Charles S. sawyer
Peirce William H. boot maker
Perkins Jonas R. lawyer, r Main
Perkins Levi, clerk
Perkins Nahum, farmer, r Summer
Perkins Samuel C. music teacher
Perkins Sidney, mechanic, r Main
Perkins Thomas C. r Spring
Perkis Amos A. r Campello
Perry Francis, shoemaker, r Main
Perry Sheldon, shoemaker, r Main
Peterson John T. carpenter, r Campello
Peterson Lewis W. shoe manuf. r Campello
Philips Anthony H. shoemaker, r Cross
Philips Caleb H. shoemaker, r Pleasant
Philips Calvin, farmer, r Chestnut
Philips Charles H. milk dealer, r Pleasant
Philips Harrison, shoemaker, bds Main
Pitts Lemuel jr., straw bleacher, r Centre
Place Darius C. r Winter
Plunket James C. laborer
Plunket John, box maker
Poole George B. r Main
Poole Thomas, clerk, Factory Village
Pope Thomas W. blacking manuf. r Belmont
Porter Ahira S. stable keeper, r Main
Porter Charles F. stitcher, r Main
Porter John W. shoe cutter, r Centre
Porter Lewis, boot manuf. r Main
Poyntz James, laborer, r Eaton
Pratt Benjamin A. shoemaker, r Ashland
Pratt Galen, farmer, r Ames
Pratt Galen E. farmer, r Ames
Proctor Samuel, stitcher, r Pleasant
Puffer Loring W. dentist, r Montello

RAMSDELL WILLIAM, farmer r Linwood
Randall George T. carriage builder, r Factory village
Raymond Benj. F. shoemaker, r West End
Reardon Daniel, shoemaker, r Main
Reed Thomas, trader, r Crescent
Remick Timothy, bootmaker, r Stone Hill
Reynolds Azel, musician, r Main
Reynolds Benj. F. farmer, r Main
Reynolds Cassander L. r Campello
Reynolds Charles T. shoemaker, r Pleasant

Reynolds Davis B. r Main
Reynolds Edmond D. machinist, Pleasant
Reynolds Edwin, farmer, r Main
Reynolds Enos H. boot manuf, r Main
Reynolds Gardner W. r Campello
Reynolds G. C. shoecutter, r Main, Campello
Reynolds Howard W. r Campello
Reynolds Isaac N. r Main
Reynolds John, r Pleasant
Reynolds Joseph, jr. shoemaker, r Pleasant
Reynolds Luke, mason, r Prospect
Reynolds Marcus H. mechanic, r Church
Reynolds Marcus V. foreman shoe factory, r Main
Reynolds Martin L. farmer, r Belmont
Reynolds Nathan, r Main
Reynolds Oliver, mason, r Pleasant
Reynolds Oliver B. machinist, r Pleasant
Reynolds Philip, organ manuf. r Main
Reynolds Thomas, r West
Reynolds Thomas T. cobbler, r Main
Rhoades Eben G. *(Howard, Clark & Co.,)*
Richards James F. physician, r Main
Richardson Chas. F. photographer, r Belmont
Richardson J. D. restaurant, r Pond
Richardson Sanford H. shoemaker, r Belmont
Richardson William, r Ash
Richmond Lucius, painter, r Lincoln
Richmond Reuel, watchman, r Main
Ridgeway Ebenezer, laborer, r School
Riley Bernard, shoemaker
Riley Cornelius, shoemaker
Roan Michael, shoemaker, r Pond
Robbins Hiram H. shoe dresser, r South
Robinson Geo. L. shoemaker, r Main
Robinson Henry W. merchant, r Main
Robinson William F. blacksmith, r Factory village
Robinson Winthrop, clerk, r Main
Rogers Harrison, horse dealer, r Main
Roripangh S. L. clergyman, r Elm
Rounds William H. shoe stitcher, r Campello
Russell Francis, laborer, r Cross
Ryder William, r Main
Ryder William, jr. wood engraver, r Main

SAFFORD GEORGE W. jobber, r Rockland
Sanford Aaron H. r Manly
Sanford Baylies, *(H. W. R. & Co.)* r Main
Sanford Samuel H. mechanic, r Belmont
Sanford Squire, shoecutter, r Main
Sanford William A. clerk, r Main
Sargent George T. painter, r Pleasant
Sargent Oliver W. painter, r Elm
Sargent Samuel A. painter, r Spring
Sawyer Clark, carver, r Elm
Sawyer George, shoe cutter
Sawyer George, 2d, fireman, r Court
Saxton Bernard, shoemaker, r Grove
Saxton James, shoemaker, r bet Elm and Belmont
Saxton Patrick, shoemaker, r Main
Scott Walter, merchant, r High
Sears Andrew, shoe cutter
Severance Alonzo C. provision dealer, r Elm
Severance Ira O. clerk, r Belmont

Policy Holders in the BERKSHIRE LIFE INSURANCE COMPANY of Pittsfield, Mass., DO NOT FORFEIT THEIR POLICIES by reason of FAILURE TO PAY their premiums. (See page 50.)

Severance L. F. provision dealer, r Wales avenue
Sewell S. E. shoemaker, r Oak
Sharp John M. painter, r Belmont
Shaw Addison, shoemaker, r Centre
Shaw Jonathan, laborer, r Pond
Shaw J. W. bds Pond
Shedd Eben A. expressman, bds Centre
Shedd Wm. M. millinery goods, r Centre
Shepard Whittier, shoe cutter, r Main
Shepardson Luther S. shoemaker, r Belmont
Sherman Job, mechanic, r Main
Sherman Joshua, laborer, r Belmont
Shiverick Thomas, r Campello
Shurtleff Lothrop, undertaker, r Main
Simmons Weston, farmer, r Pleasant
Skinner George M. shoemaker, r Belmont
Smith Charles, shoemaker, r Belmont
Smith E. Morton, shoemaker, r Cottage
Smith James A. shoemaker
Smith Jarvis D. shoemaker
Smith John F. shoemaker, r Main
Smith John T. shoemaker, r Montello
Smith Joseph S. manuf. shoes, r Prospect
Smith Robert, tin worker, r Centre
Smith Thomas, shoemaker, r Crescent
Snell Alfred, shoemaker, r Rockland
Snell Everett, mechanic
Snell Isaac, farmer, r Turnpike
Snell Isaac E. shoemaker, r Turnpike
Snell James C. farmer, r South
Snell Joseph D. r Montello
Snell Myron O. shoemaker, r Turnpike
Snell Royal, boot maker, r Main
Snell Veranus, shoe tool manuf. r Main
Snell Willard, mechanic, r Main
Snell William, mechanic, r Main
Snow Ara, shoemaker, r Centre
Snow Austin, farmer, r Rockland
Snow Barnabas, gardner, r Main
Snow David, farmer, r Rockland
Snow Dennis, shoemaker, r Rockland
Snow Francis J. r West End
Snow George G. shoe cutter, bds Main
Snow Herbert, r Main
Snow Jonathan, shoemaker, r Turnpike
Snow Lurin, shoemaker, r Rockland
Snow Martin, shoemaker, r Rockland
Snow Shepard W. cabinet maker
Snow Silas, farmer, r Rockland
Snow Silas jr., farmer, r Rockland
Snow Stephen, engineer, r School
Snow Thomas H. shoemaker, r Crescent
Soper Daniel Y. r Court
Soule Cephas, carpenter, r Pleasant
Soule Henry A. r Campello
Soule Oakes S. lumber dealer, r Main
Soule William, shoe dresser, r Main
Souther Allen, shoe cutter
Southworth Edward, farmer, r Main
Southworth Edward jr., cashier S. Bank, r Main
Southworth George, clerk, r Main
Southworth Henry, grocer, r Main
Southworth Marcus, farmer, r South
Southworth Martin, farmer, r Main
Southworth Perez, carpenter, r cor Court and Cary
Spaulding Alfred A. shoemaker, bds Main
Spaulding Edward H. r Main
Spear Charles, shoemaker, r cor. Belmont and Cottage

Sprague Chandler, last manuf. r Crescent
Sproule Charles L. shoemaker
Stetson L. C. peddler, r Wales ave
Stetson S. C. mechanic, r Main
Stevens Emery Z. tin worker, r Main
Stevens George W. shoe manuf. r Montello
Stevens George W. shoe cutter. r Centre
Stevens William, r Main st, Campello
Stoddard Enos T. shoemaker
Stoddard Henry W. mechanic, bds cor. Charles and Main
Stoddard Nathaniel W. manuf. blacking and varnish, r Main
Stoddard Robert A. shoe manuf. r Main
Stoddard William W. boot stitcher, r Main
Stone James L. insurance agent, r Campello
Stranger Edmund B. mechanic, r Main
Studley David F. jeweller, r cor. Main and Church
Studley Henry C. jeweller, r Main
Studley Luther, jeweller, r Green
Sturtevant Earl, shoe cutter, r Montello
Sullivan John, marble worker, r Crescent
Sullivan Patrick, shoemaker, r Main
Sullivan Patrick 2d, shoemaker, r Belmont
Swain Benjamin, r Campello
Swain Gideon T. shoemaker, r School
Swanton Augustus G. shoemaker, r Main
Swain Lebastin S. shoemaker
Swazey William P. r Prospect
Sylvester Algernon S. r Centre
Sylvester Charles F. clerk, r Pond
Sylvester Francis M. shoe finisher, r Court
Sylvester Frederick, shoemaker, r Centre

TABER ASA, expressman, r Pond
Taber Charles, stitcher
Taber Samuel, farmer, r Court
Thatcher George, box maker
Thatcher Rufus L. clerk, bds Belmont
Thayer El. L. boot and shoe manuf. r Pleasant
Thayer Francis A. shoe manuf. r Green
Thayer Hiram S. manuf. Scrofula remedy, bds Main
Thayer Horatio B. shoe manuf. r Green
Thayer Jarvis, carpenter, r Main
Thayer John D. shoe cutter, r Pleasant
Thayer Joseph G. shoe cutter
Thomas Harrison O. stationer, r Main
Thomas Nathan, r Summer
Thomas William E. painter, r Pond
Thompson David jr., baker, r Pleasantville
Thompson Edward, carpenter, r Court
Thompson Geo. R. shoecutter, r Montello
Thompson Henry, shoemaker, r Pleasant
Thompson Henry L. carpenter, r Ward
Thompson Nehemiah, r cor. School and Crescent
Thompson R. F. manuf. hoop skirts, bds L.
Thompson William A. farmer, r Summer
Thrasher Alexander, shoe cutter, r cor. School and Crescent
Thrasher Elias C. shoe cutter, r Main
Tilden John, provision dealer, r Main
Tilton Charles W. shoe cutter, r Pleasant
Tinkham Augustus G. shoemaker

Tinkham D. L. shoe cutter
Tinkham Ephraim, shoemaker
Tinkham George F. shoemaker, r Campello
Tinkham Oliver G. horse dealer, r Main
Tirrill Jacob, cooper, r Pond
Tirrill Jacob P. machinist, r Pond
Tobey William H. cabinet maker, r Green
Tobin Thomas, shoe finisher, r Centre
Tolman Elijah, grain and coal dealer, r Main
Tolman Harvey, r Main
Tolman John, shoe cutter, r Green
Torrey Jeremiah J. shoemaker, r Centre
Torrey Micah F. shoe finisher, r Crescent
Tower Luther, farmer, r Court
Tower S. Franklin, stitcher, r Campello
Trafton C. D. shoedresser, r Main
Trebble George H. sea captain, r Elm
Tribou Asa, shoecutter, r Main, Campello
Tribou Charles E. shoecutter, r Main
Tribou Lyman E. carriage manuf. r Factory Village
Tribou Noah D. laborer, r Crescent
Tribou Samuel, mechanic, r Crescent
Tribou Samuel F. shoecutter, r Campello
Tuck Silas V. shoe knife manuf. r Crescent
Turner Charles, shoemaker, r Main
Turner Horatio N. bootmaker, bds Main
Turner James H. bootmaker, r Albion
Tyler A. D. blacksmith, r Grove

VAUGHN ALVAN, r Campello
Vaughn Robert, shoecutter, r Pine
Vinal Nathaniel, mechanic, Centre
Vincent Joseph, shoecutter, r Campello
Vittem Edward E. teamer, r Belmont
Vose Alvan H. peddler, r Crescent
Vose Leonard, shoedresser

WADE ALBERT R. blacksmith, r Turnpike
Wade Bradford L. r Main
Wade Daniel O. laborer, r Wales ave
Wade Edmond R. physician, r Main
Wade Huram, shoecutler, r Main
Wade Isaac E. shoecutter
Wade Lewis B. confectioner
Wade Lorenzo, merchant, r cor. Turnpike and Pleasant
Wade Orin, blacksmith, r Turnpike
Wadsworth Cephas, peddler, r Pond
Wales Welcome H. town clerk, r Elm
Walker John H. shoe manuf. r Montello
Warren Alva, laborer, r Centre
Warren Azel, shoemaker, r Centre
Warren Azel H. shoemaker, r Centre
Warren Galen, farmer, r Centre
Warren Joseph G. shoemaker, r Court

Washburn Elisha, blacking manuf. r Summer
Washburn Francis B. confectioner, r Main
Washburn Lewis F. mason, r Main
Washburn Nathan H. r Main
Washburn Sidney L. mason
Waterman Sam'l. shoe cutter, r Campello
Webster Wilbor, shoe knife manuf. r Factory village
Welch John, laborer, r Grove
Welch John, 2d, shoemaker, r Grove
Wentworth John M. shoe cutter, r Campello
Wentworth Martin, shoecutt'r, r Campello
Westgate John, shoe cutter
Wheeler A. B. r Church
Wheeler Benj. F. tack manuf. r Pleasant
Wheeler Hiram N. engineer, r Pleasant
Whitcomb George T. carpenter
White Henry J. clerk, r Pleasant
White Jarvis, cabinet maker, r Pleasant
White Jonathan, lawyer, r Main
White Levi B. shoe manuf. r Pleasant
White Welcome, shoe manuf. r Elliot
Whiting William, r Ashland
Whitney George R. dentist, r L st
Whittemore David, Blacking manuf. High
Whitten Francis E. r Marshall's Corner
Whitten Geo. G. r Marshall's Corner
Whitten, Nahum W. shoemaker, Marshall's Corner
Whittier Shepard, shoe cutter, r Main
Wilbur Charles G. bootmaker, Turnpike
Wilbur Elbridge P. laborer, Belmont
Wilbur Gardner, blacksmith, r Turnpike
Wilbour Geo. E. tailor, r Elm
Wilbor Shepard B. cabinet maker
Wild Joseph A. shoemaker, Campello
Wild Martin, Campello
Wild Martin, jr., Campello
Wild Owen, boot former, r Spring
Wilde Bradford, stitcher
Wilder David, baker, r Crescent
Wilder Isaac, cabinet maker, bds Crescent
Wildes John, boot former, r Spring
Williams R. H. broker, r Crescent
Willis Daniel W. shoemaker, Belmont
Willis John, farmer, Belmont
Willis Jonathan S. bootmaker, Turnpike
Willis Mitchell, boot manuf. r Green
Willis Reuben L. shoemaker, Turnpike
Willis Wm. F. shoemaker, Belmont
Willis Wm. H. shoemaker, Belmont
Winter Sanford, butcher, r Turnpike
Wood Barzillai D. shoemaker, Montello
Wood Charles W. clergyman, Campello
Wood Geo. W. farmer, Linwood
Woodbridge E. H. r Summer
Woodward, Silas S. r Pond

YOUNG J. ALBERT, carpenter, r Summer

Pembroke General Directory.

ALLEN MORRILL, clergyman

BABIGAN JOHN, farmer
Baker Andrew H. shoemaker
Baker Calvin, carpenter
Baker Henry, shoemaker
Baker Henry, box maker
Baker Josiah H. farmer
Bailey William, shoemaker
Barker George C. teamster
Barker John, box maker
Barker Peleg, farmer
Barker Robert, farmer
Barnard Joseph S. photographer
Barstow Charles, carpenter
Barstow Thomas H. C. farmer
Bates Edward, mason
Bates Orin G. farmer
Bates William C. machinist
Beal George B. shoemaker
Beal Job H. stonecutter
Bearce Thomas, blacksmith
Bemis Ezekiel, farmer
Besse William, farmer
Besse William, jr., shoemaker
Billings Adam, anchorsmith
Blackman Allen, carpenter
Blackman Daniel, shoemaker
Blackman Thomas, farmer
Blanchard Mark M. farmer
Bonney James, farmer
Bonney James O. farmer
Bonney John C. carriage maker
Bonney J. D. carriages and harnesses
Bonney Pelham W. moulder
Bosworth Asaph, farmer
Bosworth Henry, machinist
Bosworth Nathaniel, farmer
Bonkdry John, shoemaker
Bourne James, miller
Boylston George W. peddler
Boylston Joseph, farmer
Brackett Ebenezer, shoemaker
Briggs Thomas, farmer
Briggs William, seaman
Briggs William T. box maker
Brown Samuel, farmer
Bryant Barzillai, moulder
Bryant Charles A. laborer
Bryant Hervey, farmer
Bryant Jacob M. shoemaker
Bryant John W. shoemaker
Bryant Martin, farmer
Bryant Wm. H. H. dry goods & groceries

CHANDLER DANIEL C. farmer
Chandler Jacob C. shoemaker
Chandler John B. farmer
Chandler Perez, sawyer
Chandler Philip H. shoemaker
Chandler Simeon, farmer
Chandler William E. farmer
Chapman Henry W. farmer
Church Edward R. teamster
Church George H. farmer

Church John, carpenter
Clark Charles H. shoemaker
Clark Charles N. boxmaker
Cleary James, farmer
Collamore Augustus, farmer
Collamore Francis, physician
Collamore Henry H. seaman
Collamore Horace, farmer
Collamore William, laborer
Cook John L. boxmaker
Cook Miles S. laborer
Cook Thomas L. caulker
Copeland Sidney M. conductor
Cox Isaac M. farmer
Crosley George E. shoemaker
Cushing George A. bootmaker
Cushman Julius, farmer
Curtis Albert W. mason
Curtis Isaac C. shoemaker
Curtis William, shoemaker

DAMON BAILEY D. carriagemaker
Delano Daniel, shoemaker
Delano Daniel C. shoemaker
Delano Hiram, shoemaker
Dican James, farmer
Doggett Solon, artist
Doggett Theophilus P. clergyman
Drake Augustus, shoemaker
Drake Beza, farmer
Drake Charles, shoemaker
Drake Charles F. shoemaker
Drake Thomas, tackmaker
Dwelley Charles, farmer
Dwelley George, tack maker
Dwelley James H. tackmaker
Dyer Hervey, tackmaker

FISH EUGENE, farmer
Fish Ezra W. moulder
Fish Job, farmer
Flavell John, farmer
Flavell Thomas, anchor smith
Flynn John, blacksmith
Ford Albert J. carpenter
Ford Baker, farmer
Ford Barnabas, carpenter
Ford Briggs, farmer
Ford Charles B.
Ford Charles H. shoemaker
Ford Charles L. carpenter
Ford Charles T. stone mason
Ford Edwin H. farmer
Ford Elisha W. laborer
Ford Henry, farmer
Ford James, carpenter
Ford John, carpenter
Ford Joseph P. nailer
Ford Kenelm, mason
Ford Lot, farmer
Ford Martin, farmer
Ford Peleg B. shoemaker
Ford Robert B. farmer
Ford Saunders H. shoemaker
Ford Seth, shoemaker

J. A. JACKSON 101 COURT STREET, BOSTON, DEALER IN HATS, CAPS AND FURS.

Foster Benjamin, carpenter
Foster David H. farmer
Foster John, farmer
Fuller Elbridge G. shoemaker

GARDNER BENJAMIN T. painter
Gardner Jabez M. mason
Gerrish George W. jr., shoemaker
Gerrish Samuel, farmer
Glass Thomas S. shoemaker
Goodwin Lewis, farmer
Grey Lewis T. blacksmith
Gurney Freeman J. shoemaker

HALL HORACE, farmer
Harlow Henry A. shoemaker
Hatch George F. box manuf.
Hatch John W. farmer
Hatch Seth, farmer
Hatch Leonard C. carpenter
Hatch Martin T. foreman Hatch's Mill
Hewins Marcus H. shoemaker
Hill Cushman D. shoemaker
Hill F. C. shoemaker
Hill Nahum S. shoemaker
Hinckley Charles N. pastor methodist church
Hobill Henry, anchor smith
Hobill Ralph, poultry dealer
Holmes John, shoemaker
Holmes Samuel, farmer
Hopkins Benjamin, farmer
Hopkins Benjamin jr., shoemaker
Howard Charles, laborer
Howard Charles jr., laborer
Howard Henry, farmer
Howard Nathan, shoemaker
Howe Francis, shoemaker
Howland Allen, mill wright
Howland Andrew B. moulder
Howland Augustus W. carpenter
Howland David O. carpenter
Howland Isaac W. stage driver
Howland Michael, shoe cutter
Huggins Abel H. shoemaker
Huggins Robert, shoemaker
Hyatt Joseph, laborer
Hyatt Joseph W. laborer

JENNINGS ISAAC, dry goods and groceries
Jewett John, shoemaker
Jones Amos, carpenter
Jones Amos H. laborer
Jones R. Morton, painter
Jones Seth, painter
Jones Seth L. painter
Josselyn Albert, carpenter
Josselyn Albert O. farmer
Josselyn Daniel, farmer
Josselyn David, caulker
Josselyn David A. farmer
Josselyn Edwin, mason
Josselyn Elisha, mason
Josselyn Henry, farmer
Josselyn James R. shoe express
Josselyn James M. farmer
Josselyn Marcus M.
Josselyn William B. anchor smith
Joyce Isaac, farmer

KEENE ABEL, farmer
Keene Charles, laborer

Keene Daniel, shoemaker
Keene James, farmer
Keene James S. shoemaker
Keene John A. box maker
Keene Thomas M. farmer
Keene William, farmer
Kilbrith Asa, farmer
Kilbrith Freeman, shoemaker
Kilbrith Greenleaf, dealer in Streeter's Liniment
Kilbrith John W. blacksmith

LAPHAM ALBERT, shoemaker
Lapham Caleb jr., farmer
Lapham Oliver, moulder
Lapham Otis, moulder
Lapham Samuel, farmer
Lefurgey Lemuel, box manuf.
Lewis Martin, jr. blacksmith
Litchfield L. carriage painter
Litchfield Lot, farmer
Loring Bernard, shoemaker
Loring Isaac T. farmer

MANN DAVID A. farmer
Mann John C. farmer
Mann David O. farmer
Mann George H. carpenter
Mann Jonathan O. farmer
Mann Thomas, shoemaker
Magoun Cornelius R. shoemaker
Magoun Daniel, farmer
Magoun Francis L. shoemaker
Magoun Henry S. farmer
Magoun James H. shoemaker
Magoun James L. farmer
Magoun Joseph W. farmer
Magoun Luther, farmer
Magoun Martin, shoemaker
Magoun William W. farmer
Mason Darius B. bootmaker
Mason John D. dealer Streeter's Liniment
McFarlan John, blacksmith
McFarlan John, jr. shoemaker
McLaughlin Hiram L. moulder
McLaughlin Lewis, farmer
Merritt Francis, blacksmith
Mitchell Gilman, laborer
Monroe Hector, farmer
Monroe James L. shoemaker
Morse Nathaniel, farmer
Morse Nathaniel, jr. peddler
Morton Silas, farmer

NASH ZEBULON T. farmer
Niles Samuel, shoemaker
Niles Sylvanus

OLDHAM JOHN, 2d, farmer
Osborn Leander, farmer

PACKARD ALPHEUS, stave sawyer
Parris Ambrose, farmer
Parris John T. shoemaker
Perry Charles B. farmer
Perry Horatio, farmer
Perry Nathaniel S. farmer
Perry Marcus T. shoemaker
Perry Samuel, farmer
Perry Thatcher, farmer
Peterson Calvin, box maker
Peterson Ichabod W. manuf. tin ware
Peterson John J. peddler

The terms for ENDOWMENT, and TEN ANNUAL LIFE POLICIES in the BERKSHIRE are peculiarly favorable, and rates lower than in any Note Company. 25 (See page 50.)

Peterson Thomas, carpenter
Philips Horace W. boot maker
Philips Joshua, stone mason
Philips Lemuel, farmer
Poole Andrew E. agent
Poole Willard, tack maker
Prince Charles H. shoemaker

RAMSDELL BARTLETT, farmer
Ramsdell Elbridge B. anchor smith
Ramsdell George F. carpenter
Ramsdell Levi S. anchor smith
Rand Alexander B. carpenter
Randall Ephraim, farmer
Randall Hiram, Duxbury and Abington stage
Randall Nathaniel K. carpenter
Reed Appleton, laborer
Reed Bela, farmer
Reed Calvin L. shoemaker
Reed Charles, shoemaker
Reed Cyrus, laborer
Reed Ichabod M. shoemaker
Reed Isaac T. shoemaker
Reed Isaac T. jr., shoemaker
Reed James H. shoemaker
Reed Nathaniel F. shoemaker
Rider George H. shoe stitcher
Rideout William, stone cutter

SALMOND PETER, farmer
Sampson Abijah, farmer
Sampson Alden, laborer
Sampson Alexander S. farmer
Sampson Aurora O. shoemaker
Sampson Calvin jr., caulker
Sampson Horatio C. shoemaker
Sampson Isaac, laborer
Sampson Miles, carpenter
Sampson Peleg R. carpenter
Sampson Thomas M. farmer
Sampson Thomas M. 2d, shoemaker
Sampson Thomas H. farmer
Sawin Sullivan, farmer
Scott Elias C. laborer
Scott Sanford B. shoemaker
Sears Henry W. shoemaker
Shepherd Calvin, box board mill
Shepherd Joseph R. box maker
Shepherd Nathan T. box manuf.
Sherman Joseph, engineer
Sherman Lorenzo, ship joiner
Simmons Elbridge, peddler
Simmons Ezra H. shoemaker
Simmons James T. shoemaker
Simmons Mason, carriage manuf.
Simmons Martin, stage driver
Simmons Nathan B. farmer
Smalley Adam S. sea captain
Smith John, laborer
Smith Nathaniel, book keeper
Standish Benjamin, mason
Standish Benjamin R. mason
Standish Otis, sawyer
Stetson Abel, farmer
Stetson Alexander, box maker
Stetson Charles, farmer
Stetson Edward L. shoemaker
Stetson Isaac H. laborer
Stetson Isaac O. farmer
Stetson John, farmer
Stetson John W. shoemaker

Stetson Hervey, carpenter
Stetson Martin, mill-wright
Stetson Pelham, farmer
Stetson Pelham O. farmer
Stetson Sumner, farmer
Stetson Thomas, box maker
Stetson William, trader
Stevens Hiram H. shoemaker
Stevens Thomas G. shoemaker
Streeter Barzillai, liniment
Sturtevant Ichabod, farmer
Sturtevant Isaac H. carpenter
Sturtevant John, laborer
Sturtevant Sylvanus, carpenter

TAYLOR BRIGGS, bucket maker
Taylor Charles, cooper
Taylor George A. farmer
Taylor Samuel, farmer
Taylor Samuel T. mason
Taylor William, mason
Taylor Willis, farmer
Tew Philip H. shoemaker
Thayer Charles N. agent for Selee's Hair Life
Thayer George, shoemaker
Thomas Alonzo, shoemaker
Thomas Benjamin, shoemaker
Thomas Dexter, laborer
Thomas Marcus, farmer
Thomas Oremus H. shoemaker
Thrasher Israel, dry goods and groceries
Tillson Elisha A. blacksmith
Tillson Elisha W. shoemaker
Tillson John P. shoemaker
Tillson Myron W. seaman
Torrence Henry S. shoemaker
Tucker Amariah, laborer
Turner Augustus, shoemaker
Turner Barker, carpenter
Turner Barker jr., carpenter
Turner Cyrus, shoemaker
Turner Edward E. shoemaker
Turner Edwin, shoemaker
Turner George W. shoemaker
Turner Isaiah A. shoemaker
Turner Israel H. shoemaker
Turner Thomas J. farmer

WALKER ISAIAH, farmer
West James H. box manuf.
White Benjamin F. shoemaker
White Friend, shoemaker
White Lucius, shoemaker
Whiting George W. hostler
Whiting Warren T. farmer
Whiting William, clergyman
Whiting William F. laborer
Whitman Charles H. harness maker
Whitman Henry B. harness maker
Whitman James H. attorney
Whitman Seth, carpenter
Whitman Thomas T. carpenter
Wilkinson John, laborer
Witherell Alden, farmer
Witherell Alonzo, shoemaker
Witherell John A. shoemaker
Witherell Joshua, carpenter
Witherell Martin S. farmer

J. A. JACKSON, 101 COURT STREET, BOSTON, DEALER IN HATS, CAPS, AND FURS.

Plymouth General Directory.

Streets, Places, Squares, &c.

Bartlett, foot of High to Summer
Church, from Town Sq. to Spring
Commercial, Sandwich to Union
Court, from head of North, to Kingston Line
Cushman, Court to Allerton Place
Emerald, Commercial to Water
Franklin, Pleasant to Mayflower
Tremont, from Sandwich to Stevens' Wharf
High, from Market to Bartlett
Howland, from Court to Gas Works
Jefferson, Pleasant to Mayflower
Leyden, from Town Sq. to Water
Lothrop, Court to O. C. & N. R. R
Main, from Leyden to No. Square
Market, Town Sq. to Town Brook
Massasoit, Sagamore to Mayflower
Mayflower, from Robinson to South
Middle, from Main to Cole's Hill
Mill, from Summer to Market
Mt. Pleasant, Sandwich to South
North, from North Sq. to Water
No. Green, Pleasant to Sandwich
Pleasant, from Town Brook, foot of Market to South
Prospect, from Russell to Samoset
Robinson, Pleasant to Mayflower
Russell, from Court to Bartlett
Sagamore, Robinson to Jefferson
Sandwich, from Pleasant, foot of Market, to Wellingsley Vil.
School, Town Sq. to S. Russell
South Russell, from Court to Burying Hill Cemetery
South, Sandwich to Mt. Pleasant
South Green, from Pleasant to Sandwich
Spring, from Church to Summer
Summer, Market to Sparrow's Hill
Union, Water to Tremont
Vernon, Court to Prospect
Warren, Wellingsley to Chiltonville, Lower Village
Washington, Pleasant to Mayflower
Water, Sandwich to North
Water-cure, Water to Commercial
Waverly, Vernon to Prospect
Winter, Sandwich to the Sea shore
Allerton Place, from Samoset
Bartlett Place, Russell to High
Drew Place, from Court
Highland Place, from Prospect
Ocean Place, from North
Willard Place, from Summer
Bartlett Alley, Leyden to Middle
Barnes' Lane, Sandwich to Union
Cooper's Alley, Church to High
Cox's Lane, South to Sandwich
School Lane, So. Green to South
Court Square, on Court
Monument Square, Allerton Place. Site of National Monument to the Pilgrims
North Square, junction of Main, Court and North
Plymouth Green, from Sandwich
Town Square, junction Leyden, Market, &c.
Waverly Square, from Prospect

Wharves.

Barnes' Wharf, Water
Carver's Wharf, Water
Davis' Wharf, Water
Doten's Wharf, Water
Finney's Wharf, Warren
Hedge's Wharf, Water
Long Wharf, Water
Leonard's Wharf, Warren
Morton's Wharf, Sandwich
Nelson's Wharf, Water
North Wharf, Water
Robbins' Wharf, Water
Stephens' Wharf, Union
Spooner's Wharf, Court

DIVIDENDS ADDED to the POLICY in the BERKSHIRE often exceed the premium paid; are NON-FORFEITABLE and will be redeemed in CASH ON DEMAND. (See page 50.)

ALEXANDER J. rope maker, Court
Alexander Samuel, carpenter, Spring
Alexander Samuel L. machinist, Court
Alexander Samuel T. shoemaker, Court
Allen C. B. laborer, Mt. Pleasant
Allen George, sea captain, South
Allen Joseph, farmer, Sandwich
Allen Sherman, sea captain, Warren
Allen Sherman 2d, shoemaker, Warren
Allen Winslow, seaman, Sandwich
Andrews George F. editor O. C. Memorial Court
Arthur J. P. sea captain, Court
Arthur Richard, rope maker, Court
Atwood A. J. merchant, Summer
Atwood A. P. seaman, Market
Atwood Edward B. watchmaker, Main
Atwood E. W. jeweller, High
Atwood Fred. shoemaker, Chiltonville
Atwood George H. shoemaker, So. Pond
Atwood J. M. clerk, Summer
Atwood J. R. seaman, Leyden
Atwood John, deputy sheriff, Summer
Atwood John M. merchant, Summer
Atwood Thos. jr., shoemaker, Sandwich
Atwood T. B. shoemaker, Sandwich
Atwood T. C. stonecutter, Howland
Atwood William, seaman, Russell
Atwood William, 2d, merchant, Summer
Avery Ebenezer, printer, North
Avery Winslow, printer, Pleasant

BADGER CHAS. ironsmith, Summer
Badger C. B. ironsmith, Summer
Badger E. D. ironsmith, Summer
Bagnall George, truckman, Water
Bagnall Ichabod P. seaman, Main
Bagnall Joseph, truckman, Water
Bagnall Oliver, laborer, Prospect
Bagnall Richard S. carpenter, Water
Bagnall Richard W. carpenter, Sandwich
Bailey George, seaman, Sandwich
Bailey H. P. tinsmith, Summer
Baker Edward, seaman, Russell
Baker William W. seaman, Court
Ballard S. D. saloon keeper, Main
Baldwin S. T. seaman, Water
Baldwin Wm. M. fish dealer, Spring
Bancroft Arvin N. seaman, Sandwich
Barlow George, wool spinner, Court
Barlow John, ropemaker, Court
Barnes Albert, merchant, North
• Barnes Benjamin, merchant, Sandwich
Barnes B. F. machinist, Sandwich
Barnes Bradford, fish dealer, Cole's Hill
Barnes C. C. harness maker, Summer
Barnes Charles E. clerk, Summer
Barnes Chas. E. 2d, ironworker, Howland
Barnes C. H. nailer, Sandwich
Barnes Corban, merchant, Sandwich
Barnes E. L. merchant, North
Barnes Ellis, wheelwright, Sandwich
Barnes Ellis D. shoemaker, Main
Barnes George A. shoemaker, Sandwich
Barnes Henry, cooper, Chiltonville
Barnes John C. merchant, Court
Barnes J. E. shoemaker, Franklin
Barnes Nath'l C. carpenter, Sandwich
Barnes Nath'l F. carpenter, Sandwich
Barnes R. H. farmer, Sandwich
Barnes Samuel, farmer, Tispaquin
Barnes Winslow B. carpenter, Leyden
Barnes Winslow C. shoecutter, Court

Barnes Wm. B. carpenter, Court
Barnes Wm. M. shoemaker, Howland
Barrett B. W. truckman, Middle
Barrows Ansel, ironworker, Sandwich
Barrows Asa, farmer, West District
Barrows Isaac N. farmer, West District
Barrows L. S. B. ropemaker, High
Barrows O. N. ropemaker, Leyden
Barrows Simeon H. shoemaker, Summer
Bartlett A. H. farmer, Manomet Ponds
Bartlett Alonzo S. seaman, Chiltonville
Bartlett Amasa, bookkeeper, Court
Bartlett Amasa 2d, blacksmith, Court
Bartlett A. M. wheelwright, High
Bartlett Andrew, sea captain, High
Bartlett Ansel, shoemaker, Wellingsley
Bartlett A. T. shoemaker, Wellingsley
Bartlett Caleb, farmer, S. Plymouth
Bartlett Charles, farmer, S. Plymouth
Bartlett Charles B. seaman, Main
Bartlett C. D. farmer, S. Plymouth
Bartlett Clark, farmer, S. Plymouth
Bartlett Coleman, seaman, Sandwich
Bartlett Cornelius, seaman, Wellingsley
Bartlett Cornelius 2d, seaman, Wellingsley
Bartlett Edward, harness maker, Summer
Bartlett Ephraim, shoe dealer, Bartlett Place
Bartlett E. R. carpenter, Wellingsley
Bartlett G. F. clerk, Wellingsley
Bartlett George W. shoemaker, Chiltonville
Bartlett Harvey, shoemaker, Wellingsley
Bartlett Harvey jr., shoemaker, Wellingsley
Bartlett H. C. farmer, S. Plymouth
Bartlett H. K seaman, Wellingsley
Bartlett Hiram, farmer, So. Plymouth
Bartlett Hosea, shoemaker, So. Plymouth
Bartlett Isaac, farmer, So. Plymouth
Bartlett James, iron worker, Russell
Bartlett J. L. iron worker, Russell
Bartlett Paran, seaman, So. Plymouth
Bartlett William S. farmer, So. Plymouth
Bartlett J. B. farmer, Manomett Ponds
Bartlett John, farmer, Wellingsley
Bartlett John E. manuf. patent roofing, Wellingsley
Bartlett K. R. carpenter, Wellingsley
Bartlett Lewis, nail maker, Russell
Bartlett Nathaniel, seaman, Wellingsley
Bartlett Nath'l, jr., seaman, Wellingsley
Bartlett Nath'l, 3d, seaman, Chiltonville
Bartlett R. T. seaman, Main
Bartlett S. S. farmer, Manomet Ponds
Bartlett Stephen, stable keeper, High
Bartlett T. seaman, Winter
Bartlett T. H. clerk, Manomet Ponds
Bartlett T. N. peddler, Town Square
Bartlett Thomas B. carpenter, Main
Bartlett William, seaman, Court
Bartlett William, 2d, seaman, High
Bartlett William H. clerk, Bartlett
Bartlett W. L. clerk, Manomet Ponds
Bassett Edward, seaman, Market
Bassett J. T. seaman, Market
Bassett Thomas, rigger, Market
Bragg William, rope maker, Court
Bates Andrew, laborer, Summer
Bates Benjamin, farmer, Half-way Ponds
Bates B. F. seaman, Half-way Ponds

J. A. JACKSON 101 COURT STREET, BOSTON, DEALER IN HATS, CAPS AND FURS.

Bates Jonathan, farmer, Half-way Ponds
Bates Stephen, farmer, Half-way Ponds
Bates Comfort, carpenter, Summer
Bates Clement, sexton, Market
Bates G. D. teacher, Chiltonville
Bates Hira, caulker, Mayflower
Bates James, high sheriff, Russell
Batson J. shoemaker, Howland
Battles B. L. shoemaker, Summer
Battles Caleb, merchant, Chiltonville
Battles John, surveyor of lumber, Prospect
Battles W. L. merchant, Town sq.
Baxter George L. teacher, North
Baxter J. D. policeman, Mill
Bearce Calvin, farmer, Chiltonville
Bearce Calvin jr., coachman, Chiltonville
Bearce Ichabod, nailer, Summer
Bearce Thomas, zinc worker, Chiltonville
Bearce William H. shoemaker, Chiltonville
Beckman William, shoemaker, Wellingsley
Bennett B. L. seaman, So. Ponds
Bennett L. M. seaman, Chiltonville
Bennett S. D. shoemaker, So. Ponds
Bennett S. S. seaman, So. Ponds
Benson Albert, horse trader, High
Benson Ellis, shoemaker, Summer
Benson E. F. shoemaker, Summer
Benson George, iron worker, Summer
Benson Isaac, jobber, Lothrop Place
Benson John, farmer, Chiltonville
Benson Josiah, laborer, Chiltonville
Benson Martin, blacksmith, Summer
Benson N. L. shoemaker, Summer
Benson Seth, blacksmith, Summer
Benson Timothy, farmer, Chiltonville
Blackmer A. L. wheelwright, Russell
Blackmer Branch, farmer, Wellingsely
Blackmer B. E. shoemaker, Wellingsley
Blackmer Elliot, shoemaker, Wellingsley
Blackmer E. H. farmer, South Plymouth
Blackmer I. C. farmer, Manomet Pond
Blackmer Ivory, fish monger, Wellingsley
Blackmer John, farmer, S. Plymouth
Blackmer J. W. clerk, Wellingsley
Blackmer M. B. shoemaker, Wellingsley
Blackmer S. E. farmer, Manomet Pond
Blackmer W. B. farmer, Manomet Pond
Blanchard James A. overseer cotton mill, Chiltonville
Blanchard Alvin, cotton duckmaker, Chiltonville
Blanchard George, laborer, Watson Hill
Blanchard George A. mariner, Chiltonville
Blanchard James A. overseer cotton mill, Chiltonville
Blanchard Andrew, seaman, Watson Hill
Bland John, cotton dyer, Samosett Mills
Blake G. F. shoemaker, Sandwich
Blake W. K. shoemaker, Sandwich
Booth Richard, ropemaker, North
Booth William, ropemaker, North
Bosworth D. E. merchant, Court
Bosworth J. P. merchant, Court
Bourne Charles, rope maker, Court
Bourne Francis, rope maker, Court
Bradford A. J. merchant, Court
Bradford C. C. carpenter, Cushman

Bradford Cornelius, zinc worker, Chiltonville
Bradford E. W. assessor, Sandwich
Bradford G. F. tin smith, Summer
Bradford Lemuel, collector and assessor, Court
Bradford Lemuel 2d, tack maker, Leyden
Bradford L. G. machinist, Wellingsley
Bradford N. B. farmer, Tispaquin
Bradford Samuel, nail keg manuf. Sandwich
Bradford Samuel jr., nail keg manuf. Sandwich
Bradford William, farmer, Summer
Bradford William H. nailer, Summer
Bradford Winslow, mason, Court
Bradford Zephaniah, farmer, Watson Mills
Brailey Jonathan, farmer, Obrey
Brailey J. R. laborer, Obrey
Bramhall Benjamin, shoe dealer, Russell
Bramhall George, merchant, Chiltonville
Bramhall G. W. merchant, Chiltonville
Bramhall R. E. mariner, Russell
Bremner David, clergyman, North
Brepple M. ropemaker, Court
Brewster Charles, iron worker, Summer
Brewster George B. laborer, Court
Brewster Isaac, merchant, Leyden
Brewster J. B. physician, Leyden
Brewster, Martin, shoemaker, Summer
Briggs C. farmer, So. Plymouth
Briggs Harvey, farmer, So. Plymouth
Briggs Henry, farmer, So. Plymouth
Briggs J. B. seaman, Manomet Ponds
Briggs L. B. seaman, Manomet Ponds
Briggs Samuel, seaman, Manomet Ponds
Briggs Samuel jr., seaman, Manomet Ponds
Brooks William H. clergyman, Court
Brown Benjamin, clerk, Court
Brown David, rope maker, Court
Brown Johnston, physician, Drew Place
Brown J. A. furniture dealer, Court
Brown J. L. farmer, Sandwich
Brown J. P. furniture dealer, Court
Brown Lewis, tack maker, Summer
Brown L. H. tack maker, Market
Brown Nathaniel, lumber dealer, Commercial
Brown Robert, painter, Bartlett Place
Brown S. P. merchant, Summer
Brown S. P. jr., merchant, Summer
Brown William, painter, Summer
Buckley Zedekiah, wool spinner, Court
Buhman Henry, rope maker, Court
Bumpus A. A. farmer, Summer
Bumpus Alexander, gas maker, Summer
Bumpus B. F. clerk, Summer
Bumpus L. S. brakeman, Court
Bumpus M. J. nailer, Summer
Burbank A. T. laborer, Summer
Burbank E. L. laborer, Summer
Burbank L. P. cooper, Cooper Hill
Burbank S. M. jr., merchant, So. Green
Burbank W. D. gentleman, Middle
Burbank W. S. iron worker, Summer
Burbank W. S. jr., gardener, Winter
Burt J. E. mason, Summer
Burt Wm. B. shoemaker, Leyden
Burton Charles, supt. schools, Fremont
Burgess Ezra, seaman, Wellingsley
Burgess Fred, farmer, So. Pond

Policy Holders in the BERKSHIRE LIFE INSURANCE COMPANY of Pittsfield, Mass., DO NOT FORFEIT THEIR POLICIES by reason of FAILURE TO PAY their premiums. (See page 50.)

Burgess George, laborer, So. Ponds
Burgess Henry, mariner, Wellingsley
Burgess I. S. mariner, So. Pond
Burgess I. T. mariner, So. Pond
Burgess O. W. farmer, Wellingsley
Burgess J. W. laborer, Market
Burgess J. A. mariner, Wellingsley
Burgess Phineas F. farmer, So. Pond
Burgess P. S. farmer, So. Pond
Burgess Phineas, farmer, So. Pond
Burgess Samuel, mariner, Saquish
Burgess Seth, farmer, So. Pond
Burgess S. R. mariner, Coles Hill
Burgess S. W. farmer, So. Pond
Burgess Sidney, peddler, Chiltonville
Burgess T. F. teamster, Sandwich
Burgess William, 2d, mariner, So. Pond
Burgess W. T. mariner, So. Pond
Burgess William, farmer, Chiltonville
Burgess William W. seaman, Cole's Hill
Butler Daniel, ropemaker, Court
Butsche Wm. ropemaker, Court
Byrns Wm. grocer, Court
Byrns John, ropemaker, Water

CAHOON A. F. mariner, Cedarville
Cahoon Andrew J. farmer, Cedarville
Cahoon H. H. clerk, Cedarville
Cahoon Nathan, farmer, Cedarville
Cahoon Samuel jr., farmer, Cedarville
Callahan Patrick, mariner, Spring
Calliway Geo. R. tack maker, Watson Hill
Campbell Charles, seaman, Sandwich
Carlton John, baker, Sandwich
Carnes John, mariner, South
Carr Andrew, rope maker, Court
Carr Peter, rope maker, Court
Carter Henry, baggage master, Howland
Carver Ichabod, shoemaker, Middle
Carver John, shoemaker, Leyden
Carver Josiah, shoemaker, Middle
Carver Otis, farmer, Manomet Pond
Carver William, farmer, Wellingsley
Cassady Henry, farmer, Wellingsley
Cassady James, laborer, Russell
Cassady J. S. teamster, Commercial
Cassady Michael, rope maker, Court
Caswell A. T. farmer, So. Pond Road
Caswell Thomas, farmer, So. Pond Road
Chamberlin E. steam engineer, Court
Chandler A. C. stable keeper, Court
Chandler C. B. mariner, Sandwich
Chandler D. L. mariner, Sandwich
Chandler E. C. merchant, Market
Chandler John B. mariner, Sandwich
Chandler P. C. merchant, Pleasant
Chandler S. B. mariner, Sandwich
Chandler Thomas, mariner, Sandwich
Chapman J. H. peddler, Court
Clinch M. rope maker, Court
Coffin T. M. machinist, Sandwich
Cohen John, mariner, Sandwich
Chase Allen, mariner, South
Chase George H. clerk, Pleasant
Chase John, mariner, Sandwich
Chase S. D. peddler, Court
Chase Zenas R. shoemaker, Sandwich
Churchill Amasa, carpenter, So. Green
Churchill A. R. carpenter, So. Green
Churchill Benjamin, merchant, Market
Churchill Barnabas, machinist, High
Churchill Charles, laborer, Russell
Churchill C. O. col. of customs, Russell

Churchill Daniel O. mariner, Sandwich
Churchill E. F. shoemaker, Chiltonville
Churchill F. E. mariner, Chiltonville
Churchill F. H. grocer, Summer
Churchill George, gentleman, Court
Churchill George 2d, mariner, Water
Churchill Heman, cooper, Franklin
Churchill James W. mariner, Chiltonville
Churchill J. D. shoemaker, Summer
Churchill J. F. mariner, Summer
Churchill John, trader, Water
Churchill Joseph, mariner, Commercial
Churchill Joseph 2d, mariner, Water
Churchill Josiah W. mariner, Samaria
Churchill Lionel, sea captain, Warren
Churchill Nathan, laborer, Market
Churchill Wilson, farmer, Chiltonville
Churchill R. B. machinist, High
Churchill R. H. clerk, Tremont
Churchill Rufus, merchant, Water
Churchill S. L. carpenter, Sandwich
Churchill Thomas, mason, Samaria
Churchill W. E. carpenter, Bartlett
Churchill William, carpenter, Bartlett
Churchill W. W. seaman, Chiltonville
Clark Benj. farmer, Manomet Pond
Clark David, farmer, Manomet Pond
Clark E. D. stone cutter, Chiltonville
Clark Ezra, farmer, Manomet Pond
Clark Israel, farmer, Manomet Pond
Clark Israel, 2d, farmer, Manomet Pond
Clark Ivory H. laborer, Manomet Pond
Clark James E. farmer, Chiltonville
Clark John, farmer, Court
Clark Nathaniel, farmer, Manomet Pond
Clark Nathaniel, 2d, farmer, West Dist.
Clark Robert, stone cutter, Court
Clark Samuel, farmer, Manomet Pond
Clark Seth, farmer, Manomet Pond
Clark S. P. farmer, Manomet Pond
Clark William, mercht. Manomet Pond
Clark Zoath, farmer, Court
Cobb Charles, rope maker, Court
Cobb C. S. rope maker, Court
Cobb Franklin B. trader, Warren
Cobb Franklin B. jr., clerk, South
Cobb G. W. farmer, Warren
Cobb J. K. farmer, Court
Cobb J. M. ironworker, Mayflower
Cobb Israel, iron worker, Court
Cobb W. C. clerk, Court
Cole A. B. carpenter, West Dist.
Cole C. H. farmer, West Dist.
Cole J. A. farmer, West Dist.
Cole J. B. farmer, Chiltonville
Cole Samuel, farmer, Wellingsley
Collingwood J. B. cooper, Cushman
Collins G. M. carpenter, Court
Collins James, carpenter, Court
Cooper George W. mason, Wellingsley
Cornish Aaron H. teacher, Manomet Ponds
Cornish Edwin N. farmer, Manomet Ponds
Cornish James, seaman, Wellingsley
Cornish Thomas, farmer, Manomet Ponds
Cornish Thomas, jr., farmer, Manomet Ponds
Cornish Thomas E. mariner, Wellingsley
Courtney John, farmer, Chiltonville
Courtney J. G. seaman, Ship Pond

J. A. JACKSON, 101 COURT STREET, BOSTON, DEALER IN HATS, CAPS, AND FURS.

PLYMOUTH DIRECTORY. 99

Covington William, carpenter, Summer
Cox Elias, carpenter, Sandwich
Cox William R. Chiltonville
Cox William R. jr., mariner, Chiltonville
Cox James, town treasurer, Summer
Cox W. W. mariner, Chiltonville
Cunningham G. E. baggage master, Court
Cuman John, ropemaker, Court
Cushing C. laborer, South

DAMON C. S. clerk, Court
Damond D. E. register Probate, Russell
Danforth Wm S. register Deeds, Court
Danforth Allen, Treas. Savings Bank, Main
Danforth A. B. farmer, So. Pond road
Danforth C. H. shoemaker, So. Pond road
Danforth G. F. shoemak'r, So. Pond road
Danforth Henry, farmer, So. Pond road
Daniels A. thread maker, Summer
Darling A. A. shoemaker, So. Pond
Davidson James, threadmaker, Summer
Davie Ebenezer, iron worker, Robinson
Davie Johnson, mason, Court
Davie Sylvester, clerk, Court
Davis William T. president P. N. Bank, Court
Davis Charles G. attorney, Court
Davis John R. merchant, High
Davis John R. jr., shoemaker, High
Davis F. B. mariner, Court
Deacon James, mariner, North
Deming Augustus, shoemaker, Main
Deluce G. E. engineer, Court
Devine Patrick, ropemaker, Court
Dickson C. L. shoemaker, High
Dickson J. W. shoemaker, Russell
Dickson S. R. cooper, Mayflower
Dillard Benj. mariner, Sandwich
Diman Erastus W. rope maker, Howland
Diman Ezra S. rope maker, Samoset
Diman Ezra S. jr., peddler, Samoset
Diman James, carpenter, Howland
Diman Thomas, carpenter, Court
Diman T. S. mariner, Court
Ditman Fred. ropemaker, Court
Dixon Comfort, operator in cotton duck mills, Chiltonville
Dixon Edwin, operative in cotton duck mills, Chiltonville
Dixon Graham, operative in cotton duck mills, Chiltonville
Dixon Lyman, operative in cotton duck mills, Chiltonville
Dixon Walter, operative in cotton duck mills, Chiltonville
Dorcey Wm. ropemaker, Court
Doten Chandler W. farmer, Chiltonville
Doten Charles C. merchant, Mayflower
Doten Edward, laborer, Howland
Doten Elbridge G. carpenter, Chiltonville
Doten E. S. shoemaker, Russell
Doten Everett W. merchant, Chiltonville
Doten George W. farmer, Chiltonville
Doten J. M. mariner, Chiltonville
Doten Lemuel, mariner, Chiltonville
Doten L. W. mariner, Chiltonville
Doten Prince, laborer, Sandwich
Doten Prince, mason, Sandwich
Doten Stephen, farmer, Chiltonville
Doten Stephen, jr., merchant, Chiltonville
Doten Wm. W. mariner, Chiltonville
Dotey Nathaniel, mariner, Water

Douglass A. J. farmer, Halfway Ponds
Douglass Elijah, farmer, Halfway Ponds
Douglass Elisha, farmer, Halfway Ponds
Douglass J. A. farmer, Halfway Ponds
Douglass Joshua, farmer, Halfway Ponds
Douglass Jesse, farmer, Halfway Ponds
Douglass M. V. B. farmer, Halfway Ponds
Douglass N. K. farmer, Halfway Ponds
Douglass W. S. farmer, Halfway Ponds
Downey Timothy, laborer, So. Ponds
Drew Abbot, Sup't Water Works, Middle
Drew Abijah, carpenter, Mayflower
Drew A. H. clerk, Court
Drew A. R. sailmaker, South
Drew Atwood L. clerk, Court
Drew Charles H. attorney, Mayflower
Drew David, sailmaker, South
Drew Ellis, merchant, Summer
Drew Edward W. carpenter, Drew Place
Drew George A. laborer, Water
Drew George F. shoemaker, Middle
Drew Harrison W. shoemaker, South
Drew Horace, shoemaker, Pleasant
Drew J. R. printer, Sandwich
Drew T. B. dentist, North
Drew Winslow, carpenter, Drew Place
Drew Wm. R. merchant Leyden
Dugan Patrick, ropemaker, Court
Dunham Barnabas, mariner, Mayflower
Dunham Barnabas, jr., mariner, Summer
Dunham B. F. mariner, Mayflower
Dunham D. F. peddler, Court
Dunham Ephraim, farmer, West District
Dunham George F. gunsmith, Summer
Dunham George H. mason, Court
Dunham Harvey, farmer, West District
Dunham I. T. cabinet maker, Leyden
Dunham J. A. sole leather cutter, Summer
Dunham L. S. peddler, Sandwich
Dunham Lucas, farmer, West District
Dunham Lysander, shoe manuf. Samoset
Dunham Nathan, farmer, West District
Dunham Richard B. mason, Cushman
Dunham Samuel N. shoemaker, Summer
Dunham Wm. J. mariner, Summer
Dunlap D. A. ironsmith, Summer
Dunn Wm. ropemaker, Court
Dunton S. engineer, Main
Dyer G. G. Cashier O. C. N. Bank, Summer

EATON T. T. laborer, Tispaquin
Eddy Henry H. ropemaker, Court
Eddy John, shoemaker, Summer
Eddy John, jr., shoemaker, Summer
Eddy Lewis, carpenter, High
Edes J. L. blacksmith, Edes
Edes Oliver, zinc manuf. Russell
Elliot Samuel, laborer, Cole's Hill
Ellis Abner, carpenter, Summer
Ellis Barnabas, ironworker, Jefferson
Ellis Bartlett, merchant, Russell
Ellis Clark S. farmer, Ellisville
Ellis E. B. farmer, Ellisville
Ellis E. W. farmer, Ellisville
Ellis George F. shoemaker, Summer
Ellis Hiram, farmer, Ellisville
Ellis James, wheelwright Edes
Ellis James W. farmer, Ellisville
Ellis Nathaniel, farmer, Chiltonville
Ellis Nathaniel B. shoemaker, Russell
Ellis Otis, farmer, Cedarville

ANNUAL CASH DIVIDENDS in the BERKSHIRE LIFE INS. CO., Pittsfield, Mass. Boston Office 95 1-2 Washington St. (See page 50.)

Ellis Rufus, farmer, Indian Brook
Ellis Thomas, mariner, Sandwich
Ellis Timothy, laborer, Sandwich
Ellis Watson, farmer, Manomet Pond
Ellis W. H. farmer, Manomet Pond
Ellis Ziba, farmer, Ellisville
Erland E. F. merchant, Sandwich

FARRINGTON DAVID, wool spinner, Lothrop
Farris Jeremiah, Treas. P. Mills, Main
Faulkner Dwight, Treas. Woolen Mills, Cushman
Faunce L. B. ironworker, Willard Place
Faunce Peleg, laborer, High
Faunce S. E. clerk, High
Faunce Solomon, peddler, High
Faunce Thaddeus, ropemaker, Highland
Faunce W. S. ropemaker, School
Fessenden Henry, tinsmith, Cushman
Field B. B. shoemaker, Summer
Field Benj. F. tailor, Summer
Field J. L. mariner, Sandwich
Finney Albert, soap manuf. Summer
Finney Benjamin C. grocer, High
Finney C. H. shoemaker, Howland
Finney Clark, merchant, Chiltonville
Finney David, carpenter, Chiltonville
Finney Elkanah, carpenter, Chiltonville
Finney Elkanah C. merchant, Summer
Finney Elkanah C. jr., mariner, Summer
Finney Ephraim, farmer, Chiltonville
Finney Ephraim 2d, hackman, Court
Finney Everett, farmer, Chiltonville
Finney Ezra, farmer, Chiltonville
Finney Frank, clerk, Court
Finney Frank S. clerk, Court
Finney George, farmer, Chiltonville
Finney Harrison, merchant, Pleasant
Finney James, farmer, Chiltonville
Finney John, farmer, Chiltonville
Finney Leavitt, merchant, Green
Finney L. W. clerk, Court
Finney Pelham, tackmaker, Green
Finney Robert, mariner, Chiltonville
Finney Seth, mariner, Wellingsley
Finney Wm. L. farmer, Chiltonville
Finney Wm. H. mariner, Chiltonville
Finney Walter H. mariner, Russell
Fish George H. hostler, Court
Fisher George, laborer, Emerald
Fisher M. C. farmer, Cedarville
Fisher S. C. mariner, Cedarville
Fitzgerald James, wool spinner, Lothrop
Fowler W. C. farmer, South
Frank Antonio, ropemaker, Court
Fratus Manuel, mariner, Tispaquin
Freeman B. D. baker, Sandwich
Freeman P. W. wool spinner, Court
Freeman Weston G. shoemaker, Summer
Frink C. H. barber, Sandwich
Frothingham James, ropemaker, Court
Fuller Alexander, jr., clergyman, Chiltonville
Fuller C. H. clerk, Tispaquin
Fuller George, blacksmith, Sandwich
Fuller J. C. mariner, Sandwich
Fuller J. C. shoemaker, Sagamore
Fuller Robert D. blacksmith, South
Fuller S. R. clothing manuf. Court
Fuller Wm. H., R.R. conductor, Russell
Furnside James, master weaver, Court

GALLAGHER T. G. woolen spinner, Howland
Gardener G. W. hostler, Leyden
Gardener Joseph, mariner, Commercial
Gibbs D. H. overseer duck manuf'y Chiltonville
Gibbs W. L. clerk, Chiltonville
Giles Edward, laborer, Pleasant
Gilmore C. A. gentleman, Manomet Ponds
Gleason J. G. tailor, Middle
Goddard F. J. farmer, Samoset
Goff Patrick, ropemaker, Court
Gooding B. B. watchmaker, Russell
Gooding John, gentleman, Main
Gooding Wm. merchant, Court
Gooding Wm. P. shoemaker, Court
Goodwin Charles, ropemaker, Pleasant
Goodwin Ezra S. mariner, Leyden
Goodwin Nathaniel, mariner, Leyden
Gordon Timothy, physician, North
Gould Samuel, farmer, S. Pond
Greene G. H. marble cutter, Howland
Greene Harry W. ropemaker, Court
Greene R. F. ropemaker, Court
Greene Richard, ropemaker, Court
Greene Wm. H. ropemaker, Court
Greene Wm. Harris, ropemaker, Court
Grenell D. mariner, Ebbenville
Griffin B. H. mariner, Chiltonville
Griffin Ebenezer S. ropemaker, Court
Griffin George W. ropemaker, Court
Griffin Granville, shoecutter, Leyden
Grozenger David, ropemaker, Court
Grozenger Matthias, ropemaker, Court

HABALL LEWIS, ropemaker, Court
Hadaway A. S. farmer, Chiltonville
Hadaway John B. S. ironworker, Chiltonville
Hadaway Thomas, farmer, Chiltonville
Hadaway Wm. S. farmer, Chiltonville
Hagallstine M. ropemaker, Court
Hall E. W. engineer, High
Hall Edward H. clergyman, Court
Hall Isaac T. farmer, Court
Hall James, farmer, Court
Hall John T. merchant, Main
Hall John F. farmer, Court
Hall Robert B. clergyman, Court
Hall W. C. farmer, Court
Hall Wendell, farmer, Court
Hall William, farmer, Court
Hamrose James, ropemaker, Court
Hamrose Henry, ropemaker, Court
Hape Earnest, ropemaker, Court
Harding Caleb, laborer, Summer
Harlow Abner H. cooper, Commercial
Harlow B. L. shoemaker, Court
Harlow Branch, mariner, High
Harlow C. F. mariner, Sandwich
Harlow C. G. shoemaker, Court
Harlow David L. carpenter, Franklin
Harlow E. P. machinist, Pleasant
Harlow Erastus, butcher, Pleasant
Harlow Ezra, clerk, Willard Place
Harlow Geo. H. mason, Commercial
Harlow Ivory L. carpenter, Pleasant
Harlow Ivory L. jr., carpenter, Leyden
Harlow Jesse, merchant, Summer
Harlow John, farmer, Chiltonville
Harlow John, 2d, laborer, Ebbenville
Harlow John H. merchant, Pleasant
Harlow Joseph, farmer, Ellisville

J. A. JACKSON 101 COURT STREET, BOSTON, DEALER IN HATS, CAPS AND FURS.

Harlow Lewis, ropemaker, Court
Harlow Nathaniel E. merchant, Pleasant
Harlow Richard W. mariner, Chiltonville
Harlow Samuel, merchant, Commercial
Harlow T. C. farmer, Ellisville
Harlow Thomas, farmer, Ellisville
Harlow William, seaman, Manomet Pond
Harlow Wm. J. farmer, Rocky Hill
Harlow Wm. N. wheelwright, Summer
Harriman Valentine, ropemaker, Court
Harris C. T. tinsmith, Pleasant
Harris Oliver, laborer, Pleasant
Harris Wm. O. seaman, Pleasant
Harvey Benjamin, laborer, Middle
Harvey D. O. blacksmith, Summer
Harvey Sylvanus, blacksmith, Summer
Haskell P. H. farmer, Cedarville
Haskins Alex. teamster, Court
Haskins Geo. H. laborer, Sandwich
Hathaway Allen, laborer, Leyden
Hathaway Benj. merchant, Summer
Hathaway Charles, farmer, Summer
Hathaway Chas. jr. farmer, Summer
Hathaway C. G. book-keeper, Pleasant
Hathaway Edw. harnessmaker, Pleasant
Hathaway Geo. A. neck stock manufacturer, Pleasant
Hathaway T. A. laborer, Leyden
Hattan John, ironworker, Summer
Hayden E. B. clerk, Chiltonville
Hayward C. O. farmer, Rocky Hill
Hayward P. W. clerk, Main
Hayward Wm. D. shoemaker, Rocky Hill
Hayward Wm. G. seaman, Rocky Hill
Hazzard Barney, ropemaker, Court
Heath James, ironworker, Summer
Hedge A. G. wool dyer, Vernon
Hedge Barnabas, farmer, Court
Hedge E. G. merchant, Court
Hedge Isaac L. merchant, Court
Hedge Nath'l L. seaman, Court
Heinrich Martin, ropemaker, Court
Heitze John, ropemaker, Court
Helm Louis, ropemaker, Court
Hemerlee Wm. ropemaker, Court
Henderson Geo. laborer, Russell
Hepburn John, ropemaker, Court
Hincheliff John, laborer, S. Ponds
Hincheliff Richard, wool carder, Court
Hindle James, wool spinner, Lothrop
Hobart H. M. ironworker, Summer
Hodge J. T. geologist, Cushman
Hodges Benj. seaman, Water
Hodges Benj. F. farmer, Sandwich
Hodges Nath'l, farmer, Chiltonville
Holbrook Eliphalet, seaman, Sandwich
Holbrook Gideon, sea captain, Sandwich
Holbrook Gideon, jr. cooper, Jefferson
Holbrook James S. clerk, Main
Holbrook John, farmer, Lothrop
Hollis W. T. editor, Court
Holmes Adoniram, laborer, Court
Holmes Albert, sea captain, Pleasant
Holmes Allen, expressman, Leyden
Holmes Amasa, merch't, Manomet Pond
Holmes Andrew, shoemaker, Court
Holmes A. T. clerk, Leyden
Holmes B. B. seaman, Manomet Pond
Holmes Barnabas G. laborer, Wellingsley
Holmes Barnabas H. auctioneer, Middle
Holmes Benj. cotton duck, Chiltonville
Holmes Caleb B. merchant, High
Holmes C. F. farmer, Manomet Pond
Holmes C. H. ropemaker, Court
Holmes Charles T. trader, Town Square
Holmes C. W. farmer, Manomet Pond
Holmes C. W. farmer, Manomet Pond
Holmes David, farmer, Chiltonville
Holmes David C. farmer, Court
Holmes D. S. farmer, Chiltonville
Holmes Elisha, fisherman, Manomet Pond
Holmes Ellis, laborer, Sandwich
Holmes Ephraim, painter, Jefferson
Holmes Ephraim B. shoemaker, Russell
Holmes Ezra T. cotton duck maker, Chiltonville
Holmes E. W. shoemaker, Sandwich
Holmes F. L. butcher, Manomet Ponds
Holmes Galen R. ironworker, Chiltonville
Holmes George H. mariner, Chiltonville
Holmes Geo. W. farmer, Manomet Ponds
Holmes G. F. clerk, Leyden
Holmes Harrison, butcher, Main
Holmes Henry B. hotel keeper, Manomet Ponds
Holmes I. B. baker, Leyden
Holmes I. S. watchman, Court
Holmes I. T. mariner, Watson Hill
Holmes J. F. mariner, Sandwich
Holmes Joseph, clerk, Court
Holmes Josiah, 2d, ropemaker, Court
Holmes Josiah, 3d, clerk, Court
Holmes Kendell, mariner, Sandwich
Holmes Lemuel D. clerk, Court
Holmes Marston, farmer, Manomet Pond
Holmes M. F. farmer, Manomet Pond
Holmes Micah, mariner, Sandwich
Holmes M. V. B. tinman, Market
Holmes Nathan H. blacksmith, Court
Holmes Nathaniel, farmer, Court
Holmes Nathaniel, jr., shoemaker, Court
Holmes Nelson, laborer, Samaria Place
Holmes Oliver, ropemaker, Court
Holmes Peter, gentleman, North
Holmes R. W. shoemaker, South
Holmes Samuel B. carpenter, Wellingsley
Holmes S. L. ironsmith, Summer
Holmes S. N. laborer, Court
Holmes Solomon M. farmer, So. Ponds
Holmes Stephen, farmer, Manomet Pond
Holmes Truman, farmer, Manomet Ponds
Holmes Truman C. gentleman, Sandwich
Holmes W. C. carpenter, Court
Holmes Winslow S. barber, Middle
Holmes Wm. S. carpenter, Court
Holsgrove Thos. shoemaker, Tispaquin
Hovey J. C. postmaster, Manomet Pond
Howard D. D. laborer, Willard Place
Howard Maltiah, farmer, Summer
Howard Robert, operative, Court
Howland Calvin, teamster, Chiltonville
Howland Calvin, jr., teamster, Chiltonville
Howland Chas. H. operative, Chiltonville
Howland C. H. 2d, mariner, Chiltonville
Howland F. C. mariner, Chiltonville
Howland Francis, shoemaker, Chiltonville
Howland Jacob, mariner, Sandwich
Howland Jacob, jr., shoemaker, Chiltonville
Howland John F. mariner, Chiltonville
Howland Lemuel C. mariner, Chiltonville
Howland L. C. jr., mariner, Chiltonville
Howland William, mariner, Chiltonville

The terms for ENDOWMENT, and TEN ANNUAL LIFE POLICIES in the BERKSHIRE are peculiarly favorable, and rates lower than in any Note Company. (See page 50.)

Howland Wm. H. mariner, Chiltonville
Howland W. N. mariner, Chiltonville
Hoxie Abiatha, laborer, West District
Hoxey Edward W. carpenter, Chiltonville
Hoxey N. C. shoemaker, Chiltonville
Hoxey Wm. H. mariner, Chiltonville
Hoyt J. F. mason, Sandwich
Hoyt Moses, mason, Sandwich
Hubbard Benjamin, physician, Main
Humphrey E. clergyman, Court
Hurley M. laborer, Lothrop
Hurley Timothy, laborer, Lothrop
Hutchinson Rob't, master mariner, Sandwich

IRISH C. B. twine manuf. Howland

JACKSON ALEX. physician, North
Jackson Edwin, merchant, Cole's Hill
Jackson George F. farmer, Court
Jackson Geo. H. lumber dealer, North
Jackson Henry F. merchant, Cole's Hill
Jackson Isaac C. merchant, North
Jackson J. W. clerk, Court
Jackson Thomas, farmer, Court
Jackson Thomas O. farmer, Cooper Hill
Jackson Thomas T. merchant, North
Jackson Wm. H. harness maker, Leyden
Jarvis Egbert, physician, Town Sq.
Jenkins B. F. mariner, Middle
Jennes G. H. mariner, Sandwich
Jewett R. P. mariner, South
Johnson C. W. mariner, South
Johnson Wm. H. clerk, North
Jones C. L. painter, Middle
Jones David, mariner, Emerald
Jones George, shoemaker, Federal
Jones Samuel, mariner, Sandwich
Jordan John, mariner, Sandwich
Jordan William, mariner, Sandwich

KENDRICK ASA, carpenter, Middle
Kendrick James, mariner, Water
Kendrick James F. ropemaker, Court
King E. F. mariner, Chiltonville
King Isaac B. mason, Chiltonville
King Lewis, mariner, Chiltonville
King Lothrop C. overseer, Chiltonville
King Nathan, mariner, Chiltonville
King Nathan, jr., mariner, Chiltonville
King Obadiah, farmer, Chiltonville
King Robert, mariner, Chiltonville
King R. W. mariner, Chiltonville
King Wm. mariner, Chiltonville
King Wm. 2d, mariner, Chiltonville
Kerr Michael, ropemaker, Court
Kerr Richard, ropemaker, Court
Kimball P., R. R. conductor, Court
Kingsley John, farmer, Wellingsley
Kirwin Patrick, ropemaker, Court
Klengenhaden C. H. ropemaker, Court
Kneeland J. tanner, Summer

LAMBERT W. mariner, Wellingsley
Langford John, carpenter, Chiltonville
Langford Wm. mariner, Chiltonville
Lanman Ellis T. mariner, Court
Lanman Geo. F. mariner, S. Pond R.
Lanman Henry T. carpenter, Court
Lanman H. J. shoemaker, Court
Lanman Isaac, carpenter, Court
Lanman Nath'l C. carpenter, Court

Lanman Nath'l C. jr., shoe manuf. Prospect
Lanman Samuel, carpenter, Court
Lanman S. E. farmer, Prospect
Lanman S. E. 2d, mariner, Water
Lanman W. W. expressman, Prospect
Lapham Wm. iron-smith, Summer
Lawrence John, mariner, Sandwich
Leach Allen, farmer, Chiltonville
Leach David, farmer, Chiltonville
Leach David, jr., farmer, Chiltonville
Leach Ezra, farmer, Chiltonville
Leach E. H farmer, Chiltonville
Leach F. S. mariner, Summer
Leach Lemuel, farmer, Chiltonville
Leach Lemuel, jr., farmer, Chiltonville
Leach Phineas, mariner, Summer
Leach R. B. shoemaker, Court
Leach R. H. farmer, Chiltonville
Leonard Abner, ironworker, Summer
Leonard I. W. ironworker, Chiltonville
Leonard Nath'l W. merchant, Chiltonville
Leonard Wm. M. ironworker, Chiltonville
Leonard Wm. W. ironworker, Chiltonville
Lewis F. carpenter, Franklin
Lewis Wm. carpenter, Wellingsley
Locke A. H. photographer, Sandwich
Loring Thomas, merchant, Court
Loring H. W. agent tack mill, Court
Loud Hughes, mariner, Pleasant
Loud J. H attorney, Court
Lovell James A. ironworker, Summer
Lovell Leander, town clerk, Leyden
Lucas Aug'tt H. master mariner, North
Lucas Benj. F. expressman, West Dist.
Lucas Ezra, farmer, West District
Lucas F. W. expressman, West District
Lucas Isaac J. trader, Summer
Lucas Joseph, gentleman, North
Lucas Luther, farmer, Manomet Pond
Lucas Stephen, confectioner, Summer
Lynch James, farmer, Manomet Pond
Lynch Timothy, farmer, Court
Lynes Charles, ropemaker, Court

MACOMBER W. S. mason, Pleasant
Mahler Peter, ropemaker, Court
Manter David, farmer, Chiltonville
Manter George, farmer, So. Pond
Manter George, jr., farmer, So. Pond
Manter Preston, mariner, So. Pond
Manter Prince, fish dealer, Wellingsley
Manter Timothy, mariner, Halfway Pond
Manter Wm. mariner, Halfway Pond
Manter Wm. 2d, mariner, Halfway Pond
Mason Albert, attorney, Court
Materu Fred'k, ropemaker, Court
May Charles, clerk, Middle
May Charles T. liquor agent, Middle
Maybury Joseph, moulder, Cooper Hill
Maybury J. A. moulder, Cooper Hill
McCartey Jerry, laborer, Emerald
McCartey Michael, ropemaker, Emerald
McGan Owen, mariner, Emerald
McGill Charles, laborer, Pleasant
McGreggor James, ropemaker, Court
McLean Alex. ropemaker, Court
McLean David, ropemaker, Court
McLauthlin James, farmer, Wellingsley

J. A. JACKSON, 101 COURT STREET, BOSTON, DEALER IN HATS, CAPS, AND FURS.

McLauthlin Seth, ropemaker, Watson's Hill
McMahon C. W. ropemaker, Court
McLane Richard, ropemaker, Court
McManus John, ropemaker, Court
McReady Thomas, ropemaker, Court
Mehuren Seth, farmer, Water
Merriam E. J. shoemaker, Vernon
Miller James, clerk, Summer
Millard Joseph, ropemaker, Court
Mills Henry, shoe manuf. Summer
Mitchell John, laborer, Tispaquin
Mohr Peter, ropemaker, Court
Monck Caspar, ropemaker, Court
Monks John, ropemaker, Court
Moore John, ropemaker, Court
Morey C. H. shoemaker, Court
Morey G. S. shoe cutter, Vernon
Morey Wm. shoe cutter, Court
Morey Wm. jr. shoe manuf. Court
Morissey Herbert, clerk, Main
Morrissey John, seargent-at-arms, Main
Morrissey John, jr. sea captain, Main
Morrissey W. S. clerk, Main
Morse B. W. miller, Summer
Morse C. P. student, North
Morse J. A. mariner, South
Morse John F. mariner, Summer
Morton A. G. trader, Wellingsley
Morton Amasa, farmer, Chiltonville
Morton Caleb, farmer, Chiltonville
Morton E. C. farmer, Chiltonville
Morton Edwin, merchant, Wellingsley
Morton Ellis, farmer, Chiltonville
Morton Ellis 2d, farmer, Chiltonville
Morton Ezekiel, machinist, Chiltonville
Morton F. T. student, Chiltonville
Morton George W. clerk, South
Morton Henry, thimble maker, Chiltonville
Morton Howard, seaman, Wellingsley
Morton Ichabod, merchant, Wellingsley
Morton Isaac, thimble maker, Wellingsley
Morton Isaac, jr. thimble maker, Wellingsley
Morton James, merchant, South
Morton John T. seaman, Chiltonville
Morton John jr. seaman, Chiltonville
Morton Joseph, peddler, Wellingsley
Morton Josiah, seaman, Chiltonville
Morton J. T. ropemaker, Court
Morton Lemuel, seaman, Chiltonville
Morton Levi P. sea captain, Wellingsley
Morton Lewis, seaman, Wellingsley
Morton Nath'l, merchant, Wellingsley
Morton Seth, peddler, Town Square
Morton Wm. H. carpenter, Russell
Murry Jeremiah, laborer, Court
Murry John, laborer, Court

NEAL J. O. ropemaker, Court
Nelson Charles, farmer, Court
Nelson Elisha, farmer, Court
Nelson George W. farmer, Court
Nelson Samuel, wheelwright, Russell
Nelson Wm. H. merchant, Summer
Newhall George T. ropemaker, Court
Nichols Otis, farmer, Manomet Pond
Nichols Otis E. farmer, Manomet Pond
Nickerson Ebenezer, sea captain, Chiltonville
Nickerson John, merchant, High

Nickerson Thatcher, farmer, Halfway Pond
Nickerson Thatcher jr. farmer, Halfway Pond
Nickerson Wm. carpenter, Jefferson
Nickerson Wm. T. clerk, Jefferson
Nightingale Alvan, farmer, Cedarville
Nightingale S. P. seaman, Cedarville
Nightingale Stanton, farmer, Cedarville
Nightingale Wm. sea captain, Pleasant
Noyes E. P. ropemaker, Court
Noyes Joshua B. ropemaker, Court

O'BRIEN JOHN, laborer, Howland
O'Brien William, laborer, Court
Offeman Henry, ropemaker, Court
O'Hearn Patrick, ropemaker, Court
Oldham J. B. painter, Sandwich
Olney Zabon, gentleman, Market

PAINE J. S. gentleman, Middle
Parker J. S. hotel keeper, Court
Parsons G. C. sea captain, High
Parsons John, seaman, Tispaquin
Parsons Wm. W. sea captain, Tispaquin
Paty E. T. iron worker, Prospect
Paty S. W. carpenter, Wellingsley
Paty Thomas M. carpenter, Sandwich
Paulding Daniel H. iron worker, Summer
Paulding J. T. painter, Court
Paulding Sylvanus S. ropemaker, Court
Peirce A. L. laborer, Halfway Pond
Peirce Benj. laborer, Sandwich
Peirce Benj. N. mariner, Sandwich
Peirce Broach, mariner, Chiltonville
Peirce Ezra, mariner, Indian Hill
Peirce Ignatious, mariner, Franklin
Peirce Melser, mariner, Franklin
Peirce Mendell, farmer, Manomet Ponds
Peirce Richard, miller, North Green
Peirce Thomas, stave manuf. Halfway Ponds
Peirce Thos 2d, farmer, Halfway Ponds
Peirce Tilden, farmer, Court
Peirce Wm. N. mariner, S. Ponds
Peirce Wm. P. farmer, South Ponds
Peirce W. S. mariner, Sandwich
Peirce Wm. T. mariner, Sandwich
Pettee Wm. H. shoemaker, Commercial
Phinney E. L. clerk, Sandwich
Perry Sewell, shoemaker, Summer
Pember J. H. cotton batter, Summer
Pember S. overseer cotton mill, Summer
Perkins Arad, merchant, Semmer
Perkins Gideon jr. merchant, S. Green
Perkins John, deputy sheriff, Court
Perkins John F. mason, Cooper Hill
Perkins R. H. merchant, Court
Perkins Stephen, farmer, Cooper Hill
Perkins Stephen jr. shoemaker, Summer
Perkins Wm. A. farmer, Wellingsley
Peury A. H. clerk, Summer
Perry Darius, seaman, Chiltonville
Perry H. H. shoemaker, Summer
Perry Lewis, merchant, Tremont
Perry Nath'l M. landlord, Court
Perry N. B. laborer, School
Perry Wm. laborer, Commercial
Peterson C. H. farmer, Manomet Pond
Peterson, D. P. seaman, Manomet Pond
Peterson George S. box maker, High
Peterson John C. carpenter, Manomet Ponds

DIVIDENDS ADDED to the POLICY in the BERKSHIRE often exceed the premium paid; are NON-FORFEITABLE and will be redeemed in CASH ON DEMAND. (See page 50.)

Peterson John H. mason, Manomet Ponds
Peterson Lewis, hatter, Drew Place
Peterson Wm. salesman, Drew Place
Place I. H. laborer, Summer
Pool David V. master mariner, Sandwich
Pool Geo. F. clergyman, Franklin
Pool Gridley T. ropemaker, Court
Pool Joseph, shoemaker, Court
Pope Richard, seaman, Robinson
Pope Rufus, carpenter, Robinson
Pope W. W. carpenter, Robinson
Porter J. C. cotton operator, Chiltonville
Potter J. A. cotton operative, Chiltonville
Pratt J. H. W. laborer, Russell
Pratt Jos. laborer, South Pond R.
Pratt Joshua, laborer, Russell
Pratt Lucius, merchant, Court

QUINLAN DAN. ropemaker, Court
Quinlan John, ropemaker, Court
Quinlan Patrick, ropemaker, Court
Quinlan Timothy, laborer, Commercial

RAYMOND ADONIRAM, laborer, Halfway Pond
Raymond Adoniram, jr., laborer, Chiltonville
Raymond Albert, laborer, Halfway Pond
Raymond Caleb, farmer, Halfway Pond
Raymond Calvin, farmer, Halfway Pond
Raymond Charles, cabinet maker, Cole Hill
Raymond Dennis A. laborer, Halfway Pond
Raymond Edgar C. cabinet maker, Robinson
Raymond Ed. C. farmer, Halfway Pond
Raymond E. S. blacksmith, Sandwich
Raymond E. T. farmer, Halfway Pond
Raymond Geo. baker, Watson Hill
Raymond H. G. seaman, Jefferson
Raymond H. S. shoemaker, Watson Hill
Raymond I. H. farmer, Halfway Pond
Raymond J. N. laborer, Chiltonville
Raymond Lemuel, laborer, So. Pond R.
Raymond L. H. engineer, Summer
Raymond O. H. farmer, Halfway Pond
Raymond Robert H. farmer, Halfway Pond
Raymond Shadrack A. farmer, Halfway Pond
Ready James, laborer, Court
Reckenbiel Henry, ropemaker, Court
Reed James, shoemaker, Summer
Reed Joseph A. laborer, Summer
Reed Lemuel F. laborer, Summer
Reidle Sebastian, ropemaker, Court
Reider Leopold, ropemaker, Court
Reider Matthias, ropemaker, Court
Reinhart Henry, ropemaker, Court
Rich I. B. expressman, Market
Richardson Anthony, shoemaker, Commercial
Richardson C. H. conductor
Richmond J. A. sailmaker, Samaria
Rickard F. W. farmer, Sandwich
Rickard Henry, mariner, Sandwich
Rickard Lemuel, shoemaker, Russell
Rickard Samuel, truckman, Leyden
Rickard Winslow, farmer, Sandwich
Ripley Luther, truckman, North
Robbins Alex. junk dealer, Water
Robbins Augustus, clerk, Sandwich

Robbins C. A. mariner, High
Robbins Curtis, mariner, High
Robbins Daniel, ropemaker, Court
Robbins Daniel, J., Treas. Savings Bank, Court
Robbins Edmund, rev. collector, Samoset
Robbins F. H. mason, High
Robbins Henry, gentleman, Pleasant
Robbins H. H. laborer, Summer
Robbins Heman, ropemaker, High
Robbins H. C. ropemaker, High
Robbins Horatio, laborer, Summer
Robbins Isaac M. seaman, High
Robbins J. A. trader
Robbins J. L. shoemaker, High
Robbins Leavitt T. lumber dealer, Court
Robbins Leavitt T. jr., lumber dealer, Court
Robbins Levi, mariner, High
Robbins Morton, shoemaker, S. Pond R.
Robbins Wm. S. photographic artist, 51 Summer
Robertson D. b. farmer, Sandwich
Robertson S. F. farmer, Sandwich
Rogers C. H. clerk, Robinson
Rogers Ellis, laborer, Bartlett
Rogers Francis, seaman, Chiltonville
Rogers George, laborer, Robinson
Rogers George H. seaman
Rogers George L. shoemaker, High
Rogers Stephen, farmer, Summer
Rogers Sylvanus W. baggage master, Vernon
Ross J. C. mariner, Sandwich
Ross Wm. jr., mariner, Sandwich
Ruse Manuel, laborer, Emerald
Russell Elliot, bookkeeper, Russell
Russell F. H. bookkeeper, North
Russell John J. attorney, Court
Russell Nath'l, gentleman, Court
Ryder Caleb, machinist, Court
Ryder C. E. tinman, Sandwich
Ryder Daniel, carpenter, High
Ryder Ezekiel, carpenter, Wellingsley
Ryder George, rivet maker Sandwich
Ryder George S. rivet maker, Middle
Ryder Henry, carpenter, Watson Hill
Ryder Joseph, carpenter, Watson Hill
Ryder S. T. printer, Watson Hill
Ryan James, laborer, Emerald
Ryan Thomas, seaman, Emerald

SAMPSON AARON, farmer, S. Ponds
Sampson Andrew J. farmer, S. Ponds
Sampson Ellis, farmer, South Ponds
Sampson Ellis jr. farmer, South Ponds
Sampson G. G. farmer, South Pond
Sampson Hiram, farmer, South Ponds
Sampson H. M. farmer, South Ponds
Sampson John T. shoemaker, Summer
Sampson John W. farmer, South Ponds
Sampson J. M. machinist, Chiltonville
Sampson Levi, farmer, South Ponds
Sampson L. R. farmer, South Ponds
Sampson M. R. farmer, Manomet Pond
Sampson N. B. seaman, South Ponds
Sampson N. L. farmer, South Ponds
Sampson Pelham, seaman, South Ponds
Sampson Rufus, shoemaker, Chiltonville
Sampson Samuel, ropemaker, Middle
Sampson Sylvanus, farmer, South Ponds
Sampson Sylvanus 2d, seaman, S. Ponds
Sampson Thomas, farmer, Summer

J. A. JACKSON 101 COURT STREET, BOSTON, DEALER IN HATS, CAPS AND FURS.

Sampson Truman, farmer, South Ponds
Savery J. B. farmer, Manomet Pond
Savery Nehemiah, farmer, Court
Savery N. L. farmer, Court
Savery T. G. farmer, Manomet Pond
Savery W. T. painter, Willard Place
Savery Winsor, farmer, Court
Savery Winslow T. farmer, Court
Schade Conrad, ropemaker, Court
Scheick Philip, ropemaker, Court
Scheil Peter, ropemaker, Court
Schmidt Peter, ropemaker, Court
Scott A. truckman, Sandwich
Scott Wm. S. seaman, Green
Sears Andrew C. laborer, Sandwich
Sears A. T. laborer, Sandwich
Sears Augustus, farmer, South Ponds
Sears Benj. W. laborer, Sandwich
Sears Daniel, laborer, Court
Sears E. G. shoemaker, Obery
Sears E. W. laborer, Chiltonville
Sears H. B. seaman, Sandwich
Sears Horatio, laborer, Obery
Sears H. N. laborer, Obery
Sears J. F. laborer, South Ponds
Sears J. T. laborer, South Ponds
Sears T. D. merchant, Sandwich
Sears William, light keeper, Gurnet
Sears Winslow, farmer, Sandwich
Scarson Robert, farmer, Cooper Hill
Seavey David L. hotel keeper, North
Sever Wm. R. County treasurer, Russell
Seymore H. I. seaman, Summer
Shaw DeForrest, laborer, Summer
Shaw Eleazer, mason, Summer
Shaw Gilbert, teamster, Summer
Shaw Ichabod, blacksmith, Court
Shaw Lyman E. barber, Court
Shaw J. B. blacksmith, Summer
Shaw Samuel, clerk, Summer
Sherman E. C. Pres. O. C. N. Bank, North
Sherman Elijah, operative, Chiltonville
Sherman Everett F. merchant, Court
Sherman James M. merchant, Middle
Sherman L. L. shoemaker, South
Sherman Reuben, farmer, Court
Sherman Wm. D. farmer, Pleasant
Sherman Winslow B. laborer, South
Shneider H. D. ropemaker, Court
Shubert John, shoemaker, Robinson
Simes Joseph, gentle'n, Manomet Ponds
Simmons Albert, truckman, Middle
Simmons George, truckman, Russell
Simmons George A. truckman, LeBaron
Simmons James, sea captain, Sandwich
Simmons James H. seaman, Summer
Simmons Wm. W. master mariner, Sandwich
Smith Elijah B. carpenter, Pleasant
Smith Isaiah C. farmer, Cedarville
Smith John, periodical depot, Vernon
Smith Peter W. rigger, Summer
Smith Thomas, ropemaker, Court
Smith Thomas C. sea captain, Chiltonville
Smith Wm. seaman, Cedarville
Smythe Joseph, shoe cutter, Cole's Hill
Snow D. F. station master, Court
Snow Leonard, laborer, School
Snow P. M. seaman, Long Pond
Southworth Francis, mariner, Prospect
Spear J. H. ropemaker, Court
Spear Thomas, nailer, High

Spear S. T. shoemaker, Bartlett
Spooner Bourne, treasurer cordage mills, Court
Spooner C. W. gentleman, Court
Spooner Ephraim, clerk, Samaria
Spooner H. N. ropemaker, Court
Spooner James, laborer, North
Spooner John A. clerk, Court
Spooner J. W. clerk, North
Spooner Nath'l, master mariner, Court
Spooner Nath'l B. clerk, Robinson
Spooner Thomas, farmer, Manomet Ponds
Spooner Wm. F. laborer, Court
Standish J. C. blacksmith, Russell
Standish Joshua, blacksmith, Russell
Standish Miles, blacksmith, Russell
Standish W. B. peddler, Sandwich
Steidle J. S. ropemaker, Court
Stephens Henry, ropemaker, Court
Stephens Lemuel, farmer, Fremont
Stephens T. A. engineer, Vernon
Stephens William, farmer, Fremont
Stevens Henry, ropemaker, Court
Stevens Zaccheus, farmer, Sandwich
Steward John, laborer, Court
Steward William, farmer, Obery
Stillman James E. brakeman, Emerald
Stillman J. M. laborer, LeBaron
Stoddard C. B. book-keeper, Court
Stoddard Christopher, peddler, School
Stoddard F. R. clerk, Court
Stoddard Isaac N. Cashier P. N. Bank, Court
Stoddard John T. Cashier P. N. Bank, Court
Stokes Charles, ropemaker, Court
Stone James, truckman, Spring
Straffin Wm. ropemaker, Spring
Strong B. O. merchant, Court
Sturtevant John S. laborer, Court
Sturtevant Joseph A. laborer, Court
Swan George
Sweet S. R. painter, Watson Hill
Swift Albert, mariner, Cedarville
Swift Benjamin, machinist, Leyden
Swift Edmund E. peddler, Chiltonville
Swift Eleazer E. mariner, Cedarville
Swift Elisha B. mariner, Cedarville
Swift George, mariner, Chiltonville
Swift Henry, mariner, Chiltonville
Swift Henry E. mariner, Chiltonville
Swift H. W. mariner, Cedarville
Swift I. B. mariner, Chiltonville
Swift John, blacksmith, Sandwich
Swift L. L. clerk, Chiltonville
Swift Nathaniel, farmer, Cedarville
Swift Nath'l jr. farmer, Cedarville
Swift Robert F. mariner, Cedarville
Swift Seth E. sea captain, Cedarville
Swift S. H. mariner, Cedarville
Swift Warren B. mariner, Cedarville
Swift Wm. mariner, South
Swinborn Robert, mariner, Dutch's Lane
Sylvester James A. laborer, Water
Sylvester Solomon, mariner, South

TALBOT SAMUEL, baker, Market
Taylor John, ironworker, Summer
Taylor Joseph, laborer, Leyden
Taylor Joseph jr. mariner, South Ponds
Terry Burgess, machinist, Chiltonville
Thomas Adoniram, farmer, West Dist.
Thomas Alanson, farmer, West District

Policy Holders in the BERKSHIRE LIFE INSURANCE COMPANY of Pittsfield, Mass., DO NOT FORFEIT THEIR POLICIES by reason of FAILURE TO PAY their premiums. (See page 50.)

Thomas Gamaliel, mariner, West Dist.
Thomas Joab, farmer, Court
Thomas Joshua B. attorney, Summer
Thomas Nahum, mariner, Summer
Thomas Wm. attorney, Court
Thomas Wm. H. photographer, Summer
Thrasher George, farmer, Cedarville
Thrasher George jr. farmer, Cedarville
Thrasher J. A. farmer, Cedarville
Thrasher Jonathan, farmer, Cedarville
Thrasher Joshua, laborer, Middle
Thrasher J. T. farmer, Cedarville
Thrasher L. W. farmer, Cedarville
Thrasher Reuben, farmer, Cedarville
Thurber J. D. clerk, Court
Timmerhoff W. ropemaker, Court
Tomlinson Russell, clergyman, Middle
Torrence N. S. mariner, Water
Torrence Robert, laborer, Water
Towns J. F. truckman, Tispaquin
Tribble James, mason, Tispaquin
Tribble Lorenzo, painter, Russell
Tribble W. B. painter, Samaria Place
Tripp William G. woolen operator, Court
Turner David, block maker, Leyden
Turner Ezekiel C. merchant, Sandwich
Turner F. W. mariner, Court

VALLER A. R. farmer, Cedarville
Valler Silas jr, farmer, Cedarville
Valler Simeon, farmer, Cedarville
Valler S. J. farmer, Cedarville
Valler Sylvanus, farmer, Cedarville
Valler Sylvester H. farmer, Cedarville
Valler T. J. farmer, Cedarville
Vaughan Ansel H. farmer, Manomet P.
Vaughan E. B. H. seaman, Manomet P.
Vaughan Elisha, mariner, Manomet P.
Vaughan F. H. wounded soldier, Chiltonville
Vaughan Leander, laborer, Eel River
Vaughan Lemuel, mariner, Chiltonville
Vaughan P. C. W. farmer, Chiltonville
Vaughan W. C. farmer, Chiltonville
Virgin John, clerk, Summer
Virgin G. W. gentleman, Summer
Voughtlander Herman, ropemaker, Court

WADE JOHN, mariner, Water
Wade P. S. mariner, Emerald
Wadsworth L. S. mariner, Chiltonville
Wadsworth S. D. mariner, Chiltonville
Wadsworth Wait, farmer, Court
Wadsworth W. L. mariner, Chiltonville
Warren Winslow, physician, Main
Washburn C. H. supt. gas works, Summer
Washburn Ephraim, farmer, W. District
Washburn Seth, farmer, West District
Watson A. M. mariner, Clark's Island
Watson Benj. M. revenue collector, Summer
Watson Edward W. farmer, Clark's Isl'd
Watson E. W. 2d, farmer, Clark's Island
Watson James M. farmer, Clark's Island
Watson N. B. mariner, Clark's Island
Wells W. G. S. merchant, Court
Westgate Charles, truckman, Court
Westgate C. H. laborer, Court
Weston C. H. mariner, Cole's Hill

Weston Coomer, horticulturist, Court
Weston E. C. machinist, Drew Place
Weston F. H. seaman, Shady Nook
Weston Geo. F. postmaster, Prospect
Weston Harvey, mariner, Sandwich
Weston Harvey W. expressman, Leyden
Weston Henry, carpenter, Samaria Place
Weston J. L. carpenter, Prospect
Weston Miles S. clerk, Court
Weston Wm. carpenter, North
Whall Wm. seaman, Summer
White J. B. carpenter, Summer
White T. S. Supt. Samoset Mills, Summer
Whiting Adoniram, farmer, Chiltonville
Whiting Adoniram jr. mariner, Chiltonville
Whiting Albert, mariner, Chiltonville
Whiting Benj. jr. farmer, Chiltonville
Whiting Elisha jr. farmer, Wellingsley
Whiting Ellis, farmer, Wellingsley
Whiting Ellis jr. farmer, Wellingsley
Whiting George, baker, Market
Whiting George A. stable keeper, High
Whiting Henry, mariner, Sandwich
Whiting Henry jr. mariner, Sandwich
Whiting J. B. barber, Town Square
Whiting Levi, mariner, Chiltonville
Whiting Pelham, farmer, Sandwich
Whiting Winslow, farmer, Chiltonville
Whitman, Wm. H. clerk of courts, Court
Whitmore Benj. mariner, Manomet Pond
Whitmore H. C. mariner, Manomet Pond
Whittee J. H. thread maker, Summer
Whitten Abraham, mariner, Leyden
Whitten Chas, farmer, Court
Whitten Chas. jr., carpenter, Court
Whitten F. L. mariner, Leyden
Whitten Horace C. tinsmith, Mayflower
Whitten S. M. farmer, Court
Whoorwell Wm. R. wool operative, Court
Williams J. B. iron worker, Summer
Williams Wm. rivet maker, Summer
Wilson David, twine manuf. Court
Wilson John B. cabinet maker, High
Winsor J. M. mariner, Court
Wood Alba, farmer, S. Pond Road
Wood A. N. farmer, S. Pond Road
Wood Alex. farmer, S. Pond Road
Wood Eliab, caulker, Sandwich
Wood Geo. F. sea captain, Sandwich
Wood Isaac L. mason, Russell
Wood Israel, laborer, Water
Wood Lemuel R. mariner, Sandwich
Wood L. F. mariner, Sandwich
Wood Nath'l, gentlemen, Summer
Wood Nath'l, jr., agent zinc tack manuf. Willard P'l
Wood O. T. supt alms house, Summer
Wood S. N. laborer, Summer
Wood Willard, clerk, Russell
Wright C. F. farmer, Manomet Pond
Wright Horatio, farmer, Sandwich
Wright Joseph, jr., mariner, Russell
Wright Joshua, laborer, Summer
Wright Otis, farmer, Cushman
Wright Winslow A. farmer, Chiltonville

ZAHN VALENTINE, ropemaker, Court

J. A. JACKSON, 101 COURT STREET, BOSTON, DEALER IN HATS, CAPS, AND FURS.

Plympton General Directory.

ATWOOD BENJAMIN S. box maker

BEATON HENRY F. shoemaker
Billings James, shoemaker
Billings Nathan D. shoemaker
Bisbee Elijah, farmer
Blanchard Horatio W. shoemaker
Blanchard Wm. W. shoemaker
Bonney George H. painter
Bonney James S. box maker
Bonney Wm. L. box maker
Bradford Gideon, shoemaker
Bradford Henry A. trader
Bradford Joseph W. box maker
Bradford Samuel N. shoemaker
Brewster Pelham, farmer
Briggs Herschell E. shoemaker
Briggs Lewis H. shoemaker
Briggs Nathan S. farmer
Briggs Seneca, farmer
Bryant Calvin M. mariner
Bryant Lemuel, section master
Bryant William S. farmer
Bryant Zenas, farmer

CHANDLER EDWARD, shoemaker
Chandler M. E. shoemaker
Churchill Albert S. shoemaker
Churchill Alexander, farmer
Churchill Alexander L. engineer
Churchill Ansel, jr., laborer
Churchill Bart C. farmer
Churchill Daniel, hoopmaker
Churchill Edmund F. shoemaker
Churchill Harvey, farmer
Churchill Isaiah, engraver
Churchill Isaiah F. shoemaker
Churchill Josiah, tack maker
Churchill Josiah S. shoemaker
Churchill Leander S. laborer
Churchill Lemuel P. shoemaker
Churchill Oliver, farmer
Churchill Simeon, stonecutter
Churchill Spencer, blacksmith
Churchill Timothy, farmer
Clark Hiram H. farmer
Clark Thomas H. farmer
Cobb Lemuel, farmer
Cobb Lemuel, jr., farmer
Conaway John, laborer
Cashman Zenas, harness maker

DARLING CHARLES, shoemaker
Drew Stephen, shoemaker

ELLIS EDSON, carpenter
Ellis Gustavus B. mariner
Ellis Henry K. box manuf.
Ellis James C. box manuf.
Ellis Joel, teamer
Ellis John P. shoemaker
Ellis Willard, farmer
Englestedt Charles W. mariner

FARRAR FRANKLIN P. tack manuf.
Fuller Amos, carpenter
Fuller Bildad, farmer
Fuller Charles A. sawyer
Fuller Earl, farmer
Fuller Ephraim, shoemaker
Fuller George B. peddler
Fuller Joseph H. carpenter
Fuller Lafayette, shoemaker
Fuller Lewis W. laborer
Fuller Philemau, laborer
Fuller Solomon, farmer
Fuller William, shoemaker
Fuller Zebedee C. stone cutter

GLASS GEORGE W. shoemaker
Glass Otis W. shoemaker
Glass Zenas T. peddler
Griffith Ephraim, moulder
Gurney Theron J. shoemaker*

HALEY EDWARD M. laborer
Haley William, shoemaker
Hammond Josiah P. laborer
Hammond Josiah S. physician
Harlow Jabez
Harrub George W. farmer
Harrub James M. trader
Hartford Joseph W. shoemaker
Harvey Alexander, machinist
Hayward Martin, farmer
Holmes George W. carpenter
Holmes Ira S. shoemaker
Holmes Martin E. shoemaker
Holmes Sampson, farmer

LASHURES ROBERT W. operator in Factory
Leach Ebenezer, farmer
Leach Thomas M. operator
Lobdell George B. jr., shoemaker
Lobdell Isaac F. shoemaker
Lobdell Orlando P. farmer
Loring Ezekiel
Loring Isaac, machinist
Loring Thomas E. peddler
Lovell James B. farmer
Lucas Martin B. shoemaker
Lucas Nathaniel, blacksmith
Lucas William H. shoemaker

MORSE CHARLES S. lumberman

NYE JOSEPH B. shoemaker

PACKARD PEREZ, shoemaker
Parker Gustavus, manufacturer
Parker Ira, shovel maker
Parker Oliver, shovel manuf.
Parker Zacchens, trader
Patten Moses, clergyman
Perkins Charles H. farmer
Perkins Edmund, peddler
Perkins Jonathan B. farmer
Perkins Josiah, blacksmith
Perkins Martin, carpenter
Perkins Nathan, carpenter
Perkins William, farmer

ANNUAL CASH DIVIDENDS in the BERKSHIRE LIFE INS. CO., Pittsfield, Mass. Boston Office 95 1-2 Washington St. (See page 50.)

Perkins Wilson, laborer
Phinney Beri F. laborer
Phinney Clark W. laborer
Phinney Otis, laborer
Phinney Otis W. mariner
Pope Asa F. farmer
Pratt Alphonzo, laborer
Pratt Joshua H. farmer

RANDALL GEORGE W. trader
Randall Thomas S. farmer
Randall William L. trader
Ransom Freeman B. shoemaker
Ransom John, shoemaker
Reed Joseph B. shoemaker
Rickard Giles, laborer
Rickard Isaac, farmer
Rickard James C. laborer
Rickard Jonathan, farmer
Rickard Martin, tack maker
Rickard Simeon, watchmaker
Rickard Warren, tack maker
Ripley Charles E. shoemaker
Ripley Charles H. shoemaker
Ripley Ephraim C. farmer
Ripley Ezekiel, shoemaker
Ripley Joseph S. shoecutter
Ripley Josiah W. shoemaker
Ripley Thomas S. farmer
Rogers Tully, peddler

SAMPSON JAMES L. laborer
Sampson Zebechial, physician
Sears Allen, laborer
Sears Henry A. laborer
Sherman Algernon S. farmer
Sherman Asa, farmer
Sherman Charles, blacksmith
Sherman Edward S. farmer
Sherman George W. carpenter
Sherman John, farmer
Sherman Joseph, carpenter
Sherman Nathaniel, farmer
Simmons Noah, shoemaker
Smith Martin, shoemaker
Soule Adoniram, farmer

Soule Francis, farmer
Soule William H. gentleman
Standish Thomas C. farmer
Sturtevant Isaac R. farmer
Sturtevant Lemuel, laborer
Sturtevant Samuel N. laborer

TARRY JOHN C. baker
Taylor Charles K. farmer
Taylor William, dyer
Thomas George W. shoemaker
Thomas Henry L. shoemaker
Thompson Amasa, farmer
Thompson Joshua C. farmer
Thompson Reuben, farmer

WASHBURN OSCAR E. shoemaker
Washburn Zenas M. shoemaker
Waterman James, laborer
Weston Daniel, laborer
Weston Lewis, farmer
Weston Lewis P. shoemaker
White Darius, farmer
White Ezra, shoemaker
White William S. shoemaker
Wilber Reuben A. overseer
Wilber Seth, farmer
Wright Alonzo, shoemaker
Wright Barzillai E. farmer
Wright Daniel D. farmer
Wright Eben, farmer
Wright Eben, jr., shoemaker
Wright Edward S. shoemaker
Wright Frederick, laborer
Wright George E. farmer
Wright Henry H. tack maker
Wright John B. shoemaker
Wright Newland H. laborer
Wright Roland A. shoemaker
Wright Rufus, farmer
Wright Rufus F. box maker
Wright Samuel C. laborer
Wright Winslow, farmer
Wright Winslow B. shoemaker
Wright William H. H. shoemaker

J. A. JACKSON 101 COURT STREET, BOSTON, DEALER IN HATS CAPS AND FURS.

Rochester General Directory.

ALLEY CHARLES H. farmer
Allen Daniel, master mariner
Allen Joseph, farmer
Ashley George H. mariner
Ashley Rufus M. mariner
Atwood Elias, cooper
Atwood Thornton, cooper
Atwood Warren, cooper

BARRETT WILLIAM, butcher
Bates Elijah, farmer
Bates Ephraim, farmer
Bates Rowland B. master mariner
Bearse Gershom, shoemaker
Bennett Henry H. farmer,
Bennett John, farmer
Bennett John G. farmer
Bennett Michael, farmer
Benson Benjamin, mariner
Benson Charles S. shoemaker
Benson Ephraim, farmer
Benson John A. master mariner
Benson Joseph D. farmer
Benson Rufus, farmer
Benson William, farmer
Bisbee Josiah, farmer
Bishop Alvin, farmer
Bishop Charles H. farmer
Bishop Israel S. farmer
Bishop Joseph E. farmer
Bishop Micah S. farmer
Blackmer Charles M. farmer
Blackmer Garrison B. farmer
Blackmer John, farmer
Bliss Alexander, carpenter
Bliss Ezra S. farmer
Bolton Enos, farmer
Bonney George, farmer
Bonney Nathaniel, master mariner
Bonney Selim, farmer
Bourne Thomas, farmer
Bourne William, master mariner
Bradford Henry C. farmer
Braley Abner, farmer
Braley Charles A. farmer
Braley Francis W. mariner
Braley George F. mariner
Braley Isaac V. mariner
Braley John, farmer
Braley Joseph G. farmer
Braley Lorenzo D. cigar manuf.
Braley Salmon, farmer
Braley Solomon R. shoemaker
Braley Samuel T. master mariner
Braley Thomas L. mariner
Brett Pliny, clergyman
Brightman William T. farmer
Bumpus Ansel, farmer
Bumpus Elisha M. blacksmith
Bumpus Samuel, cooper
Bumpus Samuel S. mariner

CHASE ELIAS S. farmer
Church Charles H. F. blacksmith
Church Henry W. farmer
Church Joseph E. farmer

Church Joseph W. farmer
Church Lemuel, farmer and merchant
Church Walter S. farmer and carpenter
Church Walter S. jr., mariner
Church William H. farmer
Clark Charles H. farmer
Clark Ira, farmer
Clark James H. farmer
Clark John H. farmer
Clark John H. A. farmer
Clark Joseph, farmer
Clark Nathan, jr., farmer
Clark Peleg, farmer
Clark Peleg B. farmer
Clark Peleg W. farmer
Clark Thomas L. farmer
Clark Willard, farmer
Clapp Joseph H. farmer
Clapp Nathaniel, farmer
Clapp William, farmer
Cobb Timothy, farmer
Cobb Watson T. farmer
Cole Isaac, mariner
Cole John, carpenter
Cole Joseph, marble worker
Cole Theodore W. marble worker
Crapo Francis N. farmer
Crapo Humphrey R. farmer
Crapo John A. farmer
Crapo Luther, farmer
Crapo Philip, farmer
Cromwell Joseph H. mariner
Cowing Charles E. farmer
Cowing Jonathan F. master mariner
Cowing Reuben B. farmer
Cowing Samuel, farmer
Cowing Seth, farmer
Cowing William H. carpenter
Cushing James R. clergyman
Cushman Henry P. mariner
Cushman Jesse M. merchant

DAHONEY DANIEL, laborer
Damon Charles H. painter
Davis Zenas, stone cutter
Dexter John G. master mariner
Dexter Prince, farmer
Damon John B. master mariner
Damon John B. jr., farmer
Douglass Barnabas N. farmer
Douglass James O. farmer
Douglass William M. farmer
Drake Alvin, farmer
Durfee Nathan W. farmer

ELLIOT SAMUEL, farmer
Ellis Josiah B. nailer
Ellis Thomas, farmer and mill sawyer

FIELDS DELUCE S.

GAMMONS EBENEZER K. farmer
Gammons Ebenezer K. jr., mariner
Gammons Ephraim K. farmer
Gammons Noble B. farmer
Gerrish George I. farmer

The terms for ENDOWMENT, and TEN ANNUAL LIFE POLICIES in the BERKSHIRE are peculiarly favorable, and rates lower than in any Note Company.   29   (See page 50.)

Gifford Abraham, mill sawyer
Gifford Hendrick, mariner
Gifford James, farmer
Gifford Nathan N. farmer & mill sawyer
Gurney Samuel N. nailer

HALL CLARK M. farmer
Hall Daniel H. farmer
Hall George, farmer
Haskell George W. farmer
Haskell John C. civil engineer
Haskell Joseph, physician and surgeon
Haskell Wm. C. farmer and mill sawyer
Haskell Wm. P. farmer
Haskins Charles F. mariner
Haskins Charles H. farmer
Haskins Rufus T. mariner
Hathaway Elnathan, farmer
Hathaway George W. farmer
Hathaway Jonathan, farmer
Hathaway Judah, mariner
Hathaway William H. mariner
Healy George F. trader
Hewes William L. farmer
Horr Benjamin, farmer
Humphrey George W. farmer

JEFFERSON SALEM, farmer

KING NATHANIEL, farmer
King Theophilus, merchant

LEONARD EDWIN, clergyman
Leach Lambert, mason
Leonard Theodore W. merchant
Lewis David, farmer and miller
Lewis David S. miller
Look Jacob, mill sawyer
Look James H. farmer and mill sawyer
Look James H. jr. farmer

MAXIM CHARLES M. farmer
Maxim Hosea
Maxim Marcus, farmer
Mendell Alpheus, farmer
Mendell Benjamin, farmer
Mendell Benjamin W. farmer
Mendell John, mariner
Mendell Noah F. farmer
Morris Oren, laborer
Morse Andrew
Morse John N. farmer
Morse Joseph G. machinist
Morse Josiah, farmer
Morse Josiah, jr., teamer
Morse Nahum F. farmer
Morse Newbury, farmer
Morse Thomas N. farmer
Morton Benjamin W. carpenter

NICKERSON FREDERICK W. nailer
Nickerson Hiram, nailer
Nickerson Israel F. trader
Niles Seth, farmer
Nye Charles C. cooper
Nye Elisha, farmer
Nye Henry C. farmer
Nye John L. cooper
Nye Richard B. cooper

PAINE GARDNER, carpenter
Paine James, mariner
Parlow Abraham B. farmer

Parlow Nathaniel, farmer
Peirce Dennis, farmer
Peirce Dennis A. trader
Peirce Eli, farmer
Peirce Eliphalet, farmer
Peirce George, clergyman
Peirce George H. shoemaker
Peirce John W. farmer
Peirce Joshua D. mariner
Peirce Josiah, farmer
Peirce Lucius E. farmer
Peirce Moses W. nailer
Peirce Robert, clergyman
Perkins Elbridge G. blacksmith
Perkins John, farmer
Perkins Leonard, laborer
Perkins Luke, farmer
Perkins Luke T. farmer
Perkins Thos. P. W. blacksmith & trader
Perry Andrew F. mariner
Perry Isaac F. B. peddler
Perry James E. E. farmer
Perry John O. mariner
Perry Jonathan, farmer

RANDALL CALVIN H. farmer
Randall George H. farmer
Randall George G. master mariner
Randall Jeremiah, farmer
Randall Leander, farmer
Randall Robert C. prop'r boarding house
Rankin Alexander H. teacher
Rankin William, farmer
Raymond Thomas, nailer
Reckard Ansel M. farmer
Reynolds Stephen R. farmer
Ricketson Charles, farmer
Ricketson Paul, farmer
Riley James, laborer
Rogers Mason, painter
Rounseville Alden, miller & mill sawyer
Rounseville Alden, jr. miller & mill sawyer
Ruggles James, farmer
Ryder Allen D. master mariner
Ryder Barnabas C. wheelwright
Ryder James H. mill sawyer
Ryder John S. farmer
Ryder Madison W. mill sawyer
Ryder Martin, farmer
Ryder Martin L. farmer

SAVERY RUFUS, farmer
Sears Nathaniel, carpenter
Sears Stephen C. farmer
Sears William, farmer
Shaw Lewis, farmer
Shaw William E. farmer
Sherman Bartlett, shoemaker
Sherman Dennis, farmer
Sherman Edward A. farmer
Sherman George B. master mariner
Sherman James B. shoemaker
Sherman James G. B. carpenter
Sherman John W. merchant
Sherman Kelly, farmer
Sherman Leonard, farmer
Sherman Martin, farmer
Sherman Nathaniel B. farmer
Sherman Nehemiah, shoemaker
Sherman Otis, carpenter
Sherman Thomas, carpenter
Sherman Thomas A. carpenter

J. A. JACKSON, 101 COURT STREET, BOSTON, DEALER IN HATS, CAPS, AND FURS.

ROCHESTER DIRECTORY.   111

Sherman William F. carpenter
Shockley Joseph, farmer
Shurtleff Alvah T. cooper
Silveira Jose, farmer
Smellie James, farmer
Smellie Walter, mill sawyer
Smellie William H. blacksmith
Smith Consider, farmer
Smith George F. clergyman
Smith Royal, farmer
Snell Isaiah, shoemaker
Snell Otis H. mariner
Snell Otis P. mariner
Sparrow Josiah, wheelwright
Spooner Abraham, laborer
Spooner Edward P. farmer
Spooner Noah, farmer
Staples Samuel B. miller & shingle sawyer
Stetson William, farmer
Stevens Henry, carpenter
Stevens John, farmer
Stevens Joseph B. carpenter
Stevens Joseph C. farmer
Stevens Micah W. mill sawyer
Sturtevant Charles, physician & surgeon
Sturtevant Charles H. mill sawyer

Sturtevant John B. farmer
Sturtevant William, master mariner
Surrey Henry, mariner
Swift Pelham E. wheelwright

TABER CHARLES, mariner
Taylor Benjamin, farmer
Taylor Edward B. farmer
Thompson Zebulon H. marble worker
Tillson Hiram, peddler
Townsend Silas
Tripp Handell J. mill sawyer
True Melvin H. farmer

VAUGHN HENRY L. carpenter
Vaughn Josiah D. carpenter

WALDRON GEORGE W. farmer
Waldron Hiram, farmer
West Benjamin H. carpenter
West Charles G. mariner
Wilbur Isaiah, farmer
Wilbur Isaiah T. farmer
Wild Addison A. farmer
Wrightington Orlando, laborer
Wrightington Richard, farmer

Scituate General Directory.

ALLEN GEORGE O. farmer
Allen George M. farmer
Allen Milner J.
Allen Wm. P. trader
Anderson Alexander, mariner
Anderson Alexander B. draw tender
Andrews Christopher A. A. laborer
Arnold George, shoemaker

BAILEY CHARLES E. trader
Bailey Edwin, farmer
Bailey George W. shoe manuf.
Bailey James A. shoemaker
Bailey James J. coppersmith
Bailey John W. farmer
Bailey Joseph, carpenter
Bailey Jotham W. shoe manuf.
Bailey Noah C. shoemaker
Bailey Sewall, farmer
Bailey Thomas O. shoemaker
Bailey Thomas T. carpenter
Bailey Thomas T. trader
Bailey Waterman, trader
Bailey William C. mariner
Barker Samuel P. jr., farmer
Bates Andrew, shoemaker
Bates Caleb, fisherman
Bates Caleb, 2d, fisherman

Bates Charles, farmer
Bates Coleman, fisherman
Bates George H. farmer
Bates Joseph N. fisherman
Bates Peter E. fisherman
Bates Reuben C. fisherman
Bates Reuben S. shoemaker
Bates Thomas C. fisherman
Bates William, fisherman
Beal Caleb, mason
Beal John, farmer
Bearse Ebenezer, laborer
Bearse Ebenezer, jr., peddler
Bearse Tobias, shoemaker
Bowditch Edwin, stage driver
Bonney Edward H. fish dealer
Bonney Sylvanus R. painter
Bradford Charles, shoemaker
Bradford John, shoemaker
Briggs Albert K. farmer
Briggs Barnabas W. shipwright
Briggs David, farmer
Briggs James S. shipwright
Briggs Joseph O. shipwright
Briggs Otis, farmer
Briggs Shadrach, farmer
Broughton Daniel, mariner
Brown Benjamin, laborer

DIVIDENDS ADDED to the POLICY in the BERKSHIRE often exceed the premium paid; are NON-FORFEITABLE and will be redeemed in CASH ON DEMAND.   (See page 50.)

Brown Benjamin, jr., trader
Brown Charles, laborer
Brown Charles E. mason
Brown Elisha L. shoemaker
Brown George H. ship carpenter
Brown George W. mariner
Brown Henry, shoemaker
Brown Henry L. shoemaker
Brown John, copper
Brown Joseph, farmer
Brown Joseph, jr., shoemaker
Brown Lewis, shoemaker
Brown Moses L. caulker and graver
Brown Samuel, farmer
Brown Warren L. shoemaker
Brown William, farmer
Brown William F. farmer
Bruce James R. mariner
Bryant Gridley, architect
Burrows William T. stage driver
Butterly Christopher, mosser
Butterly Joseph, mosser

CHANDLER JUDAH, gentleman
Chandler Seth, blacksmith
Chubbuck Francis G. mason
Clapp Albert, farmer
Clapp Alfred, mason
Clapp Allen, farmer
Clapp Caleb N. mariner
Clapp Chandler, farmer
Clapp Charles W. shoemaker
Clapp Elijah, blacksmith
Clapp Elijah T. blacksmith
Clapp Harvey, farmer
Clapp Henry, trader
Clapp Henry T. miller
Clapp Joseph, laborer
Clapp Luther L. shoemaker
Clapp Rufus, farmer
Clapp Thomas, farmer
Clapp William O. clerk
Cole Andrew, shipwright
Cole Augustus, farmer
Cole Augustus, jr., farmer
Cole Enoch, farmer
Cole George E. farmer
Cole George H. shipwright
Cole Henry O. engineer
Cole Joseph O. clerk
Cole Thomas O. carpenter
Coleman Joseph, shoemaker
Coleman Moses B. carpenter
Coleman Moses R. master mariner
Conroy John, mosser
Cook Francis, mariner
Cook Russell, trader
Cook Samuel W. shoemaker
Conant Thomas, clergyman
Cordis Thomas F.
Cottle Charles, miller
Cudworth James W. farmer
Cudworth Israel, carpenter
Cummings Edward, mosser
Curtis Asa F. farmer
Curtis Eli, farmer
Curtis George L. carpenter
Curtis Harvey, farmer
Curtis Henry N. shoemaker
Curtis Job E. shoemaker
Curtis Lewis N. teamster
Curtis Luther, farmer
Curtis Norton, shoemaker

Curtis Roswell, shoemaker
Curtis Rufus, peddler
Curtis Thomas, farmer
Curtis Shadrach B. mariner
Curtis Shadrach B. jr., farmer
Cushing Frederick, shipwright
Cushing John P. farmer
Cushing Nathaniel G. farmer

DAMON CALEB L. shoemaker
Damon Charles H. farmer
Damon Davis J. farmer
Damon Franklin, lumber dealer
Damon George W. farmer
Damon Henry, farmer
Damon Henry B. farmer
Damon Henry C. farmer
Damon Isaac B. farmer
Damon Israel, farmer
Damon James, farmer
Damon John, farmer
Damon John B. farmer
Damon John M. farmer
Damon Joseph, farmer
Damon Marcus M. mason
Damon Marsena, shipwright
Damon Virgil, blacksmith
Damon William, farmer
Doane Horace, farmer
Doherty Cornelius, farmer
Doherty George, mosser
Doherty John, mosser
Dolby James T. shoemaker
Dolby John, carpenter
Drew Joseph S. shipwright
Drew Theodore C. clerk
Dunbar Atwood L. laborer
Dunbar Cyrus H. mariner
Dunn Michael, mosser
Dunn Patrick, mosser

EDSON JAMES, shoemaker
Elliott George W. slop work agent
Ellms Charles, farmer
Ellms Charles O. farmer
Ellms Daniel. farmer
Ellms John B. farmer
Ellms Joseph, farmer
Ellms Melzar J. peddler
Ellms Noah, laborer
Ellms Otis J. farmer
Ellms Robert, farmer
Ellms William, fisherman

FARRAR ALLEN, farmer
Farrar Allen, jr., laborer
Ferguson Charles M. shoemaker
Ferguson William, farmer
Fittz Luke G. shoemaker
Fogg George P. farmer
Ford Daniel, trader
Ford Peleg, shipwright

GANNETT FREEMAN, farmer
Gannett Freeman H. farmer
Gannett Joseph, farmer
Gardner Enoch C. painter
Gardner Frederick U. shoemaker
Gilbert Alanson A. C. merchant
Glines Isaac, farmer
Gray Anthony, shoemaker

HATCH DANIEL, jr., farmer

J. A. JACKSON 101 COURT STREET, BOSTON, DEALER IN HATS CAPS AND FURS.

Hatch Thomas M. farmer
Hammond Frederick, sexton
Harrub Darius, farmer,
Hayes Oliver P. carpenter
Hayward John, painter
Hayward Ward L. painter
Hayward William S. clergyman
Higgins George O.
Hinckley Eben, mariner
Hoar Matthew, mosser
Hoar Richard, mosser
Holmes Lewis, clergyman
Hobson Andrew J. carpenter
Hunt Samuel J. stage driver
Hunt William E. shoemaker
Hunt Howland L. shoemaker
Hyland Isaiah, mariner
Hyland Peleg, shoemaker
Hyland Samuel, farmer

JACKSON CHARLES H. shipwright
Jackson Henry T. farmer
Jackson Roland, farmer
Jackson William T. shipwright
James Edward, stage driver
Jenkins Caleb M. shipwright
Jenkins Calvin, shoemaker
Jenkins David S. farmer
Jenkins David S. jr. miller
Jenkins Davis, farmer
Jenkins Edmund R. farmer
Jenkins Elijah,
Jenkins Harvey S. farmer
Jenkins Noah, farmer
Jenkins Perez, master mariner
Jenkins Perez T. farmer
Jones Ezekiel
Jones Ezekiel jr. post master
Jelloe Moses, mosser

LANGDON DANIEL, cooper
Lauders Edmund, tailor
Lee Francis B. carpenter
Lee George C. carpenter
Lee Stephen D. trader
Litchfield Abner, farmer
Litchfield Addison J. boat fisher
Litchfield B. B. Winsor, farmer
Litchfield Brigham D. farmer
Litchfield Caleb L. shoemaker
Litchfield Enoch, farmer
Litchfield Francis M. shoemaker
Litchfield Freeman, farmer
Litchfield Galen W. shoemaker
Litchfield George B. shoemaker
Litchfield George E. shoemaker
Litchfield George W. shoemaker
Litchfield Harvey, shipwright
Litchfield Harvey W. artist
Litchfield Horace, carpenter
Litchfield Hosea, farmer
Litchfield Howard, mariner
Litchfield Hubbard, farmer
Litchfield Ira, carpenter
Litchfield Isaac, blacksmith
Litchfield Israel, shoemaker
Litchfield James, farmer
Litchfield James 2d, shoemaker
Litchfield James C. carpenter
Litchfield James S. shoemaker
Litchfield Jarius, farmer
Litchfield John L. shoemaker
Litchfield Joseph, farmer

Litchfield Joseph H. farmer
Litchfield Joseph L. shoemaker
Litchfield Joseph W. shoemaker
Litchfield Justin, shoemaker
Litchfield Laman O. shoemaker
Litchfield Leonard, stage driver
Litchfield Lincoln, farmer
Litchfield Luther, shoemaker
Litchfield Marshall, farmer
Litchfield Marshall, jr., mason
Litchfield Marshall H. farmer
Litchfield Martin, farmer
Litchfield Melvin S. shoe manuf.
Litchfield Milton, farmer
Litchfield Nymphas, farmer
Litchfield Otis, farmer
Litchfield Paul, farmer
Litchfield Peter, farmer
Litchfield Perez L. shoemaker
Litchfield Reuben D. shoemaker
Litchfield Rufus, farmer
Litchfield Samuel, farmer
Litchfield Seth, blacksmith
Litchfield Stephen, farmer
Litchfield Stillman, farmer
Litchfield Sumner, farmer
Litchfield Sumner O. farmer
Litchfield Thaddens L. shoemaker
Litchfield Thomas, carpenter
Litchfield Turner, carpenter
Litchfield Walter, farmer
Litchfield Ward, farmer
Litchfield Warren, farmer
Litchfield Webster, farmer
Litchfield William, shoemaker
Litchfield William P. shoemaker
Litchfield Zenas H. shoe manuf.
Little Sylvens H. peddler

MANN REUBEN, mason
Mann Thomas, farmer
Mann Thomas E. farmer
Manson Ed. S. mariner
Marsh John, shoe cutter
Mason John, master mariner
Mason John L. master mariner
Mason Wm. C. master mariner
McCarty Dennis, mosser
McLaughlin Hugh, mosser
Merritt Allen, shoemaker
Merritt Allen 2d, shoemaker
Merritt Amos W. shoemaker
Merritt Asa J. carpenter
Merritt Benj. F. mariner
Merritt Cummings J. wheelwright
Merritt Dexter, farmer
Merritt Elisha L. mason
Merritt Freeman, farmer
Merritt George, carpenter
Merritt George W. farmer
Merritt Hatherly, shoemaker
Merritt Henry, carpenter
Merritt Henry 2d. mariner
Merritt Howard, farmer
Merritt Howard J. blacksmith
Merritt Israel, mariner
Merritt James H. farmer
Merritt James L. shoemaker
Merritt John A. farmer
Merritt Joseph E. mason
Merritt Kilborn B. farmer
Merritt Martin D. farmer
Merritt Monroe, shoemaker

Policy Holders in the BERKSHIRE LIFE INSURANCE COMPANY of Pittsfield, Mass., DO NOT FORFEIT THEIR POLICIES by reason of FAILURE TO PAY their premiums. (See page 50.)

Merritt Robert C. mason
Merritt Seth, farmer
Merritt Shadrack B. farmer
Merritt William O. jr., shoemaker
Mitchell Archibald, farmer
Mitchell Charles H. farmer
Morris Joseph W. shoemaker
Mott Henry W. mason
Mott Hosea B. painter
Mott Joseph, farmer
Mott Otis, shoemaker
Mott Paul, shoemaker
Mungo Elias R. farmer
Murphy Patrick, mosser
Murphy Peter, mosser

NASH EBENEZER, cooper
Nason Charles, clergyman
Neal Thomas, mosser
Newcomb Henry C. shoemaker
Newcomb Jacob C. shoemaker
Newcomb Levi, laborer
Newcomb Silas, shoemaker
Newcomb Thomas J. painter
Newcomb William J. shoe manuf.
Nichols Israel, farmer
Nichols Israel jr. carpenter
Nichols Noah B. farmer
Nichols Noah B. 2d, mason
Nightingale Isaac, butcher
Northy Henry H. farmer
Northy Joseph, farmer
Northy Harvey C. farmer
Nott Asahel F. shoemaker
Nott Hosea D. farmer

ORCUTT HOSEA V. farmer
Osborn Caleb, shoemaker
Osborn Edward H. shoemaker
Osborn Wm. H. shoemaker
Otis Job P. butcher
Otis John, shoemaker
Otis Joseph, farmer
Otis Thomas, shoemaker

Packard George, mariner
Packard Isaac, wheelwright
Parker Perry L. mariner
Peaks Martin T. shoemaker
Peirce E. Foster, farmer
Peirce John B. mason
Pettis Henry, fisherman
Poole Samuel, shoemaker
Pratt Charles B. fisherman
Pratt Elijah, fisherman
Prouty Caleb W. farmer
Prouty James L. fisherman
Prouty James L. 2d, peddler
Prouty John E. O. draw tender
Prouty Thomas L. fisherman

RICHARDSON GEO. L. mariner
Reed Horatio G. civil engineer
Rogers Nathan, farmer
Rogers Patrick, fisherman

SANBORN FRED'K S. shoemaker
Sessions Alexander J. clergyman
Severns Charles P. stitcher
Sherman Israel H. farmer
Sherman Warren H. blacksmith
Sloan John, shoemaker
Smith Charles H. shoemaker

Smith James P. shipwright
Smith John H. trader
Spooner Henry F. fisherman
Spooner Jesse W. fisherman
Stetson Benjamin, farmer
Stetson Cummings, farmer
Stetson George H. shoemaker
Stetson Peleg, shoemaker
Stevens Lewis, master mariner
Stevens Luther, farmer
Stoddard Edwin, fisherman
Stoddard Samuel, shoemaker
Stoddard Samuel, jr., shoemaker
Stoddard William, shoemaker
Stone Cyrus, clergyman
Studley Bennett D. farmer
Studley Edwin, shoemaker
Studley Henry L. farmer
Studley Homer, farmer
Studley Howland L. farmer
Studley Lewis, carpenter
Studley Libar, carpenter
Supple Edward, mason
Supple Gerritt, mosser
Sylvester Abel, peddler
Sylvester Edmund H. shoemaker
Sylvester Henry H. fisherman

TAYLOR JAMES, butcher
Taylor John S. peddler
Tilden Christopher, farmer
Tilden David, mason
Tilden James W. farmer
Tilden John, farmer
Tilden Joseph W. farmer
Tilden Thomas, farmer
Thomas Francis, physician
Thorndyke Artemus, farmer
Thorndyke T. W. farmer
Tobias Edward, mosser
Tuckman David W. farmer
Tuckman Wm. W. shoemaker
Tyrrel George E. teamster
Turner James N. shipwright
Turner John B. farmer
Turner John H. shoemaker
Turner Nathaniel, farmer
Turner Roland, peddler
Turner Samuel H. farmer
Turner William C. shipwright

VARNEY FENTON W. shoemaker
Varney Nathaniel, shoemaker
Vinal Bailey, farmer
Vinal Charles, farmer
Vinal Charles, 2d, farmer
Vinal Dexter, trader
Vinal Freeman, mason
Vinal George, shoemaker
Vinal Henry F. farmer
Vinal Henry L. farmer
Vinal Henry M. farmer
Vinal Ignatius, laborer
Vinal Jacob, farmer
Vinal Job, farmer
Vinal John, farmer
Vinal Levi, farmer
Vinal Levi, jr., mason
Vinal Leroy, farmer
Vinal Lot, trader
Vinal Lot S. farmer
Vinal Lucius H. carpenter
Vinal Nathaniel, shoemaker

J. A. JACKSON, 101 COURT STREET, BOSTON, DEALER IN HATS, CAPS, AND FURS.

Vinal Nathaniel J. farmer
Vinal Stephen D. mariner
Vinal Thomas, farmer
Vinal Warren J. shoemaker

WADE JOHN B. farmer
Wade Nathaniel, jr., mariner
Walker Charles H. fisherman
Wall Walter, farmer
Ward Arthur, mosser
Ward Daniel, mosser
Ward Daniel, jr., mosser
Ward Daniel, 2d, mosser
Ward Dennis, mosser
Ward Edward, mosser
Ward Edward, 2d, mosser
Ward Hugh, mosser
Ward John, mosser
Waterman Andrew J. tinsmith
Watson Galen, shoemaker
Webb Benjamin F. shoemaker
Webb Charles S. shoemaker
Webb Marsena, farmer
Webb Marsena, jr., carpenter

Webb Paul, farmer
Webb Seth, farmer
Webb Stephen, shipwright
Webb Stephen D. shipwright
Webb Thomas R. shoemaker
Welsh E. Parker, farmer
Welsh Michael, farmer
Wetherbee George H. merchant
Wetherbee Thomas, trader
Whearty Nicholas, mosser
Whearty Patrick, mosser
Whittiker Charles H. agent
Whittiker George H. shoemaker
Whitcomb George W. shoemaker
Whitcomb Harvey fisherman
Wilder Benjamin
Witherell Anson, farmer
Witherell Davis C. fireman

YOUNG CHARLES, painter
Young Edwin, painter
Young George M. mason
Young Henry, shoemaker
Young John H. mason

South Scituate General Directory.

BABB GEORGE, farmer
Bailey David, shoemaker
Bailey Luther C. farmer
Barker Ira, blacksmith
Barker John S. carpenter
Barker Watters B. ship carpenter
Barnes Henry, laborer
Barstow Elijah, ship carpenter
Bassford David, jr., box maker
Bates George H. shoemaker
Bates George H. 2d, butcher
Bates Harvey, butcher
Bates John B. merchant
Bates Lorenzo, express
Beal John, shoemaker
Beaslee George, Sup't Alms House
Benson Stephen, laborer
Bishop Charles D. custom shoemaker
Bowker Joseph S. laborer
Bowker Joshua, stone cutter
Bowker Nathaniel H. farmer
Bowker Parsons, laborer
Bowker Stephen C. shoemaker
Briggs Alfred B. mason
Briggs George H. ship carpenter
Briggs James P. farmer
Briggs Joseph W. shipwright
Briggs Paul D. shoemaker

Briggs Richard P. farmer
Briggs Thomas W. farmer
Brooks Edward W. farmer
Brooks Elijah F.
Brooks Nathaniel, farmer
Brooks Nathaniel M. farmer
Brown A. W. laborer
Brown Bela, shoemaker
Brown Ebenezer, farmer
Brown Ebenezer L. laborer
Brown John W. shoemaker
Brownell N. P. physician
Burrell Isaac, farmer
Burrell James M. shoemaker

CHAMBERLAIN JOSIAH W. shoemaker
Chapman Timothy, shoemaker
Church Cornelius, farmer
Clapp Allen, shipwright
Clapp Andrew, box maker
Clapp Elijah, farmer
Clapp George, shoemaker
Clapp George H. shoemaker
Clapp George H. 2d, marble worker
Clapp George P. shoemaker
Clapp Gorham, trunk maker
Clapp John, farmer

Clapp Joseph, farmer
Clapp Joseph S. farmer
Clapp Nathaniel B. farmer
Clapp Stephen, laborer
Clapp Sylvanus, farmer
Clapp Tilden, shoemaker
Collamore William W. boot crimper
Coleman Elisha, shoemaker
Coleman Elisha F. tackmaker
Coleman William, carpenter
Corlew Benjamin, grocer
Corthell John, butcher
Corthell John E. butcher
Corthell Joseph H. butcher
Cromwell Calvin, laborer
Cudworth Elijah, farmer
Cudworth Samuel C. farmer
Currill Gilbert, mariner
Curtis Frederick H. carpenter
Curtis Joseph H. shoe manuf.
Curtis Martin S. trunk maker
Curtis Peleg, carpenter
Cushing Elnathan, ship carpenter
Cushing George K. farmer
Cushing Henry W. shoemaker
Cushing John, farmer
Cushing Josiah, farmer
Cushing Martin, farmer
Cushing Parker W. shoemaker
Cushing Warren V. farmer

DAMON ALBION, shoemaker
Damon Alpheus, shoemaker
Damon Charles H. farmer
Damon Daniel, laborer
Damon Ensign B. shoemaker
Damon Freeman, carpenter
Damon Josiah A. shoemaker
Damon Luther, farmer
Damon Simeon, shoemaker
Dana Frank, peddler
Delano William H. farmer
Dunbar Amos, farmer
Dyer Samuel, laborer

ELLMES BENJAMIN T. farmer
Ellmes Lewis, shoemaker
Ellmes Lincoln, shoemaker
Ellmes Nathaniel, farmer
Ellmes Nathaniel, jr., farmer
Ellmes Rodolphus, boot maker
Ellmes Thomas, farmer
Ewell Luther, shoemaker
Ewell Luther J. shoe stitcher

FARRAR WM. H. shoe manuf.
Farrow Charles H. shoemaker
Farrow James J. farmer
Farrow Richmond, farmer
Fitz Luke, farmer
Fogg Ebenezer F. dry goods & groceries
Ford Charles J. shoemaker
Ford Coleman, farmer
Ford David B. clergyman
Ford Gideon, farmer
Ford Joseph, peddler
Ford Laban W. shoemaker
Ford Michael, shipwright
Foster Benj. P. Boston express
Foster Charles, farmer
Foster Philip, carpenter
Foster Seth, Boston Express
Foster Walter, shipbuilder

Frazer Alexander, farmer
Freeman John, laborer
Freeman Richard, shoemaker
French Benjamin W. shoemaker
French Edwin, shoemaker
French Freeman, laborer
French George, bucket maker
French Henry F. shoemaker

GARDNER AUGUSTUS, shoemaker
Gardner Hobert C. shoemaker
Gardner Horatio N. blacksmith
Gardner John, machinist
Gardner John, jr., tack packer
Gardner Marcus, Boston express
Gardner Thomas H. shoemaker
Glover Martin C. laborer
Goodrich George A. shoemaker
Goodrich Sewall H. shoemaker
Granderson Charles, farmer
Greene Andrew, shoemaker
Greene Thomas B. shoemaker
Griffith David, laborer
Griggs Augustus R. beer maker
Griggs Horace, farmer
Griggs Reuben, peddler
Groce Ansel G. farmer
Groce Charles, shoe manuf.
Groce Henry A. shoemaker
Groce John D. shoemaker
Gross John, farmer
Gross John E. trunk manuf.
Gross Lewis, farmer
Gundoway Jeremiah, pilot

HART JOSEPH T. shoe manuf.
Hart Peter, farmer
Hatch Cushing, peddler
Hatch Eleazer, carpenter
Hatch Eleazer, jr.
Hatch John W. mason
Hatch Jonathan, shoe manuf.
Hatch Joseph H. farmer
Hatch Luther, farmer
Hatch Turner, farmer
Hatch William, farmer
Hatch William S. shoemaker
Hayden George B. farmer
Hayden William, shoemaker
Hayden William J. shoemaker
Henderson Joseph M. stitcher
Henderson Lloyd G. shoecutter
Henderson Samuel A. shoemaker
Hobart Alonzo C. shoemaker
House James, wheelwright
Howland Luther, farmer
Hunt Daniel T. shoemaker
Hunt James L. shoemaker

JACKMAN GEORGE W. farmer
Jacobs Andrew F. farmer
Jacobs Barton R. farmer
Jacobs Bela T. farmer
Jacobs Benjamin, farmer
Jacobs Benjamin R. farmer
Jacobs Benjamin W. shoemaker
Jacobs Edward, brickmaker
Jacobs Edwin, farmer
Jacobs Elisha, farmer
Jacobs Franklin, teacher
Jacobs George E. auctioneer
Jacobs George F. shoemaker
Jacobs Loring, farmer

J. A. JACKSON 101 COURT STREET, BOSTON, DEALER IN HATS CAPS AND FURS.

SOUTH SCITUATE DIRECTORY. 117

Jacobs Philip C. mason
Jacobs P. farmer
Jenkins Harvey H. farmer
Jenkins Riley, shoemaker
Jenkins Riley E. car driver
Jones John H. trunk and box manuf.
Jones Gustavus, farmer
Jones Marcellus, shoemaker
Jones Thomas, farmer

KENDER WM. J. tackmaker
Kimball Estes, hotel keeper
Kimball Oliver C. trader
Knapp James B. shoemaker

LAPHAM CHARLES H. shoemaker
Lapham Elisha W. trunkmaker
Lapham William, farmer
Lawrence Thomas R. painter
Lee George, ship carpenter
Lee George H. shoemaker
Leroy Charles, shoemaker
Leslie Patrick, laborer
Lewis John, shoemaker
Lincoln George, farmer
Lincoln Washington, shoemaker
Lincoln Francis L. shoemaker
Litchfield Alfred B. shoemaker
Litchfield Amos T. baker
Litchfield Andrew J. farmer
Litchfield Benjamin, farmer
Litchfield Bernard, mariner
Litchfield Billings, farmer
Litchfield Charles A. farmer
Litchfield Charles H. shoemaker
Litchfield Cummings, farmer
Litchfield Cushing, farmer
Litchfield Elijah, shoemaker
Litchfield Elijah 2d, seaman
Litchfield Freeman, jr. shoemaker
Litchfield John R. shoemaker
Litchfield Joseph T. carpenter
Litchfield Liba, farmer
Litchfield Lot, farmer
Litchfield William C. farmer
Loring Samuel, shoemaker

McCARTY DANIEL, laborer
McCurdy John, laborer
Merritt Benjamin, farmer
Merritt Charles H. plane stock maker
Merritt Henry, farmer
Merritt James, carpenter
Merritt Joseph, ship carpenter
Merritt Joseph 2d, blacksmith
Merritt Wm. H. blacksmith
Munrow Edward D. laborer

NASH JOHN C. farmer
Nash John K. farmer
Nichols Benjamin, ship carpenter
Nichols Parker W. carpenter

OTIS DANIEL, farmer
Otis Ephraim, farmer
Otis John T. farmer

PACKARD ISAAC H. shoemaker
Packard Isaac P. shoemaker
Payne Alfred, shoemaker
Pennaman John M. laborer
Pennaman J. W. laborer
Pincin Alfred, shoemaker

Pincin Perez, shoemaker
Pratt Charles C. carpenter
Pratt Elias E. carpenter
Pratt Elias W. farmer
Pratt William B. box maker
Prouty Benjamin W. shoemaker
Prouty John H. shoecutter
Prouty Lincoln, laborer
Prouty William, farmer
Prouty William, jr., shoemaker

RANDALL ALLEN, shoemaker
Raymond Lewis, shoemaker
Raymond Thomas A. shoemaker
Reed Joshua B. shoemaker
Richardson Andrew T. shoemaker
Robbins Horace, carriage manuf.
Robertson David P. shoemaker
Rogers Jotham, farmer

SAMPSON CLARK, farmer
Sampson Gamaliel, farmer
Sampson James W. farmer
Sampson John, farmer
Sampson Thomas C. shoemaker
Sanborn Ira B. trunk maker
Savage John, farmer
Sears James I. laborer
Simmons Charles W. farmer
Simmons Walter, farmer
Snow Harvey, farmer
Southworth James, shoemaker
Sparrell Charles W. undertaker
Spencer John, ropemaker
Spencer John H. shoemaker
Sprague Amos W. shoemaker
Sprague Daniel D. laborer
Stearns George, agent
Stetson Abner, ship carpenter
Stetson Ebenezer, farmer
Stetson George F. carpenter
Stetson Luther, shoemaker
Stetson Matthew, ship carpenter
Stetson Samuel D. carpenter
Stetson Samuel O. carpenter
Stetson Roger, shoemaker
Stetson Stephen, farmer
Stevens Ebenezer, cabinet maker
Stevens Horace P. clergyman
Stockbridge Andrew, shoemaker
Stockbridge Charles, farmer
Stockbridge David, farmer
Stockbridge Hosea J. shoemaker
Stockbridge Joseph, farmer
Stoddard Cyrus, carpenter
Stoddard David shoemaker
Stoddard David T. shoemaker
Stoddard Henry, laborer
Stoddard Josiah, farmer
Stowell Edward, shoe manuf.
Studley Cushing O. shoemaker
Studley David W. ship carpenter
Studley William, wheelwright
Sylvester Charles, mariner
Sylvester Charles W. farmer
Sylvester George, laborer
Sylvester Harvey T. farmer
Sylvester Jotham T. shoemaker
Sylvester N. B. laborer
Sylvester Peter, laborer
Sylvester William, laborer

TALBOT WILLIAM H. master mariner

The terms for ENDOWMENT, and TEN ANNUAL LIFE POLICIES in the BERKSHIRE are peculiarly favorable, and rates lower than in any Note Company.   31   (See page 50.)

118 PLYMOUTH COUNTY DIRECTORY.

Thomas Alpheus, shoemaker
Thomas Seth, farmer
Thompson James, laborer
Tilden Amos H. carpenter
Tilden John, ship joiner
Tollman Edward C. farmer
Tollman James C. tack manuf.
Tollman Joseph C. farmer
Tollman Samuel, farmer
Tollman Samuel jr. tack manuf.
Tolman Thomas, dry goods & groceries
Tolman Thomas J. plane stock manuf.
Tollman William C. farmer
Tollman Wm. C. jr. shoemaker
Tolman Charles, tackmaker
Tolman George T. dry goods & groceries
Torrey David, farmer
Torrey David jr. trunk manuf.
Torrey George, farmer
Torrey George H. dry goods & groceries
Torrey George O. ship carpenter
Torrey Henry A. engineer
Torrey Willard, trunkmaker
Totman Gustavus, shoemaker
Totman John, shoemaker
Turner Asiel, farmer
Turner David W. carpenter
Turner John, farmer
Turner John 2d, farmer
Turner Henry A. farmer
Turner Nathaniel, farmer
Turner Perez, farmer
Turner Robert V. C. mason
Turner Samuel, carpenter
Turner Samuel A. farmer

Turner Shiverick, farmer
Turner Theodore, farmer

VINAL ABEL A. fisherman
Vinal Alvin D. shoemaker
Vinal Amos, trunkmaker
Vinal Ezekiel T. trunkmaker
Vinal Seth H. boxmaker
Vinal William R. laborer
Vining Israel L. shoemaker

WARNER JAMES W. engineer
Waterman James, farmer
Waterman Lemuel C. tack manuf.
Waterman Rodolph C. tack manuf.
Waterman Thomas B. ship carpenter
Waters Jacob L. wheelwright
Waters Samuel, wheelwright
Weeks James, farmer
Wilder Calvin, shoemaker
Wilder Charles, shoemaker
Wilder Harrison, shoemaker
Wilder Laban, shoemaker
Willent Dexter M. shoe manuf.
Williamson Andrew, shoemaker
Williamson Charles, shoemaker
Winslow Albert, shoemaker
Winslow Harvey, shoemaker
Winslow Rufus, shoemaker
Winslow William S. tackmaker

YOUNG BENJ. M. shoe manuf.
Young Charles, shoemaker

Wareham General Directory.

ADAMS THOMAS C. saloon keeper
Alden Addison, farmer
Alden Joseph A. farmer

BABCOCK MILTON, blacksmith
Barker Charles, carder
Barker Leonard, nailer
Barker Rufus S. mason
Barrows Abishai, depot master
Barrows Hiram, wheelwright
Barrows Hiram W. wheelwright
Barrows Isaac, nailer
Barrows Isaac F. nailer
Barrows Wm. carpenter
Bartlett John M. clerk
Bartlett Lewis H. merchant
Bartlett Zephaniah, hostler
Barnes Elmer
Bassett S. C. depot master
Bassett Washington, depot master
Bates Leonard

Bates William, Justice of the Peace
Benson Eleal, teamer
Benson Elnathan
Benson John W. farmer
Benson Lothrop W. moulder
Benson Marcus M. nailer
Benson Martin V. B. clerk
Benson William, cooper
Bent George W. shingler
Bent Isaac, blacksmith
Bent Isaac B. stove dealer
Bent Lewis, blacksmith
Besse Albert S. nailer
Besse Alden, sea captain
Besse Alvin F. mariner
Besse Augustus F. nailer
Besse Benjamin F. nailer
Besse Charles F. nailer
Besse Charles F. 2d, trader
Besse Charles H. mariner
Besse David, sea captain

J. A. JACKSON, 101 COURT STREET, BOSTON, DEALER IN HATS, CAPS, AND FURS.

Besse Earl G. nailer
Besse Edward A. laborer
Besse Elisha G. nailer
Besse Emerson F. nailer
Besse Ichabod, nailer
Besse John C. wood chopper
Besse John M. nailer
Besse Joshua B. mariner
Besse Josiah C. teamer
Besse Josiah C. jr. teamer
Besse Lothrop A. nailer
Besse Lothrop A. 2d, merchant
Besse Obed B. carpenter
Besse Rodolphus, expressman
Besse Samuel C. nailer
Besse Samuel S. nailer
Besse Seth C. sea captain
Besse Sidney C. nailer
Besse Silas, nailer
Besse Thomas, nailer
Besse Wm. H. sea captain
Billings George H. roll turner
Billings Warren, Agent Franconia Iron Works
Blackwell Ellis, puddler
Bodfish David, nailer
Bodfish Parker N. merchant
Bolles Israel B. blacksmith
Bourne Alden G. farmer
Bourne Benjamin H. mariner
Bourne Ebenezer, farmer
Bourne Heman S. nailer
Bourne John F. farmer
Bourne Josiah, sea captain
Bourne Samuel S. moulder
Bourne Silvanus, farmer
Boyd Henry, agent Tihonet Iron Works
Boyd Henry W. clerk
Brett Ezra C. clerk
Briggs Charles F. puddler
Briggs Charles G. nailer
Briggs Frederick J. nailer
Bryant Ebenezer, teamer
Bryant Ebenezer S. clerk
Bryant Hiram, puddler
Bryant Wm. R. moulder
Bumpus Benj. H. fireman
Bumpus Charles H. nailer
Bumpus Charles S. nailer
Bumpus Charles W. plate cutter
Bumpus Charles W. jr. nailer
Bumpus Daniel, carpenter
Bumpus David P. fisherman
Bumpus Eliphalet, farmer
Bumpus Eliphalet 2d, nailer
Bumpus Ezra B. paddler
Bumpus Francis D. nailer
Bumpus George W. nailer
Bumpus George W. 2d, nailer
Bumpus Henry F. mariner
Bumpus Henry W. mill hand
Bumpus Harvey, farmer
Bumpus Hiram S. farmer
Bumpus Hiram W. nailer
Bumpus Hosea C. nailer
Bumpus Ivory H. nailer
Bumpus Jonathan, farmer
Bumpus Jonathan 2d, mill hand
Bumpus Joseph W. nailer
Bumpus Julah, wood chopper
Bumpus Linus D. nailer
Bumpus Lysander N. nailer
Bumpus Reuben A. nailer

Bumpus Samuel B. school teacher
Bumpus Shem, farmer
Bumpus Watson, butcher
Bumpus Zenas F. school teacher
Burbank Walter D. stove dealer
Burgess Calvin C. nailer
Burgess Henry, farmer
Burgess James, master mariner
Burgess Joseph H. farmer
Burgess Joseph I. W. merchant
Burgess Thomas, farmer
Burgess Thomas A. nailer
Burgess Zabad, fisherman
Butland Alfred A.
Butler Ephraim D. mill hand
Butler James M. school teacher
Butler Jerome N. master mariner
Butler Patrick, farmer
Butler Patrick, jr., fisherman
Butler Patrick F. fisherman

CAHOON ISRAEL, packer
Cahoon Jesse, farmer
Cahoon Jesse, jr., mariner
Cahoon Mark H. blacksmith
Cannon Alexander B. farmer
Cannon Caleb L. farmer
Caswell Alfred, jr., nailer
Caswell William A. overseer
Chubbuck Alfred, teamer
Chubbuck Benjamin C. saloon keeper
Chubbuck Benjamin F. nailer
Chubbuck Ephraim, farmer
Chubbuck Ferdinand, farmer
Chubbuck Freeman A. mariner
Chubbuck Henry S. mariner
Chubbuck Roland, jr., farmer
Chubbuck Thomas A. mariner
Chubbuck Thomas S. master mariner
Chubbuck William E. nailer
Childs Henry E. butcher
Chipman Lloyd, gentleman
Chipman, William L. gentleman
Christie Warren M. master mariner
Churchill Benjamin, post master
Churchill Lewis, cooper
Churchill Pelham F. R.
Clary Timothy F. clergyman
Cobb James H.
Coffin Coolridge, clerk
Conroy Barnabas, heater
Covil Aaron B. nailer
Covil Enos, jr., nailer
Covil Hiram C. farmer
Crittenden Beriah D. peddler
Crittenden John F. farmer
Crittenden John F. 2d, nailer
Crittenden Wilson, peddler
Crocker Walter W. harness maker
Culworth Benjamin F. master mariner
Curran John
Cushman Jacob, blacksmith

DAMON ELIJAH
Davis Francis, carpenter
Davis William C. nailer
Dean Caleb C.
Dean Jerome C.
Dean Joshua W. miller
Dean Joshua W. jr., miller
Doggett Perez F. physician
Doty Albert, farmer
Doty Benjamin F. nailer

DIVIDENDS ADDED to the POLICY in the BERKSHIRE often exceed the premium paid; are NON-FORFEITABLE and will be redeemed in CASH ON DEMAND. (See page 50.)

Doty James M. nailer
Douglass Harrison L. farmer
Douglass Jesse, mariner
Dunham Charles R. nailer
Dunham Elijah, nailer
Dunham George W. heater
Dunham Isaac C. nailer
Dunham Joseph W. nailer
Dunham Sylvanus W.

ELDRIDGE DARIUS
Eldridge John C. puddler
Eldridge Joseph A. mariner
Eldridge Obed, nailer
Eldridge Stillman P. nailer
Ellis Charles F. cooper
Ellis Ebenezer, mill hand
Ellis Henry S. clerk
Ellis Nathan B. carpenter
Ellis Stephen, merchant
Ellis Walter, puddler
Everett John L.
Everett Josiah, farmer

FEARING ANDREW C. merchant
Fearing Andrew G. merchant
Fearing Benjamin, physician
Fearing Elbridge G. farmer
Fearing Francis H. merchant
Fearing John, farmer
Fearing Wm. H. farmer
Field Daniel L. boatman
Fish Abner C. sea captain
Franklin Emerson, nailer
Foster Barnabas, nailer
Foster Emanuel, mariner
Franklin Charles, nailer
Freeman Martin
Freeman John, nailer
Fuller John S. trader

GAMMONS EDWARD A. clerk
Gammons John W.
Gammons William, nailer
Gault David S. bread peddler
Gault John T. nailer
Gault Lysander
Gavitt John, boarding house keeper
Gibbs Abram clerk
Gibbs Albert W. shoemaker
Gibbs Alvin, merchant and town clerk
Gibbs Alvin F. depot master
Gibbs Andrew, farmer
Gibbs Augustus D. clerk
Gibbs Benjamin F. master mariner
Gibbs Elisha B. jappanner
Gibbs George F. mariner
Gibbs Jonathan, farmer
Gibbs Joseph, farmer
Gibbs Joseph G. trader
Gibbs Joshua, merchant
Gibbs Micah, nailer
Gibbs Nathan P. master mariner
Gibbs Reuel B. farmer
Gibbs Stephen, farmer
Gibbs Thomas
Gibbs William S. master mariner
Grear Charles H.
Greene Barnabas, teacher
Greene Thomas W. carpenter
Griffith George T. stone mason
Griffith William W. stone mason
Gurney Ansel A. merchant

Gurney George F.
Gurney Levi
Gurney Richard A. S. peddler
Gurney Rufus H.
Gurney Sullivan B. farmer
Gurney Sullivan B. jr., master mariner
Gurney William H.
Gurney Wilson B.

HALL HENRY W. nailer
Hall Jonathan, nailer
Hall Josiah H. Sup't Iron Mill
Hall Sylvester S. nailer
Hamblin Charles G. carpenter
Hamblin Elkanah, blacksmith
Hamblin George S. blacksmith
Hamblin John W. mason
Hamblin Lemuel H. nailer
Hammond Abiel S. nailer
Hammond Arthur H. farmer
Hammond Arthur H. jr., master mariner
Hammond Job D. shoemaker
Handy Edward F. peddler
Harding John, sea captain
Harlow James, nailer
Harlow Otis, nailer
Harris Abel T. puddler
Haskell Michael
Hatch Benj. S. nailer
Hatch Job, mason
Hathaway Albert S. carpenter
Hathaway Benjamin F. sea captain
Hathaway Charles E. nailer
Hathaway Charles H. puddler
Hathaway David, overseer
Hathaway David jr., nailer
Hathaway George H.
Hathaway Jacob E. sea captain
Hathaway John P. R. machinist
Hathaway Leander, teamer
Hathaway Matthias E. carpenter
Hathaway, Rufus F. farmer
Hathaway Salathiel
Hathaway Solomon W. nailer
Hatton John J. chair bottomer
Hatton Rowland, peddler
Hatton Wm. T. puddler
Hayden Joseph P. insurance agent
Hinckley Alpheus, shoemaker
Hinckley Robert, farmer
Hinds John, laborer
Holmes Geo. H. butcher
Holmes Henry W. butcher
Holmes Martin V. B. bar-keeper
Holmes Orin H. horse trader
Holmes Robert R. nailer
Hopkins Thomas
Horr, Henry A. laborer
Howard A. B. painter
Howard Benj. F. merchant
Howard Wm. master mariner
Howes Kimball, clerk
Hoyt Benj. rail road agent
Hoyt M. P. clerk
Hudson James S. farmer
Humphrey Galen, merchant
Hurd Joseph R. puddler

INGRAHAM WM. H. painter

JOHNSON BENJ. E. nailer
Johnson Charles H. nailer
Johnson P. S. laborer

J. A. JACKSON 101 COURT STREET, BOSTON, DEALER IN HATS CAPS AND FURS.

Johnson Urial M. nailer
Johnson Wm. T. nailer
Jones John W. stevedore

KEITH DAVID W. nailer
Keith Joseph H. nailer
Kenney Lewis, keg manuf.
Fenney John M. Agent Polls Works
Knowles Henry M. physician
King Rufus, nailer
Keyes Benjamin S. mariner
Keyes Freeman C. sea captain
Keyes Samuel S. carpenter
Keyes Wm. A. carpenter

LEONARD CHARLES S. nailer
Leonard James T. laborer
Leonard Stillman K. nailer
Leonard William L. nailer
Lincoln James F. trader
Lincoln Minor S. 2d, stevedore
Lincoln Rufus 2d, clerk
Linnel Dean S. sea captain
Linnel Joseph W. packer
Little Wm. C. S. stone mason
Long Abijah, tin peddler
Long Albert W. nailer
Long Nathan C. nailer
Long Samuel C. bluer (nails)
Longendyke Lucas, puddler
Loring William G. harness maker

MACKIE JOHN, teamer
Mackie William H. farmer
Marshall Lewis, nailer
Martin Sylvanus
Maxim Ebenezer T. mill hand
Maxim John M. nailer
May Charles H. mariner
May Francis A. nailer
May William E. nailer
McGrath Michael, laborer
McMannaman Nathan S. laborer
McMannaman Seth T. laborer
Merrifew George A.
Miles Thomas R. cashier Wareham Bank
Millard Wm. A. shoemaker
Miller Darius, farmer
Miller Seth, lawyer
Mitchell David, paper mill agent
Morse Andrew, laborer
Morse David S. farmer
Morse Edwin
Morse Oliver A. nailer
Morse Oliver E. nailer
Morse Savery A. farmer
Morse Seth C. farmer
Morse Simeon, farmer
Morse Tillson A. nailer
Murdoch Charles C. painter
Murdoch Frank W. painter
Murdoch Jason F. painter

NICKERSON IVORY H. nailer
Nickerson James, laborer
Nickerson Joseph F. overseer
Nickerson Maranda, nailer
Nickerson Watson T. hotel keeper
Nightingale Jeremiah T. nailer
Nightingale Phineas, master mariner
Nobles Jesse, carpenter
Nott Samuel, school teacher
Nye Andrew S. carpenter

Nye Thomas S. carpenter

PACKARD LEANDER L. wheelwright
Paine James
Paine Wm. J. miller
Paine Wm. R. miller
Patterson Wm. F. laborer
Peirce Anthony L. fisherman
Peirce William N.
Perkins Josiah F. painter
Perry Alexander R. nailer
Perry David, fireman
Perry David 2d, nailer
Perry Elisha D. roller
Perry Joseph W. nailer
Perry Lewis D. nailer
Pitsley Charles, nailer
Pope Joseph W. nailer
Pratt Samuel, nailer

RAYMOND FRANCIS, nailer
Raymond Henry C. laborer
Raymond Samuel D. shoemaker
Rider Benjamin
Rider Wm. W. cooper
Robbins Darius, pilot
Robinson Michael, farmer
Robinson Samuel A. oysterman
Robinson Wm. jr.
Robinson Zimri F.
Rogers Thomas, wood chopper
Rogers Thomas jr. wood chopper
Runnells Levi A. tailor
Runnells Samuel, machinist
Russell Isaac, nailer
Ryan James, laborer
Ryan Joseph jr. laborer

SAMPSON AARON, blacksmith
Sampson John, cooper
Sampson Joseph L. nailer
Sanford Ferdinand, puddler
Sanford George, merchant
Sanford Leander, puddler
Savery Adolphus, civil engineer
Savery John W. civil engineer
Savery Lemuel, farmer
Savery Thomas, civil engineer
Savery William, farmer
Savery Wm. jr. farmer
Savery Wm. 2d, peddler
Sawyer Frederick A. physician
Seaver Joseph N. nailer
Shaw Welcome, laborer
Sherman Hiram F. nailer
Sherman James R.
Sherman Jirah F. ag't Tisdale Iron Works
Sherman Joseph S. mariner
Sherman Nathaniel, farmer
Sherman Nicholas J. jeweller
Sherman Samuel T. T. overseer
Sherman Thomas J. painter
Shores Albert S. nailer
Shores Andrew H. nailer
Shores Abram W. nailer
Shurtleff Joseph, machinist
Shurtleff Lothrop, teamer
Shurtleff Seth H. nailer
Shurtleff Sylvanus, blacksmith
Smalley Charles G. fisherman
Smith Ezra N. school teacher
Smith John, puddler
Smith John, 2d, puddler

Policy Holders in the BERKSHIRE LIFE INSURANCE COMPANY of Pittsfield, Mass., DO NOT FORFEIT THEIR POLICIES by reason of FAILURE TO PAY their premiums. (See page 50.)

Smith Martin, laborer
Smith Oliver A. ship builder
Snell Alexander, puddler
Snell William H. nailer
Soule Silas T. cabinet maker
Sprague Caleb C. bookkeeper
Sprague Charles E.
Sproat Horace M. clerk
Sproat James G. lawyer
Sproat James R. merchant
Staples William F. cooper
Stevens Orlando, nailer
Stevens William, heater
Stuart Cyrus, cooper
Stuart Frederick, cooper
Stuart Frederick A. cooper
Stuart Ira C. cooper
Sullivan Cornelius, heater
Sweet Isaiah W. puddler
Sweet Samuel, puddler
Swift Alexander, stevedore
Swift Andrew J. shoemaker
Swift Ansel
Swift Asa C. mariner
Swift Clark G. stonecutter
Swift Daniel E. laborer
Swift Elisha, wood merchant
Swift Prince H.
Swift Samuel, blacksmith
Swift Stephen, farmer
Swift Stephen, jr., master mariner
Swift Timothy, farmer

TABER SALATHIEL H. mill hand
Taylor George, puddler
Thomas Henry M. nailer
Thomas Rufus H. butcher
Thompson David, hotel keeper
Thompson Edwin N. merchant
Thompson George A.
Thompson James
Tisdale Samuel T. iron manufacturer
Tobey Curtis, clerk

Tobey Joshua B. Pres. Wareham Bank
Tobey Moses S. F. postmaster
Tobey Seth F. farmer
Tobey Theodore, clerk
Tripp Jesse, laborer
Tripp John Q. A. laborer
Tripp Nathan M. carpenter
Tripp Stephen R. nailer
Turner Frank, teamer
Turner Simeon, nailer
Turner Stephen, cooper
Turner Wm. H. barber
Tyler Geo. F. laborer

VAUGHN LEONARD, carpenter

WALKER ELIJAH, iron piler
Washburn Benjamin, nailer
Washburn Charles F. carpenter
Washburn Cromwell, merchant
Washburn Gideon M.
Washburn Henry O. nailer
Washburn John B. nailer
Washburn John D. mariner
Washburn Marshall, nailer
Waters Lewis
Weaver Calvin R. civil engineer
Weeks Seth, laborer
Westgate Benjamin, nailer
Westgate Jonathan, nailer
Westgate Robert C. nailer
Westgate William
Weston Abishai B. carpenter
Weston Charles F. A. merchant
White Reuben, farmer
Wilcox George W. carpenter
Williams Joseph H. puddler
Williams Samuel, puddler
Wing George F. carpenter
Wing Joshua G.
Wood Abner
Wright Charles D. stevedore

West Bridgewater General Directory.

ALGER ALBERT L. farmer, Cochesett
Alger Chas. S. boot maker, Cochesett
Alger Cyrus, soap manuf. Cochesett
Alger Davis, farmer, Cochesett
Alger James, iron foundry
Alger Joseph, farmer, Cochesett
Alger Joseph A. stage driver
Alger Joseph W. farmer
Alger Leonard W. carpenter
Alger Martin, farmer, Cochesett
Alger Otis, farmer, Cochesett
Alger Sanford, farmer, Cochesett
Alger Ward, farmer, Cochesett
Alger Wm. farmer, Cochesett
Alger Wm. O. shoe manuf. Cochesett
Ames Charles, farmer
Ames Charles P. farmer, Cochesett
Ames David P. farmer, Cochesett
Ames John F. moulder
Ames Jonathan, farmer
Ames Thomas, farmer
Ames Willard, furnaceman
Ames Willard jr., farmer
Ames Wm. B. agent
Atwell Charles, blacksmith

BAKER DANIEL H. merchant
Bailey James S. shoemaker
Bailey Melvin, shovel welder
Bailey Sylvanus P. shoemaker
Bartlett David jr., farmer
Bartlett Horace, farmer
Bartlett Joab, farmer
Bartlett Samuel D. farmer
Burke Wm. iron worker, Cochesett
Burke Wm. H. livery stable
Burrell Jarvis D. postmaster and trader
Buttomer Andrew, laborer
Buttomer John, laborer
Bassett Keith, farmer
Beals Charles, farmer
Beals Charles R. carpenter
Benson F. T. shoemaker
Billings Edgar, boot maker
Billings Martin, shoemaker
Billings Willard, nursery.
Bird Wm. E. iron foundry
Blood Luther, farmer, Cochesett
Bowe Nicholas, shovel grinder
Brown Cyrus P. bootmaker, Cochesett

CAHILL THOMAS, forger
Callahan Dennis, shovel welder
Capen Edward, painter
Carr George G. shoemaker
Carson Lawrence, iron worker
Cashman John, forger
Caswell Henry P. shoemaker
Chaffe Nathaniel O. clergyman
Charnock Robert, engineer
Churchill Charles E. shoecutter
Cole Eleazer A. leather cutter
Colwell Charles H. shoemaker
Colwell Edgar, shoemaker
Colwell John E. shoemaker

Colwell John E. leather cutter
Colwell John H. shoemaker
Colwell Sylvanus H. laborer
Colwell Wellington, farmer
Condrick James, laborer
Conoly Patrick, farmer
Cooper John F. leather cutter, Cochesett
Copeland Albert, painter
Copeland Caleb jr. shoe manuf. North Bridgewater
Copeland Davis, farmer
Copeland Ezra S. farmer
Copeland Francis, farmer
Copeland George, leather cutter
Copeland George A. leather cutter, Campello
Copeland Heman, farmer & school teacher
Copeland James, farmer
Copeland John, cattle drover
Copeland Jonathan, farmer
Copeland Lyman, farmer
Copeland Nathan, (P. & N. Copeland), shoe manuf. Campello
Copeland Pardon. (P. & N. Copeland), shoe manuf., Campello
Copeland Uriah S. farmer
Curtis Benjamin, shoe finisher, Campello
Curtis Hiram, carpenter

DEAN THEODORE S. clergyman
Dodge Charles, leather cutter, Cochesett
Dorgan Patrick, laborer, Cochesett
Drake George R. grocery peddler, Cochesett
Dunbar Adoniram J. farmer, Cochesett
Dunbar Barnabas, farmer, Cochesett
Dunbar Chas. E. farmer, Cochesett
Dunbar Charles H. carpenter
Dunbar Daniel, farmer, Cochesett
Dunbar Daniel H. bootmaker, Cochesett
Dunbar Davis H. shoemaker
Dunbar Francis, butcher
Dunbar John S. farmer
Dunbar Lucius, bootmaker
Dunbar Mark, poultry dealer
Dunbar Martin, bootmaker
Dunbar Martin V. B. butcher
Dunbar Reuel, bootmaker, Cochesett
Dunbar Simeon, farmer
Dunbar Simeon J. teacher

EATON JOHN, grocery peddler, Cochesett
Eddy Curtis, carpenter
Edson Alanson S. painter
Edson Ephraim, shoemaker
Edson George L. farmer
Edson Melvin C. shoe manuf. & grocer
Egan Michael, shoemaker

FADDER JAMES, leather cutter
Field Perez B. bootmaker
Fish Gilmore, operator
Fisher Timothy W. laborer
Forbes Albert, fur neeman
Forbes Dwelley, iron foundry

ANNUAL CASH DIVIDENDS in the BERKSHIRE LIFE INS. CO., Pittsfield, Mass. Boston Office 95 1-2 Washington St. (See page 59.)

Forbes James A. leather cutter
Freeman Josephus S. shoemaker
French Albert W. moulder
French George M. moulder
French Jason M. laborer
Fullerton D. F. stitcher, Campello
Fullerton O. W. leather cutter, Campello
Fulton Jonathan, farmer

GALLAGHER JAMES P. shoemaker
Gardner Tillson, farmer, Cochesett
Gould Jabez, farmer
Gray Alonzo C. stitcher, Cochesett
Gray Orin T. lawyer, Cochesett
Gurney Lucius, stitcher, Cochesett.

HABBERLEY GEORGE, forgeman
Hall John W. shoemaker
Hall Josiah, operator
Hancock Elijah, farmer, Cochesett
Hartwell Jonas, farmer
Hartwell Jonas G. shoe dresser
Hartwell Joshua Q. shoe manuf. North Bridgewater
Hassett Edward, machinist
Hassett Edward F. shoemaker
Hayward Edward W. farmer
Hayward Franklin W. shoe manuf. No. Bridgewater
Hayward George, carpenter
Hayward John L. farmer
Hayward Linus, leather cutter
Hayward Lucius, carpenter
Hayward Martin, farmer
Hersey John, shoemaker, Cochesett
Hersey John T. farmer, Cochesett
Hersey Stillman W. shoemaker, Cochesett
Hobbs Nelson R. boot and shoemaker, Cochesett
Holmes Andrew B. shoemaker
Holmes Edwin, shoemaker, Campello
Holmes George T. clerk
Holmes James S. shovel maker
Holmes John B. farmer
Holbrook Ellis, shoemaker, Cochesett
Howard Alba, farmer
Howard Amasa, farmer
Howard Benjamin, shoe manuf.
Howard Benjamin B. merchant
Howard Caleb, farmer, Cochesett
Howard Elam, farmer
Howard Elbridge G. farmer, Cochesett
Howard Everett, mason
Howard Francis E. farmer
Howard Freeman, farmer
Howard Friend W. carpenter, Cochesett
Howard George L. farmer
Howard Hiram, farmer, Cochesett
Howard Horatio, cattle dealer
Howard Isaac, farmer and wheelwright
Howard James, farmer
Howard John E. music teacher
Howard Jonathan, farmer
Howard Jonathan, 2d, farmer, Cochesett
Howard Leavitt T. farmer, Campello
Howard Lewis, farmer, Campello
Howard Lewis G. carpenter
Howard M. soup peddler, Cochesett
Howard Milo, painter
Howard Nelson, cattle dealer
Howard Samuel N. farmer Cochesett
Howard Thomas, farmer

Howard Urial, farmer
Howard Waldo, farmer, Cochesett
Howard William, shoedresser
Howland Henry W. blacksmith

JENNINGS WM. H. boot & shoemaker, Cochesett
Johnson Frederic, teamer
Johnson George W. heel maker

KEITH DAVIS, farmer, Campello
Keith Henry S farmer, Campello
Keith Jonathan C. farmer and building mover, Campello
Keith Pardon, farmer, Campello
Keith Simeon C. leather cutter, Campello
Kelleher Dennis, farmer
Kenan Patrick, laborer
Kingman Joseph, farmer
Kingman Melzer, peddler
Kingman Sidney S. shoemaker

LANGLEY THOMAS, shoemaker
Leach Henry W. carpenter, Cochesett
Leonard Cyrus, fur dealer
Leonard Elihu, farmer
Leonard Jacob, carpenter, Cochesett
Leonard Jonas, stove mounter
Leonard Nahum, farmer
Leonard Philo P. shoemaker, Cochesett
Lincoln Eugene, shoemaker
Lincoln J. M. foreman pattern shop
Lineham Dennis, shoemaker
Lineham John, shoemaker
Lineham Timothy, shoemaker
Lineham William, shoemaker
Logue Michael, bootmaker
Lothrop Azel, shoemaker, Cochesett
Lothrop Caleb S. laborer
Lothrop Edwin H. shoe finisher, Campello
Lothrop John M. farmer, Cochesett

MACOMBER CHARLES A. farmer, Cochesett
Macomber Chas. A. jr, clerk, Cochesett
Marshall Benjamin, farmer, Cochesett
Marshall Bela H. leather cutter, Cochesett
Martin Charles E. shoe finisher, Campello
Martin Charles N. farmer, Campello
McAdams James, shoemaker, Cochesett
McCarty Michael, laborer
Millett Aaron, farmer, Campello
Millett John A. shoe dresser, Campello
Mitchell Isam, carpenter
Mitchell Robert, stove mounter
Morey Josiah, shoemaker
Morey Stephen, farmer
Morey Wm. L. shoemaker
Morse Charles T. peddler, Cochesett
Morse Joseph, shoe finisher, Cochesett
Morse Joshua, shoe finisher, Campello
Morse Russell W. shoemaker, Cochesett
Murphy Michael, laborer.

O'LEARY WILLIAM, laborer
O'Neil John, molder

PACKARD ABIEL, farmer
Packard Austin, lawyer, Cochesett
Packard Bradford, farmer & shoemaker
Packard Emory, stitcher
Packard Francis S. laborer

J. A. JACKSON 104 COURT STREET, BOSTON, DEALER IN HATS, CAPS AND FURS.

Packard Irving, leather cutter
Packard Japhet B. bootmaker
Packard John A. farmer
Packard Levi S. leather cutter, Campello
Packard Nahum, fur dealer
Packard Samuel, moulder
Pasco Cephas, clergyman
Peckham Alfred N. livery stable, Cochesett
Peckham C. T. *(H. E. & C. T. Peckham)* shoe manuf., Cochesett
Peckham H. E. *(H. E. & C. T. Peckham)* shoe manuf., Cochesett
Perkins Andrew W. shoemaker
Perkins Benjamin, engineer, Campello
Perkins Charles, merchant, Cochesett
Perkins Daniel, moulder
Perkins Edmond, shoemaker, Cochesett
Perkins Francis, shovelmaker
Perkins George H. shoemaker, Cochesett
Perkins Melvin O. moulder
Perkins Owen D. nailer, Cochesett
Phillips Joseph R. depot master
Pool George, junk dealer, Cochesett
Pratt George, leather cutter Cochesett
Pratt George W. moulder
Pratt Shepherd L. livery and sale stable, Cochesett
Pratt Thomas, farmer

RANDALL HEMAN, grocery peddler
Reed Charles, farmer
Richards Clarkson W. farmer
Richards Elijah E. merchant
Richards Galen R. farmer
Richards John, farmer
Richards Josiah, farmer
Richards Justin W. farmer & shoemaker
Richards Luther, farmer
Ring Joseph, shoemaker, Cochesett
Ripley Molbary, farmer
Ripley Molbary A., sawyer and wheelwright
Ripley Thos. P. leather cutter, Cockesett
Roach William, blacksmith
Round Almond, laborer, Cochesett
Rumery Henry T. shoemaker, Cochesett
Ryder George D. farmer
Ryder Joseph E. farmer
Ryder Joshua T. leather cutter
Ryder Lewis, farmer
Ryder Samuel, farmer
Ryder Samuel L. carpenter

SHAW GEO. P. stitcher, Cochesett
Shaw Horatio, stone layer
Shields James, shoefinisher, Campello
Shipman George, machinist
Simmons David, butcher, Cochesett
Simmons W. H. peddler, Cochesett
Smith William, shoemaker
Snow George, farmer
Snell Bradford, farmer
Snell Ephraim, farmer
Shipman John, machinist
Snell J. K. leather cutter
Snell Nahum, farmer
Snell Nahum P. leather cutter
Snell Thomas, farmer
Snell William Q. farmer
Sullivan Michael, shoemaker
Sullivan Timothy, shoefinisher, Campello
Swan James C. physician, Cochesett

TAYLOR DANIEL B. mechanic, Cochesett
Taylor Ebenezer, farmer
Thayer Charles C. farmer
Thayer Hiram, bootmaker
Thayer Jeremiah, farmer, Campello
Thayer Richard, farmer
Thayer Richard F. bootmaker
Tinkham David W. carpenter
Tisdale Edward, shoe manuf. Cochesett
Tisdale Mace, farmer

VOSMUS FOSTER J. shoemaker, Cochesett
Vosmus Jeffrey, shoe manuf.
Vosmus Joseph, shoemaker, Cochesett

WASHBURN ABIEL, shoemaker
Washburn Hiram G. shoemaker
Washburn Horatio L. shoe manuf.
Wheeler Eli, fur dealer
Whitman Henry H. farmer
White Herbert O. engineer, Cochesett
Wilbur George, carpenter
Wilbur Marshal, carpenter
Williams Calvin, merchant
Williams Daniel, bootmaker, Cochesett
Winship Isaac, blacksmith, Cochesett
Winship William, carpenter, Cochesett
Withington George, shoemaker
Withington Henry, shoemaker

The terms for ENDOWMENT, and TEN ANNUAL LIFE POLICIES in the BERKSHIRE are peculiarly favorable, and rates lower than in any Note Company. (See page 50.)

LIST OF BOOKS FOR SUNDAY SCHOOLS
PUBLISHED BY HENRY HOYT,
No. 9 Cornhill, Boston.

LIBRARIES.

A New and Beautiful Sabbath School Library. In a case. Price $20.

The Child's Bible Stories. A beautiful set of 4 vols. with 40 illustrations, in a case. Price $3.80.

The Hillside Library. 8 vols. embossed covers and gilt backs. Price $3.50.

The New Fireside Library. This is a charming set of 5 vols. composed of favorite works. Price $3.25.

The Gift Library. Is another set of beautiful Juvenile Works, full bound, in a handsome case. Price $2.50.

My Pet Library. 10 vols. in a neat case. 648 pages of choice reading for the little ones. Price, nett, $2.25.

The Little Home Library. 10 vols. in a neat case. 648 pp. choice reading for the little ones. Price, nett, $2.25.

Little Folks' Library. 10 vols. in a neat case. 648 pages of choice reading for the little ones. Price, nett, $2.25.

The Welcome Library. 10 vols. in a neat case. 648 pages of reading for the little ones. Price, nett, $2.25.

The Little Ones' Library. 10 vols. in a neat case. 648 pages of reading for the little ones. Price, nett, $2.25.

The Little Conqueror Series. 4 vols. in a case. Price, $2.10.

Songs for Social and Public Worship. Pronounced by critical examiners the best work extant. Price, nett, $1.15.

☞ REVISED EDITION. ☜

A new and beautiful edition of the Songs is now ready, edited by Rev. E. N. Kirk, D. D., of Boston. It is printed in large, clear type, and contains over 295 pages of hymns and tunes, including 550 hymns. The work is a model of its kind. Price, nett, 90 cents.

☞ VALUABLE QUESTION BOOKS. ☜

I. **The Explanatory Question Book**, with Analytical and Expository Notes, and an Introduction by Rev. Dr. Kirk. Price 17 cents.

II. **The Youth's Scripture Question Book on the New Testament**, adapted to Youth of both sexes, from ten to fifteen years of age. Price 15 cents.

III. **The Child's Illustrated Scripture Question Book**, containing forty-five lessons, with a new and beautiful engraving for each lesson. Price 18 cents.

IV. **Lessons on the Epistle to the Hebrews**, by a Bible Class Teacher, and an Introduction by Rev. A. L. Stone. A work of great practical excellence and unusual ability. 15 cents.

V. **A New Question Book on the Acts.** By H. HAMLIN, author of the Explanatory, Youth's, and Childs' Illustrated Question Books. Price 15 cents.

VI. **A Standard Question Book on Isaiah.** By Rev. RUFUS CLARK, D. D. Price 15 cents.

VII. **Faith and Works Harmonized.** A New Question Book on Ephesians and James. By the author of Bible Scholars' Manual. Price 15 cents.

VIII. **A New Question Book on the Epistle to the Romans.** By the author of Lessons on the Epistle to the Hebrews. In preparation. Price 15 cents.

IX. **A Christian Catechism.** Containing Popular Exposition of the Lord's Prayer, Apostles' Creed, and Ten Commandments. With Scripture Proofs. 15 cents.

X. **Lessons on the Gospel of John.** By the author of Lessons on the Acts and the Epistle to the Hebrews. Price 18 cents.

XI. **Lessons on the Gospel of John.** For Younger Scholars. Price 15 cents.

XII. **The Infant Question Book.** or Little Child's Pathway to Jesus. Price 15 cents.

XIII. **Christ the Wonderful.** A new Question Book on the Miracles. Price 18 cents.

XIV. **Lessons about Jesus.** Designated for Infant Classes. First Series. Price 10 cents.

XV. **Lessons about Jesus.** Designated for Infant Classes. Second Series. Price 10 cents.

XVI. **Heroines of the Bible ;** or the Women of Sacred History. In Three Volumes. For the Infant Class—for Children and Youth—and for Adults. Will be ready in May. Price 15 cents.

The Superintendent's Record Book.

Containing Class Register, Minute Book, Sunday School Concert Book, and a Tabular View of the Schools. Price $1.00.

PLYMOUTH COUNTY
BUSINESS DIRECTORY.

Agents.
HOLMES LEWIS J.   Bridgewater
VAIL I. B.   North Carver

Agricultural Implement Manufacturers.
Bates Caleb, (rock lifters and revolving harrows,)   Kingston
Atsatt E. S.   Mattapoisett

Agricultural Implement Dealers.
(See also Country Stores)

CLOUD H. H. No. Abington, Abington.
DYER N. N.   Abington.
FRENCH JOS.,   "
Poole F.,   "
Ripley W.   "
Soule Charles,   "
HUNT JOHN, (see page 44)
    N. Bridgewater
REYNOLDS E. D. & O. B. (Eagle Seed Sower, page 49)   N. Bridgewater
DOANE G. H. (see page 32)   Middleboro
DREW WM. R. (see page 84) Plymouth
HARLOW & BARNES,   Plymouth
WHITTEN & HOLMES, (see page 52
    Plymouth
COPELAND HEMAN, (Knife Mower, see adv.)   West Bridgewater

Anchor Manufacturers.
Barstow Edwin,   Hanover
Curtis George,   "
Holmes Alexander,   Kingston
HOLMES GAIUS,   Kingston
SIMMONS F. O.   Kingston

Apothecaries.
Nash Sylvanus,   Abington
DYER N. N. So. Abington   "
ESTES J. J. East   "   (see page 7)
CROOKER B. T. (see page 51
    Bridgewater.
Conant John A.   East Bridgewater.

Curtis Robt. S.   Hanover
Wilder Isaac M.   "
Fearing Wm. 2d,   Hingham
HUNT J. L. (see page 18)   "
Sparrow Wm. E.   Mattapoisett.
SHAW J. B. & J. (see p. 33) Middleboro
BIXBY C. C. & CO. (see page 27)
    No. Bridgewater
COBB TYLER,   No. Bridgewater
Dearborn S. Francis,   "
HUBBARD BENJ. (see p. 51) Plymouth
Egbert Jarvis,   "
Warren Winslow,   "
Baker & Williams,   West Bridgewater

Architects.
Vaughan J. C.   Carver
EATON S. K.   Mattapoisett

Artists.
Gay Wm. A.   Hingham
Hudson Wm. jr.   "

Auctioneers.
Whitmarsh A.   Abington
Cook Joshua, No. Abington   "
Whitmarsh J.   Centre,   "
Corthell W. P. So. Abington   "
Gilson L. C. East   "   "
Winslow Pelham, E.   "   "
Alden Benjamin,   Duxbury
ALDEN S. G.   East Bridgewater
SWIFT VAN R.   Bridgewater
INGLEE EDWIN,   Halifax
Cox William,   Hanson
Seymour C. W.   Hingham
Sampson A. H.   Kingston
Atsatt E. S.   Mattapoisett
Alden Milton,   Middleboro
HINCKLEY S.   "
Clapp B. R.   No. Bridgewater
Tinkham O. G.   "
HOLMES B. H. (see p. 34)   Plymouth
PROUTY C. W.   Scituate
Vinal Thomas,   "

DIVIDENDS ADDED to the **POLICY** in the **BERKSHIRE** often exceed the premium paid; are **NON-FORFEITABLE** and will be redeemed in **CASH ON DEMAND**.   (See page 50.)

Auger, Bit and Gimlet Makers.
Damon Lewis, (hollow auger.) Bridgewater
DREW C. P. & CO. (calking tools.)
(see page 36.) Kingston.

Axletree Manufacturers.
LAZELL, PERKINS & CO. (see p. 14) Bridgewater

Bakers.
Sproul G. L. South Abington.
Milliken Heard, East Bridgewater
HUNT GEO. Hingham
HUNT & WILDER, (see page 55) North Bridgewater
WASHBURN F. B. (see page 30) North Bridgewater
WHITING G. A. (see page 51) Plymouth
TERRY J. C. (see page 20) Plympton

Balance Manufacturers.
STEPHENSON LUTHER, Hingham

Beer Manufacturers.
Ramsdell Asa T. East Bridgewater

Billiard Halls.
Douglas W. East Abington
GILMAN G. N. (see p. 10) No. "
Gardner Calvin, Hingham
Davis Chas. G. Plymouth

Blacking Manufacturers.
HATHAWAY C. L. (see page 26, 27) No. Bridgewater
Washburn E. No. Bridgewater
WHITTEMORE D. (dressing, see p. 57 bis.) No. Bridgewater

Blacksmiths.
LEAN W. M. Abington
Merritt Ira "
Baker Paul East "
Bass Robert, " "
Denley W. D. " "
Kendrigan John, " "
Clift Belus, South "
Varney Geo. North "
HARLOW S. Bridgewater
LAZELL, PERKINS & CO (see p. 14) "
PRATT SETH, Bridgewater
Shaw Chas. S. North Carver
WESTGATE E. C. Carver
Delano Nath'l, Duxbury
Faunce Zenas, "
Vinal Henry G. "
Dorr Rufus B. So. Marshfield, "
Siddell Chas. W. East Bridgewater
Mitchell George, Halifax
FOSTER OTIS, Hanover
WRIGHT WARREN, "
Pool Elias C. Hanson
Cook Chas. R. Hingham
DAMON I. N. "
Merritt Henry jr. "
Murray Thomas, "
Stoddard Caleb, South "
Bailey Caleb E. Kingston
Chandler John S. "

Delano Lewis S. Kingston
Drew Job W. "
Perkins Ezra, "
Southworth Enoch, Lakeville
Winslow Asa T. "
Briggs Rufus F. Marion
Brown & Williamson, So. Marshfield
Rogers M. W. East "
Bowlm Josiah, Mattapoisett
Lincoln L. & Son, Middleboro
LITTLEJOHN A. B. Middleboro
Littlejohn O. "
Soule James, "
Southard Calvin, "
Wales Abijah T. "
Bradford & Crocker, North Bridgewater
TYLER A. D. " "
PECK HIRAM F. " "
PECK HORATIO W. N. Bridgewater
Wade Albert R. " "
Foster Otis, Pembroke
Kilberth J. Wilson, "
Bearce Thomas, North "
LEWIS MARTIN J. "
MERRITT FRANCIS, Pembroke
Gray L. T. So. Hanson, "
Merrill Francis, W. Duxbury, "
Fuller George, Plymouth
Harvey Sylvanus, "
Holmes Nathan H. "
Shaw Ichabod, "
Standish Miles, "
Morton Henry, Chiltonville, "
Lucas Nathaniel, Plympton
Perkins Josiah, "
Sherman Charles, "
Churchill Spencer, North "
CHURCH C. H. Rochester
Smellie Wm. "
Clapp Elijah, Scituate
Clapp Elijah T. "
Litchfield Isaac, "
Litchfield Seth, "
Merritt J. H. "
Sherman W. H. "
Gardner Horatio N. South "
Merritt Henry, " "
Merritt Jos. 2d, " "
Bolles Israel B. Wareham
Cushman Jacob, "
Hamblin E. "
Atwell Charles, West Bridgewater
Winship Isaac, "

Boarding House.
RANDALL R C. Rochester

Boat Builders.
Alden Samuel, Duxbury
Chandler Hiram W. "
Peterson Samuel S. "
Wadsworth Daniel, "
Denham Silas, South Hanson, Hanson
Knights E. G. Hull
Jenney Alonzo, Mattapoisett
Turner Melzar S. Scituate
Lawley Geo. & Co., N. Scituate, "

Bonnet Bleacheries.
Leonard N. W. & J. M. Middleboro
PITTS LEMUEL, JR., (see page 28) *
North Bridgewater

J. A. JACKSON, 101 COURT STREET, BOSTON, DEALER IN HATS, CAPS, AND FURS.

BOOKS AND STATIONERY—BOOT AND SHOE MAKERS. 129

Books and Stationery.

Nash Sylvanus, Abington
DYER N N So. Abington "
Dyer S. " "
ESTES J. J. E. " "
(see page 7)
BOWKER ANDREW, (see page
20) Hanson
Barnard John, Hingham
LeBaron Lemuel, Mattapoisett
J. B. & J. SHAW, (see page
33) Middleboro
BIXBY C. C. & CO., (see page 27)
North Bridgewater
DOTEN CHAS. C., (see opposite last
cover) Plymouth

Boot and Shoe Dealers.

(See also Boot and Shoe Manufacturers.)
Rosenfeld Nathan, E. Abington, Abington
Wheeler Edward A. " "
PEARSON G. H. & CO., (see page 10)
South Abington, Abington
CUSHMAN D. (see page 13) Bridgewater
GUSHEE E. (see page 17) "
WILLIS NATHAN, "
NUTTER I. N. & E. W. (see page
39,) East Bridgewater
Souther David, Hingham
Whitten E. L. "
BURGES & BAILEY, (see page
5,) Kingston
LeBaron Lemuel, Mattapoisett
Taylor Henry, "
Washburn & Andrews, Middleboro
BRIGHAM C. D. (see page 53,)
North Bridgewater
DAVIS B. P. (see p. 25) " "
Bramhall Benj. Plymouth
Bartlett Ephriam, "
Holmes Ephraim B. "
HOWLAND J. jr. (see p. 87) "
Howard D. F. Wareham
Baker & Williams, West Bridgewater
Perkins Chas. " "
Richards E. E. " "

Boot and Shoe Findings, Tools &c.

DAMON M. W. (patterns). E. Abington
Merritt Ira, (knives), East "
Pool Franklin, " "
Jenkins Bro. & Co. (shoe strings),
South Carver
KEEN SAM'L & CO. Joppa
East Bridgewater
COBB TYER, (tools) North "
Snell E. S. & Co. " "
Snell & Atherton, " "
Tuck S. V. (shoe knife manufacturer)
North Bridgewater
WEBSTER W. (shoe knives, see p.
45) North Bridgewater
Woodbridge E. H. " "
WHITTEMORE D. (pegging machines see p. 57 h) No. Bridgewater
Finney Harrison, Plymouth
May Chas. T. "

Boot and Shoe Finishers.

Damon Howard, Abington
Tregon Wm. North "

Martin P. C. West Bridgewater

Boot and Shoe Makers.

(See Boot & Shoe Manufacturers; also Boot
& Shoe Dealers)
Anderson James, Abington
Loud Charles, "
Payson B. F. "
Hibbard J. C. East Abington
Page Joseph, " "
Wheeler Edw. A. " "
ARNOLD MOSES N. No. " "
Joy B. F. " "
Noyes Cephas D. " "
Wales Cyrus M. " "
CUSHMAN D. (see p. 13) Bridgewater
GUSHEE E. (see p. 17) "
WILLIS NATHAN, "
Wood Simeon D. Bridgewater
Cole Ansel, Carver
Copeland Ralph, "
Fuller Benj. F. "
Lucas John B. "
Chandler David jr. Duxbury
Harriman Elisha A. "
Shaw Jerome B. East Bridgewater
Lyon Edwin, Halifax
Lyon C. P. "
Thompson Asaph P. "
Studley Wm. Hanover
Buffum, F. S. Hanover
Stoddard H. A. "
Young Benj. "
Callahan Job, "
Benney Josiah 2d. Hanson
Pearse Benj. H. "
Chapman Luther W. "
Cobb Theodore "
Stetson Geo. F. "
Stevens A. W. "
Josselyn Carl P. "
SOPER JEREMIAH, Hanson
Cushing Wm. C. Hingham
Dyer S. L. "
Hudson Jotham, "
Sherman Humphrey, Marion
Ames George, Marshfield
Ewell Daniel E. "
Harrington William, "
Faunce & Snow, Mattapoisett
Gammons Walter T. "
Kinney Jirah, "
Mendell Ellis, Mattapoisett
KEITH J. E. (see p. 28) Middleboro
LUIPPOLD J. M. (see p. 21) "
Bump Benj. W. Middleboro
Jones George W. "
Mitchell O. D. " "
Thomas A. C. " "
McDonnell T. W. No. Bridgewater
Skinner G. M. " "
Thayer George, Pembroke
Bartlett Ephriam Plymouth
Bramhall Benj. "
Holmes Ephraim B. "
HOWLAND J. jr. "
Perry H. H. "
Thomas George W. Plympton
Wright W. H. H. "
Peirce George H. Rochester
Merritt James L. Scituate
Hinckley Alpheus, Wareham
Moroney M. C. "
Edson L. Geo. West Bridgewater
Tisdale Edward, "

Policy Holders in the BERKSHIRE LIFE INSURANCE COMPANY of
Pittsfield, Mass., DO NOT FORFEIT THEIR POLICIES by reason of
FAILURE TO PAY their premiums.   34   (See page 50.)

Boot & Shoe Manufacturers.
(See also Makers ; also Dealers.)

ARNOLD MOSES H. Abington
BLANCHARD DANIEL H. Abington
BLANCHARD VINSON, "
BROWN H. L. "
Brown & Cushing, "
BROWN & HUNT, "
Cobb & Thompson, "
Cushing S. P. "
Cushing Sylvanus, "
Cushing W. W. "
Dunham Henry, jr. "
Faxon L. & Co. "
FLOYD & FARRAR, "
HARRIS JAMES H. "
HUNT HENRY, "
Hunt T. J. "
Jones L. S. & Co. "
Loud Charles S. "
MESERVE CHARLES, "
Nash B. T. "
Nash J. L. "
NASH M. & G. T. "
Noyes S. C. "
OSGOOD GILMAN, "
Parker David & Co. "
PERRY W. G. "
Semonin Peter, "
Shaw Jacob, "
Vaughn Joseph & Sons, "
VAUGHAN STETSON, "
Wales Cyrus M. "
WALES W. S. "
Whitmarsh James, "
Whitmarsh Joshua, "
WILKES BELA, "
Beals Nath'l E. Abington
Bigelow J. F. " "
Blanchard Leonard, " "
Clapp Geo. B. " "
Curtis Abner, " "
Curtis Geo. " "
Curtis Leander, " "
Curtis Joshua, jr. " "
Dill C. H. 2d, " "
Dill D. W. " "
Dill Joseph, " "
Fuller & Blanchard, " "
LANE JENKINS & SON, " "
Lowell Ira F. " "
REED S, jr. " "
SHAW E. A. " "
Shaw Elijah, " "
Shaw S. B. " "
Studley & Sturner, " "
TORREY C. W. " "
Whiting Jacob & Co. " "
Winslow Pelham, " "
CHAMBERLAIN ALBERT, (See p. 16,) N. Abington,
Cleverly Joseph, " "
Grose D. & Co. " "
Wales S. R. " "
WALES W. S. " "
Alden A. So. Abington,
Alden Alex. " "
ALLEN C. F. " "
Blake & Preston, " "
Gurney Davis, " "
Norton Samuel, " "
Noyes E. & E. M. " "
Prouty Charles, " "

Reed Nahum & Son, South Abington
Reed William L. " "
Vining W. R. (shoe) " "
ALLEN J. S. East Bridgewater
Bates Irving & Co. (shoes), "
EDSON FRANKLIN, "
FOLSOM GEO. W. "
Keith R. C. (shoes), "
Vinton William, "
BRYANT SETH, (shoes), Joppa, "
KINGMAN E. & E. "
Shaw S. & Son, (shoes) " "
Soule J. W. " "
VINTON, J. O. East Bridgewater
Damon Rector, Hanover
Killam & Turner, "
MORSE MARCUS, "
Studley Edwin H. "
STODDARD H. A. Hanover
Stetson George, Hanson
French George H. Hingham
Hutchins & Cloutman, "
Stoddard William D. "
Whiton & Bullard, "
Cushing & Kelley, So. Hingham, "
WHITCOMB & BATES, " "
WILDER M West "
DEAN HENRY A. & CO. Lakeville
Sherman Eli, Marion
Faunce & Snow, Mattapoisett
Kingman Calvin D. Middleboro
LEONARD GEO. jr. "
Leonard & Barrows, "
Perkins Noah C. "
Leach Geo. M. E. Middleboro,
PERKINS, E. E. & SON, N. Middleboro
Baxendale John, North Bridgewater
Brett Pliny, (boots), "
Chesman Noah & Co. "
Cross Henry, "
ELDRIDGE DAVID, N Bridgewater
Ford C. R. "
French & Packard, (boots), "
Gurney G. H. "
Herrod Sam'l (shoes), "
Hollis J. L. (Congress boots), "
HOLMES C. F. "
Holmes Marcus (shoes), "
Howard D. S. & W. A. "
HOWARD DAVID (boots), "
Howard F. O. "
Howard & Packard, "
Johnson Nahum, "
Keith C. E. "
Keith Willard, "
Leach Marcus (shoes), "
Leach O. & Son, " "
Leach O. F. "
Leach P. S. "
LITTLEFIELD HENRY, "
Packard N. R. "
Porter Lewis (boots), "
Porter & Packard, "
Reynolds Enos, "
Stoddard R. A. "
Thayer F. A. & H. B. "
Thayer E. L. "
White Welcome (boots), "
White L. B. "
Willis Mitchell, (shoes), "
Bryant Horace, Campello, "
Emerson & Keith, "
Keith A. & A. B. " "
Keith Franklin & Co. " "

LEAVITT'S FUR & HAT STORE, 91 COURT STREET, BOSTON.

BOOTS AND SHOES

Keith C. P.	North Bridgewater	Oldham J 2d,	Pembroke
Keith H. P.	" "	Shepard N T	"
Keith M. L.	" "	West & Lefurgey,	" "
Kingman Gardner J.	" "	BARNES E & J C	Plymouth
Reynolds Howard W.	" "	BONNEY JAMES S	Plympton
Reynolds Marcus V.	" "	Ellis James C	
Snell William,	" "	ELLIS THOMAS,	Rochester
Stevens George,	" "	Gross John E	South Scituate
WALKER & PETERSON,	"	Jones John H	"
Howard Capen, Northwest Bridge-		Pratt & Lapham,	"
water,	"	TORREY DAVID, JR.,	"
Bartlett Ephraim,	Plymouth	Andrews Thomas	West Bridgewater
CHURCHILL JOHN,	"	Howard Caleb, Cochesett,	"
Holmes Ephraim B.	"		
Lanman Nath'l C. jr.	"	**Bricks.**	
Mills Henry,	"	HOOPER MITCHELL (see p 12),	
MOREY WM.,			Bridgewater
	Scituate	Thompson Seth & Son,	E Bridgewater
Bailey J. W. & G. W.,N.Scituate	"	Hedge Barnabas	Plymouth
Clapp C. H.	" "	Jacobs Edward,	South Scituate
Litchfield M. S. & Z. H.	" "		
Newcomb W. J.	" "	**Brokers.**	
Sylvester E. H.	" "		
Gross Charles A.	South Scituate	Harlow Nath'l E. (fish)	Plymouth
Curtis Brothers,	"	Hathaway Benj (commercial)	"
HATCH JONA. (see page 39)	"	Nelson Wm H (fish)	"
Willcutt Dexter M.	"		
Copeland & Hartwell,	W. Bridgewater	**Butchers.**	
ERLAND THAYER, West Bridgewater		BLANCHARD VINSON,	Abington
Edson M. C.	" "	CUSHING D	"
Edson & Caldwell,	"	Studley Reuben, East Abington,	"
Howard & Washburn,	"	Alger James,	Bridgewater
Copeland P. & N.	Campello, "	WRIGHT EZRA,	Marshfield
ALGER W. O. (see p 69) Cochesett, "		Winter S.	North Bridgewater
Hayward F W	" "	Barnes Willard, Campello,	"
Peckham H E & C F	" "	BASSETT WILLIAM,	Rochester
Tisdale Edward,	" "	Otis Job P.	Scituate
		Taylor James,	"
Boot & Shoe Soles, Heels & Stiffen-		CORTHELL JOHN, (see p 47),	
ings.			South Scituate
Rochefort Francis,	Abington		
Keith & Packard (counters),		**Cabinet Makers.**	
	North Bridgewater	*(See also Furniture.)*	
Atwood J. R. (heels),	Plymouth	Willey C. B.	Abington
		Holbrook Loring, S. Abington,	"
Box Makers.		Hobart S. L.	Hingham
(See also Paper Boxes.)		Hudson Augustus L.	"
ATWOOD B. S. & E. H. (see p 10),		Leavitt A. L.	"
	Abington	RIPLEY & NEWHALL,	"
Wheeler John,	"	Cushman Edwin,	Kingston
Cushing David,	East Abington, "	NELSON THOMAS,	Mattapoisett
Keith A. W.	North " "	RAYMOND C (see p 34),	Plymouth
Pratt Z.	Bridgewater		
Cole Harrison G. & Co.,	N. Carver	**Carpenters and Builders.**	
DELANO ELISHA,	Duxbury	Brown Bela,	Abington
Goss Charles H	East Bridgewater	Keen George,	"
Damon Thomas,	Hanover	Nash William,	"
Simmons Ebenezer,	"	Singleton Richard, N. Abington,	"
Cushing Elijah,	Hanson	Bates Cyrus, S.	" "
CUSHING T & G	"	Healy Oliver G.	" "
HERSEY EDMUND,	Hingham	Keith Ambrose,	Bridgewater
LEWIS JAMES, S.	Hingham	BURT GEORGE H	Bridgewater
Lane Leavitt,	"	HOWLAND ROBERT,	"
Richmond E	Lakeville	KEITH LLOYD,	"
Hatch J & C R, W Marshfield, Marshfield		LEACH JAMES C	"
Hatch D P & J F	" "	WADSWORTH DURA,	"
Magoun & Holmes,	"	Harlow Benjamin, S. Carver,	Carver
NELSON THOMAS,	Mattapoisett	Sherman Joseph,	"
Harlow's Steam Mills (see card),		Parsons C. D. N.	" "
	Middleboro	Sherman Joseph R. "	" "
Rock Mills (see page 91), Rock,	"	Southworth Thomas,	" "
Thatcher R L	North Bridgewater	Loudon George,	Duxbury
Barker John,	Pembroke	Weston James M.	"
Hatch G F	No Pembroke,	"	

ANNUAL CASH DIVIDENDS in the **BERKSHIRE LIFE INS. CO.**, Pittsfield, Mass. Boston Office, 95 1-2 Washington St. (See page 50.)

PLYMOUTH COUNTY DIRECTORY.

Bonney Charles H.   East Bridgewater
Jackson Abner C.,   "
Leonard Hermon,   "
Holmes Darius E.   Halifax
Thompson Albert,   "
Damon Thomas,   Hanover
Hollis Silas,   "
Studley George,   "
Turner S. S.   "
Loring Joseph S.   Hanson
Taft Andrew J.   "
Josselyn Benj. W.   S. Hanson,   "
Ramsdell Sam'l D   "   "
Bailey S. G. & Son,   Hingham
Cushing Allyne,   "
Foster William,   "
Lincoln T. H.   "
NELSON WM. J.   "
Pearce John W.   "
Ripley Justin,   "
Sprague Timothy,   "
Bartlett Walter S,   Kingston
DREW C Jr.   "
Faunce George,   "
Holmes Joseph,   "
Holmes Stephen,   "
Ripley Lewis,   "
Waterman E E   "
Briggs Joseph H.   Lakeville
Sampson S W   "
Shaw Jarius H   "
Southworth Warren H.   "
Allen Silas B   Marion
Allen Webster,   "
Blankenship Warren,   "
Briggs Howard,   "
BRIGGS PAUL W.   "
Briggs William,   "
Handy Augustus H   "
HILLER B   Marion
BAKER H E   Marshfield
KENT W   "
KENT WARREN,   Marshfield.
Oakman Henry P.   "
Sprague Edward,   "
Oakman Israel,   West   "
Boodry Dennis S,   Mattapoisett
Hiller Prince,   "
Purrington George,   "
Barden John S   Middleboro
Caswell Abiather,   "
Haskins Franklin,   "
SHAW O H   Middleboro
Reed Sylvanus W.   "
Sears Ivory,   "
Sherman Joshua,   "
Sparrow James P.   "
Tinkham Joseph R.   "
Tinkham Lorenzo,   "
Eaton Lewis,   N. Middleboro,
Eaton Oliver,   "   "
Eaton Williams,   "   "
White Wm. B   "
Beal John F   North Bridgewater
FORD J W   "   "
Foye & Holmes,   "
McLaughlin Samuel,   "
Snow B   "
YOUNG A J   North Bridgewater
COBB OTIS,   Campello,
Bonney J G   Pembroke
Taylor Willis, jr,   "
Whitman Seth,   "

Whitman T T   "
Ford J.   North Pembroke,   "
FORD BARNABAS,   "   "
Howland David O.   South Hanson,   "
Barnes Nathaniel C   Plymouth
Barnes William B   "
Bartlett Thomas B   "
Bates Comfort,   "
Bradford Caleb C   Plymouth
Churchill Amasa   "
Churchill William   "
Cox Wm R   "
Diman Thomas   "
Drew Winslow   "
Eddy Lewis   "
Harlow Ivory L.   "
Holmes Wm S   "
King L C   "
Lanman Henry T   "
Peterson Charles,   "
Pope William,   "
Rider Daniel J   "
Rider Joseph,   "
Weston Henry   "
Whitten Charles,   "
Hoxie Edward,   South Plymouth,   "
Langford John,   "   "
Fuller Joseph H   Plympton
Holmes George W   "
Perkins Nathan,   "
Sherman George W   "
Sherman Joseph,   "
Cole John,   Rochester
Sherman Augustus T   "
West Benj. W   "
Lee Geo C   North Scituate, Scituate
Merritt Henry,   "   "
Foster Philip,   South Scituate
Turner David W   "
Turner Samuel,   "
Nye Andrew S   Wareham
Nye Thomas S   "
Weston Abisha B   "
Wing Geo F   "
Hayward & Mitchell,   West Bridgewater
Wilbur George,   "

Carpet Dealers.

Blanchard Ebenezer,   Hanover
Curtis Henry J   "
Robinson H W & Co   N Bridgewater

Carpet Sweeper Manufactory.

Purrington James H   Mattapoisett

Carriage, Coach and Sleigh Manufacturers.
(See also *Wagon Makers*; also *Wheelwrights.*)

Brown Pela,   Abington
Peirce M B   "
Corbett Lewis,   East Abington,   "
Eells Robert,   Hanover
Turner Thomas,   "
Whiton Pela K & Co   Hingham
Waters Samuel,   South Hingham,   "
Eldridge David,   Kingston
Washburn Salmon,   Lakeville
Brown & Williamson,   Marshfield
Damon F N,   E Marshfield,   "
HERSEY D. A.   Hingham
BONNEY J D   Pembroke
BAILEY D DAMON,

IN THE SPRING MONTHS, the system naturally undergoes a change, and HELMBOLD'S HIGHLY CONCENTRATED EXTRACT OF SARSAPARILLA is an assistant of the greatest value.

Pickens Philo H Middleboro
Crocker & Bradford, North Bridgewater
Mason A H (repairer) "
Tribou L. E "
Briggs S F N Plympton, Plympton
Merritt J C & J H Scituate
BARROWS HIRAM & SON, Wareham
Packard Leander L. "

Carriage Repositories.
White J F North Hanson, Hanson

Carriage Smiths.
(See also Blacksmiths.)
Taylor A D, North Bridgewater
Litchfield Isaac, Scituate
Atwell Charles, West Bridgewater

Carriage Trimmers.
ROGERS R S Bridgewater
Bird L T North Bridgewater
Jones Charles L Plymouth

Carvers.
Purrington Henry J Mattapoisett

Cattle Broker.
Ames Thomas, West Bridgewater

Cigar Dealers.
(See also Tobaconists.)
Coy George W. E Abington. Abington
ESTES J J (see page 7) " "
Perkins Henry F Kingston
Prince Thomas, "
JUDKINS WM. M. (see page 16)
  East Bridgewater
Calnum John, North Bridgewater

Cigar Manufacturers.
Kenney Augustus, E Abington, Abington

Civil Engineers and Surveyors.
HERSEY L Abington
Corthell W. P., S. Abington, Abington
Smith Joseph, Hanson
GURNEY E. B. K. So Hanson, Hanson
Seymour C W Hingham
STAPLES H. Lakeville
EATON S. K. Mattapoisett
Howard Albert, West Bridgewater
Howard James, "

Claim Agents.
OSBORNE WM. H. East Bridgewater
GURNEY E. B. K. So. Hanson, Hanson
Perkins Jones R. North Bridgewater

Clergymen.
ABBREVIATIONS.—B. signifies Baptist; Ch., Christian; C. T., Congregational Trinitarian; C. U., Congregational Unitarian; E., Episcopal; F. B., Freewill Baptist; M., Methodist; M. E. Methodist Episcopal; N. J., New Jerusalem; R. C., Roman Catholic; S. A., Second Advent; Uv., Universalist.
Abbe F. R. (C. T.) Abington
Dodge Benj. (C. T.) "
Pettes Joseph, (N. J.) "

ROACH A. L. (R. C.) Abington
Howe Sereno, (B.) E. Abington, "
Walker Horace D. (C. T.) " "
Darrow Geo. R. (B.) So. "
Edwards H. L. (C. T.) " "
Douglass Ebenezer, (C. T.) Bridgewater
Harris C. C. (E.) "
Hayward T. B. (N. J.) "
Leonard H. P. (C. T.) "
McGuire M. T. (R. C.) "
Leach Wm. (B.) Carver
Chase D. L. (C. T.) No. Carver, "
Coggshall S. W. (M. E.) Duxbury
Moore Josiah, (C. U.) "
Washburn Jas. A. (M. E.) W. Dux. "
Tisdale Wm. R. (W. M.) "
Farrington W. F. (M. E.) E. Bridgewater
Paine T. O. (N. J.) "
Williams F. C. (C. U.) "
Fobes W. A. (C. T.) Halifax
Ewer Seth, (B.) "
Aiken James (C. T.) Hanover
Cutler Samuel (E.) "
Freeman Joseph (C. T.) "
Reed Andrew (B.) "
Southworth Benj. (C. T.) Hanson
Watson W. H. (B.) So. Hanson, "
Lincoln Calvin, (C. U.) Hingham
Hersey Henry, "
Jones Wm. H. "
Fuller George E. (M. E.) "
Tilson J. (B.) "
Young Joshua, (C. U.) "
Sawyer ——, South Hingham, "
Peckham Joseph, (C. T.) Kingston
Phipps J. H. (C. U.) "
Tilton Josiah H (B.) "
Ward James W. (C. T.) Lakeville
Barrows Elijah W. (Ch.) "
COBB LEANDER, (C. T.) Marion
Alton Abel, (M. E.) "
Tozer William, (P. M.) "
VOSE HENRY C. (Uv.) "
Alden L. (C. T.) Marshfield
Davis Jacob, (B.) "
Leonard George, "
Snow ——, (C. U) "
Pease B. F. (M. E.) "
Williams Edward, (C. T.) E. Marshfield, "
Cleveland John P. (C. T.) Mattapoisett
Faunce William, (B.) "
ABBOTT L. A. (B.) Middleboro
DODD S. G. (C. T.) see hist. 28, "
Newell F. C. (M. E.) "
Putnam I. W. (C. T.) "
Hill E. S. (B.) Rock, "
Hutchinson J. E. (B.) North Mid. "
Little E. G. (C. T.) "
Sawyer Rufus M. (C. T.) "
Mitchell ——, (N. J.) North Bridgewater
McNulty Thomas B. (R. C.) "
Roripaugh S. L. (Uv.) "
Wood Charles W (C. T.) Campello "
Doggett T. P. (C. U.) Pembroke
Hinckley C. N. (M.) S. Hanson, Hanson
Bremner David, (C. T.) Plymouth
Brooks Wm H. (E.) "
Hall Edward H. (C. U.) "
Humprey Edward, (B.) "
Pool George F. (M.) "
Tomlinson Rassell, (Uv.) "
Fuller Alex. (C. T.) Chiltonville, "
Woodbury C. T. (C. T.) "

The terms for ENDOWMENT, and TEN ANNUAL LIFE POLICIES in the BERKSHIRE are peculiarly favorable, and rates lower than in any Note Company. (See page 50.)

Patten Moses, [C. T.] Plympton
Cushing James R. [Cong.] Rochester
Leonard Edwin, [Cong.] "
Sweet Hiram, [M.] "
Nason Charles, [M. E.] Scituate
Heywood Wm. S [C U] N. Scituate, "
Conant Thomas B [B] " "
Holmes Lewis, [B] " "
Sessions A. J. [C T] " "
Wallace J. [M E] South Scituate
Fish Wm. H. [C U] "
Cleary T. C, [C U] Wareham
Dean Theo. P. [C U] West Bridgewater
Ela Walter, [M] "
Pasco Cephas, [B] "
Pasco H. E. [B] "

Clocks.
(See also Watches, Jewelry &c.)
HEWETT E. H. *(see page 12)*
                      Bridgewater
GURNEY L. F. (see page 47) No. "
HEWETT H. *(see p. 39)* No. "
Studley Luther, dealer, " "

Clothes Wringer Manufacturer.
Packard C. H. Campello, N. Bridgewater

Clothing.
(See also Tailors.)
ESTES & WHITING, *(see page 10)*
   East Abington, Abington
Sherman Benj. East Abington, "
Howes Phineas, Bridgewater
Rogers Wales, East "
Rosenfeld G. " "
Allen S. B. Joppa, "
BLANCHARD EBEN, Hanover
Curtis Henry J. "
CURTIS R. S. "
BURGES & BAILEY, see page 5,
                      Kingston
Fuller Frank, manuf., "
TOOLE MICHAEL, see page 53,
                      Middleboro
BRETT H. A., adv. page 54,
            North Bridgewater
BRYANT G. E. & H. L. see. p 48, "
KINGMAN & HOLLYWOOD, adv.
   page 24, "
ATWOOD WM. 2d, adv. page 49,
                      Plymouth
Peterson Lewis, "

Coal and Wood.
(See also Wood and Bark.)
Noyes John N. Abington
Reed A. N. & Co., N. Abington, "
Winslow George, Duxbury
Hobart John, East Bridgewater
Bosworth Martin, Halifax
Perry Ethan, Hanover
Bassett Daniel, Hingham
MARSH CALEB D, "
LEBARON J. B. adv. page 53,
                      Middleboro
FOSS N. J. Campello, N. Bridgewater
Hayward Daniel, "
Packard E. & Co., "
Cobb F. B. Plymouth
Simmons George, "
Damon & Lewis, Scituate
Gurney Ansel S. Wareham
Richards E. E. West Bridgewater

Coffin Warerooms.
Wiley C. B. Abington
Holbrook O. B. East Abington, "
Holbrook Loring, South " "
PROPHETT WILLIAM, see page 11,
                      Bridgewater
French Daniel, East Bridgewater
Eaton A. M. Middleboro
SOULE GEO. see page 34, "
HOWARD, CLARK & CO., see
   page 25, North Bridgewater
SHUTLEFF LOTHROP, see page
   24, "
RAYMOND CHARLES, see page
   34, Plymouth
Brown Joseph P. "

Confectionery and Fruit.
Smith James E. Abington
Hull C. J. Bridgewater
RIPLEY H. C. see page 11, "
Woodward Cyrus C. East Bridgewater
Overton Francis, Hingham
Tallman Alfred S. Marion
Kinney Jireh, jr., Mattapoisett
TRIPP B. F. Middleboro
Union Saloon, "
WASHBURN F. B. see page 39,
              North Bridgewater
BALLARD S D. see card, Plymouth
DODGE, J E "
LUCAS S. see page 51, "
ADAMS T. C. Wareham
Bassett Washington, E. Wareham, "
BRIGGS E. Wareham

Conveyancers.
HOWLAND F. P. Abington
Cortheli W. P. So. Abington "
Gurney E. B. K. So. Hanson Hanson
Holmes B. H. Plymouth

Coopers.
Winsor Seth, Duxbury
Parris Jonathan, Halifax
CORTHELL NELSON, Hingham
STEWART DAVIS, Kingston
Ashley Josiah R. Lakeville
Aikens Warren, Mattapoisett
Bolles Prince, "
Bradford Samuel, Plymouth
Harlow Abner H. "
Holbrook Gideon Jr. "

Copper Founders.
LAZELL, PERKINS & CO. see page 14,
                      Bridgewater

Cordage Manufacturers.
Hingham Cordage Co Hingham
REED EDWIN, Kingston
Plymouth Cordage Co. Plymouth

Cotton Gin Manufacturers.
Bates, Hyde & Co. Eagle Cotton Gin
   Manufacturers Bridgewater
SOUTHERN COTTON GIN CO. see p.
   15, Bridgewater
E. Carver Co. East Bridgewater

Cotton Batting Manufacturers.
Chilton Batting Co. Plymouth
Old Colony Batting Co. "

LEAVITT'S FUR & HAT STORE, 91 COURT STREET, BOSTON.

Cotton Lacing Manufacturers.
Jenkins Bro. & Co. boot and corset
   South Carver,   Carver

Cotton Thread and Twine Manufacturers.
NEWCOMB THOMAS, (thread)
        Kingston

Cotton Warp Manufacturers.
Jenkins, Bro., & Co., (carpet) Plympton

Counsellors.
(See Lawyers.)

Country Stores.
Where is kept a general assortment of Dry Goods, Groceries, Agricultural Implements, Hardware, &c. Those dealing in only one kind of goods will be found under their respective heading.

Faxon B. E.	Abington
Loud Alden S.	"
Soule & Brown,	"
Whitmarsh Z. N.	"
Bigelow David,	East Abington
Curtis Abner,	" "
Torrey D. & E. P.	" "
Ford James,	North Abington
Gleason & Greenwood,	" "
Sprague Elbridge,	" "
Cook Randall,	South Abington,
DYER N. N.	" "
Perry Daniel jr.	" "
CRANE JOSHUA E.	Bridgewater
CROCKER T. W. & CO., (see page 7,)	"
HOBART CALEB,	"
ELLIS M. & CO. South Carver,	Carver
RIDER CHARLES,	" "
SAVERY WM. S. North "	"
Ford N. & Sons,	Duxbury
Protective Union Div. 654,	"
Sampson John,	"
Soule Harvey,	"
Wadsworth Henry,	"
Chandler Charles & Co., W. Dux'y,	"
High Street Union Store, "	"
Conant John A.	East Bridgewater
Hicks Jotham,	"
NUTTER I. N. & E. W. (see page 30,)	"
Rosenfeld G.	"
Churchill L. & W. K. Joppa,	"
Richard Luther,	"
Drew James T.	Halifax
INGLEE EDWIN,	"
Fuller N	"
BATES JOHN B.	Hanover
BLANCHARD EBENEZER,	"
BROOKS JOHN S.	"
Curtis Henry J.	"
CURTIS ROBERT S.	"
MAGOUN H. B.	"
STETSON I. G. (see page 18,)	"
Wilder I. M.	"
Wood Alexander,	"
BOWKER ANDREW, (see page 20,)	Hanson
DREW CYRUS,	"
HOWLAND ALBERT B.	"
Howland Luther,	"
Drayton John,	South Hanson, "
Burr F. & Co.,	Hingham
Burr M. H. & J.	"
Cain David,	"
Eldridge, Reuben,	"
Fearing William 2d,	"
Gardner Calvin,	"
HERSEY GEO. JR. & CO.,	"
HERSEY ISAAC,	"
Hunt C. S.	"
Jacobs, D. & L.	"
Whiton Royal,	"
Cushing Alonzo, South Hingham,	"
Lane Josiah,	" "
Sprague Bela T.	" "
Wilder D. & J.	" "
Pope Joseph,	Hull
BURGES & BAILEY, (see page 5,)	Kingston
COBB PHILANDER,	"
Hunt & Sampson,	"
ROBBINS CHARLES T.	"
Haskins C.	Lakeville
Delano W P	"
HADLEY A J	Marion
HALL S W	"
Mendell Jonathan,	"
Swift M H	"
BAKER GEO M	Marshfield
Crossly H T. & Son	"
Hall Elisha W	East "
Tilden Henry	" "
Tilden Wm M	" "
Weatherbee Geo H Jr	" "
Kinney Jireh jr.	Mattapoisett
Luce Wm.	"
LeBaron Lemuel	"
Mandall John,	"
Snow & Hammond,	"
Taylor Henry,	"
PEIRCE P. H. & CO.,	Middleboro
Eddy W. S. & Son,	E. Mid. "
White & Hooper,	N. Mid. "
Cobb David,	North Bridgewater
SPRAGUE C.	"
Howard & Keith,	Campello, "
Protective Union, 355,	Pembroke
Collamore Horace, N. Pembroke,	"
E. Pembroke Store Co.,	"
High St. Union Store, W. Duxbury	"
Bryant W. H. H.	South Hanson, "
Protective Union,	" "
Cobb F. B.	Plymouth
Bradford A. J.	"
Drew Ellis,	"
LORING THOS.	"
Morton Alvin G.	"
Perkins Arad,	"
Perkins R. H.	"
TURNER E. C.	"
Bramhall Geo. Chiltonville,	"
Brattles Caleb,	" "
Doten & Hoxie,	"
Clark William,	South "
Parker Z.	"
Harrub J M.	North Plympton
CUSHMAN J. M.	Rochester
LEONARD T. W.	"
SHERMAN J. W.	"
Allen Wm. P.	Scituate
Bailey H. W.	"
Ford Daniel L.	"
Smith J. H.	"
Bailey H. & Co.	North "
Turner ——,	" "

DIVIDENDS ADDED to the POLICY in the BERKSHIRE often exceed the premium paid; are NON-FORFEITABLE and will be redeemed in CASH ON DEMAND.   (See page 50.)

Brown Benjamin jr., Scituate
Litchfield M. S. & Z. H. No." "
Vinal Dexter, " "
Wetherbee Thomas, " "
Fogg E. T. South Scituate
TORREY G. H. " "
Besse L. A. Wareham
Bodfish P. N. "
Ellis Stephen, "
Gibbs Alvin, "
Thompson E. N. "
Humphrey Galen, East "
Sanford George, "
Washburn Cromwell, South "
Baker & Williams, West Bridgewater

Crockery, China, Glass and Earthern Ware.

Torrey D. & E. P., E. Abington, Abington
CRANE J. E. Bridgewater
CROCKER T. W. & CO., (see p 7), Bridgewater
CURTIS S. B. & G. E. (see p 23), No. Bridgewater
Cobb David, "
COBB L. E. "
Hayward Ambrose, "
Reed Thomas, "
DREW WM. R. (see p 84), Plymouth
Perkins Chas. West Bridgewater

Dentists.

Fontaine & Ring, Abington
Bonham G. F. E. Abington, Abington
Washburn Christian, Bridgewater
WASHBURN N. & C. (see p 12), "
Daly & Rolfe, Hingham
Leach C. W. Lakeville
Dorr Richard, Marion
Minor Westley, "
HENRY STEPHEN, Marshfield
Leach C. W. Middleboro
PACKARD J. E. (see p 21), North Bridgewater
CUFFEE L. W. (see p 26, 30), "
WHITNEY GEO. R. "
Drew T. B. Plymouth
Shumway Thomas D. "

Designer & Draughtsman.

Wilbur Winslow C. Bridgewater

Dressmakers.
(See also Milliners.)

Shaw Mary Miss, E. Abington, Abington
Studley Susan Mrs. " "
Pouldry Mary Miss, S. Abington, "
Healey Susan H. Mrs. " "
West John Mrs. " "
Hayden Sarah, Bridgewater
Howes Hannah B. Middleboro
Simmons H. A. Mrs. "
Churchill Helen Miss, No. Bridgewater
Foye E. A. Mrs. "
Knowles Emma C. Miss, "
Madison Lizzie Miss, "
Oawley Catharine Miss, Campello, "
Jones Rebecca Miss, Plymouth
Bradford Sarah Miss, "
Bugbee Orelia Miss, "
Collingwood Susan Mrs. "
Godard Harriet Miss, "
Nickerson Mary Miss, "

Dry Goods.
(See also Country Stores; also Hosiery; also Laces, Embroideries, &c.)

Smith E. J. Abington
Whitmarsh Z. N. "
Pearson G. H. & Co. S. Abington, "
Dunham C. & Co. E. Abington, "
RICE J. A. (see p 10) "
Rosenfeld Nathan, " "
Torrey D. & E. P. " "
Gleason & Greenwood, N. Abington,"
CRANE J. E. Bridgewater
CROCKER T. W. & CO., (see p 7), "
Hobart Caleb, "
NUTTER L. N. & E. W. East "
BATES J. B. Hanover
WOOD ALEX. "
BOWKER A. (see page 20) Hanson
DREW C. "
Bartlett L. A. Mrs. & Co. Hingham
LINCOLN G. jr. "
BURGES & BAILEY, (see p 5) Kingston
Hunt & Sampson, "
LePamn Lemuel, Mattapoisett
Alden A. G. Middleboro
KOLHIOK & McJENNET, see page 21, "
Rosenfeld & Toss, "
FENNER E. C. & Co. (see p 31) No. Bridgewater
BRETT BROS. see p. 29, "
Cobb David, "
Wheeler F. B. Mrs. "
Robinson B. W. & Co. "
HOWARD & KEITH, Campello
JENNINGS, L. Pembroke
THRESHER J. Pembroke
Burbank S. M jr Plymouth
CARLUTH J B Plymouth
Harlow J H & Co "
Whiting Benj "
TORREY G H South Scituate
Perkins Charles, West Bridgewater

Dyers.

Jenkins Bro & Co So Carver Carver
DODGE J E Plymouth

Eating Houses.
(See also Oysters & Refreshments)

Edge Tool Manufacturers.

Jacobs Jos & Son Hingham

Embroidery Stamping.

THOMAS H. O. (see page 26.) North Bridgewater

Expresses.

Abington, Ford, 3 Washington st. Boston
Bridgewater, Alden, 5 Congress sq.
Campello, Hancock, 5 Congress sq.
Campello, R. P. Kinsey, 11 State
East Abington, Randall, 3 Washington
East Bridgewater, Sampson & Co., 5 Congress sq.
East Pembroke, Alden 5 Congress sq.
Halifax, Rich & Weston, 5 Congress sq.
Hanover, Randall, 3 Washington
Hanover, Jones, 5 Congress sq.
Hanson, Rich & Weston, 5 Congress sq.
Hanson, Brooks, 84 Court sq

HELMBOLD'S Concentrated Extract Sarsaparilla, is the *Great Blood Purifier.*

Hingham, Cushing, 3 Washington
Hingham, Kennerson, 8 Court sq
Joppa Village, Sampson & Co., 5 Congress square
Kingston, Brooks, 34 Court sq
Marien, Paulding, 11 State
Marion and New Bedford, J. B. Barden
"   "   "   S. C. Leonard
Marshfield, Hatch, 40 Elm
Marshfield, Foster, 40 Elm
Mattapoisett, Paulding, 11 State
Middleboro, R. B. Kinsley, 11 State
Middleboro, Taunton and Providence, Davenport & Mason
No. Bridgewater, Hancock, 2 Wash.
No. Bridgewater, Joslyn, 8 Court sq
No. Duxbury, Alden, 5 Congress sq
No. Scituate, Hunt, 40 Elm
Pembroke, Randall, 3 Washington
Plympton, Rich & Weston, 5 Congress sp
Plymouth, Rich & Weston, 5 Cong. sq
Plymouth, Holmes, 8 Court sq
Scituate, Beal, 11 State
Scituate, Hatch, 40 Elm
Scituate, Hunt, 40 Elm
Scotland, Leonard, 98 Washington
So. Abington, Weston, 3 Washington
So. Hingham, Gardner, 3 Washington
So. Scituate, Foster, 40 Elm
Wareham, Witherell & Co., 34 Court sq
W. Bridgewater, Sampson, 5 Cong. sq
W. Bridgewater, R. B. Kinsley, 11 State
W. Duxbury, Randall, 3 Washington
W. Scituate, Gardner, 3 Washington
W. Scituate, Cushing, 3 Washington
W. Scituate, Foster, 40 Elm

Fancy Goods.
(See also Variety Stores.)

Nash Sylvanus, Abington
ESTES J. J. (see page 7,) East Abington,
Sherman Benj. "   "
PEARSON G. H. & CO., S. Abint'n "
Hall Curtis J. Bridgewater
CROOKER BENJ. T. (see page 51 "
RIPLEY HERVEY C (see page 11,) "
BURGES & BAILEY, (see page 5,) Kingston
Kinney Jireh, Jr., Mattapoisett
BIXBY C. C. & CO. (see page 27,) North Bridgewater
Clapp B. R. "
CURTIS S. B. & G. E. see page 23)"
COPELAND C. F. see page 30,) "
Reed Thomas, "
THOMAS H. O. (see page 26) "
Doten C. C., see opp. last cover, Plym'h
Hall J T "

Fish Dealers.

Nye John, Hingham
Spring C. "
Whiton Peter L. "
Fuller, John Kingston
Cushing Josiah C. Middleboro
Hamilton E. North Bridgewater
Baldwin Wm. M. & Co. Plymouth
Barnes Bradford, "
Manter & Blackmer, "
Bonney E. H. Scituate
Gardner Enoch C. "

Hamblin Geo. S. Wareham

Fisheries.

Delano B. & Son, Kingston
Holmes Edward, "
Atwood Jesse R. Plymouth
Barnes Corban, "
Allen Nath'l W. "
Brewster Isaac, "
Churchill John D. "
Finney Clark, "
Finney E. C. "
Harlow Nath'l E. "
Morton A. G. "
Morton James, "
Nelson Wm. H. "
Turner Ezekiel C. "
Whiting Henry, "

Florist.

HOOPER THOS. (see p 9,) Bridgewater

Flour & Grain.
(See also Produce Dealers.)

Noyes John N. Abington
Soule & Brown, "
Reed A. N. & Co., N. Abington, "
CRANE J. E. Bridgewater
CROCKER T. W. & CO. (see p 7,) "
Fobes Willard W. "
HATHAWAY W. B. (see p 22) "
HOBART CALEB, "
Keith L. M. "
Prior Allen, Duxbury
SHAW SAMUEL D. East Bridgewater
Hicks Jotham, "
Richards E. E. "
Waterman J. E. "
Bates Henry S Hanover
Curtis Robert "
STETSON I G "
Wood E F "
Howland C I. Hanson
GURNEY J R So Hanson, "
Whiton Bela Hingham
TROWBRIDGE R "
BURGES & BAILEY, Kingston
Hunt & Sampson, "
Tilden Charles I. Marshfield
Snow L & M Mattapoisett
COBB L E North Bridgewater
CURTIS S B & G E "   "
Hayward Daniel "   "
Packard E. & Co. "   "
FOSS NELSON J. Campello, "
Cobb F. B. Plymouth
Drew Ellis, "
LORING THOMAS, "
PRATT L. & CO. (see p 85), "
Leonard Chas. H. Rochester
ROUNSEVILLE ALDEN, Jr, "
Cole & Jenkins, Scituate
Besse L. A. Wareham
Gurney A. S. "
Richards E. E. West Bridgewater
Baker & Williams, "
Edson M. C. "
Perkins Charles, "
Perkins George, "

Forges.

LAZELL, PERKINS & CO. (see p 14,) Bridgewater

Policy Holders in the BERKSHIRE LIFE INSURANCE COMPANY of Pittsfield, Mass., DO NOT FORFEIT THEIR POLICIES by reason of FAILURE TO PAY their premiums. (See page 50.)

Furniture Dealers.

See also Cabinet Makers; also Furniture Manufacturers.)

Torrey D. & E. P., E. Abington, Abington
Holbrook Loring, S. "
PROPHETT WM. (see p 11), Bridgewater
French Daniel, Joppa, E. "
BURGES & BAILEY, (see p 5), Kingston
SOULE GEO. Middleboro
HOWARD CLARK & CO.
North Bridgewater
Brown J. P. Plymouth
Soule Silas T. Wareham

Furniture Manufacturers.

Nelson Thos. Mattapoisett
HOWARD, CLARK, & Co.,
North Bridgewater

Gas Light Companies.

MIDDLEBORO.—Incor. 1856. Capital $5,000. *Proprietor*, Nahum D. Wilbar.
NORTH BRIDGEWATER.—Inc. 1850. Capital, $16,000. *Treas.*, H. W. Robinson; *Supt.*, J. R. Perkins.
PLYMOUTH.—Incorp. 1853. Capital, $40,000. *Pres.*, Winslow Drew; *Treas.* Wm. S. Danforth.

General Agency.

HOLMES LEWIS J. Bridgewater

Gas Fitters and Fixtures.

DREW WM. R. (see page 84,) Plymouth

Gents' Furnishing Goods.

ESTES & WHITING, (see page10,) Abington
Sherman B. "
BURGES & BAILEY, (see page 5,) Kingston
Hunt & Sampson, "
Toole M. Middleboro
BRETT H. A. (see page 54, North Bridgewater
BRYANT G. E. & H. L. (see p 48) "
KINGMAN & HOLLYWOOD,
(see page 24,) "
SCOTT WALTER, (see page 55) "

Glaziers' Points Manufacturers.

Wood N. & Co., Plymouth

Grist Mills.

Beals N. A. jr., East Abington, Abington
Reed A. S. & Co., N. Abington, "
Carver J. E. & Co. Bridgewater
Atwood Bartlett S. Carver
Perkins Alvin. "
Cushman Stephen, South Carver, "
Richards E. E. East Bridgewater
KEEN SAM'L, Joppa, " "
Prior Allen, Duxbury
E. Carver Co. Halifax
Gardner Thomas J Hanover
Cushing Elisha Hanson
Cushing T & G "
Howland C L. Hanson
Munroe Ethan "
Whiton Bela Hingham
Hinds Sumner Lakeville
Dean Joshua W Marion

HILLER BARNABAS Marion
DUNHAM H C Marshfield
Hatch Samuel "
Lewis Charles "
Little Wm. F & S "
Hatch Ichabod West "
Bolles Solomon E Mattapoisett
Cowen Abner P "
Dexter E & Son "
Tinkham Abraham "
Town Mills, "
Namasket Manf Co Middleboro
French Merritt Bridgewater
BARNES E & J C Plymouth
Cobb F B "
Clark Wm South "
LEWIS DAVID Rochester
Clapp Thomas Scituate
Cole Jenkins & Co "
Gannett Freeman "
Gannet Joy North "
Tobey Joshua B., S. Wareham, Wareham
Ames O. & Sons, West Bridgewater

Grocers (Retail.)

(See also Country Stores.)

Dunham & Pratt, Abington
Faxon B. E. "
Ford James, "
Loud Alden S. "
Noyes John N. "
Soule & Brown, "
Whitmarsh Z. N. "
Bigelow D. E. Abington, "
Curtis Abner, " "
Curtis Henry R. " "
FRENCH JOSEPH, " "
GROVER C. H. & D. H. " "
Poole Franklin, " "
Soule Geo. C " "
Sprague E. " "
Stevens David, " "
Torrey D. & E. P. " "
Culver J. M. North Abington, "
BATES & REED, So. Abington, "
DYER N. N. " "
Noyes & Harding, " "
Packard Dan. " "
CRANE J. E. Bridgewater
CROCKER T. W. & CO., (see page 7,) "
HOBART CALEB, "
HATHAWAY, W B see (page 22) "
Keith L. M. "
Brewster Charles E. Duxbury
Freeman W S "
Hunting Amos, East Bridgewater
Keith M. M. "
BROOKS JOHN S (see p 19) Hanover
CURTIS ROBERT S. "
STETSON I. G. (see p 18), "
Bates J. B. "
HOWLAND C. L. Hanson
Sprague Nath'l, "
Howland F. W, jr. S. Hanson, "
Bowker A. "
Drew Cyrus, "
Howland A. B. "
Easterbrook Samuel, Hingham
Thayer A. E. "
TROWBRIDGE ROSWELL, "
Gardner J. 2d, "
Hersey Geo. "
Hersey J. "

LEAVITT'S FUR & HAT STORE, 91 COURT STREET, BOSTON.

GROCERS—HATS, CAPS AND FURS. 139

BURGES & BAILEY, (see p 5) Kingston
HASKINS CEPHAS, Lakeville
Atsatt John Mattapoisett
Luce William "
Snow M. & L. "
Snow & Hammond, "
PEIRCE BROS Middleboro
Thomas Ira, "
Thompson I. W. "
Waterman George, "
Cushing & Munroe, "
Cobb David, North Bridgewater
COBB L. E. "
CURTIS S. B. & G. E. (see p 23), "
Dearborne S. Francis, "
Hayward Ambrose, "
Hayward Daniel, "
Jones Nathan, "
Lovell Daniel, "
SOUTHWORTH & NOYES, (see
p 24), "
Tilden John, "
Packard Joel T. "
Baker Horace, Campello
Howard & Keith, " "
Jennings Isaac Pembroke
Thrasher I "
Atwood Adoniram J. Plymouth
Barnes Corban, "
Bosworth Daniel E. "
Bradford A. J. "
Brown S. P. "
BURNS WM. (see p 33), "
Churchill F H (see 41) "
Cobb F. B. "
Finney B. C. & Co. "
Finney E. C. "
Goodwin William, "
LORING THOMAS, "
May Charles T. "
Perkins Arad, "
Perkins Roland H. "
Robbins Josiah A. "
Sears T. D. "
Sherman E. F. "
TURNER E. C. "
Wadsworth W. "
Bradford Henry A. Plympton
Randell Wm. "
Wilbur Reuben A. "
Tollman Thomas, South Scituate
Wilder Harrison, "
Torrey Geo H "
Bartlett L. H. Wareham
Howard B. F. "
Fuller John S. W. Wareham,
Baker & Willians, West Bridgewater
Dunbar Welcome, "
Edson Melvin C. "
Perkins Charles, "
Perkins George, "
Richards E. E. "

Gun Smiths.

Merritt Ira, Abington
Dunham George F. Plymouth

Hair Dressers.

Bond John S. Abington
HOBSON R. East Abington, "
Butler J. H. South " "
Reiser Wm. H. Bridgewater
Chandler Harvey, East Bridgewater

Clary George E. Hingham
SYLVESTER S. H. (see page 21)
Middleboro
BARDEN W. H. (see page 25)
North Bridgewater
Buckley D. J. "
Jacobs W. H. "
Taylor Clary, "
Frink C. H. Plymouth
Holmes W. S. "
Spear Thomas, "
Whitney Joseph B. "
Turner William H. Wareham

Hammer Manuf.

MORTON E. S. (see p. 81) Plymouth

Hardware and Cutlery.

Ripley William, Abington
CLOUD H. H. No. Abington, "
HOBART CALEB, Bridgewater
Wilder Isaac M. Hanover
BURGES & BAILEY, (see p. 5)
Kingston
Hunt and Sampson, "
Atsatt E. S. Mattapoisett
DOANE GEO. H. (see page 32,)
Middleboro
SOUTHWORTH & NOYES, (see
page 24) North Bridgewater
Woodbridge E. H. "
DREW WM. R. (see page 84) Plymouth
WHITTEN & HOLMES, (see
page 52,) "
BENT I. B. Wareham
Perkins Charles, West Bridgewater

Harness Makers.

Folsom H. Abington
Brewster H. O. E. Abington, "
Calkins J. H. N. " "
Pownall George Abington
ROGERS R. S. (see p. 13), Bridgewater
Swift J. W. Duxbury
Gilbert Wm. E. East Bridgewater
Hersey David A. Hingham
Stetson Joseph, Kingston
Shiverick Wm. Middleboro
Bird L. T. North Bridgewater
Flagg Wm. H. "
BONNEY J. D. (see p 33), Pembroke
WHITMAN CHAS. H. "
Bartlett Edward, Plymouth
Hathaway Edward, "
JACKSON WM. H. "
Bradley Horace, South Scituate
Crocker Walton N. Wareham
Loring William G. "

Hats, Caps & Furs.

ESTES & WHITING, (see p 10),
E. Abington, Abington
FRINDSDORF EDWARD, Hanover
Whiton E. L. Hingham
BURGES & BAILEY, (see p 5) Kingston
Hunt & Sampson, "
TOOLE MICHAEL, (see p 53),
Middleboro
BRETT H. A. (see p 54), N. Bridgewater
BRYANT G. & H. L. (see p 48) "
SCOTT WALTER, "
Peterson Lewis, Plymouth

ANNUAL CASH DIVIDENDS in the BERKSHIRE LIFE INS. CO.,
Pittsfield, Mass. Boston Office, 95 1-2 Washington St. (See page 50.)

Hoop Skirts.

Conant Ira M., Bridgewater
THOMPSON R. F. (see p 69) Middleboro
THOMPSON R. F. (see p 69)
  North Bridgewater
Lucas Eldora, Plymouth

Horse Dealers.

WHITE JOSEPH, N. Hanson, Hanson
PRATT S. L., (see p 77), Cochesett
  West Bridgewater
TRIBOU N. M. Middleboro

Horse Shoers.
(See Blacksmiths.)

McNally Daniel, Abington
Bass Elisha, East Abington, "
HARLOW SOUTHWORTH,
  Bridgewater
Taylor A. D. North "
Atwell Charles, West "

Hotels.

Centre Abington Hotel, H. Ferris,
  Abington
East Abington Hotel, J. Shaw, 2d,
  East Abington, "
HYLAND HOUSE, (see history, p 132), Frank Dunphe, Bridgewater
HANOVER HOUSE, Frank Howard
  Hanover
Old Colony House, Elisha Taft, Hingham
UNION HOUSE, D. S. Norris, "
Mansion House, A. Vining, Hull
Nantasket House, Webster Hersey, "
Oregon House, L. R. Morris, "
ROCKLAND HOUSE, N. Ripley, "
Patuxet House, J. Cushman, Kingston
Sampson House, H. G. Carpenter,
  Lakeville
BAY VIEW HOUSE, J. S. Luce,
  (see page 19) Marion
Delano Hotel, Obed Delano, "
Marion House, "
Webster House, James Carr, Marshfield
Sea Side House, Eben A. Hallett,
  Mattapoisett
Namasket Hotel, S. H. Vaugan,
  Middleboro
NORTH BRIDGEWATER HOTEL,
  T. COBB, North Bridgewater
Clifford House, Smith, Hoxie & Co.,
  Plymouth
Manomet House, H. B. Holmes, "
Samoset House James S. Parker, "
Winslow House, David Seavey, "
South Shore House, Mrs Mary A.
  Torrey, Scituate
HALF-WAY HOUSE, ESTES
  KIMBALL, South Scituate
Nickerson's Hotel, W. T. Nickerson,
  Wareham
THOMPSON'S HOTEL, DAVID
  THOMPSON, "

House Furnishing Goods.

CLOUD H. H. N. Abington, Abington
Reed Thomas, North Bridgewater
DREW WM. R. (see p. 81) Plymouth

Ice Dealers.

Noyes Lorenzo D., Abington

Witherell Jabez, Bridgewater
Jenkins Merritt, East Bridgewater
Nelson James, Hingham
Howes & Sturtevant, Mattapoisett
Cleveland Walter F. North Bridgewater
Stoddard John T. Plymouth
Clapp H. T. Scituate
BURRELL J. D. West Bridgewater

Insurance Agents.

HOWLAND F. P. Abington
PIERCE H. B. (life, see page 13, 81)
  North Abington
Kingman Benj. S. Bridgewater
Kingman Philip D. "
LEACH JAMES C. "
DWELLEY J. (see page 19) Hanson
HARDING DAVID, Hingham
BAKER GEO. M. Marshfield
Robinson Everett Middleboro
Hayward S. A. North Bridgewater
DANFORTH W. S. (see p. 82) Plymouth
HALL J. T. (see page 35) "
Beal John, Scituate
Hayden Joseph P. Wareham

Iron Founders.
(See also Iron Manufacturers; also Stoves.)

LAZELL, PERKINS & CO., (see
  p 14), Bridgewater
Perkins Henry, "
Pratt Lewis & Co. Carver
ELLIS M. & CO. "
Savery Wm. "
Bird Wm. E. East Bridgewater
Old Colony Iron Foundry, Moses
  Bates, (see p 17), "
Barstow Edwin, Hanover
Curtis George, "
Howard Charles & Co. Hingham
LeBARRON JOHN B. Middleboro
Plymouth Iron Foundry, Wm. R.
  Drew, Treas., Plymouth
Franconia Iron & Steel Co., Wm.
  Hammond, Treas., office Lindall, cor. Congress st., Boston,
  Wareham
Agawam Iron Foundry (hollow-
  ware), J. F. Sherman, agent,
  E. Wareham,

Iron Manufacturers.
(See also Forges; also Iron Founders.)

LAZELL, PERKINS & CO. (see p
  14), Bridgewater

Japan, Oils & Varnish.
(See also Paints, Oils and Glass.)

SHAW GEO. H. (see p 81), Middleboro

Jewelry, Watches and Plate.

Noyes Isaiah, Abington
STUDLEY W. B. East Abington, "
HEWETT E. A. (see p 12), Bridgewater
Potter J. H. East "
LEONARD JOS. Hanson
Tower Reuben S. Hingham, Hingham
Wilder Ezra, " "
EWELL DAN'L E. Marshfield
LeBaron A. S. Mattapoisett
TINKHAM FOSTER, Middleboro
CARPENTER C. H. (see p 23), "
GURNEY L. F. (see p 47),
  North Bridgewater

THOSE WHO DESIRE BRILLIANCY OF COMPLEXION must purify and enrich the blood, which HELMBOLD's CONCENTRATED EXTRACT OF SARSAPARILLA invariably does. Ask for *Helmbold's*. Take no other.

HEWETT HERMAN, (see p 39),
                        North Bridgewater
Studley Luther,   "
ATWOOD E. W. (see p 37),   Plymouth
Gooding Benj. R.   Plymouth
SHERMAN N. J.   Wareham

Last Makers.

GILES J. H.   Abington
SPRAGUE CHANDLER, (also boot
   trees and forms) No. Bridgewater

Lawyers.

KEITH J. E.   Abington
Harris J. B.   East   "
Hobart Benj.   South   "
Whitman Jared   "   "
KINGMAN HOSEA, (see page 11,)
                        Bridgewater
LATHAM WILLIAMS, (see
   page 11)   "
STETSON SAMUEL,   Duxbury
Harris B. W.   East Bridgewater
OSBORNE W. H.   "
Simmons Perez,   Hanover
Thaxter David,   Hingham
Chamberlain G. A. W.   Hingham
Beal Joseph S.   Kingston
Robinson Everett,   Middleboro
Wood Wm. H.   "
Perkins Jonas R.   North Bridgewater
White J.   "
Damon Daniel E.   Plymouth
Davis Charles G.   "
Loud Jacob H.   "
Mason Albert   "
Russell John J.   "
Thomas Wm.   "
Whitman Wm. H.   "
Bates Wm.   Wareham
Miller Seth jr.   "
SPROAT JAMES G.   "
PACKARD AUSTIN,   W. Bridgewater
Gray Orrin T.   Cochesett, "

Liquor Agents.

Wormell J. D.   Abington
Hawes Samuel,   Bridgewater
Griffith C. W   Carver
Sherman F. P.   Duxbury
Rogers Thomas,   East Bridgewater
Vaughan C. P.   Halifax
Whiting J. S.   Hanover
Thomas O. H.   Hanson
Reed John,   Hull
Tupper Seth,   Kingston
Jenney C. E.   Lakeville
Batchelder John,   Marion
Cole W. M.   Marshfield
Damon Lincoln,   N. Marshfield
Sparrow Wm. E.   Mattapoisett
Soule George,   Middleboro
Clark George,   North Bridgewater
Cook Russell,   Scituate
Beasley George,   South Scituate
Bemis E.   Pembroke
May C T   Plymouth
Sturtevant L   Plympton
Runnells Levi A.   Wareham
Wood Thomas Mrs.   West Bridgewater
Copeland Albert,   "

Livery Stables.
(See Stables.)

Lumber Dealers.
(See also Saw Mills.)

Reed A. S. & Co. N. Abington, Abington
Alden Sam'l G.   East Bridgewater
Reed & Adams,   "
Inglee Lucius,   Halifax
THOMPSON E. B.   "
Perry Ethan,   Hanover
Studley Joshua,   "
Bourne Wm.   Hanson
Clement James F.   Hingham
Cushing David 2d,   "
Atsatt John T.   Mattapoisett
Barstow N. H. & H.   "
Dexter E. & Son,   "
Washburn P. & W.   Middleboro
Wood A. C.   "
Soule Oakes S.   North Bridgewater
Brown Nathaniel,   Plymouth
Jackson George H.   "
Lobbius Leavitt,   "
Haskell Wm. C.   Rochester
King & Lewis,   "
Rounseville Alden, Jr.   "
Damon & Lewis,   Scituate
Damon Franklin & Co.,   "
Ames Thomas,   West Bridgewater

Machinery and Tools.
(See also Machinists and Machinery Manu-
                facturers.)

LAZELL, PERKINS & CO. (see
   page 14,)   Bridgewater

Machinists and Machinery Manufacturers.

Young Jacob K.   Abington
Ellis H.   "
Kimball E. A.   "
GILES J. H.   Abington
ANDREWS M.   Bridgewater
Alden Leander M.   Bridgewater
COPELAND G. A.   "
HALL ALFRED,   "
HAYWARD EDWIN,   "
KEITH PHILO,   "
LAZELL, PERKINS & CO. (see
   page 14)   "
LEONARD ELMER,   "
LEONARD G. F.   "
MUNROE D. B.   "
PRATT EDWIN,   "
SOUTHERN COTTON GIN CO.
   (see page 15.)   "
TOWNSEND J. P.   "
UNION MACHINE CO, (see page
   23)   "
Bates Martin S.   Hanover
Merrill Isaac G.   "
Bates Caleb, (bolt machines) Kingston
Ripley C. M.   "
SNELL. E. T. & CO., (see page 44)
                        North Bridgewater
PLYMOUTH MILLS, J FARRIS,
       Agent, (see page 88,) Plymouth
SHIPMAN GEO.   West Bridgewater

The terms for **ENDOWMENT**, and **TEN ANNUAL LIFE POLICIES** in the **BERKSHIRE** are peculiarly favorable, and rates lower than in any Note Company.   (See page 50.)

Marble Workers.
(See also Stone Cutters.)
FITZGERALD, W. H. Abington
CLAPP GEO. H. (see page 17) Hanover
Bowker Davis W. Kingston
BRYANT GEO. W. & CO., (see page 53) North Bridgewater
CLARK ROBERT, (see page 57) Plymouth
Leonard Thomas, Wareham

Masons.
Bennett Nathaniel, Abington
Faunce Ichabod, "
Faunce Quincy, "
Loring Edward S. Bridgewater
Perkins Simeon, "
Standish Job, "
Barstow Henry, Duxbury
Barstow Charles, Jr., E. Bridgewater
Harris Seth L. Hanover
Everson B. Hanson
HARRIS SETH L. "
Stetson H. James, Kingston
VAIL WM. Marion
STURTEVANT N. C. Mattapoisett
Thompson Marison, Middleboro
Vaughn Harrison, "
Washburn Solomon, "
Vaughn John G. "
Elbridge Davis, North Bridgewater
Hall Domino, "
Jackson Ephraim, "
Mason Charles, "
Churchill Thomas, Plymouth
Dunham Richard W. "
Hoyt John F. "
Doten Prince, "
Macomber Warren S. "
Robbins Edmund, "
Wood Isaac F. "
Griffith George T. Wareham
Griffith Wm. W. "
Hatch Job, "
Hamblin J. W. East Wareham
Howard Everett, West Bridgewater

Melodeon Manufacturers.
REYNOLDS PHILIP, (see page 30,) North Bridgewater

Milliners and Millinery Goods.
(See also Dress Makers.)
Nash Benj. L. Abington
Stud'zy Susan Mrs. East "
Sharp E. E. Mrs. South "
CROCKER T. W. & CO. (see page 7) Bridgewater
Rider Charles Mrs. Carver
Kirby Sarah, Duxbury
Frost M. Mrs. Hanover
Thomas Christiana, Hanson
Beal Mary, South "
BURGES & BAILEY, (see page 5) Kingston
BARROWS S. F. (see p. 57) Middleboro
Briggs Roland Mrs. "
Andrews M. E. Mrs. North Bridgewater
REYNOLDS M. R. (see p. 25) "
Robinson H. W. & Co. "
Shedd W. M. "
French Mary A. Mrs. "
Studley S. H. "

Atwood J. B. Mrs. Plymouth
Olney Z. Mrs. "
Washburn & Turner, "
Howard M. S. Wareham

Millwrights.
Bonney Lucius, East Bridgewater
Phillips Mark, "
Phillips Wadsworth, "
Washburn Isaac, "
Bonney Calvin, Hanson
Stetson Thomas, "
Whitten John A. "
Phillips Lot, South "

Mowing Machines.
COPELAND HEMAN, (see adv. page) West Bridgewater

Nail Manufacturers.
(See also Tacks, Brads and Shoe Nails.)
DUNBAR, HOBART & WHIDDEN, see history, p. 33) Abington
East Bridgewater Iron Co., E. Bridgew'r
COBB & DREW, (see p. 87) Plymouth
Robinson Iron Co. (see p. 58), "
Plymouth Tack and Rivet Works, "
Kinsey Lewis & Co., S. Wareham
Wareham
Poll Mills, E. B. Tobey, Treas., West Wareham, "
Parker Mills, C. C. Sprague, agt., "
Tisdale Nail Co., J. F. Sherman, agent, East Wareham, "
Tremont Nail Co., J. B. Tobey, treas., West Wareham, "

Nurserymen, Seedsmen & Florists.
HOOPER THOMAS, see page 9) Bridgewater
Atwood E. E. Carver
Shaw E. W. "
Peterson Jabez, Duxbury
Tinkham Otis, Lakeville
Cushman Elbridge, Middleboro
MONTELLO NURSERY, L. W. PEFFER, North Bridgewater
WATSON B. M. (see p. 86) Plymouth
Weston Coomer, "
Brooks Nath'l, S. Scituate
Billings Willard, West Bridgewater

Oil and Candle Manufacturers.
JUDD L. S. (see page 18) Marion

Organ Manufacturers.
REYNOLDS P. see p 30, N. Bridgew'r
Marston A. B. Campello, "

Oysters and Refreshments.
(See Eating Houses also.)
Nash J. E. Abington
Douglas W. East "
GILMAN G. N., see p 10, No. "
Fuller John, Bridgewater
Hull J. C. "
TRIPP B. F., see card, Middleboro
Union Saloon, "
GROVER R. B., see p 57, No. Bridgew'r
Washburn and Richardson, "
PALLARD S D., see p 129 history, Plymouth
DODGE J E., see p 86, "

LEAVITT'S FUR & HAT STORE, 91 COURT STREET, BOSTON.

Painters—Carriage.

Peirce Wm M, Abington
Ford B. F., East "
Bates Asa, South "
HERSEY DAVID A., Hingham
Sprague Joseph T., "
Eldridge David, Kingston
BOOMER B. L., see p. 19) Middleboro
Southworth Rodney E., "
SPARROW J. G. (see card) "
Jones John B., North Bridgewater
Sargent Samuel, "
Thomas William E., "
Jones Charles L., Plymouth
Young Charles, Scituate
Young Edw., "

Painters, (House and Sign.)

Davis W. H., Abington
French Joseph, "
Ford B. F., East "
Gilson L. C., " "
Lawrence Thomas R., " "
Lincoln S. B., North "
Harding J. S., South "
Reed Philip, " "
Alden James S., Bridgewater
Bassman H. F. & J. G., "
Chandler Alden, Duxbury
Hathaway Joshua W., "
Sampson Alfred, "
Grow & Wentworth, East Bridgewater
Bonney E. P., Halifax
Cook John, "
Bailey Melzer, Hanover
Bryant Snow, "
Corbin Frank, "
Eells John P., "
Sturtevant George, "
Roberts John C., Hanson
Cobb David, Hingham
Cross and Lane, "
Hersey John P., "
Sprague J and S, "
Bonney Geo H, Kings on
CHURCHILL L., Lakeville
Barrows Elijah W, "
Pickens H C, "
PARLOW G. W., Marion
Rogers Wm, W. Marshfield
Dexter James W, Mattapoisett
Jones Eben, "
BOOMER B L., see p 19, Middleboro
Sparrow H A, "
SPARROW J. G., see card, "
Wood Frederick E, "
Farnham Geo, North Bridgewater
Sharp John M, "
BONNEY D. J., see p 33, Pembroke
Gardner Benj T, "
Jones E. Morton, "
Packard Alphens, No. "
Holmes Ephraim, "
Jones Charles L., Plymouth
Savery W. T., "
Tribble Wm B, "
Bonney Geo H., No. Plympton
Rogers Mason, Rochester
Bouve Sylvanus R., Scituate
Hayward John, "
Hayward Ward L., "
Young Charles, "
Young Edwin, "

MURDOCK CHARLES C., Wareham
Perkins J. F., "
Capen Edward, West Bridgewater
Copeland Albert, "
Edson Alanson, "
Howard Milo, "

Painter—Theatrical Scenery.

Wilbour Winslow C., Bridgewater

Paints, Oils and Glass.

Hathaway J W., Duxbury
Woodbridge E. H., North Bridgewater
DREW WM. R. (see p. 84) Plymouth
MURDOCK CHARLES C., Wareham

Paper Manufacturers.

Cornell Mark H., Bridgewater
Hollingsworth Lyman, "
Wheelwright G. W., West Wareham

Patent Medicines.

ESTES J. J. see p 7, E. Abington
Wadsworth H. salve plaster, Duxbury
SHAW J. B. & J. see p 33, Middleboro
BIXBY C. C. see p 27, No. Bridgewater
THAYER H. S. see p 51, "
HALL JOHN T., Plymouth
DOTEN C. C. see opp last cover, ", "

Periodicals and News Depots.

Dyer S., South Abington
Holmes Lewis, Bridgewater
Kennedy R. B., Duxbury
Ramsdell J. L., Hanover
Dean Geo H., Hingham
Shaw J. B. and J., Middleboro
COPELAND C. F. (see page 30)
  North Bridgewater
Smith John, Plymouth

Photographs, &c.

BURRELL D. T. (see page 13)
  Bridgewater
Perry Jerome, Hanover
Stetson Benj. L., "
Hudson Wm. jr. Hingham
Cornwall Henry F., Middleboro
HOWARD BROS. (see page 26)
  North Bridgewater
RICHARDSON C. F. (see page 27) "
Barnard J. S., W. Duxbury, Pembroke
Locke A. H., Plymouth

Physicians.

Dudley H. W., Abington
Harris J. T., hom. "
Hastings B. F., East "
Winslow J. A. W. Mrs., East "
Underwood J. M., East "
Tanner N. B., North "
Copeland H. F., South "
Robinson Chas. F., " "
Alden Samuel, hom. Bridgewater
Millett Asa, "
Sawyer Edward, "
Wood G. F., North Carver
Bancroft Kirk, Duxbury
WILDE JAMES, "
Chaplin Daniel, East Bridgewater
Morton Cyrus, Halifax
Pool Isaac, "
Downes Nath'l, - Hanover

DIVIDENDS ADDED to the POLICY in the BERKSHIRE often exceed the premium paid: are NON-FORFEITABLE and will be redeemed in CASH ON DEMAND. (See page 50.)

Howes W. R., Hanover
Barker Bowen, South Hanson
Whitmarsh Abby, spiritist, " "
Harlow J. E., Hingham
Stephenson Ezra, "
Spaulding H. S., (hom. see p 18, "
Chandler Ira (clairv.), Kingston
Jones Henry N. "
Nichols Paul L. "
Ransom Harvey N. (eclec.) "
Batchelder John, Marion
Vose Henry C. (homo.) "
Hagar Jos East Marshfield
Sparrow Wm E., Mattapoisett
Sweat Wm W. "
Comstock Wm W., Middleboro
Drake E. W. "
Jackson C. S. "
Sherman J. H. (hom.) see p 72, "
Robinson Morrill, North "
Snow Geo W. South "
Borden A. K. North Bridgewater
Dean E. E. (hom.), "
Kingman A. W. "
Wade E. R. (bot.), "
Richards Charles, Campello, "
Collamore Francis, N. Pembroke, Pembroke
Gordon Timothy, Plymouth
Hubbard Benj. (see p 51), "
Jackson Alex. "
Warren Winslow, "
Wood C. J. Chiltonville, "
Hammond Josiah S. Plympton
Haskell Jos. Rochester
Sturtevant C. "
Thomas Francis, Scituate
Brownell N. P. South Scituate
Doggett Perez F. Wareham
Fearing Benjamin, Jr. "
Sawyer F. A. "
Knowles H. M. (hom.), "
Swan J. C. (hom.), West Bridgewater

Plaster Mills.

BARNES E. & J. C. (see p 45), Plymouth

Printers, Book and Job.

PRATT THOS. S. & CO. (see history 134,) E. Abington, Abington
BURRELL JARVIS, E. Bridgewater
BLOSSOM & EASTERBROOK, (see history 135), Hingham
PRATT BROS. (see history 133) Middleboro
Jones Augustus T. North Bridgewater
ANDREWS G. F. (see history 135) Plymouth
Avery & Cave, "

Provision Dealers.
(See also Grocers.)

BLANCHARD VINSON, Abington
CUSHING DAVIS, East "
Moulton H. S. "
HATHAWAY WM. B. (see page 22) Bridgewater
Higgins J. L. Hingham
O'Rourke Bernard, "
Thayer Elihu, "
HERSEY ISAAC, "

Barden & Leonard, Middleboro
FIELD C. C. see p 44 North Bridgewater
SEVERANCE L. F. & A. C. (see page 28) "
Tilden John, "
Alden Lucas W. Campello, "
CHANDLER P. C. & CO., (see page 41) Plymouth
Holmes A. & Co. "
Holmes C. B. & Son, "
CORTHELL JOHN, (see page 47) South Scituate

Pump and Block Makers.

Soule L. N. Duxbury
DAVIS WILLIAM, Hingham
Leavitt John & Son, "
Turner David, Plymouth

Rivet Manufacturers.

COBB BENJ. & CO., Kingston
Old Colony Rivet Co., Hall Bros. & Co. Plymouth
COBB & DREW, (see p. 84) "
Plymouth Tack and Rivet Works, Samuel Loring, propr. "
PLYMOUTH MILLS, J. FARRIS, Agent, (see page 88) "

Rolling Mills.
(See also Iron Manufacturers.)

LAZELL, PERKINS & CO., (see page 14) Bridgewater
Rogers & Sheldon, East "
Robinson Iron Co. Plymouth
Wood N. & Co. "

Sawing and Planing Mills.

Gurney D. B. Abington
Reed B. & T. & S. East "
Reed A. S. & Co., North "
Packard E. & Co. North Bridgewater
BARNES E. & J. C. (see page 45) Plymouth
Cole & Jenkins, Scituate

Saw Mills.
(See also Shingle and Box Mills.)

DUNBAR, HOBART & WHIDDEN, (see hist, page 33,) South Abington
Hollingsworth Lyman, Bridgewater
Holmes Jacob, Carver
SAVERY WM. (steam) "
Ward Benjamin, "
Cole H. G. & Co., North "
Shurtleff L. & Co., South "
Chandler C. H. W. Duxbury
Keen Isaac, "
Peterson Stephen, "
Carver E. & Co. Halifax
Brooks John, Hanover
Gardner Thomas J. "
Bourne William, Hanson
Cushing Elijah, "
Hobart & Harding, "
Monroe Ethan, "
Hathaway Alex. Marion
HILLER BARNABAS, "
Parlow Brothers, "
Chandler Simeon B. Marshfield
DUNHAM H. C. "
Hatch Samuel, "
Bolles Solomon E. Mattapoisett

QUANTITY vs. QUALITY. HELMBOLD'S EXTRACT SARSAPARILLA. The dose is small. Those who desire a large quantity and large doses ERR.

SAWS—STABLES.   145

Dexter E. & Son,   Mattapoisett
Ellis Jarvis,   "
Ellis Thomas,   "
Tinkham Abraham,   "
Tinkham Clark,   "
Tinkham Isaac,   "
Town Mills,   "
Cox George,   Middleboro
HARLOW IVORY H. (see card
  and engraving)   "
Namasket Man. Co.   "
Benson Stillman,   South   "
Howard W. & T.   North Bridgewater
Sprague C.   "   "
BONNEY J. S.   Plympton
Hayward Martin,   "
Jenkins Bro. & Co.   "
King & Lewis,   Rochester
Clapp Thomas,   Scituate
Clapp John,   South Scituate
Jacobs B. & B.   "
Torrey D. Jr.,   "
Kenney Lewis,   South Wareham
Ames O. & Sons,   West Bridgewater

Saw Manufacturers.
ANDREWS M.   Bridgewater

Scale and balance Manuf.
CHURCHILL BENJ.   Wareham

Seed Sower.
REYNOLDS MESSRS. (see page 49)
                    North Bridgewater

Sewing Machines.
Donovan C. (also findings) East
                            Abington
Shaw Sumner,   East   "
Wheeler E. A.   "
SCOTT WALTER, (see page 55)
                    North Bridgewater

Sewing Machine Needles.
Howard Charles,   North Bridgewater
Packard J. W.   "   "

Shingle Mills.
(See also Saw Mills.)
Gurney D. B.   Abington
Chandler Charles H.   Duxbury
Keen Isaac,   West   "
Phillips & Co.   East Bridgewater
Carver E. & Co.   Halifax
Barstow Edwin,   Hanover
Curtis George,   "
Dyer Charles,   "
Stetson Thomas,   "
Monroe Ethan,   Hanson
Hinds Sumner,   Lakeville
Westgate C. T.   Lakeville
HILLER BARNABAS,   Marion
Hathaway Alexander,   "
Parlow Bros. (box boards)   "
DUNHAM HENRY C.   Marshfield
Hatch Ichabod,   West   "
Bolles S. E.   Mattapoisett
Dexter E. & Son,   "
Cowen Abner P.   "
Ellis Jarvis,   "
Tinkham Abraham P.   "
Jones Seth L.   Pembroke
BARNES E. & J. C. (see page 45)
                            Plymouth
BONNEY J. S.   Plympton

King & Lewis,   Rochester
ROUNSEVILLE ALDEN, JR.   "
Alger Warren L.   West Bridgewater
Beals & Eddy,   "

Ship Block Manufacturers.
Brown Nathaniel,   Plymouth
Turner David,   "

Ship Builders.
Keen Nath'l P.   Duxbury
Keen Wm. P.   "
Paulding William,   "
Holmes Edward,   Kingston
Barstow N. H. & H.   Mattapoisett
Cannon Brothers,   "
Holmes Josiah jr. & Bro.   "
Waterman & Barstow,   South Scituate

Ship Carpenters.
(See also Carpenters; also Ship Joiners.)
Chandler J. W.   Duxbury
Keen N. P.   "
CUDWORTH JOHN,   Hanover
Cox Wm. R.   Plymouth
Kendrick Asa,   "

Ship Joiners.
(See also Ship Carpenters.)
Boodry Dennis S.   Mattapoisett
Hiller Prince,   "

Shipsmiths.
(See also Blacksmiths.)
Faunce Zenas,   Duxbury
Barstow Edwin, (anchors)   Hanover
Curtis George,   "   "
Barton James,   "
Shaw Ichabod,   Plymouth

Ships Wheels.
Leavitt A. L.   Hingham

Soap and Candle Manufacturers.
Brown & Lawton,   Bridgewater
Pratt Isaac & Son,   South Hanson
Hammond Wm.   Mattapoisett
Alger Cyrus,   West Bridgewater

Soda Water Manufacturers.
Nash Sylvanus,   Abington

Stables.
Folsom H.   Abington
Whiting Wm. H.   "
BURRELL A.   East   "
Whiting F. T.   "   "
Shaw Jacob 2d,   "   "
Wood George W.   "   "
Randall H.   North   "
Whitmarsh F. L.   "   "
Hersey Jason,   South   "
Estes Calvin,   Bridgewater
Keith Thomas,   "
King D. Francis,   "
Dunham John,   North Carver
Sampson Eben S.   Duxbury
Witherell G. W.   "
Griffin Alfred,   East Bridgewater
Waterman John,   "
HOWARD FRANK,   Hanover
White Joseph,   Hanson
Bailey Caleb,   Hingham
BASSETT GEORGE,   "
Taft Silas W.   "

Policy Holders in the BERKSHIRE LIFE INSURANCE COMPANY of Pittsfield, Mass., DO NOT FORFEIT THEIR POLICIES by reason of FAILURE TO PAY their premiums.   38   (See page 50.)

Turner George, Hingham
Hersey W. Hull
Vining A. "
Cushman Josiah, Kingston
Foster A. B. "
Hadley Andrew, Marion
Hallett Eben A. Mattapoisett
Cole James jr. Middleboro
Fuller Marcus, "
Vaughan S. H. "
Bennett E. E. North Bridgewater
Burke E. "
COBB TYLER, "
PORTER A. S. "
Webber James, Campello.
Bartlett Stephen, Plymouth
Chandler Albert C. "
Drew George A. "
Whiting George A. "
Torrey W. S. Scituate
Brooks E. F. South Scituate
Nickerson W. T. Wareham
Fuller John S. West "
THOMPSON DAVID, "
Bates Winslow H. West Bridgewater
Bourke Wm. H. "
Holmes John, "
Peckham Altred, "
Peckham N. A. "
PRATT S. L. (see p. 77), "

Stamp and Stencil Cutters.
(See also Die Sinkers.)
THOMAS H. O. (see page 26)
North Bridgewater

Stationers.
(See also Books and Stationery.)
Clapp B. R. North Bridgewater
THOMAS H. O. (see page 26) "

Stave Mills.
Kenney Lewis, South Wareham

Steam Engine Builders.
(See also Machinists; also Boiler Makers.)
LAZELL, PERKINS & CO., (see page 14) Bridgewater

Stone Cutters and Dealers.
CLARK ROBERT, (see p. 37) Plymouth
PARLOW G. W. Marion

Stove Dealers and Tinsmiths.
Ripley Wm. Abington
Littlefield J. P. East "
CLOUD H. H. North "
Holbrook Loring, South "
Fairbanks & Poole, " "
FAIRBANKS J. H. (see page 13, 77)
Bridgewater
Jewett Charles H. "
Clark Willard, Duxbury
JOHNSON WM. (see page 16)
East Bridgewater
Gill Charles, Hingham
Loring E. & I. W. "
Myrick Wm. H. Kingston
KELLEY H. H. Marion
Atsatt E. S. Mattapoisett
DOANE G. H. (see page 32) Middleboro
Hervey L. D. (see p. 11), N. Bridgewater
DREW WM R. (see p. 84) Plymouth
HARLOW & BARNES, "
WHITTEN & HOLMES, (see p. 52) "

Waterman Andrew J. Scituate
Stoddard E. North "
BENT ISAAC B. Wareham
Burbank Walter D. "

Stove Manufacturers.
(See also Iron Founders,)
Myrick Wm. H. Kingston
PLYMOUTH IRON FOUNDRY,
(see page 84) Plymouth
Forbes D. West Bridgewater

Strawberries.
NYE J. B. B. Marion

Straw Goods Manufacturers.
BAY STATE STRAW WORKS,
ALBERT-ALDEN, (see p. 56) Middleboro

Surveyors.
Kingman P. D. Bridgewater

Tack, Brad and Shoe Nail Manufs.
(See also Nail Manufacturers.)
Gurney D. B. (also heel plates) Abington
Brigham Henry H. South "
DUNBAR, HOBART & WHIDDEN,
(see p. 33 history,) South Abington
BARTLETT ELIJAH, Bridgewater
KEITH Z. JR. & CO. (see p. 43)
East Bridgewater
SHELDON K. E. "
BARSTOW E. W. (see page 83)
Hanover
CURTIS & CO., "
PERRY E. Y. (see 1st cover) "
STETSON J. F. "
WATERMAN L. C. (see p. 45), "
SYLVESTER G. F. "
Sylvester M R. "
CUSHING & CO. (see page 12) Hanson
Howland Luther, "
COBB & DREW, see page 84, Kingston
REED ALPHONSO, "
Plymouth Tack and Rivet Works
Sam'l Loring, Propr. Plymouth
Robinson Iron Co. (see card), Plymouth
TOLMAN SAM'L. Jr. see page 47
South Scituate
PARKER MILLS, Wareham

Tailors.
(See also Clothing.)
AGNEW JOHN, see page 11, Abington
Walsh Lawrence, "
DALY C. East "
Sproul John, South "
Howes Phineas, Bridgewater
Kennedy Robt. B. Duxbury
DELANO T. B. Hanson
Todd John, Hingham
BURNS E. E. see page 21, Kingston
BURGES & BAILEY, see p 5 "
Sturtevant Perez, Marion
HARTWELL GEO. F. see card
Middleboro
BRETT H. A. see page 51, North
Bridgewater
BRYANT G. E. & H. L. see page 48.
North Bridgewater
Bumpas E. B. " "
KINGMAN & HOLLYWOOD, see page 24. North "

NOT A FEW of the worst disorders that afflict mankind arise from corruption of the blood. HELMBOLD'S EXTRACT SARSAPARILLA is a remedy of the utmost value.

SCOTT W. see p. 55, N. Bridgewater
Talbot Henry, " "
Welch & Tighe, " "
Wilbour G. E. " "
HOLMES B. H. see page 34, Plymouth
Cook Russell, Scituate
Landers Edmund, "
Runnells Levi A. Wareham

Tanners and Curriers.
Church William, Hanover
LORING ALFRED, South Hingham
Stodder Laban, " "

Taxidermist.
SYLVESTER S. H. (see page 21) Middleboro

Tap Maker.
Brozard French, Hingham

Thread Manuf.
SAMOSET MILLS, (see page next after history) Plymouth

Tin Ware Manufs.
(See also Stove Dealers.)
CLOUD H. H. Abington
Littlefield J. P. East
FAIRBANKS J. H. (see card) Bridgewater
DOANE G. H. (see p. 32) Middleboro
HERVEY L. D. (see card) North Bridgewater
Hunt John, "
WHITTEN & HOLMES, (see page 52) Plymouth

Toy Manufacturers.
Hersey Caleb, Hingham
Hersey Samuel, "

Trunk Manufacturers.
TORREY DAVID JR. South Scituate
TORREY W. "

Twine and Line Manufacturers.
Diman Ezra, Plymouth
IRISH C. B. "
Wilson David Plymouth

Undertakers.
Pratt George, North Abington
Holbrook Loring, South "
PROPHETT WM. see page 11, Bridgewater
Southworth Eli, Carver
Vaughan Thomas, "
Cobb Thomas, North Carver
Chandler Charles H. Duxbury
Weston Augustus, "
Beal George P. Hanson
Chandler Nathan, Kingston
NELSON THOS. Mattapoisett
Eaton Andrew M. Middleboro
SOULE GEO. see page 34, "
HOWARD CLARK & CO. see page 25, North Bridgewater
SHURTLEFF LOTHROP, see page 24, North Bridgewater
Jones E. Morton, Pembroke
Bates C. Plymouth
RAYMOND C. see page 34, "

Hammond F. Scituate
Newcomb Wm. J. North "
Wall Walter, " "
Sparrell C. W. South "

Varnish Manufacturers.
HAUTHAWAY C. L. (for boots, see pages 26, 27) North Bridgewater
Washburn Elisha, (for boots and shoes) "
WHITTEMORE D. (for boots and shoes, see page 57, history) "

Water Wheel Manufs.
Bates Caleb, Kingston
PLYMOUTH MILLS, J. FARRIS Agent, (see page 88) Plymouth

Weather Vane Manuf.
Howard J. & Co. West Bridgewater
Washburn L. H. & Co. "

Well Windlass.
HOLMES G. W. (see p. 22) Bridgewater

Wheelwrights.
PEIRCE M. B. Abington
Reed Abiah E. "
Darling Benjamin, Bridgewater
Edson J W "
Fobes Albert F "
Jones John, East "
Trow Bartholomew, " "
Eells Robert, Hanover
Downer Thomas, "
Clarke Thomas G Hanson
Whitten John A "
Elbridge David G. Kingston
Horr Job, Lakeville
Damon F. N. Marshfield
Simmons Hewett, "
Snow Ephriam, Mattapoisett
ATWOOD R. 2d, Middleboro
SNOW VENUS, "
VAUGHAN WM. A. "
Tribou L. E. North Bridgewater
Simmons Mason, Pembroke
DAMON BAILEY, "
Ellis James, Plymouth
Nelson Samuel, "
Rider Ezekiel, "
Sparrow Josiah, Rochester
Packard Isaac, Scituate
Litchfield Isaac, North "
Merritt J. C. " "

Wooden Ware Manuf.
Barnes Lyman, buckets, Hingham
CORTHELL NELSON, "
Hersey Caleb T. "
Hersey Cushing, "
Gardner Leonard, South "
Wilder C. & A. South "

Woollen Goods Manufs.
Star Mills, George Brayton, treasurer, (fancy cassimeres) Middleboro
Plymouth Woollen Mills, (flannels) Plymouth
West Charles E. "

Yellow Metal.
LAZELL, PERKINS & CO. (see page 14) Bridgewater

ANNUAL CASH DIVIDENDS in the BERKSHIRE LIFE INS. CO., Pittsfield. Mass. Boston Office, 95 1-2 Washington St. (See page 50.)

www.ingramcontent.com/pod-product-compliance
Lightning Source LLC
Chambersburg PA
CBHW030806230426
43667CB00008B/1081